METROPOLITAN MUSEUM JOURNAL

Volume 36 / 2001

METROPOLITAN MUSEUM JOURNAL

Volume 36 / 2001

The Metropolitan Museum of Art, New York

Distributed by BREPOLS ❦ PUBLISHERS

Editorial Board

This publication is made possible by a gift from Assunta Sommella Peluso, Ada Peluso, and Romano I. Peluso, in memory of Ignazio Peluso.

Additional support has been provided by The Adelaide Milton de Groot Fund, in memory of the de Groot and Hawley families. We are indebted to The Henry and Henrietta Quade Foundation and Annette E. Trefzer for generously supporting the publication of the technical study of the Central Asian textiles.

The members of the Editorial Board express their appreciation to Margaret Aspinwall for the four volumes of the *Metropolitan Museum Journal* that she has produced with meticulous care and sensitivity.

The *Metropolitan Museum Journal* is published annually by The Metropolitan Museum of Art
John P. O'Neill, Editor in Chief and General Manager of Publications
Margaret Aspinwall, Senior Editor

Manuscripts submitted for the *Journal* and all correspondence concerning them should be addressed to James David Draper. Guidelines for contributors are given on the last page of this volume.

For information about subscribing to the *Metropolitan Museum Journal* and to order back issues, write to the Periodicals Department, Brepols Publishers, Begijnhof 67, 2300 Turnhout, Belgium; fax + 32 14 42 89 19; e-mail periodicals.publishers@brepols.com.

ISBN 1-58839-005-5 (MMA), 2-503-51248-8 (Brepols)
ISSN 0077-8958
Library of Congress Catalog Card Number 68-28799
Copyright © 2001 by The Metropolitan Museum of Art

Laid out by Carol Liebowitz, on a format established by Peter Oldenburg and Bruce Campbell

Printed in Spain

Contents

ABBREVIATIONS

MMA   The Metropolitan Museum of Art
MMAB   *The Metropolitan Museum of Art Bulletin*
MMJ   *Metropolitan Museum Journal*

Height precedes width and then depth in dimensions cited.
Photographs, unless otherwise attributed, are by the
Photograph Studio, The Metropolitan Museum of Art.

Foreword

PHILIPPE DE MONTEBELLO

Director, The Metropolitan Museum of Art

With keen pleasure I acknowledge the generous gift that members of the Peluso family have made in memory of the late Ignazio Peluso. His widow, Assunta Sommella Peluso, and their daughter, Ada Peluso, and son, Romano I. Peluso, have thoughtfully designated their gift to subsidize the *Metropolitan Museum Journal*. It is particularly gratifying that such constant, valued friends of the Museum have chosen to recognize and sustain our scholarly endeavors in this way. As the institution's publication for specialized research on the collections, the *Journal* serves a vital function in the Museum, one bound up intimately with our raison d'être. Thanks to the Pelusos, our investigations and the dissemination of the results have acquired a much surer foundation on which to develop and flourish.

A

B

C

D

■ = azurite

■ = cinnabar

■ = charcoal

■ = Egyptian blue

■ = terre verte

■ = limestone substrate

PLATE 1. Watercolor reconstruction of the painted decoration on the Amathus sarcophagus, from Cyprus, ca. 475 B.C., with a key to the colors (drawing: Elizabeth Hendrix). See pp. 43–58

PLATE 2. Left to right: Core-formed glass aryballos; H. 5.1 cm; The Metropolitan Museum of Art, Edward C. Moore Collection, Bequest of Edward C. Moore, 1891 (91.1.1367). Core-formed glass aryballos; H. 5.1 cm; The Metropolitan Museum of Art, Gift of J. Pierpont Morgan, 1917 (17.194.309). Core-formed glass aryballos; H. 5 cm; The Metropolitan Museum of Art, Theodore M. Davis Collection, Bequest of Theodore M. Davis, 1915 (30.115.7). See pp. 59–66

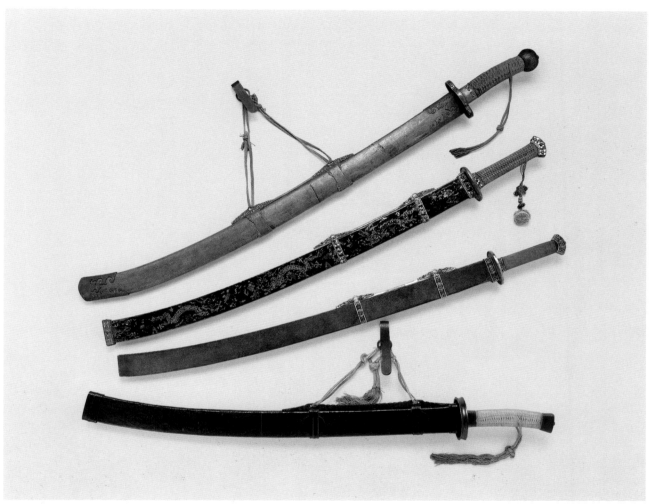

PLATE 3. Top to bottom: *Liuyedao* and scabbard, China, 18th century; blade 31¾ in. (80.6 cm), with fullers and details of dorsal spine showing European influence, mounted in gilt brass with panels of openwork and with engraved decor, the scabbard covered with polished rayskin; The Metropolitan Museum of Art, Bequest of George C. Stone, 1935 (36.25.1473a, b). *Peidao* with Japanese import blade, the mounts Chinese, ca. 1750–1800; blade 28¾ in. (73 cm), mounts gilt iron set with gemstones and mother-of-pearl, with polychrome lacquered scabbard embellished with mother-of-pearl; The Metropolitan Museum of Art, The Collection of Giovanni P. Morosini, presented by his daughter Giulia, 1932 (32.75.301a, b). *Liuyedao* and scabbard, China, 17th–18th century; blade 29⅞ in. (75.9 cm), mounted in gilt openwork iron, embellished with gemstones, with scabbard covered in brown leather; The Metropolitan Museum of Art, Rogers Fund, 1914 (14.48.2a, b). *Peidao* with blade of proto-*niuweidao* form and scabbard, China, probably 18th century; blade 28½ in. (72.4 cm), of six-row *huawengang* and stacked edge strip, fitted in iron, scabbard covered in black leather; The Metropolitan Museum of Art, Bequest of George C. Stone, 1935 (36.25.1477a, b). See pp. 207–22

PLATE 4. William J. Bennett (ca. 1784–1844). *Weehawken from Turtle Grove,* ca. 1830. Watercolor, gouache, and graphite on off-white wove paper, 15¹⁄₁₆ x 20¹⁄₁₆ in. (38.6 x 51 cm). The Metropolitan Museum of Art, The Edward W. C. Arnold Collection of New York Prints, Maps, and Pictures, Bequest of Edward W. C. Arnold, 1954 (54.90.107). See pp. 223–34

METROPOLITAN MUSEUM JOURNAL

Volume 36 / 2001

Andokides and a Curious Attic Black-Figured Amphora

MARY B. MOORE

Professor of Art History, Hunter College of the City University of New York

THE OPENING IN APRIL 1999 of the seven refurbished galleries exhibiting the Archaic and Classical Greek sculpture and painting in The Metropolitan Museum of Art was a greatly anticipated occasion. And it was well worth the wait. Exquisitely installed and bathed in light, the objects fairly sparkle in their new homes. Whereas in previous installations the large pieces, particularly the sculpture, often seemed to receive the lion's share of visitors' attention, in the new arrangement the smaller objects in metal and clay often steal the show. An Attic black-figured amphora is just such an example. The vase first came to the Metropolitan Museum in 1964 as a long-term loan from Christos G. Bastis, and in 1999 Mr. and Mrs. Bastis gave it to the museum in honor of Carlos A. Picón, curator in charge of the Department of Greek and Roman Art.[1] It has long interested me because it presents intriguing problems of epigraphy and attribution. The vase was made and signed by the potter Andokides and it should probably be dated about 540 B.C. (Figures 1–8, 23–25).

This little vase is a one-piece amphora of Beazley's Type B. The shape is characterized by a continuous-curve profile between mouth and foot, handles that are round in section, and a type of foot known as an echinus.[2] Its flaring mouth is flat on top to receive a lid.[3] On the side of the mouth is a frieze of rosettes with a white dot in the core of each. Above the figures is a band of ivy with a wavy vine and a dot between each leaf. At each handle an ornamental configuration separates the scene on the obverse from the one on the reverse: a lotus-palmette cross with a dotted chain linking the three elements (Figures 3, 4). The center of the hanging lotus at handle A/B is red, as is the heart of the right palmette; at handle B/A, part of the heart of each palmette is red and so is the center of the hanging lotus. The root of each handle is superimposed over the upper lotus so that only the leaves and fronds appear, not the cuff. There are twenty-nine rays above the foot. The lid (Figure 5), which is preserved except for its knob, has several patterns. From

the knob out they are as follows: dot band, ribbon pattern, two dot bands, each separated by three lines. On the brim are myrtle leaves with dots.[4]

On each side of the amphora there is a chariot facing to the right. On Side A (Figures 1, 6, 7, 24), the charioteer, dressed in a long, red, belted chiton and a petasos with the brim turned up in the back, stands in the box of the chariot near its back edge. He holds the reins tightly in both hands, but has no goad. A Boeotian shield hangs down his back. The horses step forward smartly, looking nervous and high-strung. The right-hand pole horse is white; the pupil of its eye is red, as is the rein where it overlaps its neck. The forelocks of the two trace horses and the left-hand pole horse are tied in topknots. Manes are red; the tails of the right-hand pole horse and the right-hand trace horse are red;[5] the breast band of the right-hand trace horse is also red, edged by a row of white dots above and below. In the field are three inscriptions (Figure 8).

Side B is similar, but there are a few differences (Figures 2, 23, 25). The charioteer wears a black chiton, his petasos is white with a red dot on the black brim near the front, and he holds a goad. The right-hand pole horse is white, but its mane is incised. As on Side A, the rein is red where it overlaps the neck. This horse's tail and the tail and mane of the right-hand trace horse are red. The girth of the latter horse is decorated with white dots. The right-hand trace horse has a small incised circle within the triangle created by the divided cheek strap of the headstall and the cheekpiece of the bit. This may be a very early rendering of a bit burr, a device that made turning a quadriga easier.[6] In front of the team, a small, nude man stands to right, holding a wreath in his lowered right hand and a palm branch in his raised left (Figure 25). His diminutive size was probably dictated by the small amount of space available for him. An eagle holding a long serpent in its beak flies to left above the croups of the horses (Figure 23).

ANDOKIDES AND THE POTTING INSCRIPTION

Writing appears very frequently on Greek vases and the letters may be painted or incised.[7] Inscriptions are

Figure 1. Side A of an Attic black-figured amphora signed by Andokides as potter, ca. 540 B.C., showing a chariot moving to the right. H. 26 cm. The Metropolitan Museum of Art, Gift of Mr. and Mrs. Christos G. Bastis, in honor of Carlos A. Picón, 1999 (1999.30a, b)

Figure 2. Side B of the amphora in Figure 1 showing a chariot moving to the right

Figure 3. Side A/B of the amphora in Figure 1 showing the configuration below the handle

Figure 4. Side B/A of the amphora in Figure 1 showing the configuration below the handle

Figure 5. Top of the lid of the amphora in Figure 1

used for various purposes. They may be the signature of the potter (as on MMA 1999.30) or of the painter; they may identify figures depicted in the illustration; or they may fall into other categories, such as signifying the purpose of the vase, citing part of a text, or naming objects.[8] The earliest known inscription on an Attic vase is incised on the shoulder of an oinochoe dated in the third quarter of the eighth century B.C., that is, in the Late Geometric period. The inscription indicates that the vase was awarded to the person who danced the most gracefully.[9] The earliest artist signatures appear on works of the late eighth century and seventh century B.C.; they give the names of potters and are not of Attic origin. The first preserved example, on a Late Geometric krater fragment found at Pithekoussai, was made by a potter whose name ends in [ ]INOΣ. The next occurs on a krater of uncertain fabric found at Cerveteri and dating about 650 B.C.; this potter's name is Aristonothos. Another potter is Kallikleas, who signed a candlestick-like object found at Ithaca that is roughly contemporary with the krater

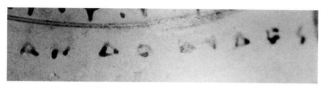

Figure 6. Detail of Side A of the amphora in Figure 1 showing the name "Andokides" in the potter's signature (photo: the author)

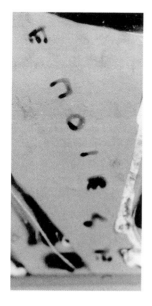

Figure 7. Detail of Side A of the amphora in Figure 1 showing the verb *epoiese* in the potter's signature (photo: the author)

Figure 8. Inscriptions on Side A of the amphora in Figure 1, behind the charioteer—nonsense inscription; in front of the charioteer's face—ANDOKIDES; beneath the horses' bellies—EPOIESE (made it); and in front of the horses—nonsense inscription (drawing: the author)

by Aristonothos.[10] In Attica, the first signatures appear about seventy years later, about 580 B.C. They are by Sophilos, who signed both as potter and as painter.[11] Next is Kleitias, who collaborated with the potter Ergotimos. The most famous of their collaborations is the François Vase in Florence,[12] but on a small stand of about 570 B.C. in the Metropolitan Museum, Kleitias and Ergotimos signed their names and the appropriate verb on the sloping surface of the stem.[13]

On Side A of MMA 1999.30, there are three inscriptions, one identifying the potter—on which we shall concentrate—and two that are nonsense. A nonsense inscription is composed of Greek letters whose sequence does not make a name or a word.[14] On the Andokides amphora, the two nonsense inscriptions

seem to be fillers, especially the one in the space in front of the team.

Of considerably more interest is the potting inscription (Figures 6–8). The name "Andokides" is written horizontally above the backs of the horses, and the verb appears vertically below their bellies; its last two or three letters seem a little too close together. This is the earliest preserved signature of Andokides.

Andokides is best known as the potter of early red-figured amphorae of Type A, the largest and the most impressive of the three variants of one-piece amphorae. The decoration of four of these amphorae is attributed to the Andokides Painter, who takes his name from the potter.[15] He is the earliest of the red-figure artists and was active about 530–515 B.C. The

Figure 9. Side A of an amphora of Type A signed by Andokides as potter and attributed to the Andokides Painter, ca. 530 B.C. H. 57.5 cm. The Metropolitan Museum of Art, Purchase, Joseph Pulitzer Bequest, 1963 (63.11.6)

Figure 10. Side A of an amphora signed by Andokides on the top of the mouth and attributed to Psiax, ca. 530 B.C. H. 39.5 cm. British Museum, London, B.M. 1980.11–29.1 (photo: courtesy the Trustees of the British Museum)

Andokides Painter is also the first red-figure painter of whose work we have enough examples to chart his chronology and establish his artistic personality.[16] The four extant amphorae of Type A signed by the potter Andokides and attributed to the Andokides Painter are these: MMA 63.11.6 (Figure 9); Berlin 2159; Louvre G 1; and Louvre F 203, a small amphora with the figures painted white instead of being left the reddish color of the clay ground, as is standard in red-figure practice.[17] This "white-figured" vase seems to be an experiment that was not repeated.

Figure 11. Detail of the amphora in Figure 10 showing the signature of Andokides on the top of the mouth (photo: courtesy the Trustees of the British Museum)

A fifth amphora of Type A signed by Andokides as potter is the bilingual one in Madrid attributed to Psiax, a versatile painter active in the Athenian Kerameikos from about 530 until 510 B.C.[18] A bilingual vase is decorated in both black-figure and red-figure and each technique is confined to one side of the vessel. The Madrid amphora is generally dated about 520 B.C. or possibly a little later. Each of these five signatures is incised on the torus of the foot in precise, neat letters and placed so that the initial **A** begins at the axis on the obverse (Figure 9).[19]

There is one more incised potting signature by Andokides. It occurs on the foot of a red-figured calyx-krater in the Villa Giulia, which also bears the incised signature of the painter Epiktetos written above the heads of the komasts on Side A.[20]

More pertinent to this article and to our amphora are two potting signatures of Andokides that are painted instead of incised. The first is written on the top of the mouth of a neck-amphora of special type once in the collection at Castle Ashby and now in the British Museum (Figures 10, 11).[21] This black-figured neck-amphora is attributed to Psiax, who also decorated

Figure 12. Side A of a bilingual cup signed by Andokides as potter and attributed to the Lysippides Painter, showing a fight under the handle, ca. 525 B.C. Diam. 53.5 cm. Museo Nazionale, Palermo, V 630 (photo: after *CVA* Palermo 1 [Italia 14], pl. 1 [658], 1)

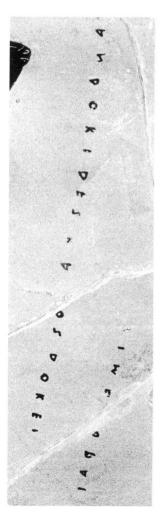

Figure 13. Detail of a hydria signed by Timagoras as potter and praising Andokides as *kalos*, ca. 550 B.C. H. 42 cm. Musée du Louvre, Paris, F 38 (photo: Louvre)

the signed bilingual in Madrid, and it is dated about 530 B.C. or a little later. The signature of Andokides is centered directly above the figures on Side A, which shows Dionysos holding a vine in his left hand and a drinking horn in his right. The god walks to the left between two cavorting satyrs, looking back at one of them.

The second painted signature of Andokides appears on an odd bilingual cup in Palermo, Museo Nazionale, V 650 (Figure 12), a collaboration between the Andokides Painter, who did the red-figured decoration, and his colleague the Lysippides Painter, who was responsible for the black-figured painting.[22] This is an eye-cup, so-named because a pair of apotropaic eyes appears on each side of the exterior.[23] Normally on bilinguals, each technique appears on just one side of the vessel, divided front and back as on the Madrid amphora just discussed. In part, this is the case with the Palermo cup. Black-figured archers appear between outline eyes on one side, and part of a red-figured archer is seen next to a red-figured eye on the other (the right half of this side is missing, but it would have had a similar eye). A most unexpected feature of this cup, however, is that the two techniques *overlap* in the handle zone, where combats take place between well-matched warriors fighting over a fallen comrade or enemy. In both fights, the injured man is drawn in black-figure against the light background, but his round shield is in red-figure with its emblems in black.[24] The effect is as peculiar as it is unique. On this cup, the signature of Andokides appears on the black-figured side above the left eyebrow, written retrograde, that is, from right to left, not left to right (see Figure 12).

The name "Andokides" appears on two other vases. The first is on a black-figured hydria attributed to the Taleides Painter, an artist active in the third quarter of the sixth century B.C.[25] The vase is signed by the potter Timagoras, and his inscription is painted vertically along the left side of the panel. Complementing it on the right is an inscription in which Timagoras praises Andokides: ΑΝΔΟΚΙΔΕΣΚΑ[Λ]ΟΣΔΟΚΕΙ and retrograde ΤΙΜΑ[Γ]ΟΡΑ / (Andokides seems *kalos* to Timagoras) (Figure 13). This hydria is usually dated soon after 550 B.C., a little earlier than MMA 1999.30, and the *kalos* name is one of the earliest. *Kalos* names praise youths, very likely well known or at least handsome young Athenians, in this case, Andokides. These names appear on Attic vases only; they begin around the middle of the sixth century B.C. and continue into the third quarter of the fifth, with the greatest concentration occurring in the late sixth and early fifth centuries B.C. The length of time a youth was considered *kalos* was about ten years or a little longer, though on occasion ancient authors refer to a man as *kalos*.[26]

The last instance in which the name of Andokides occurs is on a marble pillar for a bronze statue dedicated on the Athenian Akropolis about 530 B.C., thus a decade later than our amphora. There, his name appears with that of a potter named Mnesiades. The inscription, written vertically down the center, reads: M]ΝΕΣΙΑΔΕΣΚΕΡΑΜΕΥΣΜΕΚΑΙΑΝΔΟΚΙΔΕΣΑΝΕΘΕΚΕΝ (Mnesiades [the] potter and Andokides dedicated me).[27] On the Athenian Akropolis in the sixth century B.C., there were hundreds of dedications. They ranged from simple gifts made of inexpensive materials to monumental sculptures in bronze and marble and small objects made of precious materials. Understandably, most of these dedications have not survived. For the large sculptures, especially bronzes, the main evidence is epigraphical, gleaned from the inscribed bases, columns, and pillars that supported them.[28]

The Mnesiades-Andokides dedication is the earliest preserved potter dedication from the Athenian Akropolis that is inscribed on stone,[29] and since it supported a bronze statue, it may reflect the economic status enjoyed by these two potters as a result of their lucrative business.[30] This important dedication raises a number of interesting questions and issues that cannot be answered for lack of sufficient evidence but are worth considering. Other than its material, we can say very little about the statue that surmounted the pillar. Raubitschek, whose interest was epigraphical, not sculptural, simply says that the statue was fastened to the top of the pillar by means of the Samian technique; he describes the cuttings to receive the statue as four grooves forming a rectangle with an estimated length of 22 centimeters parallel to the front edge and an estimated depth of 36 centimeters. The surface between the grooves was left roughly picked.[31] Scheibler, following Raubitschek's description, suggests that the pillar probably supported an under-lifesize seated bronze statue of Athena.[32] The potter Peikon's dedication (mentioned above in note 29), a pedestal with part of a column shaft remaining, has a rectangular socket (not grooves) carved in its top surface; this feature prompted Raubitschek to suggest that the statue surmounting this column was "a seated figure rather than a standing kore," which would have a circular or generally oval base leaded into a socket of similar shape.[33] This may lend some credence to Scheibler's suggestion that the figure on our pillar was seated, though it may have been male, not female. On the analogy of the potter relief discussed in note 29 above, the statue surmounting the Mnesiades-Andokides column may have been a bronze statue of a seated potter. More than this, one cannot really say.

The wording of the inscription clearly links Mnesi-

ades with the word "potter" (κεραμεύς) and by implication also includes Andokides as a potter, thus assuming that they worked together.[34] I disagree with the interpretation by Vickers and Gill that the word κεραμεύς refers to Kerameis, a deme or township in ancient Attica, rather than to Mnesiades' occupation, and also with their suggestion that Andokides is not the same person as the potter who signed our vase and later codedicated the statue on the Akropolis.[35] For me, Beazley's and Raubitschek's judgments remain entirely persuasive. Beazley writes: "[M]nesiades is otherwise unknown, but Andokides must be the famous potter in whose workshop the red-figure technique was probably first employed."[36] Raubitschek thinks that Mnesiades may very well have been a potter who worked with Andokides and concludes: "It is certain, however, that the word κεραμεύς refers to the dedicator's occupation, not to the deme, Kerameikos."[37] So far, the signatures of Mnesiades and Andokides do not appear together on the same vase, but this is no reason to dismiss their collaborative dedication on the Akropolis.[38] Scheibler thinks that Mnesiades may be the older because he is named first, and she wonders if the two might be father and son.[39] I find the idea that Mnesiades was older than Andokides attractive because the two known signatures of Mnesiades are earlier than the Akropolis dedication and MMA 1999.30, as well as all the other known signatures of Andokides. They occur on vases of about 550–540 B.C. and thus are contemporary with the hydria in the Louvre mentioned above that is signed by Timagoras as potter and praises Andokides as *kalos* (Figure 13).

The first known signature of Mnesiades appears on the shoulder of a black-figured hydria in the collection of Herbert Cahn in Basel.[40] The potting inscription, which is complete, is written vertically next to the right side of the panel, behind a figure crouching to left: ΜΝΕΣΙΑΔΕΣΕΠΟΙΕΣΝ. This warrior holds a large, round shield emblazoned with the hindquarters and tail of a horse drawn in accessory white with incised details. In front of the warrior's face is written: ΑΡΙΣΤΟΜ[ΕΝΕΣΚΑΛΟΣ], retrograde.[41] The second potting signature of Mnesiades is less well preserved, for only the first four letters of the name remain: ΜΝΕΣ[ΙΑΔΕΣ, retrograde. It occurs on a fragmentary Panathenaic Prize amphora dedicated on the Athenian Akropolis by an unknown victor in the games honoring Athena and is attributed by Beazley to the manner of the Princeton Painter.[42] This is a precanonical prize vase because Athena (fragment *a*) does not appear between columns. Also, this Panathenaic amphora has a potting signature, and fragment *b* (from the reverse) bears an inscription that tells us the subject was a race for men called the *diaulos*.[43]

On canonical prize Panathenaics, potting signatures do not appear before the end of the fifth century B.C.

As for the more tantalizing question raised by Scheibler, whether Andokides could be the son of Mnesiades, there is no proof one way or the other, and barring the future discovery of an inscription with a patronymic or a filial noun, we shall never know for sure. Still, chronological factors do not rule out the possibility.

As mentioned above, Andokides is praised as *kalos* by the potter Timagoras on a hydria that may be dated shortly after 550 B.C., and the length of time for a youth to be considered *kalos* was about ten years or a little longer.[44] If Andokides was in his mid-to-late teens at this time—that is, the early 540s—it would mean that he was probably born about the middle of the 560s. If this Andokides is the same Andokides who took up potting, it would strengthen the suggestion that he was younger than Mnesiades. The two vases signed by Mnesiades may be dated about 550–540 B.C. and thus are more or less contemporary with Timagoras's hydria. The evidence strongly suggests that at this time Mnesiades was already established as a potter and, if so, would have reached maturity, having been born in the late 590s or early 580s.

Although we really know nothing about the training of potters in the Athenian Kerameikos, presumably they began young.[45] It is very possible that Andokides was a youth when he began his apprenticeship as potter. At this time he would have developed the strength and coordination needed to shape a pot from a lump of heavy clay centered on a rapidly turning wheel. If Mnesiades was the older man, as he seems to be from the epigraphical evidence, he could have provided the proper instruction to the young Andokides. MMA 1999.30 not only is the earliest preserved vase signed by Andokides but also exhibits features that suggest he had not yet acquired the potting skills on which his fame would later rest (Figures 1, 2). Our amphora lacks the crisp, tight contours of the potter's later vases, such as MMA 63.11.6 (Figure 9). The proportions are top-heavy, for the mouth is 2 centimeters wider in diameter than the foot. This difference would be negligible in a vase 60 centimeters or more in height, but it is quite noticeable in one that stands only 26 centimeters high, including its lid. The elevation of the mouth as well as the rosettes decorating its side add to the top-heaviness. Yet the attention to details such as the precise tooling of the edges of the mouth and foot reveals the care with which Andokides applied the finishing touches to his vase before the clay dried and the pot was fired. The potting of this amphora suggests someone who has learned his lessons but has not yet mastered his craft. Is it possible,

nevertheless, that for Andokides, this vase was significant enough an achievement at this stage of his career that he proudly signed his name to it?[46] We probably shall never know for sure, but it is tempting to think so.

The next vases bearing the signature of Andokides are wholly accomplished. These are the London neck-amphora of special shape decorated by Psiax (Figure 10), and MMA 63.11.6 (Figure 9) and Berlin 2159 both by the Andokides Painter.[47] Each vase reveals the considerable potting skills that Andokides exhibited until about 520–515 B.C., when his latest preserved signature is recorded.[48] The London and New York vases may be dated about 530 B.C., the one in Berlin a little bit later.[49] These three vases are about contemporary with the bronze dedication on the Akropolis. Raubitschek thinks that "most of the potters must have made their dedications towards the end of their career."[50] He is referring specifically to Euphronios's dedication, made long after that artist ceased to paint and had become a potter (see note 29 above), but in view of the chronology offered here for Mnesiades, the latter could have made his dedication with Andokides late in his career. None of these observations, of course, can answer the question raised by Scheibler as to whether Mnesiades and Andokides were father and son, respectively, but their chronology and the frequent occurrence of father-son potting associations during the third quarter of the sixth century favor such a possibility.

In any case, given the information known to us and presented here, it seems to me that the Andokides named in the *kalos* inscription and in the Akropolis dedication could well be the potter of our amphora.[51]

For more than a century, various scholars have thought the amphorae of Type A by Andokides indicate that for a time he worked with Exekias, who favored the shape and signed as both potter and painter the earliest known canonical example, the famous amphora in the Vatican of about 530 B.C.[52] Exekias signed this vase on the top of the mouth. Andokides also signed the London neck-amphora on the top of the mouth. The two vases are roughly contemporary. Did Andokides get the idea from Exekias?[53] As early as 1887, Wilhelm Klein linked Andokides with Exekias: "Der Meister [Andokides] ist in den Traditionen der archaischen Technik aufgewachsen. Exekias blickt als Vorbild überall durch, so dass die Vermuthung, er wäre sein Lehrer gewesen, sehr nahe liegt. Schon die Gefässformen und die beträchtlichen Dimensionen erinnern an ihn."[54] In his publication of the Metropolitan Museum's red-figured amphora signed by Andokides, Dietrich von Bothmer remarked: "As a potter, Andokides is in the tradition of Exekias and may be considered his follower."[55] Bothmer went on to suggest that some of the late works attributed to Exekias but not signed by him as potter may have been made by Andokides. He stopped short of citing specific examples. In 1978 Beth Cohen noted peculiar features shared by some of the two potters' signatures,[56] namely, the omission of the iota from *epoiesen,* the verb for "potting." This occurs in all of Andokides' *incised* signatures and twice in Exekias's painted ones: Berlin 1720 (see note 11 above) and Munich 2044 (see note 24 above). She thought that "Exekias was probably the potter Andokides' master,"[57] but did not elaborate. In 1991, Cohen restated her belief that the potter Andokides was a pupil of Exekias and later wrote that she thought Andokides learned from Exekias how to incise his signature.[58] Webster went so far as to say that Andokides "seems to have taken over the workshop of Exekias."[59] Later, he modified this: "Andokides[9] made an early amphora for a member of Group E and carried on the Exekias potting tradition into the red-figure period."[60] Having Andokides take over Exekias's shop may be stretching things a good bit, though it would be perfectly possible, since the signatures of Andokides seem to outlast both the potting and painting ones of Exekias, at least as they are known at the present time.

Following is a summary of the chronology and career of Andokides as suggested above. Andokides is praised as *kalos* by Timagoras on a hydria in the Louvre of about 550–540 B.C. His name next appears as the potter of MMA 1999.30, which may be dated on stylistic grounds to about 540 B.C.; for reasons given above, I believe it is an early work by a potter destined for greater fame as attested by his signature on the splendid later vases. In the late 530s, Andokides may have begun to work with Exekias and to learn from him how to make amphorae of Type A and to incise his signature on the glazed torus foot so it would stand out clearly and sharply. MMA 63.11.6 (Figure 9) and Berlin 2159, both early works by the Andokides Painter, are signed on the foot in crisply incised letters, a manner of signing that Andokides made his own, as indicated by his other signatures discussed briefly on page 20. Also, about this time, Andokides made the Akropolis dedication with Mnesiades.

Admittedly, all of our hypotheses are predicated on the supposition that the Andokides who was praised as *kalos* was the same person who became a famous potter and not a young Athenian of the same name belonging to a wealthy family. Furthermore, while each of these bits of evidence (*kalos* name, early potting signature, mature potting signatures, dedication on the Akropolis, activity with Exekias and also, as we shall see, probably with Nikosthenes), if taken by

itself, does not tell us very much about Andokides, when considered together, they help to map his career.

One more aspect of our signature needs consideration, namely its placement within the figural composition (Figures 1, 6, 7). We do not know for sure if the potter himself always signed his own name or if he delegated the task to the painter, who would be more adept with brush and glaze.[61] It is worth while, however, to consider the question. In the case of potters who were also painters, it seems reasonable to assume that they wrote their own names and verbs plus any other inscriptions. Sophilos, Nearchos, and Exekias are obvious examples, and in each case the character and quality of their letters complement the drawing.[62] Comparison of each painted signature of Andokides with the drawing on the vase reveals stylistic similarities between the two. On the London amphora attributed to Psiax (Figures 10, 11), the position of the inscription and the carefully written letters are in keeping with the precise drawing on the neck. On the Palermo cup (Figure 12), the letters are not so neat, nor is the drawing.[63] On MMA 1999.30, the situation is similar. The letters are a little sloppy and so is some of the drawing (see pp. 26–27 below for a discussion of the letters and p. 31 below for the drawing). After studying in detail the drawing and the inscriptions on these three vases, I have concluded that in each case the painter was responsible for both the figures *and* the inscriptions. On the other hand, I think the potter probably indicated to the painter the place in which he wanted his name and the verb to appear.

As we have seen, a potting signature normally appears in one of two places. It may be written completely apart from the figural decoration, as on the London neck-amphora attributed to Psiax (Figure 11) and on Andokides' amphora of Type A in the Metropolitan Museum (Figure 9).[64] More often, however, particularly on Attic black-figured ware, the signature appears within the figural composition. It is this latter placement that is pertinent to our amphora, for it may provide another workshop connection for Andokides. Normally, signatures within the figural decoration are written so that the name and the verb appear together, either in one line or in two. Good examples are on the François Vase signed by Ergotimos and Kleitias and the Akropolis kantharos by Nearchos with the double signature.[65] Contemporary with Andokides, the most important signatures are those of Amasis and Exekias, who carefully relate name and verb to the figures; in their signatures the name is *never* separated from the verb.[66] There are not too many exceptions to this arrangement in general,[67] but the signature of one potter is especially significant. He was Nikosthenes, who ran a very successful pottery

Figure 14. Detail of the top of the mouth of a black-figured volute-krater signed by Nikosthenes as potter, ca. 530 B.C. H. 37.5 cm. British Museum, London, B.M. 1842.4–7.17 (B 364) (photo: courtesy the Trustees of the British Museum)

shop during the third quarter of the sixth century and later (545–510 B.C.), with his largest output occurring between 530 and 515 B.C., at exactly the time when Andokides enjoyed his greatest fame as a potter.[68]

The name "Nikosthenes" appears on vases more often than that of any other Greek potter known.[69] The signatures are usually placed within the figural composition or, infrequently, elsewhere on the vase. Usually the name and the verb are not separated by figures, but on seven known vases they are.[70] One more possible Nicosthenic link with Andokides is the placement of the latter's signature above the left eye on the black-figured side of his cup in Palermo (Figure 12). A review of the eye-cups bearing the signature of Nikosthenes[71] reveals that the inscription may be written in various places, but most often appears in the area of one or both eyes. Nikosthenes' cup in Malibu, which is contemporary with the Palermo cup, has the inscription written above the left eyebrow, but from left to right, not retrograde.[72]

Thus, the evidence suggests that Andokides worked with three potters. One, of course, is Mnesiades, though the actual potting evidence is slender due to the lack of surviving material. A second may be Nikosthenes. Besides the comparable placement of the signatures within the figural decoration, another link between the two may be the signatures on the top of the mouth of two vases in London, the neck-amphora signed by Andokides (Figure 11) and the volute-krater signed by Nikosthenes (Figure 14), as well as the latter's signed psykter in Houston.[73] This unusual placement of a potting signature is known so far three times in the work of Exekias, who as potter may have exerted the greatest influence on Andokides, teaching him to create the splendid amphora of Type A with all its subtle nuances and perhaps instructing him how to incise fine and sure letters through the black glaze.

Admittedly, these observations are based solely on the artistic and epigraphical evidence; still, the conclusion should not be dismissed for mere lack of historical fact. Artists are often gregarious individuals who enjoy communicating with and learning from one another, and there is no good reason to think they were any different in the Kerameikos of the sixth century B.C. than they are in Soho and Chelsea today.

THE PAINTER

The inscription on Side A of MMA 1999.30 says that Andokides potted our amphora, but who painted it? In order to attribute a vase, it is necessary to consider its general appearance, the choice of ornament, and the style of drawing. It is possible that the potter, not the painter, chose the ornamental patterns, since these frequently emphasize details of shape, but it is quite likely that the painter executed them, since he would wield a brush more skillfully. Subject matter may also be a factor in determining who painted a vase. Some vases may be attributed very easily to a painter because the style of drawing is clearly his. Others require longer study before their painters can be recognized, and some appear destined to remain orphans.[74]

Many of the potting peculiarities of MMA 1999.30, in particular the relatively large size of its mouth and its top-heavy look, have already been discussed. Another oddity concerns the choice of ornaments to articulate sections of the vase and to frame the figures. A brief description and an illustration of a typical amphora of Type B contemporary with MMA 1999.30 will reveal how elaborately decorated the latter is by comparison. MMA 56.171.12, by a painter from Group E, may serve as an example (Figure 15).[75] The

Figure 15. Side B of an amphora of Type B attributed to Group E, ca. 540 B.C. H. 40 cm. The Metropolitan Museum of Art, Fletcher Fund, 1956 (56.171.12)

Figure 16. Side A of a Nicosthenic amphora signed by Nikosthenes as potter and attributed to Painter N, ca. 540 B.C. H. 29.5 cm. Villa Giulia, Rome, 20863 (photo: after Tosto, *ΝΙΚΟΣΘΕΝΕΣΕΠΟΙΕΣΕΝ*, pl. 91)

side of the mouth is glazed, not decorated with ornament. On each side, the figures are set in a panel surrounded by black glaze and framed by ornament at the top only, usually by a lotus-palmette festoon or a lotus-palmette chain, or even by a simple chain of palmettes. There is no ornamental configuration beneath each handle separating obverse from reverse. Rays appear above the foot. The general effect is restrained and sober, in marked contrast with MMA 1999.30.

This observation holds true for the lids of Type A and Type B amphorae as well as for the lids of neck-amphorae. Most often, lid and pot do not survive together; sometimes they do but have become separated. In some cases, just the lid remains, and in lucky instances, both components stayed together.[76] In spite of the relative dearth of lids compared with vessels, we have enough lids belonging to one-piece amphorae and to neck-amphorae to make clear that their systems of decoration are normally very different from the lid of MMA 1999.30. In general, their appearance is rather conservative. Often the knob is in the shape of a pomegranate and glazed. A zone of rays encircles

the base of the knob and the only other pattern is the one that decorates the brim, often a frieze of ivy.[77] By comparison, the lid of MMA 1999.30 is very ornamental and complements the colorful appearance of the pot quite well.

In the section on potting signatures, connections with the workshops of Exekias and Nikosthenes were discussed, but these concern the making, not the decorating of vases. There is nothing Execian in the drawing on MMA 1999.30, but there are connections with the Nikosthenes Workshop, the painters of Group E, the Princeton Painter, and his close colleagues.

Let us begin with Nikosthenes. The inscriptions on MMA 1999.30, which I think were written by the painter, share certain features with those by Nikosthenes. The signatures of Nikosthenes are always legible, but in general they lack the precision of placement and the perfect letter forms of those by his famous contemporaries Amasis and Exekias. The letters are quite often rather messy and lack uniformity, much as if they had been drawn with an old brush that had worn or missing bristles. Sometimes there is not quite enough space for all the letters, so the inscrip-

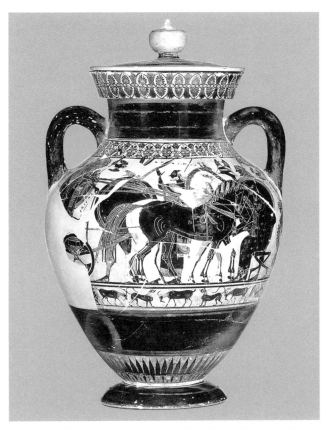

Figure 17. Side B of an amphora of Type B attributed to Group E, ca. 540–530 B.C. H. 47.5 cm. British Museum, London, B.M. 1839.11–9.1 (B 147) (photo: courtesy the Trustees of the British Museum)

Figure 18. Detail of handle B/A of the amphora in Figure 17 (photo: after Paul Jacobsthal, *Ornamente griechischer Vasen* [Berlin, 1927], pl. 18b)

tion may have to take a sharp turn to fit in. At other times, the letters are not spaced uniformly, but grouped as if to form units or syllables, and this results in a somewhat fragmented appearance. The signature of Andokides on MMA 1999.30 exhibits all of these features, but not to the degree that they appear on vases signed by Nikosthenes.[78]

The colorful character of MMA 1999.30 makes it comparable to the products of the Nikosthenes Workshop, and some of the patterns also find parallels there, notably the lotus-palmette configuration, which our painter placed below each handle. A similar ornament appears on the neck of quite a few of Nikosthenes' amphorae of the special type known as Nicosthenic.[79] This pattern, a lotus-palmette cross, is characterized by addorsed vertical lotuses flanked by horizontal palmettes. It is an old motif, reaching back to the early decades of the sixth century B.C.[80] The painters in the Nikosthenes Workshop gave it their own interpretation, mainly by leaving the hearts of the palmettes relatively plain instead of decorating them with incision, by linking the units horizontally with tangential circles that are either plain or dotted, and

by drawing tendrils that terminate in tightly wound spirals that often have more than one revolution. The pattern is not found on vases elsewhere, and it was used throughout the life span of the Nikosthenes Workshop.[81] The configuration at each handle of MMA 1999.30 compares with two contemporary examples by Painter N, the most prominent and prolific artist of the Nikosthenes Workshop: Kurashiki, Ninagawa Museum, formerly Paris, André Jameson collection; and Rome, Villa Giulia 20863 (Figure 16).[82]

The rosettes on the side of the mouth and the ivy above the figures on MMA 1999.30 deserve consideration. The idea of decorating the side of the mouth of an amphora of Type B with a frieze of rosettes started with the Gorgon Painter, who was active in the opening years of the sixth century,[83] but it is more common in the work of the Painter of London B 76, who flourished during the second quarter of the century.[84] Still, its appearance on the mouths of amphorae is the exception in Attic painting. As far as I can tell, a frieze of rosettes is not an ornamental pattern favored by Nicosthenic painters: I have found it once, on the back of each handle of Louvre F 100 by Painter N, and its appearance there is as unexpected as it is on the mouth of our amphora.[85] One further link with the Nikosthenes Workshop is the ribbon pattern on the lid of MMA 1999.30 (Figure 5), an ornament that appears on many different shapes produced in the workshop.[86]

The use of ivy on our amphora, where it continues around the neck without interruption, including under the handles, is rare.[87] Ivy appears most often on the brims of lids and on the handle flanges of volute-kraters and amphorae of Type A (Figure 9). These always have the leaves back-to-back, with or without stems—sometimes with dots between the leaves, more often without—and the separating stem may be wavy or straight.

The comparisons cited above suggest that the painter of our amphora was quite familiar with the products of the Nikosthenes Workshop, particularly some by Painter N. But there also appear to be links with painters of Group E, artists who were active during the third quarter of the sixth century and were, as Beazley once put it, "the soil from which the art of Exekias springs."[88] Webster claimed authorship of our New York vase for a painter from Group E, but without offering details.[89] Much of the output of the Group E Workshop is rather conservative, and the amphora described above on page 26 illustrates this very well (Figure 15). But some of their vases are pertinent to MMA 1999.30. One is London, B.M. 1839.11–9.1 (B 147),[90] an amphora of Type B that has an elegant lotus-palmette chain on the side of the mouth, a frieze of animals below the figures that continues around the vase, and stacked rays above the foot (Figures 17, 18). While both vases share one obvious feature—the side of the mouth is ornamented rather than left black—other details may be more significant. First of all, the figures on the London vase are not set in panels, but extend to the handles, where the two sides are separated by a lotus-palmette cross placed below the handle root. The upper tendrils of the cross wind around the root itself, which is superimposed over the cuff of a lotus, as it is on MMA 1999.30. There is a palmette painted below the upper handle attachment. The palmettes of the London configuration have large hearts, mostly reserved, similar to those on our amphora, and while the chain linking the elements is more elaborate on the London amphora, each link has a large dot in it, just like ours. The lotus-palmette chain above the figures extends to the handles and even a bit under them, a curious feature almost like the ivy on our amphora.

The dots in the links of the palmette-lotus crosses on MMA 1999.30 introduce one other contemporary painter who frequently used large dots in the links of his chains. This is the Princeton Painter, and a good

Figure 19. Side A of a neck-amphora of Panathenaic shape by the Princeton Painter, ca. 530 B.C. The Art Museum, Princeton University, Trumbull-Prime Collection, 1889, Princeton 169 (photo: Clem Fiori)

example of such detail occurs on his name piece, a neck-amphora of Panathenaic shape (Figure 19).[91] This is also a vase where the pattern immediately above the figures, in this case black tongues, continues around the neck without interruption. Figures, not ornament, appear below the handles. The arrangement of figures and ornament recurs on a neck-amphora of Panathenaic shape by a painter of Group E, Tarquinia RC 1061.[92]

These comparisons between the ornaments on MMA 1999.30 and those on some contemporary vases suggest that our amphora was painted by an artist who absorbed much of what he saw around him without copying slavishly and without following the conventions governing the ornamental decoration of most amphorae of Type B. That he was very much his own man is borne out by the figure drawing, which has an eclectic character to it.

We may begin with the horses, which are much better drawn than the human figures and look as if they would quickly provide criteria for identifying our painter. They have small, well-bred looking heads, proudly arched necks, muscular bodies, and slender, clean-boned legs. They look well fed and cared for. The closest counterparts to the chariot team on MMA 1999.30 are found on two Group E amphorae of Type B of about 540 B.C. The first is Munich 1396, which shows a chariot scene on its obverse.[93] These horses have the same small, refined heads, strongly arched necks and filled-out bodies, but there is no white pole horse and the animals' hindquarters are not as powerfully built as are those of MMA 1999.30. Closer to our horses are those on London, B.M. B 160 (Figure 20).[94] The team holds their heads in almost exactly the same position as our horses, and their bodies are plump and healthy-looking; moreover, the right-hand pole horse is white and has a red rein crossing its neck. But because their legs are longer than the legs of the horses on MMA 1999.30, the proportions are more pleasing overall.

Details of equine anatomy as well as of harnessing reveal further links between MMA 1999.30 and painters of Group E and the Princeton Painter. Foremost in importance are the concentric arcs on the hindquarters of both of our right-hand trace horses (Figures 1, 2); sometimes two similar arcs appear on the inside of the left hind leg (Figure 2). This treatment of the hindquarters is standard for horses of Group E and appears frequently in the work of the Princeton Painter—his name piece, for example (Figure 19), or London, B.M. 1843.11–3.100 (B 212).[95] See also Munich 1376, an amphora attributed to the manner of the Princeton Painter.[96] Here, however, the lines do not continue to the inside of the left hind leg. By the end of the 530s B.C., two converging lines became the conventional means of showing the musculature of equine hindquarters.

More difficult to parallel are the two biconcave arcs

Figure 20. Side A of an amphora of Type B attributed to Group E, ca. 540 B.C. H. 41.1 cm. British Museum, London, B.M. B 160 (photo: courtesy the Trustees of the British Museum)

Figure 21. Detail of a hydria probably in the manner of the Princeton Painter, ca. 540 B.C. H. 38 cm. Museo del Palazzo dei Conservatori, Rome, 158 (photo: after *CVA*, Musei Capitolini 1 [Italia 36], pl. 26 [1626], 1)

Figure 22. Side A of an amphora of Type B attributed to the Princeton Painter, ca. 540 B.C. H. 38.4 cm. The Metropolitan Museum of Art, Fletcher Fund, 1956 (56.171.9)

Figure 23. Detail of the eagle on Side B of the amphora in Figure 1 (photo: the author)

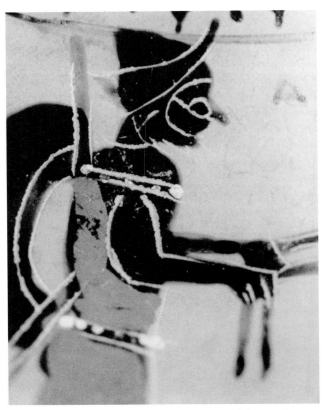

Figure 24. Detail of the charioteer on Side A of the amphora in Figure 1 (photo: the author)

on the shoulders of our trace horses (Figures 1, 2). The formula used by painters of Group E consists of two biconvex arcs, with or without a short stroke between (Figure 20). I have been able to find this odd biconcave motif only once elsewhere, on the horses wheeling around on an unattributed hydria in the Museo del Palazzo dei Conservatori in Rome (Figure 21).[97] The hydria is probably by the same hand as Munich 1376, attributed to the manner of the Princeton Painter, and both of them bring MMA 1999.30 a little closer to him, for they depict harness details not known in Group E work. An oddity of our amphora is that the headstalls of the trace horses on Side A have *both* throatlatches *and* browbands. Throatlatches, which prevent the headstall from slipping off the head of the animal, are the norm in both art and life. Browbands are decorative and also help to hold the headstall in place but may be dispensed with as they often are today in American Western riding. Browbands *and* throatlatches are common features on horses executed by the Princeton Painter, whether they are mounts or chariot teams (Figure 22), and as far as I know, he is the only artist to include these harness parts consistently. They are also worn by the two trace horses on Rome, Conservatori 158, mentioned above, which may be in the manner of the Princeton Painter (Figure 21).[98] Also, each trace horse on this hydria has small circles at the mouthpiece of its bit, much like the circle on the bit of the right-hand trace horse on Side B of MMA 1999.30 (Figure 2), which I think represents a bit burr.[99]

Another harness detail takes us back to horses by painters of Group E, and to a lesser extent to those by the Princeton Painter and his manner. This is the

girth, visible on each right-hand trace horse, a harness part that went out of fashion in vase painting during the 530s B.C. The painters of Group E treat this strap in a very distinctive manner (Figure 17). It is always knotted at shoulder level so that the loop hangs down next to the start of the rib cage, the ends overlap the shoulder, and the section of the strap above the knot is slightly wider than the part below it. This is exactly the configuration on MMA 1999.30 (Figures 1, 2). The Princeton Painter varies his drawing of this harness part. Sometimes, it may be a single line, as on MMA 56.171.9 (Figure 22); it may be a double line as on Rome, Villa Giulia 910; or it may be omitted altogether, as on the artist's name piece (Figure 19).[100] When the girth is included, the loop of the tie overlaps the shoulder and the ends extend toward the hindquarters. In other words, in this feature it is exactly the opposite of Group E and our amphora. Also, when the girth is indicated by a double line, the strap is of equal width throughout. Exceptions to this

Figure 26. Detail of a pyxis probably by Exekias, ca. 540 B.C. Brauron, no number (photo: after Eleni Manakidou, Παραστάσεις με άρματα [8ος–5ος αι π.Χ.] [Thessaloniki, 1994], pl. 11, γ)

Figure 25. Detail of the man in front of the chariot team on Side B of the amphora in Figure 1 (photo: the author)

occur, however, on Munich 1376, in the manner of the Princeton Painter, and on Rome, Conservatori 158 (Figure 21), perhaps by the same hand. On both of these, the section of the girth above the knot is wider than the section below it, as on our amphora, but the knot is tied according to the preference of the Princeton Painter, not of the painters of Group E.

There is one further link with Group E, though perhaps a minor one. An eagle flying to left with a snake in its beak is tucked away in the upper right of the composition on Side B of London, B.M. 1839.11–9.1 (B 147) (Figure 18). It compares with our eagle (Figure 23), though our snake is considerably longer than the one on the Group E amphora.

If we had only the horses to consider for attributing MMA 1999.30, we would make a case for a painter from Group E or the Princeton Painter or one in his manner. But the drawing of the human figures and the composition on each side tell a different story.

In the *comparanda* discussed above, the scenes are

full, often with densely overlapping figures. Good examples are London, B.M. 1839.11–9.1 (B 147) and London, B.M. B 160 (Figures 17, 20) from Group E, the name piece of the Princeton Painter (Figure 19), and the hydria in the Museo del Palazzo dei Conservatori that may be in his manner (Figure 21). By comparison, the arrangement of the figures on MMA 1999.30 seems timid, with only the horses forming a tight group. The drawing of the horses on MMA 1999.30 is, by contrast, quite accomplished and sure, suggesting to me that the painter may simply have "copied" a conventional composition standard in Attic vase painting beginning with the Gorgon Painter.[101]

By comparison, the drawing of the human figures and even that of the eagle with the snake in its mouth are far inferior. The incision is rather coarse and the glaze and accessory color are carelessly applied. This is particularly apparent in the case of the charioteer on Side A (Figure 24). He has a huge eye but no mouth, the drawing of his hands is quite inarticulate, one contour of his upper right arm is partly redrawn (without significant improvement), and the red is applied to his chiton in a slapdash manner. The charioteer on Side B is comparable. He, too, has a large eye, and his arm and hands are carelessly executed.

On the other hand, the small man in front of the horses on Side B (Figure 25)—far more accomplished in its drawing—is somewhat reminiscent of the youths leading the horses of Stesagoras's victorious team on a pyxis probably by Exekias that is datable to about 540 B.C. (Figure 26).[102] The body build is similar: broad shoulders with torso tapering to a thin waist, ample thighs, slender calves, and long feet. The man on MMA 1999.30 is slightly more animated than

Exekias's youth, for he holds a branch aloft, probably waving it slightly.[103] But this is a marginal difference. The idea of showing a male figure walking in front of a horse, not standing before it, is the same.

Examination of our painter's ornamental patterns and details of his drawing leads to connections with workshops, but not to an outright attribution. The painter of MMA 1999.30 seems to have been influenced by some of the painters he saw around him, most specifically, Painter N from the workshop of Nikosthenes, painters from the Group E Workshop, the Princeton Painter and those in his immediate circle, and perhaps the young Exekias. Our amphora is not by one of these artists, and I have not been able to find any vases that are undeniably by the same hand.

There remains one option to consider, namely, that Andokides himself decorated this amphora. There is no tangible evidence from his later work as a mature potter that Andokides ever tried his hand at decorating one of his vases. One may not, however, exclude this possibility in the case of his earliest preserved, signed vase. The chronology for Andokides, as I have tried to establish it, indicates that he was young and still learning his craft when he made and signed MMA 1999.30. Its top-heavy proportions and small size, compared with the elegant refinement and large size of the signed vases of his maturity, suggest a young man at work, applying lessons he has not yet perfected. Furthermore, the young Andokides must have been aware of the beautiful vases decorated by Exekias and the painters of Group E, or the Princeton Painter and his companions, perhaps even the Amasis Painter. Might it be that, fresh with enthusiasm for his youthful potting achievement, Andokides picked up brush and stylus to try his hand at painting? Such a bold idea may seem completely fanciful, even far-fetched. Still, everything about MMA 1999.30 convinces me that Andokides painted it, not another artist. This would explain, especially, the variation in the quality of the drawing: the painstaking attention to the ornament, both chariot teams, and the man in front of the horses on Side B, on the one hand; and the rather careless execution of the charioteers and the eagle, on the other. When Andokides had a model to guide him, his results were quite respectable. When he wanted to see what he could do on his own, here and perhaps elsewhere on pieces that have not survived or are not yet recognized, his eagerness to become an accomplished painter greatly surpassed his ability to fulfill his ambition. When Andokides realized this, he chose to perfect his innate potting skills and leave the decorating to others. The rest, as they say, is history.

ACKNOWLEDGMENTS

I particularly wish to thank Joan R. Mertens for reading a draft of this article, for making very many helpful suggestions, and also for encouraging me to draw sharper and stronger conclusions. I also wish to thank Martine Denoyelle, Jasper Gaunt, Elfriede R. Knauer, Heide Mommsen, and Stephen P. Tracy for their help in various ways.

ABBREVIATIONS

ABV
John D. Beazley. *Attic Black-Figure Vase-Painters.* Oxford, 1956.

*Addenda*²
Thomas H. Carpenter. *Beazley Addenda: Additional References to ABV, ARV², and Paralipomena.* Oxford, 1989.

Agora XXIII
Mary B. Moore and Mary Z. Philippides. *The Athenian Agora.* Vol. XXIII, *The Attic Black-Figured Pottery.* Princeton, 1986.

AJA
American Journal of Archaeology

*ARV*²
John D. Beazley. *Attic Red-Figure Vase-Painters.* 2nd ed. Oxford, 1963.

Beazley, *Development*
John D. Beazley. *The Development of Attic Black-Figure.* 1951; 1964; 3rd ed., Berkeley, 1986.

Beazley, *Potter and Painter*
John D. Beazley. *Potter and Painter in Ancient Athens.* London, [1946].

Bothmer, "Andokides"
Dietrich von Bothmer. "Andokides the Potter and the Andokides Painter." *MMAB* 24 (1966), pp. 201–12.

BSA
British School at Athens Annual

Cohen, *Attic Bilingual Vases*
Beth Cohen. *Attic Bilingual Vases and Their Painters.* New York, 1978.

Cohen, "Literate Potter"
Beth Cohen. "The Literate Potter: A Tradition of Incised Signatures on Attic Vases." *MMJ* 26 (1991), pp. 49–95.

CVA
Corpus Vasorum Antiquorum

Immerwahr, *Attic Script*
Henry R. Immerwahr. *Attic Script: A Survey.* Oxford, 1990.

JHS
The Journal of Hellenic Studies
Paralipomena
John D. Beazley. *Paralipomena: Additions to Attic Black-Figure Vase-Painters and to Attic Red-Figure Vase-Painters.* Oxford, 1971.

Raubitschek, *Dedications*
Antony E. Raubitschek. *Dedications from the Athenian Akropolis.* Cambridge, Mass., 1949.

Scheibler, "Künstlervotive"
Ingeborg Scheibler. "Griechische Künstlervotive der archaischen Zeit." *Münchner Jahrbuch der bildenden Kunst* 30 (1979), pp. 7–39.

Scheibler, *Töpferkunst*
Ingeborg Scheibler. *Griechische Töpferkunst: Herstellung, Handel und Gebrauch der antiken Tongefässe.* Munich, 1983.

Tosto, *ΝΙΚΟΣΘΕΝΕΣΕΠΟΙΕΣΕΝ*
Vincent Tosto. *Black-Figure Pottery Signed ΝΙΚΟΣΘΕΝΕΣΕΠΟΙΕΣΕΝ.* Allard Pierson Series 11. Amsterdam, 1999.

Webster, *Potter and Patron*
Thomas B. L. Webster. *Potter and Patron in Classical Athens.* London, 1972.

NOTES

1. L.64.31a, b; acc. no. 1999.30a, b. Bibliography: Christie's, London, sale cat., July 15, 1948, lot 12, ill.; Parke Bernet, New York, sale cat., December 7, 1951, lot 8, ill.; *ABV*, p. 253, top; Cornelius C. Vermeule and Dietrich von Bothmer, "Notes on a New Edition of Michaelis, *Ancient Marbles in Great Britain, Part Two,*" *AJA* 60 (1956), p. 346, pl. 112, figs. 34, 35; D. von Bothmer, *Ancient Art from New York Private Collections* (New York, 1961), p. 51, cat. no. 198, pl. 73; Bothmer, "Andokides," p. 207, fig. 8; Enrico Paribeni, "Attici Vasi," *Enciclopedia dell'arte antica classicae orientale,* suppl. 1970 (Rome, 1973), p. 100, fig. 103; *Paralipomena,* p. 113; Cohen, *Attic Bilingual Vases,* p. 3, pl. 1,2; *Addenda²,* p. 65; Beazley, *Development,* p. 69 and pl. 79,1; Diana Buitron-Oliver, in *Antiquities from the Collection of Christos Bastis,* Emma Swan Hall, ed. (New York, 1987), pp. 248–50, cat. no. 150.

   Dimensions and condition: Height to top of lid 26 cm; to top of mouth 24.7 cm; diam. of mouth 11.5 cm; width of rim 1 cm; diam. of body 14.7 cm; diam. of foot 9.6 cm; width of resting surface 1 cm. Knob of lid missing. Both handles and the foot reattached. A few chips on edge of mouth, on brim of lid, and on edge of foot. Some of the accessory white on each of the pole horses and on the charioteer's petasos on Side B has flaked.

2. A continuous curve between neck, shoulder, and body distinguishes the one-piece amphora from the neck-amphora, which has a distinct break between the neck and the shoulder. Sir John D. Beazley was the first to classify the three types of one-piece amphora. Type A is large and showy, with flanged handles decorated with ivy and a foot in two degrees, a vertical member above a torus (Figure 9). Type B, the most common, has an echinus foot and handles that are round in section. Type C looks like Type B, except that it has a torus mouth that is glazed and, unlike the other two types, it was not lidded. It is the rarest of the three. See Beazley, "Citharoedus," *JHS* 42 (1922), pp. 70–71, for the three types. For the actual potting of an amphora, see Toby Schreiber, *Athenian Vase Construction: A Potter's Analysis* (Malibu, 1999), pp. 72–83.

3. An unusual feature of this amphora is that the top of the mouth is glazed. Normally, this is not the case with lidded vases. There is also a reserved line on the top of the mouth at the outer edge. The neck is glazed on the inside to a depth of 2.5 cm. Red lines are drawn in the following areas: one above the ivy on each side; two below the figures that continue around the vase and two more above the rays that also continue around the vase, one on the top of the foot and another at the lower edge.

4. Certain Greek vase shapes were designed to receive a lid. These are vessels intended for storage, the one-piece amphora and the neck-amphora being the principal examples pertinent to this article. A lid always complements its pot in both shape and system of decoration. The outer diameter of the lid equals the diameter of the mouth of the pot, and the thin side of the brim should continue the flare of the side of the mouth or be vertical to it, as on MMA 1999.30. See Dietrich von Bothmer, "Lids by Andokides," *Berliner Museen* 14 (1964), pp. 38–41. This article is mainly concerned with red-figured amphorae of Type A signed by Andokides as potter or attributed to the Andokides Painter, but Bothmer sets out the general principles for establishing whether a lid and a pot belong together.

   For a good example of a vase from which an alien lid was removed, see Cab. Méd. 222, attributed to the Amasis Painter and signed by Amasis as potter (*ABV*, p. 152, no. 25; *Paralipomena,* p. 63, no. 25; *Addenda²,* pp. 43–44). The diameter of this lid (14 cm) is much less than the diameter of the mouth of the amphora (16.8 cm). For a good color illustration showing the alien lid in place, see Paolo Arias, *A History of Greek Vase Painting* (London, 1962), color pl. xv. See also Dietrich von Bothmer, "Lids by the Amasis Painter," *Enthousiasmos: Essays on Greek and Related Pottery Presented to J. M. Hemelrijk,* Allard Pierson Series 6 (Amsterdam, 1986), pp. 83–91. For a well-fitting lid, see MMA 17.230.14, the Museum's neck-amphora attributed to Exekias (*ABV*, p. 144, no. 3; *Paralipomena,* p. 59, no. 3; *Addenda²,* p. 39; for good photographs that illustrate the unity of lid and pot, see *CVA*, Metropolitan Museum 4 [USA 16], pls. 16, 17 [744, 745]).

5. The system for harnessing a four-horse team in the ancient Greek world hitched two of the animals to a yoke that rested on their backs and was bound to the chariot pole. They are called the pole horses and they supplied the main draft. The two outside horses were attached to the vehicle by a trace line that may have run directly from each horse to the chariot or may have passed through a ring on the girth of each pole horse before extending back to the vehicle. These two horses are called trace horses, or outriggers, and their function may have been to help with pulling or turning, or perhaps in setting the pace. In real life the four horses were probably abreast. In Greek art, however, when a quadriga is shown in profile, as on MMA 1999.30, the two trace horses appear to be slightly ahead of the two pole horses. This is very likely an artistic convention devised to clarify an otherwise dense composition. This may also be the reason why a white horse is usually the right-hand pole horse if the

chariot moves from left to right. The first to identify this harnessing arrangement were Aldis Hatch Jr. and Christine Alexander in Gisela M. A. Richter, *Archaic Attic Gravestones* (Cambridge, Mass., 1944), pp. 56–58. See also the colored drawing by Lindsley F. Hall of MMA 36.11.13, a grave stele datable ca. 530–520 B.C., in G. M. A. Richter, "Polychromy in Greek Sculpture with Special Reference to the Archaic Attic Gravestones in the Metropolitan Museum," *AJA* 48 (1944), pp. 321–33, pl. VIII. For ancient harnessing, see Jean Spruyette, *Early Harness Systems: Experimental Studies,* trans. Mary A. Littauer (London, 1983), passim, but esp. pp. 52–72 for the Greek chariot.

6. The bit burr was a small metal plate with spikes on the inside. It slipped onto the mouthpiece of the bit next to the cheekpiece and pressed against the animal's mouth. Its function seems to have had to do with control and turning. For bit burrs, see J. K. Anderson, *Ancient Greek Horsemanship* (Berkeley, 1961), pp. 48–49 and pls. 20–22; P. Vigneron, *Le cheval dans l'antiquité gréco-romaine* (Nancy, 1968), p. 65, pls. 18, 20c; also, Mary B. Moore, *The Athenian Agora,* vol. XXX, *Attic Red-Figured and White-Ground Pottery* (Princeton, 1997), pp. 147–48, under cat. no. 96.

7. The most comprehensive study is Immerwahr, *Attic Script,* passim. For incised inscriptions, see Cohen, "Literate Potter," pp. 49–95.

8. Naming the purpose of the vase: The Panathenaic Prize amphora offers the best example. See, e.g., two in the Metropolitan Museum: MMA 14.130.12, a canonical Panathenaic on which the prize inscription is given in front of Athena alongside the left column (*ABV*, p. 322, no. 6; *Paralipomena*, p. 142, no. 6; *Addenda*², p. 87); and MMA 1978.11.13, a precanonical Panathenaic that has, in addition to the prize inscription in front of Athena, the signature of the potter Nikias in back of the goddess and, on the reverse, an inscription naming the athletic event for which the vase was awarded as the prize, in this case the sprint for men (see Mary B. Moore, "'Nikias Made Me': An Early Panathenaic Prize Amphora in The Metropolitan Museum of Art," *MMJ* 34 [1999], pp. 37–56, figs. 5–8).

Lines of a text: A good example occurs on the pyxis found at Aigina and attributed to the Amasis Painter, where part of a verse is preserved on one leg (Martha Ohly-Dumm, "Appendix IV: Tripod-Pyxis from the Sanctuary of Aphaia on Aigina," in Dietrich von Bothmer, *The Amasis Painter and His World* [New York and London, 1985], pp. 236–38); another is on the cup in Malibu, J. Paul Getty Museum 86.AE.324, attributed to the Akestorides Painter (*ARV*², p. 1670 to p. 781, no. 4 *bis*; Henry Immerwahr, "More Book Rolls on Attic Vases," *Antike Kunst* 16 [1973], pp. 143–44, pl. 31,1–3; Mary B. Moore, *CVA*, Malibu 8 [USA 33], pp. 51–52, pl. 440 [1717],2).

Objects: See those in the scene of Achilles pursuing Troilos on the François Vase by Kleitias, Florence 4209 (*ABV*, p. 76, no. 1; *Paralipomena*, p. 29, no. 1; *Addenda*², p. 21; Mauro Cristofani, *Materiali per servire alla storia del Vaso François,* Bollettino d'Arte, serie speciale 1 [Rome, 1981], passim)—the fountain (KPENE), Cristofani, fig. 84; the hydria dropped by Polyxena (HYΔPIA), ibid., fig. 86; the block seat on which Priam sits (ΘAKOΣ), ibid., figs. 87, 88.

9. The oinochoe is in the National Museum in Athens, N.M. 192. It is attributed by J. Nicolas Coldstream (*Greek Geometric Pottery: A Survey of Ten Local Styles and Their Chronology* [London, 1968], p. 32, cat. no. 36) to the Dipylon Workshop and designated by him as a minor piece from this workshop. See the remarks in

Cohen, "Literate Potter," pp. 50–51, with bibliography, p. 86, n. 10; and in Immerwahr, *Attic Script,* p. 7. For a good color photograph, see Stavroula Kourakou-Dragona, Κρατήρ Μεστός Εὐφρόσυνης (Athens, 1998), p. 86. See also Immerwahr, *Attic Script,* p. 18, n. 21, on the so-called Cup of Nestor from Pithekoussai, which bears an inscription, a graffito or a poem. This cup may be nearly contemporary with Athens N.M. 192, and Antony Raubitschek (review of Immerwahr, *Attic Script,* in *Gnomon* 65 [1993], p. 615) thinks it may even predate it. In any case, these are the earliest preserved inscriptions on Greek vases.

10. For the Pithekoussai inscription, see Giorgio Buchner, "Recent Work at Pithekoussai (Ischia), 1965–71," in *Archaeological Reports for 1970–71,* no. 17 (Athens, 1971), p. 67, fig. 8; and Margherita Guarducci, *L'epigrafia greca dalle origini al tardo imperio* (Rome, 1987), p. 433, fig. 149. Aristonothos's name occurs on Rome, Conservatori, no no. (see Paolo Arias, *A History of Greek Vase Painting* [London, 1962], pls. 14, 15; also, Lilian Jeffery, *The Local Scripts of Archaic Greece: A Study of the Origin of the Greek Alphabet and its Development from the Eighth to the Fifth Centuries B.C.* [Oxford, 1961], p. 241, cat. no. 24). For Kallikleas, see Martin Robertson, "Excavations in Ithaca, V: The Geometric and Later Finds from Aetos," *BSA* 43 (1948), pp. 88–89, cat. no. 534 and pls. 38, 39; Jeffery, *Local Scripts,* p. 234, no. 2, pl. 45. For the term "candlestick," rather than "torch," see Robertson, "Excavations in Ithaca, V," *BSA* 43, p. 88. For these early signatures, see Beazley, *Development,* p. 7, and Scheibler, *Töpferkunst,* pp. 112, 204–5 nn. 72, 73; see also Dyfri Williams, "Potter, Painter, and Purchaser," in *Culture et cité: L'avènement d'Athènes à l'époque archaïque,* ed. Annie Verbanck-Piérard and Didier Viviers (Brussels, 1995), pp. 139–40, which illustrates (p. 140, fig. 1) a painting signature on a sherd from Naxos (only five letters of the verb remain). For a signature of Istrokles, who may be a potter or a painter (the verb is missing), see Lilian Jeffery, "Old Smyrna: Inscriptions on Sherds and Small Objects," *BSA* 59 (1964), p. 45, cat. no. 1, and pp. 48–49 for a brief discussion of early signatures, these as well as a few others. Debatable is the fragment of a plaque found on Aigina, Athens N.M. 18872 that preserves]ΣONOΣEΠIΣT[. It was restored by John M. Cook to read: Λυσιάδης Λύ]σωνος ἐπιστ[αμένως ἐποησεν (in his review of Eva T. H. Brann, *The Athenian Agora,* vol. VIII: *Late Geometric and Protoattic Pottery, Mid 8th to Late 7th Century B.C.,* in *Gnomon* 34 [1962], p. 823). It dates ca. 700 B.C. Immerwahr (*Attic Script,* p. 9, cat. no. 9), however, thinks the inscription was a dedicatory one because it was found in the Apollo Sanctuary on Aigina.

11. See *Agora* XXIII, p. 79 and n. 53, for the tabulation of the signatures as well as previous bibliography. Artists who signed as both potter and painter are rather rare. In Attic black-figure, only two others are known. Nearchos signed a kantharos found on the Akropolis, Athens N.M. 15155, ex Akrop. 611 (*ABV*, p. 82, no. 1; *Paralipomena*, p. 30, no. 1; *Addenda*², p. 23). The painting verb (*egrapsen*) is preserved and two letters of KAI (and), indicating that the signature was a double one: NEAPXOΣMEΓPAΦΣENKA [ΠOIEΣEN] (Nearchos painted and made me). Exekias signed three times as potter and painter, twice on the top of the mouth: Berlin 1720, a neck-amphora (*ABV*, p. 143, no. 1; *Paralipomena*, p. 59, no. 1; *Addenda*², p. 39), and Vatican 344, an amphora of Type A (*ABV*, p. 145, no. 13; *Paralipomena*, p. 60, no. 13; *Addenda*², p. 40). This is odd because each vase had a lid, which means that the inscription would have been covered. I have no explanation for this. On Vatican 344, Exekias signed again as

potter on Side A behind Achilles. For the signatures of Exekias, see Beazley, *Development*, p. 58. The third double signature by Exekias occurs on his amphora in Taranto (to be published by Heide Mommsen in her contribution to the forthcoming Festschrift for Dietrich von Bothmer). On this amphora, the potting signature is separate from the painting signature, and each is written in the panel, not on the top of the mouth. I wish to thank Andrew J. Clark for this information.

12. Florence 4209 (see note 8 above). The signatures occur on the front of the vase in the main scene, the Wedding of Peleus and Thetis. Kleitias's name appears in the vertical space between Peleus and Chiron (Cristofani, *Materiali* [note 8 above], figs. 82, 83); that of Ergotimos in the comparable space in front of Zeus and Hera's chariot, between it and the Horai (ibid., fig. 81)

13. MMA 31.11.4 (*ABV*, p. 78, no. 12; *Paralipomena*, p. 30, no. 12; *Addenda*², p. 22; Cohen, "Literate Potter," p. 52, fig. 3). For a good illustration, see Immerwahr, *Attic Script*, figs. 20, 21. For a list of other signed collaborations between potters and painters, see Scheibler, *Töpferkunst*, pp. 205 n. 81, 206 n. 85.

14. This is a little different from imitation inscriptions, which may or may not be letters and sometimes are just a row of dots placed between the figures in a composition to suggest the appearance of inscriptions. For another example in which the letters do not make words, see MMA 41.162.179, a neck-amphora attributed to the Group of Würzburg 210 (*ABV*, p. 373, no. 174; *Addenda*², p. 99; *CVA*, Metropolitan Museum 4 [USA 16], p. 43, for a facsimile). For a true imitation inscription, where the letters are a row of dots between the figures, see Agora P 1261 from the Group of North Slope AP 942, dated in the third quarter of the 6th century B.C. (*ABV*, p. 89, no. 1; *Addenda*², p. 24; *Agora* XXIII, pl. 37, cat. no. 375). For nonsense and imitation inscriptions, see Immerwahr, *Attic Script*, pp. 44–45. For a good example of sense and nonsense inscriptions on the same vase, similar to MMA 1999.30, see the Museum's aryballos by Nearchos, MMA 26.49 (*ABV*, p. 83, no. 4; *Paralipomena*, p. 30, no. 4; *Addenda*², p. 23; see especially, Gisela M. A. Richter, "An Aryballos by Nearchos," *AJA* 36 [1932], pp. 272–75).

15. In Greek vase painting, one cannot assume that the potter is also the painter, not even when several vases signed by one potter may be attributed to a single artist. Therefore, in lieu of a painter's signature, and to be on the safe side, we name that painter after the potter. Besides the Andokides Painter, the Amasis Painter offers a good example of this practice. For the latter artist, see *ABV*, pp. 150–58; *Paralipomena*, pp. 62–67; *Addenda*², pp. 42–46. Some of the other ways modern scholars name painters who do not sign their vases are these: after a ΚΑΛΟΣ inscription praising a youth, e.g., London B.M. 1851.8-6.15 (B 211), the name vase of the Lysippides Painter (*ABV*, p. 256, no. 14; *Paralipomena*, p. 113, no. 14; *Addenda*², p. 66); for kalos inscriptions, see pp. 21–22; after the present location of the vase, e.g., Princeton 169, the name piece of the Princeton Painter (*ABV*, p. 298, no. 6; Figure 19 in the present article); after a subject, e.g., Louvre F 60, which depicts a girl on a swing and gives the Swing Painter his name (*ABV*, p. 308, no. 74; *Paralipomena*, p. 133, no. 74; *Addenda*², p. 82; Martine Denoyelle, *Chefs-d'oeuvre de la céramique grecque dans les collections du Louvre* [Paris, 1994], pp. 84–85, cat. no. 37).

16. A basic bibliography on this artist includes: *ARV*², pp. 2–6; *Paralipomena*, pp. 320–21; *Addenda*², pp. 149–50. The most comprehensive study of the painter is Cohen, *Attic Bilingual Vases*, chap. 3. Cohen not only clearly defined the style and the artistic person-

ality of the Andokides Painter, traced his development, and pointed out his close ties with the sculptures of the Siphnian Treasury at Delphi but also settled—once and for all, I think—the question that has tantalized scholars for generations: are the Andokides Painter and the Lysippides Painter different artists or are they a single man working in both red-figure and black-figure? Cohen made the strongest possible case for keeping the two artists separate, even though they collaborated on several bilingual vases, i.e., vases decorated in both techniques (see pp. 20–21).

17. MMA 63.11.6: *ARV*², p. 1617, no. 2 *bis*; *Paralipomena*, p. 320, no. 2 *bis*; *Addenda*², p. 149. Berlin 2159: *ARV*², p. 3, no. 1; *Paralipomena*, p. 320, no. 1; *Addenda*², p. 149. Louvre G 1: *ARV*², p. 3, no. 2; *Paralipomena*, p. 320, no. 2; *Addenda*², p. 149; Denoyelle, *Chefs-d'oeuvre de la céramique grecque*, pp. 92–93, cat. no. 41. Louvre F 203: *ARV*², p. 4, no. 13; *Addenda*², p. 150; Denoyelle, *Chefs-d'oeuvre de la céramique grecque*, pp. 94–95, cat. no. 42. For the signatures of Andokides, see Immerwahr, *Attic Script*, p. 58; and, for a briefer account, see Beazley, *Development*, p. 69.

18. Madrid 11008: *ABV*, pp. 253 no. 1, and 294 no. 24; *ARV*², p. 7, no. 2; *Paralipomena*, pp. 128 no. 24, and 321 no. 2; *Addenda*², p. 150. For Psiax, see *ABV*, pp. 292–95; *ARV*², pp. 6–9; *Paralipomena*, pp. 127–28, 321; *Addenda*², pp. 76–77, 150–51.

19. Dietrich von Bothmer was the first to point this out, in his 1966 article "Andokides," p. 202. See also Cohen, "Literate Potter," p. 60.

20. Rome, Villa Giulia, no no. (*ARV*², p. 77, no. 90; *Addenda*², p. 169). Cohen ("Literate Potter," p. 89, n. 68) thinks the foot may not belong to this krater: "In reexamining my notes, I notice no preserved join between this calyx-krater's body and the foot, and I am now inclined to believe that the foot does not belong. The foot's profile suggests it may have come from a lost amphora—a sibling of the Metropolitan's amphora [63.11.6]." Calyx-kraters and amphorae of Type A have similar feet, a vertical member above a torus, and it can be quite difficult to determine to which vase shape a foot belongs without a break-to-break join. Nevertheless, the signature on this foot is not in doubt.

21. London B.M. 1980.11-29.1 (*ABV*, pp. 253,— no. 2, 293, no. 7; *ARV*², p. 6; *Paralipomena*, p. 127, no. 7; *Addenda*², p. 76). The amphora displays several oddities. It has ridged handles with side flanges and rotelles that attach each handle to the mouth (usually, three ropes of clay joined together form the handle of a neck-amphora; see Schreiber, *Athenian Vase Construction*, p. 79). Neck-amphorae have ornamental patterns on the neck and figures on the body. On the London vase, the figural decoration appears on the neck only; the rest of the pot is black, except for the triple net pattern on the side of the mouth (normally this area is black). An elegant palmette configuration appears below a key pattern on the root of each handle instead of below it. Also peculiar is the absence of rays above the foot.

22. For the cup, see *ABV*, p. 256, no. 21; *ARV*², p. 5, no. 14; *Paralipomena*, pp. 114 no. 21, 321 no. 14; *Addenda*², p. 150. On the collaboration between the two painters, the best and most thorough discussion is Cohen, *Attic Bilingual Vases*, pp. 163–91.

23. For bilingual eye-cups, the basic study is Cohen, *Attic Bilingual Vases*, pt. 2.

24. For a good illustration of the red-figured side of the cup, see *CVA*, Palermo 1 [Italia 14], pl. 1 [658], 2. See the discussion by Cohen (*Attic Bilingual Vases*, pp. 247–49), who also remarks (p. 247) that the depiction of combats at the handles of this cup

very likely reflects the similar concept on the somewhat earlier eye-cup in Munich signed by Exekias as potter and attributed to him as painter (Munich 2044: *ABV*, p. 146, no. 21; *Paralipomena*, p. 60, no. 21; *Addenda²*, p. 41). Exekias signed on Side A of the foot, the letters centered below the eyes. For a good illustration, see Arias, *A History of Greek Vase Painting*, pl. 59, above; also, Cohen, "Literate Potter," p. 56, fig. 8.

25. Louvre F 38 (*ABV*, p. 174, no. 7; *Paralipomena*, p. 72, no. 7; *Addenda²*, p. 49). For the Taleides Painter, see *ABV*, pp. 174–77; *Paralipomena*, pp. 72–74; *Addenda²*, pp. 49–50.

26. The basic study is still David M. Robinson and Edward J. Fluck, *A Study of Greek Love Names* (Baltimore, 1937), pp. 1–14, for a general discussion with bibliography as well as a history of the various interpretations of the meaning of *kalos* on vases. See also the brief remarks by Gisela M. A. Richter and Lindsley F. Hall, *Red-Figured Athenian Vases in The Metropolitan Museum of Art* (New Haven, 1936), pp. xxix–xxx; and G. M. A. Richter, *Attic Red-Figure Vases: A Survey* (New Haven, 1946), pp. 43–45; Webster, *Potter and Patron*, pp. 43–44; Brian A. Sparkes, *Greek Pottery: An Introduction* (Manchester, England, and New York, 1991), p. 53. For a list of *kalos* names on black-figured vases, see *ABV*, pp. 664–76; *Paralipomena*, pp. 317–19; *Addenda²*, pp. 391–92.

27. See Raubitschek, *Dedications*, pp. 213–16, cat. no. 178; also the illustration by Bothmer in his "Andokides," p. 206, fig. 7; Scheibler, "Künstlervotive," p. 9; and the brief remarks by Williams, "Potter, Painter, and Purchaser," pp. 147–48 (see note 10 above). For other potter dedications on the Akropolis, see note 29 below.

28. The source for these is Raubitschek, *Dedications*, passim.

29. Beazley, *Potter and Painter*, p. 21; Webster, *Potter and Patron*, p. 5; Scheibler, "Künstlervotive," p. 9. The potter dedications inscribed on marble are discussed in some detail by Beazley in *Potter and Painter* (pp. 21–25), who cautiously separated those he thought were certainly dedications by potters from those that were uncertain or improbable (for these, see ibid., pp. 23–24, n. 1; and Scheibler, "Künstlervotive," pp. 12–13). See the brief discussion in Webster, *Potter and Patron*, pp. 5–6, and in Scheibler, "Künstlervotive," pp. 9–11, both with references to the pertinent catalogue numbers in Raubitschek, *Dedications*; also Scheibler, *Töpferkunst*, pp. 124–28. The most recent account of potter dedications, stone as well as clay, is by Claudia Wagner, "The Potters and Athena: Dedications on the Athenian Acropolis," in *Periplous: Papers on Classical Art and Archaeology Presented to Sir John Boardman* (New York, 2000), pp. 383–87. The negative assessment of them by Michael Vickers and David Gill, who for the most part discard them as dedications made by potters, seems excessive (*Artful Crafts: Ancient Greek Silverware and Pottery* [Oxford, 1994], pp. 93–95). Besides the Mnesiades-Andokides monument, there are four other assured potter dedications inscribed in marble from the Athenian Akropolis.

1. Akropolis 681, the kore dedicated by Nearchos and made by Antenor, son of Eumares (Beazley, *Potter and Painter*, p. 21; Raubitschek, *Dedications*, pp. 232–33, cat. no. 197; Gisela M. A. Richter, *Korai: Archaic Greek Maidens* [London, 1968], pp. 69–70, cat. no. 110; Scheibler, "Künstlervotive," pp. 9–10). The noun κεραμεύς (potter) is restored in the inscription on the basis of the presence of Nearchos's name (Beazley, *Potter and Painter*, p. 21). The kore is dated ca. 520 B.C., which would be compatible with the career of the potter Nearchos, who flourished about the middle of the 6th century B.C. and whose two sons, Ergoteles and Tleson, signed as potters of Little-Master

cups well into the third quarter of the century (see *ABV*, p. 162 for Ergoteles, pp. 178–83 for Tleson; see also note 39 below). By this time, the workshop (and family) might well have been wealthy enough to make such a large dedication in honor of Athena. The inscription also contains the word ἀπαρχέν (firstfruits), which refers to the offering of an unspecified portion of the best that one has earned (see Scheibler, "Künstlervotive," p. 10).

2. Akropolis 1332, E.M. 6520, and Agora I 4571, the famous relief that shows a man seated to left on a diphros holding in his lowered left hand two drinking cups, one by a handle, the other by its foot and stem (Beazley, *Potter and Painter*, pp. 22–23; Raubitschek, p. 75, cat. no. 70 with extensive bibliography, esp. his article "An Original Work by Endoios," *AJA* 46 [1942], pp. 245–53, where he restores the name of Endoios as the sculptor of the relief; Scheibler, "Künstlervotive," p. 10). The relief may be dated in the last decade of the 6th century B.C. That the dedicant was a maker of cups is suggested by the subject, hence the inclusion of this relief in the list of assured marble dedications by potters. The inscription also tells us that he gave a tithe, a tenth (δεκάτην), of his annual earnings in honor of Athena, a more precise percentage than "firstfruits" (ἀπαρχέν; see Scheibler, "Künstlervotive," p. 10). But only the last three letters of the potter's name remain (]ΙΟΣ), not enough to link him definitively with a known potter, although Beazley speculated that the name might be Pamphaios (*Potter and Painter*, p. 22). Also, the better preserved of the two cups he holds may not be matched detail for detail with a known variant. Its offset lip reminds one of the Little-Master cups, but the offset is too sharp and the bowl is too deep. Several authors, starting with Hansjörg Bloesch (*Formen attischer Schalen von Exekias bis zum Ende des strengen Stils* [Bern, 1940], p. 144), link it with a rare variant called the Acrocup, short for "Acropolis-cup" (Beazley, *Potter and Painter*, pp. 22–23); however, it lacks the thick fillet between bowl and stem that is a defining feature of the Acrocup, for which see Brian A. Sparkes and Lucy Talcott, *The Athenian Agora*, vol. XII, *Black and Plain Pottery of the 6th, 5th and 4th Centuries B.C.* (Princeton, 1970), pp. 92–97.

3. Athens, Epigraphical Museum, E.M. 12750, a fragment of a pedestal with the start of a column shaft and part of a cutting on top for a statue (O. Broneer, "Excavations on the North Slope of the Acropolis," *Hesperia* 4 (1935), p. 150, cat. no. 2, fig. 38; Beazley, *Potter and Painter*, p. 23; Raubitschek, *Dedications*, pp. 46–47, cat. no. 44; Scheibler, "Künstlervotive," pp. 11–12). The inscription reads that a potter named Peikon, whose name is otherwise unknown, dedicated a tithe to Athena. The monument is dated by Raubitschek to ca. 500–490 B.C.

4. Athens, Epigraphical Museum, E.M. 6278, three fragments of a pillar monument (Beazley, *Potter and Painter*, pp. 21–22; Raubitschek, *Dedications*, pp. 255–58, cat. no. 225; Scheibler, "Künstlervotive," pp. 10–11). The inscription says that Euphronios the potter made the dedication to Athena as a tithe. Raubitschek dates the inscription to ca. 480 B.C., well after Euphronios turned from painting large vases to fashioning drinking cups, of which several are decorated by Onesimos, who was active during the time of the Persian Wars and perhaps a bit beyond. For Euphronios as potter, see *ARV²*, pp. 313–14; also Dyfri Williams, "Euphronios: vom Maler zum Töpfer," in *Euphronios der Maler*, exh. cat., Sonderausstellungshalle, Staatlichen Museen Preussischer Kulturbesitz, Berlin-Dahlem (Milan, 1991), pp. 47–51, with previous bibliography.

These are the dedications in stone. For vases dedicated by potters, which are not pertinent to this article, see Webster, *Potter and Patron*, pp. 4–5, and Wagner, "The Potters and Athena," pp. 385–86.

30. The inscription does not specify whether this is a dedication of "firstfruits" or a "tithe." For these portions of annual earnings as dedications, see note 29 above. Scheibler (*Töpferkunst*, pp. 125–26) says that a dedication could have been an offering as the fruits of work of several years.

31. Raubitschek, *Dedications*, p. 213. For bronze statues mounted on marble bases by the Samian technique, see Anton Raubitschek, "Zur Technik und Form der altattischen Statuenbasen," *Bulletin de l'Institut Archéologique Bulgare* 12 (1938), pp. 134–35. According to this technique, four channels or grooves are drilled on the top of the base, forming a rectangle. The statue is joined to a flat base with down-turned edges that fit into the channels, where they are secured with lead. On some of the examples, traces of lead remain. The bronze statue of a striding warrior represented on the name piece of the Foundry Painter, Berlin 2294, seems to stand on such a base, as noted by Raubitschek ("Zur Technik und Form," p. 135, n. 1). For the Berlin cup, see *ARV²*, p. 400, no. 1; *Paralipomena*, p. 370, no. 1; *Addenda²*, p. 230.

32. Scheibler, "Künstlervotive," p. 9.

33. Raubitschek, *Dedications*, p. 47. For korai and their bases, see Richter, *Korai*, passim.

34. See the remarks in note 29 above. Vickers and Gill (*Artful Crafts*, p. 94, n. 114) write: "*Kerameus* is linked to [M]nesiades and need not be associated with Andocides." This seems to me to be a willful and arbitrary dissociation.

35. Ibid., p. 94. Their sole reason for rejecting the Mnesiades-Andokides monument as a potter dedication seems to be that the noun κεραμεύς (potter) appears without the definite article *ho* (the); thus, they think it should refer to the deme Kerameikos to which Mnesiades may have belonged, not to his occupation. See the more measured remarks by Alan Johnston, in *Papers on the Amasis Painter and His World*, Colloquium Sponsored by the Getty Center for the History of Art and the Humanities and Symposium Sponsored by the J. Paul Getty Museum (Malibu, 1987), pp. 135–36: "Where *kerameus* is assuredly preserved, on less prestigious bases, two of the three dedicants appear to be known potters, Mnesiades and Euphronios, while Andokides is associated with Mnesiades. It would be a striking coincidence if they were from the deme Kerameis and yet none of them were the potters known to us by that name from the relevant period. . . . We can conclude therefore that some potters did accede to modest wealth, and that is a measure, however unsatisfactory, of the financial success, if not social status, of the members of the Athenian Kerameikos in the years following the career of our particular artist [the Amasis Painter]." Williams ("Potter, Painter, and Purchaser," p. 147) thought that the dedication might have been made to record "the transfer of ownership or direction of the business from Mnesiades to Andokides" or even the "merging of two smaller operations into one larger workshop." He then concluded somewhat awkwardly (pp. 147–48): "Whatever the circumstances, the chances against the two men named on the inscription not being potters must be very high—for the obvious metrical reasons *kerameus* appears only once." Most recently, Claudia Wagner has reviewed these dedications and concluded ("The Potters and Athena," p. 387): "The case for identifying the *kerameus* as potter is indeed strong.

We have shown motive and opportunity, as well as the strong circumstantial evidence of names known from the potters' quarter. The possibility of a misinterpretation seems to be minute."

36. Beazley, *Potter and Painter*, p. 21. Beazley wrote this before he learned of the hydria fragment signed by Mnesiades that was once in the Riaz collection in Cairo and is now in the Cahn collection in Basel. For the fragment, see *ABV*, p. 314; *ARV²*, p. 2; *Paralipomena*, p. 136; *Addenda²*, p. 85; Bettina Kreuzer, *Frühe Zeichner 1500–500 vor Chr.: Ägyptische, griechische und etruskische Vasenfragmente: der Sammlung H. A. Cahn, Basel* (Freiburg im Breisgau, 1992), p. 64.

37. Raubitschek, *Dedications*, p. 216.

38. Collaborations between potters whose signatures appear on the same vase are rare. Thus far, it seems to occur only twice, each on a Little-Master cup. Archikles and Glaukytes both signed Munich 2243, Archikles under one handle, Glaukytes under the other (*ABV*, pp. 160,— no. 2, 163,— no. 2; *Paralipomena*, p. 68,—, no. 2; *Addenda²*, p. 47). Anakles and Nikosthenes both signed Berlin 1801, one potter on each side (*ABV*, pp. 159,— no. 4, 230,— no. 1; *Paralipomena*, p. 108,—, no. 1; Tosto, *ΝΙΚΟΣΘΕΝΕΣΕΠΟΙΕΣΕΝ*, pp. 230–31, cat. no. 158. This cup has been missing since World War II [*pace* Tosto]). See also Beazley (*Potter and Painter*, pp. 26–27), who remarks that it is difficult to see how the potting responsibilities could be divided on such a small vase and why such a division of labor would have been recorded. Also Webster (*Potter and Patron*, p. 14), who suggests that the presence of the two signatures "may merely mean that an older master is allowing a younger potter to sign with him." Collaborations between potters and painters are more common; see, for example, the list given by Dietrich von Bothmer, "'Ἄμασις, Ἀμάσιδος," *J. Paul Getty Museum Journal* 9 (1981), p. 1, which names those collaborations known before the middle of the 19th century. I have already mentioned Ergotimos and Kleitias. For others, see also Webster, *Potter and Patron*, pp. 11–14. Collaborations between *painters*, however, as opposed to those between potters and painters, are known only from attributions, one of the most famous being that between the Lysippides Painter and the Andokides Painter (see note 16 above). For others, see Beazley, *Potter and Painter*, pp. 27–30; Webster, *Potter and Patron*, pp. 15–18.

39. Scheibler, "Künstlervotive," p. 9. Inscriptions on vases attest that sons of potters sometimes became potters themselves. Since there are not very many, it is worth reviewing them. The names of two, Ergotimos and Nearchos, have already been mentioned. Ergotimos had a son named Eucheiros, who signed two cups with his patronymic. One is London, B.M. 1847.8-6.44 (B 417) (*ABV*, p. 162,—, no. 2; *Paralipomena*, p. 68, no. 2; *Addenda²*, p. 47), signed on Side A: ΕΥΧΕΡΟΣ:ΕΠΟΙΕΣΕΝΜΕ (Eucheiros made me); signed on Side B: ΗΟΡΓΟΤΙΜΟΗΥΙΗΥΣ (son of Ergotimos). The other is Berlin 1756 (*ABV*, p. 162,—, no. 3), signed on Side A, below the female head in outline: ΕΥΧΕΡΣΕΠΟΙΟΕΣΕΝ. ΗΟΡΓΟΤΙΜΟΗΥΙΗΣ (Eucheiros made me. Son of Ergotimos). Eucheiros, in turn, had a son, who signed a lip-cup in the Vatican, frr (*ABV*, p. 163,—; *Paralipomena*, p. 68), but only the patronymic and the filial noun remain in the inscription, on Side A: ΕΥΧΕΡΟΗΥΙΗΥΣ (son of Eucheiros); on Side B: ΗΟΕ[ ]ΗΥΙΗΥΣ (the [ ] son of). Better known are the two sons of Nearchos, Ergoteles and Tleson, especially the latter. Ergoteles signed two cups, each with the name of his father written after the potting verb. One is Berlin 1758 (*ABV*, p. 162,—, no. 1; *Addenda²*, p. 47), signed on each side: ΕΡΓΟΤΕΛΕΣΕΠΟΙΕΣΕΝΗΟΝΕΑΡΧΟ (Ergoteles

made [me], the son of Nearchos). The second is a cup formerly on the Florence art market (*ABV*, p. 162,—, no. 2), signed in the handle zone: ΕΡΓΟΤ . . . , . . . ΣΕΠΟΙΕΣΕΝ . . . , . . . ΕΝ ΗΟΝ[ΕΑΡΧΟ (Ergoteles . . . made [me], the son of Nearchos). Tleson signed many cups, too numerous to list here, always using the formula that places the potting verb after the patronymic (*ABV*, pp. 178–83; *Paralipomena*, pp. 74–76; *Addenda*², pp. 50–51): ΤΛΕΣΟΝΗΟΝΕΑΡΧΟΕΠΟΙΕΣΕΝ (Tleson, the son of Nearchos made [me]). In both inscriptions, the name of Nearchos is in the genitive case. Two inscriptions have revealed that the potter Kleophrades was the son of Amasis. One is on Malibu, J. Paul Getty Museum 80.AE.54, signed on the side of the foot, the rest of the cup lost:]ΣΙΔΟΣΗΥΥΣ (son of [Ama]sis). The other is on Malibu, J. Paul Getty Museum 83.AE.217, a cup signed in the tondo by Douris, and on the side of the foot: ΚΛΕΟΦΡΑΔΕΣ: ΕΠΟΙΕΣΕΝ:ΑΜΑΣΙΔΟΣ (Kleophrades made [me] of Amasis); for this cup, see Diana Buitron-Oliver, *Douris: A Master-Painter of Athenian Red-Figure Vases*, Kerameus 9 (Mainz, 1995), p. 75, cat. no. 38, pl. 24. For Kleophrades as the son of Amasis, see Bothmer, "'Ἄμασις, 'Ἀμάσιδος," pp. 1–4, which sets out the history of the problem and establishes the father-son relationship. Until this new evidence came to light, Kleophrades was known from his signature on the foot of a cup in Paris, Cab. Méd. 535, 699, that is his name piece (*ARV*², p. 191, no. 103; *Addenda*², p. 189): ΚΛΕΟΦΡΑΔΕΣ:ΕΠΟΙΕΣΕΝ: ΑΜΑΣ[. . .]Σ (Kleophrades made [me]: of Amasis); and on a cup attributed to Douris, Berlin 2293 + Rome, Astarita 134 (*ARV*², p. 429, no. 21; *Addenda*², p. 236; Buitron-Oliver, *Douris*, p. 74, cat. no. 34): ΚΛΕ[Ο]ΦΡΑ[ΔΕΣΕΠΟ]ΙΕΣΕ[Ν (Kleophrades made [me]).

Scheibler (*Töpferkunst*, p. 114) remarks that it is probably no accident that the largest number of potting signatures on Attic black-figured vases occurs on drinking cups, and she suggests that this may be because they were difficult to make. She does not elaborate but implies this may be due to their small size and delicate features. There may also be a simpler answer. The handle zone of most drinking cups is a plain, narrow reserved band (elaborate cups like Munich 2243 by Archikles and Glaukytes, with its full frieze of figures, would be an exception), and this undecorated zone provides the perfect space for a signature.

40. See note 36 above.

41. This *kalos* name is also known on a slightly later neck-amphora by an artist formerly included with painters near Group E, Louvre F 218 (*ABV*, p. 139, no. 9; *Paralipomena*, p. 57, no. 9: the attribution withdrawn; *Addenda*², p. 37).

42. Akropolis 921 (*ABV*, p. 300, 16; Martin Bentz, *Panathenäische Preisamphoren: Eine athenische Vasengattung und ihre Funktion vom 6.–4. Jahrhundert v. Chr*, Achtzehntes Beiheft Antike Kunst [Basel, 1998], p. 124, cat. no. 6.011, pl. 7).

43. For precanonical Panathenaic prize amphorae, see note 8 above.

44. See pp. 21–22 and note 26. One *kalos* name that appears on pottery for well over ten years is "Onetorides" (*ABV*, p. 672). The earliest of these that has been preserved occurs on Berlin 1720, a very early work by Exekias (ca. 540 B.C.) that he signed as both potter and painter (see note 11 above). The latest examples occur in the second half of the 520s, e.g., MMA 14.105.10 by the Mastos Painter (*ABV*, p. 261, no. 37; *Addenda*², p. 68).

45. An exception, of course, to this generalization is Euphronios, who turned to potting after a successful career as a painter. For Euphronios as potter, see note 29 above. Dietrich von Bothmer ("Andokides," p. 202) suggested that during the career of

Timagoras, Andokides must have been a boy, and this may have been when he served as an apprentice to Mnesiades.

46. Scheibler (*Töpferkunst*, p. 128) suggests that, in general, signatures on pottery are a mark of pride. This may be true, not only for young potters but also for established ones. For example, Exekias signed as potter certain shapes that were new to the repertory, such as the Munich eye-cup (see note 24 above) or the Vatican amphora (see note 11 above), or old shapes that offered new features that would become standard, such as London, B.M. 1836.2-24.127 (B 210) (*ABV*, p. 144, no. 7; *Paralipomena*, p. 60, no. 7; *Addenda*², p. 39). See the tabulation in *Agora* XXX (see note 6 above), p. 81, n. 3. The striking exception seems to be Nikosthenes, who signed more than one hundred vases. Perhaps this was a case of "company policy"; see Klaus Stähler, "'Exekias bemalte und töpferte mich,'" *Jahreshefte des Oesterreichischen Archäologischen Institutes* 49 (1968–71), p. 112. For the signatures of Nikosthenes, see notes 69 and 70 below.

47. See above, p. 22 and note 17; p. 22 and note 21.

48. This is probably Madrid 11008, the bilingual amphora by Psiax (see p. 22 and note 18 above). For a discussion of this amphora and the problem of dating it, see Cohen, *Attic Bilingual Vases*, pp. 233–39, esp. p. 237.

49. Bothmer ("Andokides," p. 202) suggests that by this time Andokides was probably a prosperous citizen.

50. Raubitschek, *Dedications*, p. 258.

51. Other than Vickers and Gill, the main dissenter from this interpretation was Gisela M. A. Richter, who in 1936 expressed doubt: "If this Andokides was the well-known potter, as has been thought, we should obtain support for dating the vases signed by him about 525–520. But as we have records of a distinguished Athenian family from about the middle of the 6th century on in which this rare name also occurs,²³ it seems more likely that the Andokides praised as *kalos* was a young scion of that family than that he was a potter" (Richter and Hall, *Red-Figured Athenian Vases*, p. 11). The work cited in Richter's n. 23 is Johannes Kirchner, *Prosopographia Attica* (Berlin, 1901), pp. 62–63.

Richter probably had in mind the Athenian family whose first attested historical member, Andokides (I), is among those possessing land that produced 500 measures of corn yearly; his name appears on a bronze plaque recording a dedication on the Athenian Akropolis by the treasurers. The plaque, N.M. 6975, is dated ca. 550 B.C. See John K. Davies, *Athenian Propertied Families, 600–300 B.C.* (Oxford, 1971), pp. 27–28. For the plaque, see Jeffery, *Local Scripts*, p. 77, cat. no. 21, pl. 3, and p. 401, cat. no. 21, for the transcription. Besides Andokides, the inscription mentions Anaksion, Eudikos, and Lysimachos, as well as an individual whose name is preserved only in the initial letter Σ.

Davies (*Athenian Propertied Families*, p. 28) writes: The Andokides "named on a Bf. hydria of ca. 540 . . . is at least a generation younger than Andokides (I). He may be identical with the potter of the name, but could equally well be a younger relation of Andokides (I)."

Richter's conclusion that the Andokides described as *kalos* is not the same person as the potter was echoed by Robinson and Fluck (*Greek Love Names*, p. 82): "This Andokides is probably not the well-known potter, though the vase [the hydria in the Louvre signed by Timagoras: see note 25 above] (c. 540 B.C.) dates from his time but probably a young member of a distinguished family of this name, known from the middle of the sixth century on."

52. Vatican 344 (see note 11 above).

53. Usually signatures appear within the figured compositions or on the side of the foot. There are not many vases signed by a potter on the top of the mouth. Besides the Vatican amphora, the following are the ones I have been able to find. Berlin 1720, the very early neck-amphora by Exekias that has the double signature (see note 11 above). Vienna, formerly Klein, a fragment of an amphora or a neck-amphora with the first five letters of Exekias's name (*ABV*, p. 146,—, no. 1). Eleusis 280, ex 4267, a long-necked amphora signed by Kleimachos and dating ca. 570 B.C. (*ABV*, p. 85, —; *Paralipomena*, p. 32). London, B.M. 1842.4–7.17 (B 364), a volute-krater by Nikosthenes of ca. 530 B.C. (Figure 14); (*ABV*, p. 229; *Paralipomena*, p. 108; Tosto, *ΝΙΚΟΣΘΕΝΕΣΕΠΟΙΕΣΕΝ*, p. 227, cat. no. 136). Finally, Houston, De Menil Foundation 70.53DJ, a psykter also signed by Nikosthenes but attributed to the Antimenes Painter (*Addenda²*, p. 401; Tosto, *ΝΙΚΟΣΘΕΝΕΣΕΠΟΙΕΣΕΝ*, p. 234, cat. no. 183, pl. 152). The attribution is Bothmer's (see M. B. Moore, "The Gigantomachy of the Siphnian Treasury: Reconstruction of the Three Lacunae," in *Études delphiques, Bulletin de correspondance hellénique*, suppl. IV, 1977, p. 314, n. 38). Oddly, Tosto merely mentions the unusual placement of these two potting inscriptions (*ΝΙΚΟΣΘΕΝΕΣΕΠΟΙΕΣΕΝ*, p. 182).

54. Wilhelm Klein, *Die griechischen Vasen mit Meistersignaturen* (Vienna, 1887), p. 188.

55. Bothmer, "Andokides," p. 204.

56. Cohen, *Attic Bilingual Vases*, pp. 3–4.

57. Ibid., p. 4, n. 9.

58. Cohen, "Literate Potter," pp. 59, 63. In the same article (pp. 53–59), Cohen also discusses the incised signatures on Attic black-figured vases, which do not occur very often, probably because it was so easy to find an unglazed space in which to paint a signature. Exekias seems to have incised his signature only once, on his fragmentary dinos in Rome, Villa Giulia 50599 (*ABV*, p. 146, no. 20; *Addenda²*, p. 41; Cohen, "Literate Potter," p. 56, fig. 9). This is, if not the first, one of the first dinoi to have the body glazed black and the figures (in this case, sleek warships) painted on the inside of the mouth. The large area of black glaze may have prompted Exekias to sign his name as potter in precise letters on the shoulder above the carefully painted tongue pattern. He also incised the name of the buyer (Epainetos) and the person for whom the dinos was purchased (Charopos). For this inscription, see Cohen, ibid., p. 56, fig. 10. According to Beazley (*ABV*, p. 146, no. 20), the inscriptions were incised after firing. This dinos may be dated ca. 530 B.C., about the time Andokides may have started working with Exekias.

59. Webster, *Potter and Patron*, p. 7.

60. Ibid., p. 12. The bibliographic citations in Webster's n. 9 in this quotation are the Beazley references for MMA 1999.30.

61. See Cohen, *Attic Bilingual Vases*, p. 4: "There is evidence to show that while the painted potter-signatures may have been executed by the vase-painters, those incised on the feet of the vessels are by a *single* distinctive hand, almost certainly the potter's own." In 1984 Henry Immerwahr ("The Signature of Pamphaios," *AJA* 88 [1984], p. 341) put the idea more strongly: "There can be no doubt that *epoiesen* signatures painted in the scenes together with other inscriptions are the work of the painters. Exceptions are of course possible, given the large cor-

pus of vase inscriptions, but I am not aware of any at this point."

62. The following are good examples. Athens, N.M. 15499 by Sophilos (*ABV*, p. 39, no. 16; *Paralipomena*, p. 18, no. 16; *Addenda²*, p. 10); the exuberant, somewhat rough-and-ready drawing complements the letters, and one word (ΑΤΛΑ: "games") is even misspelled (it should be ΑΘΛΑ). Athens, N.M. 15155, ex Akrop. 611 by Nearchos (see note 11 above), and Berlin 1720 and Vatican 344 (see note 11 above), both by Exekias. On these three, the fine, precise letters of the inscriptions parallel the elegant draftsmanship.

63. There is one further point to be made concerning the potting inscription on this cup. The name "Andokides" appears on the black-figured side—the one attributed to the Lysippides Painter—not on the red-figured side, which is by the Andokides Painter. Cohen (*Attic Bilingual Vases*, pp. 3–5) noticed that the Andokides Painter never includes inscriptions in his compositions, but the Lysippides Painter does. She also makes the point (ibid., p. 5) that there are no inscriptions on their bilingual amphorae. See also the remarks in note 61 above.

64. See pp. 18–19 above. This placement of the inscription starts with the very earliest vase signatures, which are non-Attic, the one from Pithekoussai ending in [ ]ΙΝΟΣ and the one from Ithaca, by Kallikleas (for both, see note 10 above).

65. See notes 8 and 11 above.

66. These are a few examples by each potter. Amasis: Boston, M.F.A. 01.8026, the signature written vertically between the two figures on each side (*ABV*, p. 152, no. 26; *Paralipomena*, p. 63, no. 26; *Addenda²*, p. 44); Boston, M.F.A. 01.8027, written behind and above the figure of Apollo on Side A (*ABV*, p. 152, no. 27; *Paralipomena*, p. 63, no. 27; *Addenda²*, p. 44); Cab. Méd. 222, written between Athena and Poseidon on Side A (see note 4 above); and London, B.M. 1849.6–20.5 (B 471), written vertically behind Perseus in such a way that the hero seems to be reading it (*ABV*, p. 153, no. 32; *Paralipomena*, p. 64, no. 32; *Addenda²*, p. 44). On Würzburg 332, by the Amasis Painter, the inscription is written vertically between the two central figures, and a spear separates the name from the verb (*ABV*, p. 152, no. 30; *Paralipomena*, p. 63, no. 30; *Addenda²*, p. 44).

Exekias: Vatican 344, the signature written horizontally behind Achilles' spear on Side A (see note 11 above); London, B.M. 1836.2–24.127 (B 210), written vertically behind Achilles on Side A and behind Oinopion on Side B (see note 46 above); and Louvre F 53, attributed to a painter from Group E, the potting signature of Exekias written vertically behind Herakles on Side A (*ABV*, p. 136, no. 49; *Paralipomena*, p. 55, no. 49; *Addenda²*, p. 36). It is perhaps worth noting that on MMA 1999.30, Andokides placed the two nonsense inscriptions in a similar vertical framing position. Might this be a further link with the Exekias Workshop?

In each of these examples, even the last, and in many others, the placement of the inscription enhances the composition. In view of this, see Tosto's odd remark that "a signature was simply not considered by Greek potters and painters on the whole to be an integral part of the finished product" (*ΝΙΚΟΣΘΕΝΕΣΕΠΟΙΕΣΕΝ*, p. 182).

67. Several exceptions occur on band cups by Hermogenes, where a chariot to left separates the name from the verb: Cambridge GR 41.1864 (63) (*ABV*, p. 165, no. 1; *Addenda²*, p. 47); Florence 70996 (*ABV*, p. 165, no. 2); Munich 2232 (*ABV*, p. 165, no. 2); Melbourne, ex Castle Ashby (*ABV*, p. 165, no. 4; *Addenda²*, p. 47); Oxford G. 244 ex 231 (*ABV*, p. 165, no. 5; *Addenda²*,

p. 47); probably also the fragment Louvre C 10261, which preserves the name on the left, then a chariot wheeling round, and in the missing section on the right presumably the verb (*ABV*, p. 165, no. 6). Other exceptions are the following. The oinochoe Athens N.M. 1045, signed by Xenokles as potter and by Kleisophos as painter, where the two names appear together at the far left of the panel, the potting verb between the second and third figures, and the painting verb at the far right (*ABV*, p. 186,—; *Addenda²*, p. 51). Pamphaios signed his name as potter above the figures on Cab. Méd. 254, a hydria by the Euphiletos Painter, and here the crest of Athena's helmet interrupts the letters of the name (*ABV*, p. 324, no. 38; *Addenda²*, p. 88). The heads of two goats separate Theozotos's name from the potting verb on a kyathos in Paris, Louvre F 69 (*ABV*, p. 349,—; *Paralipomena*, p. 159,—; *Addenda²*, p. 95). Thrax signed a band cup in Taranto in the same manner as those by Hermogenes (I.G.6222: *ABV*, p. 178,—; *Paralipomena*, p. 74,—).

68. See the new study by Tosto, *ΝΙΚΟΣΘΕΝΕΣΕΠΟΙΕΣΕΝ*, passim.

69. Ibid. lists 139 in black-figure and 10 in red-figure (see p. 1 and especially chap. 11, "The Signatures in Nikosthenic Black Figure and the Catalogue of Signatures" [pp. 173–92]).

70. Ibid., pp. 175–76. It is worth listing them:

1. Berlin 1801, the cup cosigned with Anakles (see note 38 above), on which the name and the verb are separated by Herakles and the Hydra.

2, 3. Two amphorae of Type B of ca. 540 B.C.: Rome, Villa Giulia 63643 and 63644 (*ABV*, p. 229, V; *Paralipomena*, p. 108; Tosto, *ΝΙΚΟΣΘΕΝΕΣΕΠΟΙΕΣΕΝ*, p. 233, cat. no. 176, pl. 151, 1), the verb written between the legs of the left warrior and the name between the right warrior and the onlooker; Leiden I.1956/11.2 (Tosto, *ΝΙΚΟΣΘΕΝΕΣΕΠΟΙΕΣΕΝ*, p. 233, cat. no. 177, pl. 151, 2), the verb written between the first two figures and the name between the second and the third.

4, 5, 6. Three cups dated by Tosto between 525 and 520 B.C.: Louvre F 124 (*ABV*, p. 232, no. 15; *Paralipomena*, p. 109, no. 15; *Addenda²*, p. 60; Tosto, *ΝΙΚΟΣΘΕΝΕΣΕΠΟΙΕΣΕΝ*, pp. 228–29, cat. no. 145), the name and the verb divided by an upright lotus (for an illustration, see Joseph Clark Hoppin, *A Handbook of Greek Black-Figured Vases* [Paris, 1924], p. 263); Louvre F 121 (*ABV*, p. 231, no. 7; *Paralipomena*, p. 108, no. 7; *Addenda²*, p. 59; Tosto, *ΝΙΚΟΣΘΕΝΕΣΕΠΟΙΕΣΕΝ*, pp. 232–33, cat. no. 171, pl. 148, 2), the name written between eye and eyebrow of the left eye, the verb below the upper contour of the right eye; San Antonio 86.134.56 (Tosto, *ΝΙΚΟΣΘΕΝΕΣΕΠΟΙΕΣΕΝ*, p. 233, cat. no. 172, pl. 149, 2), the name written between eye and eyebrow of the left eye, the verb in the same space in the right eye.

7. Rome, Conservatori 57 (*ABV*, p. 220, no. 29; *Paralipomena*, p. 104, no. 29; Tosto, *ΝΙΚΟΣΘΕΝΕΣΕΠΟΙΕΣΕΝ*, p. 215, cat. no. 38), a Nicosthenic amphora dated ca. 515 B.C. by Tosto, the name and the verb separated by a lotus-palmette cross, the first four letters of the name written between the legs of the left panther (for a good illustration, see Hoppin, *Handbook*, p. 269). This inscription may also be counted among those where name and verb are divided more or less syllabically between the figures. For three good examples, see these: Florence 76931, a pyxis on which the signature is divided between Herakles, Zeus, and Athena (*ABV*, p. 229, VII; *Paralipomena*, pp. 108, 109; *Addenda²*, p. 59; Tosto, *ΝΙΚΟΣΘΕΝΕΣΕΠΟΙΕΣΕΝ*, pp. 227–28, cat. no. 139, pl. 135, 2); Louvre F 106, a Nicosthenic amphora on which the inscription is divided between the hind legs of the Nemean Lion, the legs of Iolaos, and the lotus bud at the handle (*ABV*,

p. 218, no. 13; *Addenda²*, p. 57; Tosto, *ΝΙΚΟΣΘΕΝΕΣΕΠΟΙΕΣΕΝ*, p. 210, cat. no. 7, pl. 89); MMA 14.136 (*ABV*, p. 232, no. 13; *Addenda²*, p. 60; Tosto, *ΝΙΚΟΣΘΕΝΕΣΕΠΟΙΕΣΕΝ*, p. 229, cat. no. 148, pl. 141, 2—here, the image is reversed), the signature written below the rim between the heads of the figures.

For a discussion of the signatures of Nikosthenes as well as of the different hands that wrote them, see Tosto, *ΝΙΚΟΣΘΕΝΕΣΕΠΟΙΕΣΕΝ*, pp. 176–82. It is a great pity that Tosto did not illustrate a sample of them in detailed photographs.

71. Conveniently collected in Tosto, *ΝΙΚΟΣΘΕΝΕΣΕΠΟΙΕΣΕΝ*, pp. 229, 231–33.

72. Malibu, J. Paul Getty Museum 86.AE.170 (*ABV*, p. 231, no. 10; *Paralipomena*, p. 109, no. 10; *Addenda²*, p. 60; *CVA*, Malibu 2 [USA 25], pl. 111 [1285], 2, and pl. 112 [1286], 1; Tosto, *ΝΙΚΟΣΘΕΝΕΣΕΠΟΙΕΣΕΝ*, p. 232, cat. no. 166, pl. 149).

73. For London B.M. 1980.11-29.1, see note 21 above. For the volute-krater and the psykter signed by Nikosthenes, see note 53 above.

74. Here are some examples of vases, all of good quality, by painters who do not seem to have left us other work. Athens, N.M. 353 by the Piraeus Painter, a neck-amphora of ca. 620 B.C., depicting two chariot teams (*ABV*, p. 2; *Paralipomena*, p. 1,— no. 1; *Addenda²*, p. 1). Eleusis 280, ex 4267, a loutrophoros of ca. 570 B.C. signed by Kleimachos as potter, with a man and a women on the neck (see note 53 above). Athens, N.M. Akropolis 2134, a fragmentary kantharos of ca. 560–550 B.C. that shows a very large-scale battle between the Olympian Gods and the Giants (*ABV*, p. 347,—; *Addenda²*, p. 94); the vase was signed by the potter, but his name is lost. Louvre F 69, a kyathoid vase of ca. 540 B.C. signed by Theozotos and depicting a goatherd (see note 67 above). Oxford 189, a small standed dish dated ca. 520 B.C., signed by Oikopheles as potter and painter. It shows a Gorgoneion in a small tondo surrounded by a frieze consisting of four themes: a hare hunt, a sphinx, a satyr and a maenad, and Herakles and a Centaur (*ABV*, p. 349,—; *Paralipomena*, pp. 159–60).

75. *ABV*, p. 134, no. 22; *Paralipomena*, p. 55, no. 22.

76. Bothmer, "Lids by the Amasis Painter," pp. 83–91 (see note 4 above).

77. Examples include Zurich ETH 7 (*CVA*, Zürich 1 [Schweiz 2], pl. 16 [58], 2); and four lids in Brussels (*CVA*, Bruxelles 3 [Belgique 3], pl. 24 [118], 1–4). For a lid still in place, see MMA 98.89, an unattributed amphora dated early in the 5th century B.C. (*CVA*, Metropolitan Museum 3 [USA 12], pl. 23 [555], 2, and p. 19 for a description of it). For a neck-amphora with extant lid, see MMA 17.230.14 by Exekias (note 4 above and the illustration in *CVA*, Metropolitan Museum 4 [USA 16], pl. 19 [747], 1).

78. Tosto (*ΝΙΚΟΣΘΕΝΕΣΕΠΟΙΕΣΕΝ*, p. 178, n. 824) gives a list of signatures he describes in the text as follows: "the lettering is careless and the line disorderly. Thickish strokes are the rule, often blotted and ragged, as if written with a brush clogged with clay-paint . . . ; the horizontal bars of many epsilons, for instance, have run together." Most of the examples cited by Tosto are later than MMA 1999.30. One signature, however, seems to me particularly relevant to that on our amphora. This is on Brussels R 388, an early Nicosthenic amphora that incorporates fragments once in the Fogg Art Museum, Cambridge, Mass., and in Florence (*ABV*, p. 217, no. 11). The illustration in Tosto, *ΝΙΚΟΣΘΕΝΕΣΕΠΟΙΕΣΕΝ*, p. 209, cat. no. 4, pl. 88, does not depict the side of the amphora with the inscription, which is preserved

on the fragment once in the Fogg; for a good illustration, see Hoppin, *Handbook,* p. 193. Compare especially, the thickness of some of the letters, particularly, the epsilons and the meandering of the inscription.

79. The shape of these neck-amphorae, which is not pertinent to the present discussion, was borrowed from Etruria but given a distinctive Attic stylistic flavor. See the discussion by Tosto, *ΝΙΚΟΣΘΕΝΕΣΕΠΟΙΕΣΕΝ,* chap. 1, "Nikosthenic Amphorae: An Etruscan Vase-Form 1–127," pp. 17–41.

80. Examples of its early-6th-century use, all by the Gorgon Painter, are the following: Louvre E 817 (*ABV,* p. 9, no. 7; *Paralipomena,* p. 6, no. 7; *Addenda²,* p. 2); Tübingen 5445/28 (*Paralipomena,* p. 7, no. 11; *Addenda²,* p. 3); London, Russell (*ABV,* p. 9, no. 17)

81. Briefly discussed in Tosto, *ΝΙΚΟΣΘΕΝΕΣΕΠΟΙΕΣΕΝ,* pp. 83–84. Tosto (ibid., p. 83) mentions the rarity of this configuration as it appears here, in particular the treatment of the hearts of the palmettes: "Most strikingly, about two-thirds of the palmettes in crosses, unlike those in chains, have bipartite cores, that is, the core is divided into two curving sections by an inner arch (*c–d*). The type is extremely rare in Attic painting. Insofar as I am aware, it recurs in the panel of an olpe by the Gorgon Painter, about 590; in the crosses at the handles of the black-figure type B amphora with an *epoiese*-signature of Andokides [MMA 1999.30], about 540; and next to the handles of a black-figure eye-cup, about 540–530." The last example, in the Jacques L. Theodor collection in Brussels, bears no resemblance to MMA 1999.30 (see Pieter Heeson, with contributions by Herman A. G. Brijder and J. L. Kluiver, *The J. L. Theodor Collection of Attic Black-Figure Vases,* Allard Pierson Series 10 [Amsterdam, 1996], p. 182).

82. Kurashiki, Ninagawa Museum (*ABV,* p. 217, no. 9; Tosto, *ΝΙΚΟΣΘΕΝΕΣΕΠΟΙΕΣΕΝ,* pp. 208–9, cat. no. 1, pl. 85); Rome, Villa Giulia 20863 (*ABV,* p. 218, no. 14; *Paralipomena,* p. 104, no. 14; Tosto, *ΝΙΚΟΣΘΕΝΕΣΕΠΟΙΕΣΕΝ,* pp. 210–11, cat. no. 11, pl. 91).

83. See Louvre E 817 (note 79 above).

84. See the tabulation of this ornament in his work and remarks in *Agora* XXIII, p. 100, under cat. no. 6. Rosettes also appear on the sides of the mouths of loutrophoroi during this time. See, e.g., Charikleia Papadopoulou-Kanellopoulou, Ἱερό τῆς Νύμφης. Μελανόμορφες Λουτροφόροι (Athens, 1997), no. 246, pl. 48, nos. 280–81, pl. 55, and no. 291, pl. 58. All of these are significantly earlier than MMA 1999.30.

85. *ABV,* p. 216, no. 2; *Paralipomena,* p. 104, no. 2; *Addenda²,* p. 57; Tosto, *ΝΙΚΟΣΘΕΝΕΣΕΠΟΙΕΣΕΝ,* p. 215, cat. no. 43, dated ca. 535 B.C. (p. 14), so perhaps marginally later than MMA 1999.30. For a hardly legible illustration, see *CVA,* Louvre 4 [France 5], pl. 33 [199], 7 and 11. For earlier occurrences of rosettes on the backs of handles, see *Agora* XXIII, p. 121, under cat. no. 147.

86. See the brief discussion by Tosto (*ΝΙΚΟΣΘΕΝΕΣΕΠΟΙΕΣΕΝ,* pp. 79–80), who shows that the pattern on Greek vases begins in East Greek ware.

87. I have only been able to find this treatment of ivy on an unattributed amphora of Type B dating from ca. 540 B.C. that was once on the Paris art market (Koutoulakis): Side A, showing a mounted youth leading a riderless horse, between two men; Side B, showing two mounted youths; in the field on each side, nonsense inscriptions. I know this piece from Bothmer's photographs. Similar is Würzburg 258, also unattributed, but on this amphora the upper half of the pattern is a border of esses, not ivy (Ernst Langlotz, *Griechische Vasen in Würzburg* [Munich,

1932], pl. 78). On these, the ivy leaves alternate red and black.

88. J. D. Beazley, "Groups of Mid-Sixth Century Black-Figure," *BSA* 32 (1931–32), pp. 3–4.

89. See note 60 above.

90. *ABV,* p. 135, no. 44; *Paralipomena,* p. 55, no. 44; *Addenda²,* p. 36. Probably ca. 540 B.C. or a little later. The similarity between the two amphorae was briefly noted by Beazley (*ABV,* p. 253).

91. See note 15 above. A neck-amphora of Panathenaic shape, as the name implies, has the shape of the prize vase but not its subjects. It may be decorated in black-figure or in red-figure. See *Agora* XXIII, pp. 10–11, and *Agora* XXX (see note 6 above), pp. 9–11. For the dotted links, see also the Princeton Painter's handsome neck-amphora in London, B.M. 1843.11–3.100 (B 212) (*ABV,* p. 297, no. 1; *Paralipomena,* p. 129, no. 1; *Addenda²,* p. 78). One further, if perhaps minor, link with the Princeton Painter's Workshop may be included here. In note 3 above, it was stated that the top of the mouth of MMA 1999.30 is glazed, instead of reserved. This is also true of Princeton 29.192 in the manner of the Princeton Painter (*ABV,* p. 300, no. 9; *Paralipomena,* p. 130, no. 9).

92. *ABV,* p. 137, no. 63; *Paralipomena,* p. 55, no. 63; *Addenda²,* p. 37.

93. *ABV,* p. 135, no. 39; *Addenda²,* p. 36.

94. *ABV,* p. 134, no. 15.

95. See note 90 above.

96. *ABV,* p. 300, no. 12; *Paralipomena,* p. 130,—, no. 12.

97. Rome, Conservatori 158: *CVA,* Musei Capitolini 1 [Italia 36], pl. 26 [1626], 1. This hydria is probably in the manner of the Princeton Painter. See Mary B. Moore, *Horses on Black-Figured Greek Vases of the Archaic Period: Ca. 620–480 B.C.,* Ph.D. diss. New York University, 1971 (Ann Arbor, 1972), p. 96, cat. no. 643. This biconcave pair of arcs occurs on the necks of the pole horses on Würzburg L 415, a Droop cup attributed to the Group of Toronto 289 (*ABV,* p. 196,—, no. 1; *Addenda²,* p. 53).

98. Since this is a chariot wheeling around, the heads of the pole horses are frontal, and a throatlatch would not be visible. These horses have browbands.

99. See note 6 above.

100. MMA 56.171.9 (*ABV,* p. 299, no. 15; *Paralipomena,* p. 129, no. 25; *Addenda²,* p. 78). Rome, Villa Giulia 910 (*ABV,* p. 298, no. 9; *Paralipomena,* p. 129, no. 9). For the name piece, Princeton 169, see note 15 above.

101. See his name vase, Louvre E 874 (*ABV,* p. 8, no. 1; *Paralipomena,* p. 6, no. 1; *Addenda²,* p. 2). For the convention, see note 5 above. This arrangement for a four-horse team in profile was also used for relief sculpture. A particularly good example is MMA 36.11.13 (see note 5 above). See also Athena's and Aphrodite's chariot teams on the west frieze of the Siphnian Treasury at Delphi (Pierre de La Coste-Messelière, *Delphes* [Paris, 1957], figs. 66, 67). Each of these examples may be dated ca. 530 B.C. or a little later.

102. *Paralipomena,* p. 61; Eleni Manakidou, *Παραστάσεις με ἄρματα (8ος–5ος αι π.Χ.) Παρατηρήσεις στην εικονογραφία τους* (Thessaloniki, 1994), pp. 58–61 and pl. 11; see also Immerwahr, *Attic Script,* p. 34, cat. no. 144.

103. For this feature, though it is less animated, see the figure of Stesagoras himself on Exekias's pyxis (Manakidou, *Παραστάσεις,* pl. 11, γ).

Polychromy on the Amathus Sarcophagus, a "Rare Gem of Art"

ELIZABETH A. HENDRIX

Assistant Conservator, Sherman Fairchild Center for Objects Conservation, The Metropolitan Museum of Art

THE ELABORATELY SCULPTED and painted limestone sarcophagus on display in the new Cypriot galleries at The Metropolitan Museum of Art was brought to New York in 1872–73 by General Luigi Palma di Cesnola, who was to become the Museum's first director in 1879. Cesnola and his family had arrived in Cyprus on December 25, 1865, to serve as American consul.[1] The British and French consuls were already in place and, in fact, were already digging for antiquities.[2] Cesnola followed their lead, exploring the areas around Dali (ancient Idalion), Athienou (Golgoi), and later Amathus. He published the results of his efforts in 1877 (*Cyprus: Its Ancient Cities, Tombs, and Temples*), combining anecdotes of his adventures and descriptions of the local inhabitants with a brief history of the island and the report on his archaeological discoveries.

Amathus is situated on an acropolis on the southern coast of the island, northeast of modern Limassol (Figure 1). Near the sea, in a well-watered valley and close to forests as well as rich copper sources in the Troodos Mountains,[3] the site offered many advantages to the artisans and traders who settled there. According to Cesnola (whose opinion has more recently been expressed by others), the town was founded by Phoenicians, who also settled at nearby Paphos and Kition and whose traditions persisted in the region, especially at Amathus.[4] Cesnola was equally interested in the city's Homeric associations, reminding his readers that Agamemnon was said to have installed a colony of Greeks at Amathus on his return from Troy.[5]

Associated with the ancient settlement were three groups of tombs. One of them, with graves ranging in date from the period known as Cypro-Geometric II (ca. 950–850 B.C.) to the Greek Classical era (ca. 500–350 B.C.), was located in a field east of the north aqueduct, just outside the city wall (see Figure 1).[6] Within this group of about one hundred tombs was the one that contained the painted sarcophagus under discussion (Colorplate 1, Figures 3–6), recovered in fragments by Cesnola sometime in the early 1870s, possibly before his first reported campaign at Amathus in 1874–75.[7]

The one-, two-, and four-chambered tombs unearthed by Cesnola northeast of Amathus were built of fine ashlar masonry; he described the individual blocks as measuring on average 14 feet by 7¼ feet by 2 feet.[8] He stated that the tombs were buried more than 40 feet deep in the earth;[9] however, subsequent visitors to the area noted that the remains lay just below the surface of the ground.[10] Although the great majority of tombs at Amathus were disturbed by the time Cesnola got there, nearly all still contained sarcophagi of local limestone or of marble.[11] The so-called Amathus sarcophagus at The Metropolitan Museum of Art is the most elaborate and arguably the most interesting example found by Cesnola on Cyprus. The four-chambered tomb where it was found —one of two in the group—was described by Cesnola as follows: "This tomb consisted of a square room used as an antechamber, and three lateral rooms, to the right and left, and opposite the entrance door. The sculptured sarcophagus was in the centre of the inner room, facing the entrance, and lay there in a heap broken to pieces by the vandals who centuries ago had opened this tomb, and being perhaps disappointed in not finding the treasure they sought, wreaked their vengeance on this rare gem of art."[12]

He continued: "In the chambers adjacent to that in which the great sarcophagus was found were two plain sarcophagi, one in white marble and the other in calcareous stone, both of which had been greatly damaged."[13] A picturesque tale of Crusader knights (the aforementioned "vandals") discovering the tomb—which provides a romantic pedigree for Cesnola's efforts—follows this passage, from which we gather that there were three sarcophagi, including one of imported marble, in the large, elaborate and carefully constructed tomb. There can be little doubt that the occupant was an important personage in the city of Amathus.

© The Metropolitan Museum of Art 2001

METROPOLITAN MUSEUM JOURNAL 36

The notes for this article begin on page 57.

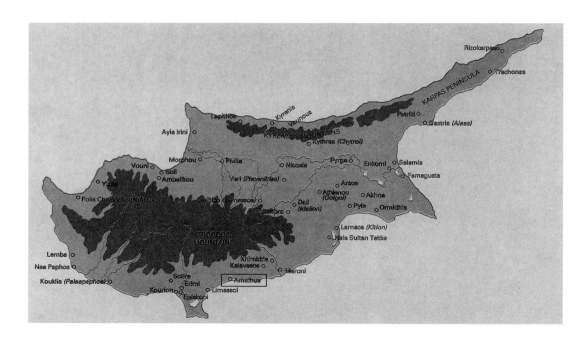

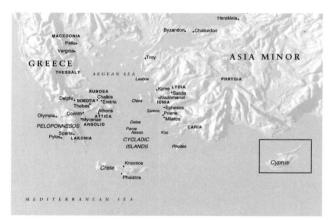

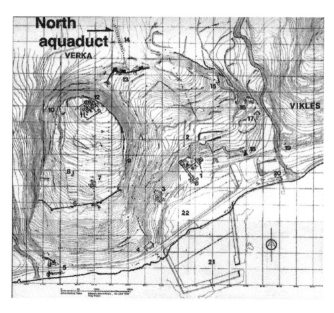

Figure 1. Maps of Cyprus, the eastern Mediterranean, and Amathus (map of Cyprus: after Veronica Tatton-Brown, *Ancient Cyprus*, 2nd ed. [London, 1997], p. 12, ©British Museum; map of the eastern Mediterranean: detail of *Ancient Art from Cyprus* [New York, 2000], p. xiv; map of Amathus: courtesy Pierre Aupert)

Although Cesnola did not mention it in his 1877 publication, all four sides and probably much of the lid of the sarcophagus were painted in red, green, black, and two shades of blue. Almost every centimeter of stone was highly colored, with the exception of the symbolic figures on the short ends of the sarcophagus, where only details were picked out in color. The background of each side was patterned in blue and red, and the bands of decoration above and below the figural scenes were also painted in contrasting shades (a reconstruction of the polychromy on the sarcophagus is illustrated in Colorplate 1, and the subject is discussed in detail below).

DATE AND ICONOGRAPHY

According to Cesnola, the approximate date of the sarcophagus is suggested by comparing it with a Lycian frieze from Building G at Xanthus, tentatively dated by Henri Metzger to the second quarter of the fifth century B.C., just after the destruction of the city in about 470 B.C.[14] In particular, Cesnola noted the similarity between the "topknots" on the horses' bridles in the two works.[15] John L. Myres first suggested a date for the sarcophagus, based on style, of about 550–500 B.C., but after comparing the sphinxes on the lid to examples from the Archaic period he eventually

44

Cyprus provided some of the fields on which the struggle between East and West was played out. Amathus, alone among Cypriot cities, remained loyal to the Persians when the island was invaded by Ionian Greeks.[20] In time, other cities, too, such as Kourion, turned the tide of battle on Cyprus against the Greeks and in favor of the Persians. All the while, Greek imports and influence seem to have continued to flow into the island, alongside those of the Phoenicians (major suppliers of luxury goods to the East), testifying to the mixed allegiances of communities throughout Cyprus since at least the sixth century B.C.[21]

The scenes and figural types presented on the Amathus sarcophagus would be consistent with the hand of a sculptor and/or the taste of a patron who was in some respects familiar with art of both the East and the West. As will be discussed below, the iconography and ornament have parallels in the Near East; however, the faces depicted on the sarcophagus are decidedly not Oriental—nor are they even Cypriot in appearance. Compare them with the visages of Assyrians on Ashurbanipal's relief sculpture from Nineveh,[22] for example, and the rest of the Cypriot-looking sculpture at Amathus.[23] Their very "Greek" aspect, reminiscent of the faces of late-sixth-century-B.C. statues from the Athenian Acropolis,[24] hints at types familiar to the sculptor, who may well have been following models from Greece in fashion a couple decades or so before the sarcophagus was carved.

The iconography and style of certain elements are much older, suggesting that some Phoenician traditions at Amathus were as deeply rooted as they were strong. Already in the fourteenth and thirteenth centuries B.C., ivory workers at Ugarit, on the Levantine coast opposite Cyprus, were producing figural scenes bordered by the same stylized-tree formation that was carved on the piers of the long sides of the Amathus sarcophagus more than seven hundred years later. This vegetal motif also persisted in Syrian and Phoenician ivories—for example, in a carving of two sphinxes from Arslan Tash of the second half of the ninth century B.C.,[25] and in an eighth-century plaque exported to Nimrud in Mesopotamia (Figure 2), where the products of Phoenician ivory carvers were highly prized.

The procession scenes on each long side of the sarcophagus are not unusual in their iconography (see Figures 3, 4). As Cesnola himself noted, such scenes appear on the frieze of horsemen and chariots recovered at Xanthus from a sepulchral monument.[26] Procession scenes frequently occur in nonsepulchral contexts on wall reliefs in Assyria and Persia. Those from the reign of Ashurbanipal (ca. 630 B.C.) in the palace of his predecessor Sennacherib, include representations of very similar horse tack, especially the

arrived at a date in the early fifth century B.C.[16] Also basing her judgment more on style than on iconography, Veronica Tatton-Brown concluded in 1981 that the sarcophagus fits best in the second quarter of the fifth century B.C., somewhere between 460 and 450 B.C.[17] In 1996 Pierre Aupert brought the date back to the time favored by Myres, the first decades of the fifth century B.C.[18] Most recently curators in the Metropolitan Museum Carlos A. Picón and Joan R. Mertens have concurred with Vassos Karageorghis that the sarcophagus should be dated to about 475 B.C.[19]

The beginning of the fifth century B.C. was a time of momentous conflict between Greece and Persia, and

Figure 3. Side A of the Amathus sarcophagus, from Cyprus, ca. 475 B.C. Limestone, 147.3 x 228.8 x 109.5 cm overall sarcophagus. The Metropolitan Museum of Art, The Cesnola Collection, Purchased by subscription, 1874–76 (74.51.2453)

Figure 4. Side B of the Amathus sarcophagus

Figure 5. Side C of the Amathus sarcophagus

Figure 6. Side D of the Amathus sarcophagus

details of the harness. However, the liveliness of the figures on the Amathus sarcophagus—both their postures and their facial expressions—is unlike anything from the Near East (where a shallower type of relief carving was used to render both animated and more sedate scenes).[27] Cesnola suggested that the figures in the parasol group on Side A of our sarcophagus may represent a Persian satrap and his attendant, as does a similar group on the Nereid Monument, of about 400 B.C., also from Xanthus. [28] Amathus was, in fact, part of the Persian satrapy under Darius at the end of the sixth century B.C.; the motif may therefore acknowledge Persian traditions of wall-relief carving. But, as Cesnola observed, the processions on the Amathus sarcophagus "would seem to have been part of funeral obsequies," not parades of tribute bearers, such as those that decorated palace walls at Nineveh and Persepolis.

The naked women on one short side of the sarcophagus (Figure 5) have been identified as figures representing the Phoenician goddess Astarte,[29] although their posture and gesture have a long history in the Near East. In Cyprus, tradition holds that Astarte became Aphrodite, the preeminent deity of the island.[30] A cult center devoted to Astarte/Aphrodite was located at Amathus in the vicinity of Vikles (see Figure 1), possibly about 500 B.C. and, if so, was contemporary with the Amathus sarcophagus.[31]

Egyptian influence is apparent on the other short side of the sarcophagus, where four figures of the god Bes appear (Figure 6). A horned deity, sometimes in the form of an anthropomorphized bull but sometimes in the guise of the Near Eastern Humbaba or the Egyptian Bes, was second in importance only to Astarte/Aphrodite in Cyprus. The presence of both deities on the Amathus sarcophagus suggests an attempt to ward away evil on the one hand (ensuring the deceased a safe journey to the next world?)[32] and to conjure fecundity on the other. The representation of male figures on one side and female figures on the other emphasizes the idea of fertility.[33]

RESTORATION AND CONSERVATION HISTORY BEFORE 1999

In his *Handbook of the Cesnola Collection of Antiquities from Cyprus,* published by the Museum in 1914, John L. Myres stated that the Amathus sarcophagus was restored before it was shipped to New York,[34] and an analysis of the mortar lining of the interior supports this claim.[35] At that time the fragments of stone Cesnola had found scattered about the tomb chamber were reattached to each other and to the mortar lining with a plasterlike substance of varying hardness. The sarcophagus was cleaned and then completely coated

Figure 7. Detail of Side D of the Amathus sarcophagus showing old plaster restoration when it was being removed

with a yellow-tinted limestone wash, which obscured much of the original polychromy, though the coating may also have protected it from the damaging effects of light (see below, p. 53).[36]

When Cesnola's "rare gem of art" arrived at the Museum, it was placed on display in the main hall, and there it remained, probably undisturbed, for more than eighty years. Myres mentions that it was cleaned in 1909, but I have been unable to find any record of this in the Museum's files.[37]

In 1958 the lid was removed, and red lines tracing the borders of the major fragments of stone were observed on the mortar lining. It is not clear if the sarcophagus was examined or treated after 1958, but there are no records to indicate that it was. It was displayed in 1987 until the "Cypriot Corridor" was disassembled in August of 1997.

THE 1999–2000 CONSERVATION CAMPAIGN

In preparation for the reinstallation of Cypriot art in the Metropolitan Museum, the Amathus sarcophagus

was scrutinized by conservators as well as curators. We determined that a thorough examination and treatment would improve our understanding of the piece and its appearance. The latest conservation campaign thus began in August of 1999. Six conservators worked on the sarcophagus for nearly a year, two of us continuously. Our goals were to ensure that the sarcophagus was structurally stable, to identify any modern materials used in previous restorations, and to reveal as much of the original surface as possible. We also decided that the treatment on all four sides should be simple and consistent in method and materials.

After consolidating some old repairs that had deteriorated and determining that the overall structure was sound, we turned to a consideration of the surface. The greatest amount of previous restoration was found to be the additions of plaster over broken or weathered stone surfaces, and the thin limewash toned with raw sienna (a golden color) that covered plaster restoration, original stone, and in some cases the original polychromy, grossly distorting the visual effect in those areas. Tests showed us that warm water brushed on the surface loosened the raw sienna and its limewash vehicle without disturbing original polychromy, and so this procedure was carried out over the entire surface to diminish the yellow effect. As we reduced the yellow limewash, we also mechanically removed areas of plaster restoration that had been applied as a skim coat over areas of original stone. Most often, the stone was sound underneath this coating, and in some cases the original pigments were intact as well; wherever it seemed feasible to do so, the original surface was exposed (see Figure 7).

Little by little, we were able to determine which elements of the relief were originally painted with which colors, but except for some of the raw sienna, all pigments were left on original stone surfaces. Had we attempted to remove the modern blue paint from the horses' hooves, for example (see below, pp. 49, 52), we would have risked removing some ancient pigments as well. In some areas raw sienna had been painted on top of the restored blue, suggesting the order of these two restoration efforts.

A hard gypsum crust had formed over some areas of the sarcophagus while it was still buried (see below, p. 53). We cleaned the disfiguring areas of this crust away, except where it covered cinnabar, a brilliant but capricious red pigment. In those areas, we removed only enough of the crust to determine which details were red. (The information thus obtained later enabled me to prepare the color reconstructions illustrated in Colorplate 1.) Most of the patches of exposed cinnabar were sealed with a dilute clear acrylic coating in an attempt to keep the red from darkening (discussed below, pp. 53–54). In addition, we covered some small areas of red with opaque Japanese tissue paper painted the color of the stone so that future conservators might compare them with the areas that were given clear coatings.

RECONSTRUCTION OF THE POLYCHROMY

An important part of the most recent conservation program was to determine the color scheme and the pigments on the sarcophagus as accurately as possible. To this end, our team of conservators mapped the colors that were visible on each side, with the exception of the yellow limewash that coated everything. We then took microscopic samples from different areas of each side in order to identify the colors, both ancient and modern, that had been applied to individual sculptural elements on the sarcophagus; sixty-seven samples were taken in all. As a rule, except for the background of the figurative panels, each color follows the sculptural elements closely. Some fine details in black were also noted, such as the stripe on the parasol bearer's shirt. A map was created for each side with "flags" showing exactly where the samples had been taken. Another map, also for each side, was made to document precisely where pigments were still preserved. Pigments were sampled from both original surfaces and restored areas in order to determine whether modern materials differed from the ancient ones. The results also indicate that some colors were applied over original surface in modern times. Colorplate 1 shows, as far as can be determined, how the original polychromy looked on each side.

With the exception of Cesnola's *Cyprus,* most of the important earlier descriptions of the sarcophagus mention the polychromy, some with more accuracy than others. Describing the stone fragments in his *Handbook* of 1914, Myres wrote: "They were loaded originally with a hard limewash richly coloured with black, red, yellow, and blue. The last has mostly turned to green; but the green is so thick and loose that it may in part result from the decay of gilded copper-foil. Most of the colour which remains is ancient, except about the plastered fractures."[38] Myres correctly observed that black, red, and blue had originally been applied. He may have thought Cesnola's golden overall wash was at least partially ancient, and he was also mistaken about the reason behind the blue-to-green shift.

Tatton-Brown described the sarcophagus as originally painted with vivid colors; she mentioned in particular the "green" that could be observed on the lozenges ("scales") behind the figures, the beads of the Astartes' necklaces, the harnesses of the horses on the long sides, the chariots, and the parasol.[39] None of these details was originally meant to appear green, however; a color shift occurred over time that will be discussed below. Although Aupert characterizes the sarcophagus as richly decorated, he does not elaborate further on the polychromy.[40] Following are a description of the colors we found on the sarcophagus, an identification of the pigments used, and the conclusions we drew regarding the antiquity of the colors. The optical, elemental, and compositional analyses were carried out with polarizing light microscopy (PLM), X-ray fluorescence spectroscopy (XRF), Fourier-transform infrared spectroscopy (FTIR), X-ray diffraction (XRD), and energy dispersive X-ray spectrometry (EDS). These techniques are briefly described in the Appendix.

Many of the decorative elements common to all four sides were painted the same color (see Table 1). Two different blues were used on the sarcophagus in antiquity: azurite, a strong medium-to-dark blue, and Egyptian blue, which is paler, and closer to a robin's egg in hue (see Colorplate 1). Azurite was chosen for most of the architectural elements; for example, in the ornamental frieze that runs around the top of the sarcophagus box every other cone in the upper band and every other ball in the lower is painted with azurite. Azurite was also used to decorate every other "egg" above and below the figurative panels on each of the four sides and as one of the two colors on the background scale pattern on each side. In addition, every other "plume," the central line of the arching motif, the curling elements, and the outer parts of the bud motif (but not the stems) on the piers that border the long sides were decorated in this color. The paler Egyptian blue was used to paint the vertical bands that frame the corner piers and the horizontal groundlines beneath the four figurative scenes.

A cooler, almost midnight blue was also found on the sarcophagus. This color, identified as Prussian blue, was first made in 1704 and in use by 1750, but it did not become common until the late eighteenth century.[41] We found that it had been consistently applied over the plaster restorations where blue was required by the design; it also served to enhance some of the original blue-painted areas, such as the horses' hooves (where azurite was also found) and some of the volutes on the piers. In addition, Prussian blue decorated some elements of the horse tack that had originally been painted red.

During the cleaning process it became apparent that red had been applied almost as generously as blue. The pigment was identified by PLM, XRD, XRF, and EDS as cinnabar, known to have been used in the

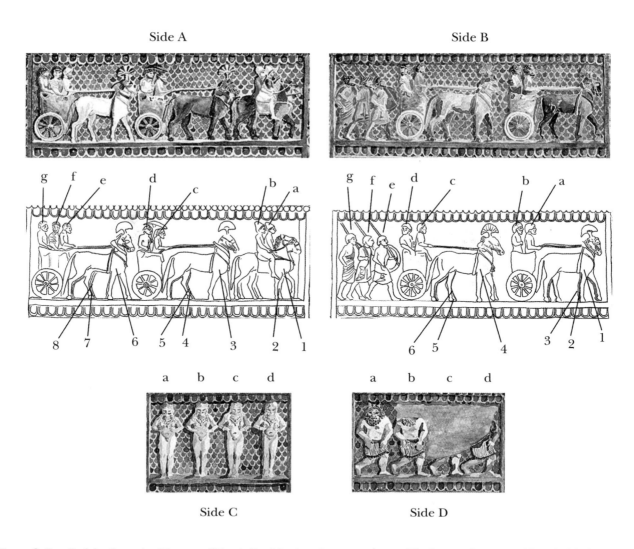

Figure 8. Detail of the figurative friezes on Sides A–D of the Amathus sarcophagus. The human figures are identified by lowercase letters and the horses by numbers (drawing: the author)

eastern Mediterranean since at least the Early Bronze Age.[42] The decorative motifs of the continuous frieze were colored with azurite, as we have seen, in alternation with cinnabar. In addition, the background of the lotus-blossom and lotus-bud band was painted with this vibrant red. Azurite and cinnabar were also alternated along the egg motif above and below the figurative panels on the long sides, and across the scale pattern on the background of all four sides. Relatively fewer details were picked out in red on the piers of the long sides: these include the alternating plumes, the arches, the bud centers, and the teardrop-shaped "tendrils" suspended from the curly vegetal forms. On the short sides, red was used as the background color on the vertical piers. Like the Prussian blue, a modern vermilion paint had been used to continue areas of

the design covered by the plaster restoration. Because of the chemical similarity between cinnabar and vermilion (both are mercuric sulfides), it was difficult to determine whether vermilion had been applied over original stone in conjunction with the ancient cinnabar.[43]

A true green appears in the lotus band that encircles the sarcophagus (see Colorplate 1). The optical properties of the pigment are consistent with terre verte, "high-quality deposits" of which are still being exploited on Cyprus.[44] On the long sides, vestigial traces were found only on the vine at the base of the flowers, but on the short side with the Bes figures green was also located in the center of the blossoms and the buds. We are working under the assumption that green was used all the way around the sarcopha-

TABLE 1. COLORS USED ON ELEMENTS OF THE AMATHUS SARCOPHAGUS

(for the colors, see Colorplate 1; for identification of the figures in the friezes, see Figure 8)

ELEMENTS ON THE SARCOPHAGUS	BLUE	RED	GREEN	BLACK
Common to two or more sides				
alternating cone shapes at top of sarcophagus box	azurite	cinnabar		
alternating balls at bottom of frieze	azurite	cinnabar		
alternating egg shapes in horizontal bands above and below figurative panels	azurite	cinnabar		
alternating scales in backgrounds of figurative panels	azurite	cinnabar		
alternating plumes in piers flanking long sides	azurite	cinnabar		
alternating arches above "stretched" volutes in piers flanking long sides	azurite	cinnabar		
"stretched" and compact volutes, and buds in piers flanking long sides	azurite			
vertical borders of piers	Egyptian blue			
horizontal groundline in figurative panels	Egyptian blue			
background and vegetal ornaments on piers of short sides	Egyptian blue (vegetal motifs)	cinnabar (background)		
centers of buds and tendrils depending from "stretched" volutes in piers flanking long sides		cinnabar		
background of lotus-blossom and bud band in surrounding frieze		cinnabar		
center of and below lotus-blossom and bud motif			terre verte	
Side A				
incisions in horses' tails	azurite			
incisions in manes of horses A2, A6	azurite			
girth, yoke, and bridle side straps of horse A6	azurite			
girth of horse A3	azurite			
breast strap and most of bridle of horse A1	azurite			
hooves of horses A1, A3	azurite			
top of parasol	azurite			
stripes in horses' crests	Egyptian blue			
short-sleeved shirt of rider Ab and undergarment of rider Aa	Egyptian blue			
chariots	Egyptian blue			
hooves of horse A2		cinnabar		
tunic of rider Aa		cinnabar		
saddlecloth of horse A1		cinnabar		
yoke of horse A3	Prussian blue (modern overpaint)	cinnabar (below overpaint)		
spokes of parasol		cinnabar		
yoke pad of horse A6		cinnabar		
spaces between chariot-wheel spokes		cinnabar		
chariot cars	Egyptian blue (main part)	cinnabar (behind horses' tails)		
hair and beards of figures Ac, Ad, Af, Ag				charcoal
horses A1, A3				charcoal
thin lines around chariot wheels				charcoal
thin, seamlike lines in parasol bearer's shirt (figure Ad)				charcoal
Side B				
girth, tassels, bridle, blinker, and hooves of horse B4	azurite	cinnabar (edges of girth)		
stripes in horses' crests	Egyptian blue			
chariot cars	Egyptian blue (main part)	cinnabar (behind tail)		
tunic of shield-bearing soldier Be	Egyptian blue			
vertical element above yoke pad of horse B4		cinnabar		
spaces between chariot-wheel spokes		cinnabar		
shield interiors		cinnabar		
incisions in tail of horse B4		cinnabar		
horse B1				charcoal
hair and beards of all men				charcoal
Side C (Astarte figures)				
alternating beads of necklaces	azurite			
hair				charcoal
Side D (Bes figures)				
alternating fringe of Da's skirt	azurite	cinnabar		
interior of Da's ears		cinnabar		
hair and/or beard of Da, Db				charcoal
circles around irises of Da's eyes				charcoal
Lid				
alternating balls around base of gabled roof	azurite	cinnabar		
alternating vegetal motifs on preserved sculpted end above Side C	azurite	cinnabar		
alternating feathers of sphinxes, front and back	Egyptian blue	cinnabar		
circles around irises of sphinxes' eyes				charcoal

gus both in the heart of the flowers and on the band that links the vine with the flowers. It seems safe to do this because as a general rule details in the figurative elements were colored with some consistency from side to side.

Carbon black (charcoal) seems not to have been used on the areas of the sarcophagus decorated with architectural and vegetal motifs. Black does appear, however, in the four figurative panels, whose polychromy will be described fully below for each side. These descriptions will mention only what our analyses suggest were the original colors, not modern pigments.

Side A, one of the long sides, depicts a procession of two chariots led by two equestrian figures (see Figures 3, 8; Table 1). By counting the legs, one can determine that three horses were meant to be depicted as drawing each chariot, with another for each rider, totaling eight on this side. The incised lines in the tails of all the horses and the manes of horses A2 and A6 were painted azurite blue, as were the girth, yoke, and side straps of the bridle of horse A6, the girth of horse A3, and the breast strap and most of the bridle of horse A1. Azurite was used for the top of the parasol and for the hooves of horses A1 and A3.

Egyptian blue was identified on the short-sleeved shirt of the equestrian figure Ab, and on the undergarment of Aa. The chariots were painted Egyptian blue, as were the stripes on the horses' crests.

The hooves of horse A2 were red, as were the tunic of the equestrian figure Aa, the saddlecloth of horse A1, the yoke of horse A3, the spokes of the parasol, the yoke pad of horse A6, the spaces in between the spokes of the chariot wheels, and those parts of the chariot cars directly in back of the team. All samples of this color could be identified as cinnabar.

Black pigment (charcoal) was found in the hair and beards of figures Ac, Ad, Af, and Ag. Traces were also found on horses A1 and A3, suggesting that the coats of these animals were originally black. Thin lines of black filled the light incisions encircling the chariot wheels, and also described seams on the shirt of the parasol bearer.

The other long side of the sarcophagus, Side B, shows a similar procession, with two chariots preceding a group of foot soldiers bearing shields (see Figures 4, 8; Table 1). There are six horses on this side: two teams of three, each team drawing a chariot. Azurite blue decorated the girth, tassels, bridle, blinker, and hooves of horse B4. As on Side A, Egyptian blue was used to delineate the chariot cars and the stripes on the crests fanning above the horses' bridles. The tunic of the leading shield bearer, Be, was once also Egyptian blue.

Red (cinnabar) was painted on the front of the chariot directly behind the first team of horses, the edges of the blue girth of horse B4, the vertical element on top of the yoke pad of horse B4, and the spaces in between the spokes of the chariot wheels. The shield interiors, too, are red—as are those depicted in reliefs at the Siphnian Treasury at Delphi and at Building G at Xanthus.[45] Red was also used, interestingly enough, in the incisions defining the strands of the tail of B4 (perhaps indicating that this horse was chestnut-colored).

Charcoal black was identified on the hair and beards of all the figures on this side, as well as on most of horse B1.

The Astarte figures of Side C seem to have had relatively few painted details; there may have been a conscious choice to leave the stone as naked as the subject (see Figures 5, 8; Table 1). Azurite was used to color every other bead of the necklaces on each figure, and although no traces of cinnabar have been found, it would be consistent with the rest of the color scheme if red beads had alternated with the blue ones. Traces of black remain on the hair of the Astarte figures, but no color, if there ever was any, is left on the bracelets.

Nor does much color remain on the figures of the god Bes depicted on Side D (see Figures 6, 8; Table 1). Cinnabar red was found on every other string of Da's skirt, and in his ears. Carbon black (charcoal) was identified on the hair and beard of figure Da and the beard of figure Db (the upper part of the head is not preserved) and was used to describe the fine circles outlining the irises of Da's eyes.

Finally, we must also imagine the lid with its corner sphinxes brightly painted (see Figures 3–6; Table 1). The balls running in a band around the foot of the lid were done in azurite and cinnabar; but unlike those at the base of the frieze on the sarcophagus proper, the ones at either end of Side C are not both blue, but blue on the left and red on the right. This anomaly cannot be ascribed to erroneous restoration, since the lid is well preserved on this side. The face of the gable was in all likelihood painted over the entire decorated surface. Only a few of the elements preserve any pigment, but where there is color, azurite alternates with cinnabar on the vegetal motifs. The sphinxes were also painted. The creatures' wing feathers were colored front and back with alternating cinnabar and Egyptian blue, and the irises of their eyes were defined by thin black circles, as on the Bes figures. Since nothing original remains from the long sides of the lid, or from Side D save the damaged sphinxes (which preserve enough traces to show that they were painted in a way similar to the better-preserved examples), it is not possible to know how these sides may have been colored.

Discussion of the Color Shifts in Azurite and Cinnabar

Among the many questions raised during our examination of the sarcophagus were why the pigment identified as azurite often appears green and why the pigment identified as cinnabar sometimes appears black. In the case of azurite, the greenish hue associated with much of this blue can be explained by the presence of malachite, a pigment that has been used since antiquity in its own right. Under the microscope, at 400x magnification, the most predominant characteristic of the green particles after the hue is the fibrous or broken structure typical of malachite,[46] whereas the azurite particles are blue with a clean conchoidal fracture. Were these two colors deliberately mixed together in varying proportions on the sarcophagus to create a graded color effect? We noticed that the greenest blue-green was often found in deeply cut areas of the stone while the bluest shade tended to predominate on the high relief. This suggested that the artist might have been trying to achieve a special effect with the color application. However, blue-green could sometimes be found in a random distribution, such as on some parts of the vegetal motifs on the piers of the long sides. Furthermore, true azurite blue was occasionally preserved over an entire surface, whether flat or three-dimensional, and so we finally concluded that the two-color effect was accidental, the result of weathering or other natural conditions rather than of human agency.

The explanation for this color shift on the sarcophagus seems to lie in the chemical similarity between azurite and malachite. Water collected in the crevices of broken chunks of the sarcophagus or mere dampness in the tomb could have hydrated the copper carbonate of the azurite, transforming it directly into malachite. Gettens and Fitzhugh, who have published studies on both pigments, indicate that such shifts are common in old paintings kept in damp conditions: "There is hardly a medieval Italian church where azurite in mural paintings does not show evidence of being transformed to malachite."[47]

Earlier, I described the ancient red pigment on the sarcophagus as capricious. Chemical and compositional analyses by powder XRD, XRF, and EDS have identified the red as mercuric sulfide, or cinnabar/vermilion, and PLM has confirmed the optical properties of cinnabar. However, XRD and XRF analyses have also identified as cinnabar a black pigment that occurs on some of the patterns that appear red elsewhere on the sarcophagus, such as the scales that alternate with blue in the figurative panels.

More surprisingly, we noticed that the red we were

revealing underneath the thick modern limewash coating became gradually darker if it was left unconsolidated after cleaning. Why was the color turning now, after existing for thousands of years as a brilliant cherry red? The answer to this question, we think, is that for the first time in the long life of the sarcophagus, its surfaces were being exposed to light without protection. The sarcophagus was probably shut up in the dark tomb chamber soon after it was sculpted and painted. Whoever smashed it to pieces, perhaps in medieval times, apparently did so without removing the roof of the tomb, so the painted surfaces were exposed to daylight only in the nineteenth century, when Cesnola removed the fragments from their original context. Within a relatively short time, evidently before the sarcophagus left the island, Cesnola had it skim-coated with the yellow-toned limewash that has frequently been mentioned above. This covered stone, polychromy, and plaster restoration about equally. In addition, the hard gypsum deposit that we found on some areas of the surface must have kept the underlying paint from direct contact with daylight. This crust could have formed before the sarcophagus was broken, if water was able to seep through the calcareous walls of the tomb chamber and drip onto the lid or stone fragments. It may also have formed later, if the pieces were in direct contact with moisture, causing the calcium from the limestone to leach out of the fragments, combine with sulfur in the atmosphere, and form calcium sulfate (gypsum) on some surfaces.

This brief digression provides the background for our attempt to explain the shift that has occurred in the cinnabar. The darkened form of this red pigment, referred to as metacinnabarite or metacinnabar, was described as early as the first century B.C. by the Roman architect Vitruvius:

Though it keeps its colour perfectly when applied in the polished stucco finish of closed apartments, yet in open apartments, such as peristyles or exedrae or other places of the sort, where the bright rays of the sun and moon can penetrate, it is spoiled by contact with them, loses the strength of its colour, and turns black. Among many others, the secretary Faberius, who wished to have his house on the Avetine finished in elegant style, applied vermilion to all the walls of the peristyle; but after thirty days they turned to an ugly and mottled colour. He therefore made a contract to have other colours applied instead of vermilion.

But anybody who is more particular, and who wants a polished finish of vermilion that will keep its proper colour, should, after the wall has been polished and is dry, apply with a brush Pontic wax melted over a fire and mixed with a little oil; then after this he should bring the wax to a sweat by warming it and the wall at close quarters with charcoal enclosed in an iron vessel; and finally he should smooth it all off by rubbing it down with a wax candle and clean linen cloths, just as naked marble statues are treated.

This process is termed *ganosis* in Greek. The protecting coat of Pontic wax prevents the light of the moon and the rays of the sun from licking up and drawing the colour out of such polished finishing.[48]

We may gather from this text that the presence of a barrier layer can in some cases prevent the darkening of cinnabar and also that heat apparently does not affect the color adversely.

Descriptions in Dana's *System of Mineralogy* (compiled between 1837 and 1892) indicate that small amounts of zinc and selenium may substitute for mercury and sulfur, respectively, in naturally occurring samples of metacinnabar.[49] Since EDS analysis of samples taken from the sarcophagus did not identify either zinc or selenium,[50] substitution by these elements in the original ore is not the reason we have metacinnabar here. The pigment was applied in its red form and was meant to be red, never black (important when considering the red hooves and tail incisions).

Besides mercury and sulfur, we identified traces of iron in a sample taken from a restored section of the decoration, which may indicate that an iron oxide was used to extend the red pigment. No iron was found in the samples taken from areas that we judged were ancient (either because they were under a gypsum crust or because they were part of the original pattern overlaying intact stone). On the other hand, traces of silver, in one case significant, were found in the three ancient samples analyzed by EDS but not in the restoration sample. As silver sulfides and mercury sulfides can occur together, the explanation for this discovery may lie in the composition of the ore from which our cinnabar came.

The darkened form of cinnabar has the same chemical elements as the red variety, but a different crystal structure. Because the change from one form to the other takes place on the surface of a sample, XRD, which analyzes the bulk of the material, is not able to detect metacinnabar on samples that have not thoroughly converted.[51] Feller, in his "Studies on the Darkening of Vermilion by Light" (1967), measured the

rate of darkening with an instrument designed to detect changes in the wavelength absorbed by the pigment, rather than reflected by it.[52] When absorption was measured against time in a carbon-arc Fade-Ometer, the resulting straight line showed that the rate of formation of metacinnabar is directly related to time of exposure to light. Changes in the rate of darkening could be manipulated, however, by changing the medium in which the cinnabar was suspended, a relationship that Vitruvius had already noted. The early studies of Alexander Eibner, which had inspired Feller to look into this phenomenon, were confirmed by Feller's own work, which showed that cinnabar darkened more quickly in oil than in watercolor (presumably gum arabic was the binder) or acrylic emulsion. One implication is that the absence of medium of any sort leaves the pigment most vulnerable of all to darkening in the presence of light. The procedures we devised for treating areas of red paint on the sarcophagus (see above, pp. 49–52) are based on Feller's conclusions.

The kinetics of this color shift are not well understood; however, a recent study of the effects of light-aging on samples of cinnabar and two forms of synthetic vermilion has been undertaken at the Courtauld Institute in London by Rachel Grout and Aviva Burnstock.[53] Their study confirmed the conclusions of Eibner and Feller but also suggested that impurities in the pigment may affect darkening by altering the way light energy is absorbed in localized points.

The recent course of treatment in the Sherman Fairchild Center for Objects Conservation has restored to the carving on the Amathus sarcophagus something of its original character, now that the coating of plaster and limewash has in some areas been removed and in others diminished. In addition, the long and careful examination of the polychromy has made it possible to create a watercolor reconstruction of each side, reproductions of which hang on the wall opposite the sarcophagus in the Museum's new permanent installation of Cypriot art. With these nearby, the viewer can appreciate how astonishingly rich was the full effect and with careful inspection can find more than a little of the evidence for the reconstruction still visible on the stone.

APPENDIX: ANALYTICAL METHODS USED ON THE AMATHUS SARCOPHAGUS DURING THE 1999–2000 CONSERVATION CAMPAIGN AT THE METROPOLITAN MUSEUM

POLARIZING LIGHT MICROSCOPY (PLM)

With its high magnification capability (100x–400x), the polarizing light microscope has made it possible to identify the morphological and optical properties of a pigment and thereby gain valuable information about the manufacture and even the origin of a given sample. When an unidentified pigment is examined by PLM, the following properties are observed: (1) the sample's color/transparency in plane polarized light; (2) its color/transparency when polars are crossed; (3) its extinction characteristics under crossed polars; (4) its shape; (5) the sizes of its particles (average, plus smallest and largest); (6) its aspect ratio (long axis relative to short axis); and (7) its refractive index relative to the mount medium. PLM can also help determine whether or not the sample is still associated with particles that suggest its geological source.[54]

Under low magnification (8x–20x), samples are prepared by removing a few particles with a scalpel and placing them between two glass microscope slides. The slides are pressed together, crushing the particles. The particles are then scraped onto one of the slides and sealed with a cover slip to which a droplet of a mounting medium of known refractive index has been applied (the mounting medium fixes the particles between the glass slide and the cover slip). The mounted sample is then ready for examination under the higher-powered polarizing light microscope. The instrument utilized for the Amathus sarcophagus pigment analyses at the Sherman Fairchild Center for Objects Conservation was a Zeiss Axioplan 2; the mounting medium was Aroclor, with a refractive index of 1.66.

X-RAY FLUORESCENCE SPECTROSCOPY (XRF)

XRF is used to identify the elements that make up a sample of inorganic material, such as mineral pigments, metals, or salts. A beam of X rays is fired at the sample, causing atoms at the surface to emit fluorescent X rays (also called secondary-emission X rays). The particular wavelengths of the fluorescent X rays correspond to specific elements. A detector converts these X rays into electric pulses, which can be analyzed by software in the instrument's computer. The X-ray spectrometer at the Sherman Fairchild Center is set up in a lead-lined room, where even very large objects can be analyzed without removing a sample; a video camera reveals a tiny area that contains the target location.

A database in the instrument's computer contains known emission lines of the chemical elements, from the heaviest down to potassium (atomic number 19), the present limit of the detector; elements lighter than potassium, such as sulfur, will not be detected. As sulfur is one of the elements constituting the red pigment cinnabar (or vermilion), it is important to remember when interpreting the results of XRF analysis that the absence of sulfur in the analysis does not preclude the presence of cinnabar in the sample. Since no other red pigments contain the element mercury (atomic number 80), its detection is sufficient for an identification of cinnabar or vermilion. Hematite, an iron oxide, and red ocher, composed of silicates and iron oxides, will yield very similar results by XRF analysis; red lead, however, will produce clear peaks corresponding to the lead component.

Blue pigments cannot always be identified by this technique with certainty. The silicon and aluminum that occur as impurities in most samples of azurite will not be detected by XRF analysis, although the major element, copper, will be.[55] Egyptian blue, which is a mixture of calcium-copper silicates,[56] might be confused with azurite on a calcitic substrate if analyzed by XRF alone, as would the modern pigment phthalocyanine blue, which also contains copper. Lapis lazuli, a silicate containing sodium (atomic number 11) and/or potassium, and rich in sulfur, will be essentially invisible to XRF. The presence of cobalt blue, on the other hand, will be detected (as the element cobalt), and modern pigments such as Prussian blue, which contains iron, can also be spotted in XRF analysis.

The detection limits in XRF need to be considered when interpreting the results of analysis. The absence of certain elements may be a function of the instrument capabilities, or it may reflect the composition of the sample. Other questions must therefore be raised when a sample is analyzed—primarily, which elements are likely to be present, and which are not?

ENERGY DISPERSIVE X-RAY SPECTROMETRY (EDS)

As in XRF analysis, a beam of X rays is aimed at a sample and the specific photons thus emitted are collected and analyzed. When electrons of a certain energy strike electrons in the inner shells, or orbitals, of atoms in a specific element of the sample, the inner shell electrons will be displaced. Electrons from the next orbital will drop down to fill the vacancies. Since they are dropping to a lower energy level, they give off excess energy in the form of X rays, emitted at specific energies corresponding to the difference in energy between the shells; these energies are characteristic for each element. Thus, measurements of the energies of the X rays enable the identification of the element(s) from which they derive. A semiconductor detector captures the energy emitted by each X ray, then converts the energy to a voltage pulse and finally to a digital signal that is saved and plotted in a computer. The source for the impinging electron in the Sherman Fairchild Center is a scanning electron microscope outfitted with a Kevex Model Delta IV EDS instrument operated by Mark T. Wypyski.

FOURIER-TRANSFORM INFRARED SPECTROSCOPY (FTIR)

The component atoms of a molecule exist in states of vibrational motion with respect to each other. These modes of vibration are distinguished according to their spatial geometry and frequency, which are determined by the relative masses of the atoms and their arrangement in the molecular structure. Infrared spectroscopy is based on the principle that molecular vibrations can absorb energy from incident electromagnetic radiation having the same frequencies as the vibrational modes in the molecule; many of the vibrational modes occurring in materials comprising works of art have frequencies that occur in the infrared region of the electromagnetic spectrum, and so it is this region that is found to be specifically diagnostic.

In general, when infrared radiation is passed through an unknown sample, selective absorption by the many different molecular groups produces a spectrum of bands that can either be identified individually as to the specific molecular components that they represent or compared as an assemblage to spectra of known compounds in an effort to find an acceptable match.

FTIR permits all frequencies of absorption to be measured simultaneously—thus, much more quickly and efficiently than a so-called dispersive instrument, which measures frequencies in sequence. The FTIR instrument operated at the Museum by Dora Henel, a volunteer research scientist in the Sherman Fairchild Center, is a BIO-RAD FTS-40 spectrometer. The samples were mounted in a Spectra-Tech diamond cell and placed in a BIO-RAD UMA 500 infrared microscope. The spectra were collected at four wavenumber resolution, with a total of fifty scans each.

X-RAY DIFFRACTION (XRD)

Most ancient pigments are minerals, naturally occurring crystalline materials composed of atoms arranged periodically in three dimensions. Such arrangements define sets of parallel lattice planes that have the property of being able to diffract X rays at specific angles according to the wavelength of the impinging radiation and the spacing of the lattice planes in the sample. A crystalline material such as a mineral pigment is characterized by the spacings between its lattice planes; the pattern formed by the impinging X rays, as recorded on film or with an instrument detector, can be used to determine these spacings and thereby identify the mineral itself. This method is particularly useful when combined with XRF or other analytical means that can identify the elemental composition of an unknown sample. Ground pigment samples and film were loaded into a Philips Debye-Scherrer powder camera, mounted on a Philips PW 1840 X-ray diffractometer, and exposed for three hours at 35 KV, 20 ma. The results were interpreted using Micro Powder Diffraction Search/Match software (PSI International) on a Gateway 2000 GP5-200 Personal Computer.

ACKNOWLEDGMENTS

I am grateful to James H. Frantz and Dorothy H. Abramitis of the Sherman Fairchild Center for Objects Conservation at The Metropolitan Museum of Art for entrusting me with the study and conservation of the Amathus sarcophagus, and to Karen Stamm, Sarah MacGregor, Dylan Smith, and Shinichi Doi. The information gleaned from this remarkable work of art could only be assembled by the efforts of an outstanding team. As ever, Tony Frantz (whose assistance was particularly helpful with the Appendix), Dora Henel, Mark T. Wypyski, and George Wheeler, all of the Sherman Fairchild Center, were generous with technical expertise. I would also like to thank Carlos A. Picón and Joan R. Mertens, curators in the Department of Greek and Roman Art, for much valuable advice during the treatment of the sarcophagus and for encouraging me to prepare reconstructions of its polychromy and to make the results of our study available to a wider audience. This paper is dedicated to Catherina Emmen-Aalders.

NOTES

1. Luigi Palma di Cesnola, *Cyprus: Its Ancient Cities, Tombs, and Temples,* 1877, reprint ed. with foreword by Stuart Swiny (Limassol, 1991), p. 41. Once established, he took on additional consulships—for Russia, Greece, and an unspecified country—in order to supplement his income (p. 2).

2. John L. Myres, *Handbook of the Cesnola Collection of Antiquities from Cyprus* (New York, 1914), pp. xiii–xiv.

3. Pierre-Yves Péchoux, "La situation géographique," in Pierre Aupert, *Guide d'Amathonte,* École française d'Athènes, Sites et monuments 15 (Paris, 1996), p. 9.

4. Cesnola, *Cyprus,* pp. 249, 251; Aupert, *Guide d'Amathonte,* pp. 24, 39.

5. Cesnola, *Cyprus,* p. 5; see also Aupert, *Guide d'Amathonte,* p. 19, n. 6.

6. On the disposition of tombs, and dates of the Cypro-Geometric and Classical periods, see Aupert, *Guide d'Amathonte,* pp. 23, 41–43, 46, 151.

7. Ibid., pp. 14, 46, 151. See also Elizabeth McFadden, *The Glitter and the Gold: A Spirited Account of The Metropolitan Museum of Art's First Director, the Audacious and High-Handed Luigi Palma di Cesnola* (New York, 1971), pp. 143ff.

8. Cesnola, *Cyprus,* p. 256.

9. Ibid., p. 255.

10. Myres, *Handbook,* p. 228.

11. Since there is no marble on Cyprus, the sarcophagi of this material must have been carved locally from imported stone or manufactured elsewhere and brought to the island. See Joan B. Connelly, *Votive Sculpture of Hellenistic Cyprus* (Nicosia, 1988), p. 3.

12. Cesnola, *Cyprus,* p. 259, and see pp. 256, 260, for plans and elevations.

13. Ibid., p. 269. The king of Cyprus joined the Fifth Crusade of A.D. 1218, and throughout that century Cyprus was an important rallying point for the Latin knights; it is possible that this is the period Cesnola was thinking about. See Maurice Keen, *The Pelican History of Medieval Europe* (London, 1968), pp. 179–81.

14. Henri Metzger, *L'acropole lycienne,* Fouilles de Xanthos 2 (Paris, 1963), pp. 60–61. Frederick N. Pryce gave a somewhat earlier date for the Xanthus reliefs, of ca. 500 B.C. in his *Catalogue of Sculpture in the Department of Greek and Roman Antiquities of the British Museum,* vol. 1, pt. 2, *Cypriote and Etruscan* (London, 1931), pp. 118, 144–46. This may have been the approximate date Cesnola had in mind for the sarcophagus. See also William A. P. Childs, "Lycian Relations with Persians and Greeks in the Fifth and Fourth Centuries Reexamined," *Anatolian Studies* 31 (1981), pp. 55–80.

15. Cesnola, *Cyprus,* p. 264. Pryce also compares the horses' crests on the Lycian monument to the horses' gear at Persepolis; see Pryce, *Catalogue,* p. 145, and, for an illustration of the horse harness on the Lycian frieze, pl. 30.

16. Myres, *Handbook,* p. 233.

17. Veronica Tatton-Brown, "Le 'sarcophage d'Amathonte,'" in Antoine Hermary, *Amathonte II: Les sculptures découvertes avant 1975,* Recherche sur les grandes civilisations, Mémoire 10; Études chypriotes 5 (Paris, 1981), pp. 81–83.

18. Aupert, *Guide d'Amathonte,* pp. 41–46.

19. Vassos Karageorghis, in collaboration with Joan R. Mertens and Marice E. Rose, *Ancient Art from Cyprus: The Cesnola Collection in The Metropolitan Museum of Art* (New York, 2000), p. 201.

20. Herodotus, *The Histories,* ca. 425 B.C., 5.104 (trans. Aubrey de Sélincourt, rev. with introductory matter and notes by John Marincola [London, 1996], p. 319).

21. Aupert, *Guide d'Amathonte,* p. 36; see also pp. 41–43. Herodotus (*Histories,* 5.114 [trans., 1996, pp. 319–22]) tells of a Cypriot soldier named Onesilus who laid siege to Amathus for siding with the Persians (and Phoenicians) against the rest of the Cypriots (allied with the Ionians and the Athenians). After Onesilus fell, his head was hung in triumph over the city gates. In time, bees colonized the head and filled it with honey. An oracle advised the people of Amathus to bury the head and worship Onesilus thenceforth. It seems that Herodotus's legend attempts to account for Amathus's traditional alliance with the East as well as its more recent ties to people west of Cyprus.

22. Pierre Amiet, *Art of the Ancient Near East* (Paris 1977; New York, 1980), pl. 120; see also the procession relief at Persepolis, built by Darius and his son Xerxes at about the same time as the Amathus sarcophagus was carved, pls. 684–91.

23. Hermary, *Amathonte II,* pls. 2, 3, 7.

24. John Boardman, *Greek Sculpture, the Archaic Period: A Handbook* (New York, 1978). pls. 151–53, 166.

25. For the ivory carving of two sphinxes from Arslan Tash/Hadatu, of ca. 850–800 B.C., see Harvey Weiss, ed., *Ebla to Damascus: Art and Archaeology of Ancient Syria. An Exhibition from the Directorate-General of Antiquities and Museums, Syrian Arab Republic,* Smithsonian Institution Traveling Exhibition Service, in association with the J. Paul Getty Trust (Washington, D.C., and Malibu, 1985), no. 175; see, in the same catalogue, fig. 67, and "ivory bed or chair panel from Nimrud, 8th–7th c. B.C."

26. Cesnola, *Cyprus,* p. 260.

27. See Amiet, *Ancient Near East,* pl. 120, top register, "Assyrian general leads Ummanigash, the new king imposed on Elamites, by the hand."

28. See William A. P. Childs and Pierre Demargne, *Le monument des Néréides: Le décor sculpté,* Fouilles de Xanthos 8 (Paris, 1989), vol. 1, pp. 263, 265–66, vol. 2, pl. 57.2 (British Museum 879).

29. Hermary, *Amathonte II,* p. 12; Aupert, *Guide d'Amathonte,* p. 46.

30. Tatton-Brown, "Le 'sarcophage d'Amathonte,'" p. 78. See also Aupert, *Guide d'Amathonte,* p. 36.

31. Aupert, *Guide d'Amathonte,* p. 39.

32. The possible apotropaic function of the Bes figures on the sarcophagus is mentioned in Aupert, *Guide d'Amathonte,* p. 37.

33. Ibid., p. 41.

34. Myres, *Handbook,* p. 228.

35. A thin section taken from the mortar lining of the sarcophagus shows stressed feldspar, schist, and brownish, grainy, hornblende aggregate in a micrite cement (lime-rich matrix). The proportion of aggregate to binder—about two to one—is common in restoration mortars (personal communication, George Wheeler, April 2000). The aggregate is very heterogeneous in both particle size and composition, and there are indications that some of it may have come from a volcanic source. The fact that it contains a few marine shells and other fossils increases the likelihood that it was obtained in a marine environment, such as Cyprus's. A thin section of the stone shows about 40% porosity; the rest is calcitic and fossiliferous—there are no noncarbonaceous inclusions. "Thin sections" are samples of material ground exactly 30 μm (0.000003 m) thick and mounted on glass microscope slides. The optical properties of minerals at a known thickness are diagnostic. My thanks are due to Leonard Cannone for preparing the thin sections of the mortar and stone of the Amathus sarcophagus.

36. The yellow pigment was identified by PLM and FTIR as raw sienna.

37. Myres, *Handbook,* p. 228.

38. Ibid.

39. Tatton-Brown, "Le 'sarcophage d'Amathonte,'" p. 76. The scale pattern on certain areas of the west frieze of the Siphnian Treasury at Delphi provides another datable parallel to the Amathus sarcophagus; see Vinzenz Brinkmann, *Beobachtungen zum formalen Aufbau und zum Sinngehalt der Friese des Siphnierschatzhauses* (Ennepetal, 1994), pls. 142, 143. Brinkmann (p. 73) dates the sculpture on the treasury to just after 480 B.C. The pattern appears on the mantle of Athena, and it is made by alternating blue and red, with green interspersed. Brinkmann does not identify the pigments definitively but mentions (pp. 49, 51) azurite, red ocher or cinnabar, and malachite green as likely pigments.

40. Aupert, *Guide d'Amathonte,* pp. 45–46.

41. Rutherford J. Gettens and George L. Stout, *Painting Materials: A Short Encyclopedia* (1942; corrected republication, New York, 1966), pp. 149–51.

42. Elizabeth Hendrix, "Painted Ladies of the Early Bronze Age," *MMAB* 55 (Winter 1997–98), p. 8.

43. See Rutherford J. Gettens, Robert L. Feller, and W. Thomas Chase, "Vermilion and Cinnabar," *Studies in Conservation* 17, no. 2 (1972), pp. 45–69, esp. pp. 50–52, where the similarity in appearance between ground natural cinnabar and dry-processed vermilion, even under very high magnifications, is discussed.

44. Carol A. Grissom, "Green Earth," *Artists' Pigments: A Handbook of Their History and Characteristics,* vol. 1, ed. Robert L. Feller (Washington, D.C., 1986), p. 141.

45. Pryce, *Catalogue,* p. 127.

46. Rutherford J. Gettens and Elisabeth W. Fitzhugh, "Malachite and Green Verditer," in *Artists' Pigments: A Handbook of Their History and Characteristics,* vol. 2, ed. Ashok Roy (New York, 1993), p. 186.

47. Rutherford J. Gettens and Elisabeth W. Fitzhugh, "Azurite and Blue Verditer," *Artists' Pigments,* vol. 2, p. 27. For example, Gettens and Fitzhugh ascribe changes in Cimabue's fresco on the ceiling of the Upper Church of Saint Francis, Assisi, to the transformation of azurite to malachite.

48. Vitruvius, *The Ten Books on Architecture,* 1st century B.C., 9.2–4 (trans. Morris Hicky Morgan [Cambridge, Mass., 1914; New York, 1960], pp. 216–17).

49. *The System of Mineralogy of James Dwight Dana and Edward Salisbury Dana, Yale University, 1837–1892,* vol. 1, *Elements, Sulfides, Sulfosalts, Oxides,* 7th ed., rewritten and enlarged by Charles Palache, Harry Berman, and Clifford Frondel (New York and London, 1944), pp. 215–17, 251–54.

50. Performed by Mark T. Wypyski in the Sherman Fairchild Center for Objects Conservation.

51. Alternatively, an amorphous form of metacinnabar may be responsible for the darkening. This form would not be detected by XRD. See Rachel Grout and Aviva Burnstock, "A Study of the Blackening of Vermilion," *Zeitschrift für Kunsttechnologie und Konservierung* 14, no. 1 (2000), pp. 15–22.

52. Robert L. Feller, "Studies on the Darkening of Vermilion by Light," *National Gallery of Art: Report and Studies in the History of Art* (Washington, D.C., 1967), p. 99, with reference to Alexander Eibner, *Über lichtechte Zinnober* (Munich, 1914).

53. Grout and Burnstock, "Study of the Darkening of Vermilion," pp. 15–22.

54. For minerals associated with naturally occurring cinnabar, for example, see Gettens, Feller, and Chase, "Vermilion and Cinnabar," p. 46.

55. For the composition of azurite and its history as a pigment, see Gettens and Fitzhugh, "Azurite and Blue Verditer" (and bibliography therein).

56. W. Thomas Chase, "Egyptian Blue as a Pigment and Ceramic Material," in *Science and Archaeology,* ed. Robert H. Brill (Cambridge, Mass., 1971), p. 80.

The Pendant Possibilities of Core-Formed Glass Bottles

C. S. LIGHTFOOT

Associate Curator, Greek and Roman Art, The Metropolitan Museum of Art

CORE-FORMED GLASS was produced in the Mediterranean area between the sixth and first centuries B.C. The industry follows on from those developed in Egypt and western Asia in the Late Bronze Age (1600–1200 B.C.), which created the first glass vessels, principally small containers for expensive perfumes, oils, and cosmetic creams. The making of glass vessels was revived in Mesopotamia in the Iron Age (ca. 725–600 B.C.). Monochrome cast-glass bowls, jars, and palettes are some of the more spectacular products of this industry, but it was the renewed production of core-formed bottles that stimulated the growth of glass industries elsewhere in western Asia and the eastern Mediterranean. The manufacture of a core-formed bottle was relatively simple and straightforward; the hot glass could be worked easily around the core (probably a mixture of clay, sand, and an organic binder), while the core itself could be both made and removed by an unskilled worker.[1] The predominant shape of Mesopotamian core-formed glass was the alabastron, a tall cylindrical bottle, imitating vessels made in other media, notably alabaster itself. This shape was eagerly adopted by the new production centers farther west, and the alabastron became a standard form in the repertoire of Mediterranean core-formed glassmaking until the industry's final demise in the first century B.C. But, in addition to the alabastron, the Mediterranean industry produced a number of other shapes—principally the aryballos, the amphoriskos, and the oinochoe—which were adapted from forms commonly used by Greek potters. As time went on, a greater variety of shapes and sizes was produced, and three new forms were introduced—the stamnos, the hydriske, and the unguentarium.[2]

Modern scholarship divides Mediterranean core-formed vessels into three chronological groupings. Group I is dated to between the mid-sixth and the end of the fifth century B.C. There then comes a gap of some fifty years or more before the reemergence of the core-formed industry in the late fourth century B.C.[3] Groups II and III both date to the Hellenistic period

(332–31 B.C.); the division between them, in terms of chronology and style, is harder to define. Although there does appear to be a gap in the archaeological record between the late third and mid-second centuries B.C. in some of the standard forms, other forms such as the amphoriskos and unguentarium show some continuity and overlap of production. Essentially, however, Group II is dated to the late fourth and first half of the third century B.C., while Group III represents production in late Hellenistic times from the mid-second century B.C. onward.

The three small aryballoi in the Metropolitan Museum that are the subject of this article have been assigned to Group II, although there is no firm archaeological evidence for dating them to this period. The first of these bottles was acquired by the Museum in 1891 as part of the bequest of Edward C. Moore (91.1.1367; Figure 1). It is broken into three pieces, and a small fragment is missing from the neck.[4] Because of this damage, it has been possible to observe that the interior retains a layer of fine, deep reddish brown grit from the core. The second example was part of the bequest of Theodore M. Davis in 1915, although it was only accessioned in 1930 (30.115.7; Figure 2). It is intact but has a milky iridescent surface. The third bottle, also intact, was acquired by J. Pierpont Morgan as part of the Gréau Collection and came to the Metropolitan Museum with the Morgan bequest in 1917 (17.194.309; Figure 3), along with approximately seven thousand other objects.[5] Since their acquisition, these small aryballoi have attracted little attention, and all have remained unpublished for seventy years or more.

The three vessels are very similar in shape and size. Each stands only about 2 inches (about 5 cm) high and has a broad, horizontal or inward-sloping rim-disk, a short cylindrical neck, and a small circular body. Although the bottles are described as lentoid aryballoi because their bodies are wider than they are deep, it is misleading to say that their sides have been "flattened"; rather, they have convex, rounded profiles quite unlike later-blown glass lentoid bottles.[6] Two small ring handles, set vertically on the shoulder of each vessel, suggest that these bottles could have

© The Metropolitan Museum of Art 2001
METROPOLITAN MUSEUM JOURNAL 36

The notes for this article begin on page 65.

Figure 1. Core-formed glass aryballos. H. 5.1 cm. The Metropolitan Museum of Art, Edward C. Moore Collection, Bequest of Edward C. Moore, 1891 (91.1.1367). See also Colorplate 2

Figure 2. Core-formed glass aryballos. H. 5 cm. The Metropolitan Museum of Art, Theodore M. Davis Collection, Bequest of Theodore M. Davis, 1915 (30.115.7). See also Colorplate 2

been suspended from a chain or string of some sort.

The most interesting and distinguishing characteristic of these core-formed vessels is the amount of decoration applied to them, for it is seemingly quite out of proportion to their size and importance. This ornamentation generally comprises four elements:[7] a prominent twisted thread in two contrasting colors of glass that runs from beneath the ring handles under the body in a graceful U-shape; a fine trail of light-colored glass wound around the neck; a circular blob of differently colored glass, pressed and smoothed into each side of the body using a technique known as marvering; and a single trail wound around the outer edge of the rim. The body of the first bottle (Figure 1) is in a translucent honey brown glass, while the rim trail and marvered blobs are opaque white. The twisted thread around the body is translucent honey brown and opaque white. The body of the second piece (Figure 2) is also translucent honey brown, but the marvered blobs and applied trails are in an opaque yellow glass. The badly weathered twisted thread comprises one honey brown thread intertwined with a finer, possibly opaque yellow thread. The body of the third vessel (Figure 3) is a translucent deep blue glass with numerous opaque white speckles. The twisted thread is blue and opaque white, while the marvered

Figure 3. Core-formed glass aryballos. H. 5.1 cm. The Metropolitan Museum of Art, Gift of J. Pierpont Morgan, 1917 (17.194.309). See also Colorplate 2

blobs and the trails around the rim and neck are also opaque white glass. The uniformity of the three vessels in size, shape, and decoration indicates that they were produced at roughly the same time and probably in a single workshop.

Relatively few core-formed vessels of this distinctive type are known. Fossing referred to two examples, both in London, one in the Victoria & Albert Museum (1019-1868), the other in the British Museum (GR1856.12-26.1143).[8] The latter was subsequently published by Harden, along with a third example, also in the British Museum (GR1867.5-8.585).[9] The two British Museum bottles are very similar in size to the three aryballoi in the Metropolitan; the V&A piece (Figure 4) is somewhat larger, measuring just over 2½ inches (6.5 cm) in height, but it shares the same characteristics as the rest of the group. Three other examples were published by Froehner in 1903 as once forming part of the Gréau Collection.[10] One of these is noted by Harden as "not in the MMA, NY, and its whereabouts is unknown."[11] Froehner indicated that the piece was in the Louvre in Paris, but this seems not to be the case, and it has proved impossible to find any trace of the vessel. The second of the Gréau aryballoi certainly did pass into the Morgan Collection and from there into the Metropolitan Museum; it is one of the three pieces under discussion here (Figure 3). The present whereabouts of the third vessel illustrated by Froehner is unknown.

Harden was able to cite only three additional examples—one in Tunisia (at the National Museum, Carthage) and two in Spain (one in a private collection in Barcelona, the other in the Museo Nacional de Artes Decorativas, Madrid).[12] Five more can now be added: one is in the Corning Museum of Glass; the second formed part of the Hans Cohn collection, exhibited at the Los Angeles County Museum of Art; and the third was formerly in the Kofler-Truniger collection.[13] Only two additional examples have come to light in the past twenty years. One, in the Alfred Wolkenberg collection, was sold at auction in 1991.[14] The other has recently been published in a new catalogue of the core-formed glass collection in the Louvre.[15] This makes a grand total of sixteen known examples of the type.

Other than minor variations in size and color, these vessels are remarkably similar in overall design and decoration. The majority are made of blue glass, but two of the examples in the Metropolitan are in honey brown, an unusual ground color for core-formed vessels.[16] The applied trails are either opaque yellow or opaque white. Opaque yellow predominates for the marvered blobs, while the twisted thread decoration around the body is made of one thread in the ground color combined with one yellow or white thread. Opaque turquoise blue, common on many other core-formed vessels, does not seem to have formed part of the repertoire of colors for small lentoid aryballoi. Also, the vessel said by Froehner to be in the Louvre lacks the blobs on either side.[17]

The distinctive characteristics of these sixteen aryballoi set them apart from the mainstream of core-formed glass production. While their uniformity may suggest a single workshop, the lack of a good provenance for most of them adds to the problem of placing them within a stylistic and chronological framework. Regrettably, no intact or fragmentary examples have surfaced on an archaeological excavation (or, if they have, they have not been recognized for what they are). Only one of the vessels cited above (BM GR1856.12-26.1143) is given a site provenance—from Ruvo (ancient Rubi) in Apulia, southern Italy. The examples now in Spain and Tunisia were presumably found in their respective countries. It is significant, perhaps, that none of the vessels can be said to have come from the eastern Mediterranean, although they are frequently described as having been produced there.

The placement of these small aryballoi in the corpus of Mediterranean core-formed glass relies,

Figure 4. Core-formed glass aryballos. H. 6.5 cm. The Victoria & Albert Museum, London, 1019-1868 (photo: V&A Picture Library)

Figure 5. Core-formed aryballos. H. 8.8 cm. The Metropolitan Museum of Art, Edward C. Moore Collection, Bequest of Edward C. Moore, 1891 (91.1.1348)

and allied hydriskai" to the same class of vessel as the lentoid aryballoi, pointing out various similarities between these vessels and the lentoid aryballoi.[22] Although not found on every example, the distinctive feature that links them most closely with the aryballoi is the use of twisted bichrome threads for the handles.[23] Twisted threads are generally not found on other types of core-formed vessels, either as handles or as decorative elements.[24] They may, therefore, be regarded as a trademark of a particular workshop or production center. The creation of these threads would have required the glassmaker to add an extra stage to his work, and so this feature is indicative not just of a preference for one shape or style of decoration over another, but of a deliberate choice that increased the complexity of the manufacturing process. In all other cases of core-formed vessels, monochrome threads or trails were applied singly to the body. Known examples of stamnoi and hydriskai with bichrome twisted-thread handles are rare, but it is interesting to note that two of them that have provenances come from Italy: a fragmentary stamnos in the British Museum (GR1873.8-20.413) is from Tarquinia, and a fine hydriske, now in the Royal Ontario Museum, Toronto, was found near Perugia, together with an Etruscan bronze mirror.[25] There is no direct evidence of an eastern Mediterranean origin for any example of this group of stamnoi and hydriskai.

The stylistic links between these other core-formed vessels and the group of small aryballoi help to provide some indication of the latter's date. However, the evidence is meager in the extreme: the Etruscan mirror associated with the hydriske just mentioned is said to be of a type dated to the fourth–third century B.C., while Fossing refers to a lentoid aryballos without twisted bichrome threads as coming from a grave in the Great Bliznitsa burial mound in south Russia, dated to about 300 B.C. or just before.[26] Nevertheless, it is now generally accepted that the whole class of core-formed stamnoi, hydriskai, and lentoid aryballoi belongs to Group II and dates to the early Hellenistic period. Harden was probably right to conclude that production of the lentoid aryballoi lasted for only a short time, "not more than thirty or forty years during the late 4th and the early 3rd century."[27]

Moreover, Harden attributed several Group II vessels, including the two lentoid aryballoi and the stamnos in the British Museum, to a production center in southern Italy.[28] Grose has since questioned the validity of Harden's argument that the presence of white speckling on the surface of the glass used for these vessels is proof of Italian manufacture.[29] Nevertheless, in terms of their stylistic affinities and distribution, the southern Italian attribution would seem to remain convincing.

therefore, on stylistic considerations and on comparison with groups of similar vessels. Fossing was the first to point out that they are most closely related to the other main group of lentoid aryballoi, both in terms of their shape and in some of their decorative features.[18] In particular, there is a striking similarity in the use of twisted and applied threads down the sides of vessels in both groups—consistently in the case of our small aryballoi, but only on certain examples of the larger variety. Fossing illustrated one such example in the Staatliche Museen, Berlin, and referred to another, presumed to have been found at Carthage.[19] The latter is shown in the Toledo (Ohio) Museum of Art catalogue, together with a third example, said to have been acquired in Italy.[20] The Metropolitan also has one of these larger aryballoi (Figure 5), but it is of unknown provenance.[21] Such vessels all have small ring handles, which are attached to the shoulder above two twisted threads that run down the sides of the body. This decorative feature recalls the twisted thread that runs continuously under the body between the ring handles on the smaller aryballoi. Other details, however, are dissimilar—most notably, the bodies of the larger aryballoi are invariably decorated with marvered threads tooled into a feather pattern.

Grose tentatively assigned a "novel series of stamnoi

Another line of inquiry may provide new insight into both the origins and the use of the present group. As noted above, three lentoid aryballoi are to be found in Tunisia and Spain, areas that lay within the Carthaginian sphere at the time the vessels were being produced. There is good reason to believe that many of the classes of rod-formed glass head-pendants are of Carthaginian origin (see below). Some of these pendants are decorated with a headband of bichrome or polychrome twisted threads.[30] It suffices to mention two examples, both now in the Toledo Museum of Art; one, belonging to the Archaic period (late 7th–5th century B.C.), has a headband of twisted threads in dark blue and opaque white, and the second, dated to the third century B.C. or later, has a twisted-thread headband in dark blue and opaque yellow.[31] As already noted, to make such colored threads required adding a special stage to the manufacturing process. There should, therefore, be some link between its use on our lentoid aryballoi and on the head-pendants.

In addition, the technique of making and applying separate spiral ringlets to form the hair and beards on larger and more elaborate head-pendants is not dissimilar to that used for the small ring handles on the aryballoi. Both display a certain dexterity in the working of small trails of hot glass.[32] A fine example of a head-pendant with such curls is in the Metropolitan Museum, acquired as long ago as 1906 but previously unpublished (Figure 6).[33] Seefried dated this type of head-pendant to between the mid-fourth and the end of the third century B.C., the same period as that to which the aryballoi are attributed, and she considered it very probable that such head-pendants were produced at Carthage.[34] Certainly, the overwhelming majority of examples with find-spots come from the western Mediterranean.[35] It may also be noted that, despite the iridescent film covering most of its surfaces, the Metropolitan's head-pendant is made of translucent honey brown glass. The most obvious explanation for the technical similarities between the head-pendants and the lentoid aryballoi is that both groups were products of the same industry. As yet, however, there is insufficient evidence to prove such a hypothesis, and for the present it may be better to regard the presence of similar decorative elements on the core-formed vessels, traditionally regarded as Greek, and on the rod-formed head-pendants of "Carthaginian" manufacture as an indication of cross-cultural influences. The island of Sicily, where Greek and Punic communities lived in close, and not always hostile, proximity, may be the bridge across which these exchanges were made.

The small lentoid aryballoi, like other classes of

Figure 6. Rod-formed glass head-pendant. H. 5.2 cm. The Metropolitan Museum of Art, Rogers Fund, 1906 (06.1126)

core-formed glass, were made as containers for various sorts of rare and expensive perfumes, lotions, and medicines. As a vessel form, the aryballos was designed to be portable; many examples both in other media and from other periods have survived complete with a swing handle or chain attachment.[36] In the case of the core-formed glass examples, Fossing suggested that the twisted threads applied to the sides of some of the larger aryballoi represent a carrying cord that had become purely ornamental.[37] Fossing also referred to the twisted thread that runs around the body of the small lentoid aryballoi as a "carrying cord."[38] On the three Metropolitan Museum examples, the ring handles on the shoulders have all been carefully pierced with a hole through which a string or a fine metal chain could easily have been threaded. It is not inherently impossible, therefore, that these small lentoid aryballoi were meant to be carried, and it seems likely that they were intended to be worn around the neck like pendants.

Pendants shaped as miniature vessels were a popular form of Greek jewelry throughout the Classical and Hellenistic periods (5th–1st centuries B.C.). Examples of such pendants—made principally of gold, although other luxury materials such as rock crystal were also used—are widespread, and finds are recorded from sites in Italy, Greece, and Cyprus.[39] The fact that many

Figure 7. Gold and garnet pendant amphora. H. 3 cm. The Metropolitan Museum of Art, Purchase, Mr. and Mrs. Christos G. Bastis Gift, 2000 (2000.9a)

Figure 8. Gold and garnet pendant amphora. H. 5.9 cm. The Metropolitan Museum of Art, Gift of Mr. and Mrs. Stephen Kellen, 1999 (1999.289.9)

of these pendants were made with accompanying lids or stoppers clearly indicates that they were not just ornaments but served also as receptacles for small amounts of precious substances such as exotic oils or perfumes. Although some of the pendants are considerably smaller than the present group of lentoid aryballoi, others are of comparable size. The Metropolitan Museum recently acquired two such pieces of jewelry. A small gold amphora, decorated with patterns of twisted gold wire and a facetted garnet set into its base, measures 1 9/16 inches (3 cm) in height (Figure 7) and comes complete with a lid, suspension chain, and tripod stand.[40] The other piece is a larger amphora, measuring 2 5/16 inches (5.9 cm) in height, also decorated with garnets and twisted gold wire (Figure 8).[41] An example of a rock crystal bottle that has a gold lid and suspension chain is presently on loan to the Museum.[42] The main difference between these pendant vessels and the small glass aryballoi is that the former have full, rounded shapes, whereas the latter have lentoid bodies with the two broad faces divided by narrower sides decorated with the ring handles and the "cord" of twisted threads. This lentoid shape would naturally allow the vessels to hang flat against a surface (such as the wearer's chest), preventing them from spinning around and getting their hanging strings or chains twisted. Perhaps this shaping was the

maker's conscious attempt to ensure the safety of the glass bottles, which were more fragile than pendant vessels in other media.

It is noteworthy that head-pendants were worn principally as apotropaic amulets, and consequently size and visibility were important factors.[43] The type mentioned above is particularly large and attractive, comparable in size to the lentoid aryballoi. The Metropolitan's example (Figure 6) is only a fraction over the 2 inches of the bottles, but a particularly splendid head-pendant in the British Museum (GR1906.6-27.33) measures a full 2½ inches (6.2 cm) in height.[44] The present group of core-formed aryballoi also has a special feature which may suggest that they, like the rod-formed head-pendants, had an amuletic function. All three of the Metropolitan Museum examples have a blob of opaque white or yellow glass marvered on to their front and back surfaces. Each blob stands out sharply against the dark blue or honey brown background of the vessel's body. It is easily recognizable as an "eye," a powerful symbol for warding off evil, which was popular in antiquity and remains in use today in many societies.[45] The "eye" on these vessels finds its closest parallel in the stratified eye used to decorate glass beads, some of which are attributed to the Carthaginian glass industry of the fourth–third centuries B.C.[46] Thus it may be argued that the small bottles served a dual purpose—as containers for precious ointments and as apotropaic pendants.

The three lentoid aryballoi in the Metropolitan's collection may, therefore, be credited with a greater importance than has previously been recognized. They belong to a group of vessels that, although rare and imprecisely dated, would seem to offer a new insight into the glass industry in the early Hellenistic period. It has been suggested here that they provide a link between glass production in the Greek and Carthaginian worlds, between the use of glass for vessels and for ornaments, and between a purely functional application and a symbolic meaning. In addition, one may speculate that some details of ancient glass production—notably the use of twisted threads of glass as decoration—may have been influenced by gold working techniques. This particular group of small but fascinating core-formed glass bottles thus opens up the possibility of a wider study into the relationship between workshops making glass, jewelry, and pottery.

ACKNOWLEDGMENTS

I am grateful for the help, advice, and encouragement that I have received from numerous colleagues at the Metropolitan Museum during the preparation of this study. I wish to thank most especially Carlos A. Picón and Joan R. Mertens. Véronique Arveiller-Dulong also very kindly supplied details of the piece in the Louvre in advance of its publication.

NOTES

1. For details of the technique, see D. F. Grose, *Early Ancient Glass: Core-Formed, Rod-Formed, and Cast Vessels and Objects from the Late Bronze Age to the Early Roman Empire, 1600 B.C. to A.D. 50* (New York: Hudson Hills Press in association with the Toledo Museum of Art, 1989), p. 31; E. M. Stern and B. Schlick-Nolte, *Early Glass of the Ancient World, 1600 B.C.–A.D. 50* (Ostfildern-Ruit: Gerd Hatje, 1994), pp. 28–30, 39–40.

2. Grose, *Early Ancient Glass*, pp. 110–25.

3. M. C. McClellan, "Core-Formed Glass from Dated Contexts," Ph.D. diss., University of Pennsylvania, Philadelphia, 1984, pp. 77–79.

4. An old repair, made presumably before the vessel was acquired by the Metropolitan Museum, was dismantled, and the pieces were rejoined by Lisa Pilosi and Melpomene Yale of the MMA Sherman Fairchild Center for Objects Conservation in June 2000. This work revealed that the body of the bottle had been broken into two unequal pieces, while a third fragment comprised the neck and rim. A small sample of the glass was retained for future analysis.

5. J. Strouse, "J. Pierpont Morgan: Financier and Collector," *MMAB* 57, no. 3 (Winter 2000), pp. 58–59.

6. D. B. Harden, *Catalogue of Greek and Roman Glass in the British Museum*, vol. 1, *Core- and Rod-formed Vessels and Pendants and Mycenaean Cast Objects* (London: British Museum Press, 1981), p. 100; Grose, *Early Ancient Glass*, p. 128.

7. In rare cases, on individual pieces one or another element is absent. For example, 91.1.1367 does not have a trail around the neck.

8. P. Fossing, *Glass Vessels before Glass-Blowing*, trans. W. E. Calvert (Copenhagen: Ejnar Munksgaard, 1940), p. 94 and fig. 63.

9. Harden, *Greek and Roman Glass*, p. 113, nos. 297, 298; see also V. Tatton-Brown and C. Andrews, "Before the Invention of Glass-blowing," in *Five Thousand Years of Glass*, ed. H. Tait (London: British Museum Press, 1991), p. 44, fig. 48 (right).

10. W. Froehner, *Collection Julien Gréau: Verrerie antique, émaillerie et poterie appartenant à M. John Pierpont Morgan* (Paris: Imprimerie alsacienne, 1903), pl. XXIII,4; p. 29, no. 135, pl. XXII,6; and p. 12, no. 46, pl. IX,3.

11. Harden, *Greek and Roman Glass*, p. 169, n. 93.

12. Ibid., p. 112.

13. S. M. Goldstein, *Pre-Roman and Early Roman Glass in the Corning Museum of Glass* (Corning, N.Y.: Corning Museum of Glass, 1979), pp. 128–29, no. 266—not, apparently, one of the Gréau pieces, as cited; A. von Saldern, *Glass 500 B.C. to A.D. 1900: The Hans Cohn Collection, Los Angeles/Cal.*, exh. cat. (Mainz: Philipp von Zabern, 1980), p. 38, no. 26; *3000 Jahre Glaskunst: Von der Antike bis zum Jugendstil*, exh. cat. (Lucerne: Kunstmuseum, 1981), p. 53, no. 101 (= Christie's, London, sale cat., March 5–6, 1985, lot 305).

14. Christie's, London, sale cat., July 9, 1991, lot 181.

15. V. Arveiller-Dulong and M.-D. Nenna, *Les verres antiques: I. Contenants à parfum en verre moulé sur noyau et vaisselle moulée, VIIe siècle avant J.-C.–Ier siècle après J.-C.* (Paris: Réunion des Musées Nationaux, 2000), p. 127, no. 156.

16. The use of honey brown as a ground color is not, however, entirely without precedent; see Grose, *Early Ancient Glass*, pp. 114, 138, no. 80 (a 5th-century alabastron whose ground color is described as "golden brown").

17. This piece, as illustrated (Froehner, *Collection Julien Gréau*, pl. XXIII,4), seems to be made of an opaque green glass for the body. However, one of the honey brown examples at the Metropolitan (30.115.7) appears to have a similar green hue in reflected light. Since the ex-Gréau bottle has not been traced, it is impossible to clarify its exact color.

18. Fossing, *Before Glass-Blowing*, pp. 93–94; see also Harden, *Greek and Roman Glass*, pp. 100–101, 112—Form 1; Grose, *Early Ancient Glass*, p. 119—Form II:1.

19. Fossing, *Before Glass-Blowing*, p. 93 and fig. 62; see Harden, *Greek and Roman Glass*, p. 112.

20. Grose, *Early Ancient Glass*, p. 118, fig. 75, and pp. 164–65, no. 154. For another example, see also Arveiller-Dulong and Nenna, *Les verres antiques*, p. 126, no. 155.

21. Acc. no. 91.1.1348, The Edward C. Moore Collection, Bequest of Edward C. Moore, 1891, H. 3¼ in. (8.8 cm); unpublished. What may be a second example of the larger lentoid aryballos at the Metropolitan Museum (91.1.1327) has been excluded from the present discussion because it is very fragmentary and heavily

restored. Until further conservation work on the piece has been completed, it is impossible to state exactly the nature of this vessel.

22. Grose, *Early Ancient Glass*, p. 119, figs. 76, 78, 79, and pp. 165–66, nos. 155–57.

23. The hydriske at the Toledo Museum of Art, for example, does not have this feature; see Grose, *Early Ancient Glass*, pp. 165–66, no. 157.

24. A rare exception would appear to be an oinochoe of the mid-4th through early 3rd century B.C. that has a handle made of cobalt blue and opaque white twisted threads; see Sotheby's, New York, sale cat., December 17, 1997, lot 3A. Most other examples of this type have a plain blue handle; see Grose, *Early Ancient Glass*, pp. 161–62, nos. 146–49.

25. Harden, *Greek and Roman Glass*, p. 114, no. 299; J. W. Hayes, *Roman and Pre-Roman Glass in the Royal Ontario Museum: A Catalogue* (Toronto: ROM, 1975), p. 12, no. 21, and pl. 43.

26. Fossing, *Before Glass-Blowing*, p. 92; see also Harden, *Greek and Roman Glass*, p. 112.

27. Harden, *Greek and Roman Glass*, p. 112.

28. Ibid., pp. 103, 114.

29. Grose, *Early Ancient Glass*, p. 116; *contra* Harden, *Greek and Roman Glass*, pp. 103, 106, 112–16.

30. Grose, *Early Ancient Glass*, pp. 82–83.

31. Ibid., pp. 88–99, no. 42, and p. 90, no. 50; see also pp. 90–92, nos. 51–62.

32. I owe this observation to Dr. Carlos Picón. For the technique, see M. Seefried, *Les pendentifs en verre sur noyau des pays de la Méditerranée antique* (Rome: École française de Rome, 1982), pp. 18–19.

33. Acc. no. 06.1126, Rogers Fund, 1906, H. 2¹⁄₁₆ in. (5.2 cm); no provenance. It may be attributed to Tatton-Brown's Type G, and to Seefried's Type C III; V. Tatton-Brown in Harden, *Greek and Roman Glass*, pp. 147–48, 150–51, nos. 423–26; Seefried, *Les pendentifs*, pp. 105–16, nos. 1–69.

34. Seefried, *Les pendentifs*, pp. 28–29, 29. It should also be noted, however, that Tatton-Brown (in Harden, *Greek and Roman Glass*, pp. 143, 147) argued against Seefried's view that Carthage was the center of production for these head-pendants.

35. Seefried, *Les pendentifs*, fig. 45—showing that 72 out of 79 provenanced examples come from North Africa (Carthage), Spain, the Balearics, Gaul, Illyria, Sardinia, Italy, and Sicily. *Pace* Seefried's own remark that this type is "found only on the eastern side of the Mediterranean"; M. Seefried, "Glass Core Pendants found in the Mediterranean Area," *Journal of Glass Studies* 21 (1979), p. 20.

36. For example, a Roman blown-glass oil flask with a U-shaped bronze handle, now in the Corning Museum of Glass (CMG 55.1.96); D. Whitehouse, *Roman Glass in The Corning Museum of Glass*, vol. 1 (Corning, N.Y.: Corning Museum of Glass, 1997), p. 201, no. 351. The Metropolitan also has two Roman glass aryballoi with metal handles (17.194.191 and 17.194.193), both unpublished.

37. Fossing, *Before Glass-Blowing*, p. 93.

38. Ibid., pp. 93–94.

39. For example, two amphora-shaped pendants found in Tomb 10 at Marion, Cyprus; D. Williams and J. Ogden, *Greek Gold: Jewelry of the Classical World*, exh. cat. (New York: Harry N. Abrams, 1994), p. 246, nos. 181, 182. Compare also two gold pendants described as Parthian earrings in the British Museum (WAA 135207 and 132933); *Jewellery through 7000 Years*, ed. H. Tait (London: British Museum Press, 1976), pp. 122–23, nos. 180(a)–(b).

40. Acc. no. 2000.9a, b, Purchase, Mr. and Mrs. Christos G. Bastis Fund, 2000; unpublished. For parallels, see E. B. Dusenbery, "A Samothracian Necropolis," *Archaeology* 12 (1959), pp. 163–70, esp. p. 167 and fig. 5; S. G. Miller, *Two Groups of Thessalian Gold* (Berkeley: University of California Press, 1979), pp. 30–31 and pls. 15a–16a; E. M. De Juliis, *Gli ori di Taranto in età ellenistica* (Milan: A. Mondadori, 1984), pp. 232–33, no. 163.

41. Acc. no. 1999.289.9, Gift of Mr. and Mrs. Stephen Kellen, 1999; see Paul Cassirer, Berlin, sale cat., December 11, 1928, lot 101; *Ancient Art in American Private Collections*, exh. cat. (Cambridge, Mass.: Fogg Art Museum, 1954), p. 38, no. 318, pl. XC.

42. L.1997.56, Anonymous loan, H. 2 in. (5.1 cm); unpublished. There is a similar piece in the Berlin Antikenmuseum; see W.-D. Heilmeyer, "Salbgefäss aus Bergkristall mit goldener Montage," *Jahrbuch Preussischer Kulturbesitz* 18 (1972), pp. 165–68. For another example, see Sotheby's, New York, sale cat., December 17, 1998, lot 154.

43. Seefried, *Les pendentifs*, pp. 56–59.

44. Harden, *Greek and Roman Glass*, p. 150, no. 423; see also Grose, *Early Ancient Glass*, p. 82 and fig. 53.

45. See, for example, G. Eisen, "The Characteristics of Eye Beads from the Earliest Times to the Present," *American Journal of Archaeology* 20 (1916), pp. 1–27, esp. pp. 1–2; Ö. Küçükerman, *Göz Boncuğu* (Istanbul: Türkiye Turing ve Otomobil Kurumu, 1987).

46. See, for example, Stern and Schlick-Nolte, *Early Glass of the Ancient World*, p. 195, no. 39, and pp. 198–99, no. 41; E. Kypraiou, ed., *Greek Jewellery: 6,000 Years of Tradition*, exh. cat. (Athens: Archaeological Receipts Fund, 1997), p. 98, no. 84; V. Karageorghis, J. R. Mertens, and M. E. Rose, *Ancient Art from Cyprus: The Cesnola Collection in The Metropolitan Museum of Art* (New York: MMA, 2000), p. 287, no. 469.

A Roman Sarcophagus and Its Patron

JEAN SORABELLA

Assistant Museum Educator, The Metropolitan Museum of Art, and Assistant Professor of Art History, Providence College

THE FUNERARY ART of ancient Rome is remarkable for its variety of styles and subjects and also for the insight it provides into the thoughts and emotions of private individuals. The marble sarcophagi that came into widespread use in the second century A.D. are among the most artistically impressive sepulchral monuments, for their large surfaces are often elaborately carved with scenes from Greek mythology. Scholars have searched the episodes portrayed for allegorical meanings and signs acknowledging a life after death. This line of inquiry has illuminated various systems of belief but rarely addressed the persons who made, commissioned, and selected sarcophagi. Since the death of a loved one and the task of consigning him or her from experience into memory are personal responsibilities only partly circumscribed by custom, every Roman sarcophagus represents an individual confrontation with tradition and conventional practice. With this in mind, it seems wise to heed Hellmut Sichtermann's warning not to seek universal or official meanings for Roman sepulchral imagery.[1] Close analysis of specific examples can reveal personal concerns that might have influenced ancient choices. When something is known about the actual buyer, occupant, or context of a sarcophagus, it is possible to consider what particular myths might have meant to an otherwise undocumented personage in antiquity.[2] Scholars have used funerary inscriptions in several useful studies of Roman society, but often the focus on epigraphy excludes analysis of the images that accompany the texts.[3] As Guntram Koch points out, inscribed sarcophagi have much to impart about private patronage, social structures, and personal relationships among the Romans.[4]

A Roman sarcophagus of the early third century in The Metropolitan Museum of Art is particularly promising for a study of this kind, for it bears an inscription identifying both the deceased and the patron (Figures 1, 2).[5] On the lid is a portrait of the deceased with a coiffure made fashionable by the empress Julia Domna, beside which these lines appear: ANINIA HILARA / CL · ARRIAE MARI / · INCONPARABILE / FECIT · VIXIT · / ANN · L · MEN / · X.[6] The inscription is conventional, yet it distinguishes the sarcophagus—one of very few known to have been dedicated by a daughter of the deceased—as a case of unusual patronage and a rare document of such a familial relationship.[7] Commemorative inscriptions appear infrequently on Roman sarcophagi with mythological decoration, where the panels prepared for them are often left blank. On other types of grave monuments where inscriptions are more abundant, grieving parents, husbands, and wives are the usual dedicants.[8] In standard fashion, the inscription here gives the names of the dedicant and of the deceased, as well as the latter's age at death. The word MARI is generally read as a dative for mother, *matri*, in the same case as the name of the deceased.[9] The spelling of the word is irregular and represents a scribal error not without parallel in Latin epigraphy.[10] Modifying MARI is the word INCONPARABILE, one of several flattering adjectives routinely applied to the dead in Latin epitaphs; some others are *dulcissimo* (sweetest), *carissimo* (dearest), and *piissimo* (most faithful). Again, the orthography deviates from the standard with the substitution of *N* for *M*, but the variant is common and seems to reflect contemporary pronunciation.[11] The form resembles the accusative, but there are examples in epigraphy of datives that end in *E*, and the conventional application of the adjective to the deceased suggests that third-century Roman readers would not have understood the monument itself as the incomparable object of the verb *fecit*.[12]

Aninia Hilara, the dedicant, may have been able to read both her own name and her mother's in the inscription. The CL beside ARRIA stands for "Claudia," an imperial name more commonly abbreviated than spelled out by the second century A.D.; the name of the deceased woman was Claudia Arria. Aninia Hilara, the daughter, is the subject of the verb FECIT, which embraces a range of meanings including "to make," "to do," and "to have made." Although the word sometimes identifies the artist who created the work, in this case, as in other funerary dedications, it designates

The notes for this article begin on page 79.

Figure 1. Marble sarcophagus of Claudia Arria. Roman, ca. A.D. 220, from Ostia. The Metropolitan Museum of Art, Rogers Fund, 1947 (47.100.4a, b)

Figure 2. Center front of the sarcophagus in Figure 1

68

Figure 3. Left end of the sarcophagus in Figure 1

Figure 4. Right end of the sarcophagus in Figure 1

Figure 5. Back of the sarcophagus in Figure 1

Aninia Hilara as the one who paid for the monument, the inscription, and other aspects of the burial. In the fourth line of the inscription, the daughter's action, FECIT, is juxtaposed with the mother's, VIXIT—that is, that she lived for fifty years and ten months. The wording has a conventional grace in contrast to the awkward spacing of the letters and the irregular forms of the words, which show the hand of a carver less skilled than the one or ones who executed the relief decoration. The difference in quality between the ornament and the inscription may indicate that to the dedicant

the first mattered more than the second, yet she made a deliberate choice not to leave the monument uninscribed. There is nothing to suggest the social class of mother and daughter except the magnificence of the sarcophagus itself, which may have cost Aninia Hilara the best part of her fortune. The source of her wealth is unknown, and her existence unattested in other Ostian inscriptions—unless she is to be identified with a freedwoman commemorated simply as "Aninia" on a modest funerary plaque set up by her husband and master.[13] The fact that she alone is named as responsible

69

for her mother's memorial may suggest that Claudia Arria's husband died before she did or that Aninia Hilara was her sole heir or that the daughter had other reasons for preferring to act alone.[14]

The sarcophagus, which is in excellent condition, was intact when recovered from a chamber tomb in Ostia in 1825.[15] It was believed to have burned in a fire at Warwick Castle in 1871; Carl Robert included it in his corpus as a lost work known only from old engravings. The sarcophagus appeared on the art market in London in 1913 and entered the Museum's collection in 1947.[16]

Remarkable for the refinement of its sculptural decoration, the sarcophagus shows numerous figures, animals, and landscape elements carved in high relief, examples of the daring and sophistication of the Severan style in Roman sculpture. The *lenos* form of the box, which approximates a wine trough complete with lions' heads where spouts would be, allows the movement and action of the frieze to extend from the front around the curved ends and even to cover the back, where there is a pastoral scene in low relief (Figures 3–5). The decoration overall presents an outstanding richness of subject matter. The box depicts the tale of Endymion and Selene, other myths are illustrated in the small panels on the lid, and a host of figures spread throughout personify Sun, Moon, Earth, Ocean, and various other elements of the atmosphere.

No complete retelling of Endymion's tale survives in classical literature, and scattered textual references vary in their details.[17] The images, however, relate a largely consistent version of the story. Endymion was a hunter or shepherd who spent his time outdoors on Mount Latmus in Caria. His beauty attracted Selene, the goddess of the Moon, as she drove her chariot across the sky. Eager to make him her lover, she acted only after granting him eternal sleep. Like other depictions of the myth on sarcophagi, Claudia Arria's monument shows the moment just before Selene takes Endymion for herself. He reclines on the right, nude but for the cloak typical of a huntsman, with his right arm bent above his head in a pose that is associated with sleep in Greek art.[18] Selene steps from her heavenly chariot onto the Earth, a personification of which lies beneath the horses, while a winged female figure wearing boots and a short garment holds their bridles.[19] Another female figure with a kindly face, a variation of Selene's own, appears above Endymion with a stalk of poppies and pours a potion on him that probably relates to his immortal slumber.

The story of Endymion is found on some 120 sarcophagi made in Roman workshops.[20] Robert first outlined the typology and chronology of the corpus, and subsequent scholars have refined his categories

and his conclusions.[21] The earliest examples, dated to about A.D. 130, have spare compositions animated by the movement of Selene, who is often depicted walking from right to left. In representations of the theme by the next generation of carvers, Selene is portrayed walking from left to right, a change some have associated with the direction in which Greek and Latin text is written and read.[22] Some sarcophagi show a single episode, the arrival of Selene before her sleeping lover, and others include the next scene, when she drives away in her chariot. In the early third century, the single scene becomes most common, and a multitude of cupids, personifications, and pastoral characters join the protagonists.

There is a great deal of dispute about the meaning of the Endymion myth and the judgment of the second- and third-century Romans who considered depictions of it suitable for sarcophagi. The appropriateness of the theme for funerary monuments seems, perhaps, immediately apparent, for the myth distilled to its essence describes the elimination of barriers between mortality and divinity and proposes sleep and love as alternatives to death. The analogy between sleep and death was a commonplace in classical literature as early as the Homeric epics, in which Hypnos and Thanatos, Sleep and Death, are described as twin brothers.[23] Disagreement persists, however, as to whether the comparison permits a wishful equation between everyday waking life and life after death. The early Christians referred to their dead as asleep and awaiting certain resurrection, yet R. A. Lattimore regarded the parallel as drawn in poetry and epitaphs as a descriptive metaphor without reference to belief.[24] Ancient thinkers themselves confronted Endymion as a paradox of possible existential significance. The everlasting sleep that he is meant to enjoy seems to exclude the possibility of both death and waking, yet in the *Phaedo*, a discourse on the relevance of death to life, Plato has Socrates say, "But what if there were such a thing as falling asleep without the waking up to answer it in kind. You know, in the end, that would show up Endymion as a lot of silly talk, and he would seem to be nowhere through his sleeping, and everything else would seem to be in the same state, sound asleep."[25] Franz Cumont associated the myth of Endymion in Roman sepulchral art with Pythagorean and Stoic ideas about the moon as a resting place for the dead and as an Elysian haven for their souls.[26] A. D. Nock countered that allegorical interpretations of mythology vary among ancient commentators and cited the dream book of Artemidorus, in which coupling with the moon can portend a consequence as banal as dropsy.[27]

Scholars have also explained the myths depicted on

Roman sarcophagi as glosses on the manner of death and the character of the deceased.[28] Thus, Persephone violently abducted by Hades might be chosen to decorate the tomb of a girl who died before her prime, and Adonis killed while hunting and mourned by Venus perhaps suggests a parallel with the death of a handsome young man. Comparing the deceased with appropriate mythological figures seems to have been common practice at Roman funerals, and it is not unlikely that surviving family members made and recalled such comparisons.[29] In both Greek and Latin, "to sleep Endymion's sleep" was an idiom meaning to sleep well and long, literally or metaphorically in death, and a family might think of a dead relative in such terms.[30] If such ideas influenced those who selected sarcophagi, the sex of the deceased seems not to have mattered, since women as well as men, children, and married couples were buried in coffins decorated with scenes of Endymion and Selene.

There are those who explain the prevalence of the Endymion myth as a simple matter of decoration without allegorical significance. Robert Turcan points out that this view presumes the existence of art for art's sake in antiquity and reminds us how little in Greek or Roman art was completely devoid of meaning.[31] A further shortcoming of the idea is the difficulty of accounting for the tremendous expense and effort Roman craftsmen and patrons lavished on scenes with clear narrative value. Sculptors in workshops in and near Rome were carving sarcophagi with the myth of Endymion for more than five generations, from about A.D. 130 well into the fourth century, yet the later examples show a continuing understanding of the story and not a reduction to mere pattern. Indeed, the imagery of the tale of Endymion persisted into the Early Christian period, when it furnished a model for the portrayal of Jonah in art.[32] At least part of Endymion's appeal to the buyers of sarcophagi seems to have been his story.

The search for what Endymion might have meant to ordinary Romans of the second and third centuries hinges largely on the interpretation of texts. Ovid and Apollodorus omitted the tale from their mythological compendia of the first centuries B.C. and A.D., which might suggest that the tale had been forgotten by then. Michael Koortbojian imagines ancient artists attempting to reconstruct a little-known myth from the casual and incomplete references to Endymion in classical literature, which offered them "scarcely more than the bare remnants of a myth from which to work."[33] One wonders, however, how a forgotten story could have captivated so many Roman patrons, or why workshops would have focused on an arcane myth when there were so many well-documented ones that

do, indeed, appear on sarcophagi. It is important to remember that no story needs an author to enshrine it in tradition and that in antiquity Ovid and Apollodorus did not have the authoritative status they now possess. High rates of illiteracy among the Romans seem to rule out the possibility that many individuals knew of mythological tales from having read them.[34] The lack of literary versions of Endymion's story cannot be interpreted to mean that it was unknown to the ancients.

The numerous sarcophagi with mythological ornament made near Rome in the second and third centuries suggest instead a widespread awareness of Greek myths. It has been proposed that the theater exposed a broad audience to the themes represented on sarcophagi, yet the story of Endymion appears not to have furnished material for the contemporary stage.[35] Educated people had occasion to encounter Greek myths at school, in exercises that required the composition of speeches for familiar characters.[36] Lucian's dialogue between Aphrodite and Selene, composed about A.D. 160, has the flavor of such an assignment, as well as a touch of irreverent humor:

> To me, indeed, he seems, Aphrodite, beautiful in every way, and most of all when he sleeps on a rock with his cape thrown under him, holding his javelins in his left hand and just now slipping out of his grasp, and his right arm bent up around his head, placed around his passing fair face, and he breathes that ambrosial breath, held fast in sleep. Then, let me tell you, I noiselessly step down, treading on the tips of my toes so that he isn't thrown into a fright should he wake—you understand. Why tell you then the things that happen after? For you know I'm all but dying of love.[37]

Some of Lucian's other writings tell of his training in a sculptor's workshop, and his description of Endymion conforms to the figure types depicted on sarcophagi. Although the majority of marble carvers cannot have possessed Lucian's level of erudition, there is reason to believe that they might have been just as familiar with Endymion's tale as the well-to-do Romans who bought sarcophagi.

The elliptical references in classical literature imply that the myth was so familiar as not to need retelling—the sort of tale that one might even have heard in childhood. The Sophist Philostratus, writing about A.D. 230, reminds a ten-year-old listener that the myth of Ariadne is one he "heard even from your nurse, perhaps, for those women are wise about such things and cry about them when they wish."[38] Plutarch, writing about A.D. 110, shortly before the first Endymion sarcophagi, reports the tale of Numa, Rome's first king, consorting with the nymph Egeria and so gaining wisdom and happiness. "It is most certain," he continues, "that these things resemble many of the very ancient tales which the Phrygians hand down and love to tell of Attis, the Bithynians of Herodotus, the Arcadians of Endymion, and others of other fortunate souls who seemed to have become gods' lovers."[39] Plutarch implies that the story is a common matter of popular tradition, whatever the names of the characters. Cicero, writing nearly two centuries earlier, offers further insight into the transmission of Endymion's myth. Mourning his grown daughter Tullia, he writes, in an argument against fearing death:

> If we wish to hear fairy tales, Endymion, indeed, fell asleep I know not when on Latmus, which is a mountain in Caria, and, I think, he has not yet awakened. You don't think then that he worries when the Moon is in travail, the Moon who is thought to have made him sleep, that she might kiss him while he slept? Why then should he worry, who, indeed, has no sensation? You have sleep, the image of death, which you put on every day, and still you doubt that there is no sensation in death, although you see in its counterfeit that there is none?[40]

The words have the colloquial quality of a remembered anecdote, even of a bedtime story meant to calm a child. The implicit parallel between bedtime ritual and mortal concern suggests the affinities between death and sleep and the solace that being dead might be no more fearful than being asleep. At the same time, the passage casts Cicero as a storytelling parent, comforting himself in his grief even as he once might have soothed his daughter when she was young. Another reference in Cicero's writings presents Endymion as an incarnation of the inactivity human beings repudiate all through their lives, even in babyhood; it is tempting to imagine the sleepless child and the unsuccessful bedtime story that might lie behind the association.[41] Greek mythology and its trappings have figured so frequently in the learned traditions and high culture of the West that it is easy to forget the fundamental simplicity of many of the tales and the spontaneous entertainment they offered to listeners and storytellers in any setting in antiquity.[42]

The elements of Endymion's tale—sleep, night, a tranquil landscape, and perpetual romance—could have been variously embellished by countless occasional storytellers, including the craftsmen who made sarcophagi, those buried in them, and the families who visited the tombs of their relatives in remembrance. The one essential scene all the sarcophagi include features the goddess arriving and the youth asleep. The details vary within the formula over time and from object to object, however, so that each presents a slightly different version. The similarities have

prompted statements about possible prototypes. Some scholars trace the source of the Endymion figure to monumental sculpture and compare the lifesize marbles in Saint Petersburg and in Stockholm, which date to the second century A.D. but may reproduce compositions of the second century B.C.[43] The large sleeping youths bear some resemblance to the Endymions on sarcophagi, but the poses are not identical, and the figure of Selene is lacking. The weightless shimmer of her moonlight is a better theme for painting, and scholars accordingly have proposed a connection between the sarcophagi and a lost picture like the one from which Campanian wall paintings are thought to derive.[44] Although these, too, differ in their details, most of them fit within a square frame, and include Endymion and Selene, if not alone then accompanied only by Endymion's dog and a cupid or two.[45] The illusionistic rendering of space seems to give them room to breathe, and a single rock or tree suggests the landscape.

The latest Campanian paintings were executed at least fifty years before the first representations of Endymion on sarcophagi, and no painted examples survive from the second or third centuries A.D. A child-sized coffin carved about A.D. 135 and now in the Museo Capitolino, Rome, bears an early adaptation of the scene (Figure 6). If, in fact, the sculptor was working from a square composition, he added considerable detail to fill the oblong format. At the left, a tree extends into the scene, and a dog with its ears pinned back sits before a rocky ledge. A bearded, barechested male figure—the personification of Sleep—holds the recumbent Endymion on his lap and lifts his drapery as though to peer underneath. The effect perhaps results from the horizontal position of Endymion, modified for the narrow band of the relief. Selene, in the middle of the scene, approaches Endymion, with her skirt billowing behind her and a single cupid preceding her, while, on the right-hand side, two horses draw her chariot toward an arch. The hypothetical prototype for the image is less apparent than the way in which the sculptor has altered it for his own medium, as nearly contemporary mosaicists were also doing, but with different results.[46] Plastic details abound in the textures of the bark, cloth, and rock, the representations of relief decoration on the chariot and arch, the little herm that protrudes from the tree, and the snake that coils on the ground. The figures are surrounded by space as in paintings, but here it is the shallower space appropriate to a frieze. Although the sarcophagus probably was enhanced with paint in antiquity, the marble carvers naturally brought their own craft to the design.[47] The various versions of the story on later sarcophagi probably

Figure 6. Marble sarcophagus. Roman, ca. A.D. 135, from Rome. Museo Capitolino, Rome, 325 (photo: Deutsches Archäologisches Institut, Rome)

Figure 7. Marble sarcophagus. Roman, ca. A.D. 160. The Metropolitan Museum of Art, Fletcher Fund, 1924 (24.97.13)

represent the innovations of individual workshops within the limits of the standard formula.[48]

The adaptation of the scene to a horizontal format raises both formal and narrative considerations. On the Capitoline sarcophagus, for example, Selene is smaller than Endymion, perhaps because she stands upright in the narrow space. Here, Endymion is more voluptuous than in other portrayals, with his arched back, spread legs, soft chest, and slight smile. His right arm hangs down in the relaxation of sleep, and his left arm is bent above his head in a gesture that the two cupids with the chariot are imitating. Selene, before him, looks small and childlike, endowed with a round belly, small breasts, and chubby legs. Her pose, with her shoulders behind her hips, suggests some reluctance, as though she were pulling back from the cupid leading her. The depiction is unusual, for Selene normally appears with more maidenly proportions and often leans forward so as to fit into a restricted space without a reduction in size. Here, the cupid seems to hurry her toward an erotic encounter she is too young to seek for herself; one thinks of the many ancient epitaphs that express sadness at the prospects of adulthood unattained and marriage denied by death. The

sarcophagus itself is child sized, and at some time subsequent to its initial carving, it contained the body of a little girl; her name, Gerontia, appears in the inscription, which is dated to the fourth century.[49]

Differences in the depiction of Endymion and Selene change the story within the limits imposed by the form of the sarcophagus and the elasticity of the myth itself. An example in the Metropolitan Museum, made about A.D. 160, heightens the pastoral aspects of the story and alters the attitudes of the participants (Figure 7). Selene leans slightly forward toward Endymion, her dress slips from her right shoulder to bare her right breast, and the mantle she holds above her forms a crescent-shaped billow appropriate to her identity as the personification of the Moon. Endymion's body is almost completely exposed, revealed by a cupid who lifts his cloak. His head leans back so that he faces up toward Selene, his long hair falls over his neck, and his legs are crossed. The personification of Sleep is a less sensuous and less obtrusive character than his counterpart on the Capitoline sarcophagus. He is represented smaller than the lovers, bearded, draped, and equipped with the butterfly wings typical of images of Psyche in ancient art, and he hovers or stands above Endymion without touching him. Selene is walking from left to right, but this is not the only direction of the movement in the scene, for her horses face left and so does the shepherd asleep on a rock, who rests his head in his hand; his flock, seen on a ledge above him, perhaps is meant to occupy the space behind him. A pair of cupids, sleeping upright as they lean on inverted torches—common types in Roman sepulchral art—frame the narrative without taking part in the scene, conveying a mood of quiet melancholy.[50] They seem to belong to a foreground nearer to the observer, and the tale of Endymion and Selene unfolds between them like a romantic shadow play. Whereas the Capitoline carving implies childhood and maturity denied, the New York example suggests a more intimate bond between Selene and Endymion and a pastoral atmosphere rather than merely an out-of-doors setting. The differences likely reflect not only changes in compositional style but also distinct perspectives on the story.

In comparison with earlier examples, Claudia Arria's sarcophagus presents a more populous scene, remarkable for its greater movement, drama, and eroticism (see Figures 1, 2). Variations in style and workmanship help create this new effect. In a manner typical of Severan sculpture, extensive use of undercutting and the drill increase the depth of the relief, while the densely figured composition leaves no space empty. One horse's leg is physically in front of the female figure holding the bridle, and the personification of Earth places her elbow literally beside the foot of the seated shepherd to the left. The scene is filled with motion of all kinds: the horses rear, their guide lunges forward and twists her head back, and the shepherd reaches out to stroke his dog's neck. The wheel of the chariot, a perfect circle nearly centered on the scene's groundline, seems to serve as the fulcrum for the motion surrounding it. Selene herself performs the most significant action. In a rush of breezes that press her skirt against her legs, lift the overfold of her chiton, and blow her mantle overhead, she has descended from the chariot and places her foot between Endymion's crossed legs. Her movement determines the direction and focus of the entire scene, for all the other participants face right as she does, including the figure in front of the horses, Endymion himself, and the cupids who turn to look back while their bodies press forward.

The heightened activity and the increased population of the scene on the sarcophagus again transform the mood and the impact of the story. An air of prenuptial festivity and pastoral abundance replaces the intimate quiet of earlier versions of the subject. The tree in fruit above the horses' heads, the bearded

and muscular shepherd, and the ram and the ewe nestled against each other, above him, all belong to the idyllic landscape, as represented in ancient painting, poetry, and romantic prose.[51] A flock of cupids, who seem to radiate directly from Selene, fills her surroundings with suggestions of love and lights her way with torches, as wedding parties did for Roman brides. She is shown, as erotic figures commonly are in Greco-Roman art, with her right breast bared, and the bit of fabric across Endymion's thigh heightens his sensuality. Although his pose is typical of that seen on sarcophagi, it is unknown in three-dimensional sculpture and would be difficult to maintain in sleep. Perhaps the artist rotated the body from a recumbent posture in order to offer the viewer the perspective that Selene would have enjoyed.

In addition to the primary scene, the sarcophagus features several others, all with themes of love. One of the ten arched panels on the lid, just to the left of the inscription, depicts a later moment in the romance of Endymion and Selene, shown seated together on a rock: Endymion turns his body away from Selene, who twists her face toward her as though to kiss him. The subject is unique on Roman sarcophagi, but as Sichtermann has demonstrated, it is adapted from images of Venus and her wounded and dying mortal lover Adonis.[52] The young man's air of refusal in each case seems to acknowledge a divide between mortality and divinity, and the goddess's gesture is an effort to nullify it. The scene has less narrative and more symbolic value than the one on the coffin itself and is like a moral to the tale illustrated below.

Another panel on the lid shows a second couple, Cupid and Psyche, in a visually comparable but existentially opposed image. Psyche reaches for Cupid's chin while he turns away, but here he is the god and she is the mortal. The most extensive literary version of the myth dates to the second century and occurs in Apuleius's novel *Metamorphoses*, where an old woman tells the story to calm a girl roused by a bad dream.[53] Unlike the tales of Endymion and Adonis, which end ambiguously, Psyche's has a happy ending, for the gods allow her to awake from a magic sleep and welcome her into their midst forever as Cupid's bride. Cupid and Psyche appear again in an embrace under the left lion-head spout, presumably having surmounted the impediments intimated in the scene above (Figure 8).

The division of the various narratives into scenes on the box and lid moves the focus of the storytelling in various directions. To trace the myth of Endymion and Selene, the sequence reads from the right, and then up; for Cupid and Psyche, the order of the scenes is from top to bottom. Three other panels on

Figure 8. Detail of Cupid and Psyche on the sarcophagus in Figure 1

Figure 9. Terracotta antefix. Roman, 27 B.C.–A.D. 14. The Metropolitan Museum of Art, Purchase, 1896 (96.18.162)

the lid depict events involving Venus: in one, she stands, partly draped, among cupids, with a staff and an apple in hand; in the next scene, to the right, she is nude and sits beneath a tree on rocky ground while cupids frolic around her. The missing but implied protagonist of these narratives is the male figure, who occupies his own frame to the left; nude but for a helmet, he carries a spear and a sword and gazes toward the two images of Venus. He may represent the god Mars, who often appears as Venus's paramour in Roman art, as on a terracotta antefix in the Metropolitan Museum's collection (Figure 9). The intention might have been for the viewer of the sarcophagus to associate him with Venus in a straightforward love affair, but the apple that Venus holds suggests another possibility, proposed by Sichtermann, that the man is the Trojan prince Paris, who judged the beauty contest among Juno, Minerva, and Venus.[54] In that case, the scene of Venus seated on the rocks would show her preparing for the contest, and the one beside it depicts her as the winner with the golden apple as her prize. J. Engemann reminds us that the ancients probably could interpret iconographic signs that are indiscernible to us, yet the possibility exists that different viewers in antiquity understood the male figure on the sarcophagus as either Mars or Paris and completed the story according to their various interpretations.[55]

The rest of the figures on the sarcophagus signify natural phenomena and aspects of the settings for the stories. The panels on the extreme right and left of the lid show male figures seated in landscapes, extensions of the pastoral scenery of the box and personifications of the place—perhaps Latmus—where Endymion is supposed to have lived.[56] In the panels one in from each end, cupids appear with fruits and animals—attributes apposite to the seasons or to Dionysus, god of wine.[57] Whatever their intended identity, they personify the abundance and fecundity of the earth. Helios, the Sun, drives his four-horse chariot over the personification of the Ocean on the right end (Figure 4), and Selene proceeds in the same direction on the left end, riding over the recumbent Earth (Figure 3). As though chasing each other around an oval track, they personify the movement of the cosmos and place the myths on the sarcophagus within the circuit of time. The decoration continues around to the back, where horses and cattle are shown grazing beneath the trees and male and female figures

Figure 10. Marble sarcophagus. Roman, ca. A.D. 220, from Saint Médard d'Eyran, near Bordeaux. Musée du Louvre, Paris, Ma 1346 (photo: Alinari/Art Resource, NY)

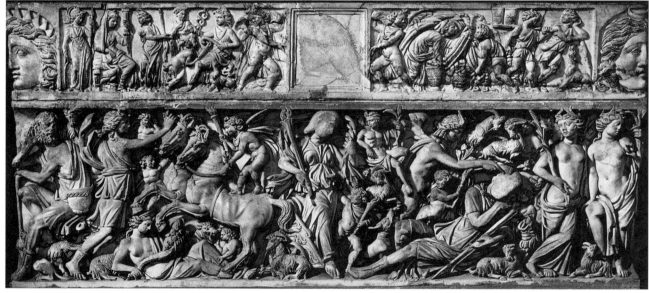

Figure 11. Marble sarcophagus. Roman, ca. A.D. 230, from Saint Médard d'Eyran, near Bordeaux. Musée du Louvre, Paris, Ma 1335 (photo: Alinari/Art Resource, NY)

assume relaxed poses in their midst (Figure 5). Although the back was probably not visible when the sarcophagus was placed in the chamber tomb, its ornamentation shares the spirit of idyllic romance prevalent on all sides.

The bust-length portrait of Claudia Arria seems to depict her at a window, as a witness to the many tales of love; her expression is stern but need not imply an unwillingness to countenance them. Indeed, her

daughter Aninia Hilara, the dedicant specified in the inscription, probably chose the sarcophagus from among several adorned with different subjects. The market for sarcophagi in antiquity is incompletely understood, but there is reason to presume that workshops did not specialize in single subjects, although individual craftsmen might have done so.[58] F. Matz found stylistic grounds to associate Arria's monument with five others decorated with scenes depicting the

Figure 12. Marble sarcophagus. Roman, ca. A.D. 310. Palazzo Doria Pamphilj, Rome (photo: Deutsches Archäologisches Institut, Rome)

Judgment of Paris, the Indian triumph of Dionysus, a battle, a grape harvest (*vindemia*), and episodes from a child's life, respectively.[59] As A. M. McCann has observed, stylistic inconsistencies obtain within the group, which may be the product of different workshops.[60] Ostia was probably home to some skilled marble carvers, and many more would have worked in Rome, slightly farther afield.[61] Aninia Hilara could have visited several of these workshops until she found what she wanted. In all likelihood, she bought the sarcophagus in a nearly finished state, since the effort required to carve it completely to order would not have allowed for a timely burial. Claudia Arria's conventional gesture and generalized costume seem made to suit any sitter, and tool marks around the head indicate the roughed-out form from which the portrait later was cut.[62] The completion of Claudia Arria's portrait indicates a choice, for several comparable sarcophagi include unfinished portraits; one appears, for example, on the vertical face of the lid of a sarcophagus carved about 220 and now in the Louvre (Figure 10). The addition of Claudia Arria's facial features probably made her monument more expensive and may have been understood by her daughter as a means of recording her appearance and, like the inscription, of guaranteeing her identity against anonymity and obscurity.[63]

Nothing about Claudia Arria's sarcophagus makes explicit reference to a belief in any particular god or philosophy. In the early second century A.D., Ostia was a cosmopolitan port city where numerous religions and philosophies flourished, among them Christianity and the eastern cults of Cybele, Isis, and Mithras, which all promise life after death.[64] Cumont argued that the proliferation of these faiths and their propen-

sity to teach by allegorical interpretation of visual images helped invest myths like Endymion's with eschatological significance.[65] To the modern observer, the complexity and vitality of the carvings on the sarcophagus may suggest a mood closer to anxiety than to faith. Indeed, the riot of personifications, cupids, and animals detracts from the impact of the two main characters and dilutes their symbolic potential.

The decoration on the sarcophagus does not attribute immortality to Claudia Arria or associate her with any specific character. It departs from a trend common on other monuments, where a portrait likeness of the deceased often completes the image of a divinity or a hero.[66] On a sarcophagus found near Bordeaux in 1805 and now in the Louvre, the faces of both Endymion and Selene have been left incomplete along with the space reserved for the inscription (Figure 11). Selene carries her own torch, and Endymion sleeps fully clothed in a naturalistic pose unusual on sarcophagi. The shape of Selene's head as preserved seems to have allowed for a hairstyle like those popular about A.D. 230—that is, for a particular coiffure rather than the Greek-inspired one seen on the Metropolitan's sarcophagus.[67] A much-restored sarcophagus carved about A.D. 310 and now in the Palazzo Doria Pamphilj, Rome, displays the impact of portraiture on a mythological scene destined for the tomb (Figure 12).[68] Endymion's "bowl" haircut and cowlick and Selene's distinctive face, with full lips and dimples at the corners of her mouth, identify the figures in the story with specific individuals; the myth could have inspired personal retellings, including the concept of a marriage to last through eternity. When only a single figure bears a portrait likeness, it is usually Endymion, as on a sarcophagus of A.D. 150–70 in the Museo

Capitolino, and on another, in Copenhagen, with an inscription identifying the deceased as a young man and the dedicants as his parents.[69] The analogy between Endymion and the dead youth seems obvious, and the portrayal of Selene without individualized features appears to have been an attempt to substitute the goddess herself to comfort the young man in place of the earthly wife he never had.

The straightforward resemblance between Endymion and a particular male figure does not obtain on Claudia Arria's sarcophagus. Had the dedicant desired to make such a comparison between her mother and a sleeping female figure, she might have chosen a sarcophagus decorated with the myth of Dionysus and Ariadne, another subject popular in Roman funerary art. The Louvre sarcophagus discussed displays the many compositional similarities between scenes of Endymion and Ariadne (see Figure 10). The sleeping figure reclines on the right, the god alights from a chariot near the center, and an abundance of figures creates an atmosphere both festive and tranquil, a setting for both the maenad with her cymbals and the centauress with her child. The story is in some respects parallel to the tale of Endymion, for Ariadne was a mortal princess who fell asleep on the island of Naxos and Dionysus was the god who married her. The two myths do not have the same existential value, however, for Endymion's sleep may be endless, and Ariadne's culminates in waking. Visitors to the tomb in which the Ariadne sarcophagus was deposited could readily have observed the similarity between the two stories—a comparison that may have been intended by the carvers as well as the dedicants, for the Louvre's Endymion sarcophagus occupied the same chamber (see Figure 11). It has been suggested that the young woman whose body the coffin contained was the wife of the man buried in the Endymion sarcophagus.[70] Since his monument postdates hers by about ten years, he may have outlived her and selected both sarcophagi.[71] If so, he might have been inclined to imagine himself as his wife's Endymion but not as her Dionysus, for the images of both protagonists on the Endymion sarcophagus are prepared for the addition of portrait likenesses, while on the other example this is true only of Ariadne. The god appears with a finished, idealized head, but the features of the husband—who is portrayed on the lid above, outside the scene like a spectator or listener—might have been deliberately left incomplete, to be added later, in order to personalize the portrait bust.

In mythological scenes that do not include portraits, the narrative itself may confer immortality on the dead in the certainty that the story will be retold repeatedly as the dead themselves are remembered.

On Claudia Arria's sarcophagus, her likeness and her name, along with the depiction of stories that Aninia Hilara may first have heard from her mother, preserve her memory. The images associate her with scenes of Venus, Cupid and Psyche, and Endymion and Selene, which appear not as metaphysical fables but as romances ripe for retelling in the light of personal recollection. When those who mourned Claudia Arria visited the tomb on holidays and anniversaries, they also encountered these myths in the flickering light.[72] By observing the sarcophagus and retelling the stories depicted, they perpetuated her memory and that of her daughter, the dedicant. The sarcophagus and its decoration forged an enduring bond between mother and daughter—one of reflection and active remembrance.

Epitaphs for and by women, which give some indication of what the Romans saw fit to commemorate and to remember, often compare the deceased to mythological figures and combine reflection on personal traits, sometimes idealized, with wishes for comfort and love.[73] A Greek inscription found in Rome refers to a dead woman as "this dark-eyed muse," and a funerary altar for a woman named Laberia Daphne bears an image of Daphne, beloved of Apollo, being transformed into a laurel tree.[74] A remarkable epitaph for the freedwoman Allia Potestas credits her with legs lovelier than Atalanta's and a steady routine: "First she was to leave her bed in the morning, and she again was the last to bring herself to bed to rest once she had put things in order."[75] A second-century Greek inscription found in Rome praises the dead and comforts the living: "Say that Popilia is asleep, sir; for it would be wrong for the good to die; rather, they sleep sweetly."[76] A Latin epitaph from a young wife for her husband affirms a wish for love in the hereafter: "So I beseech you, most holy shades, take my dear husband whom I commit to your care; and desire to prove most indulgent to me, that I may see him in the hours of night; he also wishes that I may sway fate and come to him sweetly and quickly."[77] The emphasis on the continuing alternation of sleeping and waking, as in life, seems to express a popular belief in timeless repetition, which is a theme implicit in the myth of Endymion. When the story is actually depicted, as on Claudia Arria's monument, the invitation to retell it over and over heightens the calming thought of an unending routine.

As John Boardman and Donna Kurtz note in their study of Greek burial customs, "When man disposes of his dead he is usually trying to satisfy the emotional and even physical needs of the living, faced by a puzzling sense of loss or even danger, haunted by memories or dreams of the dead as still alive."[78] The psychologist Simon Grolnick extends this idea when he states, "A complex continuum exists between the bedtime rituals of infants and children and the rituals and art of a culture's burial practices."[79] A child craves reassurance before he will fall asleep, and the grieving need to be soothed in order to face death. In either situation, a story is a ritual instrument of solace, a series of known events to replace a threatening void. The myths of Endymion and Selene and of Cupid and Psyche end happily and feature the themes of sleep and love. Classic bedtime stories, they offered comfort to Roman patrons in childhood and in mourning, and calmed the dead before their final sleep.

ACKNOWLEDGMENTS

I am grateful to the many people who discussed this paper with me in its two earlier forms, as presented in 1999 at the conference "Women Art Patrons and Collectors Past and Present" and as part of my dissertation, "Sleep That Rouses: Naturalism and the Observer in Greco-Roman Art," Columbia University, 2000. I wish especially to thank Aileen Ajootian, John Bodel, Richard Brilliant, William Harris, Evelyn Harrison, Natalie Kampen, Barbara Kellum, Clemente Marconi, Joan Mertens, Marice Rose, Suzanne Said, Emma Scioli, and Amy Smith. All translations from the Greek and Latin are my own unless otherwise noted and are based on the texts established for the Loeb Classical Library, published by Harvard University Press.

NOTES

1. H. Sichtermann, *Die mythologischen Sarkophage,* vol. 2, Die antiken Sarkophagreliefs 12 (Berlin: G. Mann, 1992), p. 52.

2. For a brief but exemplary consideration of a sarcophagus and its patron, see the analysis of the Alcestis sarcophagus from Ostia, now in the Vatican, by K. Fittschen, "Über Sarkophage mit Porträts verschiedener Personen," in B. Andreae, ed., *Symposium über die antiken Sarkophage* (Marburg: Verlag des kunstgeschictlichen Seminars, 1984), pp. 141–43.

3. For example, T. Frank, "Race Mixture in the Roman Empire," *American Historical Review* 21 (1916), pp. 689–708; L. R. Taylor, "Freedmen and Freeborn in the Epitaphs of Imperial Rome," *American Journal of Philology* 82 (1961), pp. 113–32; R. P. Saller and B. D. Shaw, "Tombstones and Roman Family Relations in the Principate: Civilians, Soldiers, and Slaves," *Journal of Roman Studies* 74 (1984), pp. 124–56.

4. G. Koch, *Sarkophage der römischen Kaiserzeit* (Darmstadt: Wissenschaftliche Buchgesellschaft, 1993), p. 4.

5. I thank John Bodel for generously helping to interpret the inscription.

6. *Corpus Inscriptionum Latinarum* 14.565.

7. Dedications by mothers to children outnumber those by children to mothers by a margin of about five to three, according to S. Dixon, *The Roman Mother* (London: Croom Helm, 1988), pp. 214, 229. Funerary inscriptions recording dedications by daughters to mothers amount to only 3 percent of the examples from Rome and Latium examined by Saller and Shaw, "Roman Family Relations," pp. 147–48.

8. Saller and Shaw, "Roman Family Relations," pp. 133–39.

9. J. Bodel and S. Tracy, *Greek and Latin Inscriptions in the USA: A Checklist* (Rome: American Academy in Rome, 1997), p. 196.

10. Dessau lists examples of the omission of the *T* in the middle and at the end of words. See H. Dessau, ed., *Inscriptiones Latinae Selectae* (Berlin: Weidmann, 1916), vol. 3, pt. 2, p. 833.

11. For examples, see Dessau, *Inscriptiones,* vol. 3, pt. 2, p. 827.

12. For examples in inscriptions of an *E* as a dative singular ending for nouns and adjectives of the third declension, see Dessau, *Inscriptiones,* vol. 3, pt. 2, p. 848.

13. *Corpus Inscriptionum Latinarum* 14.564; H. Thylander, *Inscriptions du port d'Ostie* (Lund: C. W. K. Gleerup, 1952), p. 238, B 14, and pl. 95, 1.

14. On the obligation of relatives to pay for a burial, see Saller and Shaw, "Roman Family Relations," p. 126. On daughters' responsibilities to their mothers, see Dixon, *The Roman Mother,* pp. 221–23.

15. On the few restorations, see A. M. McCann, *Roman Sarcophagi in The Metropolitan Museum of Art* (New York: MMA, 1978), p. 39.

16. C. Robert, *Die antiken Sarkophagreliefs,* vol. 3, *Einzelmythen,* pt. 1 (Berlin: G. Grote, 1897), no. 83, pp. 103–6, pl. 26; F. Matz, "An Endymion Sarcophagus Rediscovered," *MMAB* 15 (1956–57), p. 128.

17. For the variants, see H. Gabelmann, "Endymion," *Lexicon Iconographicum Mythologiae Classicae,* vol. 3, pt. 1 (Zürich: Artemis, 1986), pp. 726–28; M. Koortbojian, *Myth, Meaning, and Memory on Roman Sarcophagi* (Berkeley: University of California Press, 1995), pp. 63–64.

18. On the origins and meaning of the gesture, see P. J. Connor, "Dead Hero and the Sleeping Giant by the Nikosthenes Painter: At the Beginnings of a Motif," *Archäologischer Anzeiger* (1984), pp. 387–94; E. J. Milleker, "The Statue of Apollo Lykeios in Athens," Ph.D. diss., Institute of Fine Arts, New York University, 1986, pp. 58–69.

19. The female figure was identified as Aura, the personification of Breeze, by Robert, *Sarkophagreliefs,* vol. 3, pt. 1, pp. 54–60, and many scholars have followed him, including G. M. A. Richter, "A Roman Sarcophagus," *MMAB* 20 (1925), p. 78, and McCann, *Roman Sarcophagi,* p. 42. Without identifying the figure otherwise, Sichtermann, *Sarkophage,* vol. 2, pp. 36–38, casts doubt on the identification and points out that a similar figure appears with the chariot of Hades on the Persephone sarcophagi. There is reason to associate the female figure more with darkness than with air, a point that I will address in a forthcoming paper.

20. For the count, see Koch, *Sarkophage der römischen Kaiserzeit,* p. 74.

21. Robert, *Sarkophagreliefs,* vol. 3, pt. 1, pp. 53–59.

22. Koortbojian, *Myth, Meaning, and Memory,* p. 68.

23. For more on the comparison between sleep and death in poetry, see P. Boyancé, "Le sommeil et l'immortalité," *Mélanges d'archéologie et d'histoire* 45 (1928), pp. 97–105; M. Ogle, "The Sleep of Death," *Memoirs of the American Academy in Rome* 11 (1933), pp. 81–117; Jean-Claude Eger, *Le sommeil et la mort dans*

la Grèce antique (Paris: Éditions Sicard, 1966); E. Vermeule, *Aspects of Death in Early Greek Art and Poetry* (Berkeley: University of California Press, 1979); C. Mainoldi, "Sonno e morte in Grecia antica," in *Rappresentazioni della morte*, ed. R. Raffaelli (Urbino: Quattro Venti, 1987), pp. 9–46.

24. P. Ariès, *L'homme devant la mort* (Paris: Éditions du Seuil, 1977), pp. 30–32; R. A. Lattimore, *Themes in Greek and Latin Epitaphs* (Urbana: University of Illinois Press, 1942), pp. 164–65.

25. Plato *Phaedo* 72b–c: "ἀλλ' οἶον εἰ τὸ καταδαρθάνειν μὲν εἴη, τὸ δ' ἀνεγείρεσθαι μὴ ἀνταποδιδοίη γιγνόμενον ἐκ τοῦ καθεύδοντος, οἶσθ' ὅτι τελευτῶντα πάντ' ἂν λῆρον τὸν Ἐνδυμίωνα ἀποδείξειεν καὶ οὐδαμοῦ ἂν φαίνοιτο διὰ τὸ καὶ τἆλλα πάντα ταὐτὸν ἐκείνῳ πεπονθέναι, καθεύδειν."

26. F. Cumont, *Recherches sur le symbolisme funéraire des romains* (Paris: Paul Geuthner, 1942), pp. 246–50.

27. A. D. Nock, "Sarcophagi and Symbolism," *American Journal of Archaeology* 50 (1946), pp. 150–52, 159–61; Artemidorus *Interpretation of Dreams* 1.80.

28. R. Turcan, "Les sarcophages romains et le problème du symbolisme funéraire," *Aufstieg und Niedergang der römischen Welt*, vol. 2, no. 16, pt. 2 (Berlin: W. de Gruyter, 1978), pp. 1728–29; R. Brilliant, *Visual Narratives* (Ithaca: Cornell University Press, 1984), p. 150.

29. F. G. J. M. Müller, *The So-Called Peleus and Thetis Sarcophagus in the Villa Albani* (Amsterdam: J. C. Gieben, 1994), pp. 145–46.

30. The idiom in Greek is Ἐνδυμίωνος ὕπνον καθεύδειν. For citations, see Gabelmann, "Endymion," p. 727. On the Latin idiom *Endymionis somnum dormire*, see Cicero, *Tusculan Disputations*, J. E. King, trans. (Cambridge, Mass.: Harvard University Press, 1971), p. 110, n. 3.

31. Turcan, "Le problème du symbolisme," p. 1701.

32. On the iconography of Jonah, see M. Lawrence, "Three Pagan Themes in Christian Art," in M. Meiss, ed., *De Artibus Opuscula XL: Essays in Honor of Erwin Panofsky* (New York: New York University Press, 1961), pp. 324–27.

33. Koortbojian, *Myth, Meaning, and Memory,* pp. 63–65.

34. W. V. Harris, *Ancient Literacy* (Cambridge, Mass.: Harvard University Press, 1989), pp. 259–67, estimates the average level of literacy in Italy during the Roman Empire at about 15 percent.

35. Turcan, "Le problème du symbolisme," pp. 1721–26.

36. Such a speech is actually inscribed on the grave monument of a Roman schoolboy, now in the Palazzo dei Conservatori, Rome. See Müller, *Peleus and Thetis*, pp. 150–51; A. E. Gordon, *Illustrated Introduction to Latin Epigraphy* (Berkeley: University of California Press, 1983), pp. 130–33, pl. 33.

37. Lucian *Dialogues of the Gods* 19: "Ἐμοὶ μὲν καὶ πάνυ καλός, ὦ Ἀφροδίτη, δοκεῖ, καὶ μάλιστα ὅταν ὑποβαλλόμενος ἐπὶ τῆς πέτρας τὴν χλαμύδα καθεύδῃ τῇ λαιᾷ μὲν ἔχων τὰ ἀκόντια ἤδη ἐκ τῆς χειρὸς ὑπορρέοντα, ἡ δεξιὰ δὲ περὶ τὴν κεφαλὴν ἐς τὸ ἄνω ἐπικεκλασμένη ἐπιπρέπῃ τῷ προσώπῳ περικειμένη, ὁ δὲ ὑπὸ τοῦ ὕπνου λελυμένος ἀναπνέῃ τὸ ἀμβρόσιον ἐκεῖνο ἆσθμα. τότε τοίνυν ἐγὼ ἀψοφητὶ κατιοῦσα ἐπ' ἄκρων τῶν δακτύλων βεβηκυῖα ὡς ἂν μὴ ἀνεγρόμενος ἐκταραχθείη—οἶσθα· τί οὖν ἄν σοι λέγοιμι τὰ μετὰ ταῦτα; πλὴν ἀπόλλυμαί γε ὑπὸ τοῦ ἔρωτος."

38. Philostratus *Imagines* 1.1, 15: "τάχα που καὶ τίτθης διακήκοας· σοφαὶ γὰρ ἐκεῖναι τὰ τοιαῦτα καὶ δακρύουσιν ἐπ' αὐτοῖς, ὅταν ἐθέλωσιν."

39. Plutarch *Life of Numa* 4.2: "ὅτι μὲν οὖν ταῦτα πολλοῖς τῶν πάνυ παλαιῶν μύθων ἔοικεν, οὓς οἱ Φρύγες τε περὶ Ἄττεω καὶ Βιθυνοὶ περὶ Ἡροδότου καὶ περὶ Ἐνδυμίωνος Ἀρκάδες ἄλλοι

τε περὶ ἄλλων εὐδαιμόνων δή τινων καὶ θεοφιλῶν γενέσθαι δοκούντων παραλαβόντες ἠγάπησαν, οὐκ ἄδηλόν ἐστι."

40. Cicero *Tusculan Disputations* 1.92: "Endymion vero, si fabulas audire volumus, ut nescio quando in Latmo obdormivit, qui est mons Cariae, nondum, opinor, est experrectus. Num igitur eum curare censes, cum Luna laboret, a qua consopitus putatur, ut eum dormientem oscularetur? Quid curet autem, qui ne sentit quidem? Habes somnum imaginem mortis eamque cotidie induis, et dubitas quin sensus in morte nullus sit, cum in eius simulacro videas esse nullum sensum?"

41. Cicero *De Finibus* 5.55: "Itaque nisi iucundissimis quidem nos somniis usuros putemus, Endymionis somnum nobis velimus dari, idque si accidat mortis instar putemus." (And so, even if we thought we might enjoy the most delightful dreams, we should not want the sleep of Endymion to be given us, and would think it if it happened identical to death.)

42. For a sensitive discussion of storytelling at home in antiquity, see S. C. Humphreys, "Women's Stories," in *Pandora: Women in Classical Greece*, ed. E. D. Reeder (Baltimore: Walters Art Gallery, 1995), pp. 102–10.

43. Sichtermann, *Sarkophage*, vol. 2, p. 34. For the Saint Petersburg and Stockholm types, see Gabelmann, "Endymion," p. 735, nos. 92, 93.

44. Matz, "An Endymion Sarcophagus," p. 127.

45. For the list of examples, see Gabelmann, "Endymion," pp. 729–31, nos. 14–27.

46. The mosaics tend to retain square compositions and to focus on the two protagonists. Third-century polychrome examples include the mosaic from the House of the Laberii in Oudna, now in the Bardo, Tunis, and another from a house in El Jem, now in the archaeological museum there. A similar composition, also in black-and-white mosaic, is in the 2nd-century tomb 87 in the Isola Sacra cemetery at Ostia. See N. Blanchard-Lemée et al., *Sols de la Tunisie romaine* (Paris: Imprimerie nationale, 1995), p. 242; G. Becatti, *Mosaici e pavimenti marmorei*, Scavi di Ostia, vol. 4 (Rome: Istituto Poligrafico dello Stato, 1961), pp. 307–8, pl. 105.

47. On the relationship between craftsmen's traditions and their output, see J. B. Ward-Perkins, "The Role of the Craftsman in the Formation of Early Christian Art," in *Atti del IV congresso internazionale di archeologia cristiana* (Rome: Pontificio Istituto di archeologia cristiana, 1978), vol. 1, p. 651. On the painting of sarcophagi, see G. Koch and H. Sichtermann, *Römische Sarkophage* (Munich: Beck, 1982), pp. 87–88.

48. Sichtermann, *Sarkophage*, vol. 2, pp. 39–40.

49. Ibid., p. 104: D M / GERONTIAE / FILIAE KRM.

50. For more on the type of the sleeping cupid, see J. B. Hartmann, "Die Genien des Lebens und des Todes: Zur Sepulkralikonographie des Klassizismus," *Römisches Jahrbuch für Kunstgeschichte* 12 (1969), pp. 11–38; McCann, *Roman Sarcophagi*, pp. 51–52; N. Blanc and F. Gury, "Eros / Amor / Cupido," *Lexicon Iconographicum Mythologiae Classicae*, vol. 3, pt. 1, pp. 971–72, 1047.

51. Compare, for example, Statius's address to Sleep, *Silvae* 5.4.3–6: "Tacet omne pecus volucresque feraeque / et simulant fessos curvata cacumina somnos, / nec trucibus fluviis idem sonus; / occidit horror / aequoris, et terris maria adclinata quiescunt." (Every beast lies quiet, and birds and wild animals, / And curved treetops look undone in slumber, / And raging rivers have not the same sound; the rising of the sea / Gives way, and the waters leaning on the earth are still.)

52. Sichtermann, *Sarkophage*, vol. 2, pp. 135–36. For an example of

a scene with Venus and Adonis, see the sarcophagus Louvre Ma 347, ex coll. Borghese, in F. Baratte and C. Metzger, *Catalogue des sarcophages en pierre d'époque romaine et paléochrétienne* (Paris: Éditions de la Réunion des Musées Nationaux, 1985), no. 16, pp. 55–57.

53. Apuleius *Metamorphoses* 4.28–6.24.

54. Sichtermann, *Sarkophage*, vol. 2, p. 136.

55. J. Engemann, *Untersuchungen zur Sepulkralsymbolik der späteren römischen Kaiserzeit* (Münster: Aschendorffsche Verlagsbuchhandlung, 1973), p. 30.

56. Sichtermann, *Sarkophage*, vol. 2, p. 137.

57. McCann, *Roman Sarcophagi*, p. 43, interprets them as personifications of Spring and Fall; Sichtermann, *Sarkophage*, vol. 2, p. 137, prefers to identify them as Bacchic figures.

58. On the artisanal tendency to specialize, see Ward-Perkins, "The Role of the Craftsman," p. 368.

59. F. Matz, *Ein römisches Meisterwerk: Der Jahrzeitensarkophag Badminton–New York* (Berlin: Walter de Gruyter, 1958), pp. 166–67.

60. McCann, *Roman Sarcophagi*, p. 44.

61. Inscriptions found at Ostia record the existence of numerous trade guilds, and it is likely that there were also more. Among those recorded are the *corpus traiectus marmorariorum* (the marble importers) and the *collegae pingentes* (the painters) (*Corpus Inscriptionum Latinarum* 14.425; Suppl. 4699). See R. Meiggs, *Roman Ostia* (Oxford: Clarendon, 1960), pp. 311–36.

62. The gesture is widespread in Roman Republican funerary portraits. For examples and discussion, see R. Brilliant, *Gesture and Rank in Roman Art* (New Haven: Connecticut Academy of Arts and Sciences, 1963), pp. 45–49; D. E. E. Kleiner, *Roman Group Portraiture* (New York: Garland, 1977), pp. 80–83.

63. On inscriptions and the immortality they may promise, see Ariès, *L'homme devant la mort*, pp. 201–15; Harris, *Ancient Literacy*, pp. 221–22.

64. Meiggs, *Roman Ostia*, pp. 354–80.

65. Cumont, *Recherches sur le symbolisme*, pp. 2–16.

66. The classic study of the phenomenon in Roman art is H. Wrede, *Consecratio in Formam Deorum* (Mainz: Philipp von Zabern, 1981).

67. On the hairstyle and date, see R. Turcan, *Les sarcophages romains à représentations dionysiaques* (Paris: Boccard, 1966), pp. 278–80.

68. On restorations to the sarcophagus, see Robert, *Sarkophagreliefs*, vol. 3, pt. 1, no. 77, p. 92; Sichtermann, *Sarkophage*, vol. 2, no. 93, pp. 142–43.

69. On the Capitoline sarcophagus, no. 725, see Robert, *Sarkopha-greliefs*, vol. 3, pt. 1, no. 61, pp. 76–78, pl. 16; W. Helbig, *Führer durch die öffentlichen Sammlungen klassischer Altertümer in Rom*, ed. H. Speer, 4th ed. (Tübingen: Ernst Wasmuth, 1966), vol. 2, no. 1406, pp. 213–14; Sichtermann, *Sarkophage*, vol. 2, no. 51, pp. 114–15. On the Copenhagen example, Ny Carlsberg - Glyptotek 848, see Robert, *Sarkophagreliefs*, vol. 3, pt. 1, pp. 68–69; Sichtermann, *Sarkophage*, vol. 2, no. 35, p. 109. The inscription, *Corpus Inscriptionum Latinarum* 14.622, reads, "D.M. / AURELIO.LUCANO / GRATUS.CAES.ET / SULPICIA.LASCIBA / PARENTES.FILIO / DULCISSIMO."

70. Robert, *Sarkophagreliefs*, vol. 3, pt. 1, p. 87.

71. Turcan, *Sarcophages dionysiaques*, pp. 278–80.

72. On visits to the tomb, see J. M. C. Toynbee, *Death and Burial in the Roman World* (Baltimore: Johns Hopkins University Press, 1971), pp. 61–64. For a brief description of the cemeteries of Ostia, see Meiggs, *Roman Ostia*, pp. 455–70.

73. For several samples with commentary, see D. E. E. Kleiner and S. Matheson, eds., *I Claudia: Women in Ancient Rome* (New Haven: Yale University Art Gallery, 1996), pp. 199–213.

74. For the epitaph, see Lattimore, *Themes*, p. 175. For the altar, in the Palazzo Ducale in Urbino, see D. E. E. Kleiner, *Roman Imperial Funerary Altars* (Rome: Giorgio di Bretschneider, 1987), no. 75, pl. 42.

75. *Corpus Inscriptionum Latinarum* 6.37965. For commentary, see Lattimore, *Themes*, pp. 298–99; Gordon, *Latin Epigraphy*, pp. 145–48.

76. For the translation, see Lattimore, *Themes*, p. 164; G. Kaibel, *Epigrammata Graeca* (Berlin, 1878), p.559, ll. 7–8: "καὶ λέγε Ποπιλίην εὕδειν, ἄνερ· οὐ θεμιτὸν γὰρ / θνήσκειν τοὺς ἀγαθούς, ἀλλ' ὕπνον ἡδὺν ἔχειν."

77. *Corpus Inscriptionum Latinarum* 6.18817.9–18: "Ita peto vos, manes sanctissimae, / commendatum habeatis / meum carum et vellitis / huic indulgentissimi esse, / horis nocturnis / ut eum videam, / et etiam me fato suadere / vellit, ut et ego possim / dulcius et celerius / aput eum pervenire." For commentary, see Lattimore, *Themes*, p. 277; Koortbojian, *Myth, Meaning, and Memory*, p. 108.

78. D. C. Kurtz and J. Boardman, *Greek Burial Customs* (London: Thames and Hudson, 1971), p. 332.

79. S. Grolnick and A. Lengyel, "Etruscan Burial Symbols and the Transitional Process," in *Between Reality and Fantasy: Transitional Objects and Phenomena*, ed. S. Grolnick and L. Barkin (New York: Jason Aronson, 1978), p. 381.

A Man's Caftan and Leggings from the North Caucasus of the Eighth to Tenth Century: Introduction

PRUDENCE O. HARPER

Curator Emerita, Ancient Near Eastern Art, The Metropolitan Museum of Art

IN SEPTEMBER 1995 the Metropolitan Museum was offered by a dealer in London a linen caftan trimmed with silk and fur and a pair of silk leggings with linen feet. They had been recently restored, and they date in all probability to the eighth to tenth century A.D. The garments had been auctioned in an unrestored condition in 1994 at the Stuttgarter Kunst-Auktionhaus Fritz Nagel, where they were described as Tang dynasty textiles.

To any student of Near Eastern and western Central Asian art it was immediately apparent that the textiles described above belong to a unique body of material recovered over several decades beginning at the start of the twentieth century from the site of Moshchevaja Balka, in the northwest Caucasus Mountain region. Most recently, similar types of garments decorated with identical silk pieces have been recovered from this site, which lies above the Bolshaja Laba River near the Laba Pass leading over the mountain range. Four seasons of excavations were carried out between 1969 and 1976 by Anna A. Ierusalimskaja, curator since 1962 of northern Caucasian antiquities in the Oriental Department of the Hermitage Museum in Saint Petersburg. All the materials excavated at Moshchevaja Balka by Ierusalimskaja and her predecessors at the beginning of the twentieth century are now gathered together in the Hermitage Museum's Oriental Department collection.

Correspondence in 1995 with Anna Ierusalimskaja, a friend and colleague of many curators at the Metropolitan Museum, confirmed Moshchevaja Balka as the probable place of origin for the caftan and leggings being offered to the Museum and revealed the century-long history of excavation and looting of graves at the site. This information, which was published in her book *Die Gräber der Moščevaja Balka: Frühmittelalterliche Funde an der nordkaukasischen Seidenstrasse* (Munich, 1996), explained the appearance on the art market of the examples offered to the Museum. In the final report, Ierusalimskaja also offers a detailed history of the excavations and of the subsequent transfer of Moshchevaja Balka materials between various museum collections in Russia before their ultimate disposition in the Hermitage Museum.

The significance of the caftan and leggings acquired by the Trustees of The Metropolitan Museum of Art in 1996 at the recommendation of the Department of Ancient Near Eastern Art is immense. Textiles and complete garments are almost never recovered from excavations in the Near East, where climatic conditions lead to the destruction of most perishable organic remains. Quite exceptional are a few fragmentary textiles of Sasanian seventh-century date excavated by David Stronach at Shahr-i Qumis in northern Iran, an archaeological project supported by the Metropolitan Museum. A share of the finds from Shahr-i Qumis is now part of the Department of Ancient Near Eastern Art's collection, and the proposed acquisition of the Moshchevaja Balka caftan and leggings, of slightly later date than the Shahr-i Qumis textiles, was therefore of particular relevance. In the effort to acquire the pieces, the department was enthusiastically supported from the start by the head of the Museum's Textile Conservation Department, Nobuko Kajitani, who assisted us in the examination leading to their purchase, and by the specialist in the history and development of the caftan garment in Asia and Europe Elfriede R. Knauer. These two colleagues subsequently agreed to take on the complex task of correctly restoring and publishing the caftan and leggings. The results appear in this volume: by Kajitani, "A Man's Caftan and Leggings from the North Caucasus of the Eighth to Tenth Century: A Conservator's Report," pages 85–124; and by Knauer, "A Man's Caftan and Leggings from the North Caucasus of the Eighth to Tenth Century: A Genealogical Study," pages 125–54.

A final event in the history of this acquisition occurred in 1999, when Jacqueline Simcox, a well-known dealer in textiles based in London, wrote to the Department of Ancient Near Eastern Art offering as a gift forty-three objects including garments and fragments of decorative textiles as well as items made of wood, leather, bone, shell, bronze, and gold (see Kajitani, Figures 5–18). Many of these items had either exact or close parallels with published finds from Moshchevaja Balka. These objects, of considerable archaeological and ethnographic significance, had been offered for sale at the Stuttgarter Kunst-Auktionhaus Fritz Nagel on November 15, 1996, but went unsold. Enquiries at that time by the Department of Ancient Near Eastern Art revealed that the material was still available but at a price higher than what the Museum felt prepared to pay. Our delight, therefore, on receiving the offer of Jacqueline Simcox a few years later was considerable, and we are indebted to her for making possible this important addition to the department's collection of objects that provides a cultural context for the caftan and leggings.

An expression of appreciation and respect for the archaeological fieldwork and scholarly study of the Moshchevaja Balka site and finds by Anna Ierusalimskaja is appropriate here. Without her investigations the extraordinary remains now preserved in the Hermitage Museum would have remained lost to the world of scholarship. While discussions of the textiles and related materials, their place of original manufacture, and their proper cultural context will inevitably continue, the importance of the meticulous and thorough documentation of Anna Ierusalimskaja cannot be overestimated. Working under often austere conditions in a difficult period of modern history and under financial restrictions, she published the results of her studies and made available to scholars for consideration the extraordinarily rich archaeological heritage of this remote region. Throughout the long period of her researches, Ierusalimskaja never hesitated to share her unique materials and preliminary ideas with colleagues in a generous fashion; she remains in this and in many other respects a model for us all.

The following articles by Nobuko Kajitani and Elfriede R. Knauer describe the site of Moshchevaja Balka and the nature of the finds from the shallow graves situated above the mountain river valley. The environment in which the graves were found, on rock terraces overhung by a cliff face, naturally protected and preserved the fragile materials. While the location of Moshchevaja Balka on trade routes linking Central Asia, the Near Eastern lands, southern Russia, and the Black Sea explains in part the varied nature of the finds, questions remain: who were the people buried in these graves; and what role did they play in the acquisition and transfer of the goods that have been discovered? Local merchants and foreign traders appear to have come together at this site near the Laba Pass, and their possessions continue to be fascinating and enigmatic.

A Man's Caftan and Leggings from the North Caucasus of the Eighth to Tenth Century: A Conservator's Report

NOBUKO KAJITANI

Conservator in Charge, Textile Conservation, The Metropolitan Museum of Art

THE LINEN CAFTAN embellished with elaborate silk borders (Figures 1–3) and the pair of silk leggings with linen feet (Figure 4) that accompanies it are immediately recognizable as parts of a coordinated set of garments made for a horseman. Although the once brilliant colors of the silks and the whiteness of the linen have archaeologically discolored and the fur lining is mostly gone, material evidence such as the patterned silks relates the set to a large corpus of mortuary offerings excavated at Moshchevaja Balka, located in the northwestern Caucasus Mountains (between the Black and Caspian Seas), now in the collections of the State Hermitage (Saint Petersburg) and other museums in Russia.[1] It is possible that the caftan and leggings could have come from the same or a related site. If so, the wearer might have been an Alan who lived in an outlying settlement ruled by the Khazars in the vicinity sometime during the eighth to tenth century (see Elfriede R. Knauer, "A Man's Caftan and Leggings from the North Caucasus of the Eighth to Tenth Century: A Genealogical Study," pp. 125–54 below).

Our study of the caftan and leggings was aided by a hands-on comparison with the following three groups of objects—Reference Groups I, II, and III—excavated at or attributed to the Moshchevaja Balka site.

Reference Group I: A large corpus of a variety of objects in the Hermitage representing the Moshchevaja Balka group with secure excavation provenance that has been published (for selected pieces, see Knauer, Figures 5, 11–13, 30).[2] (The proportionately smaller groups in other Russian museums, for the most part, have not been published.)

Reference Group II: Three garments—the Metropolitan's caftan, the leggings, and a caftan made of Chinese Tang dynasty silk damask—attributable to the Moshchevaja Balka group, auctioned in 1994.[3] Referred to here as the Reference Silk Caftan (Figures 19, 20),[4] the silk damask caftan was in a London collection and was generously lent to the Metropolitan Museum for this study.

Reference Group III: A corpus of forty-six objects related to those in Reference Group II, similarly attributable to the Moshchevaja Balka group, was auctioned in 1996.[5] All items in the lot except three became a most welcome gift to the Metropolitan Museum in 1999 (Figures 5–18). Among the objects, an undecorated linen caftan (Figure 5; extant part consisting of an entire lower section and a small portion of the upper sections) and a pair of leggings (Figure 6; complete) were extremely helpful for this study.

The fifty-six auctioned objects of Reference Groups II and III plus seven not referenced (see note 3) and three missing from Reference Group III (see note 5) exhibit common traits indicating that they make up full or partial finds removed from burials at the same site as the objects in Reference Group I or from one nearby.[6] Of these, comprehensive and comparative visual and technical assessment was directly possible on thirteen items, enabling me to characterize the group's materials, weaving, design, cut, style, tailoring, state of preservation, and material fatigue.

When the Metropolitan Museum acquired the caftan and the pair of leggings at the recommendation of the Department of Ancient Near Eastern Art, the garments came with distinctive physical attributes we interpret as indicating they had been preserved in a burial site: their overall state; interrelated evidence of losses, creases, discolorations, organic brown staining, and encrustation penetrating through or deposited on the obverse and reverse in a somewhat dissimilar way; and masses of embedded dried-up, empty insect cocoons. The caftan and leggings have survived in reasonably fair physical condition, given their age, despite the fact that approximately 35 percent of the caftan and 10 percent of the leggings have suffered environmental deterioration associated with burial

© The Metropolitan Museum of Art 2001
METROPOLITAN MUSEUM JOURNAL 36

The notes for this article begin on page 117.

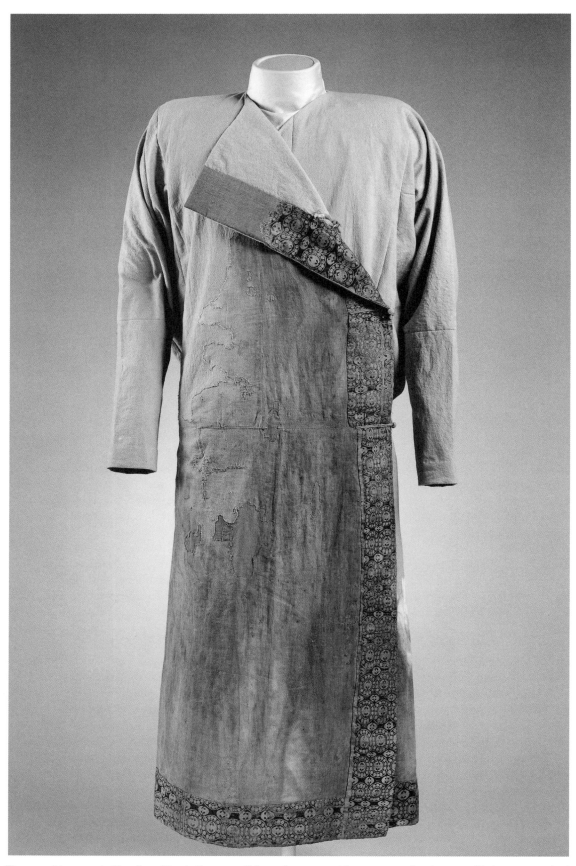

Figure 1. Linen and silk caftan. North Caucasus, 8th–10th century. After conservation in 2000. H. (reconstruction) 142 cm. The Metropolitan Museum of Art, Harris Brisbane Dick Fund, 1996 (1996.78.1)

Figure 2. Proper left side of caftan in Figure 1

Figure 3. Back of caftan in Figure 1

conditions, which are detrimental to organic materials. Most of the polychrome patterned silks on both legs of the leggings and on the proportionately sparse borders of the caftan, which constitute the visibly significant design features of the set, have miraculously survived. The examination and interpretation of these materials and design features gave us an adequate understanding of their original form as well as their surroundings during the time they were used as functional items.

At the initial stage of the burial, slightly acidic moisture must have exuded from the body, staining and damaging the buried objects. Concurrently, oxygen and acid-oriented mildew and keratin-infesting insects thrived for one or two generations in the earliest, slightly acidic burial period, as evidenced by the loss

Figure 4. A pair of silk and linen leggings. North Caucasus, 8th–10th century. After conservation in 2000. H. 81 cm. The Metropolitan Museum of Art, Harris Brisbane Dick Fund, 1996 (1996.78.2 a [right], b)

of the fur lining and countless numbers of cocoons found embedded in adjacent layers of the silks and linens. (The moth-eaten, shredded fur lining presumably remained in the burial site but must have been removed at the time of unearthing.) As the bodily substances changed into an alkaline state, the chemical reaction discolored the alkaline-sensitive safflower-dyed red color of the silk to beige and the indigotin blue to a gray-blue brown, whereas the breakdown of the acid-sensitive iron mordant in the brown was prevented. (A brown or black color commonly dyed with tannin and iron would have completely deteriorated through oxidation caused by acidification by air.) Subsequently, over the duration of a long-term burial, the presence of alkalinity fostered by the limestone reported at the site (instead of common acidic earth burial), the low humidity (the site was above ground), the severely limited fresh oxy-

gen supply (the burying space was contained), and the low temperature (oxidation was slowed down) allowed the two contrasting media—cellulosic linens and proteinaceous silks, wool, and fur—to survive side by side. In assessing the state of the textile culture in the region, therefore, one should not interpret the general lack of items woven with proteinaceous wool yarn in the lot to indicate its paucity in the region, as it was used instead of cotton as wadding, and a thoroughly developed fiber-spinning method was known. Cotton, the same cellulose-based fiber as the linen in the burial site, however, is absent, which may indicate that it was not yet used in the region.

It is no longer possible to estimate the precise condition of the caftan and leggings at the time of their unearthing, and no doubt the rest of the caftan and leggings had deteriorated in the burial site. But it can be conjectured that there was a quantity of unavoid-

Figure 5. Back of a portion of a linen caftan, showing the join of the proper left sleeve at the waist. North Caucasus, 8th–10th century. H. 112 cm. The Metropolitan Museum of Art, Gift of Jacqueline Simcox, 1999 (1999.153.37)

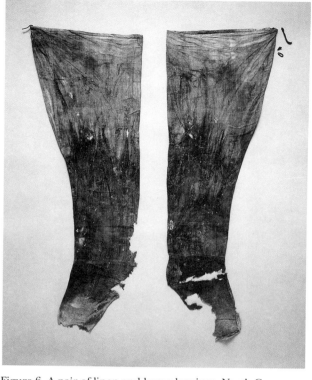

Figure 6. A pair of linen and hemp leggings. North Caucasus, 8th–10th century. H. 89 cm. The Metropolitan Museum of Art, Gift of Jacqueline Simcox, 1999 (1999.153.38)

able archaeological staining, soiling, and oxidative products that had accumulated and interacted with the linen, silk, and fur/skin in the burial site over a millennium. No sooner were the garments brought out of the burial site than much of the in situ information was lost, as usually occurs with all archaeological dyes, fibers, yarns, cloth, and other items. With certain exceptions, their postexcavation treatment appears to have included rinsing in water in the same way at the same time, and then all were stored within the same length of time. Among the garments in Reference Groups II and III, the Metropolitan's caftan (Figure 1), and Reference Silk Caftan (Figure 19), both Reference Group II, and an undecorated caftan (Figure 5) from Reference Group III share nearly identical indications of loss and preserved areas as well as similar burial stains, causing one to wonder if they had been layered on the same deceased body. From the evidence of the parts of the garments that survived and that were stained, the deceased appears to have been laid in a dorsal position with the legs and proper left side of the body positioned higher than the right side, and with the right arm and torso slanting down toward the head.

The first treatment after excavation appears to have been a quick rinsing in water shortly after removal

Figure 7. A woman's tunic of linen and nettlelike fibers. The neckline and cuffs are embellished with a rural-type patterned silk (similar to our Silk A) and with loops and buttons and an appliquéd square of two kinds of mainstream-type patterned silk. North Caucasus, 8th–10th century. H. 122 cm. The Metropolitan Museum of Art, Gift of Jacqueline Simcox, 1999 (1999.153.35 [appliqué], 36 [tunic])

Figure 8. A pair of leather mitts. North Caucasus, 8th–10th century. H. 17 cm. The Metropolitan Museum of Art, Gift of Jacqueline Simcox, 1999 (1999.153.1a, b)

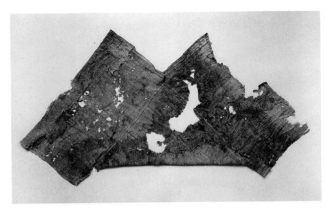

Figure 9. A pair of short linen and hemp trousers. North Caucasus, 8th–10th century. H. 58 cm. The Metropolitan Museum of Art, Gift of Jacqueline Simcox, 1999 (1999.153.40)

Figure 10. Portion of a pair of short trousers of nettlelike fiber. North Caucasus, 8th–10th century. H. 52 cm. The Metropolitan Museum of Art, Gift of Jacqueline Simcox, 1999 (1999.153.43)

Figure 11. A rural-type patterned silk similar to our Silk A, probably a tunic collar. North Caucasus, 8th–10th century. H. 80 cm. The Metropolitan Museum of Art, Gift of Jacqueline Simcox, 1999 (1999.153.34)

Figure 12. Portion of a linen caftan sleeve. North Caucasus, 8th–10th century. L. 57 cm. The Metropolitan Museum of Art, Gift of Jacqueline Simcox, 1999 (1999.153.41)

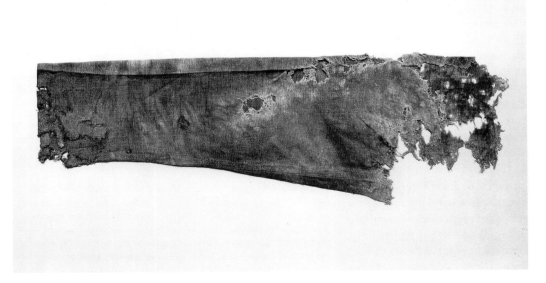

Figure 13. Pillow with ends (only one end extant) of a rural-type patterned silk (similar to our Silk A), stuffed for exhibition. North Caucasus, 8th–10th century. L. 54 cm. The Metropolitan Museum of Art, Gift of Jacqueline Simcox, 1999 (1999.153.39)

from the burial site. The treatment must have reduced the odor associated with burial and aging and made the set biologically cleaner while removing the visible surface soils and oxidative products. The immersion in water, however, even if it was for only one minute, not only caused a certain amount of loss but also irreversibly altered the quality of the material:[7] the weight became lighter; the sheen decreased; the texture roughened; the tactile character, or hand,[8] softened; the unraveling yarns along cut edges became matted during drying; and as for the fur, the water gelatinized the oxidized protein while contracting and stiffening the skin, thus causing it to crack under any straining. The treatment also dispersed, redeposited, and saturated the heavy gelatinized body decomposition products, soils, and stains, and thus they still remain.[9] The creases that occurred in the burial and the wrinkles created by washing appear to have been ironed out. Hundreds of empty lepidopteron cocoons are still scattered over the surface of both the interior and exterior of the linen and silk cloths as well as on the inside layers of the wool wadding. Despite the loss of portions in the burial, what remains at present of the linen and silk is in a remarkably good state of preservation for its age and material chemistry. In particular, the condition of the silk fibers is notably good—the good condition of the dark brown is unusual despite the nature of the mordant used.

The second treatment on our caftan and leggings occurred between the auction in 1994 and the Museum's acquisition. For presentation on the art market, the disassembled scattered parts of the caftan

Figure 14. Rectangular length of linen. North Caucasus, 8th–10th century. H. 36 cm. The Metropolitan Museum of Art, Gift of Jacqueline Simcox, 1999 (1999.153.42)

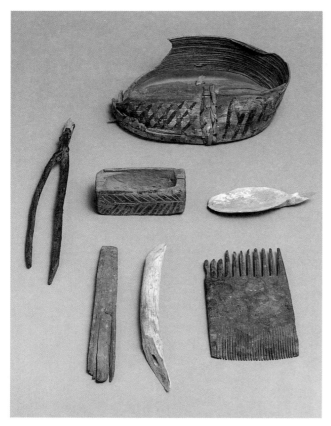

Figure 15. Top row: oval wooden container, side bound with twine, decorated with black, red, and white paint in a crisscross pattern (1999.153.2), L. 15.5 cm. Middle row: forked wooden twig (1999.153.13); small hollowed-out wooden container with channel for lid (1999.153.4); wooden spoon with broken handle (1999.153.18). Bottom row: hardwood knife sheath (?) (1999.153.16); curved wooden handle (1999.153.15); fruit-wood comb (1999.153.14). North Caucasus, 8th–10th century. The Metropolitan Museum of Art, Gift of Jacqueline Simcox, 1999

Figure 16. Clockwise from top: circular container of burl wood with pierced handle (1999.153.5), L. 13.7 cm.; decorated rectangular wooden container with channel for lid (1999.153.3); decorated wooden lid (1999.153.9); wooden disk (1999.153.10); fruitwood comb (1999.153.8); decorated rectangular wooden container with lid (1999.153.7a, b). North Caucasus, 8th–10th century. The Metropolitan Museum of Art, Gift of Jacqueline Simcox, 1999

were reconstructed by stitch-mounting them onto conservation backing cloths (see Figure 19 for the style in which the Metropolitan Museum's caftan was reconstructed when acquired). After the Museum's acquisition in 1996, the examination of the context of the caftan and leggings in comparison to a portion of an undecorated linen caftan (Figure 5) and a pair of undecorated linen and hemp leggings (Figure 6) in Reference Group III, strengthened by field experience and Reference Group I publications, led me to conclude that the preacquisition reconstruction of the caftan and the leggings was incompatible with their original styles. In 1999–2000 they underwent a third phase of conservation in the Department of Textile Conservation, which, despite our concern at exposing them to yet another round of treatment, included

disassembling the previous reconstruction, cleaning, straightening, and then reconstructing.

To assist the gallery visitors' perception of the garments in the context of an art museum's collection, the caftan and leggings were reconstructed based on our subjective but informed assumptions.[10] Even though we had the remarkable objects from Reference Groups II and III as models at our side, it was agonizing, as usual during a reconstruction, to have to choose a single way to proceed in preference to several other conceivable options while working with the minute details of the garment's cutting and tailoring.

On completion of our conservation work, the caftan and the leggings together with a pair of mitts (Figure 8) and a pillow (Figure 13) from Reference Group III were displayed in the Museum's newly reor-

Figure 17. Top row: brass earring (1999.153.33), 3.2 x 1.3 cm; brass pendant (1999.153.31); copper disk with spoked design and suspension loop at the top (1999.153.30). Second row: tinned brass mirror with crisscross design, loop (broken) in center (1999.153.22); copper bracelet (a child's?) (1999.153.21). Third row: brass spoon with flat disk bowl (1999.153.17); two brass hooks with holes for suspension (toilet articles?) (1999.153.20a, b); bow of brass fibula (1999.153.23); brass beaded strip (1999.153.25). Fourth row: iron pointed object (1999.153.24). Bottom row: gold earring (1999.153.32); gold circular disk with repoussé pattern (imitation coin?) (1999.153.12); brass comb-shaped object (1999.153.11); pierced mother-of-pearl disk (1999.153.26). North Caucasus, 8th–10th century. The Metropolitan Museum of Art, Gift of Jacqueline Simcox, 1999

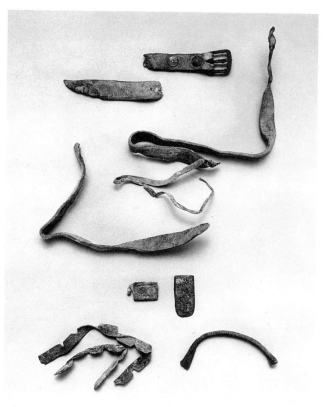

Figure 18. Top group: leather strap with iron and copper buckle in four pieces (1999.153.6a–d), portion with buckle L. 20.6 cm. Second row from bottom: tinned copper belt plaque decorated with a design of bunches of grapes (1999.153.29); tinned copper belt plaque with relief design (1999.153.19). Bottom row: notched leather strips (1999.153.28a, b); curved leather band (1999.153.27). North Caucasus, 8th–10th century. The Metropolitan Museum of Art, Gift of Jacqueline Simcox, 1999

ganized Ancient Near Eastern Art Galleries. The rest of the Reference Group III textile objects are stored in boxes made specifically for each item, for the most part with the encrustation and dried-up empty cocoons left as they were when the Museum acquired the objects, and are available for future study and conservation.

In the following discussion, overall features of the caftan and the pair of leggings will be described based on our reconstruction, and the many fragmentary extant original features associated with the caftan and leggings and from the three reference groups will be noted as necessary.

THE PRIMER OF THE CAFTAN AND THE PAIR OF LEGGINGS

Based on representations depicting the steppe peoples of the period (e.g., Knauer, Figure 20), the caftan probably reached the mid-calf of the wearer. It could have been worn as one of several layers, with a functional, undecorated linen caftan[11] underneath and a sheer, decorated caftan, such as the Reference Silk Caftan, over it perhaps during the day, with a third layer such as our heavy, fur-lined one worn in the cold. Over this caftan, an ornate, multipurpose belt, and headgear, a pair of leather mitts,[12] and boots would

Figure 19. Reference Silk Caftan of silk damask, Chinese Tang dynasty, trimmed with rural-type patterned silk (similar to our Silk A). North Caucasus, 8th–10th century. Unlined. Reconstruction by the owner in 1995. H. 132 cm. Rossi and Rossi Ltd., London (photo: courtesy Rossi and Rossi)

Figure 20 (below). Design of the Tang dynasty silk damask of the Reference Silk Caftan in Figure 19. H. roundel 14.5 cm. (drawing: Barbara Teague)

have been part of the wearer's accoutrements. For vigorous hunting and combat, an appropriate set of protective gear must have been worn over the caftan.

The caftan was worn double-breasted style, with the proper left front closing toward the right and the right front overlapping it. Modeled according to the reference undecorated linen caftan (Figure 5), the triangular sidepieces on the front push the side seams toward the back, causing the broad-shouldered back to narrow toward the waistline (Figures 1–3, 21) and making the sleeves emerge from the back like a pair of huge wings. This style provided considerable room to accommodate the height and breadth of the mounted wearer's upper body even in full motion. The narrow wrist openings of the sleeves helped to retain the wearer's body heat. For easier movement of the lower body, two long slits, bordered with decorative silks,

were left in the back below the hipline. When the wearer was in a standing position, the slits would slightly reveal the leggings, and with the wearer's knees bent in a seated position, as on a chair or in a saddle,[13] the entire elaborate leggings would be visible. At the top of the seamed part of each of the embellished slits, a rounded hump conspicuously sticks out on the narrow back waistline.[14] Three sets of button-and-loop fastenings hold the caftan closed. The garment was completely lined with fur (see Figures 1, 37), although, owing to the loss, it cannot be ascertained whether the sleeves were originally fur-lined as well.

The coordinating leggings were made of a polychrome patterned silk like those depicted in full view in pictorial representations (see Knauer, Figure 18). Each legging is composed of two standard units (Figures 4, 22; see The Construction: The Pair of Leggings, p. 98). The upper parts are a single layer of silk, soft and pliant without a lining or stiffener or any visible attachments. This characteristic suggests that the leggings were more decorative than protective and that they might have been worn over a pair of undecorated functional leggings (Figure 6).

The silks and linens used in the coat and leggings came from bolts of cloth woven as a length to be cut into required shapes and sizes (not an easy task at that time).[15] The type of pattern cutting practiced in the region was semistraight. Representing a long-established local craft convention, the semistraight pattern cutting was designed with precision to be suitable for the wearer's activities. In tailoring, the cut pieces were neatly seamed with the finest stitches using sturdy linen sewing threads and, no doubt, finely forged sharp iron needles. Overall, the high quality of the linen cloth, garment design, cutting, assembling, and sewing demonstrated remarkable professional coordination in comparison with contemporaneous examples from other cultures, attesting to this region's elevated standards in artistic and technical achievements regarding textile culture and perhaps even social decorum.

THE CONSTRUCTION: THE CAFTAN

The caftan was made of a densely woven plain-weave cloth of undyed white[16] fine linen (Figure 23) with a medium hand (Figure 24). The linen's plainness was decorated effectively with broad strips of two different polychrome patterned weft-faced samit silks (Figure 26)[17] along the edges, both exterior (Silk A, Figures 28–30) and interior (Silk B, Figures 31–33). It was lined with fur. Collar, cuffs, and other elements, if any, are unknown.

The caftan was composed of the twelve standard units (Figure 21) of linen cloth (of which six units in thirteen pieces are extant) plus the embellishing silks, the three buttons made of linen cloth, and two lengths of linen double cording (bias cut) used for the three button-fastening loops. Each of the twelve standard units could be made up of a number of pieces seamed depending on the original width of the bolt or the size of the remnants or old garments that were used. Each of the triangular sidepieces (4, 5) in our caftan is composed of two pieces instead of the standard one. The lower fronts (10, 11) and the back (12) are composed of three pieces each, with narrow strips placed along the sides, mostly hidden under the border silks. The upper sleeves (6, 7) are composed of two pieces, discussed below. All the units and decorative borders are actually composites of small to large similar pieces of cloth with traces that indicate that they had been used previously.[18] This must have been the result of either the talismanic use of old clothes associated with a respected person or the reuse of precious hand-worked materials, a common practice in many cultures throughout history then and now.

The overall measurements of the caftan come to a total height of 142 centimeters (reconstruction), with the upper half to the waistline measuring 65 centimeters (reconstruction), and the lower half 77 centimeters (extant). The entire shoulder line, from wrist to wrist, is 184 centimeters (reconstruction). With the two overlapping front panels (one-half extant) closed in a double-breasted manner, the waistline is 105 centimeters (extant), and the entire fanned-out hemline 164 centimeters (extant, with actual open waistline 151 centimeters and hemline 210 centimeters). (See The Construction: The Pair of Leggings, p. 98, for measurements of the leggings.) Based on these measurements, which are an approximation of the space afforded within the garment's fur-lined interior, it can be deduced that the coat and leggings were made for a male equestrian approximately 180 centimeters tall but assuredly slender and perhaps young. The degree of wear and soiling indicates that the set had been worn only slightly before becoming mortuary items.

All the units of linen including the lower sleeves were cut with the direction of the warp consistently aligned vertically when the coat is arranged with the arms stretched out straight. There is no shoulder seam along the line from wrist to shoulder to wrist. The units were assembled for the most part by neatly stitched flat-fell seams, which were folded and finished toward the center of the units.[19]

In tailoring the coat, the units were prepared, the upper and the lower halves were each assembled and for the most part embellished, then the two halves

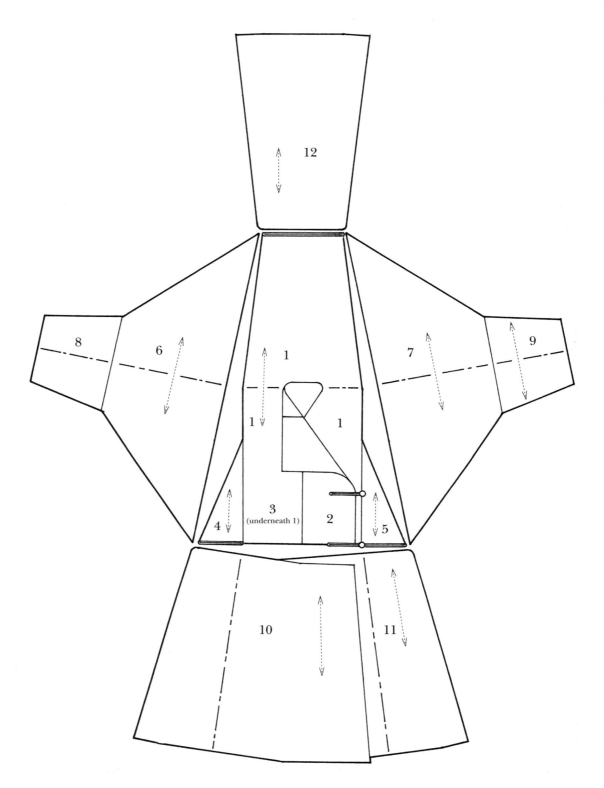

Figure 21. Diagram of the twelve standard units of a caftan like the MMA caftan (Figure 1), an undecorated linen caftan (Figure 5), and the Reference Silk Caftan (Figure 19): 1) contiguous unit of upper right front, upper left front, and back; 2) right and 3) left fronts' extended overlaps seamed to center cuts of 1); 4) right and 5) left triangular sidepieces attached to the body's front underarm areas; 6) right and 7) left upper sleeve pieces, shoulder to elbow, front and back continuous; 8) right and 9) left lower sleeve pieces, elbow to wrist, front and back continuous; 10) right and 11) left lower halves of front; and 12) lower half of back (drawing: the author and Daniel Kershaw)

were seamed together along the waistline. For the upper part of the body (1), the cloth was cut in one continuous panel for the front and back, and folded in half at the wider shoulder line. A slit was made in the center of the front half, and a neck opening (reconstruction, 15 x 6 cm) was cut out. To each side of the slit in the front, an overlap panel (2, 3; reconstruction) was sewn, creating the double-breasted front. The triangular sidepieces (4, 5; reconstruction) were seamed to the outer edges of the front; the edges of the sidepieces and the outside edges of the back would be seamed to the upper sleeves later. Adding the sidepieces pushes the side seams of the caftan toward the back, making the back narrower than the front.

To prepare the upper sleeves (6, 7; reconstruction), two rectangular panels were cut diagonally at one end. The cut-off triangular pieces were each seamed to the other straight-cut end of the panels, forming trapezoidal pieces whose bias-cut edges became the lower edges of the upper sleeve units. Then the five units making up the upper half of the caftan were seamed to each other in the direction of the warp, the sleeve units (8, 6 and 7, 9) flanking the central unit (1–5). The assembled flat upper body section was then folded in half in the direction of the weft, creating a shoulder line from wrist to wrist. The lower edges of the joined upper and lower sleeves were sewn together. Unable to verify the lost original but following the model of reference caftans, tunic, and sleeve,[20] we reconstructed the Metropolitan's caftan with a simple hem at the wrists, without embellishing borders.

The refinement and embellishment of the assembled upper body section followed. To create a lapel on the extended overlap of the outer right front (the left front was lost), a border of Silk A was first attached to the exterior extending to midway in the panel (26 cm, extant). The obverse of the border was overlaid onto the obverse of the linen and sewn. After the border was folded back to expose its obverse, the opposite edge and the top were turned under and sewn to the linen, completing the exterior border. To finish the interior, first a strip of wool wadding and then a border of Silk A (63 cm, of which 50 cm extant) were placed on the linen and stitched. Examining the remaining proper right front panel with a decorated lapel and a small part of proper left front panel, it was clear that the caftan had an asymmetrical lapel closure (see Knauer, Figure 17). The presence or absence of embellishment for the neckline is unknown, however, for those sections, as well the neckline portions of the comparable undecorated (Figure 5) and Reference Silk (Figure 19) caftans, were totally lost. We therefore stabilized the original decorated lapel on

the proper right front, and we left the neckline plain.

Each of the three lower panels (10–12, all extant) is a composite of three pieces. After seaming the nine pieces into three panels, the panels were assembled for the lower half of the caftan. The two front panels, wider than the back panel, extend 7 centimeters around each side of the body toward the back (33 cm at the waistline, plus the humps). To facilitate movement of the lower body, the two front panels were seamed to the back panel (almost all extant) only down to the hipline (27 cm, extant), leaving the rest of the lower portion (49 cm, extant) as slit openings for the ease of the wearer seated on horseback. The outer edges of the three panels were embellished by stitching borders of Silk A on the exterior and Silk B on the interior. In attaching the borders (8.5 cm wide), the two-directional designs, whether Silk A or Silk B (see Figures 28–33), were meticulously oriented vertically long or horizontally wide in their proper upright position—never sideways, even when tiny pieces were used. (Under magnification, it can be seen that the direction of the weaving, not otherwise recognizable, was not respected in these borders.) The assembled and silk-trimmed upper and lower body sections were then joined at the waistline.

The final refinement was the attachment of button-and-loop fasteners. To hold the double-breasted front closed, three sets of button-and-loop fasteners were strategically placed: 1) on the waistline at the proper right interior; 2) on the waistline at the proper left exterior; and 3) at breast height on the proper left exterior. The buttons, 7 millimeters in diameter and 4 millimeters thick, were made of linen cloth covering an undetermined hard core. For the loops, cording (19 cm extant) was made of bias-cut linen, stitched, and turned inside out (3 mm diam.), with loops at both ends. It was sewn doubled onto its position around the back outside waistline of the caftan. The loop at the proper right (3 cm, extant) was pushed through a gap in the waistline seam to the inside of the caftan and securely stitched to meet the button (1; reconstruction) attached to the right side of the left front panel. The other loop (reconstruction) placed at the proper left side meets the button (2; reconstruction) attached to a short doubled cording (reconstruction) placed on the left side of the right front. Another button (3; extant) at the end of a short doubled cording (extant) attached at breast height to the right front was positioned to meet the loop (reconstruction) attached to the edge of the proper left front.

A prepared fur lining[21] (lost, not simulated in reconstruction) was stitched along the inside edge of the silk borders through the layer of linen.

A knot of heavy black thread, pierced through the layers of silks and wadding at each of the lower corners of the front panels, remains. The reason for the knots cannot be conjectured.

For our reconstruction, an unbleached muslin (cotton)[22] was selected because it is a texture close to the original linen. It was dyed with a mixture of four dyes from the Solophenyl series by Ciba-Geigy with Glauber's salts under normal pressure. A practical test for color fastness, which involved exposing the dyed muslin to simulated gallery light for a time calculated to be the equivalent of eight hours per day for three years at fifty lux, showed no visible fading.

THE CONSTRUCTION: THE PAIR OF LEGGINGS

The major parts of the leggings were constructed of decorative Silk C for the leg section and of durable linen cloth for the foot section (Figure 4). Each legging was composed of two standard units (Figure 22). The leg section, reaching from the ankle to above the knee, is a single layer of Silk C (extant), soft and pliant without a lining or stiffener.[23] On these leggings, a separate piece was added to the ankle area, also of Silk C, perhaps because the silk length was not sufficient. Linen reinforcing strips (cut in the direction of the warp) were stitched around the interior of the leggings' tops. The foot section (partial reconstruction)—covering the foot from below the ankle to the toes—was constructed of tiny random-size bits of linen cloth ingeniously seamed with curves and darts to form three-dimensional interiors.[24] In the middle of the front edges of the tops of the leggings, small

leather disks with holes (extant) were sewn through all layers of linen strips and silks. The leggings, probably worn over undecorated ones, must have been held up by means of strings (missing)[25] threaded through the leather disks and probably anchored to a belt worn inside the coat.

The dimensions of the leggings are 81 centimeters in height (extant), 59 centimeters around the knee (extant), 32 centimeters around the ankle (extant), and 24 centimeters from heel to toe (extant).

It cannot be ascertained from the silk leggings whether there were distinctions between the right and the left foot, since seams for the toe only partially remain. However, the Metropolitan's undecorated linen and hemp leggings (Figure 6) clearly do not distinguish between right and left feet. Only the creases caused by tying and dark staining from the burial suggest whether the leggings were worn on the right or left foot.

UNDECORATED LINEN CLOTH

Structure (applicable to all the composite pieces)
Predominantly warp-faced plain weave. Structurally reversible

Materials
Warp: Undyed, bleached linen, Z (spun). Count: 27–29 per centimeter
Weft: Undyed, bleached linen, Z (spun). Count: 19 per centimeter

A close examination of the weaves reveals that the somewhat irregular thick-and-thin diameter off-white

Figure 22. Diagram of the two standard units of a pair of leggings like the ones in Figure 4: 1) leg section; 2) foot section (drawing: the author and Daniel Kershaw)

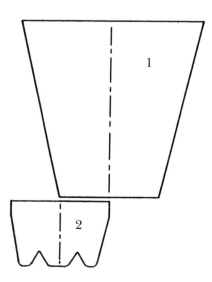 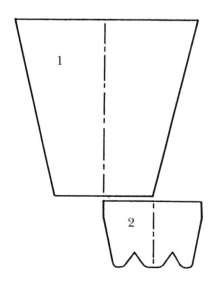

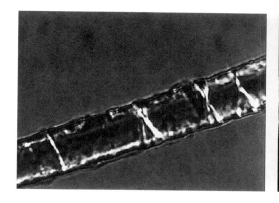

Figure 23. Flax fiber of the caftan in Figure 1, longitudinal (left) and cross-sectional views, 1000x (microscopy: Florica Zaharia)

Figure 24. Surface of the linen cloth of the caftan in Figure 1, 17x (microphotograph: the author)

linen yarn is sporadically mixed with slightly darker fibers[26] running in both warp and weft directions, creating a subtle surface effect distinctive to the region (Figure 24). Unlike most linen fabrics from other cultures, there is no streaking or striped discoloration in the warp or weft or weft irregularity, attesting to the high level of quality control in the area. The hand of the cloth can be described as soft, bending, clinging, and draping but with a fairly dense, integral strength. This visual impact and hand of our linen, which was woven as a bolt of cloth, distinguish it from woven-to-shape items produced in the environs of Egypt, Syria, and Iraq in the Late Antique period.

THE POLYCHROME PATTERNED SILKS

Three polychrome patterned silks, Silks A, B, and C, of related types, embellished and adorned the caftan and leggings: Silk A was used as a border on the lapels and the exterior of the lower panels of the caftan; Silk B was used as a border in the interior of the lower panels of the caftan; and Silk C was used as the leg section of the leggings.

Patterned Silk A (same pattern from more than one bolt)

Design
Pattern of pearled-border roundels and interstitial fillers, both filled with a double-axlike design. Pattern repeats straight horizontally and vertically without distinct top and bottom (Figures 28–30).

Structure common to Silks A, B, and C
Weft-faced samit: weft-faced 1\2 twill weave compounded with inner warps and complementary wefts. Four colors compose the design, of which two- or three-color complementary wefts interlace per passage depending on the colors called for in the design. The weft order (g is the ground weft, and a and b are the pattern wefts) is as follows: two-color weft passages, a,g/g,a/...; three-color weft passages, a,b,g/a,b,g/ ... The pattern step is one binding warp. It is not reversible.

Materials
Binding warp: Undyed silk (spun), **Z**. Count: 21 per centimeter
Inner warp: Undyed silk (spun), **Z** x 2. Count: 21 per centimeter
Weft: Dyed and undyed silk (reeled). Colors: dark brown, undyed? or red?, yellow? Count: 24–51 per centimeter

99

Figure 25. Silk filament of the border of the caftan in Figure 1, longitudinal (left) and cross-sectional views, 1000x (microscopy: Florica Zaharia)

Figure 26. Weft-faced samit of Silk A, the border of the caftan in Figure 1, showing weft-faced 1\2 twill with thickness compounded by inner warps, and three-color (10th, 11th weft passages from the bottom) and two-color (the rest) weft orders; 17x (microphotograph: the author)

The pattern organization is based on the circle-and-cross repeat of Sasanian origin and is oriented in two directions along the warp, without a distinct top and bottom of the design. Across a row, roundels abut horizontally without interstices whereas between roundel rows, space accommodates interstitial patterns. Both the interstitial patterns and the roundel fillers are stylized double-axlike motifs. The border of each roundel contains fourteen pearls. An odd feature is that at the center of the loomed width, an off-white 4-millimeter stripe was woven abutting the two center roundels as if dividing the woven width of the cloth in half.[27]

One complete pattern unit, composed of two minimum units, is symmetrically repeated horizontally, with the complete units aligned vertically in columns (not offset). The interstitial patterns extend 3 millimeters into the space between the roundels' tops and bottoms. Although the roundels were supposed to be woven to a consistent size, approximately 4 by 4 centimeters, they vary greatly from row to row and

somewhat from column to column. The average dimensions of the roundels woven is 4 centimeters high by 3.5 centimeters wide (Figure 28). The minimum repeat units are 4.5 by 1.8 centimeters, and the complete, maximum units are 4.5 by 3.5 centimeters. The width of the roundels overlaps 2 millimeters with the interstices.

At present, the pattern appears as an off-white color on a dark brown ground. Examination of the structure, however, reveals that the pattern was executed in polychrome. Within one pattern unit, at the center of the axlike motif in both the roundels and the interstices, aside from the dark brown ground there are four weft passages of two-color pattern wefts, while all the rest is in one color. A light yellow is faintly identifiable in one of the pieced borders.[28] Because analogous colors of yarns cannot be easily differentiated by their physical characteristics alone, in the absence of visible colors and with the reverse of the selvage inaccessible, it is not possible to ascertain whether a third or fourth color might have been present.

Selvages, about 1 centimeter wide, were continuously woven with a pattern weft on the obverse over the last regular warp in the same weft-faced 1\2 twill samit weave. The stripe in the center, the graduating widths of the roundels becoming symmetrically narrower toward the selvages, and the extant two selvages indicate that the full-loom width of the fabric was 64 centimeters, accommodating sixteen complete roundels. Since the roundels at both the right and left selvages are complete, the starting point of the pattern heddle arrangement on the loom could have been either side.[29]

Patterned Silk B (same pattern from more than one bolt)

Design
Repeated pattern of pearled-border roundels with interstitial fillers, both filled with a rosette. Pattern repeats straight horizontally and vertically without distinct top and bottom (Figures 31–33).

Structure—see Silk A

Materials
Binding warp: Undyed silk (spun), Z. Count: 21 per centimeter
Inner warp: Undyed silk (spun), Z x 2. Count: 21 per centimeter
Weft: Dyed and undyed silk (reeled), no twist. Colors: dark brown, undyed?, blue, yellow?, red? Count: 18–27 per centimeter

The pattern organization is based on the circle-and-cross repeat and is oriented in two directions along the warp, without a distinct top and bottom of the design. Across a row, roundels abut horizontally without interstices, whereas between the roundel rows, the space accommodates interstitial patterns. Both interstitial patterns and fillers of the roundels are rosettes. Depending on cut pieces, each roundel border contains sixteen, seventeen, or eighteen pearls, indicating that the pieces of Silk B were cut from at least three different bolts. (Full-width reconstruction of Silk B from two pieces indicates that each bolt was obviously woven with a consistent number of pearls.)

One unit of the pattern is symmetrically repeated along the horizontal axis aligned vertically in columns (not offset). The minimum repeat unit is 8.5 centimeters high by 2.5 centimeters wide, and the maximum unit 8.5 by 5 centimeters. One complete pattern unit is composed of two minimum units in a horizontal symmetrical repeat. The vertical repeat is a straightforward repeat of the maximum unit, with the rosettes in the interstices extending 1.2 centimeters into the space between the adjacent roundels' top and bottom. Greatly varying from row to row and column to column in size, the average dimensions of the roundels are 7 centimeters high by 5 centimeters wide, and the interstice filler measures 4 by 4 centimeters (Figure 32).

At present, the pattern appears to be solely an off-white color on a dark brown ground. Originally polychrome, within one repeat unit, apart from the dark

Figure 27. Obverse (left) and reverse of weft-faced samit Silk B of the interior border of the coat in Figure 1. The reverse shows three-color areas (in three bands at each rosette's center of the large petals) and two-color areas (the rest—dark and light reversal of the obverse) (photo: the author)

Figure 28. Silk A, showing one repeat unit (photo: the author)

Figure 29. Silk A, showing vertical repeat units. The heights of the roundels change from shorter to taller every three-roundel repeat

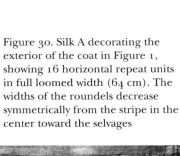

Figure 30. Silk A decorating the exterior of the coat in Figure 1, showing 16 horizontal repeat units in full loomed width (64 cm). The widths of the roundels decrease symmetrically from the stripe in the center toward the selvages

brown for the ground, one- and two-color pattern weft passages are evident, as called for by the design. One of the off-white colors shows a brownish yellow tint, and another a bluish gray, originally a blue. Other than that, for the most part, the original colors of the yarns are indistinguishable by their physical characteristics. The pearls in the border were likely red, the center of the rosettes blue, and the tips of the petals accented by yellow against a dark brown ground. Whether the one-color pattern wefts were off-white or red cannot be determined. In the pattern unit, there are ten bands of two-color pattern areas: five bands in the roundels, each with four or eight passages of weft; and five bands in the interstitial pattern, each with six or ten passages (Figures 27, 32) that alternate with one-color pattern areas.

Selvages, about 1 centimeter wide, were continuously woven with a pattern weft on the obverse over the last regular warp in the same weft-faced 1\2 twill samit weave. The graduating width of the roundel suggests the loomed width was about 64 centimeters (the maximum width with one selvage extant is 53 cm), accommodating ten roundels with the first and the last roundels complete at the selvages.

Patterned Silk C

As a rare example, Silk C has two different consecutively woven patterns, C1 and C2: the first pattern, C2 (Figure 36), of isolated large rosettes, was woven as a short beginning length (only present in legging 1996.78.2a; see Figure 4). Along the same length of warp, the second pattern, C1 (Figure 34), constitutes the rest of the entire cloth composing the pair of leggings.

Design
Patterned Silk C1: repeated pattern of pearled-border roundels and interstitial fillers, each filled with a confronted pair of highly stylized birds or boar's heads between stemmed dish or compotelike devices, the smaller one above and the larger one below. The pattern repeats straight horizontally and vertically with distinct top and bottom (Figures 34, 35).
Patterned Silk C2: repeated pattern of isolated large rosettes. Pattern repeat is organized offset, in vertical alignment without distinct top and bottom (Figure 36).

Figure 31. Silk B, showing vertical repeat units. The heights of the roundels change from shorter to taller every three-roundel repeat

Figure 32. Silk B, showing one repeat unit (photo: the author)

Figure 33. Silk B decorating the interior of the caftan in Figure 1, showing six horizontal repeat units with a selvage at right. The widths of the roundels decrease toward the selvage (reconstructed full loomed width is 64 cm, fitting ten roundels)

Structure—see Silk A

Materials

Binding warp of C1 and C2: Undyed silk (spun), Z. Count: 18–24 per centimeter

Inner warp of C1 and C2: Undyed silk (spun), Z. Count: 18–24 per centimeter

Weft of C1: Dyed and undyed silk (reeled). Colors: dark brown, no twist; undyed?, no twist; red?, no twist; yellow, no twist; blue (spun), Z. Count 18–30 per centimeter

Weft of C2: Dyed and undyed silk (reeled), no twist. Colors: dark brown, undyed? Count: 18–30 per centimeter

In Silk C1, the pattern organization is based on the circle-and-cross repeat and is oriented in a single direction with a distinct top and bottom of the design. The pattern is composed of horizontal rows of major pearled-border roundels connected by inset minor roundels without interstices, and of vertical columns (not offset) of major roundels connected by abutting minor roundels separated by interstices with fillers. The major roundels and interstices are filled with highly stylized, confronted pairs of birds or heads of

boars[30] placed between two compotelike devices,[31] the smaller one above and the larger one below (Figure 34). Each minor roundel is filled with a single pearl. Pearls fill the borders of all roundels, eighteen in each major roundel, twelve in each inset minor roundel, and eleven in each interstitial minor roundel.

The pattern is oriented along the warp with a distinct top and bottom, unlike Silks A and B. Following the convention of draw-loom weaving applicable for this type of textile,[32] the weaving direction can be postulated as conforming to the direction of the pattern, beginning at the bottom of the design and weaving toward the top (see weft order, below). Silk C, with its conspicuous design orientation, was used in the leggings for the most part with the design upside down, suggesting that the people who used the silk were not reading the design clearly.

At present, the pattern appears to be an off-white color on a dark brown ground. Examination of the structure, however, reveals that although the colors are no longer present, the pattern had originally been polychrome. Within one repeat unit, besides the dark

Figure 34. Silk C1, showing one repeat unit (photo: the author)

Figure 35. Silk C1 of the legging at right in Figure 4. Used upside down in the legging. The widths of the roundels decrease toward the selvage at right. The heights of the roundels change from shorter to taller per every three-roundel repeat (reconstructed full loomed width is 64 cm, fitting nine roundels)

brown for the ground, one- and two-color pattern weft passages appear as called for by the design. In one area, one of the off-white colors shows a discolored yellow and another a light greenish brown reduced from the original blue. Beyond these two, other colors, if any were used, are indistinguishable because the physical characteristics of the yarns are visually similar. While the off-white may have been the original color of the pearls, the other colors cannot be determined. It is likely that yellow and/or red were used in combination in the two-color pattern areas (besides the dark brown ground color). Within the height of the minimum pattern repeat unit, and alternating with single-color areas, there are eight two-color pattern areas: five in the roundels, each with two, four, or six passages of weft; and three in the interstices, each with two or four passages.

Although actual woven dimensions of the pattern vary greatly from row to row and somewhat from column to column, the major roundels were intended to be 7.5 centimeters high by 7.5 centimeters wide; the minor roundels 1.5 by 1.5 centimeters; and the design

in the interstices 2.3 by 4.5 centimeters. In the horizontal organization of the pattern, one complete unit is composed of two symmetrical minimum units; the vertical organization consists of one complete unit in straight repeat, with the interstitial pattern overlapping each roundel's top and bottom by 3 millimeters (Figure 34). The minimum unit is 9 centimeters high by 3.8 centimeters wide, and the maximum unit is 9 by 7 centimeters.

Selvages, about 1 centimeter wide, were continuously woven with a pattern weft on the obverse over the last regular warp in the same weft-faced 1\2 twill samit weave. The maximum width extant is 43 centimeters with one selvage present. The graduating

Figure 36. The two different continuously woven patterns of Silk C on the rim of the right legging in Figure 4, showing half of a pattern unit of C2 at the beginning of weaving followed by C1. Used upside down in the legging. (photo: the author)

width of the roundels suggests the full loomed width was about 64 centimeters, which would accommodate nine complete major roundels.

In Silk C2, the weaving begins with an undecorated dark brown section (3 mm extant). After that, a pattern oriented in two directions, without a distinct top and bottom, was woven with only one-half of a complete repeat unit (3.5 cm), perhaps as an experimental run on the new warp or section. Not enough fabric was woven for us to estimate the size of a complete repeat unit, but it appears that the pattern was intended as a two-directional, straight repeat, with one complete unit composed of two symmetrical minimum units arranged horizontally and offset in columns vertically. This type of pattern repeat with a singular design in offset columns is unusual in the eighth to tenth century, but it becomes increasingly common in later periods. Even though the patterns in C1 and C2 were set up with the same repeat-unit organization on the same warps,[33] the pattern in C2, being too large to fit into either the roundels or interstices of C1, can be considered an independent design. The shift in pattern from Silks C2 to C1 is evidence that the loom in use in this weaving locality was devised for interchangeable sets of patterning cords.[34]

The pattern against the dark brown ground is in two colors, off-white with tiny dots in four of the petals that are the same dark brown color as the ground. As with Silk C1, the rosette is 7 centimeters high by 7.5 centimeters wide and the space between the rosettes is 5 by 2 centimeters. The minimum repeat unit is 6 centimeters high, and the design overlaps 1 centimeter

with the next row. The minimum unit is 3.8 centimeters wide, and the design overlaps 5 millimeters with the design in the next column.

THE WOOL WADDING

When the caftan was worn, the interior silk borders were meant to be visible. The fur lining, therefore, extends only to the inside edge of the silk borders. To replicate the thickness of fur, a wadding of loose, hairy wool fibers (not felted) was placed between the linen and the exterior and interior silk borders at the lapels and around all the panels of the lower section. The use of hairy wool fibers as wadding suggests that wool was less precious than cotton. Perhaps cotton was not raised as an agricultural product, and it may have been imported to the area only as yarn and cloth, not as fibers.

THE FUR LINING

The fur lining is now totally lost and indicated only by several tiny remnants left sewn at the edge of the interior border (Figure 37). The fur consists of yellow, long curly hair (ca. 2.5 cm) still on the skin or hide, which is now stiff, dark brown, and cracking. The fur lining was probably removed at the time of unearthing owing to its state of decomposition. It had likely been far too infested and shredded by keratin-starved insects, a common fate for this type of animal sub-

Figure 37. Remnant of the fur lining in the coat in Figure 1; see the inside edge of the opened lapel in that photograph (photo: Emilia Cortes)

stance in a burial site. The type of animal and method of tanning have not been investigated.

EARLY LINENS AND THEIR INHERENT QUALITIES IN HISTORICAL PERSPECTIVE

The entire caftan and the foot section of the leggings, as well as the majority of the other items in the reference groups, were constructed of cloth woven with flax fiber yarn,[35] indicating that linen was historically the most common textile fiber in the region. The softer and pliable fine fibers for the caftan were taken from the source plant in the middle of its growth cycle, while the stiff and sturdy fibers for the items that required strength to withstand abrasive use, such as the foot sections of the leggings, were from an over-matured stage of growth. Although linen constitutes the major component among the bast fiber-made items in Reference Group III, a smaller quantity of hemp and nettlelike fibers was also found making up all or part of those items that were expected to withstand vigorous, abrasive use.[36]

The degree of uniformity and fineness of all bast fiber yarn in the garments under discussion here shows that fiber preparation and spinning in the region were expertly practiced. As is common in professional weaving, the warp yarns were slightly finer and more consistent than the weft. Effects observable in the yarns include the Z-twist spinning direction,[37] degree of twist, amount of fiber fed into the yarn while twisting, constancy of diameter, full rotation through the innermost fibers, and others. These features indicate that the spinning practice in the region during the eighth to tenth century likely consisted of using a spinning shaft with fibers fed to its end in a clockwise motion.[38]

Variations among cloths woven in different regions can be largely attributed to different source plants (or animals) and processing methods. Contributing factors include the stage of growth of the plant at the time of harvest and the method of fiber extraction (influenced by the quality of the local water and the variability of the weather). The linen and other bast fiber yarns associated with the caftan, leggings, and other garments from the Moshchevaja Balka group were spun, not spliced or knotted. This allows speculation that the linen cloths were local or Middle Eastern products[39] and not imported either from Central Asia (where in this period, a bolt of cloth would have been woven with ramie and hemp yarns[40] that were spliced, probably up to the time of Muslim influence) or from Egypt.[41]

The regional convention for weaving a long length or bolt of undecorated utilitarian linen cloth was to produce a predominantly but not highly warp-faced,[42] not weft-faced, weave.[43] All the cloths used to make garments, whether cut from new bolts or from already used garments or remnants, were flawless products. This indicates that the tension of the warp was kept constant throughout its length except for the negligible shortening caused by the take-up of the weave, which enabled the weft to be inserted uniformly. When the weaving was completed, any variation in the compactness of the weft was gradual and, if uneven, scattered in random areas. The total absence of sudden increases and decreases in the density of the wefts, in contrast to the patterned silks discussed below, allows us to conjecture that the type of loom used to weave this linen maintained an open warp, fully extended for its entire length, and rules out the loom types that required rolling and unrolling of stored lengths of warps during weaving. A bolt of plain-weave linen in this region in this period was most likely woven on a staked-out loom, the type traditionally set up outdoors in the Middle East.[44] The two warp sheds were created by a counter-shed arrangement, and the weft was beaten with a sword,[45] not a reed. Indeed, examination of the fabric in microscale (Figure 24) supports this hypothesis: alternate warps are considerably straighter or tighter than the intervening ones,[46] and the fabric's density is irregular from warp to warp and area to area across the width, since thick and thin yarn contours are made to accommodate or adjust to each other. The overall uniform compactness of all the cloths also indicates that the warps and wefts had been wetted during weaving,[47] a process that was more conveniently done if the loom was set up in houses with mud floors or outdoors.

Selvages were present in some of the pieces that were simply woven with the one-shuttle weft returning over the last regular warp. Since none of the cloth in our caftan is a selvage-to-selvage width, the original loomed width cannot be determined. The widest width extant in the Metropolitan's caftan is 48 centimeters with one selvage present.[48]

Linen can be dyed only with a limited variety of natural dyes since most natural dyes are not chemically compatible with cellulosic bast fiber. In this region, we can postulate that linen was dyed in brown from a combination of tannin coming from a variety of trees and from water that contained iron and blue from a plant containing indigotin. Faint yellow from a variety of plants and perhaps a light pink from safflower, madder, and/or henna might have been used, but since each of these dyes has a short duration, we do not expect to see these colors today.[49] In the Museum's caftan, leggings, and all other linen items in Reference Group III, no dyed colors, if there were any originally, remain visible today.

No finishing treatment on the linen cloths composing the caftan, such as flattening or glazing, is detectable, if it had ever been applied to the cloth after weaving was completed.[50]

EARLY SILKS AND THEIR INHERENT QUALITIES IN HISTORICAL PERSPECTIVE

The world's different textile cultures developed various looms in response to regional requirements for transforming specific types of yarn into cloth.[51] In broad terms, two types of looms evolved: warp- and weft-oriented. The regions in which long, smooth silk or spliced bast fiber (linen, ramie) were the major textile materials—primarily China and Egypt—developed the warp-oriented weaving technology, in which warps were set close together. Looms could be used either indoors or outdoors, depending on the environment. Nomadic and pastoral weavers who used spun wool and bast fiber yarn also developed a warp-oriented weaving technology that required the warps to be highly twisted. Their looms were used outdoors, fitting their lifestyle. The sedentary people in the regions where short, resilient wool and cotton as well as spun bast fibers were the major textile materials, most of the regions west of China, developed a weft-oriented weaving technology, in which warps were set with spaces between them. Their looms were made for working indoors.

Over time, motivated by the desire to wear decorated textiles, weavers succeeded in weaving patterned fabrics, regardless of the primary orientation of warp or weft. At the outset, monochromatic warp- and/or weft-float patterns were created, and colored yarns were used as stripes (vertically, in warps) and bands (horizontally, in wefts) or added as supplementary sets of patterning warp and/or weft.

The development of fiber-dyeing technology, an application of practical organic and inorganic chemistry, paralleled the development of weaving and enabled weavers to create polychrome patterns on the loom. Because of the chemistry between the two types of available fibers (proteinaceous silk and wool, and cellulosic cotton and bast fibers) and the restrictive coloring matter or dye sources at hand (which need to bond chemically with the two types of fibers), dyeing technology supported the production and defined the regional character of the textiles produced. In the regions where proteinaceous fibers were available, particularly silk in China and wool in other temperate-to-cold regions, weavers were able to work with a variety of colors because dyes bond with proteinaceous fibers more readily than with cellulosic fibers such as linen and cotton. It is understandable that by the eighth to tenth century in the Moshchevaja Balka region only the colorful imported silk textiles were available to ornament the locally produced bleached white linen garments.

As weaving technology matured worldwide, weavers in both warp- and weft-oriented cultures developed loom mechanisms that created patterns in an interlacing principle that would today be called warp-faced (Figure 38) and weft-faced (Figure 40) taquete (binding in a plain-weave sequence) and warp-faced (Figure 39) and weft-faced (Figure 41) samit (binding in a twill-weave sequence) structures.[52] The selective manipulation of the sets of polychrome patterning warps or wefts to create the pattern in warp- or weft-faced plain or twill weave was initially done manually with simple tools in narrow widths. Eventually, as loom engineering developed,

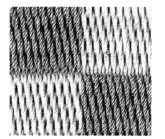

Figure 38. Warp-faced taquete, two-color warps alternated, obverse (left) and reverse (weaving: the author and Sandra Sardjono)

Figure 39. Warp-faced samit (2\1 twill), in two-color warps alternated, obverse (left) and reverse (weaving: the author and Sandra Sardjono)

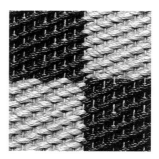

Figure 40. Weft-faced taquete, in two-color wefts alternated, obverse (left) and reverse (weaving: the author and Sandra Sardjono)

Figure 41. Weft-faced samit (1\2 twill), in two-color wefts alternated, obverse (left) and reverse (weaving: the author and Sandra Sardjono)

greater widths of fabric could be woven mechanically, which had the advantages of reducing the breakage of warps, increasing productivity, and allowing a variety of design units to be repeated—motivated first by the desire to weave a better-quality product and later to make the task less labor-intensive.

In warp-faced taquete or samit structure (Figures 38, 39), three sets of elements are used: 1) one set of complementary warps composed of two or more colors to create the pattern and form the structure; and two sets of wefts, 2a) one set that functions as structural binding (in a plain- or twill-weave binding sequence); and 2b) a second set of wefts, referred to as inner wefts, that functions as a color separator for the complementary warps. The inner weft allows the selected warp color making the pattern to be visible on the obverse of the cloth, while the other elements remain on the reverse, thereby creating an obvious distinction between obverse and reverse of the cloth. Depending on the colors called for in the design in vertical relationship, at least two, generally three, and up to six complementary warps or colors in varying combinations from area to area have been used in warp-faced taquet or samit textiles. Unlike a weft-faced structure, colors in warps, once set on the loom, cannot be changed.

In weft-faced taquete or samit structure (Figures 40, 41)—such as the fabrics associated with the Moshchevaja Balka group finds—three sets of elements are used: two sets of warps, 1a) one set that functions as structural binding (in plain- or twill-weave binding sequence), and 1b) the second set of warps, referred to as inner warps, that functions as a color separator for 2); and 2) one set of complementary wefts composed of two or more colors to create the pattern and form the structure. The inner weft allows the selected weft color making the pattern to be visible on the obverse of the cloth, while the other colors remain on the reverse, making an obvious difference between obverse and reverse. Depending on the colors called for in the design in horizontal relationship, at least two, generally three, and up to six complementary wefts or colors in varying combinations from row to row or area to area have been used in weft-faced taquete or samit textiles. Of the complementary sets, at least two wefts must traverse selvage to selvage. Otherwise, any number of complementary wefts in different color combinations, continuous or, unlike warp-faced taquete and samit, discontinuous,[53] were used per passage of weft from one horizontal repeat of design to the next. Each additional complementary weft increases the fabric's thickness, and in some weft-faced samit textiles, in order to accommodate them as substitutions, the unused wefts floated on the back, unbound in the structure (not discontinuously brocading). Silks A, B, and C from the Moshchevaja Balka group were woven during a four-hundred-year period, from the seventh to the eleventh century, in which weft-faced taquete and samit developed, improved, matured, and eventually were replaced by another type of pattern-weave principle, lampas.[54]

As with the process of yarn twisting, looms are made to work efficiently by exploiting human physical capacities and the earth's gravity. To insert a weft that creates a pattern on a common bolt-weaving pattern-weaving loom, a shed is opened by mechanically raising[55] the selected warps from the stationary straight web plane. Only the warps raised from the web plane are thus strained, crucially distinguishing the two faces of freshly woven cloth: the face on the underside, which remained unmoved, comes out as a flatter surface and is considered the obverse side of the finished cloth; the upper side, because it was disturbed by the raising of warps for structure and pattern as randomly and frequently as needed, is bumpy and is considered the reverse side of the finished cloth. The weaver must deal frequently with many loose pieces of yarn—ends of broken warps, joins of overlapping ends of weft yarns, and unused carryover brocading wefts—and leaves them on the easier-to-work-on upper side. In addition, the upper side can easily be soiled by the many small tools and shuttles placed there until they are next needed (they cannot hang between and down below the warps because they would drop to the floor).[56]

In warp-oriented weaving, to weave, for example, warp-faced 2-1 twill samit in four colors (using a complementary set of warps) with the reverse (weft-faced) shown at the upper side on the loom, each shed for one twill binding weft of three threaded in three shafts in the twill-weave system unit is facilitated by raising one shaft. To create the pattern, while the single selected color warp stays on the web plane as the obverse (underside), the remaining two warps are raised and the inner weft is inserted—only once—to keep them separated as the reverse. Since the weave is warp-faced, the insertion of the weft can be tighter, thus easier and more evenly spaced, and allows faster weaving than weft insertion in the weft-faced weaves.

In weft-oriented weaving, to weave, for example, weft-faced 1\2 twill samit—the structure of Silks A, B, and C—using a complementary set of weft with the reverse

(warp-faced) shown at the upper side on the loom, in the twill unit each shed for one twill-weave binding warp of three threaded in three shafts is made by raising two shafts. To create the pattern, selected inner warps are also raised: the single selected color weft for the pattern is laid on the web plane to appear on the obverse (underside), separated from the other two yarns laid above the inner warp. Thus, for example, to weave a pattern that requires three colors per passage, shuttles each with a different color must be thrown three times to complete one weft passage.

Another crucial and time-consuming skill required in loom weaving is the laying of the weft in the opened shed. For a warp-faced weave, the tighter the weft tension, the easier, and therefore the faster, it is to lay the wefts in the shed evenly as required. For a weft-faced weave, the looser the weft tension, the more difficult it is to lay the wefts in the shed as required. In creating weft-faced weaves, as in the weft-faced samit of Silks A, B, and C, while maintaining the warp tension taut, the tension of the weft inserted must be loose and even to allow the weft to meander compactly around the warp. The weft tension can differ from weaver to weaver and from insertion to insertion by the same weaver. A bobbin winder's skill in smoothly unwinding the weft yarn from a shuttle also contributes to the evenness and looseness of the inserted weft. In addition, if the wefts are inserted taut, selvages will be pulled inward, narrowing the width of the cloth—a common problem faced by weavers—as exemplified by Silks A, B, and C. Hence, weft-faced samit is the type of weave that is the most time-consuming to produce, and even when done by a skilled weaver, the faults that require post-weaving correction are disproportionately greater than when producing a warp-faced weave.

During the international trade and thus communication among nations of the fifth through the eleventh century, weaving technology was one of the major exchanges. By the seventh century, using available materials of each region to participate in this lucrative exchange, weavers competed to produce patterned silks solely in the unprecedented weft-faced samit structure. As the world reached the stage of early medieval "fancy silk" consumerism in approximately the tenth and eleventh centuries, the demand increased. As a result, time-consuming production of weft-faced samit-weave silks was replaced by more elaborate and colorful patterned lampas-weave silks that were easier to weave. While lampas-weave structures allowed more efficient production compared to the superb weft-faced taquete and samit weaves, the quality was inferior. Consumers, however, were unaware of the differences.

Figure 42. Silk, weft-faced samit (1-2 twill), from the Church of Saint-Leu-Saint-Gilles, Paris. Woven in a Byzantine dominion, ca. A.D. 600–800. Musée de la Mode et du Textile, Paris, 16364 (photo: Laurent-Sully Jaulmes)

By the eighth- to tenth-century period in which the Metropolitan's caftan was made, contacts between East and West through trade on the Silk Routes had already existed for over a millennium.[57] While the routes shifted from place to place and from time to time because of political and territorial conflicts, bandits, and geological changes, the extant archaeological objects are evidence that trade, even if interrupted, never ceased completely. From the earliest times, among the most sought-after trade goods were particularly colorful patterned cloths. Those woven of silk were cherished by wool cultures,[58] those made of cotton were desired by bast fiber, wool, and silk cultures,[59] and vice versa.[60] Increased encounters with exotic and refined foreign goods not only aroused awe and curiosity at each destination but also encouraged rural weavers to imitate new products through trial and error. That, in turn, created competition among the weaving centers. In due course, various technologies developed for the efficient production of salable products, the result of which was a decline in quality.

Initially, craftsmen must have used local materials, but to achieve better or new products, they chose the best of the portable trade goods—fibers, yarns, dyed yarns, dyes, auxiliary agents, seeds, tools, and other essentials—produced in different parts of the world. At the same time, they were dependent on their local water, environment, and climate. Increased production due to commerce led to the migration of textile professionals. The skills of craftsmen[61] had expanded and become specialized to such an extent that traders and suppliers of basic materials responded to the specific demands of their clients, sometimes unaware of the end purpose of their goods. The desire for elaborate textiles, on both the supply side as an achievement and the demand side as a luxury—from the courts of Byzantium to Sasanian Iran, and from the Tang dynasty in China to the Nara court in Japan—accelerated regardless of cost, with the result that between the eighth and the twelfth century, textile culture reached an unparalleled height. The patterned silks found in the Moshchevaja Balka group were woven in the first half of this epoch of textile achievement. Later, as demand decreased or ceased—whether because of a patron's whim or tribal conflict, or as supply was reduced or interrupted by natural disasters[62]—the quality of textile production declined and shifted to such an extent that the once high material-technological level was never achieved again.

To weave a patterned cloth in a weft-faced structure on a loom, a mechanical device to control the pattern and increase production was developed. A design to be woven is normally drawn in a small unit. To transpose it efficiently to a large surface, weavers in both the East and the West, perhaps concurrently (present evidence favors a date about the fourth to fifth century), laid out the design following a basic repeat system, while devising a mechanism to convert it into a woven structure. In the East, with its predisposition for warp-faced taquete and samit silk weaving,[63] the pattern was laid out vertically, a technique that remained common until the eighth century.[64] In the Western, Roman world, with weft-faced taquete/samit weaving, the horizontally organized pattern was repeated vertically up to the sixth century.[65] Silks woven with this type of pattern repeat with roundels and interstices are, coinciding with the overall development in many facets of technology, far more elaborate, detailed, and colorful than their warp-faced counterparts. They became common from the seventh century and evolved with the technical development associated with the structure of weft-faced samit and the pattern-loom mechanism.

Coincidentally, at the outset, both East and West employed a similarly organized one-directional pattern repeat system, attesting to similar solutions when working with manually operated looms. In the seventh century, along with the gradual disintegration of the Chinese sericulture monopoly, the repeat system changed to one that is symmetrically organized, using the Sasanian pearled-border roundel design,[66] indicative of the power and expansion of both the Sasanian and Byzantine Empires. As history moved forward, so did design and the loom mechanism.

Contact through trade between East and West is apparent in extant contemporaneous textiles fortuitously preserved in burial sites in Egypt and in a documented repository of the imperial house of Japan. In China, this epoch coincided with the transitional period in which loom technology shifted from warp- to weft-oriented weaving with the advent of pattern weaving. Such a shift was a fundamental technological breakthrough, but in China it was an adaptation

Figure 43. Silk, weft-faced samit (1/2 twill), probably from a site in the Taklimakan desert, Xinjiang. Woven in a Sasanian dominion in Central Asia, ca. A.D. 700–800. Private collection (photo: Bruce Schwarz)

rather than an invention. Warp-faced samit for bolt weaving had already been used in the warp-oriented weaving culture in China in ancient times, from the Warring States period to the Sui and Tang dynasties. The warp-faced structure that was conventionalized over a millennium under China's silk monopoly was cumbersome and restrictive. In contrast, the weft-faced taquete/samit weave system,[67] which was based on the weft-oriented looms that had developed in the culture of the regions from Persia/Iran westward using short-fiber wool, was less cumbersome, more versatile, and material-saving.[68]

In the West, wool cultures had already developed the taquete/samit system for both warp-faced (for narrow-band weaving)[69] and weft-faced (for wide-width weaving)[70] cloth. Recently reported archaeological evidence has added documentation for the concurrent or even earlier occurrence of weft-faced wool taquete (estimated as a wide-width bolt weaving) from a wool-based textile culture in the Roman world.[71] To produce traditional samit in highly sought-after silk,[72] the wool, linen, and wild silk[73] weavers of the West had only to learn how to handle the traded silk yarn—most likely with its colors already dyed. They did not have to change the orientation of weaving, the loom mechanisms, or the weave structure, nor did they need to learn the labor-intensive and costly cultivation of mulberry trees, silkworms, yarn-making processes, and dyeing chemistry.

In the East, in the Sasanian domain, a weft-faced samit in red wool and white cotton (initially two, later three colors per passage of weft) of superb quality with the pattern of Sasanian pearled-border roundels had been woven.[74] A rare example in silk with a similar design but in one-quarter scale is extant.[75] Sometime in the seventh century, at a weaving workshop within the Sasanian Empire, local and Chinese weavers seem to have collaborated on a different version of the samit in polychrome and with silk for Sasanian patrons. Extrapolating from the Chinese polychrome warp-faced samit technology (more than three colors per passage of weft), the weavers interpreted the Sasanian design from a Chinese perspective.[76]

The convention of the repeat pattern of a combination of roundels and interstices (Figures 42, 43; Knauer, Figure 5) began at this time.[77] Soon, all textile cultures were producing the elaborate polychrome samit silks, copying the Sasanian roundels with pearled borders in a circle-and-cross repeat. In this patterning system in the mainstream, the large major roundels, sometimes with connecting roundels, are filled with senmurv, elephants, winged horses, or horsemen. These designs, favored by Sasanian and Byzantine patrons, were placed in the roundels oriented in an upright direction. In each roundel a single design faces in the same direction, alternating direction row by row or column by column. If two motifs appear within a single roundel, they confront or oppose each other symmetrically. Fillers in the interstices are, for the most part, oriented in four directions but in exceptional cases in only one direction. With diameters commonly measuring about 20 centimeters or as much as 50 centimeters,[78] these mainstream silks' perfectly circular roundels required a weaver of remarkable skill and aesthetic sensibility, and provided viewers a magnificent object to look at.

To produce warp- and weft-faced taquete and samit, technologies integrally related to the structure, the pattern repeat, and the mechanical organization of the loom were developed at silk-weaving centers in the East and West at various times. In brief, the development of warp- and weft-faced taquete and samit structures can be postulated to have evolved progressively through stages of an experimental period.

- In China, as a long-fiber culture (silk and spliced ramie/hemp), weaving of a vertically oriented warp design for a warp-faced taquete and samit was done on a back-tensioned loom with closely set warps without a reed. The weft was beaten with a wooden sword, thereby creating a textile that becomes warp-faced. A bolt width of cloth was produced.[79] In the seventh-century adaptation of the Sasanian circle-and-cross design, the orientation allowed half-inverted patterning to appear.

- In the regions west of China or in the spun short-fiber cultures (wool and cotton), weaving of a horizontally oriented weft design for weft-faced taquete and samit weaves (developed in a region under the Sasanian Empire or some earlier patronage) was done on an upright or high loom. The looms were equipped with or without a spacer/reed, and the weft was inserted into moderately spaced warps loosely in tension and compactly in space (the time-consuming characteristic of weft-oriented weaving) by beating with a pointed stick or reed. A bolt width of cloth was produced.

- In the regions farther west in spun-fiber cultures (spun linen and wool), weaving of a horizontally oriented weft design for a weft-faced taquete weave (a structure that originated in the region) was done on an upright loom with moderately spaced warps and wefts inserted loosely and compactly by beating with a pointed stick. A short, garment-shaped cloth was produced.

Contacts between the East and West eventually caused evolutionary modifications to traditional Chinese silk weaving technology.

- Weaving of a design for a weft-faced samit weave was done on a back-tensioned loom. The weft was compacted with a sword beater while a bolt-width weft-faced samit was being woven. (This was not a successful method for creating weft-faced weaves, as the setup, in principle, tends to create warp-faced weaves.)

- Weaving on the back-tensioned loom continued, but the sword beater was changed to a reed as the warp-separator/weft-beater. This involved the creation of specialized professions, including bamboo splitter and reed maker. With less effort, weft-faced weaves can be created with this method.

- An innovative cloth beam tensioner—a rope wrapped around the cloth beam and tied to the loom structure—was invented. This enabled the weaver to adjust the tension of the warps at any point during weaving with or without a back beam (for example, bundled warps can be tied to a post). Its introduction terminated the use of back-strap tensioning and made weft-faced weaves possible, if the weft was laid loosely enough to meander around the taut warps, and allowed weavers to perfect the technique of weaving weft-faced taquete and samit.

- To achieve the clearest design on the obverse, weaving workshops further developed a mechanical system of double back beams on the loom. This system enabled the two independently functioning warps to be taken up each according to its own requirements as weaving proceeded, one for the binding warps (which loosely meander between multiple wefts) and the other for the inner warps (which lie tautly between the two groups of separated wefts, the single weft for the obverse and the rest of the multiple wefts for the reverse).

- Beginning about the tenth century, the time-consuming weft-faced taquete and samit weaving were gradually replaced, first by double-faced weft-faced samit[80] (pseudo–weft-faced) for a short while in the East, and by lampas. Weft-faced taquete and samit were continued only in isolated regions[81] that are far removed from the original places of manufacture of weft-faced taquete and samit weaving.

Over time, along with the dissemination of lampas weave,[82] weft-faced samit from the early medieval period that is structurally associated with the circle-and-cross repeat pattern stopped being produced owing to cultural shifts that were occurring at an even faster pace than the transition of lampas loom technology. Against this background, the Moshchevaja Balka group of weft-faced samit silks represents the product of a rural technology of the eighth to tenth century, imitating the mainstream circle-and-cross repeat pattern.

THE MOSHCHEVAJA BALKA GROUP OF PATTERNED SILKS

The homogeneity of Silks A, B, and C and all others of the same type in the three reference groups allows us to identify the group as a specific rural type. They share the same traits in fibers, yarns, dyes/colors, method of fabrication, structure, pattern repeat organization, and finishing. Whether the similarity stems from demand (for example, the cloth could have been restricted to designated wearers as in military ranks) or limited supply (possibly through the lack of designers or pattern cord plotters), each piece was evidently woven in the same rural weaving center. Nonetheless, details vary from piece to piece. Silk A, for example, is represented in all three reference groups in many dissimilar versions, and Silk B, which appears in the strips used as the border in the interior of the Metropolitan's coat, can be identified in at least three versions in the reference groups. Further details, such as the common state of soiling, fading, physical condition, and material fatigue, support the conclusion that the silks come from a group with the same provenance. All the patterned silks are more pliable than mainstream weft-faced samit[83] even from later periods, being soft to the touch and able to drape in all directions despite the

fact that the weave was compounded with two sets of warps and frequently three complementary wefts (Figures 25, 26). These silks are not only more numerous than the mainstream high-quality weft-faced samit[84] among the Moshchevaja Balka group finds but are also unique to this site. Since not even a single piece of this type from the same period has so far been associated with any other sites where similar mainstream-type silks were also found, we can conjecture that they were manufactured in a region west of the Caspian Sea, not far from Moshchevaja Balka.[85]

The production of polychrome patterned silks, whether by a large- or small-scale mainstream or rural workshop, requires the well-coordinated and time-consuming labor of craftsmen responsible for material, tools, and equipment. Silks A, B, and C, individually and collectively, evince the standards of craftsmen using a minimally equipped loom to weave a samit structure and whose goal seems to have been only to finish the task, with little concern for the quality of the finished product.

In early times, each warp or weft yarn was individually and collectively handled after being made into yarn until it was transformed into cloth. Adding twist,[86] therefore, to individual reeled yarn for ease of dyeing, warping, threading, beaming, and weaving was an essential part of the process, even though it is arduous and time-consuming. In the silks under consideration, the wefts are dyed reeled silk yarns[87] without additional twist,[88] whereas the warps are tightly twisted undyed spun yarns (Figure 26). For weavers in rural workshops, inexperienced in handling reeled-out silks that catch on anything they come into contact with, such as other yarns, hands, and surroundings, spun silk yarns and twisted reeled silk yarns were easier to handle. Weavers outside the mainstream used the less-costly, easier-to-handle spun silks. The choice of yarn was also dictated by cultural or religious beliefs. For instance, followers of Buddhism and Islam produced only spun yarns from moth-hatched cocoons, so that they did not have to kill the pupae, which occurs when reeling out the filaments. Whether motivated by religious beliefs or for other reasons, the makers of these silks' spun yarns came from outside the mainstream of silk producers. At this time, it is not possible to identify where the two types of yarns were processed and where the entire cycle of raising the silkworms, harvesting the cocoons, reeling out or preparing floss, spinning from the floss, and adding the additional twist took place.

All the reeled silk weft yarns without twist are the same off-white and brown colors. As these silks are obviously expensive and luxury goods, such unpretentious colors cannot be taken as original. From the well-preserved colors of the Sasanian woolen textiles excavated in Iran and Egypt,[89] we are able to conjecture that colors conventionally used by the Sasanians, besides undyed cotton for white, were intense red, blue, yellow, brown, and, in a later period, green.[90] No colors were in pastel tones. The sources of dyes for these colors are as follows: red, the root of madder[91] with alum mordant or an insect with alum mordant; blue, an indigo-containing plant; yellow, a plant source with or without alum mordant; and brown-black, a tannin-containing wood with iron mordant. Since silk and wool are both proteinaceous, the dyes used for these materials can generally be the same. For silk, an additional dye used was a red color from safflower, popular for its intensity. Since ancient times, in many parts of the Old World, the safflower plant was cultivated for its seeds that produced oil and its flower petals that were used in infusions to cure ailments and from which a pigment/dye was extracted as a cosmetic to color lips as well as a dye to color cotton, linen, and, most commonly, silk (though not wool). Since the annual plant grows everywhere and is thus inexpensive, the colorant was used ubiquitously and abundantly. To dye silks red in the most coveted intensity, dried safflower petals were traded to dyers living in specific regions where water was relatively uncontaminated. The bright red is, however, acutely unstable and extremely reactive to light and acidity/oxidation and alkalinity that come from common household sources—air, water, food, or discharges. The colorant degrades, appearing faded faster than any other colorant through inevitable exposure to destructive elements during use and over time, even in storage, frequently disguising the once strong visual impact of the red color.[92] The burial conditions of the Moshchevaja Balka group site, with a decaying body and limestone enclosure, accelerated the garments' color loss from brilliant red to light beige to off-white with a yellowish orange hue.

That the dyes used in the yarns of Silks A, B, and C were from inferior sources is proved by the even fading of the cloth in its entirety, regardless of whether the areas were with or without burial stains or in good or bad condition. Good craftsmen generally choose those dye colors that will last as long as their products. It is, therefore, possible that the weft yarns in these silks reached the weavers already dyed brilliant red. The weavers chose them for their weaving unaware of the source of the dye or its rapid fading quality. For example, if the equally pervasive but more fast madder red (since its hue is a brownish subdued tone and more costly, the weavers must have opted for the more brilliant but cheaper safflower red)[93] had been used, Silks A, B, and C would still be red today, even after having been buried. Alternatively, if the weavers knew

that safflower's brilliant red had a short life, they may have intended to weave the silks for sale.

The color that was originally blue, being indigotin, became gray through chemical reduction in the burial site. The yarn that had the traces of blue was the only weft composed of spun yarn (in Silk B); as the dye was common and used for cellulosic fibers, the regional specialty, the yarn could have been dyed locally to save money in preference to the purchase of already dyed yarn. The loss of colors made from safflower and indigo as well as the unusually good state of the dark brown dye and its substrate silk yarn (which normally we would expect to have deteriorated by accelerated oxidation of iron mordant) indicate that the burial environment acted as an alkaline buffer.

At a glance, the pattern repeat in these silks looks the same as those of refined, mainstream weft-faced samit silks following the circle-and-cross repeat pattern. There are, however, differences. Far smaller in scale (4–7 cm high), these are simplified versions. In terms of pattern layout in a repeat unit, the roundels abut horizontally repeating row by row, and vertically with interstices between the roundel rows. The interstices are filled with a design. In Silks A and B, the design is oriented in two directions without distinct top and bottom, whereas in Silk C1 the design is oriented in one direction with distinct top and bottom and with additional small connecting roundels located at each juncture, horizontally inset and vertically abutted. The major designs contained in the roundels, unlike their mainstream counterparts, are identically repeated in the interstices in almost the same scale. Further, the design was taken from the minor connecting roundels sometimes associated with a type of larger-scale mainstream silk (e.g., Figure 42). For the adapted pattern, we see evidence of simplification, a clever accommodation by rural weavers working on a loom equipped with a basic pattern-control mechanism and operated by the simplest technology. This pattern organization was based on a timesaving preparation common to Silks A, B, and C.

The numbers of weft passages in each pattern repeat unit are: Silk A, 138; Silk B, 174; and Silk C1, 230. The reduced size of the pattern, the repeat type, and the restrictive use of one- (Silk C2) and two-color design wefts (in several rows of Silks A, B, and C1) besides the ground color made production less time-consuming and labor-intensive. The count of warps per centimeter is irregular, averaging 21, with the center of the width of cloth having fewer than the areas toward the selvages. The count of wefts varies from 18 to 30 per centimeter, with Silk A, the finest in count, having up to 54 wefts per centimeter.

To repeat the pattern unit that runs upward as the

weaving progresses, a set of pattern-controlling heddles was used in rotation. In Silk C and portions of Silks A and B (coming from different bolts), the pattern repeats vertically in one straight unit, in a one-directional rotation. In some of Silks A and B (but not in all of them), four dark and light wefts alternate in the center of the roundels. In Silk B, the relationship of the pearled-border roundels and the palmette design contained within the roundels is inconsistent roundel to roundel.

In Silk A, because of the change in density of the warps, the sixteen roundels gradually decrease in width, the ones in the center being 4.5 centimeters wide and the ones closest to the selvages, the smallest, 3.2 centimeters wide. An even slightly tight weft can cause an excessive narrowing of the loom width, especially with this weft-faced samit when the weaver hastily throws a shuttle without taking the time to lay the weft loosely at each insertion into a shed.

All the Metropolitan's silks are in weft-faced samit weave structure with the binding system of 1\2 twill weave. Binding warps were threaded in three shafts in sequence, and inner warps were threaded in the pattern-controlling device. From various features inherent in these silks, we can deduce that the looms, beginning from the weaver's end, must have been equipped with a front cloth beam, a tenter stretching over the freshly woven cloth, a reed, three shafts, and a set of pattern-controlling devices, and that without a back warp beam, the binding and inner warps were held in two separate bundles. The pattern-controlling device for inner warps was probably the type in which a series of draw cords selectively raises the warps in sequence, separating above at least two- and sometimes three-color complementary wefts (that were not patterning) for the reverse, and leaving one for the obverse, which faces downward on the loom. Seated at the loom, the first weaver treadled the shafts to create the structure, raising the first set of warps in a twill binding sequence that did not bind pattern wefts on the obverse. After the second weaver manipulated the draw cords of the patterning device to lower the warps not patterning for a color, the first weaver threw a shuttle. This procedure was arduously repeated for each of the multiple colors that composed one of three passages of weft within a unit of 1-2 twill weave structure. The team moved on to the next two twill binding sequences using the same procedure. For example, in a three-color per weft, 1-2 weft-faced samit, to complete the weaving of one three-weft unit of twill structure (1–2 mm of cloth is woven), the shed opening for twill structure was required three times. At each opening an additional three were needed, for a total of nine pattern shed openings that alternated

with nine shuttle throwings (as opposed to a monochrome standard weft-faced 1-2 twill weave, which required only three sequences). To smoothly roll out the weft from the shuttle, a professional bobbin winder wound the bobbins, and an assistant did chores around the loom.

All the roundels in a circle-and-cross pattern should have been woven in perfect circles throughout a bolt. Instead, in Silks A, B, and C, the height of the roundels gradually row by row became elongated from circles to ovals. This is not intentional to achieve a particular design but rather results from the change in compactness of the weft caused by the weaver's lack of sensitivity toward his goal.

In the rural regions of the Middle East and as far east as Central Asia, the length of warps prepared for weaving a length of bolt was conventionally chained and/or bundled, not wound on a roller.[94] This method not only saved manpower during the setting up of warps on the loom but also avoided their becoming tangled since they were handled only once after warp preparation was completed on a warping board. (In later centuries, engineering improvements produced an efficient, uniform rolling system on a warp beam, eliminating tangling and obvious traces of tension or beam unit renewal in the resultant cloth.)[95] After the rest of the warping procedures were done—arduous threading into heddles and reed, and setting onto the front beam to create the weaving plane under the tension necessary for weaving—the chained warp was placed at the back of the loom and weighted down to keep it dangling or stretched out.[96] As the weaving progressed, in order to advance weaving approximately 5 centimeters further, the warps had to be forwarded. The bundled warps would first be released from the tension, and then only the required length of the warps would be unchained. The remainder of the warps would be repositioned at the back, while the subtle tension of the beam would be simultaneously adjusted and the weaving could then be resumed.[97] In order to weave on a loom equipped with this type of warp storage, the weaver would have been required to spend a considerable amount of time whenever the warp was forwarded. The weavers of our silks were obviously in haste and so unrolled the bundled warps less frequently than necessary.

What is more, our silks indicate that the force used to beat in the weft at each insertion in weaving was less than adequate. On the loom, the reed/beater frame hangs (or, later, stands) in the area where weft beating takes place. A straight and narrow rigid beater swinging from a fixed point can function properly only when the just inserted weft is beaten within a 10- to at most 15-centimeter space against the already woven section near the front or cloth beam. Although the position of the beater can be adjusted on an advanced loom, on the loom on which our silks were woven it was apparently not moved toward the back as the weaving progressed. As our silks indicate extra-long beam units, the weaver must have beaten in the wefts for the entire 30- to 50-centimeter length of beam unit while the beater was hanging pivoted in one position. (One "beam unit" constitutes the weaving space possible between the last weft in the woven portion that is rolled up onto the cloth beam and the front of the reed/beater when it is pushed against the foremost shaft.) At the beginning of weaving, with the warps under proper tension and the beater in a proper relationship to the area being woven, the wefts were correctly compacted by the beater in a standard position creating the first row of roundels in circles, as intended in the design. As weaving progresses, each insertion incorporates a certain length of warp into the weave, thereby shortening the length of the remaining warps on the beam unit and increasing their tension. In weft-faced weaves, the looser the warp tension, the less compact the weave becomes; conversely, the tighter the warp tension, the more compact the weave becomes.[98] In our silks, as the weaving continued without renewing the warps and the wefts were beaten in by the beater beyond its functional capacity and so not able to compact the wefts, the spaces between the wefts began to increase, resulting in an elongated height of a row of roundels. Only after weft insertion reached the far end of the maximum length of the beam unit—in Silk C an astonishing 51 centimeters—where there was no more space for the inserting weft, was the warp tension released and the woven area rolled onto the cloth beam. As a result, in our silks, the roundels are circular at the outset of the beam unit but gradually—not abruptly—become elongated and finally become ovals. The next row of roundels is suddenly circular again, indicating the boundary line at which as yet unwoven warps were unrolled and the woven portion was rolled onto the cloth beam. The indicated direction of weaving conforms to the conventional order of weft insertion (see note 32). Even in the better-executed Silk A, the length of the beam unit that contains three or four rows of graduated roundels is 20 to 25 centimeters. In the worst executed Silk C, the length of the beam unit containing four rows of graduated roundels is an astonishing 40 to 50 centimeters: the tallest row of 9.7 centimeters with a loose weft count of only 15 per centimeter gradually changes to the shortest row of 7.5 centimeters with a weft count appropriately compacted to 27 per centimeter.

Although these technical matters required con-

certed planning for the type of yarns and densities of the warp and weft, ultimately the all-important adjustment of tension at the time of weaving is solely dependent on the attentiveness of the weaver. Had the weaver of Silks A, B, and C kept the proper warp tension throughout by adjusting it each time three to five centimeters of the bolt's length was woven, releasing a length of warp from the bundled warp (or moving the positions of the weights, an advanced mechanism), and inserting each weft loosely (which requires considerable skill and takes time), the roundels would have come out the perfect circles the designer intended.

The weaving of Silks A, B, and C was done hastily, perhaps for export and, because of its unrefined character, presumably was not made for someone in the community. No weaver would let such inferior products be sold locally, in particular, such a laboriously fashioned polychrome patterned cloth of expensive silk. The irregularities in weaving, which could have been better regulated, suggest that the weaver was pressured to finish the bolts, perhaps for a waiting merchant or a unknown client.

After being woven, the cloth was mechanically flattened to add glossiness. Silk cloths were laid on a hard surface, moistened with water with or without additives such as sizing or an alkaline agent, and beaten with a wooden beater. The sheen[99] that was present at the time of burial is slightly noticeable even now, though the postexcavation washing reduced it to a degree.

Throughout history, the development of a textile culture has been a fruitful outcome of concerted responses to the disposition of natural materials in the environment by craftsmen, each pursuing various specialties in search of the ultimate achievement through ingenuity and tenacity. By their efforts, the foundation for today's aesthetics, arithmetic, chemistry, and engineering was formed. Whether motivated by simple awe, genuine joy, critical needs, or impossible demands, the same search continues today by individuals in the field of preservation. Art historians and conservators cooperate in interpreting the material and technological context of items from the remote northwestern Caucasus Mountains, just as those who directly and indirectly made the coat and leggings pursued it a millennium ago. By studying their material nature, ethnographic features, and the particular environment that contributed to their survival today, our integrated technical and scientific perception and knowledge have been broadened. The Museum's collection will assist us to elucidate, if only fractionally, the knowledge of a distant culture of the past and to formulate a preservation strategy for future generations.

ACKNOWLEDGMENTS

I am most grateful to have participated in this great project and to have had assistance from professional friends. Prudence O. Harper's and Joan Aruz's continual encouragement brought the project to its best realization. The generosity of Anna Maria Rossi, Jacqueline Simcox, and Elfriede R. Knauer enabled me to come up with crucial information by physically comparing other examples right in our conservation laboratory. Midori Sato's technical skill and endurance in performing conservation work, gallery installation, and assisting the Museum photographer were pivotal to the project. Discussion, analysis, and structural reproduction with Sandra Sardjono on loom technology refined my perspective. Florica Zaharia's fiber microscopy enhanced my conclusions. Emilia Cortes, Melanie Hatz, Paul Lachenauer, Arlene Olivar, Shawn Osborne, Elena Phipps, Gemma Rossi, Cynthia Vartan, and Cynthia Wilder participated in the project with their expertise. Funds from an anonymous donor covered the cost of my three study travels abroad and of materials for this article. I am also especially grateful for support from The Henry and Henrietta Quade Foundation and Annette E. Trefzer.

NOTES

1. Moshchevaja Balka is in the southern part of the Russian Soviet Federated Socialist Republic. The first recorded academic fieldwork was conducted in 1900–1901. Alternating with postexcavation research and publication, intermittent fieldwork continued most actively in the 1960s–1970s and is still ongoing by Russian museums. For publications, see note 2.

2. See Anna A. Ierusalimskaja, *Die Gräber der Moščevaja Balka: Frühmittelalterliche Funde an der nordkaukasischen Seidenstrasse* (Munich, 1996); Anna A. Ierusalimskaja and Birgitt Borkopp, *Von China nach Byzanz,* exh. cat. (Munich, 1996); Valery Golikov et al., "Experimental Research of Polychrome Sogdian Silk of the VIIIth–IXth Centuries from the Tcherkessk Museum Collection," in *Interdisciplinary Approach about Studies and Conservation of Medieval Textiles,* preprints for the Interim Meeting, ICOM Conservation Committee, Palermo, October 22–24, 1998, ed. Rosalia Varoli-Piazza (Rome, 1998), pp. 133–39.

3. The first of three lots of the Moshchevaja Balka group of objects was sold at the Kunst-Auktionshaus Dr. Fritz Nagel, Stuttgart, May 7, 1994, lot 18; it consisted of the Metropolitan's leggings and the fragments that were reconstructed as the Metropolitan's caftan and the Reference Silk Caftan. The second lot, seven textile fragments, was sold at Kunst-Auktionshaus Dr. Fritz Nagel, May 6, 1995, lot 1; the present whereabouts are unknown. For the third group, see note 5.

4. The Reference Silk Caftan warrants further research. It is conceivable that this lightweight silk caftan embellished with polychrome silk borders similar to those on the Metropolitan's caftan was one of the garments in a set that was worn interchangeably with the MMA caftan. The silk composing the entire caftan is a late Tang dynasty 2-1 twill damask (in two opposing twill alignments: warp-faced for ground and weft-faced for pattern, which reverse at a point) dyed in golden yellow. It is one of the securely identifiable Chinese silks among the other silks in the Moshchevaja Balka finds, which came from an area reaching as far west as the northern Caucasus in the 8th–10th centuries. See note 58.

5. The third lot of material from the Moschevaja Balka group, 46 objects, was auctioned at Kunst-Auktionshaus Dr. Fritz Nagel, November 15, 1996, lot 262. Of these, three textile fragments are purported to have been in a Paris collection, but their whereabouts are uncertain in 2001, and 43 crafted objects of wood, metal, shell, leather, and textiles were given to the Metropolitan Museum by Jacqueline Simcox (Figures 5–18).

6. A silk illustrated in Ierusalimskaja, *Gräber,* pl. 11, fig. 25 (Reference Group I), Reference Silk Caftan (Figures 19, 20; Reference Group II), and MMA 1999.153.43, worn-out pants (Figure 10; Reference Group III), all show unusually large holes of embroidery stitches made with a blunt needle or heavy threads, indicating that the three groups previously shared a common use before they were reused and made into these items.

7. Post-unearthing contamination (primarily from touching, washing, and X-raying) prevents an accurate measurement by the radiocarbon-dating method without applying still inconclusive adjustments.

8. *Hand* is professional jargon to describe subjectively a tactile physical quality of fabrics, e.g., stiff, sturdy, soft, pliable, etc.

9. A sufficient amount of body decomposition remains to allow for future DNA analysis that could confirm association between the burial lots and the past and present people of the region.

10. I propose that excavated objects should be preserved intact in museums in a condition as close as possible to their state at the time of burial, including food stains, sweat marks, and, in some cases, earth (but not postexcavation dust). Since these alien substances present, singly and in combination, valuable intrinsic information about the objects' past and excavation, they should not be thoughtlessly removed (these alien materials would no longer be harmful, and some substances have protected the fibers throughout the burial period). The level of cleanliness we demand for a facial towel today is not appropriate to museological preservation and conservation. Essentially, an archaeological object must be preserved in an environmental condition identical to or approximating its findspot, provided with physical/mechanical support while shielded from exposure to air, incompatible pH conditions, all types of light, and mechanical movements. All invasive treatments including washing and attachment of conservation materials should best be avoided; these are frequently, and paradoxically, the causes of additional damage in the long run.

11. For example, an undecorated lower half of a caftan (Figure 5).

12. For example, a pair of leather mitts (Figure 8).

13. When seated, the wearer sits on the back panel. The 27-cm side seams between the waistline and rider's panels do not allow the lower back panel to flip out backward.

14. A pair of humps on the back at the waistline recurs in all three subject and reference caftans under discussion: the Metropolitan Museum's caftan (one extant, decorated with silk border, Figure 2), Reference Silk Caftan (one extant, decorated with silk border), and the undecorated lower half of a caftan (a pair extant, Figure 5).

15. As opposed to extant contemporaneous garments that were woven, from Mesopotamia to the Mediterranean coastal regions as well as in some other parts of the world, in the specific shape of a straight-seamed garment that required little sewing. See notes 65 and 72 for fancy versions.

16. The original whiteness remains in the lower half of the left front (hidden under the right front panel; Figure 2) and in sections of the back panels (Figure 3) of the caftan.

17. See note 52 for terminology use in this article.

18. For example, a tunic for a woman (Figure 7) is also a composite of several different used linen and hemp cloths.

19. In seaming the Reference Silk Caftan (Figure 19), the last warps in the full 1-cm-wide plain-weave selvages were butted and stitched. At the edges of the wrist openings, raw selvages were used.

20. A portion of a linen tunic sleeve (Figure 12). The wrist opening was finished with straightforward hemming without a border. Since the Metropolitan's caftan is also of linen, its sleeves would have been finished the same way. The original wrist openings of the Reference Silk Caftan (Figure 19) had no patterned silk borders, whereas a woman's tunic (Figure 7) was embellished at the wrists with silk borders.

21. Many tiny remnants, mostly without hair, are extant in the interior along the seams of the border silks.

22. Modern linen fibers are extracted from flax stalks by the use of strong chemicals to speed up the process. The chemicals' residues and/or overprocessing affect the bast fiber's ability (see note 26) to withstand oxidation/acidification or longevity in our environment, much less than the fibers processed in the natural environment of the archaeological period. For our conservation work, cotton cloth was used for the coat for easy identification of the original and the conservation materials. The 8th–10th-century linen could have greater longevity than the industrially hybridized 20th-century cotton grown in a polluted environment.

23. The Reference Silk Caftan made of very sheer silk damask is, with borders altogether, also unlined.

24. The foot parts of all other leggings in the reference groups were composed of a single piece with the seam in the heel. Each foot part of the undecorated leggings (Figure 6) and, according to the photograph, Ierusalimskaja, *Gräber*, pl. 25, fig. 55 (Reference Group I), was of a nettlelike fiber cloth, coarser and darker in color than the linen cloth used for their leg sections.

25. Leather disks (triangle, 1.5 cm) attached at the front rim of a pair of linen leggings (Figure 6) retain the leather strings (6 cm).

26. Dark streaks in bast fibers are commonly interpreted as evidence of the presence of lignin (an acidic compound inherent in the source plant) that turns brown as it oxidizes over time. The presence and amount of lignin differ not only by plant species but also according to when and where the plants were harvested. Since the acidic lignin accelerates oxidation of cellulose, bast fibers weaken and break faster than those with less or no lignin. Flax contains much less lignin than other bast fiber plants. Since the linen fibers in our objects are still in good condition for their age, our caftan, from the time the thread was spun and to the burial, must have been evenly off-white (see note 16).

27. This recurs with the pillow (Figure 13). Also Reference Group I; see Ierusalimskaja, *Gräber*, pl. 94, fig. 156 II.

28. Also a tunic collar (Figure 11) of the same type of silk but from a different bolt, retains high-value yellow wefts in the center of the axlike pattern.

29. In executing a repeated design oriented either upright or sideways in the weft direction across the full width of cloth on the loom, the beginning and end of a repeat unit are, for the most part, regionally conventionalized. In the Eastern tradition, in medieval silks, almost all units were completed at both right and left selvages—as ours is—whereas in areas west of China, a unit would be complete at the left but frequently remained incomplete at the right selvage. Since weaving had to be done with the reverse side up on the loom, the incomplete pattern units indicate that the pattern heddle threading of warps started at the right side of the loom.

30. In earlier and contemporaneous textiles of all types and provenances, the design of a boar's head—never the whole animal—is consistently depicted alone in a roundel. See, for example, a Sui dynasty samit silk in a private collection (Figure 43); a Tang dynasty samit silk (Xinjiang Uygur Autonomous Regional Museum), *Archaeological Treasures of the Silk Road in Xinjiang Uygur Autonomous Region*, exh. cat. (Shanghai: Shanghai Translation Publishing House, 1998), cat. no. 47; a wool embroidery attributed to the 7th century, Textile Museum, Washington, D.C., inv. no. 3.304, Carol M. Bier, "Textiles," in Prudence Oliver Harper, *The Royal Hunter: Art of the Sasanian Empire* (New York: Asia Society in association with John Weatherhill, 1978), cat. no. 53; and a wool tapestry attributed to the 7th century, Cleveland Museum of Art, inv. no. 50.509, *Woven Treasures of Persian Art*, exh. cat. (Los Angeles: Los Angeles County Museum of Art), cat. no. 4. If the design in Silk C1 can be interpreted as a pair of confronted boar's heads, the heads are considerably stylized (see Knauer, Figures 11–13), perhaps because the motif was not in the convention of their locality. The lack of clarity in the motif is another reason to think that this rural group of weft-faced samit silks was woven after the 7th century by copying a copy of a copy, in a weaving center remote from the mainstream.

31. This motif is derived from the tree of life that was naturalistically rendered in the 7th century and gradually became stylized. See, for example, a wool and cotton samit, Textile Museum, inv. no. 73.623, Bier, "Textiles," cat. no. 57; a silk samit, Musée National du Moyen Âge (Cluny), Paris, inv. no. Cl. 22513 (see note 75).

32. The direction of the weaving is established following the conventional order of three-color wefts, the two design wefts first, followed by the ground weft.

33. To weave a cloth on a mechanical loom, for example a polychrome samit on a draw-loom, each warp in the set(s) of the massive number of warps has to be threaded in strict order through each dent of the reed, each hole in a heddle in the shaft, and, with a draw-loom, each hole in a pattern lash according to the complex sequence required by the structure. As such, the threading of the warp in dressing a loom requires a greater understanding of loom technology and weave structure than skill at simply tying the ends of two fine warp threads. Thus weavers saved a length of already threaded leftover warps on the loom and tied them with the new warps one by one. Once the warps were arranged in a particular structure, the arrangement would be continuously used to weave many bolts in the same structure; the pattern could be changed by choosing from a variety of patterning cord arrangements that were coordinated with the type of structure.

34. For an example of the use of interchangeable patterning cords, see Museum of Fine Arts, Boston, inv. no. 40.45; Dorothy G. Shepherd, "Medieval Persian Silks in Fact and Fancy," *Bulletin*

du CIETA, nos. 39–40 (1974), pts. 1 and 2, figs. 49a, b. Also see Biblioteca Apostolica Vaticana, Museo Sacro, inv. no. 6953a–g; Odile Valansot, "Un tissue islamique de la Bibliothèque Apostolique Vaticane: Étude technique," *Bulletin du CIETA,* no. 70, (1992), fig. 3.

35. At present, reports on archaeological finds of the Linum family plant's seeds (for oil) and fibers (including yarns and fabrics) that indicate the early cultivation in the regions closer to the Moshchevaja Balka include Çatal Hüyük, Turkey, 6000 B.C., and Jordan, 4000 B.C. *Linum bienne,* a wild perennial, grows today in steppes such as the southern slope of the Caucasus Mountains. The manufacture date of our coat suggests that its linen was likely by then a widely cultivated annual, *Linum usitatissimum L.,* which must have been grown in the alluvial soil plains in the greater Caucasus region. Under the Soviet system, flax cultivation was terminated in present-day Georgia and Armenia.

In textile jargon, the word *flax* connotes the plant, whereas *linen* refers to both the fiber that was extracted from the stalk of the plant and the cloth that was made of it.

36. Hemp was identified in the foot parts of a pair of undecorated linen leggings (Figure 6) and a pair of short trousers (Figure 9). Nettlelike fiber was used in a pair of short trousers (Figure 10) that were severely battered by use, even after being patched in many places.

37. To obtain a yarn in the large quantity required for weaving (as opposed to a limited-length twine for tying or a single thread for stitching, for example), time-consuming, labor-intensive yarn-making procedures evolved into regionally specific methods.

To transform short fibers into a single yarn and, further, to form more than two single yarns into plied yarn or re-plied yarn for strength and thickness, the fibers must be spun. Spinning is a technology for making a continuous yarn in which short fibers of all kinds and types (including shortened and/or bundled long fibers such as flax and silk) are prepared into a loose mass from which a portion is pulled out while in a rotation. The process can be done with the fingers (the slowest), sticks, spindles, a wheeled apparatus, or a flyer-attached spinning wheel (the fastest). A draw of even quantity (dictated by the degree of fiber preparation) and a steadiness in speed and force (dictated by the spinner's dexterity and apparatus) are the essential factors in making a yarn of infinite length with even diameter, twist, and strength that results in good cloth. See Allen Fannin, *Handspinning: Art and Technique* (New York: Van Nostrand Reinhold, 1970). Spinning requires a few seconds of ceaseless repeated motion with hands or tools to continuously draw and twist the fibers and yarns. (In describing yarn-making, "spinning" implies only fibers that are actually spun, whereas long fibers, e.g., silk and bast fibers that undergo each specific process in the first stage of transforming fibers into yarn, are reeled or spliced/knotted and then plied.)

The physiology of the human hand determines the way in which something is twisted, rolled, or rotated—as in this case, a shaft of a hand spindle or a spinning wheel. For the right-handed majority of people, it is natural to hold the shaft of a spindle with the right palm facing the body. To roll the shaft while holding it between the thumb and the rest of the fingers, one moves the thumb to the left (toward the right requires an unnatural effort), pushing against the other fingers; then the thumb returns to its original position and repeats the action. If viewed from the upper end of the rolling shaft, the rotation is in a clockwise direction that imparts what is called a Z-twist to the yarn being spun. The same rotation if seen from the bottom up is in a counterclockwise direction. If the fiber is tied from the bottom of the shaft, an S-twist results.

To make yarns, while continuously rotating a spindle with the right hand, fibers must be constantly fed to the end of the spindle shaft by the left hand. If the spindle is held vertically, the only direction fibers can be supplied is from above downward, resulting in a Z-twist yarn. If the spindle is held horizontally (with the palm upward), the only direction the left hand can supply the fibers is from the left, resulting in as S-twist yarn. Likewise, if working on the lap or on the proper right thigh (for right-handed people), it is more natural for the right hand, palm down, to roll the hand away from the body. If two ends to be spliced are laid horizontally on the lap or a vertically held spindle shaft is placed against the outside of the right thigh and rolled, with the fibers being supplied from the left side, the splicing area or the spun yarn twists in an S direction. With a so-called spinning wheel equipped with a belt, S- or Z-twist directions can be chosen by the way the belt goes around the wheel (in a circle as a figure 0 or with a twist as a figure 8) without changing the right-handed person's clockwise rotation.

Since such spinning actions force resilient fibers to change from their natural state into an unnatural twisted state, the fibers try to return to their original state. Plying, which combines two or more yarns twisted in the same direction by retwisting them together in the opposite direction, adds stability and strength to the yarn by exploiting the opposing inherent forces, as 2 Z-spun yarns plied in an S twist, 3 S-spun yarns plied in a Z twist, and so forth.

Following the initial yarn making, the plying process forces all spinners to perform a physically unnatural, tiresome reverse twisting motion. Or were left-handed people specifically brought into the process? In some regions, spinners have come up with solutions to lessen the work of plying by adapting different methods (first, working with a drop spindle, then rolling on the thigh) or have avoided plying altogether (doubling the yarn but not twisting it). The application of two opposite directions of twist applies only to resilient wool, cotton, bast, and prepared natural and synthetic fibers. Less or nonresilient materials of long to infinite length, such as plant stem, hard leaf, sheath, some synthetic, and metal (e.g., steel cables), are twisted and plied in the same direction.

As a result, depending on the type of fibers available at the early stage of technological development, a regionally distinctive convention of fiber preparation (one of the most time-consuming processes in spinning) and of spinning methods was established. Such conventions may or may not have been modified by the introduction of unfamiliar fibers or of unfamiliar yarns through trade.

38. The options for spinning apparatus used include a spindle that rotates on the ground or in the air, a team of a fixed rotator and a mobile fiber-feeder, or a wheel-operated apparatus. Four spindle whorls were included in the report of Reference Group I (Ierusalimskaja, *Gräber,* pl. XLVII, figs. 111 and 112; those with a single hole in the center were captioned "ornaments" together with those with two holes), but that does not exclude the possibility of a wheel-operated apparatus in this context.

39. The paucity of surviving archaeological textiles from the Caucasus and neighboring regions in the Middle East makes such assessment somewhat insecure.

40. See, for example, Tomoyuki Yamanobe, *Shiruku-rōdo no Sen-*

shoku: Sutain Korekushon, Nyūderī Kokuritsu Hakubutsukan-zō (Kyōto: Shikō-sha, 1979), pl. 100. The detail of a bolt illustrated is captioned as "hemp," a common questionable translation from Japanese. Although it could be hemp, the original Japanese *asa* connotes "a bast fiber" that includes ramie as well as all other visually similar plant fibers.

41. In Egypt, during the period of colonization by the Romans (30 B.C. through A.D. 395), in making yarns from linen fibers, the conventional Dynastic splicing method, in which two or more single plies were twisted together in the same direction, changed completely into the spinning method traditional to the regions north of the Mediterranean Sea, at the same time that the Dynastic wraparound garment style changed to the Roman tunic. Woven of spun yarns, 4th–12th century linens excavated in Egypt (so-called Coptic group), Syria (Palmyra, Dura Europos), and Iraq (At-tar) resemble each other but do not resemble those found at Moshchevaja Balka. Rather, the linens used in the Metropolitan's caftan are closer to the medium-hand, high-quality linens woven of spun yarns by the Tiraz of Arabs who adopted the mode of Late Antique linen culture in the period following their invasion of Egypt (A.D. 750). Excavation of contemporaneous counterparts from Middle Eastern regions has scarcely been reported.

42. It is in every weaver's interest to weave as fast as possible, and warp-faced weaving can be done faster than weft-faced weaving. The technical issues involved include the relationship of diameter, elasticity (largely dependent on the degree of twist), and tension of the warp yarns in one direction and the weft yarns in another, how the yarns withstand the weaving process, which is a function of the locality or the type of fibers used, and how they were put together as individual yarns.

   In the web plane on the loom, a warp-faced weave results when closely set warps are maintained at a loose tension (enhanced if the loom has an adjustable warp tension setup), and the inserted weft yarns lie taut or straight with spaces between them (a natural phenomenon). In particular, in the initial period, when a wooden sword was used to beat in the weft (without a reed), the closely set warps meander over the taut, straight wefts, creating warp-faced weaves, including warp-faced taquete and samit in bolt-length, wide-width weaving. Once the custom of warp-faced weaves is established, looms and techniques conform to it. Today, a handweaver in China, for example, can no longer weave a weft-faced samit as true weft-faced, since no weavers allow loosely inserted uneven wefts in their products, and the space available on the loom (ca. 30 cm as opposed to the required 50 cm) does not permit a weft to lie diagonally. The time-consuming insertion of wefts in scallops as in the manner of tapestry weavers was beyond the concept of a handweaver mechanically weaving a pseudo–weft-faced satin samit on a draw loom that was constructed for warp-faced weaves.

43. In the web plane on the loom, a weft-faced weave results when spaced warps (with a reed) are kept under taut tension, and the inserted weft yarns meander around the warps compactly, an effect that is obtained only with effort. Inserting a weft loosely so that it successfully meanders around the warp to achieve a weft-faced weave consumes more time and skill than simply throwing straight and taut weft into an open shed.

   In producing polychrome-patterned cloth such as weft-faced taquete and samit, although the warp preparation for the warp-faced Chinese counterpart (or narrow-band weaving in many cultures) was cumbersome, the ability to use any number of colors called for in the design was achieved by exchanging the roles of warp and weft. This was also time-consuming even though the slowness might not have been a serious concern in the production of luxurious textiles. By the 13th century the weft-faced taquete/samit weave system was virtually replaced by the lampas-weave system (see note 54). Weft-faced taquete/samit weaves were continued in Iran (see Nancy Andrews Reath and Eleanor B. Sachs, *Persian Textiles and Their Technique from the Sixth to the Eighteenth Centuries Including a System for General Textile Classification* [New Haven: Pub. for Pennsylvania Museum of Art by Yale University Press; London: H. Milford, Oxford University Press, 1937], figs. 9, 10; Jon Thompson and Hero Granger-Taylor, "The Persian Zilu Loom of Meybod," *Bulletin du CIETA*, no. 73 [1995–96], pp. 27–53), Egypt (see M. M. El-Homossani, "Double-Harness Techniques Employed in Egypt," *Ars Textrina* 3 [May 1985], pp. 229–68), and perhaps a few other areas. The development of the lampas-weave system—for the most part, satin weave as a warp-faced weave foundation—eventually brought about the invention of a sectional warping method, which totally eliminated the time-consuming twisting of warp yarns.

44. See examples of outdoor weaving in Ann Hecht, *The Art of the Loom: Weaving, Spinning, and Dyeing across the World* (New York: Rizzoli, 1990), pl. 56, pp. 62–63; Shelagh Weir, *Spinning and Weaving in Palestine* (London: British Museum, 1970), pls. 8–11; Eric Broudy, *The Book of Looms: A History of the Handloom from the Ancient Times to the Present* (New York: Van Nostrand Reinhold, 1979), pls. 3–22, 27. For the contrasting warp arrangement for an indoor loom, see El-Homossani, "Double-Harness Techniques Employed in Egypt," pp. 229–68.

45. If wool yarn was used, which needs to be tightly twisted, a pointed stick could have aided in beating in the weft.

46. Other types of two-shaft loom could cause the same phenomenon, but are more likely to be inconsistent within the width of the loom.

47. During the yarn-making and weaving processes of bast and leaf fibers, the fibers are kept considerably moist or wet. This is because, unlike resilient wool and cotton fibers that inherently cling to each other when transformed into yarn, nonresilient smooth bast and leaf fibers stretch when moistened and shrink back after drying. Thus, the physical manipulation of bast fibers, yarns, or cloth—splicing, spinning, plying, weaving, tying, knotting, and stretching—is traditionally done by moistening the fibers. Because these fibers lack resiliency when dry, if processed in that state, the spun or spliced yarn would come apart, a tied knot would slip, weaving would produce a cloth with a loose weave that would shrink over 30% when wet later, and a stretched painting canvas would get wrinkles.

48. A width of 56 cm was measured in the panels (edges are folded inside seams, so the selvages are not determinable) making up the lower half of a coat (Figure 5).

49. In isolated regions of the world, a shellfish secretion was used to dye cellulosic and proteinaceous fibers purple (also brown and dark green). The dyeing of pink to red shades of madder on cotton in India by an extraordinarily complex method was uncommon in other parts of the world in early times.

50. In contrast, the excavated contemporaneous Egyptian linens used by the Muslim culture attest to the practice of a glazed finish for a new bolt as well as at each laundering.

51. For looms, see, for example, Broudy, *The Book of Looms*; Cheng

Weiji, chief compiler, *History of Textile Technology of Ancient China* (Rego Park, N.Y.: Science Press, 1992).

52. In this paper, the following four terms are used: warp-faced taquete (Figure 38), warp-faced samit (Figure 39), weft-faced taquete (Figure 40), weft-faced samit (Figure 41). These patterning structures involves a set of binding elements and a complementary set of patterning elements in opposing directions interlacing either warp-faced or weft-faced in plain weave (taquete) or twill weave (samit, most commonly 1/2, 1\2, 2/1, or 2\1 twill). Another set of elements, an inner set in the direction of the first set, separates one or the other of the complementary sets on the obverse for the pattern and on the reverse for the rest within the structure. For a discussion of warp- and weft-faced samit, see p. 108. For further reading, see Irene Emery, *The Primary Structures of Fabrics: An Illustrated Classification* (Washington, D.C.: Textile Museum, 1966), pp. 150–53; Shinzaburō Sasaki, *Nihon Jōdai Shokugi no Kenkyū* (Kyōto, 1976); Milton Sonday Jr. and Nobuko Kajitani, "A Second Type of Mughal Sash," *Textile Museum Journal* 3, no. 2 (1970), pp. 6–12.

    Although warp-faced and weft-faced taquete/samit textiles are structurally different, the general appearance of the two is indistinguishable to laymen.

53. For example, for one of the earliest discontinuous wefts in the set of complementary wefts in 9th-century weft-faced samit silk, see Biblioteca Apostolica Vaticana, Museo Sacro, inv. nos. 1231 and 1258, in Maria Teresa Lucidi, *La seta e la sua via*, exh. cat. (Rome: De Luca, 1994), nos. 68, 69. The varied uses of discontinuous wefts in silk, wool, and cotton in weft-faced taquete/samit are the subject of a future research paper.

54. *Lampas* is broad terminology for a loom-controlled pattern-weave system (after the 10th century) and also connotes textiles woven using this method. It is a compound structure in which a compact warp-faced weave such as satin weave (after the 13th century) is used for the ground, and a spaced-warp, weft-faced weave such as plain or twill weave is used for the pattern; they are fully or partially interconnected. The pattern stands out against the background not only because of the colors used but also because the warp-faced surface reflects and the weft-faced surface absorbs light, showing the pattern distinctly, as in damask weave. It is essential for a description of lampas to include the visual impact of the two structures, their structural relationship, and the varied types of yarns used. Because the ground weave of a lampas structure is warp-faced, which is much less time-consuming to weave than the weft-faced samit, it resulted in greater productivity and replaced weft-faced samit systems relatively quickly. The lampas system began to appear in the 10th–11th century and matured by the 12th century in weaving centers. Whether the lampas system originated in the Arab or Chinese cultures, or both, cannot be determined.

55. Sinking and counterbalanced shafts are outside the scope of this discussion. Upright looms that share the same principles of interlacing weft-faced taquete/samit but developed in the regions weaving with spun yarn must also be left out of this discussion.

56. The underside, obverse of cloth inevitably displays many weaving faults. After removal from the loom, a freshly finished bolt of patterned silk and the extra yarns used for it are taken to a craftsman who specializes in structural and material refinement for time-consuming correction by needlework, and a finisher for steaming, pounding, rolling, and stretching.

57. See Ernest Pariset, *Histoire de la soie*, 2 vols. (Paris: A. Durand, 1862–65); Luce Boulnois, *La Route de la soie* (Paris: Arthaud,

1963). The essays in these books are informative, but readers must trace the sources of references and make their own interpretations.

58. For evidence of trade from the East to West in the earliest periods, see, for example, R. Pfister, *Textiles de Palmyre*, 3 vols. (Paris: Les Éditions d'art et d'histoire, 1934–40); R. Pfister and Louisa Bellinger, *The Excavations at Dura-Europos: The Final Report*, vol. 4, pt. 2, *The Textiles* (New Haven: Yale University Press, 1945); Hero Granger-Taylor and John Peter Wild, "Some Ancient Silk from the Crimea in the British Museum," *Antiquaries Journal* 61, pt. 2 (1981), pp. 302–6.

59. For evidence of trade from cotton culture to linen culture, see Carl Johan Lamm, *Cotton in Mediaeval Textiles of the Near East* (Paris: Librairie orientaliste P. Geuthner, 1937).

60. For evidence of trade from the West to East, see, for example, *Archaeological Treasures of the Silk Road in Xinjiang Uygur Autonomous Region*; Yue Feng et al., "Special Issue of the Achievements of Archaeological Work in Xinjiang," *Chien Shang Chia* (Connoisseur), no. 8 (April 1998), pp. 62–85; Feng Zhao and Zhiyong Yu, eds., *Legacy of the Desert King* (Hong Kong: ISAT, 2000); Kaneo Matsumoto, *Jōdai-gire: 7th and 8th Century Textiles in Japan from the Shōsō-in and Hōryū-ji* (Kyōto: Shikōsha, 1984).

61. These included the mulberry farmer, silkworm grower, basketry worker, boiling pot maker, cocoon reeler, unreeling tool maker, floss spinner, silk winder, warper, weft winder, reed maker, bobbin maker, shuttle maker, bamboo craftsman, carpenter, metalsmith, rope maker, structural finisher, wet finisher, and so on. The Industrial Revolution, particularly since the mid-19th century, destroyed the professions that had sustained the culture for three millennia.

62. It is known that beginning at the turn of the 10th century, previously warmer global temperatures gradually began to drop, finally reaching their lowest average point in the 12th century, at approximately 3° C. The paucity and poor quality of extant silks produced in the mid-10th to mid-11th century that coincides with these low temperatures suggest that this natural phenomenon may have affected the entire chain of sericulture, yielding inferior mulberry leaves, which, when fed to silkworms, resulted in thin and weak silk. See R. W. Fairbridge, "Eustatic Changes in Sea Level," *Physics and Chemistry of the Earth* 4 (1961), pp. 99–185; Zu Kezhen, "Zhongguo Jin-wuqiannianlai Qihou Bianqian de Chubu Yanjia," *Kaogu Xuebao*, no. 1 (1972), pp. 15–38.

63. Thought at this time to be the earliest examples of warp-faced taquete extant are a series of silks excavated as garments from the Mashan site, Jiangling, attributed to 3rd–2nd century B.C., Middle Warring States period. See Jingzhou diqu bowuguan, *Jiangling Mashan Yihao Chumu* (Beijing: Wenwu Chubanshe, 1985). See also Calvin S. Hathaway and Jean E. Mailey, "A Bonnet and a Pair of Mitts from Ch'ang-Sha," *Chronicle of the Museum for the Arts of Decoration of the Cooper Union* 2, no. 10 (1958), pp. 315–46.

64. See, for example, *Archaeological Treasures of the Silk Road in Xinjiang Uygur Autonomous Region*, cat. nos. 32–41, 43. The layout in silk cat. no. 44 demonstrates a transition.

65. See, for example, weft-faced taquete fragments from: Iraq, Dura-Europos, Yale University Art Gallery, New Haven, inv. no. 1933.486, spun silk, 3rd century (Pfister and Bellinger, *The Textiles*, no. 263); Iran, Shar-i-Qumis, MMA 69.24.35, wool and cotton, 6th century; Egypt, woven in tunic shapes with the design in weft direction, MMA 09.50.2304 (stitched on a later

tunic); and Victoria and Albert Museum, London, inv. nos. 1264-1888, 1286-1888, T188-1976, linen/wool, and many wool tunics and blankets, 4th–5th century (A. F. Kendrick, *Catalogue of Textiles from Burying-Grounds in Egypt* [London: V&A, 1920–21], vol. 2). For succeeding weft-faced samit, see note 72.

66. A single or double row of solid circles as decorative borders, particularly of roundels, is already observable on 4th-century Sasanian monochromatic architectural, metal, and wood objects. See, for example, Harper, *Royal Hunter*. Whether the circles can be attributed to "pearls" or should be described differently, the extant polychrome wool or silk textiles from and attributed to Iran from the 6th to 8th century were consistently woven in white. For example, the earliest dated two-weft weft-faced taquete is MMA 69.34.8, wool and cotton, excavated with a coin dated A.D. 587–88 at Shar-i-Qumis (Iran). Attributed to the 7th–8th century is MMA 48.43, wool and cotton, and to the 9th century, Musée du Louvre, Paris, inv. no. E 29187, silk sewn on wool tunic sleeves. Also, for example, see Bier, "Textiles," pp. 119–40, and Matsumoto, *Jōdai-gire*. As the design and the weft-faced samit loom technology spread internationally from the Sasanian weaving centers, pearls began to appear partially in white and later totally in other colors. For example, Abegg-Stiftung, Riggisberg, inv. no. 9, wool weft-faced samit, 9th century, in blue and red; Cooper-Hewitt National Design Museum, Smithsonian Institution, New York, inv. no. 1902–1-222, silk weft-faced samit, 11th century, in blue.

67. See Krishna Riboud and M. Gabriel Vial, *Tissus de Touen-Houang* (Paris, 1970); Matsumoto, *Jōdai-gire*.

68. The dissemination of the weft-faced samit weave system—the first polychrome loom-patterning technology—was swift in the 7th century. Since the compound structure was based on plain- and twill-weave binding systems to which weavers were accustomed, they were able to participate in the international market by adopting only the patterning apparatus with no need to change the basic mechanism of their looms. Since the weft-faced samit silks that were woven at the various workshops in widespread regions of manufacture throughout the 7th to 12th century appear, for the most part, to resemble each other visually, attribution of provenances remains so (as opposed to the succeeding lampas-weave system [see note 54] for which the loom, but not the patterning apparatus, had to be changed). This is because weft-faced samit was woven in the identical structure, with similar pattern repeat (as opposed to the lampas-weave system that produced a variety of weaves, pattern organizations, and designs), even though materials—particularly colors—and technical details differed.

69. Fragments of two narrow bands of superb quality, Byzantium, 5th century, wool and silk warp, and linen weft, excavated in Egypt, are known: MMA 90.5.11a–e (width 10 cm); see Nobuko Kajitani, "Koputo-gire," *Senshoku-no-Bi*, no. 13 [Early Autumn 1981], pl. 49, and *Textiles of Late Antiquity*, exh. cat. [New York: MMA, 1995], cat. no. 26, p. 38. The second band is in two pieces, the larger portion (width 6 cm) in the Städtische Kunstsammlungen, Düsseldorf, inv. no. 13095 (see Leonie von Wilckens, *Die textilen Künste: Von der Spätantike bis um 1500* [Munich, 1991], fig. 14), and the smaller fragment, MMA 90.5.9, unpublished.

70. For weft-faced taquete in wool/linen or wool, see note 65, and weft-faced samit (silk), note 72.

71. See *Archaeological Treasures of the Silk Road in Xinjiang Uygur Autonomous Region*, pp. 228–29, "VIII. Male Mummy of Yingpan"; Li Wanying and Zhou Jinling, "Fine Woolen Robe

Unearthed from an Ancient Tomb of Yingpan," *Chien Shang Chia* (Connoisseur), no. 8 (April 1998), pp. 62–67. The excavation context is dated to Han 206 B.C.–A.D. 8 through Jin A.D. 265–420, from a site in Yingpan, Yuli (north of Khara-khoto), Xinjiang Uygur Autonomous Region, People's Republic of China (excavated in 1995).

The plate on p. 66 in the latter publication shows a close-up of the lower part of the overlapping proper left front of the superbly preserved man's coat made of wool double cloth (slightly weft-faced). At its edge (seen in the center of the plate) is a triangular piece of wool cloth in weft-faced taquete most likely cut from a bolt. As illustrated, the warp runs horizontally. Wefts are in two sets, one a solid red and the other graduated blue to pink and pink to white, a typical feature in the attributed context. The narrow solid blue area is the heading of the cloth. Exquisitely executed, all yarns are of the finest wool. The graduated-color yarns were first fleece-dyed, then mixed and carded before being spun. On the underside of the front panel, not shown, is a second small weft-faced taquete cloth in another design similarly organized. I would also note that these three loom-patterned textiles do not incorporate the circle-and-cross format, even though the pattern organization in symmetrical and offset row arrangements (like the Roman weft-faced samit in silk in note 72) was capable of creating such a design (see note 77). The entire corpus of textiles associated with the Yingpan mummy would rewrite textile history. It again demonstrates how little we know about human potential and ingenuity in history. On the other hand, it is gratifying that even a tiny example survived and that we are afforded a glimpse into the ancient world. I am most grateful for having been given the opportunity in 1997 by the Archaeological Institute of Xinjiang to study the garment closely firsthand.

72. The following silk weft-faced samit examples in fragments with a profusely repeated pattern of Roman origin, none related to Sasanian pearl roundels, are estimated to have been woven in tunic shape (with the direction of the design oriented in the weft direction), attributed to the 4th–6th century. In two-color wefts: Cathedral Treasury, Sens, inv. no. AB (*Age of Spirituality*, ed. Kurt Weitzman [New York: MMA, 1979], cat. no. 413); Mechthild Flury-Lemberg, *Textile Conservation and Research*, Schriften der Abegg-Stiftung Bern 7 (Riggisberg: Abegg-Stiftung Bern, 1988), no. 72, pp. 412–22, and no. 94, pp. 367–69, 381–83; Museum of Fine Arts, Boston, inv. no. 11.90 (Adèle Coulin Weibel, *Two Thousand Years of Textiles: The Figured Textiles of Europe and the Near East* [reprint, New York: Hacker, 1972], pl. 50); Monique King and Donald King, *European Textiles in the Kier Collection, 400 B.C. to 1800 A.D.* (London: Faber, 1990), cat. no. 7; Cooper-Hewitt National Design Museum, inv. no. 1902–1-210 (Weibel, *Two Thousand Years of Textiles*, pl. 48); MMA 2000.374; from the same tunic, Royal Museum of Scotland, Edinburgh, inv. no. 1975.299; King and King, *European Textiles in the Kier Collection*, cat. no. 6; a private collection, Antwerp, no. 795; Newark Museum, inv. no. 77.29, 39. In three-color wefts: Cleveland Museum of Art, inv. no. 50.520. For an earlier-period linen/wool weft-faced taquete, see note 65.

73. In the technological history of weaving with silklike filaments in the West, for a considerably long period, local wild silks (see King and King, *European Textiles in the Kier Collection*, cat. no. 149, which may be one of them) were used. Then, with the advent of international contact, traded silk yarns (from *Bombyx mori*) were used by weavers already familiar with weaving with wild silk.

From China reaching westward as far as Western Europe, probably as early as 100 B.C., the use of traded silk yarns—including dyed yarns—long preceded the introduction of sericulture. This extremely complex, time-consuming, labor-intensive undertaking involved raising sensitive silkworms and mulberry trees, compatible climate, soil, and water, as well as cultivating the knowledge and skill of workers. The 6th-century myths apparently fantasized by C. H. Yule in 1898, based on an anecdote in *De bello gothico* (ca. A.D. 550) by Procopius, that sericulture began in the West after silkworm eggs were smuggled out of China could be a factor, but that alone, without the lead time of the use of local wild silk and then traded silk yarns, cannot initiate and support the system of sericulture. See R. J. Forbes, *Studies in Ancient Technology,* vol. 4 (Leiden and New York: E. J. Brill, 1987), pp. 50–53. For example, the following two textiles, unearthed in Egypt, contain filaments that appear not to be from *Bombyx mori:* yellowish filaments in wool and linen tapestry-weave design, a 3–4th-century belt, MMA 33.10.36, from the Kharga Oasis (unpublished; the author is preparing a manuscript for publication); beige color filaments in a polychrome silk tapestry-weave in a 4–5th-century polychrome silk tunic decoration, MMA 90.5.154, (*Textiles of Late Antiquity,* cat. no. 14, p. 35), and from the same piece, Victoria and Albert Museum, inv. nos. 334-1887, 335-1887 (Kendrick, *Catalogue of Textiles from Burying-Grounds in Egypt,* vol. 1, no. 62, pl. XIV), and Museum of Fine Arts, Boston, inv. no. 35.87 (Weibel, *Two Thousand Years of Textiles,* cat. no. 7).

74. See, for example, MMA 1974.113.11, 12; Textile Museum, inv. nos. 73.623, 73.34, in Bier, "Textiles," cat. nos. 57–59. For others, see Lamm, *Cotton in Mediaeval Textiles,* pp. 17–52. Also blue and white, and green and white examples have been reported.

75. Musée National du Moyen Âge (Cluny), inv. no. Cl. 22513 (see note 31).

76. See, for example, Matsumoto, *Jōdai-gire,* pl. 38, with the pattern of four horsemen each aiming at a lion under the Tree of Life within Sasanian roundels with pearled borders, which was documented to have belonged to a prince in the court of Nara in the last half of the 7th century. Others of the exact type have been excavated in China and Egypt; for example, see Bier, "Textiles," cat. no. 56; Lamm, *Cotton in Mediaeval Textiles,* pp. 17–52. The sudden appearance of this type in superb quality among other experimental, rural types as well as its distribution seen in extant examples as far west as Egypt and as far east as Japan is a marvel in the history of textiles.

77. For the earliest Western counterpart of circle-and-cross repeat pattern—not yet including the Sasanian pearled roundels and before the invention of symmetrical organization of filler designs—of the 4th century or earlier, see a Roman silk weft-faced samit in fragments: Royal Museum of Scotland, Edinburgh, inv. no. 1975.299; King and King, *European Textiles of the Kier Collection,* cat. no. 6. For further development in loom technology, see MMA 2000.374, not yet published.

78. Matsumoto, *Jōdai-gire,* pl. 44.

79. Preceding bolt-width weaving, narrow belt-width weaving must have been practiced using highly twisted yarns of all types of fibers with the loom with or without string heddles and patterning shed sticks, a sword beater (seldom a reed), and sticks to hold bundled warps up at working position. The setup of the loom created a variety of warp-faced structures, including warp-faced taquete (note 69) and samit. The weavers of the world also initially wove narrow belt-width warp-faced weaving that endures today.

80. At a glance, the surface of double-faced, weft-faced samit, or Liao samit, looks like a basic weft-faced samit of the later period. Extra fine yarns for binding and inner warps alternate, and extra thick yarns for complementary wefts form the body of the fabric with weft colors mixed on the reverse. Unlike the basic weft-faced samit, the reverse is not warp-faced but weft-faced, thus double-faced—both faces structurally the same. In the structure, one of the complementary wefts patterns the obverse in 1-2 weft-faced twill, or interlaces over two binding and three inner warps and under one binding warp. The rest of the mixed color weft interlaces, with their binding points offset one binding warp, over one binding warp and under two binding and three inner warps, in effect becoming warp-faced. In this structure, however, both the obverse and the reverse have the appearance of being weft-faced since the sole weft-faced-patterning weft slides or expands over to the other warp-faced area. Hence it is a pseudo–weft-faced twill surface. To weave this patterning structure, different from the original weft-faced samit in which patterning is achieved by manipulation of inner warps, the advanced heddle threading mechanism that had earlier been developed for damask weaving must be incorporated in the loom. Since the warps and wefts do not fully interlace as in true weft-faced samit, all double-faced, weft-faced samit weave silks lack structural integrity, compromising rigidity and longevity. Still a time-consuming weft-faced weave, double-faced, weft-faced samit twill advanced next to be woven in a satin-weave based structure leading the technology into a much less time-consuming warp-faced weave, and finally arrived at a lampas weave. It is understandable that the historically short-lived double-faced, weft-faced twill and satin samit weave structure emerged and disappeared quickly and was replaced by lampas. See, for example, MMA 1996.103.1 (in 1\2 twill binding), in "Recent Acquisitions, a Selection: 1995–1996," *MMAB* 54, no. 2 (Fall 1996), p. 77. See Sasaki, *Nihon Jōdai Shokugi no Kenkyū,* pp. 91–93 (in 1\2 twill binding); Zhao Feng, "Satin Samite: A Bridge from Samite to Satin," *Bulletin du CIETA,* no. 76 (1999), pp. 46–63 (in 1-2 twill and 1-4 satin bindings).

81. For example, Persia/Iran, Egypt, and others. See El-Homossani, "Double-Harness Techniques Employed in Egypt," pp. 229–68.

82. There are no lampas silks in the Moshchevaja Balka group finds.

83. There are several small pieces of two types of mainstream-type patterned silk in Reference Group III. They are heavily grave-stained but retain yellow, dark green, and faded beige colors with dark brown pattern outlining, and are in fair condition.

84. For example, in Reference Groups II and III, only a woman's linen tunic (Figure 7) was embellished with mainstream- as well as rural-type weft-faced samit silks. All the rest—the subject caftan, leggings, Reference Silk Caftan (Figure 19), tunic collar (Figure 11), and an extant end of a pillow (Figure 13)—are decorated with rural-type weft-faced samit silks.

85. At present, several regions can be considered locations for the sericulture that could have included the production of the rural-type weft-faced samit silks associated exclusively with the Moshchevaja Balka group textiles. The most likely is the area of fertile valleys along the south side of the Caucasus Mountains in today's Georgia and Azerbaijan, where silk weaving was said to have been in practice by the 4th century, but whether it was full sericulture then is uncertain. Silkworms are no longer raised, but the endless lines of mulberry trees, for the most part still

trimmed in the style peculiar to leaf harvesting, and the old houses that are windowless on two sides of the ground floor strongly indicate the practice in the region perhaps until the advent of the Soviet system. Other regions that can be considered are in Armenia, Turkey, northwestern Iran, Syria, and Iraq. The author has not been able to survey the regions located on the north side of the Caucasus Mountains.

86. Twisting a yarn, particularly reeled-out silk yarn, not only strengthens it but also makes it possible to manipulate the yarns without tangling—as when weaving, stitching, and doing all other craftwork. Warp yarns, which are under tension and exposed to friction during weaving, require stronger yarns and time-consuming twisting. If warp yarns are not twisted, filaments catch on each other and disturb the order of thousands of warps during the process of warping and transferring them from the warping pegs and threading them into different parts of the loom.

Weft yarns—which are simply laid between warps in opened sheds without tension and friction—do not require twist and can consist of any type of lesser-quality fibers.

Paradoxically, yarn with a twisted surface, which does not reflect light, dulls the surface of an otherwise highly desired glossy silk fabric. Sometime in the 14th–15th century, because of consumers' preference and weavers' increased skill, a warp-faced satin weave (prior to its development about the 13th century, a warp-faced four-shaft broken twill weave had been the major warp-faced weave) became prevalent, though the use of twisted warps prevented a highly glossy surface. By the 15th century, the introduction of the sectional warping method allowed all warps to be prepared without twist. This development made it possible for all silk cloths to be lustrous, but weak. The diffusion of both this method and the satin weave was similar to the diffusion and disappearance of weft-faced samit in both the East and the West.

87. Reelable silk filament is a little more than half the full length of silk (ca. 1,500 m) that forms a cocoon. The remaining filaments and deformed cocoons (ca. 40% of the harvest) are unreelable. They are transformed into floss pads, which can be used as wadding or from which yarns are spun. Reeled-out silks are often overly degummed for easier dye penetration and a glossy effect in bolts. Consequently, they are expensive and used by selective weavers, although the resulting products often lack the strength and longevity of spun silks. Because the fiber source of spun-silk products was considered "waste" and because the simpler yarn-making process resulted in a heavier yarn with better durability that was more easily handled by novices, spun-silk products were always marketed more cheaply and thus as "inferior" quality goods.

88. Except for a blue weft in Silk C1, which is the same spun yarn as the undyed warps.

89. For example, MMA 69.24.35, 5th-century wool/cotton fragments, excavated in Iran; MMA 48.43, 51.85.3b, 1974.113.11, 1974.113.12, 6th–8th-century wool/cotton fragments, believed to have been excavated in Egypt. There are no known Sasanian weft-faced samit silks excavated in the heartland of the Sasanian Empire.

90. Colors that were selectively applied to ethnographic objects are always associated with cultural significance. With textiles, however, the manifestation of a particular color was not initially possible simply by the whim of an individual. The development—often accidental—of dyes and dyeing technology necessarily precedes such selection of a color. A dye compound in nature must be discovered, then a time-consuming complex treatment must be developed to cause the dye (impurities included) to chemically bond with the fibers. The establishment of cultural significance comes afterward.

91. See Robert Chenciner, *Madder Red: A History of Luxury and Trade* (Richmond, Surrey: Curzon, 2000).

92. The earliest safflower red identifiable from its visual appearance would be, generally speaking, in 15th-century textiles that have not been exposed to air and light. In daily conservation routines, the criteria can be applied in estimating the date of textiles as "before the 15th century" if there is a suspected beige in an unexposed area or "after the 15th century" if a UV-exposure fluoresces a reddish beige to pink shade in an exposed area in silks. If already faded, the textile can be exhibited, whereas unfaded, particularly light shades of pink should, in principle, never be allowed to be on view, exposed to air and light.

93. The madder plant is a perennial, and several years must pass before the best dye can be harvested.

94. The use of a roller on the loom required the invention of a device that would prevent the roller from unrolling when under tension.

95. Being extremely sensitive to climatic changes, silk has to be woven indoors so that throughout the weaving, the length of warps have to be accommodated in a limited space. Hence, in some parts of the world, warps were chained and dangled at the back of the loom. See, for example, Broudy, *Book of Looms*, pls. 6–12.

96. On a back-strap loom, tension can be adjusted at will. To weave on a high loom emancipated from the back-strap system, commonly a roller (infrequently a thick, flat board) was used to wind and release warps to be woven at the back of the loom (thus eliminating the bundling system) and another was used to roll the cloth just woven in the front. Since the roller system unrolls the wound item(s) too easily when tensioned, a device had to be invented to secure the roller(s) in a desired position for the necessary tension of the warp plane. The invention and introduction of the rope-and-lever or ratchet-and-wheel system in high looms made the subtle adjustment of tension in the warp plane possible.

97. See El-Homossani, "Double-Harness Techniques Employed in Egypt," pp. 229–68.

98. In warp-faced weaves, the phenomenon reverses.

99. Yarns and washable types of silk cloth (frequently plain or monochrome patterned cloths) to be dyed were degummed in the same way.

A Man's Caftan and Leggings from the North Caucasus of the Eighth to Tenth Century: A Genealogical Study

ELFRIEDE R. KNAUER

DEDICATED TO RUDOLF AND UTTA KASSEL

THE METROPOLITAN MUSEUM'S Department of Ancient Near Eastern Art has, over a period of years, acquired a number of textile fragments of no evident glamor and of unknown provenance. Among the better-preserved pieces are a caftan and a pair of leggings. Closer investigation reveals that they are testimony to the historic, cultural, and economic interconnections between Europe and Asia that have existed for millennia. This study focuses on the period between the sixth and the tenth centuries that corresponds to the early medieval period in Europe. The overthrow of the Roman Empire was prompted by the ascendancy of Germanic, Iranian, and Altaic tribes, whose gradual assimilation of the remnants of Late Roman culture in the West and aspects of the emerging Byzantine civilization in the East directly pertain to our concerns here. The epoch was as crucial to the formation of national identities in Western Europe as it was for the eastern part of the Classical world. Less well known are conditions in the Near East, where the alternation of confrontation and cohabitation between sedentary populations and the nomadic world differs from conditions in the West. This article investigates the historical background of the coat and the leggings (Figures 1, 2), as well as the related issues of geography, costume history, and commerce. A number of features, specifically the cut and the materials employed in the outfit, make it possible to approximate the date and to pinpoint the region where it may have been produced. Climate plays a major role in the preservation of perishable fibers, and, in general, desert conditions are most conducive to their preservation.[1] As we shall see, the Museum's garments do not come from regions of extremely dry conditions, making their conservation all the more astounding.

Since Nobuko Kajitani presents a comprehensive technical analysis of the caftan and the leggings in "A Man's Caftan and Leggings from the North Caucasus of the Eighth to Tenth Century: A Conservator's Report" (pp. 85–124 above), I shall give only a brief description of their salient features. Measuring about 142 centimeters in length, the coat must originally have come down to the mid-calves of a tall male (Figure 1; Kajitani, Figures 1–3). Unlike modern coats, the caftan is composed of a tight-fitting portion over the chest to which a skirtlike lower part is attached at the waistline. The garment closes at the proper left side of the body and is fastened with frogs.

The basic fabric of the caftan is finely woven bleached linen, cut into pieces that were stitched together. The two front panels of the skirt and the one of the back are composed of three pieces each: a wider central length of linen is flanked by narrower gussetlike pieces that widen progressively toward the lower edge. Two deep slits in the coat's skirt are positioned at either side of the back—not (as one might expect) at the sides below the arms. The solution is practical for a coat that was worn for horseback riding, since the rather narrow back panel of the skirt permitted the wider front panels to better protect the horseman's legs.[2] A minute fragment of skin—as yet unidentified—preserved on the caftan's interior attests to a fur lining.

The riding coat's most spectacular feature is its trimming of patterned "Sogdian" silk, which originally ran along all its edges, including the slits in the back, both outside and inside (Silks A and B; Kajitani, Figures 28–33). They consist of two different patterns of samit—that is, weft-faced compound twill—pieced together to form strips about 8 centimeters wide. On the lapel of the right panel, which is preserved up to the neck, only the outward-turned underside of the lapel is trimmed, not the outside, since it was turned toward the body and was therefore invisible, thus saving a bit of the precious material. On the back of the coat, although the slits do not run up to the waist, their trimming does, as confirmed by the preserved part at the right side of the back. Instead of smoothly disappearing in the seam at the waistline, the ends of the two trims bordering the slits are doubled up face

METROPOLITAN MUSEUM JOURNAL 36

The notes for this article begin on page 145.

Figure 1. Linen and silk caftan. North Caucasus, 8th–10th century. The Metropolitan Museum of Art, Harris Brisbane Dick Fund, 1996 (1996.78.1)

Figure 2. A pair of silk and linen leggings. North Caucasus, 8th–10th century. The Metropolitan Museum of Art, Harris Brisbane Dick Fund, 1996 (1996.78.2a, b)

The leggings, which were worn with the riding coat, measure 65 centimeters in height (Figure 2; Kajitani, Figure 4). The leg portion, which is funnel-shaped, consists of patterned silk (Silks C1 and C2)—differing in design from the caftan's borders—as far as the ankle, while the feet are tailored from sturdy linen. The stitching is meticulous throughout.[4]

PROVENANCE OF THE METROPOLITAN MUSEUM'S CAFTAN

Recent publications have shed considerable light on fabric finds made intermittently throughout the twentieth century in the northwestern part of the Caucasus Mountains and their piedmont, modern Karachayevo-Cherkesskiya and Kabardino-Balkarskiya. The set of garments in the Metropolitan Museum's possession certainly comes from the same region. The main site, Moshchevaja Balka, is situated in a ravine, high above a mountain stream. Densely wooded and situated at an altitude of about one thousand meters, not far from the confluence of the rivers Beskes and Bolshaja Laba, a left-hand tributary of the mighty Kuban, the site is hard to reach even today (Figures 3, 4).[5] Exten-

to face, sewn together, and thus jut out like little humps that accentuate the waist and hip (Kajitani, Figures 2, 3). An additional practical purpose of this detail may have been to hold the obligatory belt of the riding coat in place.[3] Most likely, the missing (and presumably extremely long) sleeves, too, were embellished with silk at the cuffs.

sive burial grounds were laid out on limestone terraces with overhanging ledges. The tombs are either built up from slabs on these terraces or hollowed out in the rock face. Favorable microclimatic conditions helped to preserve garments and burial furnishings in the harsh climate. The local population seems to have picked over these cemeteries long before the first scholarly investigation of this important find spot ever took place in 1900–1901, and they have continued to do so. The name of the site, Moshchevaja Balka, that is, Ravine of the Mummies or Relics, indicates the significance of the site to the local people.[6]

The noted Russian archaeologist N. I. Veselovskii briefly reported on his 1900–1901 investigations of the region to the Archaeological Commission without, however, specifying the exact location. Because his finds were well preserved, he considered them of recent date and relegated them to the Ethnographic Section of the Russian Museum in Saint Petersburg. An amateur archaeologist, N. I. Vorob'ev, followed in Veselovskii's footsteps in 1905. The eight hundred objects collected by Vorob'ev were consigned to the former Kunstkammer of Czar Peter I (today's Museum of Anthropology and Ethnography of the Academy of Sciences). They were transferred to the Oriental Department of the Hermitage in 1935, a move that rescued them from total oblivion. The Veselovskii finds joined them there in 1951. However, some rare pieces were lost during World War II. The stylistic identity of the two groups of materials puts their common origin from Moshchevaja Balka beyond doubt. The site was again visited and adequately described for the first time by the scholar A. A. Iessen in 1950. By then, about one thousand objects were preserved in the Hermitage, ready at last to be conserved and studied.[7]

In 1962 Anna A. Ierusalimskaja was appointed curator of the North Caucasian antiquities in the Hermitage. Thanks to her tireless and painstaking examination of the largely fragmentary materials from Moshchevaja Balka, to which she added considerably thanks to four excavation campaigns of her own between 1969 and 1976, we can now appreciate their intrinsic importance.[8] In close to thirty articles, written with few exceptions in Russian (and thus not easily accessible to readers in the West), she elucidated the multifarious problems the materials posed. Her two latest publications, in German, not only represent the sum of almost four decades of work but conveniently illustrate the results to a public unfamiliar with Ierusalimskaja's mother tongue.[9] The benefits are immeasurable for the present study.

Besides garments, shoes, caps, veils, napkins, rugs, and small bags, some made of silk from China or the eastern Mediterranean, materials from the Moshchevaja Balka cemetery consist mostly of ceramic jugs and bowls, trinkets, amulets, knives, agricultural tools, occasional weapons (e.g., bow and arrows with their receptacles), and wooden containers, particularly small lidded boxes (see Kajitani, Figures 15–18).[10] Much of these materials were apparently destined for burial since metal objects were rarely recovered. Clearly, metal was too costly a substance to be wasted, and cheap substitutes were fashioned for funerary purposes. Objects made of precious metals are lacking; they must have fallen victim to local looters. Few imported objects from the eastern Mediterranean and Asia Minor were found (glass, beads, bracts, and Arabic coins used as amulets, etc.), indicating that this was not an affluent society, a fact corroborated by the scant remains of a walled settlement on the plateau above the cemetery. In addition to the objects of foreign manufacture, Ierusalimskaja uses the ceramic finds from the larger North Caucasian region to date the burial grounds and the settlement to the eighth and ninth centuries. However, the chronology of neither the imported objects nor the ceramics is as well established as she maintains.[11] In view of the present state of information, closer dating seems premature. Neither the age and places of manufacture of the majority of Chinese silks nor of those from the eastern Mediterranean recovered at the North Caucasian sites can as yet be defined with absolute certainty. In the absence of further criteria, Ierusalimskaja's dates can only be accepted with caution.[12]

A great number of tribes seem to have shared a fairly uniform and—were it not for the textile finds—unspectacular material culture, known as the Saltovo-Majaki culture.[13] Fragments of silk were recovered in tombs in the foothills and plains north of the Caucasus, too.[14] But none are as striking as the clothes found at Moshchevaja Balka, most notably a blue-green silk caftan with a senmurv pattern. Dated to the early ninth century, it may have belonged to the chief of a tribe. It has been exhibited at various international venues over the last decade (Figure 5).[15]

THE HISTORICAL AND GEOGRAPHICAL
CONTEXT OF THE ADYGO-ALANIC TRIBES

The mountain chains that stretch from the Black to the Caspian Sea, with two peaks, Elbruz and Kasbek, over five thousand meters high, virtually block access from the South Russian steppes to Anatolia, the highlands of Iran, and the Fertile Crescent (see Figure 4).[16] Yet, since prehistoric times, waves of peoples succeeded in surmounting these ranges, attracted by the

Figure 3. The site of the cemetery at Moshchevaja Balka seen from across the ravine (after Anna A. Ierusalimskaja, *Die Gräber der Moščevaja Balka* [Munich, 1996], pl. 1, fig. 1)

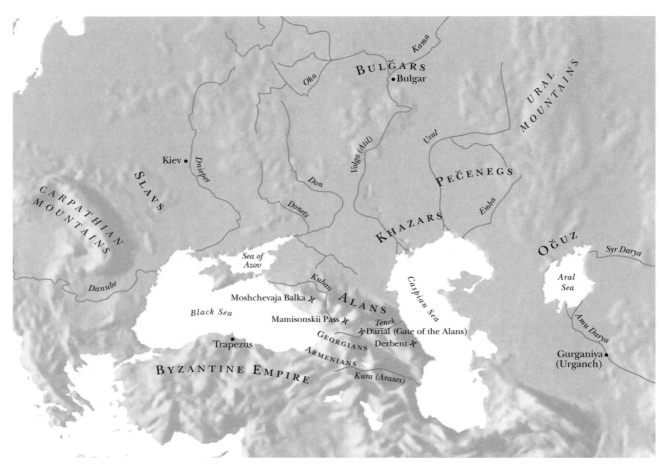

Figure 4. Map of the larger Caucasus region (map: Anandaroop Roy)

Figure 5. Blue-green fur-lined silk caftan with senmurv pattern from Moshchevaja Balka. State Hermitage, Saint Petersburg, Kz 6584 (photo: W. Haberland, courtesy Bayerisches Nationalmuseum, Munich)

wealth and culture of the civilizations in the south. Ever since Milesian settlers founded colonies on the eastern shores of the Black Sea, for example, Dioscurias/ Sebastopolis (today's Sukhumi) in the seventh century B.C., the Caucasus was known to the Greeks—at first somewhat vaguely—as adjacent to the land of Colchis.[17] The region's strategic importance was not lost on the Romans; they gained dominion over Armenia, which was, next to Georgia, the most powerful regional kingdom in the first century A.D. Armenia functioned as an outpost, first against the Parthians, then against the

Sasanians. Later on, as part of the Byzantine empire and an early adherent of Christianity, it served the same purpose. Over time, the Caucasus also provided refuge for the remnants of successive invading tribal confederations that headed west from the depths of Asia: Huns, Alans, Avars, Khazars, and many more. Hence, the ethnic spectrum was vast, including indigenous races, Indo-Iranians, and Turkic and Mongolian groups. Pockets of linguistically well-defined areas are relevant in our context. The Alans, who had roamed the Pontic steppe since the first century A.D., were

Figure 6. Ascent to the Krestovaya Gora, the highest elevation of the Darial (Gate of the Alans), the main pass of the Central Caucasus (photo: the author)

Figure 7. The upper Terek River leading to the Darial (Gate of the Alans); note the medieval watch tower (photo: the author)

swept along by the Huns in the fourth century A.D. and found refuge in the central portion of the mountain chain, in the modern Republic of North Osetiya–Alaniya.[18] They have been identified as constituting the Adygo-Alanic tribes responsible for the Moshchevaja Balka settlement and cemetery.[19]

Four photographs will illustrate the arduous passages through the Caucasus chains (Figures 6–9). Of the many passes, we have chosen the central and most important one, which was among the three that were critically important in antiquity and medieval times.[20] While the defile at Derbent close to the Caspian coast served the eastern Caucasus, it was the Darial (Iranian: Dar-i Alan = Gate of the Alans = Porta Alanica) that carried the main traffic and still does today. When Russia wrested Caucasia from the Persians and the obstinate mountain tribes during the eighteenth and nineteenth centuries, she made use of the Porta Alanica for the so-called Military Gruzinian Highway built in 1811–64. Our sequence approaches the pass from Georgia, that is, south of the range. The road ascends the denuded and eroded flanks of the Krestovaya Gora (Mountain of the Cross) to the most elevated point of its course (at ca. 2,400 m; Figure 6). It then descends into a valley formed by the upper reaches of the river Terek (Figure 7). The rare villages are still dominated by medieval watchtowers that once served to spot approaching caravans or to provide shelter for the inhabitants during all too frequent invasions. The road then skirts mighty Mount Kasbek (Figure 8) and

literally squeezes through a forbidding ravine, together with the waters of the Terek, to emerge finally into the foothills of Transcaucasia at Vladikavkaz (Hold the Caucasus!; Figure 9). In antiquity, the narrow defile seems to have been closed by actual iron-clad gates. Yet it remained a genuine Highway of Peoples through the ages.

CURRENT INTERPRETATION OF THE MOSHCHEVAJA BALKA TEXTILES

One of the most pressing questions posed by the fine textiles from Moshchevaja Balka is why silks of such varied provenances and value found their way to this remote and unhospitable area at all. Anna Ierusalimskaja has argued that the prevaling political constellations in the Caucasus region from the sixth through the ninth century necessitated a northward shift of the established routes used by the caravans through the Caucasian passes on their way between China or Central Asia and Iran and Byzantium. Control and high taxation by the Sasanian authorities, who continued a practice already enforced by their predecessors, the Parthians, during the first three centuries of the common era, compelled the traders to find other roads. Therefore, the passes of the eastern Caucasus were neglected in favor of inconspicuous yet perilous transit routes across the western stretch of that formidable mountain barrier. One of them led through the Laba

Figure 8. Mount Kasbek seen from the Military Gruzinian Highway leading to the Darial (Gate of the Alans) (photo: the author)

Figure 9. The ravine of the Terek River, the proper Darial (Gate of the Alans) (photo: the author)

(or Tsegerker [*sic*]) Pass in the immediate vicinity of Moshchevaja Balka.[21] After this pass, the caravans must have followed the short courses of some of the Abkhazian rivers, for example, the Bzyb', the Kodori, and the Enguri, or the larger Rioni (Phasis) to ports on the Black Sea (Pitsunda [Pityus], Sukhumi [Dioskurias], Poti [Phasis]).[22] From there, the merchandise was shipped to Byzantium and elsewhere. This transit trade required local guides, carriers, and pack animals; such services were provided by the tribes who commanded the defiles. Tolls and rewards were paid in kind, that is, with various textiles, among them silk. That this type of remuneration continued can be gathered from eighteenth- and nineteenth-century travelers' accounts from the same region, when the payment mostly consisted of lengths of linen, tailored shirts, or leather. The porters' teams cut the fabric into individual pieces right after receiving their lengths as payment (which may account for the patchwork character of many of the garments found). The practice was continued until early in the twentieth century (see Figure 10). Ierusalimskaja uses these circumstances to explain the evidence from the burial grounds.[23] It should be noted that similar situations are attested for Bohemia in the tenth century and for the northern Crimea and southern Ukraine in the mid-thirteenth century. Textiles were the usual currency of predominantly rural societies.[24]

Except for the few outstanding pieces of apparel that must have belonged to the upper crust of the tribe, linen garments from Moshchevaja Balka are often embellished with only the tiniest snippets of silken material. Although the patterns or designs hardly ever match, care was taken to match colors. Sorting the textiles according to their place of origin, Ierusalimskaja assigns the majority of the silk finds to "Sogdian" workshops, about 150 samples with more than 40 different patterns. Next in number comes the group of Far Eastern silks. There are about 100, mostly monochromatic or simply patterned, some with resist-dye printing; many have parallels in finds from Dunhuang in western Kansu and the Turfan Oasis (Xinjiang). Finally, there are silks from the Mediterranean realm, Byzantium, Syria, and Egypt—more than 50 smallish samples with about 20 different patterns.[25] The finds, therefore, clearly reflect the gamut of textiles traded along the Silk Routes, even if this branch was only a minor one among many others. The vicissitudes of survival have singled out Moshchevaja Balka as a paradigm of the large-scale exchange of goods and cultural contacts. A wealth of artifacts recovered in excavations of sites on the Asian trade routes over the last decades indicate that mercantile transactions were already initiated in a fairly organized way early in the first millennium A.D.[26]

A number of Chinese and western—that is, Byzantine or Syrian—silks found at Moshchevaja Balka can be matched with fabrics recovered in excavations in Chinese Central Asia, found in western collections, or incorporated into European church treasures as

Figure 10. Caravan of porters, Persia, early 20th century (after *A Treasury of Early Iranian Photography*, compiled by Iraj Afshar [Tehran, 1992])

relics. However, among the "Sogdian" silks, which form the majority of the silk textile finds, one group seems to represent an entirely local phenomenon.[27] Fragments of this very circumscribed group have so far not been unearthed beyond sites in the northwestern Caucasus. This is surprising and invites a number of reflections. Within the range of "Sogdian" silks, they are technically much inferior to the rest of the material, in both dyeing and weaving.[28] Their formerly bright colors have largely faded, reducing the spectrum to the brown of the background and the eggshell-colored pearl roundels with their double-ax, star, or blossom motifs (see Figures 11–13; Kajitani, Figures 28–36). However, the original color scheme must have been striking and powerful, with red, yellow, and blue bands framing the images within the roundels as well as the smaller motifs in the interstices. The brown ground may have been black initially, the pearl roundels and central motifs a creamy white.

The double-ax motif has received particular attention from Ierusalimskaja and provides additional, significant evidence for characterizing the local silks. As Ierusalimskaja astutely recognized, the double-ax is a stylized version of confronted boars' heads.[29] The

source of the motif is to be found in Sasanian textiles, stucco panels, wall decoration, and metalwork. There, the boars' heads occur mostly as individual heads within roundels, not as two facing ones as in the majority of the "Sogdian" silks from Moshchevaja Balka.[30] In the latter a split palmette frames the heads below and above, rendering their orientation ambivalent. However, once one understands the source, the eyes and snouts of the confronted heads can still be discerned in the less stylized examples. Ierusalimskaja suggests that the local Adygo-Alanic tribes had a special affinity with the motif, based on age-old beliefs—analogous to, and derived from, the significance of the boar in Sasanian royal ideology. This may well be so in view of the fixation on the image in its various permutations.

Only four different patterns occur in the caftan and leggings at the Metropolitan Museum (Kajitani, pp. 99–105). There are two variations of the boars' head, that is, the double-ax motif. In the first, more complex, form, pearl roundels are linked by miniature ones, in both the warp and the weft direction (Silk C1; Kajitani, Figure 34). The large orbs encompass confronted heads between split palmettes while heads without palmettes fill the spandrels. In the second, entirely stylized, pattern, the pearl roundels just touch in the weft direction but are not linked in that of the warp; there are simple double-axes within the orbs and in the spandrels (Silk A; Kajitani, Figures 28–30). The third pattern has horizontally linked pearl roundels containing star-shaped blossoms and smaller ones in the spandrels (Silk B; Kajitani, Figures

Figure 11. "Sogdian" silk with boar's head in spandrel, found at Moshchevaja Balka in 1905. Note the off-white strip at the right edge, also found on the Metropolitan Museum's caftan (see Kajitani, Figure 30). State Hermitage, Saint Petersburg, Kz 4675 (photo: W. Haberland, courtesy Bayerisches Nationalmuseum, Munich)

Figure 12. "Sogdian" silk with confronted boars' heads in spandrel, found at Moshchevaja Balka in 1974. State Hermitage, Saint Petersburg, Kz 6984 (photo: W. Haberland, courtesy Bayerisches Nationalmuseum, Munich)

Figure 13. "Sogdian" silk with star pattern in pearl roundels and spandrels and confronted boars' heads in pearl roundels in the bottom row, found at Moshchevaja Balka in 1905. State Hermitage, Saint Petersburg, Kz 4879 (photo: W. Haberland, courtesy Bayerisches Nationalmuseum, Munich)

31–33). Finally, the piece of fabric at the top of the better-preserved of the two leggings shows an unexpected change of design; the more complex boars' heads/double-ax pattern is here replaced by one of unframed dotted blossoms with rounded petals (Silk C2; Kajitani, Figure 36). Despite crucial disparities between the technically and artistically highly refined silks, which seem to have originated in Sogdia proper—specifically in Buchara and Samarkand—and the distinct double-ax group from Moshchevaja Balka, Ierusalimskaja includes them under the heading "Sogdian." This does not appear very convincing.[31] The iconographic peculiarities, the technical mediocrity, and the limited diffusion combine to suggest that the "Sogdian" silks were not produced in Sogdia proper as deliberately inexpensive fabrics with which to pay the transport tax or tariffs levied by the hill tribes, but were manufactured locally for home consumption or regional export. As we shall see, the draw looms required for that type of fabric can hardly have stood in the exposed settlements high up in the mountains. The looms may, however, have existed in any of the many fortified communities of the Saltovo-Majaki and Proto-Bulgarian cultures that are attested through excavations in the North Caucasian foothills and plains. All that was needed was silk yarn, which must have been considerably less expensive than woven patterned fabric and was probably levied as tax. The coveted products of Chinese or western looms, which were accessible only to individuals of status or as snippets by the poor, could have been imitated at lower cost and decorated with symbols and patterns that fitted local traditions. Ierusalimskaja briefly considers this scenario but dismisses it as implausible.[32]

The garments from Moshchevaja Balka are of exceptional interest not only for the textiles but also for the way in which they were cut. Here again, Ierusalimskaja's work has been fundamental. We summarize her conclusions. While female attire seems to have taken some of its inspiration from eastern Mediterranean models, the outfit of males follows Persian and Central Asian traditions.[33] The garb of the steppe nomads also exerted some influence. Ierusalimskaja stresses, however, a strong local component, distinctive of the Adygo-Alanic tribes of the central Caucasus, whose descendants, the modern Ossetians, are still settled there today.[34] Their ancestral garb, the caftan with wide skirt, was worn in the region until recently. Ierusalimskaja refers to the "karts," a fur coat of similar design common among the Ossetians in the central Caucasus. The Ossetians are of Alanic extraction

Figure 14. "Cherkeska," Caucasian coat with tightly fitted frogged upper part and skirtlike lower part, still worn locally (after Nancy Lindisfarne-Tapper and Bruce Ingham, eds., *Languages of Dress* [Richmond, Surrey, 1997], fig. 22; for description of the frogging in the illustration, see note 36 below)

and still speak an Iranian language. A lighter unlined linen caftan with frogging is called the "kurta," also an Iranian term.[35] Though cut without a collar, the well-known "cherkeska" must be of the same Iranian parentage (Figure 14).[36] An older yet seminal study provides the required wider perspectives.[37]

A Reappraisal of the Textiles from Moshchevaja Balka

Ierusalimskaja's emphasis on the domination of trade and its obstruction by the Sasanians as the compelling factors for the transfer of caravan routes to out-of-the-way passes of the northwestern Caucasus may be pertinent for the sixth and early seventh centuries.[38] But by the eighth to tenth century, to which the finds from Moshchevaja Balka and other sites in Ciscaucasia can be assigned with some degree of confidence, different political circumstances prevailed. The Arabs had subdued and replaced the Sasanians and had made deep inroads into Central Asia, which they finally con-

quered in the eighth to tenth century.[39] The North Caucasian and Transcaspian steppes up to the Aral Sea were part of the Khazar empire that also comprised the lower course of the Volga and the North Pontic plains. Of Turkic stock, the Khazars had embraced Judaism as their state religion.[40] They ruled over a great number and variety of tribes and they encouraged a highly lucrative trade. Most of the peoples subject to them and the groups of merchants they taxed appear in the sources either as already well known or as relative newcomers: Avars, Oguz, Bashkirs, Bulgars, Slavs, Varangians, and Rus. The culture and artifacts of these tribes became amalgamated into the existing traditions. Moreover, the political resurgence of Byzantium made itself felt in the region. Slowly emerging from the throes of iconoclasm, the Byzantine emperors reasserted control of parts of the Crimea and the northern shores of the Black Sea during the ninth century. Thus, contact with the Transcaucasian regions intensified, and mercantile patterns followed suit. At that time, one may indeed speak of a diversion of trade, however not in the sense stressed by Ierusalimskaja. The cause was Arab dominance of the Levant and northern Africa. It significantly curtailed seaborne commerce in the eastern Mediterranean but furthered it in the Black Sea and along the great Russian rivers, the Volga, Don, and Dnieper.

Among the most informative sources on the activities of those tribes, on political alliances and commercial activities between the late sixth and tenth centuries are literary documents. We shall refer to two that are especially enlightening for the period and the region under consideration. The first report is part of the *History* of Menander the Guardsman, a Byzantine author writing under the patronage of the emperor Maurice (582–602) who seems to have had access to the imperial archives.[41] The main Caucasian pass, the Darial/Porta Alanica, is at the heart of a sixth-century diplomatic mission conducted by the West Turkish ruler (khagan) of the name Istämi (Greek: Sizaboulos) to his western neighbors on behalf of Sogdian silk manufacturers and merchants, who had recently become his subjects and whose lucrative trade he strongly supported. The Western Turks had at first been allies of the Sasanians in defeating the Hephthalites or White Huns—a confederation of Iranian and Turkic groups—who had held sway over Central Asia for more than one hundred years. Under energetic and talented rulers, the Western Turks replaced the Hephthalites in Central Asia in the sixth century. Ongoing warfare between Byzantium and the Sasanians allowed the Turks to occupy Sasanian Afghanistan. They were now as powerful as both empires. Nomads by tradition, they incorporated into their policy fruitful collaboration with their sedentary subjects.

As mentioned, Istämi/Sizaboulos, the khagan of the Western Turks, sponsored a Sogdian embassy to the Sasanian court in 568 to obtain permission for the merchants to trade raw silk freely within Sasanian territory. The Sasanians tightly controlled the transit trade at the western end of the Silk Routes, as had the Parthians before them. The khagan's request was declined, and as a powerful signal, the Sasanian king bought the silk the Sogdians had brought and had it burned in the presence of the ambassadors. Greatly annoyed, the khagan now promoted a mission "via the Caucasus" to the Byzantine court asking for the same privilege, since the Sogdians knew that "they [the Romans = Byzantines] made more use of it [i.e., silk-yarn] than other people." Silk production had by then been established in Byzantine lands, but demand remained high. The Byzantine emperor responded by sending a return embassy under the general Zemarchos to Sogdia and to the khagan's itinerant court in Central Asia, where a deal was struck. Zemarchos's description of the most lavishly decked-out tent-residence demonstrates the importance of silk fabrics as a status symbol. Not only does his report represent a superb piece of early ethnography, it also vividly evokes the dangers and vicissitudes to which caravans or embassies were exposed. On the arduous way back into Byzantine lands, across waterless deserts and along "that enormous, wide lake"—it is not clear whether the Aral or the Caspian Sea is meant—the ambassador, protected by the khagan's guides and anxiously avoiding a Persian ambush, was finally kindly received by the king of the Alans in Ciscaucasia. To deceive the watchful Sasanians, the Alans advised Zemarchos to send the porters with their load of silk across the Caucasus through the region called Miusimia and—though it required a detour—to use himself the "Dareine road." Whether the "Miusimian" defile can be identified with today's Mamison Pass[42] that carries the Ossetian Highway is uncertain; the "Dareine road," however, clearly designates the Darial/Porta Alanica. Zemarchos safely reached the Black Sea, took one boat to Phasis and another one to Trapezus, and returned to Byzantium on horseback, provided by the imperial postal service. One cannot wish for a more informative sketch of the circumstances at a time when considerable amounts of raw silk were traded. As pointed out above, we believe that "Sogdian" silk was produced locally from imported raw materials. Menander's narration seems to support our hypothesis concerning silk weaving in the "land of the Alans." By the seventh century, the Chinese in their most daring westward foray ever, annihilated the empire of the Western Turks. It was replaced by that of the Khazars. Here, our second historical source gains relevance.

In 921–22, Ibn Fadlan, an expert in matters of Islamic religion, served as secretary of a large embassy sent from Baghdad by the Abbasid Khalif al-Muqtadir to and through the Khazar empire.[43] Bulgar, then still an encampment at the site of the yet to be built city, was located south of the confluence of the rivers Volga and Kama. At this northernmost point of the voyage, Ibn Fadlan had to present the khalif's message and gifts to the king of the Volga Bulgars, who was a Muslim. The Volga Bulgars were the most populous of the many tribes subject to the Khazars.[44] Ibn Fadlan's matter-of-fact yet very vivid report, completed in 923, attests to an ambitious political attempt on the part of the Abbasid empire to enter into friendly relations with the Khazars and the Turks. Access to the middle reaches of the Volga with its potential for trade was of great importance to the Arabs. It was the Khazars who had—exactly as during earlier attacks by the Sasanians—blocked the Arab advance across the Caucasus in the middle of the seventh century, and they continued to do so for almost one hundred years. The Arabs never gained lasting military access to the North Pontic plains, which definitely prevented them from attacking eastern Europe, while western Europe stood open to the Muslim armies after their capture of Spain. However, the constantly changing battlegrounds on either side of the Caucasus chains deeply affected the local mountain tribes.

As in the case of Zemarchos's mission, Ibn Fadlan's travelogue is a marvel of acute observation. Having proceeded from Baghdad via Hamadan, Rayy, and Bukhara to Gurganiya (Urganch) in Khwarizm, he and his companions joined a caravan of three thousand men and five thousand animals headed for the future town of Bulgar on the Volga.[45] These figures attest to the enormous volume of merchandise traded by the Arabs for northern goods: primarily slaves, but also furs, wax, honey, weapons, and other commodities. Tangible proof of the amount of exchange are the some hundred thousand Arabic dirhams of the early medieval period found on the island of Gotland and elsewhere in Scandinavia, in the Baltics, and in Russia.[46] The Russian rivers served as arterial roads for the northmen (Varangians) and, soon, for the Rus who established their kingdom in Kiev. They would topple the Khazar empire in the later tenth century.

Nothing escapes Ibn Fadlan. He comments on the climate, on the lay of the land, on trade, currency, and religion, and—most important in our context—on the customs and costumes of the multitude of tribes encountered along the way. Warned by the locals of the harsh winter, he provides his group with victuals for three months, and he lists the array of clothes considered necessary for the trip: "Everybody put on a qurtaq, then a caftan, above it a bustin (sheepskin coat) and on top of it a coat made of felt, together with a fur cap that left nothing but the eyes uncovered; simple underpants, quilted ones, followed by trousers; boots of soft leather and real boots. When mounting our camels, we were hardly able to move."[47] Moreover, Ibn Fadlan points out local differences of some interest for our study. The long or full "qurtaq" is worn by the Khazars, the Bulgars, and the Petchenegs, while the short one is characteristic of the Rus.[48] Qurtaq means "jacket," apparently available in various lengths. Caftan is an upper garment with overly long sleeves, often worn with a belt. Among other precious pieces of attire, Ibn Fadlan presents a Turkish commander—on whose hospitality he had to rely—with two qurtaqs which he has especially made for him out of "two suits of clothes from Merw."[49] We do not know what those suits looked like, but it seems that our ambassador felt they were not appropriate for the military man and had them adapted to local fashion. During his stay at the tent city of the king of the Volga Bulgars, he reports a conversation with "a tailor of the king, a man from Baghdad who had come to this region."[50] Ibn Fadlan's travelogue culminates in the description of the funeral of a trader of the Rus on the banks of the Volga.[51] He admires their build: "They are tall like date trees, blond and with such good circulation that they do not need qurtaqs or caftans but wear instead a kisa [= sleeveless woolen vest]." However, in death, the merchant from the north is decked out in costly oriental garments and fabrics especially tailored for the occasion: two pairs of trousers, qurtaq and caftan of brocade with gold buttons, a brocade cap trimmed with sable. According to custom, a young Rus servant girl is killed and cremated with the merchant to serve as his companion in the beyond. His boat functions as pyre. As a Muslim, the eyewitness Ibn Fadlan is simultaneously fascinated and appalled.

It is notoriously difficult to pinpoint the exact meaning of the various Persian, Arabic, or Turkic terms for attire used by contemporary authors.[52] However, the terminology reflects the ubiquity of garments developed and worn in the Asian steppe since at least the first millennium B.C. and destined to spread very widely. Originally fashioned of leather, felt, wool, or hemp, by late antiquity and in the early medieval period these garments were made of silk, by then a coveted material. A number of studies have traced the background of those "nomad" garments—sleeved coats and leggings specifically—which differ radically from the untailored clothes of the ancient Near East and the Classical world.[53] Over the last decades, this quest has been greatly furthered by spectacular textile finds. They generously supplement attempts to recreate the gamut of oriental clothes based on contemporary or later depictions.[54]

The few passages concerned with clothes that we have chosen from Ibn Fadlan's text are indicative of the international flavor of Khazar civilization. Commerce was its motor and its contacts were truly global. The apex of the Khazar khaganate partly coincided with that of the Chinese Tang dynasty in the eighth century, when Silk Route trade was at its height and firmly linked east and west. With Chang'an and Byzantium at the ends of that well-established axis, another one was added under the Khazars. Ibn Fadlan's voyage traces it at least up to the middle course of the Volga. It extended—upriver—north- and northwestward via the Volkhov, Neva, and Dvina during the eighth and ninth centuries and included the Don and Dnieper as of the tenth century. A network of portages and smaller rivers draining into the Baltic joined these routes with Northern Europe. Through excavations at various Scandinavian and Frisian sites, we are well informed about the Baltic and North Sea trade that handled the oriental merchandise. Settlements such as Birka, Kaupang, Hedeby/Haithabu, Ribe, and Dorestad served as entrepôts and meeting grounds for a truly international crowd. Many objects of eastern provenance have been recovered from sites and cemeteries, and evidence of a sartorial nature from tombs attests to the presence of Central Asians in the trading communities of the Norsemen.[55] They, in turn, adopted foreign fashions, among them sleeved jackets and lapelled coats. On their far-flung voyages, whether as raiders, traders, or mercenaries—for example at the Byzantine court—the Scandinavians and the Rus had ample opportunity to comprehend and appreciate garments that were splendid as well as serviceable. In the late tenth century, when the Kievian Rus overthrew the Khazar khaganate, trade along the Russian rivers diminished greatly.[56] Continuous warfare, the decline of the khalifate's central authority, and the depletion of the Central Asian silver mines were to blame. Frankish silver currency replaced the dirham in the North, and the improved European road system redirected traffic.[57]

THE METROPOLITAN MUSEUM'S CAFTAN: ITS LARGER CONTEXT AND ITS SPECIFIC FEATURES

It is time to return to our Caucasian coat. As shown above, it can be assigned approximately to the eighth to tenth century by the archaeological context of closely related finds. Having established the contemporaneous environment of the garment, we must now go beyond its immediate context to place the caftan in a larger setting. We shall attempt to trace the most characteristic features—the trimming, the lapels, and the frogs—to their earliest occurrence and follow their development over time. Our main sources in this process are two- or three-dimensional depictions. The three features we singled out are age-old, basic components of the accoutrements of peoples with varied ethnic backgrounds but a lifestyle dictated by the harsh steppe environment. The Museum's caftan is clearly a descendant of this nomadic apparel.

Fundamentally unchanged in cut and decoration for centuries, the traditional steppe costume, also worn by Parthians and Sasanians, spread widely when East Germanic peoples settled in the Pontic and Danube regions during the second to fourth century. Converts to local sartorial steppe traditions, these tribes were swept west by the invasion of the Huns in A.D. 375 and were soon recruited into the Roman army or assigned land at the eastern frontiers to defend them against further nomadic invasions.[58] Consequently, the importance of Germanic and Iranian military men and administrators in both East and West Rome rose steadily. As a consequence, their "barbarian," that is, their recently adopted steppe attire, became acceptable in the ancient centers of the classical world. The proximity of the Parthians to the Romans, and later the Sasanians to the Byzantine Empire, led to rivalry as well as alliances between them over extended periods. Inevitably, large-scale cultural cross-fertilization occurred. In other words, transmission of the steppe apparel was effected by the cohabitation of Germanic as well as Iranian powers within the later Roman Empire. Byzantium's nomadic neighbors were mostly of Turkic stock. Shared borders in the North Pontic and Caucasian plains also led to shared fashions.

The Silk Trimming

The silk trimming certainly has one of its roots in the embellishment of leather jackets or coats with rare furs so clearly depicted on fourth-century precious metal vessels with Scythian themes. The edges of the garments shown are adorned with costly pelts—easily distinguishable from the sheepskin body of the coats—and with embroidery and metal roundels (Figure 15).[59] The jackets are belted and close, Iranian fashion, on the proper left side of the body. They have no lapels. Woven garments received the same treatment. The rare full-length coats do not overlap at the front as documented by the example from Katanda (Figure 16).[60] Before silk was widely available in Central and Western Asia, the specific zones of jackets or coats—that is, seams, edges, and cuffs—were decorated with strips of embroidery or with woven bands.[61] By the time of the Western Han dynasty (206 B.C.– A.D. 8), silk trimming was a ubiquitous feature in the steppe environment.[62]

Silk had reached the nomad tribes from China by exchange or as "gifts"—in other words, as tribute extorted by them—late in the first millennium B.C. It became a commodity once the Silk Routes were established and commerce developed in an organized way. As demonstrated by the historical sources quoted above, trade between China and the West was controlled and directed by a succession of Iranian and Altaic dynasties who all had their roots in a nomadic environment: the Parthians (247 B.C.–A.D. 227), the Kushans,[63] the Sasanians (A.D. 227–651), the Chionites/Hephthalites (4th–6th centuries), the Turks (A.D. 552–742), and the Khazars (ca. A.D. 630–1016). Piping or trimming of the traditional steppe outfit, that is, jackets and coats of silk or other fabrics, was a standard feature under each of these empires, for garments of the upper class as well as for those of the common man.[64] Such trimming remained in fashion throughout the early medieval period in the Near East and Central Asia.

The Lapels

Lapels are not a feature found on Parthian, Kushan, or Sasanian caftans.[65] They do, however, occur in many variants on monuments in Central Asia, situated either in Hephthalite sites both north and south of the Hindukush (present-day southern Uzbekistan and Afghanistan), in Sogdian cities involved in the silk trade, or in Buddhist settlements at oases on the more southerly branches of the Silk Routes that ran through Chinese Central Asia (Xinjiang).[66] The wealthy appear in wall paintings, either feasting or as donors in sanctuaries from about A.D. 500 to about 800. A few examples must suffice. An important source is the large banqueting scene in the residence of a local grandee at Balalyk-tepe, north of Termez in southern Uzbekistan (Figure 17).[67] The large urban centers and the residences of the Sogdian nobility and merchant aristocracy in Afrasiab (Samarkand), Pendjikent, and other sites also furnish abundant depictions of both sexes in either single- or double-lapelled caftans and in sleeved coats, worn draped about the shoulders.[68] Farther south, in the oases at the edge of the Taklamakan desert, we once again see the native aristocracy and foreign merchants in comparable

Figure 15. Scythians in fur-trimmed leather coats with metal studs (clasps or buttons?) tied with strings. 4th century B.C. chased gold vessel from Kul Oba kurgan (Crimea). State Hermitage, Saint Petersburg, GE KO 11 (photo: Bruce White)

Figure 16. 5th–4th-century B.C. leather coat studded with gold-covered wooden ornaments, from Katanda kurgan (Altay). State Historical Museum, Moscow, 54660/1801 (after *The Oasis and Steppe Routes: Grand Exhibition of Silk Road Civilizations* [Nara, 1988], no. 137)

Figure 17. Mural with banqueting couples from a ruler's residence at Balalyk-tepe near Termez (Uzbekistan), early 7th century A.D. (after L. I. Albaum, *Balalyk-tepe: K istorii materialnoj kultury i iskusstva Tocharistana* [Tashkent, 1960], pl. 105)

outfits, now including leggings.[69] They are represented as donors and devotees in Buddhist cave sanctuaries (Figure 18).[70]

To resolve the question of the possible origin of the lapels, we briefly return to Menander's mission of 568 to the khagan of the Western Turks discussed above. The report makes evident that Sasanian predominance in the region had been replaced by ascendant Turkic confederations at approximately that time. Though differing ethnically from the native Iranians, the Turks were steppe dwellers, too, and wore the appropriate outfit. There is general agreement that regional fashions in Sogdia as well as in Xinjiang where the Turks held sway had been strongly influenced by the sartorial models of the long dominant Sasanian court. There are, however, important differences, notably that there is no evidence for the lapelled coat in the Sasanian realm. We are not yet in a position to state where the (eminently practical) lapels were first added to the age-old nomad outfit. It may have originated in a Turkic ambient. A fresh source of images has recently been investigated thoroughly and may corroborate our assumption: the stone statues of seated and standing males on grave mounds or in memorial monuments of Turkic tribes spread over a wide area between the Altay and Mongolia. They are dated to the sixth to eighth century (Figure 19). The authenticity of these costumes is validated by textile finds from Turkic burials (Figure 20).[71] The appearance and diffusion of the lapelled caftan seem to coincide with the ascendancy of the Turkic tribes as successful builders of empires.[72] It is worth remembering that it was the khan of the Western Turks who lived the life of a nomad ruler but supported and sponsored the activities of the Sogdian merchant aristocracy. Such contact zones facilitated assimilation.

The Frogs (Proto-Buttons)

The final, and perhaps most elusive, feature that requires consideration is the frog closing. From our modern perspective, frogging seems intimately connected with East Asian clothes. In the Far East, buttons and loops, both fashioned from fabric, appear to be a hallmark of traditional garment fastening. A closer look, however, reveals that frogging seems unattested before the Tunguse Jurchen state—known as the Northern Song dynasty in China—in the early twelfth century (Figure 21).[73] This observation is corroborated by the absence of a term for frogging in the traditional Chinese lexica. It may indicate the age-old Chinese contempt for the habits of "barbarians" who had not reached the necessary level of civilization

to qualify as partners of the Central Kingdom. The modern Chinese colloquial term, *panniu*, "twisted fastener," is purely descriptive and does not reveal anything etymologically or historically.[74] We may thus assume that frogs were an alien feature, introduced into China comparatively late from the nomad realm. Being a relatively minor detail, they are not easy to pinpoint in their Central Asian avatar. It appears that they are shown on some of the "balbals" mentioned above. They are attested in depictions of foreign (Sogdian?) merchants in the Buddhist cave paintings at the northern edge of the Tarim Basin, specifically in Cave 20 at Bezelik near Turfan. They become a salient feature of the finds at Moshchevaja Balka and similar sites. Despite a dearth of depictions, a virtual explosion in the use of frogs must have taken place among the Bulgars, the Rus, and the Slavs (Figure 22), all subjects of the Turkic Khazars. The latter were probably the propagators of certain sartorial features of the New York caftan and its relatives.

The multicultural character of the Khazar empire that was entirely based on trade created ideal circumstances for the dissemination of cultural artifacts. Its influence extended to neighboring Byzantium. The so-called scaramangion, a splendid court dress often mentioned in the "Book of Ceremonies" by the emperor Constantine VII Porphyrogenetus (912–959), seems to have been cut like the Museum's caftan and fitted with froglike features.[75] Practical and decorative at the same time, frogging is found somewhat later in abundance[76] and as a permanent feature in late medieval Russia on caftans and sleeved coats. These frogs no longer resemble the simple contraptions found on the New York garment; instead, they are rather elaborate mechanisms fashioned from precious metal threads. Not content with the functional double strap, embroidery and studs are added, resulting in the characteristic "galloons." As decorative features, they took Western Europe by storm in the sixteenth century and became known under the name "brandebourgs" from the seventeenth century on. The term is indicative of Eastern descent, even if, as we have seen, it comes from regions much more remote than the realm of the Elector of Brandenburg. He and his counterparts in Central and Eastern Europe, whose attire drew heavily on "oriental" models because of the proximity and long cohabitation with peoples originating from the steppe, became the mediators of an age-old functional device (Figure 23).[77] Precious metal frogs on caftans and related upper garments are a standard feature in post-Mongol Persia, best documented in a multitude of miniatures, which often extol the heroic history of the country (Figure 24). An early twentieth-century photograph attests to the

Figure 18. Mural with family of noble donors and Buddhist monks. The older males wear caftans with double lapels, the younger ones with single lapels (perhaps an indication of lower rank) and leggings, from Cave 19, Qumtura, Xinjiang (China), 7th century A.D. (?) (after Albert von LeCoq, *Bilderatlas zur Kunst und Kulturgeschichte Mittel-Asiens* [Berlin, 1923], fig. 11)

Figure 19. Stone statue of seated Turkic grandee in belted patterned silk caftan with two lapels from memorial monument in Mongolia, 6th–8th century A.D. (after Dovdoin Bayar, *Turkic Stone Statues of Central Mongolia* [Ulan Bator, 1997], p. 124, fig. 79; courtesy of Gleb Kubarev)

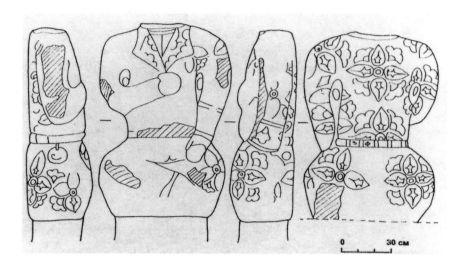

Figure 20. Reconstruction by G. V. Kubarev and D. V. Pozdnyakov of two Old Turkic caftans on the basis of textile finds at Yustud XXIV, barrow 13 (left), and at Altai-Barburgaza I, barrow 20 (right), (after G. V. Kubarev, *Archaeology, Ethnology and Anthropology of Eurasia* 3, no. 3 [2000], fig. 4)

Figure 21. Group of Mongolian entertainers in frogged caftans from tomb of Jiao Zuojin in Xifengfeng, Henan Province (China), Jin Dynasty (1115–1234) (after Shen Congwen, *Zhongguo gudai fushi yangjiu* [Hong Kong, 1992], p. 429, fig. 203)

persistence of the frogged caftan in the Near East until modern times (Figure 25). The Turkic Ottomans played an important role as mediators. Encroaching ever more on Central Europe during the sixteenth and seventeenth centuries, their presence also contributed to the adoption of frogging in the West. For Western Europe, the exotic "galloons" clearly became a mark of wealth and distinction (Figure 26). Both the Persian Il-Khans and the Ottomans were largely of Turkic stock and thus heirs to the sartorial tradition we have been investigating.[78]

CONCLUSION

At the end of this inquiry into seemingly minor features, we should ask whether the Metropolitan Museum's caftan and its North Caucasian relatives

Figure 22. Heathen Bulgar in frogged caftan slaying Christian martyrs. Detail of miniature in the Menologion of the Byzantine emperor Basil II (r. 976–1025). Byzantine (Constantinople), ca. 985. Tempera and gold on vellum, 36.5 x 28.5 cm. Biblioteca Apostolica Vaticana, Vat. gr. 1613, fol. 345 (photo: Vatican)

Figure 23. Hungarian nobleman in frogged caftan. Woodcut (after Cesare Vecellio [1521–1601], *Vecellio's Renaissance Costume Book: All 500 Woodcut Illustrations from the Famous Sixteenth-Century Compendium of World Costume* [reprint, New York, 1977], fig. 403)

Figure 24. The first Sasanian king Ardashir (r. 226–41) recognizes the royal descent of his grandson Hormuzd by the way the latter recovers the hockey ball from under the horse. Persian miniature of the 16th century. Bayerische Staatsbibliothek, Munich, Persian MS 10, fol. 533v (photo: Bayerische Staatsbibliothek)

were—in view of their special cut—indeed a local phenomenon. Anna Ierusalimskaja, to whom we owe immense gratitude for making this material accessible and intelligible, sees the caftan, because of its long survival in the region, essentially as an indigenous product that differs from other Eastern examples in having a skirtlike lower part attached to a tight-fitting top. Indeed, at first sight it appears to lack obvious convincing parallels. However, a few specimens invite comparison, first from the Byzantine realm. Depictions of the wide array of garments we know were worn at the Byzantine court are limited. The strictness of the protocol and the quasi-religious context of the extant images deprive us of detailed representations. Yet the splendor and variety of the costumes worn by the emperors and their bureaucracy are evident from the written sources.[79] As in the case of Persian, Turkic, and Arab terminology, the Greek sartorial vocabulary can rarely be reconciled with the few surviving images or garments. In a number of significant cases, however, the impact of foreign models can be demonstrated. It is noteworthy that they are dated to the Khazar khaganate, that is, to the post-Sasanian period to which the caftan in New York belongs.[80] A somewhat later chance find furnishes tangible proof. The recently discovered caftan of red silk, with splendid golden embroidery and studs along the front, the

Figure 25. 'Abbas 'Ali Khan, supervisor of the Royal Photography Studio (left) with Mohammad Baqer (right), a page of 'Ayn al-Molk. Early 20th century (after *A Treasury of Early Iranian Photography*)

Figure 26. Aelbert Cuyp (Dutch, 1620–1691). *Starting for the Hunt: Michiel (1638–1653) and Cornelis Pompe van Meerdervoort (1639–1680) with Their Tutor and Coachman.* Oil on canvas, 109.9 x 156.2 cm. The Metropolitan Museum of Art, The Friedsam Collection, Bequest of Michael Friedsam, 1931 (32.100.20)

Figure 27. King Saul in belted, single-lapelled caftan that closes on the left; he is pointing at David and Goliath. Relief from the south façade of the Armenian church of the Holy Cross at Aght'amar (eastern Turkey), 10th century (after Sirarpie der Nersessian, *Armenian Art* [London, 1978], fig. 87)

Figure 28. Giorgi IV Lasha and his mother, Thamar, queen of Georgia; he wears a belted trimmed caftan, and she wears Byzantine court dress. 13th-century mural in the church of Betania (Georgia) (after Rusudan Mepisashvili and Vakhtant Tsintsadze, *The Arts of Ancient Georgia* [London, 1979], p. 199)

edges, and the sleeves and with a gathered skirt, from the burial mound of a Polovcian khan in Ukraine, has all the features of the more modest New York garment.[81] According to the excavators, it was fashioned in Byzantium in the thirteenth century and reached the North Pontic steppe as a gift or tribute. That may well be the case. Yet Byzantine manufacture does not contradict the basic steppe background of this caftan. As part of the trade network that connected it with Central and East Asia, the Byzantine civilization was subject to influences from that zone over time, but it also dispatched its own cultural messages into it. As close neighbors of Byzantium, the Christian Armenians and Georgians evince such influences. Between the seventh and the thirteenth centuries, the sculpted or painted donor figures on their churches display a variety of caftans and draped, sleeved coats (Figures 27, 28).[82] Another observation may reinforce this analysis. Though mostly closing Chinese fashion on

the right and lacking lapels, the caftans worn by the Mughal emperors and their retinue (Figure 29) are constructed exactly like the one in New York.[83]

As a last point, to demonstrate the multiple links that connect the Metropolitan's caftan with the wider world of Central Asia, mention should be made of a set of miniature garments recovered at various times in the Moshchevaja Balka cemetery and called "doll's clothes" by Ierusalimskaja (Figure 30).[84] Since no remains of dolls were ever found at the site, a different function for these miniature outfits should be considered. During recent excavations of a burial ground at Yingpan in the Lop Nor region of Xinjiang, China, a mummified male, wearing a mask, was found with all his clothes preserved. Exceptionally precious, these garments are neither of local nor of Chinese manufacture but clearly point to Central Asia, if not the eastern Mediterranean, as their place of origin. At the belt of the man's caftan was placed a superbly tailored

Figure 29. Mughal period (1526–1857) courtiers in white caftans, some closing on the left, others in the center of the body. *Maharaja Sidh Sen Receiving an Embassy*, ca. 1700–1710, by the Mandi Master (Punjab Hills). Ink and opaque watercolor on paper, 37 x 27 cm. The Metropolitan Museum of Art, Purchase, Florence and Herbert Irving Gift and Rogers Fund, 1995 (1995.39)

natural that a region deeply involved in the transit trade should take sartorial inspiration both from the commodities it handled and from the foreign traders who passed through. An extraordinary set of eighth- to ninth-century documents from the burial ground at Moshchevaja Balka epitomizes the truly global connections of the site. These are papers and objects that may have belonged to a Chinese merchant.[87] They include a list of locally made purchases of victuals, a Buddhist text (sutra), and religious images painted on silk and fragments of a small Buddhist votive banner. Contrary to a widely held belief that merchants from either end of the Silk Routes rarely traveled the entire way but rather used middlemen to execute transactions in stages, these documents attest to exceptions. Seen in the light of this evidence, the complex ancestry of the Metropolitan Museum's caftan that we have tried to trace in this study appears quite persuasive. Each individual feature of this splendid coat can be shown to belong to the vast realm of the nomads whose contribution to world history and culture is becoming ever more apparent.[88]

Figure 30. "Doll's clothes" from Moshchevaja Balka; note the frogged linen kaftan with "Mandarin" collar and the trimmed coat. State Hermitage, Saint Petersburg, Kz 6726–6728 (caftan, dress, and trousers found in 1972), Kz 4872 (coat found in 1905), Kz 6718 (boot found in 1974) (photo: W. Haberland, courtesy Bayerisches Nationalmuseum, Munich)

miniature silk outfit, suggesting a "change of clothes" for the beyond. This is not an isolated feature in Chinese Turkestan (Xinjiang). The drawing of the miniature clothes reveals the upper garment—though closing on the right side and secured with ribbons, not with frogs—to be constructed exactly like the Metropolitan Museum caftan.[85] The deceased may have been a wealthy merchant from Sogdia or even from the late Roman East. The find is certainly earlier than the objects from the Moshchevaja Balka cemetery. Perhaps similar ideas were current among the "heathen" Adygo-Alans. However this may be, the "doll's clothes" from Moshchevaja Balka also confirm that a variety of options for the cut of caftans and caftan collars was available locally, among them "Mandarin" and "kimono" types (see Figure 30).[86] The famous senmurv caftan from the site mentioned earlier has lapels on both sides (see Figure 5). It seems only

ACKNOWLEDGMENTS

I would like to thank Prudence O. Harper for entrusting me with the publication of the Caucasian coat. Nobuko Kajitani has been a source of inspiration for the textile technology and conservation neophyte. I am, as so often, deeply grateful to Joan Mertens, whose sense of style and proportion has saved this study from many infelicities. Responsibility for the opinions expressed here rests with me alone.

ABBREVIATIONS

Barber
  Elizabeth W. Barber. *The Mummies of Urümchi.* New York and London, 1999.

Ierusalimskaja
  Anna A. Ierusalimskaja. *Die Gräber der Moščevaja Balka: Frühmittelalterliche Funde an der nordkaukasischen Seidenstrasse.* Ed. Bayerisches Nationalmuseum, Munich, and State Hermitage, Saint Petersburg. Munich, 1996.

Ierusalimskaja and Borkopp
  Anna A. Ierusalimskaja and Birgitt Borkopp. *Von China nach Byzanz: Frühmittelalterliche Seiden aus der Staatlichen Ermitage Sankt Petersburg.* Ed. Bayerisches Nationalmuseum, Munich, and State Hermitage, Saint Petersburg. Munich, 1996.

Otavsky
  Karel Otavsky. "Zur kunsthistorischen Einordnung der Stoffe." In *Entlang der Seidenstrasse: Frühmittelalterliche Kunst zwischen Persien und China in der Abegg-Stiftung,* pp. 119–214. Riggisberger Berichte 6. Ed. Karel Otavsky. Riggisberg, 1998.

PW
  Paulys Realencyclopädie der classischen Altertumswissenschaft. Ed. Georg Wissowa, and Wilhelm Kroll et al. Stuttgart, 1894–1980.

Roth
  Helmut Roth. Review of Ierusalimskaja. *Byzantinische Zeitschrift* 92, no. 2 (1999), pp. 523–29.

Tilke 1923
  Max Tilke. *Orientalische Kostüme in Schnitt und Farbe.* Berlin, 1923.

Tilke 1925
  Max Tilke. *Osteuropäische Volkstrachten in Schnitt und Farbe.* Berlin, 1925.

Togan
  A. Zeki Validi Togan. *Ibn Fadlān's Reisebericht.* Abhandlungen für die Kunde des Morgenlandes 24, no. 3. Leipzig, 1939; reprint Nendeln, Liechtenstein, 1966.

Werbart
  Bozena Werbart. "Khazars or 'Saltovo-Majaki Culture'? Prejudices about Archaeology and Ethnicity." *Current Swedish Archaeology* 4 (1996), pp. 199–221.

Widengren
  Geo Widengren. "Some Remarks on Riding Costume and Articles of Dress among Iranian Peoples in Antiquity." In *Arctica: Essays Presented to Åke Campbell,* pp. 228–75. Studia Ethnographica Upsaliensia 11. Uppsala, 1956.

von Wilckens
  Leonie von Wilckens. Review of Ierusalimskaja, and Ierusalimskaja and Borkopp. *Kunstchronik* 50, no. 6 (1997), pp. 249–57.

NOTES

1. For well-preserved garments from the deserts of Central Asia, see, e.g., Barber; J. P. Mallory and Victor Mair, *The Tarim Mummies: Ancient China and the Mystery of the Earliest Peoples from the West* (London, 2000); *Archaeological Treasures of the Silk Road in Xinjiang Uygur Autonomous Region,* exh. cat. (Shanghai, 1998).

2. A 4th-century A.D. text attesting to this feature so specific to mounted tribes is Ammianus Marcellinus's comment on the dress of the Persian (Sasanian) adversaries of the Romans under Emperor Julian the Apostate during his Mesopotamian campaign in 363: they wear bright-colored tunics open (that is, not sewn up) in front and at the sides (*indumentis . . . sinus lateraque dissuta; Rerum gestarum libri* 23.6.84). A disposition of the Abbey of Beaulieu near Limoges, France, of A.D. 971 decrees that a serf or his descendants cannot be promoted to the rank of an arms-bearing soldier (*miles*) and must not wear a garment slit in front or behind (*non habeant vestem scissam de antea et de retro*), a privilege of the mounted nobility; *Cartulaire de l'abbeye de Beaulieu en Limousin,* Maximin Deloche, ed. (Paris, 1854), pp. 91–93, cited by Franco Cardini, *Alle radici della cavalleria medievale* (Florence, 1981), p. 324. The feature is documented in countless representations of knights and members of the upper social strata on horseback in the medieval West as well as of eastern horsemen, be they depicted by their own artists or seen by Westerners. As a practical device, the riding coat with slits clearly was adopted and retained in the West during the Migration Period. The term *redingote* (= riding coat), that is, a long, double-breasted coat with a slit, encapsulates the concept. The slits are clearly visible in a number of early Sasanian grafitti at Persepolis depicting mounted nobility; see Peter Calmeyer, "Zur Genese altiranischer Motive, V, Synarchie," *Archäologische Mitteilungen aus Iran,* n.s. 9 (1976), pp. 63–95, figs. 3, 4.

3. Similar designs are found in Near Eastern, Baltic, and Eastern European folk costumes; see, e.g., Tilke 1923, pls. 54, 57, 61; and Tilke 1925, pls. 36, 51. Also Ilmari Manninen, "Die Kleidung," *Kansatieteellinen Arkisto* 13 (1957)—a very useful survey of the costumes of the Finno-Ugric peoples—figs. 113, 117f., 120f., 131, and pp. 132–35.

   The humplike accent at the hip occurs as a constant feature

in a great many of the splendid silk caftans worn by the Ottoman sultans between the late 15th and the 18th centuries and preserved in Istanbul. They also close on the left with multiple buttons—attached to the edge of the right breast—and frogs, not unlike the Metropolitan's caftan. We shall see that this tradition seems to be a legacy of early medieval Turkic tribes. See Hülye Tezcan and Selma Delibaş, *The Topkapi Saray Museum: Costumes, Embroideries and Other Textiles,* trans. and ed. J. M. Rogers from Turkish (New York, 1986); and *Palace of Gold and Light: Treasures from the Topkapi, Istanbul,* exh. cat., Corcoran Gallery of Art (Washington, D.C., 2000).

4. Although the pair has feet, we prefer the term *leggings* to *stockings,* because the use of precious silk suggests a decorative function. See, in this volume, Kajitani, p. 98. Low boots must have been worn with them, perhaps of the kind found at Moshchevaja Balka; see Ierusalimskaja and Borkopp, no. 25; and Ierusalimskaja, pp. 54–56, 156–57, nos. 336–347, and pl. 77, fig. 204.

5. See Ierusalimskaja, 343 pp., 88 pls. with 228 figs., 18 line drawings in the text; and Ierusalimskaja and Borkopp, 108 pp. with black-and-white and color figs. The first volume is a catalogue and interpretation of the most important objects found at this site and preserved in the Hermitage; the second is the catalogue of an exhibition in Munich (October 25, 1996–January 26, 1997) presenting only the choicest objects from Moshchevaja Balka and other North Caucasian sites in the Hermitage. This catalogue presents excellent technical analyses of the textiles. For a review of both works, see von Wilckens; and for an important review of Ierusalimskaja, see Roth, who provides an English military map giving the exact location of the site.

6. See Ierusalimskaja, p. 17; the local population apparently considered the tombs to be those of Christian saints.

7. For the history of the investigation of the site, see Ierusalimskaja, pp. 17–20; Ierusalimskaja and Borkopp, pp. 9–12; and Roth, pp. 523f.

8. She has augmented the holdings in the Hermitage by one-third. Other scholars have continued the exploration of the site, and the objects found are kept in various North Caucasian museums. They remain unpublished; see Ierusalimskaja, p. 20; and Roth, p. 524.

9. See note 5 above. Unfortunately, in Ierusalimskaja the original Russian titles of her rich bibliography were translated into German. Her sources thus cannot be traced. In addition, she did not summarize the findings of the scholars she refers to. Access to information of primary importance is thus effectively blocked for the non-Russian-speaking reader. Except for a bare handful of titles, there is no bibliography in Ierusalimskaja and Borkopp.

10. The detailed categorization and interpretation of the various kinds of objects in Ierusalimskaja is useful but tends to be somewhat repetitive; it also entails many inconsistencies. Roth, pp. 525–29, draws attention to them in detail.

11. See Roth, pp. 527f., who favors dates between the 8th and 10th centuries, against Ierusalimskaja's 8th to 9th century.

Besides the vessels published in Ierusalimskaja and in Ierusalimskaja and Borkopp, see Alexander Leskov, *Grabschätze der Adygeen: Neue Entdeckungen im Nordkaukasus* (Munich, 1990), no. 262, fig. 213; and Werbart, fig. 6, p. 214.

12. See Ierusalimskaja, pp. 234ff. For the uncertainties of dating and locating silks, see von Wilckens; Roth, p. 526. See also the review by David Jacoby, *Byzantinische Zeitschrift* 92, no. 2 (1999), pp. 536–38, of Anna Muthesius, *Byzantine Silk Weaving AD 400 to AD 1200* (Vienna, 1997). Muthesius, p. 95, accepts Ierusalimskaja's dates as firmly based on archaeological evidence—clearly a risky assumption. However, the valiant attempt to define the character and date of a group of "Central Asian" textiles recently acquired by the Abegg Foundation in Riggisberg, Switzerland, demonstrates what can be achieved by a concerted effort: *Entlang der Seidenstrasse: Frühmittelalterliche Kunst zwischen Persien und China in der Abegg-Stiftung,* Riggisberger Berichte 6, ed. Karel Otavsky (Riggisberg, 1998). Apparently recovered from Tibetan burials, these silks emulate Sasanian patterns and may have been produced in China (Sichuan) in the 7th to 8th century. The results of an interdisciplinary colloquium at the Abegg Foundation, "Textile Art between Persia and China in the Early Middle Ages," October 7–8, 1999, to be published as Riggisberger Berichte 9, will throw additional light on the problem.

13. Ierusalimskaja varies in her designation of that culture: Alano-Saltovan or Adygo-Alanic, probably to indicate the circumscribed region of the northern Caucasus. The culture, which encompassed a wide area, takes its name from the hill fort Verchneje Saltovo on the Donets, not far from Charkov (Ukraine) and the Majaki hill fort near the river Don; see Werbart, p. 201. A. Belinsky and H. Härke, "Cemetery Excavations at Klin Yar, North Caucasus, 1993–94," *Newsletter of the Centre for the Archaeology of Central and Eastern Europe* 3 (1995), pp. 4–5, report on one hundred excavated Alanic tombs containing many Khazar metal objects. For the Alans, see below, note 18; for the Khazars, note 40.

14. The most important findspot there is Khasaut, southwest of Kislovodsk. For examples, see Ierusalimskaja and Borkopp, where the concordance (pp. 106–8) facilitates identification of the pieces.

15. See Ierusalimskaja, no. 24, pls. 73f., figs. 196f., where an early-9th-century date is convincingly argued (confirmed by von Wilckens, pp. 252f.); Ierusalimskaja and Borkopp, no. 1, figs. 1 and 1a; see also Krishna Riboud, "A Newly Excavated Caftan from the Northern Caucasus," *Textile Museum Journal* 4, no. 3 (1976), pp. 21–42; Anna A. Jeroussalimskaja, "Le cafetan aux simourghs du tombeau de Mochtchevaja Balka (Caucase Septentrional)," *Studia Iranica* 7, no. 2 (1978), pp. 183–211, pls. 1–14. The caftan is occasionally figured closed on the wrong side—a regrettable mistake, e.g., *Cultural Contacts between East and West in Antiquity and Middle Ages from USSR* (in Japanese), exh. cat., Tokyo National Museum; Museum of Art, Osaka (Tokyo, 1985), no. 121; and—strangely—Anna A. Ierusalimskaja, *Kavkaz na shelkovom puti* (The Caucasus on the Silk Road), exh. cat. (Saint Petersburg, 1992), no. 1, figs. 1f., p. 35. A line drawing of the caftan in Csanád Bálint, *Die Archäologie der Steppe: Steppenvölker zwischen Volga und Donau vom 6. bis zum 10. Jahrhundert* (Cologne, 1989), p. 29, fig. 7, 2, shows the relevant features more clearly than a black-and-white photo. A senmurv is a mythical animal: a winged dog's forepart with a peacock's tail.

16. Although focused on the Black Sea, the article "Pontos Euxeinos," *PW,* suppl. 9 (1962), cols. 866–1175 (Danoff), contains a wealth of information on every aspect of the region. See also *PW* 11, 1 (1921), s.v. "Kaukasos," cols. 59–62 (Herrmann). For a conspectus of archaeological finds in the western Caucasus, see Leskov, *Grabschätze der Adygeen* (note 11 above). See also *National Treasures of Georgia,* ed. O. Z. Soltes (London, 1999); and Kristin M. Romey, "Land of the Golden Fleece: Legendary Colchis Lives On in the Republic of Georgia," *Archaeology* 54, no. 2 (March–April 2001), pp. 28–35.

17. See *PW* 5, 1 (1903), s.v. "Dioskurias," cols. 1123–25 (Tomaschek); David Braund, *Georgia in Antiquity: A History of Colchis and Transcaucasian Iberia 550 BC–AD 562* (Oxford, 1994); Gocha Tsetskhladze, *Die Griechen in der Kolchis (historisch-archäologischer Abriss)* (Amsterdam, 1998); idem, "Cultural History of Colchis (6th–1st Centuries B.C.)," Ph.D. diss., University of Oxford, 1998 (British Library Document Supply Center), was not accessible to me. In our context, it is worth noting that Colchic linen was much appreciated in antiquity, as was hemp, endemic in the North Pontic plains, and mentioned already by Herodotus (4.74) as a Scythian material. He comments on the difficulty of distinguishing between linen and hemp. It was much used for garments (however, only occasionally in the finds from Moshchevaja Balka, where linen prevails). See *PW* 6, 2 (1909), s.v. "Flachs," cols. 2435–84, esp. col. 2450 (Olck); *PW*, suppl. 9 (1962), cols. 1001f.; and Victor Hehn, "Der Flachs: Der Hanf," in *Kulturpflanzen und Haustiere in ihrem Übergang aus Asien nach Griechenland und Italien sowie in das übrige Europa,* 9th ed. (Leipzig, 1963), pp. 164–93.

18. For Armenia, see A. E. Redgate, *The Armenians* (Oxford, 1998); for the Alans, Vladimir Kouznetsov and Iaroslav Lebedynsky, *Les Alains: Cavaliers des steppes, seigneurs du Caucase* (Paris, 1997); *Dal mille al mille: Tesori e popoli dal Mar Nero,* exh. cat. (Milan, 1995), chaps. 4–6; and Michel Kazanski and Anna Mastykova, "Le Caucase du nord et la région méditerranée aux 5ᵉ–6ᵉ siècles," *Eurasia Antiqua* 5 (1999), pp. 523–73, for trade and foreign contacts as documented in the Alan region in the vicinity of Kislovodsk. For a rich documentation on the Alans, see Gherardo Gnoli, "Il nome degli Alani nelle iscrizioni sassanidi: Considerazioni linguistiche e storiche sul tema dell'opposizione tra Iran esterno e Iran interno," in *Il Caucaso: Cerniera fra culture dal Mediterraneo alla Persia,* Settimane di studio del Centro italiano di studi sull'alto medioevo 43 (Spoleto, 1996), pp. 831–66.

19. Ierusalimskaja, passim; Ierusalimskaja and Borkopp, p. 12.

20. See *PW* 11, 1 (1921), s.v. "Kaukasiai Pylai," col. 58 (Adler); *PW* 4, 1 (1900), s.v. "Δαρεινὴ ἀτραπός," cols. 2183f. (Tomaschek). See also *Encyclopaedia Britannica* (1957), s.v. "Caucasus." Braund, *Georgia in Antiquity,* provides a map (no. 2) of the Caucasian passes with some of their names.

21. Ierusalimskaja, pp. 119f. and passim.

22. Ierusalimskaja, p. 120, misspells the antique names. Roth, p. 524, corrects the name of the pass: Tsagekhulir. Braund, *Georgia in Antiquity,* provides the Greek names on map 3, the names in the Roman period on map 6. Maps 2 and 3 give the present names of the rivers. For a micro-analysis of the dense network of trade routes across and along the Caucasus chain, see H. A. Mamandian, *The Trade and Cities of Armenia in Relation to Ancient World Trade,* 2nd rev. ed., trans. Nina G. Garsoian, Armenian Library of the Calouste Gulbenkian Foundation, no. 12 (Lisbon, 1965), reference owed to Helmut Roth.

23. Ierusalimskaja, pp. 120f. For another report on such payment practices, see Sir Robert Ker Porter, *Travels in Georgia, Persia, Armenia, Ancient Babylonia etc. etc. during the Years 1817, 1818, 1819 and 1820* (London, 1821), p. 80, with a suggestive engraving (pl. 3) of the Darial defile (Terek gorge). Von Wilckens, p. 252, questions Ierusalimskaja's concept by referring to the widespread European habit of furnishing the deceased with used and mended clothes instead of new ones. Hence, the patchwork might rather be the result of funerary clothes being put together from worn garments. I wish to thank William Hanaway for his translation of the Persian captions for Figures 10 and 25.

24. For Bohemia, see Georg Jacob, *Arabische Berichte von Gesandten an germanische Fürstenhöfe aus dem 9. und 10. Jahrhundert* (Berlin and Leipzig, 1927), p. 13. The 11th-century author Al-Bekri, drawing on information by the 10th-century Jewish merchant Ibrahim Ibn Jaqub, reports on the "currency" of the country: small, loosely woven pieces of cloth, which are the inhabitants' assets and are useless for any other purpose than payment for goods. For Ukraine, a country famous for its linen and hemp, see "The Journey of William of Rubruck," in *The Mongol Mission: Narratives and Letters of the Franciscan Missionaries in Mongolia and China in the Thirteenth and Fourteenth Centuries,* ed. Christopher Dawson (New York, 1955), pp. 87–220, esp. p. 93: "cotton" serves as payment ("dant duas telas de cotone"). Cotton had been introduced from India to Europe by the Arabs; see Hehn, *Kulturpflanzen und Haustiere,* pp. 515f.; and *PW* 3, 1 (1897), s.v. "Baumwolle," cols. 167–73 (Wagler). Rubruck was apparently familiar with the designation. Whether cotton was grown in Ukraine already in the 13th century, I cannot judge; the Franciscan may have mistaken hemp for cotton. Rubruck returned from his mission to the Great Khan in Mongolia via the pass of Derbent at the Caspian, of which he gives a gripping description.

25. Ierusalimskaja, pp. 233–38.

26. The literature on this topic is vast; for a recent summary, see Elfriede R. Knauer, *The Camel's Load in Life and Death: Iconography and Ideology of Chinese Pottery Figurines from Han to Tang and Their Relevance for Trade along the Silk Routes* (Zurich, 1998), pp. 30–33; and Otavsky.

27. This is not the place to enter into the ongoing discussion on "Sogdian" silk. Ierusalimskaja, p. 116 (see also pp. 131, 237), bases her arguments mainly on two studies by D. G. Shepherd: Shepherd and W. B. Henning, "Zandanījī Identified?" in *Aus der Welt der islamischen Kunst: Festschrift für Ernst Kühnel,* ed. Richard Ettinghausen (Berlin, 1959), pp. 15–40; Shepherd, "Zandanījī Revisited," in *Documenta textilia: Festschrift für Sigrid Müller-Christensen,* ed. M. Flury-Lemberg and K. Stolleis (Munich, 1981), pp. 105–22; but see von Wilckens, p. 256, and Roth, p. 526. Otavsky, in his magisterial analysis (p. 201), convincingly summarizes the problem by questioning the validity of the "Zandanījī" concept: "Es scheint eher, dass es sich um einen Stil handelt, der sich im 8. und 9. Jahrhundert zwischen Kansu und Chorasan als eine späte, vulgarisierte Abwandlung des sasanidischen Textildekors entwickelte, möglicherweise im Zusammenhang mit der Verbreitung und Verbilligung der entsprechenden Webtechniken. Varianten dieses Stils, die schon A. A. Ierusalimskaja und Dorothy Shepherd beobachtet haben, *spiegeln wahrscheinlich weniger seine chronologische Entwicklung als die geographische Streuung seiner Zentren wider*" (my emphasis). The problem will be discussed in detail in Riggisberger Berichte 9 (note 12 above). See also Chris Verhecken-Lammens, "Weft Sequence and Weave Direction in 'Byzantine,' 'Egyptian' and 'Sogdian' Silk Samits of the 6th–10th Century," *Bulletin du CIETA* 77 (2000), pp. 34–44.

28. See the technical analysis, Kajitani, pp. 99–105, and Valery Golikov et al., "Experimental Research of Polychrome Sogdian Silk of the VIIIth–IXth Centuries from the Tcherkessk Museum Collection," in *Interdisciplinary Approach to the Study and Conservation of Medieval Textiles,* preprints for the Interim Meeting, ICOM, Palermo, October 22–24, 1998, ed. Rosalia Varoli-Piazza (Rome, 1998), pp. 133–39 (reference supplied by Nobuko Kajitani). Since the textile holdings from old and more recent excavations of many different cemeteries in the North Caucasian

museums remain unpublished, it seems premature to assume that the silk patterns of the Metropolitan Museum's caftan occur only at Moshchevaja Balka.

29. Ierusalimskaja, p. 267 (text to no. 86); also pp. 116, 131. For another sample with a single boar's head, see Golikov et al., "Experimental Research"; cf. Figure 11.

30. Still basic: Kurt Erdmann, "Eberdarstellung und Ebersymbolik in Iran," *Bonner Jahrbücher* 147 (1942), pp. 345–82. For examples of textiles or on wall paintings, see, e.g., Otavsky, figs. 89, 92, 94, 100, and Kajitani, Figure 43. In Sasanian iconography, the boar symbolizes the god of victory, Verethragna; see the contribution by A. D. H. Bivar, in Riggisberger Berichte 9 (note 12 above).

31. See note 27 above.

32. Ierusalimskaja, p. 131. Cf. Kajitani's suggestions, pp. 99–105.

33. Ierusalimskaja, chap. 3, "Kleidung": pp. 41–45, "Frauengewänder"; pp. 45–54, "Männerkleidung"; and pp. 57f., the summary; on p. 53, she declares—among other features—as unique the construction of the women's shirts from narrow pieces. However, interesting parallels to these shirts are to be found in the linen garments of Finno-Ugric tribes. The silk trimming is here replaced by embroidery; there also occur comparable asymmetric neck openings of shirts composed of narrow pieces of material; see Manninen, "Die Kleidung," p. 107, who hints at the range of the type (Caucasus, Persia, Turkistan, Afghanistan, Kashmir, Egypt, and Morocco); see his figs. 86f., 91f. See also Tilke 1923, pls. 51, 82, 90; and Tilke 1925, pls. 64, 67, depicting shirts with asymmetrical necklines, very reminiscent of female shirts from Moshchevaja Balka. According to him, the asymmetrical neck opening is a typical "Persian" trait. Since he pictures "modern" garments, this is correct; in the context of our study, one would speak of "Iranian." This puts the women's shirts into a much wider frame, perhaps less dependent on Mediterranean than on "steppe" models. It is helpful to remember that the Byzantine official and historian Priscus, in his report on the embassy he led to the court of Attila the Hun in 449, describes a visit he pays to Kreka, the wife of Attila. He finds her in her beautifully carved wooden abode, resting on a kind of sofa, surrounded by women seated on the floor who embroider linen pieces to be sewed on garments "of the barbarians." The memoir is preserved in the *Excerpta de legationibus* of the emperor Constantine VII Porphyrogenetus. I have used the annotated translation of E. Doblhofer, *Byzantinische Diplomaten und östliche Barbaren: Aus den Excerpta de legationibus des Konstantinos Porphyrogennetos ausgewählte Abschnitte des Priskos und Menander Protektor* (Graz, Vienna, Cologne, 1955), p. 48. Ierusalimskaja (p. 53) deplores the lack of regional evidence for the survival of features of female attire that occur at Moshchevaja Balka. There are, however, striking parallels available from the Caucasus as well as Central Asia, documented as being worn into the early 20th century, for instance the elaborate female headgear. See Ierusalimskaja, pl. 78, figs. 205f., and p. 158, figs. 10 and 12, with the identical *kulutapushak* caps worn by women in Bukhara and Samarkand. The caps are fitted with baglike extensions for the pigtails and are covered with veils and tiara-like bands, exactly like the early medieval models from the Moshchevaja Balka; see *Facing West: Oriental Jews of Central Asia and the Caucasus*, exh. cat., Joods Historisch Museum, Amsterdam; Russian Museum of Ethnography, Saint Petersburg (Zwolle, 1997), p. 41 and nos. 30–32, 52. The last venue of this exhibition was the Jewish Museum in New York, fall 1999. The catalogue text repeatedly states that the Jewish communities adopted indigenous dress

(that is, of peoples mostly of Muslim persuasion) to such a degree that distinctions are impossible to make.

34. Ierusalimskaja's emphasis is on ethnogenesis; see Ierusalimskaja, p. 38 and passim, an approach that clearly has its limits. For a good analysis of such hypotheses, see Werbart.

35. Ierusalimskaja, p. 52. Cf. Widengren, p. 231: "kurät" (jacket), "kärc" (sheepskin coat).

36. See *Languages of Dress*, ed. N. Lindisfarne-Tapper and B. Ingham (Richmond, Surrey, 1997), fig. 22, which gives a good description of the garment with its frogs ("Fastened at the centre with five fasteners, not buttons . . . but bobs of braid . . . which fit into cotton loops serving as button-holes"); the Georgian and Abkhazian terminology are on p. 94. Noblemen prefer the coat to be white. See also George Hewitt and Zaira Khiba, "Male Dress in the Caucasus with Special Reference to Abkhazia and Georgia," in ibid., pp. 93–106. The cartridge holders at the chest are, of course, a relatively late addition to the traditional outfit. A splendid collection of traditional Caucasian and kindred coats is in Tilke 1923, pls. 49f., 54, 56f., 59, 61, 65, 69, 83; and Tilke 1925, pls. 65, 89. They show many of the salient features of the Metropolitan Museum's caftan. The American Museum of Natural History, New York, has a fine collection of Caucasian costumes where the relevant features can be studied.

37. Widengren, in his linguistic and art-historical study, on the basis of still current Ossetian dress terminology, traces the remarkable constancy of the basic steppe garments—in cut and vocabulary—from the Scythians to the Persians, the Parthians and Palmyrans, the Kushans, the Sasanians, the Sogdians to modern times. See also Elfriede R. Knauer, "Le vêtement des nomades eurasiatiques et sa postérité," in *Académie des Inscriptions et Belles-Lettres: Comptes Rendus des Séances de l'Année 1999* (Paris, 2001), pp. 1141–85; and Andreas Schmidt-Colinet et al., *Die Textilien aus Palmyra: Neue und alte Funde*, Damaszener Forschungen 8 (Mainz, 2000), p. 92.

38. Ierusalimskaja, p. 120 and passim.

39. For an outline of the development with respect to textile history, see Otavsky, pp. 190–95, "Arabische Expansion nach Zentralasien." For the political history, see *Cambridge History of Iran*, vol. 3, pt. 2, *The Seleucid, Parthian and Sasanian Periods*, ed. Ehsan Yarshater (Cambridge, 1983), and vol. 4, *The Period from the Arab Invasion to the Saljuqs*, ed. Richard N. Frye (Cambridge, 1975); also Richard N. Frye, *The Heritage of Central Asia* (Princeton, 1995), chaps. 10–15, pp. 153–232. For the economy of the region, see E. Ashtor, *A Social and Economic History of the Near East in the Middle Ages* (London, 1976). See also Roth, p. 527.

40. See the thorough study of D. M. Dunlop, *The History of the Jewish Khazars* (New York, 1967), with the important review by Vladimir Minorsky, "A New Book on the Khazars," in *The Turks, Iran and the Caucasus in the Middle Ages* (London, 1978), pp. 122–44; Peter B. Golden, *Khazar Studies*, Bibliotheca Orientalis Hungarica 25, nos. 1–2 (Budapest, 1980); and idem, *An Introduction to the History of the Turkic Peoples: Ethnogenesis and State-Formation in Medieval and early Modern Eurasia and the Middle East* (Wiesbaden, 1992), pp. 233–44. The most useful feature of Kevin A. Brook, *The Jews of Khazaria* (Northvale, N.J., and Jerusalem, 1999) is its bibliography. For the archaeological evidence, see S. A. Pletneva, *Die Chasaren: Mittelalterliches Reich an Don und Wolga* (Leipzig, 1978); eadem, *Ocherki Khazarskoi Archeologii* (Moscow and Jerusalem, 1999). See also Werbart for an excellent analysis of the "multicultural" character of the Khazar state. For the technical aid provided by Byzantine engineers, see

Gennady Afanassiev, "Les forteresses du royaume Khazare," *L'Archéologue*, no. 46 (February–March 2000), pp. 44f. In early December 2001, the Second International Colloquium on the Khazars, organized by the Jewish University in Moscow and the State Historical Museum, will take place at the State Historical Museum (Kremlin) accompanied by a special exhibition of Khazar materials.

41. See R. C. Blockley, *The History of Menander the Guardsman: Introductory Essay, Text, Translation and Historiographical Notes* (Liverpool, 1985), pp. 110–27; also Doblhofer, *Byzantinische Diplomaten*, pp. 88–141.

42. The Mamisonskij Pereval does not figure in M. Vasmer, *Russisches geographisches Namenbuch* (Wiesbaden, 1964–). For its location, see Braund, *Georgia in Antiquity*, map 2.

43. See the translation and commentary of Togan. For a brief account see Judith Gabriel, "Among the Norse Tribes: The Remarkable Account of Ibn Fadlan," *ARAMCO World*, November–December 1999, pp. 37–42. See also Thomas S. Noonan, "What Can Archaeology Tell Us about the Economy of Khazaria," in *The Archaeology of the Steppes: Methods and Strategies*, Papers from the International Symposium, Naples, November 9–12, 1992, ed. Bruno Genito (Naples, 1994), pp. 331–45.

44. For the role of the Bulgars, see Dunlop, *History of the Jewish Khazars*, passim; and Golden, *Introduction to the History of the Turkic Peoples*, passim.

45. Togan, pp. 136f. The numbers are probably somewhat exaggerated.

46. For a comprehensive interpretation of dirham finds in European Russia and the Near East, see Noonan, *The Islamic World, Russia and the Vikings: The Numismatic Evidence*, Variorum Collected Studies Series (Aldershot, 1998), a collection of articles written between 1981 and 1986. A catalogue of dirham hoards from throughout western Eurasia compiled by Noonan will be published by the Numismatic Institute of the University of Stockholm; see Gabriel, "Among the Norse Tribes," p. 42. Still useful is Georg Jacob, *Der nordisch-baltische Handel der Araber im Mittelalter* (Leipzig, 1887; reprint, Amsterdam, 1966).

For maps of East Central Europe in the 7th–8th centuries and the 9th century, see Paul R. Magocsi, *Historical Atlas of East Central Europe* (1993), pp. 8–12.

47. Togan, p. 16.

48. Ibid., pp. 226f., 240f.

49. Ibid., p. 29.

50. Ibid., pp. 53f.

51. Ibid., pp. 82–97. Understandably, Ibn Fadlan does not distinguish between Swedes and Rus, see note 55 below. For the international makeup of these groups of enterprising traders, see the highly suggestive introduction by Omeljan Pritsak, *The Origin of Rus'*, vol. 1, *Old Scandinavian Sources Other than the Sagas* (Cambridge, Mass., 1981). Pritsak calls them "fluvial nomads," p. 21.

52. Still valuable is Reinhart P. A. Dozy, *Dictionnaire détaillé des noms des vêtements chez les Arabes* (Amsterdam, 1845); Leo Ary Mayer, *Mamluk Costume: A Survey* (Geneva, 1952); Yedida Kalfon Stillman, *Arab Dress from the Dawn of Islam to Modern Times*, ed. Norman A. Stillman (Leiden, 2000); Karl Lokotsch, *Etymologisches Wörterbuch der europäischen (germanischen, romanischen und slavischen) Wörter orientalischen Ursprungs* (Heidelberg, 1927). See also, for the various terms, *Encyclopedia of Islam*, new ed. (Leiden, 1960–).

53. Still fundamental: Henry Seyrig, "Armes et costumes iraniens de Palmyre," *Syria* 18 (1937), pp. 4–31; Widengren; Elfriede R. Knauer, "Towards a History of the Sleeved Coat: A Study of the Impact of an Ancient Eastern Garment on the West," *Expedition* 21, no. 1 (1978), pp. 18–36; eadem, "Ex oriente vestimenta: Trachtgeschichtliche Beobachtungen zu Ärmelmantel und Ärmeljacke," *Aufstieg und Niedergang der Römischen Welt*, pt. 2, vol. 12, sec. 3 (Berlin and New York, 1985), pp. 579–741; eadem, "Le vêtement des nomades eurasiatiques."

54. See, e.g., Barber; Mallory and Mair, *Tarim Mummies*. More, as yet scarcely known materials will be presented in Riggisberger Berichte 9 (note 12 above).

55. E.g., silk garments, metal frogs, buttons, and other oriental accoutrements were certainly the possessions of resident foreign members of the international trading houses. Only a choice of publications dealing with such textile finds will be listed. Agnes Geijer, *Die Textilfunde aus den Gräbern, Birka, Untersuchungen und Studien 3* (Uppsala, 1938); eadem, "The Textile Finds from Birka: Birka III. Die Textilfunde aus den Gräbern," revised by the author, *Acta Archaeologica* 50 (1980), pp. 209–22; Valdemārs Ginters, *Tracht und Schmuck in Birka und im ostbaltischen Raum: Eine vergleichende Studie* (Stockholm, 1981), reviewed by Elfriede R. Knauer, *American Journal of Archaeology* 87 (1983), p. 125f.; Inga Hägg, "Mantel och kjortel i vikingatidens dräkt," *Fornvännen* 66 (1971), pp. 141–53 (with German résumé p. 153); eadem, *Die Textilfunde aus dem Hafen von Haithabu* (Neumünster, 1984); Hildegard Elsner, *Wikinger Museum Haithabu: Schaufenster einer frühen Stadt* (Neumünster, n.d.), pp. 45–54, "Bekleidung." The important but elusive trading post of Reric on the Baltic has apparently just been located on the east coast of the Bay of Wismar (Germany): Gerd Lobin, "Wir haben Reric entdeckt," *Frankfurter Allgemeine Zeitung*, June 19, 1999; and Wolfgang Korn, "Die Hanse der Nordmänner," *Bild der Wissenschaft* 3 (2000), pp. 22–27. The population of these "viks" (traders, shippers, craftsmen), consisting of Norsemen, Wends (Slavs), Balts, or Finns and others, relied on slave labor. Caught in razzias in the Central Asian steppes and the North Pontic plains, slaves (Arabic: Ṣaqāliba) were also their main "merchandise," coveted in both the Carolingian and the Abbasid empires. While the slave trade had been in the hands of Jewish merchants—who traveled unhindered through the Mediterranean to the Khazars even after the Arabs dominated its eastern part—during the 8th and early 9th centuries, it was taken over by the Norsemen—whose access to the same markets was via the Baltic and the Russian rivers—as of the middle of the 9th century; see Pritsak, *The Origin of Rus'*. It is also worth consulting the entry "Birka at the Silkroad! A Town of 'Vikings' or Merchants?" (1997) on the web (Mats Philip and Björn Axelson, eds., http://home1.swipnet.se/~w-14723/birka/birke010.html). The Birka excavations have also yielded Khazar pottery: M. Bäck, "Importkeramiken i Birka," *Medeltidsarkeologisk Tidskrift* (1995) was inaccessible to me. For reports by oriental traders on the Rus, see Heinz-Joachim Graf, *Orientalische Berichte des Mittelalters über die Germanen: Eine Quellensammlung* (Krefeld, 1971), pp. 28–105. For a discussion of the debated etymologies of Rus, Varangian, or Ṣaqāliba, see ibid., nn. 26–28; see also Pritsak, *The Origin of Rus'*, pp. 24–28, who localizes the Rus near Rodez, France, and makes them the descendants of the Ruteni or Ruti of Celto-Roman times. Togan's addendum on the Ṣaqāliba, pp. 295–331, has been challenged by Vladimir Minorsky, *A History of Sharvan and Darband in the 10th–11th Centuries* (Cambridge, 1958), pp. 108–16. For more recent overviews, see *Les Viking . . . les scandinaves et l'Europe 800–1200*, 22^e exposition

d'art du Conseil de l'Europe (Paris, 1992), pp. 74–83, 126–31; and Thomas S. Noonan, "Scandinavians in European Russia," *The Oxford Illustrated History of the Vikings*, ed. Peter Sawyer (Oxford, 1997), pp. 134–56; there, the name Rus is derived from the West Finnic name for Sweden: Ruotsi.

56. The Rus modeled their state after the Khazar khaganate; see Pritsak, *Origin of Rus'*; Golden, *Introduction to the History of the Turkic Peoples*, passim. For the interaction in the field of art, see Vladimir J. Petrukhin, "The Early History of Old Russian Art: The Rhyton from Chernigov and Khazarian Tradition," *Tor* 27, no. 2 (1995), pp. 475–86.

57. For the economic reasons for the dearth of silver currency in the Arab realm, see Carl Brockelmann, *Geschichte der Islamischen Völker und Staaten*, 2nd ed. (Munich and Berlin, 1943), pp. 133–35. It seems that the silver mines of Central Asia, exploited by the Samanids of Buchara, gave out. See the reference to Noonan's forthcoming catalogue in Gabriel, "Among the Norse Tribes," p. 42. The silver mines in the Harz Mountains provided a new source for Northern Europe, and the demand for silk of the Franks was satisfied by shipments along the Russian rivers. See Marc Blackburn, "Money and Coinage," *The New Cambridge Medieval History*, vol. 2, *C. 700–c. 900*, ed. Rosamond McKitterick (Cambridge, 1995), pp. 538–59; *Transit Brügge–Novgorod: Eine Strasse durch die europäische Geschichte*, ed. Ferdinand Seibt et al., exh. cat., Ruhrland Museum Essen (Bottrop, 1997), notably the chapters "Wege der Mächtigen: Herrscher-Itinerare auf der Strasse Brügge–Nowgorod in den mittelalterlichen Jahrhunderten" (E. Müller-Mertens), "Jüdische Gemeindebildung und Fernhandel an der Strasse von Brügge nach Nowgorod im Mittelalter" (M. Toch), and "Zur Frühgeschichte Nowgorods: Von den Anfängen bis gegen Ende des 12. Jahrhunderts" (E. Mühle); and Jean Blankoff, "Letters from Old Russia," *Archaeology* 53 (November–December 2000), pp. 30–35, esp. pp. 32f.

58. It appears that glorified versions of the steppe garb even reached and inspired wealthy chiefs in Scandinavia to emulate its distinctive features in the 5th century. See Margareta Nockert, "Vid sidenvägors ände: Textilier från Palmyra till Birka," in *Palmyra: Öknens drottning* (Stockholm, 1988), pp. 77–112, and eadem, in her publication of the chieftain's tomb in Högom, Sweden: *The Högom Find and Other Migration Period Textiles and Costumes in Scandinavia. Högom Part II* (Umeå, Sweden, 1991), "Oriental Tunics and Trousers," pp. 116–22; also pp. 112–14. The decorative bands of the tunics are tablet-woven; horsehair serves as weft, which gives them a silky sheen. They were stitched onto fine woolen jackets of vermilion color. Another Eastern feature are the splendid metal clasps or buttons. Apparently copied from Parthian or Sasanian clasps, which served to close coats at the neck: one circular "button" fastened at both edges of the neckline and tied together with ribbons; the Scandinavian clasps were used on cuffs, at side slits of tunics, and at the ends of narrow trousers. They went out of fashion after the Migration Period. For Parthian and Sasanian clasps, see Friedrich Sarre, *L'art de la Perse ancienne* (Paris, 1921), fig. 57; and Roman Ghirshman, *Iran: Parthians and Sasanians* (London, 1962), p. 170. Buttons do not reappear in Western Europe en masse before the 14th century, certainly again inspired by Eastern models. The adaptation is probably due to crusader contacts with Byzantium and its eastern neighbors. Fine series of silver gilt buttons attached to a decorative woven metal band from the 13th–14th centuries have been excavated in North Caucasian

tombs (see Leskov, *Grabschätze der Adygeen*, fig. 216), bell-shaped ones are known from Moshchevaja Balka (Ierusalimskaja, p. 82; from a man's caftan, attesting that metal buttons coexisted with the textile samples from frogs), and other North Caucasian cemeteries. To the best of my knowledge, there exists no "History of the Button." My own attempt at a survey is Knauer, "Ex oriente vestimenta," pp. 652–54. I would suggest that the button fad (mostly attested in late medieval paintings) was mediated to Western Europe by, among others, Italian merchants settled in the East, e.g., in Kaffa (Crimea) in the 14th century. Actual series of buttons fashioned of cloth were found in excavations in London; see Elisabeth Crowfoot, Frances Pritchard, and Kay Staniland, *Textiles and Clothing c. 1150–c. 1450*, Medieval Finds from Excavations in London 4 (London, 1992), figs. 141–47. They are dated to the 14th century and confirm the widespread use also among the common people. Contemporary paintings mostly depict the upper classes and show metal buttons.

59. The jackets of the Chertomlyk vase are trimmed with fur, with only the seam in the back appearing to be covered with embroidery (see Widengren, fig. 2); the Scythians on the Kul Oba bottle, however, show a wealth of embroidery on their garments, combined with rows of metal (?) roundels (see Figure 15). Isolated buttonlike roundels on the chest may have served to secure the closing of the jacket in addition to the belt. To judge from later examples, strings must have connected the "buttons" across the chest. I assume that the hooklike ornaments at the chest of the Scythians' jackets on the vessel from the Gajmanova Mogila served as closing devices, too ("proto-frogs"); they are used only above the belt (see *Gold der Steppe: Archäologie der Ukraine* [Schleswig, 1991], no. 96a. Besides embroidery, the jackets display a double trimming of precious fur. Interestingly, the legs of the lambskins have not been cut off the jackets but serve as additional protection for the thighs—waste was not in the nature of nomad societies.

Herodotus (4.110, trans. Aubrey de Sélincourt [Harmondsworth, 1954], p. 306), speaking of the Budini and Geloni, neighbors of the Scythians, reports that "otters and beavers are caught in the lake and another sort of creature . . . whose skin they use for making edgings for their jackets."

60. The leather-mosaic coat from the 4th-century B.C. kurgan in Katanda (Altay) (Figure 16) and the Persian kandys, also fashioned of leather and best known from the Persepolis reliefs, are almost contemporaneous; see Henry Frankfort, *The Art and Architecture of the Ancient Orient*, 2nd ed. (Harmondsworth, 1958), fig. 182. They are fastened with ribbons at the neck and were worn draped over the shoulders with very narrow dangling sleeves. Some of the finds from the permafrost burials in the Altay evince strong Achaemenid influence. It should be kept in mind that the more "civilized" Persians—before creating an empire—shared a steppe background with the tribes in the Altay which includes traditional clothing.

61. This fashion persisted as demonstrated by the passage from Priscus describing the activities of the servants of Attila's spouse (note 33 above, trans. Doblhofer, *Byzantische Diplomaten*, p. 48).

62. See the garments from the 1st-century A.D. Hsiung-Nu tumuli in northern Mongolia; S. I. Rudenko, *Die Kultur der Hsiung-nu und die Hügelgräber von Noin Ula* (Bonn, 1969); also the trimmed silk "caftan" from Niya (Xinjiang) of the Han period, no. 49, in *Archaeological Treasures of the Silk Road in Xinjiang Uygur Autonomous Region*; and *Wen Wu* 1 (2000), pp. 4–40 (English

résumé, p. 40). The importance of braided bands as decoration of garments becomes apparent from clothes either stitched together entirely from woolen ones or decorated with them (see Barber, pls. 6A, 6B, and 7A, 7B); they both date from the 1st millennium B.C. See also the recently discovered tapestry bands found in Xinjiang, *Fabulous Creatures from the Desert Sands: Central Asian Textiles from the Second Century B.C. to the Second Century A.D.*, Riggisberger Berichte 10, ed. Dominik Keller and Regula Schorta (Riggisberg, 2001).

63. The nomadic Yüeh-chih, of Indo-European extraction, who called themselves Kushans, after they had wrested Bactria (northern Afghanistan) from the Greeks and created a powerful state in northwest India during the 1st to 3rd century A.D., continued wearing a refined version of the steppe outfit. Embroidered (?) bands with floral motifs are visible on King Vima Kadphises' jacket (closing in the center) and are studded with metal roundels; B. Rowland, *The Art and Architecture of India: Buddhist-Hindu-Jain* (Harmondsworth, 1959), pl. 43. The ones lined up at the jacket's edges may have been linked by strings (no longer visible) to hold the tight-fitting garment in place. See Widengren, figs. 26f.; fig. 28 shows a Kushan grandee with banded and girt caftan, without lapels, that closes on the left side of the body. See also Knauer, "Ex oriente vestimenta," pp. 629–31; and eadem, "Le vêtement des nomades eurasiatiques," pp. 1152–55.

64. See, e.g., the trimmed coat of an ancestor of King Antiochus of Commagene, 1st century B.C., from Nimrud Dağ, Turkey; Knauer, "Le vêtement des nomades eurasiatiques," fig. 14. The rather flimsy (silk?) material of the Parthian warrior's jacket seems to be strengthened with a wide trimming of firmer stuff; see *Propyläenkunstgeschichte*, vol. 2 (Berlin, 1967), pl. 392. This bronze statue from Shami in Khuzistan is dated to the first half of the 2nd century B.C. He wears baggy leggings. A similarly trimmed Sasanian example is found on the monumental statue of King Shapur I (sculpted from a stalactite) in the Mudan cave near Bishapur, of the later 3rd century A.D.; see ibid., pl. 412. An open trimmed silk coat, tunic, and leggings are worn by the Palmyrene Makkai; see Widengren, figs. 9–11 (Shami) and 8 (Palmyra). See also Knauer, "Ex oriente vestimenta," pp. 631f.; and the trimmed and belted coat with side slits of an Umayyad khalif's statue from Khirbat al-Mafjar (second quarter of the 8th century) in Jerusalem, Janine Sourdel-Thomine and Bertold Spuler, *Die Kunst des Islam*, Propyläen Kunstgeschichte (1966) 4 (Berlin, 1973), pl. 58.

65. In a single instance, the late Sasanian king Khosrau II in the relief at Taq-i Bustan, near Kermanshah (Iran), which shows him hunting boars from a boat, wears a belted caftan closing at the left side of the body but with a high neckline. If opened, the upper right part might have formed a lapel, but it is not shown that way; see *Bulletin du CIETA* 74 (1997), p. 24, fig. 10.

66. Compelling evidence for single lapelled and trimmed Hephthalite caftans comes from murals at Dalverzin-tepe in the Surkhandarya valley (southern Uzbekistan); see Irina T. Krouglikova, "Peinture murale de Delbarjin," Sovetsko-afganskaia arkheologicheskaia ekspeditsiia (1969–73) *Drevnaia Baktriia* (Moscow, 1976), pp. 185–87, fig. 56, specifically in rooms N 12 and N 15. For parallels, the author rightly refers to the Hephthalite murals in the niche of the 35-m-high Buddha at Bamiyan, recently destroyed, and to those of the cave temple in Kizil (Xinjiang); for an instructive juxtaposition of the relevant images (Hephthalite "knights" in trimmed, single-lapelled caftans that close

on the left and Tocharian "knights" in similar outfits from the Cave of the Sixteen Sword-Bearers in Kizil, dated between 600 and 650), see Takayasu Higuchi, "Studies on Buddhist Sites in Northern Central Asia," *Silk Roadology* 4, Bulletin of the Research Center for Silk Roadology (1997), p. 188, fig. 7-1; see also Knauer, "Le vêtement des nomades eurasiatiques," figs. 18, 19. For the political history and the numismatic evidence, see Roman Ghirshman, *Les Chionites-Hephthalites* (Cairo, 1948).

67. The site is not closely dated. (7th century? Some Russian authors prefer a date between the 5th and 6th centuries; however, Boris Marshak opts for the very early 7th century, oral communication.) If the copies of the fragmentary wall paintings from the site can be trusted, there is a single participant whose outfit is distinguished by a jacket with double lapels and sleeves; coming down only to the elbows worn over a patterned undergarment—all the other males sport just one lapel and long sleeves, see L. I. Albaum, *Balalyk-tepe: K istorii materialnoj kultury i iskusstva Tocharistana* (Tashkent, 1960), figs. 106f. He may be the most honored member of the gathering and the lapels a sign of rank, and he also balances by far the largest cup among the banqueters. For an interpretation of the "Sasanian" textiles depicted in Balalyk-tepe, see Otavsky, pp. 165–67. A feature that has, to the best of my knowledge, never been addressed is the cut of the female coats on these murals. They are worn draped over the shoulders, giving them the semblance of a cape with a single lapel on the right; ribbons to close them are attached on either side at the height of the breast. In rare instances, however (Albaum, *Balalyk-tepe*, figs. 101f.: a line to the left of the ribbons under the lapel indicates the empty sleeve), it becomes obvious that these are coats worn with dangling sleeves, like the Old Persian kandys, also favored by females during Sasanian times. See also the ladies on a 7th–8th-century mural from Kalai Kafirnigan (Tokharistan), *Cultural Contacts*, no. 101. Identical coats—worn in the same fashion, but not recognized for what they are—are found on wall paintings in 12th-century Buddhist temples in western Tibet depicting high-ranking laypeople, male as well as female. See, e.g., Deborah E. Klimburg-Salter, *Tabo, a Lamp for the Kingdom: Early Indo-Tibetan Buddhist Art in the Western Himalayas* (Milan, 1997), figs. 229f. and passim; for male lapelled sleeved coats, see figs. 40 and 137 and passim. The 13th-century Nepalese temple in Alchi provides other examples; see P. A. Pal, *A Buddhist Paradise: The Murals of Alchi, Western Himalayas* (Hong Kong and Basel, 1982), fig. LS 30, a ruler on horseback, in a draped sleeved coat. For a survey of the phenomenon, see Knauer, "Le vêtement des nomades eurasiatiques."

68. For Afrasiab, see L. I. Albaum, *Zivopis Afrasiaba* (Tashkent, 1975); Boris I. Marshak, "Le programme iconographique des peintures de la 'Salle des ambassadeurs' à Afrasiab (Samarkand)," *Arts Asiatiques* 29 (1994), pp. 5–20; Markus Mode, *Sogdien und die Herrscher der Welt: Türken, Sasaniden und Chinesen in Historiengemälden des 7. Jahrhunderts n. Chr. aus Alt-Samarqand* (Frankfurt-am-Main, 1993); on the cover is a drawing of two Turkish soldiers in lapelled caftans. The one on the right has shed the top of his caftan and knotted the sleeves like a belt, the silk-trimmed cuffs are visible, middle of the 7th century A.D. For Pendjikent, A. M. Belenitskii, *Monumental'noe iskusstvo Pendzhikenta* (Moscow, 1973), note, e.g., pl. X, the mural with female and young male donors in draped sleeved coats and a caftan who worship a god, from a Sogdian residence in Pendjikent (Tajikistan), second half of the 7th century; Boris I. Marshak

and Valentina I. Raspopova, "Wallpaintings from a House with a Granary: Panjikent, 1st Quarter of the Eighth Century A.D.," *Silk Road Art and Archaeology* 1 (1990), pp. 123–76; and the single-lapelled, trimmed, and belted long coats of two musicians on a Sogdian ossuary from Sahr-i Sabz, Frantz Grenet, "Trois nouveaux documents d'iconographie religieuse sogdienne," *Studia Iranica* 22 (1993), pp. 55–59, pl. v, fig. 7. Guitty Azarpay, *Sogdian Painting: The Pictorial Epic in Oriental Art,* with contributions by A. M. Belenitskii, B. I. Marshak, and M. J. Dresden (Berkeley, 1981). See also Cheng Yue, "A Summary of Sogdian Studies in China," *China Archaeology and Art Digest* 1 (1996), pp. 21–30. For a survey of Sogdian garments, see *Encyclopaedia Iranica,* ed. Ehsan Yarshater (Costa Mesa, 1992), vol. 5, pp. 754–57, s.v. "Clothing VI, of the Sogdians" (Aleksandr Naymark), reference owed to the author of the entry.

69. A peculiarly shaped single lapel is worn by the painters in the Cave of the Painters in Kizil, dated ca. A.D. 500 (see Albert von LeCoq, *Bilderatlas zur Kunst und Kulturgeschichte Mittel-Asiens* [Berlin, 1925], fig. 7)—but cf. the new dates suggested by Ma Shichang, "Dating of the Kizil Caves," in *In the Footsteps of the Buddha: An Iconic Journey from India to China,* exh. cat., Department of Fine Arts and University Museum and Art Gallery, University of Hong Kong (Hong Kong, 1998), p. 92. Leggings are more in evidence in Xinjiang than in Central Asia. Their history has been expertly documented by Seyrig, "Armes et costumes iraniens de Palmyre," and Widengren. Actual boots with strings at the top, of the 5th century, were found by Folke Bergman at grave 10 at Kroraina; see Mallory and Mair, *Tarim Mummies,* p. 222 and fig. 133. Similar models are still being used in Asia today; see Tilke 1923, pl. 103 and p. 29 (from Tibet), and the Mongolian boy victors in a horserace wearing leggings tied to the belt, second quarter of the 20th century, Carl Diem, *Asiatische Reiterspiele* (Berlin, 1942), fig. 14, p. 45. There are two kinds: stocking-shaped or without feet. Poor-quality silk was fashioned into leggings for the Byzantine army in the 10th century; see David Jacoby, "Silk in Western Byzantium before the Fourth Crusade," *Byzantinische Zeitschrift* 84–85 (1991–92), p. 474, n. 118. The majority of "Sasanian" leggings comes from the excavations in Antinoë, Egypt; they are dispersed over many European museums. For one in Berlin, see Tilke 1923, pl. 28 and p. 13. The latest survey is by Dominique Bénazeth and Patricia Dal-Prà, "Quelques remarques à propos d'un ensemble de vêtements de cavaliers découverts dans des tombes égyptiennes," *L'armée romaine et les barbares du IIe au VIIe siècle,* ed. Françoise Vallet and Michel Kazanski (Rouen, 1993), pp. 367–82. The leggings of the kneeling Sogdians (?) are apparently held up with two strings; see the mural from Buddhist Temple 9 at Bezeklik near Turfan, Xinjiang (China), 8th century A.D. (?), *Kunst und Kultur entlang der Seidenstrasse,* ed. H. G. Franz (Graz, 1986), p. 53. The pair of leggings in the Metropolitan Museum (Figure 2) may have been fashioned for funerary purposes. The unlined silk could hardly have withstood daily use.

70. Albert von LeCoq, participant in the four German missions to Chinese Turkestan between 1902 and 1914, was the first to analyze thoroughly the pedigree of costumes depicted in those murals, in his *Bilderatlas zur Kunst und Kulturgeschichte Mittel-Asiens.* His astute observations are still valid today, while some of his conclusions need revision in the light of many new finds. For the German involvement in the exploration of Central Asia, see M. Yaldiz, "The History of the Asian Collection in the Museum für Indische Kunst in Berlin," in *In the Footsteps of the Buddha,*

pp. 41–50. See also *Along the Ancient Silk Routes: Central Asian Art from the West Berlin State Museums,* exh. cat., MMA (New York, 1982). For the Tocharians in Central Asia, see *The Bronze Age and Early Iron Age Peoples of Eastern Central Asia,* ed. Victor H. Mair (Washington, D.C., 1998); also Barber, and Otavsky, pp. 173–84, for textiles from the region. The dates of the (stylistically more Western) murals in the Buddhist sanctuaries at Kizil are still debated; see Ma Shichang, "Dating of the Kizil Caves," p. 92. Tests conducted by the Leibnitz Laboratory in Kiel in 1999 on behalf of the Museum für Indische Kunst, Berlin, will certainly lead to a revision of some of the murals' dates (Marianne Yaldiz, oral communication).

71. Though often badly abraded, these so-called balbals are dressed in belted and lapelled caftans that occasionally display Chinese silk patterns. These features are confirmed by actual finds of garments fashioned from Chinese silk in contemporaneous regional Turkic cemeteries. Frogging is attested. The majority of the caftans shown have either one or two lapels and are closed on the proper left side. A few others close, Chinese fashion, on the right, a feature that is probably to be explained by the proximity and frequent contacts of those tribes with the Celestial Empire. I am much indebted to Dr. Gleb Kubarev, Novosibirsk, who outlined the results of his excavations and analyses for me and provided a number of images; his dissertation, "The Culture of the Ancient Turks of the Altay (on Materials of the Burial Monuments)" (in Russian), Novosibirsk, 1997, 445 pp., was not accessible to me, but see his "The Robe of the Old Turks of Central Asia According to Art Materials," *Archaeology, Ethnology and Anthropology of Eurasia* 3, no. 3 (2000), pp. 81–88. He also drew my attention to Dovdoin Bayar, *The Turkic Stone Statues of Central Mongolia* (in Mongolian) (Ulan Bator, 1997), equally beyond reach as yet. However, Dr. Kubarev kindly sent a summary and some images from his and the latter work. Interestingly, the caftans were closed with either ribbons or frogs (Russian: *galuny* = galloons, from French "galon" and mediated via Poland; see Max Vasmer, *Russisches etymologisches Wörterbuch* [Heidelberg, 1953–], reference supplied by Rainer Stichel). These stone "balbals" have Bronze Age and Scythian predecessors in the vast steppe region between the Danube and the Altay; see Alexej Kovalëv, "Die ältesten Stelen am Ertix: Das Kulturphänomen Xemirxek," *Eurasia Antiqua* 5 (1999), pp. 135–78; and P. B. Belozor, "Stone Statues in the Context of the Scythian Ethnographic Problems" (in Russian, with brief English summary), *Archeologia* 4 (1996), pp. 41–50. They are sartorially less informative than the Turkic statues. For the latter, see Vladimir D. Kubarev, *Kamennye izvaianiia Altaia* (Novosibirsk, 1997), with English summary. An interesting passage from the early Tang annals illustrates the sinification of the inhabitants of the Turfan oasis in today's Xinjiang. Its (Turkic) ruler rendered homage to the Chinese court and, returning home with a Chinese noblewoman as his consort, he decreed: "Formerly, since our dynasty was in a savage frontier country, we wore our hair hanging down the back and buttoned our garments at the left. . . . Let the people and all above them undo their braids or knots of hair and do it in the Chinese fashion, and change the lapel which crosses to the left on their garments." Edouard Chavannes, *Documents sur les Tou-Kiue occidentaux* (Saint Petersburg, 1903), pp. 102f.; English trans., in Jane Gaston Mahler, *The Westerners Among the Figurines of the T'ang Dynasty of China* (Rome, 1959), pp. 26f. Long braided hair and garments closing on the left are typical for the Turkic tribes, as well as among the

residents of multicultural Turfan. China herself, moreover, did not remain unaffected by the fashions of this newly occupied province. The lapelled coat became a fad, even for ladies, in this most internationally minded period of Chinese history. See also Joachim Hildebrand, *Das Ausländerbild in der Kunst Chinas als Spiegel kultureller Beziehungen (Han-Tang)* (Stuttgart, 1987); and Knauer, "Le vêtement des nomades eurasiatiques," pp. 1156–59. Chinese statuettes of Central Asians often show them with single buttons at the end of the lapel, indicating that they could be closed high on the neck.

72. For the early Turks, see Golden, *Introduction to the History of the Turkic Peoples,* pp. 79–83 and passim. Gyula Moravcsik, *Byzantinoturcica,* vol. 1, *Die Byzantinischen Quellen der Geschichte der Türkvölker,* 2nd ed. (Berlin, 1958), pp. 69, 76, and passim. See also Wolfgang-Ekkehard Scharlipp, *Die frühen Türken in Zentralasien: Eine Einführung in ihre Geschichte und Kultur* (Darmstadt, 1992).

73. The result of consultation of the splendid volume by Shen Congwen, *Zhongguo gudai fushi yanjiu* (Hong Kong, 1992)—reference to this work kindly supplied by Xinru Liu. The statuettes of performers (p. 429, fig. 203), chiseled from baked brick, come from the tomb of Jiao Zuojin in Henan Province, see *The Quest for Eternity: Chinese Ceramic Sculptures from the Peoples Republic of China,* ed. Susan L. Caroselli, exh. cat., Los Angeles County Museum of Art (Los Angeles, 1987), pp. 147f., nos. 92–94. The statuettes we picture are part of the group but were not shown in that exhibition.

74. For this information I am grateful to Victor Mair, who also refers to *Hanyu Da Cidian* (Shanghai, 1993), vol. 3, p. 73a, s.v. "kòu" (knock), which gives us the last definition *kouzi* (button; Yüan period). There is no entry for the word in Ulla Cyrus-Zetterström, *Fang chi shu yü: Chung wen-Ying wen-Fa wen-Jui wen, Textile Terminology Chinese-English-French-Swedish* (Boras, 1995). Alide Eberhard and Wolfram Eberhard, *Die Mode der Han- und Chin-Zeit* (Antwerp, 1946), do not mention this type of fastener. See also Richard Ettinghausen, "Chinese Representations of Central Asian Turks," in *Beiträge zur Kunstgeschichte Asiens* (Istanbul, 1983), pp. 208–22, who mistakes the multiple frogs on figs. 11 and 16 for belts.

75. The first to address the problem of the "scaramangion" was N. P. Kondakov, "Les Costumes orientaux à la Cour Byzantine," *Byzantion* 1 (1924), pp. 7–49. Many of his observations are still valid. I do not think that the type of riding coat presented by A. Geijer, "A Silk from Antinoë and the Sasanian Art," *Orientalia Suecana* 12 (1963 [1964]), pp. 3–36, fig. 2 (flopped; the coat should close on the left), could be called a "scaramangion" since it is neither constructed from several parts nor does it display frogs. These are the salient features described in Du Cange, *Glossarium ad scriptores mediae et infimae Graecitatis* (Lyon, 1688; reprint, Graz, 1958), s.v. "ΣΚΑΡΑΜΑΓΚΟΝ/ΣΚΡΑΝΙΚΟΝ," pp. 1382f., and idem, *Glossarium mediae et infimae Latinitatis,* ed. G. A. L. Henschel (Paris, 1840–50), s.v. "Scaramanga." I have discussed the garment and its etymology in Knauer, "Ex oriente vestimenta," pp. 657f., esp. n. 231. See also F. Cumont, "L'uniforme de la cavalerie orientale et le costume byzantin," *Byzantion* 2 (1925), pp. 181–91.

76. For precious metal braids and frogs from tombs in Birka, see Hägg, "Mantel." For a summary of closing devices, including frogs, in the early medieval period, see Knauer, "Ex oriente vestimenta," pp. 651–55 and 683, n. 331. In Europe, embroidery with precious metal threads is documented since the late 10th

century; see Kay Staniland, *Medieval Craftsmen: Embroiderers* (London, 1991), pp. 7f. For Byzantium, see *The Oxford Dictionary of Byzantium* (Oxford, 1991), s.v. "embroidery" (A. Gonosova); and Angelike Chatzemichale, "Ta chrysoklabarika-syrmateina-syrmakesika kentemata," *Mélanges offerts à Octave et Melpo Merlier,* Collection de l'Institut Français d'Athènes 92–93 (Athens, 1956), vol. 2, pp. 447–98 (reference supplied by Rainer Stichel). As a specialized craft it is called "passementerie" in French (a guild was established in Paris in 1588), "passamaneria" in Italian, and "Posamentierarbeit" in German.

77. See Knauer, "Ex oriente vestimenta," pp. 683 (with n. 331), 705–11.

78. A rare pictorial document of the 11th century—a period otherwise devoid of images—are the murals in the Ghaznavid palace of Lashkari Bazar in northern Afghanistan. Mahmud of Ghazni, the founder of this Turkic dynasty and conqueror of northern India, and his grandees must have worn single-lapelled, trimmed, and belted caftans that closed at the left and were fashioned of magnificent post-Sasanian silks. This is what can be perceived on the walls of the audience hall where the "corps d'élite" of the ruler is depicted; see Daniel Schlumberger, "Le Palais Ghaznévide de Lashkari Bazar," *Syria* 29 (1952), pp. 251–70, pl. 32, 1. For the history, see Clifford E. Bosworth, *The Ghaznavids: Their Empire in Afghanistan and Eastern Iran* (Edinburgh, 1963). Tilke 1923, passim, refers to frogs always as a Turkic feature.

79. Foremost is the "Book of Ceremonies" of Constantine Porphyrogenetus; for it, see *Constantin VII Porphyrogénète: Le Livre des Cérémonies,* ed., trans., comm. Albert Vogt, 4 vols. (Paris, 1935; 1939; 1940). For the author and the textual transmission, see Moravcsik, *Byzantinoturcica,* vol. 1, pp. 356–90. J. L. Ball at the Institute of Fine Arts, New York University, is preparing a dissertation with the title "Byzantine Dress" (reference supplied by Rainer Stichel).

80. Still fundamental in our context is the work of Gyula Moravcsik, *Byzantinoturcica,* vol. 1, *Die Byzantinischen Quellen der Geschichte der Türkvölker,* and vol. 2, *Sprachreste der Türkvölker in den Byzantinischen Quellen,* 2nd ed. (Berlin, 1958). Military and matrimonial alliances between the Byzantine and the Khazar courts are well attested (see ibid., vol. 1, pp. 81–83): the emperor Heraklius offers his daughter in marriage to the Khazar khagan in 626; they unite forces against the Sasanians. Exiled from his capital to the Crimea, the emperor Justin II flees to Khazaria in 704 and marries the sister of the khagan. The emperor Constantine V (r. 741–75) marries the daughter of the khagan. As empress, she takes the name Eirene and introduces a Khazar garment into Byzantium. Its name, Tzizakion—from Turkish *čiček* = "flower"—is suggestive without our being able to visualize it; see Gyula Moravcsik, "Die Herkunft des Wortes Tzitzakion," *Seminarium Kondakovianum* 4 (1931), pp. 69–76 (German résumé, p. 76); he suggests that the Khazar princess's name was "Flower." Under the emperor Theophilus (r. 829–42), Byzantine architects construct the Khazar stronghold Sarkel on the river Don. In the 9th and 10th centuries, Khazars serve as imperial bodyguards in the capital and Khazars participate in Leo VI's war against the Bulgars in 894. It is only in the early 11th century that collaboration ceases. Basil II, supported by the Russians, conquers the remnants of the Khazar khaganate, already threatened in the east by the Kumans (Polovtsy)—yet another tribe from the depth of Asia (the genuine "officina gentium aut certe velut vagina nationum," the "manufactory of peoples

and certainly like the vagina of nations," as the 6th-century author Jordanes calls remote Scandinavia, which had just sent forth the Gothic tribes; see *Iordanis Romana et Getica,* ed. Theodor Mommsen, Monumenta Germaniae Historica, Auctorum Antiquissimorum 5 [Berlin, 1882], p. 60, ll. 6f.).

81. See *Gold der Steppe: Archäologie der Ukraine,* ed. Renate Rolle et al. (Schleswig, 1991), no. 208b; see pp. 274f., fig. 1, and pp. 418f. Remains of three caftans were found in the kurgan.

82. See, e.g., Rusudan Mepisashvili and Vakhtang Tsintsadze, *The Arts of Ancient Georgia* (London, 1979), pp. 86: Demetre, founder of the Ivari church in Mtskheta (early 7th century); and 245: Ashot II, founder of the early-10th-century church at Tbeti. Closest to the Metropolitan's coat is the caftan worn by King Saul in the scene of David and Goliath, a relief on the church of the Holy Cross at Aght'amar, 10th century. It closes on the left, has a single lapel on the right breast, and is girded (see Figure 27). See also Knauer, "Le vêtement des nomades eurasiatiques," p. 1165 and fig. 15.

83. Of Turco-Persian stock, the Mughals invaded India in the 15th century and imposed their—by now highly refined—civilization on the venerable culture of large parts of the subcontinent. The garment has survived until today, e.g., among the cattle-breeding Rabaris in Ahmadabad in the north Indian state of Gujarat and other "foreign" groups in this country. See Aditi Shah, Mitu Banga, and Erol Pires, *The Rabari of Ahmedabad: A Study of Their Costumes* (Paldi, Ahmedabad, 1992), figs. 17A and 18. The cotton garment is called "kediu." It closes on the left, at the neck with a cloth button and loop and at the waist with ribbons; it also features a "hidden" inside fastening. The authors are unaware of the costume-historical connections. For similar garments, see Tilke 1923, pls. 95f., and the Parsee cotton coat, pl. 97, closing on the left and with shirred skirt. The Parsees arrived in India in the 10th century as refugees from Iran, where they had been persecuted since the overthrow of the Sasanians by the Arabs in 766.

84. Ierusalimskaja, pl. XXIII, fig. 51, nos. II 79, II 106, II 201, II 338; Ierusalimskaja and Borkopp, nos. 28–32. They are exact copies of full-size garments.

85. *Archaeological Treasures of the Silk Road in Xinjiang Uygur Autonomous Region,* nos. 132–35, and pp. 228–33. The miniature set is only visible in the photo on p. 132; the date is given as between A.D. 265 and 420. See now *Wen Wu* 1 (1999), pp. 3–16; the drawing is on p. 15. The author of the article, Xiu Xing Guo, presented the find at the Abegg Foundation colloquium, October 7–8, 1999, mentioned in note 12 above; she dates Tomb 15 to the 2nd century A.D. See also Knauer, "Le vêtement des nomades eurasiatiques," pp. 1178–87. Von Wilckens, p. 252—unaware of this recent find—rightly refers to similar miniature garments found in tombs from the same region: Vivi Sylwan, *Investigation of Silk from Edsen-Gol and Lop-Nor and a Survey of Wool and Vegetable Materials,* Reports from the Scientific Expedition to the North-Western Provinces of China under the Leadership of Dr. Sven Hedin 32, VII, Archaeology 6 (Stockholm, 1949), pp. 57f. Add to this the miniature objects, bolts of silk, etc., found in the tomb of Lady P'eng in Astana; Valerie Hansen, "The Path of Buddhism into China, the View from Turfan," *Asia Major,* 3rd ser., vol. 11, no. 2 (1998), p. 48. Miniature articles of clothing of the Tang dynasty (618–907) were also found in the underground rooms of the Famen temple (Shaanxi); see *XI'AN: Legacies of Ancient Chinese Civilization,* 2nd ed. (Beijing, 1997), p. 190 bottom. The objects will be presented by Han Jinke in the forthcoming colloquium publication Riggisberger Berichte 9 (note 12 above).

86. The until now unpublished caftan (see Kajitani, Figure 19) that guided the reconstruction of the Metropolitan Museum's garment shows that single lapel models were current, too.

87. Ierusalimskaja, pp. 127–29, figs. 21f.; Ierusalimskaja and Borkopp, pp. 101f, no. 120. Again, this is not an isolated case in our context: a Chinese inscription, dated as early as the 2nd–3rd century A.D., was found in the Crimea; see B. I. Staviskii, "Central Asian Mesopotamia and the Roman World: Evidence of Contacts," *In the Land of the Gryphons* (Florence, 1995), pp. 191–202, esp. p. 192, with reference to *Sovetskaia Arkheologiia* 1972, 2, pp. 135–45, fig. 3 (p. 137), and p. 140 (I was unable to find the report at the indicated spot).

88. Topics relevant for costume history were broached at the Third International Archaeological Conference, "The Cultures of the Steppes of Eurasia of the Second Half of the 1st Millennium A.D.," in Samara, Russia, in March 2000. I am grateful to Dr. Gleb Kubarev for alerting me to the meeting and to Dr. D. Stashenkov, Regional Museum, Samara, for providing me with a preliminary program.

Armor Made in Basel: A Fifteenth-Century Sallet Attributed to Hans Blarer the Younger

PIERRE TERJANIAN

Adjunct Associate Curator in European Arms and Armor, Carl Otto von Kienbusch Collection of Arms and Armor, Philadelphia Museum of Art

ARMOR WAS MADE in hundreds of locations throughout Europe during the fifteenth century. Although this is substantiated by contemporary documents, very little armor surviving today can be attributed to a specific place of origin other than a handful of large, well-researched production centers. Most of the many smaller and less prominent sites have been overlooked. This article attempts to attribute a fifteenth-century German sallet (helmet) to an armorer active in Basel, thereby identifying a previously unknown maker in a city whose armor-manufacturing capacity has long been forgotten.

The majority of extant German armor cannot be ascribed to specific makers. Among the obstacles to identification is insufficient scholarly attention to the documentation of armorers and manufacturing sites. A few cities have been studied in detail, notably Augsburg, Nuremberg, and Landshut in southern Germany, and Innsbruck/Mühlau and Vienna in Austria, but other centers in the German-speaking core of the former Holy Roman Empire remain largely unresearched. The problem is compounded by the frequent absence of maker's marks or the inability to associate existing marks with known craftsmen or workshops. As a result, attributions of German armor are often based on subjective stylistic comparison with the few examples that bear identified makers' or town marks.

Armorers' marks stamped into the steel surface of helmets and other armor are clues essential to ascertaining their origin, provided that the marks can be securely linked to a specific craftsman or his workshop. For example, marks have provided indisputable grounds for ascribing sallets to no fewer than ten different master armorers active in Innsbruck and neighboring Mühlau in the years 1450–1500.[1] This was made possible by the extensive surviving records of these makers in the Innsbruck archives, and their

voluminous publication under the auspices of the former Austro-Hungarian monarchy.[2] Given the lack of comparable published material for most of the former Holy Roman Empire, few other makers active during the same period have been identified to date.

The subject of this article is a late-fifteenth-century sallet stamped with a hitherto unidentified maker's mark (Figures 1, 2). Preserved in the Metropolitan Museum, the sallet was included in a recent exhibition of European helmets at the Museum.[3] It is first recorded in the collection of Count Hans Wilczek (d. 1922) at Kreuzenstein Castle, near Vienna.[4] It was acquired from Kreuzenstein in 1927 by Bashford Dean (1867–1928), curator of arms and armor at the Metropolitan Museum, for his private collection, and it was purchased by the Museum in 1929.[5] No details are known about its provenance before it was acquired by Count Wilczek.

The form of the sallet suggests a south German origin and a date in the 1470s or the mid-1480s. Notable features are the slightly crested bowl, the moderately extended tail, and the pivoting visor that locks by a spring pin located on the right side. The flukelike conformation of the visor's upper edges, although infrequently encountered on preserved examples, is well documented in contemporary funeral effigies.[6]

The armorer's mark stamped on the right side of the sallet's tail depicts a rooster (cock) facing to the sinister in a shield (Figure 2). This mark corresponds to the heraldic emblem used by the Blarers (also spelled Blarrer, Blaerer, Plorer), a family of armorers documented at Basel throughout the fifteenth century.[7] Their existence was accidentally discovered in the Basel Staatsarchiv while the author of this paper was researching the armor production of early modern Europe.

The earliest member of the Blarer family was Hans, an armorer ("harnascher") from Constance who became a burgher of Basel on *Martinstag* (November 11) 1409.[8] Little is known of Hans Blarer's life and career other than the fact that he eventually became influential in

METROPOLITAN MUSEUM JOURNAL 36

The notes for this article begin on page 158.

Figure 1. Visored sallet, attributed to Hans Blarer the Younger (documented Basel, 1453–83), ca. 1470–85. Steel. The Metropolitan Museum of Art, Bashford Dean Memorial Collection, Funds from various donors, 1929 (29.158.11)

Figure 2. Maker's mark stamped on the tail of the sallet in Figure 1

the smiths' guild to which he belonged. In 1432 he was first appointed *Sechser*, a member of the committee of six masters overseeing the guild's normal business. In 1434 he became a *Kieser*, a position that probably conferred a say in specific guild or municipal matters (*kiesen*, archaic = to select, choose, elect).[9] Members honored with such positions were identified in a special volume compiled by the guild in the seventeenth century and now preserved in the Historisches Museum Basel. Their coat of arms, their name, and the date of their first appointment were carefully recorded; the thirty-first entry reads: "M[eister] Hans Plorer / Sechser 1432."[10] The master's coat of arms—Argent, a cock gules facing to the sinister—appears above the inscription (Figure 3).[11] The similarities

between this coat of arms and the mark on the Metropolitan's sallet are obvious, although Hans Blarer himself cannot have been the sallet's maker. He was active in the first half of the fifteenth century and therefore was unlikely to have made armor as late as the date of this sallet, about 1470–85.

Another possible candidate is Heinrich Blarer, who became a burgher of Basel in 1425. Heinrich was probably a relative of Hans Blarer, but he also appears to have been active too early in the century to qualify as the maker of the sallet.

The most likely owner of this mark is another Hans Blarer, documented from 1453 to 1483 and quite certainly related to the older armorer of the same name. This Hans Blarer's membership in the smiths' guild indicates that he had burgher status. Since he cannot be found in the burgher books recording the admission of new citizens, he was evidently born into the family of a Basel burgher of the same name. A master armorer in 1453, he could not have been born later than about 1437, when the elder Hans Blarer, probably his father, was still alive. His use of the heraldic emblem of a rooster, which appears on his personal seal on a 1482 document preserved in the Basel archives, conclusively demonstrates that he was directly related to the elder Hans Blarer (Figure 4).[12]

The identification of the younger Hans Blarer as the owner of this armorer's mark remains unequivocal despite a minor variation between his emblem and

Figure 3. Coat of arms of Hans Blarer the Elder, in entry 31 in a volume compiled in the 17th century by the smiths' guild of Basel. Historisches Museum Basel, 1882.169 (photo: Peter Portner, Historisches Museum Basel)

Figure 4. Wax seal of Hans Blarer the Younger, from a charter dated August 20, 1482. Staatsarchiv des Kantons Basel-Stadt, Urkunden, 2116 (photo: Staatsarchiv des Kantons Basel-Stadt)

that of his elder relative. In the former, the rooster is facing to the dexter, thus appearing reversed when compared to the elder Blarer's coat of arms and to the mark stamped on the Metropolitan's sallet. However, German and Swiss heraldry often permitted the reversal of positions, and such changes were sometimes dictated by mere aesthetic reasons and *courtoisie*. In any case, such reversals were not seen as significant alterations and should not be given undue weight when considering the identity of the arms' owner. The younger Blarer's wax seal depicting a rooster facing to the dexter actually follows the conventional position for animal charges, perhaps because seal engravers may have been more familiar than others with heraldic rules and conventions. It was also a common mistake to forget to reverse the emblem's position when cutting a seal or a punch—which wore out quickly and frequently had to be replaced—and all too often the emblem turned out to be reversed when stamped. As Helmut Nickel points out, a well-known inspection mark stamped on firearms, the hen of the town of Suhl (canting arms of the county of Henneberg), shows that a reversed position was not regarded as a matter of great importance. Although this was an official mark, hundreds of examples of the Suhl mark reveal that the hen could be facing either way.[13]

Deriving from the Blarer family coat of arms, the rooster mark securely identifies the younger Hans Blarer as the likely author of the Metropolitan's sallet.

For his maker's mark, he could certainly have used the family emblem in the same position as that of his ancestor, as it appears on the Metropolitan's sallet (Figure 2). No other contemporary armorer is known to have employed a similar device. Furthermore, there is no evidence that armorers of the Blarer family were active at places other than Basel during the fifteenth century, not even at Constance, where the elder Hans Blarer originated.[14]

Like his elder relative, Hans Blarer was a prominent craftsman who held several prestigious offices at the smiths' guild. He was *Sechser* from 1453 to 1467, then *Kieser* from 1468 to 1473.[15] Blarer seems to have obtained municipal offices as well. A document of 1459, in which he is referred to as an armor maker ("harnescher"), reveals that he was also a rent master ("der reten ze Basel zinsmeister"), that is, a collector of revenues on behalf of the city council.[16] These many responsibilities suffice to indicate that Hans Blarer had a reputation beyond the guild. A married man, Blarer had several children who were still minors when he was last mentioned in 1483; nothing else is known of them.[17]

In his book on Swiss arms makers, *Schweizer Waffenschmiede*, Hugo Schneider identified two distinct master armorers named Hans Blarer, probably father and son, active in Basel during the second half of the fifteenth century. According to Schneider, one is documented from 1456 to about 1460, the other from

1469 to 1479.[18] No evidence has been found in Basel archives, however, to confirm this distinction.

The attribution of the Metropolitan's sallet to Hans Blarer the Younger identifies a surviving armorer's work from Basel. During the fifteenth century, Basel was an important staple market on the busy trade routes connecting northern Italy to the Low Countries. This capacity promoted a flourishing trade in armor, enabling domestic armorers, in turn, to achieve considerable wealth.[19] In the early fifteenth century, for example, a mail maker, Heinrich Kupfernagel, acknowledged a fortune of some 2,000 florins.[20] During the younger Blarer's active years, Basel was an armor-making center esteemed by foreign princes. Although the duke of Lorraine employed several armorers at his court, he commissioned an armor for his personal use at Basel in 1493.[21] At that time, Basel was still an imperial city; it became part of the Swiss Confederation in 1501.

Hans Blarer's influential position in the smiths' guild must have reflected, beyond his social status, a relative material success as well. Further archival research would certainly uncover more details on his career as a master armorer. No other armor pieces bearing his mark have been identified to date, but some may be found in the future.[22] Hans Blarer's sallet serves as a reminder of the existence of notable armor-manufacturing cities whose history still needs investigation.[23]

ACKNOWLEDGMENTS

I am greatly indebted to Stuart W. Pyhrr, Arthur Ochs Sulzberger Curator in Charge of the Department of Arms and Armor at the Metropolitan Museum, for his encouragement and support in the preparation of this article. I am also very grateful to Sonya Terjanian, my wife, for reviewing the initial manuscript and suggesting many useful revisions to the text. I would like to thank Helmut Nickel for his helpful advice and useful suggestions on heraldic issues, and Thom Richardson, Keeper of Armour and Oriental Collections at the Royal Armouries Museum, Leeds, for consulting the de Cosson files about Hans Blarer's mark.

NOTES

1. The Innsbruck/Mühlau masters in question are: Konrad, Jörg, Adrian the Elder, and Christian Treytz; Hans Vetterlein; Christian Schreiner the Elder; Kaspar Rieder(er); Christian Spor; Jörg Wagner; and Hans Prunner.

2. This literature is listed in Bruno Thomas and Ortwin Gamber, *Die Innsbrucker Plattnerkunst*, exh. cat. (Innsbruck, 1954), pp. 49–50.

3. Stuart W. Pyhrr, *European Helmets, 1450–1650: Treasures from the Reserve Collection*, exh. cat., MMA (New York, 2000), no. 12, ills.

4. The construction of Kreuzenstein Castle from existing ruins began in 1879. See Alfred Ritter von Walcher, *Burg Kreuzenstein an der Donau* (Vienna, [1914]). On Count Wilczek and his arms and armor collection, see Graf Wilczek, *Erinnerungen eines Waffensammlers* (Vienna, 1908), pp. 9, 21–24; "Mittelalterliche Helme aus dem Besitz Sr. Exz. des Grafen Hans Wilczek: Sammlung Schloss Kreuzenstein," *Zeitschrift für historische Waffen- und Kostümkunde* 6, no. 2 (1912–14), pp. 41–47. A brief obituary is in *Zeitschrift für historische Waffen- und Kostümkunde* 9, no. 4 (1922), p. 148.

5. Acc. no. 29.58.11, Bashford Dean Memorial Collection, Funds from various donors; Pyhrr, *European Helmets, 1450–1650*, no. 12; Stephen V. Grancsay and Carl Otto von Kienbusch, *The Bashford Dean Collection of Arms and Armor in The Metropolitan Museum of Art* (Portland, Maine, 1933), no. 39, pls. I no. 39 and IV no. 39.

6. A comparable cut of the visor's upper edges can be found on a sallet in the Historisches Museum der Stadt, Vienna, inv. no. 126.014; another sallet in the Armeria Reale, Turin, inv. no. E 4; and on many funeral effigies in southern Germany, for example, those of Ulrich Staufer zu Ernfels, Pfarrkirche, Sünching; of Heinrich von Nothaft (d. 1471), Karmeliterkirche, Straubing; of Heinrich von Staudach (d. 1483), Sankt Jodokskirche, Landshut. Illustrated in Philipp Maria Halm, *Studien zur süddeutschen Plastik*, vol. 1, *Altbayern und Schwaben* (Augsburg, 1926).

7. The rooster in the Blarer family coat of arms seems to be "canting," i.e., forming some sort of wordplay with the owner's arms. *Blaerer* refers to one that crows, or makes strident noises, which would describe the cry of a rooster (*plärren* = to crow, blubber, bawl, cry). Helmut Nickel suggested this possibility to Stuart Pyhrr, later directly to the author of this article in a letter of May 27, 2000.

8. Staatsarchiv des Kantons Basel-Stadt, Ratsbücher P 7, 1, Chron. Verz. der Bürgerannahmen I: Vor 1530. In southwestern Germany, *Harnischer*, a contraction of armor maker (*Harnischmacher*), was a label commonly used for the makers of plate armor until the mid-16th century, when they became increasingly referred to as *Plattner*. In Basel this equivalence is explicitly indicated in records of the smiths' guild, with the following entry: "Hans Saur, the armor maker or plate armorer . . ." (Hans Saur der harnister oder plattener hat ein Ehrer Zunfft zue den Schmieden empfangen. . . . Actum Sonntag Trinitatis A[nn]o etc. 1551); Staatsarchiv des Kantons Basel-Stadt, Zunftakten, Schmiedezunft 28, fol. 119v.

9. Staatsarchiv des Kantons Basel-Stadt, Zunftakten, Schmiedezunft 22.

10. Historiches Museum Basel, inv. no. 1882.169, entry no. 31.

11. The description in heraldic language was kindly provided by Helmut Nickel in a letter to the author, May 27, 2000.

12. Staatsarchiv des Kantons Basel-Stadt, Urkunden, no. 2116, August 20, 1482; cited in Rudolf Thommen, ed., *Urkundenbuch der Stadt Basel*, vol. 8 (Basel, 1901), no. 633.

13. Letter to the author, May 27, 2000.

14. The name and coat of arms of the Blarer armorers of Basel, together with the geographical origin of the elder Hans Blarer, suggest the possibility that they were indirectly related to the Blarer patrician family of Constance. See, for instance, the portrait of Heinrich Blarer of Constance, dated 1460, with his coat

of arms (Argent, a cock gules facing to the sinister), preserved at the Rosengartenmuseum Konstanz, inv. no. M 15; Bernd Konrad, *Rosengartenmuseum Konstanz: Die Kunstwerke des Mittelalters* (Constance, 1993), no. 1.05, pl. 4.

The Constance Blarers belonged to the social elite of the city—the patricians—and some of them sat in the city council. While a few, like Heinrich Blarer, collected memberships in knightly orders and participated in jousts, others took a very different path in the 16th century—for example, as abbot of Saint Gall, or as religious reformers.

The nature of the relationship between the elder Hans Blarer and the Blarers of Constance remains unclear. Precedents allow us to speculate that he belonged to an ancient line of armorers whose most distinguished members entered the ranks of the Constance patriciate in the 14th century or even earlier. The case of the Brun(lin) mail makers at Strasbourg demonstrates well the potential of the armorer's profession for considerable social advancement in the 14th century. See Martin Alioth, *Gruppen an der Macht. Zünfte und Patriziat in Strassburg in 14. und 15. Jahrhundert: Untersuchungen zur Verfassung, Wirtschaftsgefüge und Sozialstruktur* (Basel and Frankfurt am Main, 1988), vol. 1, p. 293. Members of the patrician Blarers also lived in Augsburg. See Eduard Zimmermann, *Augsburger Zeichen und Wappen* (Augsburg, 1970), no. 5638, ill.

15. Staatsarchiv des Kantons Basel-Stadt, Zunftakten, Schmiedezunft 22.

16. *Urkundenbuch der Stadt Basel*, vol. 8, no. 117.

17. Staatsarchiv des Kantons Basel-Stadt, Gerichtsarchiv A 34, fol. 362v.

18. Hugo Schneider, *Schweizer Waffenschmiede: Vom 15. bis 20. Jh.* (Zurich, 1976), p. 61.

19. On a Basel merchant importing armor from Milan in 1473, see Emilio Motta, "Armaiuoli milanesi nel periodo visconteosforzesco," *Archivio Storico Lombardo* 41, no. 5 (1914), entry no. 113. For a reference to Basel's role in the importation of foreign armor in France, see Jean-Pierre Reverseau, "The Classification of French Armour by Workshop Styles, 1500–1600," in Robert Held, ed., *Art, Arms, and Armour: An International Anthology*, vol. 1, *1979–80* (Chiasso, 1979), p. 203.

20. See on this topic Katharina Simon-Muscheid, *Basler Handwerkszünfte im Spätmittelalter: Zunftinterne Strukturen und Innerstädtische Konflikte*, Ph.D. diss., University of Basel, 1986; Europäische Hochschulschriften, Bd. 348 (Bern, 1988).

21. Archives Départementales de Meurthe-et-Moselle, Nancy, B 8339: Compte de Claude d'Ainvaux, receveur de Raon.

22. Personal communication from Stuart W. Pyhrr to the author, February 1, 2000. I am also grateful to Thom Richardson for checking records of armorers' marks compiled by Baron Charles Alexander de Cosson (1846–1929) and later by Royal Armouries staff after the so-called de Cosson dictionary entered the collections of the Tower of London. This investigation did not reveal the existence of another piece with Hans Blarer's mark. Personal communication to the author, February 24, 2000.

For an example of subsequent discoveries of medieval plate armor with marks of Innsbruck and Mühlau masters, see Bruno Thomas, "Die Innsbrucker Plattnerkunst—Ein Nachtrag," *Jahrbuch der Kunsthistorischen Sammlungen in Wien* 70 (1974), pp. 179–220.

23. Medieval mail shirts signed by Basel mail makers have survived. One is in the Schweizerisches Landesmuseum, Zurich (signed FRANZ KLUSEMAN); the other was in the armory of Churburg Castle, ex T1 (signed BTL: STADLER V BASEL). See Schneider, *Schweizer Waffenschmiede*, p. 162; and Thom Richardson, "The Archibald hauberk," *Royal Armouries Yearbook* 4 (1999), p. 30.

Signorelli's *Madonna and Child:* A Gift to His Daughter

Oxford Brookes University

L UCA SIGNORELLI'S *Madonna and Child* in the Metropolitan Museum (Figure 1) is an exquisite picture, eloquently and intelligently appreciated by Roger Fry in 1910:

> [Signorelli's] *Madonna* is a great and profoundly original creation. At first sight one is inclined to complain that the elaborately decorated gold background, an imitation apparently of a gilded leather hanging, is too assertive, that the rich golden flesh tones are not sufficiently relieved; but as the eye gets accustomed to the unusual treatment one not only gains intense satisfaction from the marvellous drawing of the gold decoration, with its *intreccia* of aggressive *putti* and scroll-work, but one realizes that the figures of the Madonna and Child maintain their due predominance by the unparalleled amplitude and simplicity of their forms. The simplification here is such as only a few of the greatest draughtsmen have ever attained to. It is as surprising as Piero della Francesca's, and yet the line seems to imply the control of a more tumultuous, nervous force. The color, too, with its suggestion of archaic and Byzantine originals, is one of the most daring and successful experiments in Italian art.[1]

The painting measures 51.4 by 47.6 centimeters and was first recorded in the Tommasi collection in Cortona in 1857.[2] It had been sold to Robert Benson by 1893 and passed (via Duveen) to Jules Bache in 1928. The Metropolitan Museum acquired the picture in 1949, as part of the Bache Collection, and it is frequently referred to as the *Bache Madonna*. The painting has been accepted as an autograph work by Luca Signorelli (ca. 1450–1523) in most modern scholarship and is generally dated about 1505–10.[3]

One can read biographies of fifteenth-century artists without ever learning whether they married or had children. In the case of the *Bache Madonna*, however, Signorelli's private life sheds light on his picture. An overlooked, but not unknown, document in the State Archives in Florence effectively establishes that the *Bache Madonna* was given by Luca Signorelli to his daughter Gabriella in April 1507.[4] This provides a

charming provenance, a confirmation of the date, and some explanation of the appearance of the picture. It is also one of the rare occasions in the history of Italian Renaissance art in which a domestic picture can be related to a contemporary document.

Luca Signorelli was born in Cortona about 1450 and died there in October 1523.[5] He married Galizia Carnesecchi soon after 1470 (when Galizia was described as still unmarried),[6] and she predeceased him in September 1506.[7] Four of the couple's children lived into adulthood: Antonio, Tommaso, Felicia, and Gabriella.

The eldest, Antonio, appeared before the Priors in Cortona in 1490 to explain his father's absence elsewhere (almost certainly in Volterra).[8] He became an assistant to his father, and in 1494 he apparently collected a payment for Signorelli in Città di Castello.[9] In February 1497 Antonio witnessed a document in his father's workshop in Cortona,[10] but his only documented activity as a painter was a pair of candelabra, which had been commissioned from Luca in 1495.[11] Kanter has cautiously advanced that Antonio's hand might be found in the *Assumption of the Virgin* in the Metropolitan Museum (acc. no. 29.164), and in the earliest frescoes at Monteoliveto Maggiore, painted about 1498–99.[12] But before Antonio could develop into an independent artist he died, almost certainly of the plague.[13] He was still alive on July 2, 1502, but was dead by July 23, when Signorelli, acting as his heir, returned some land which had been part of the dowry that Antonio's wife had brought to the Signorelli estates.[14] Signorelli's second son, Tommaso, was not a painter, but was named as the artist's heir from 1502 onward (following the death of his elder brother). He duly inherited his father's property in 1523 and died in 1529.[15]

Signorelli also had two daughters, both of whom married and had children. The elder, Felicia, married Luca Boscia in October 1500 with a dowry of 220 florins.[16] She had a daughter, Bernardina, but died before Signorelli drew up his first surviving will, in August 1502.[17] If, as seems likely, she died in the same bout of plague that claimed Antonio Signorelli, we can probably infer that Luca's will, which he made on

© The Metropolitan Museum of Art 2001
METROPOLITAN MUSEUM JOURNAL 36

The notes for this article begin on page 167.

Figure 1. Luca Signorelli (Italian, ca. 1450–1523). *Madonna and Child*, ca. 1505–7. Oil and gold on wood, 51.4 x 47.6 cm. The Metropolitan Museum of Art, The Jules Bache Collection, 1949 (49.7.13). See also front cover

August 1, 1502, was a response to this family tragedy (both at the level of the morbid thoughts that were probably provoked by the death of his children and to vary the terms of his will in order to install Tommaso Signorelli as his universal heir).[18]

Signorelli's second daughter, Gabriella, married Mariotto di Antonio Mazza (also from Cortona) sometime before August 1502, and the couple had three daughters. There are a few scattered references to Gabriella. The first is oblique. In December 1492, Signorelli bought new dresses for his daughters from a Cortonese tailor, Pavolino di Mariotto, and one of these was probably for Gabriella.[19] She was mentioned in his will of 1502, and when Signorelli renewed his will in October 1504, Gabriella was bequeathed a mourning dress worth 7 florins (the same value, inci-

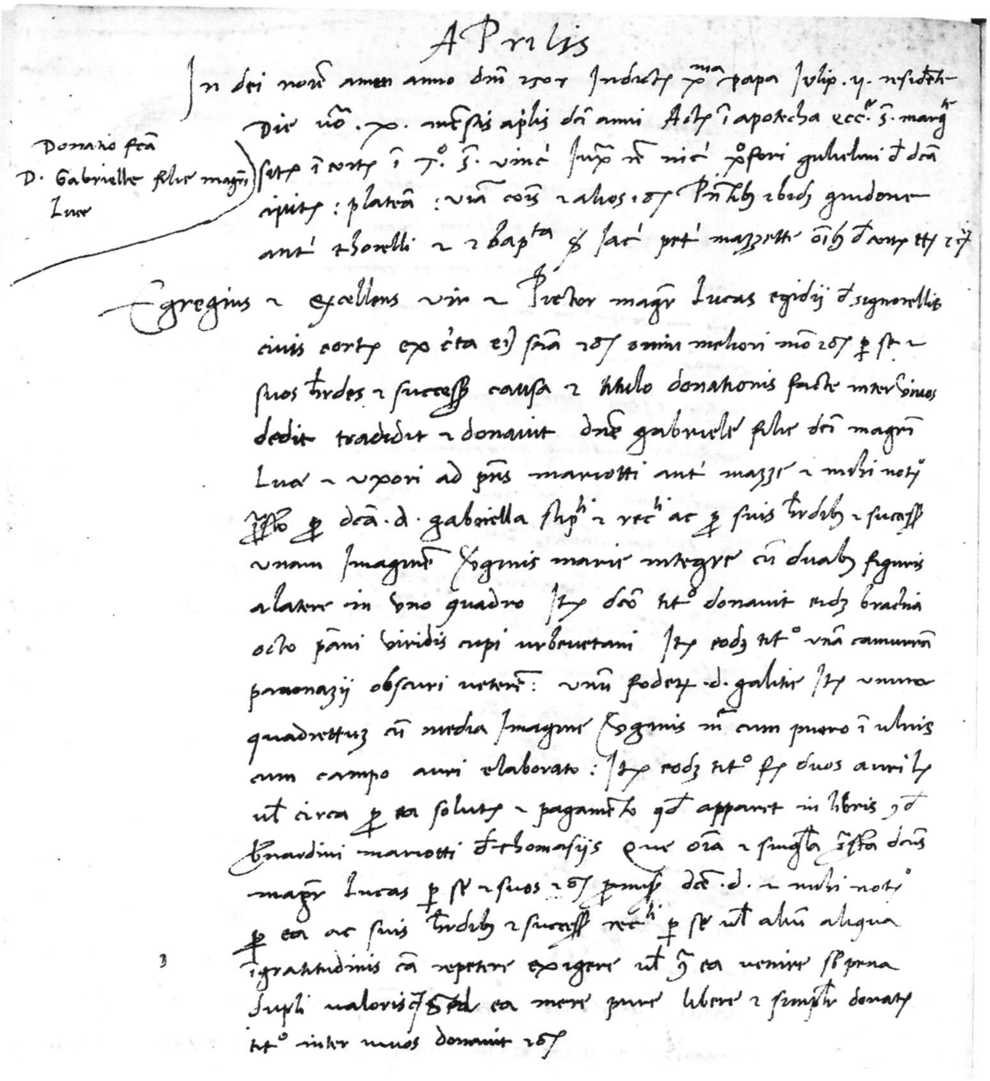

Figure 2. Notarial act of April 10, 1507. Archivio di Stato, Florence, Notarile Antecosimiano 11417 (formerly L 51), Noferi Laparelli, 1501–7, fol. 271v (photo: Archivio di Stato, Florence)

dentally, as a tondo that he painted in 1505).[20] In Signorelli's final will of October 1523, this bequest to Gabriella was extended to mourning dresses for her two unmarried daughters, Felicia and Diana.[21] And Gabriella was also remembered in her mother's will, in which she was left 4 florins.[22]

The gifts to Gabriella that concern us are not, however, these items of cash and clothing, but some paintings that the artist gave to his daughter on April 10, 1507. In a notarial act (Figure 2) which was drawn up in the church of Santa Margherita in Cortona by Ser Noferi Laparelli, Signorelli gave his one surviving daughter various possessions.[23] The reason for this gift was not stated, but the death of Luca's wife (and Gabriella's mother) in the previous year may provide the context of the gift. Alternatively it may have been intended to celebrate the birth of a child. The gift included a length of green cloth from Orvieto, a dark purple cloak (camurra), a coverlet that had belonged to Gabriella's mother, and 2 gold florins, which were owed to Bernardino di Mariotto (Cortonesi).

The gift also included two paintings. The first is unidentified. It was "an image of the Virgin Mary, full-length with two figures to the side."[24] No indication of scale is given, except that it was called a quadro and was presumably larger than the second picture (which was described as a quadrettum). The only surviving picture which fits this description is a fragment of an altarpiece at Lucignano, but this picture does not have a provenance that can reasonably be traced to Signorelli's family and it is unlikely to have been a domestic picture.[25] It was probably not the same picture that was given to Gabriella.

The second painting was a "small picture with a

163

Figure 3. Luca Signorelli. *Four Standing Figures* (fragment of the Matélica altarpiece), 1504–5. Oil and gold on wood, 71 x 88.4 cm. Private collection, England (photo: National Gallery, London)

half-length image of the Virgin Mary with her son in her lap with an elaborate gold background" (unum quadrettum cum media imagine Virginis Marie cum puero in ulnis cum campo auri elaborato). There is little doubt that this picture was the *Bache Madonna.* Although the document does not state that Signorelli was the author of this picture, the implication seems reasonable, and this painting is Signorelli's only known gold-backed Madonna. The *Bache Madonna* is also surprisingly small, given the forceful impact of the figures. The extraordinary gilded background points to a specific moment in the artist's career: the first decade of the sixteenth century. Although it has been dated as early as the 1480s (Van Marle) or the 1490s (Dussler),[26] most commentators (Salmi, Scarpellini, Zeri, and Kanter) have associated the *Bache Madonna* with the decorative tendency seen in the Cortona *Lamentation,* the Matélica altarpiece, and the Arcevia polyptych and have plausibly dated the picture about 1505–7.[27] The Matélica altarpiece is securely dated 1504–5, and there is a clear connection between the *Bache Madonna* and the severe profile and the glazed putti painted on a gold background in the draperies of one fragment from this altarpiece, the *Four Standing Figures* in an English private collection (Figure 3; foreground left).[28] There are also connections with the *Virgin and Child* of the Arcevia polyptych

of 1507 (Figure 4). The decorative motifs of the Virgin's draperies in this picture can again be compared with the *Bache Madonna,* and the Virgin and child are closely comparable, although I would argue that this group at Arcevia develops out of the solution for the *Bache Madonna* (and not vice versa).

The unique gold background and the stylistic dating both support the conclusion that the *Bache Madonna* was Signorelli's gift to his daughter, and the provenance of the picture may support this view (and certainly does not undermine it). We do not know how the picture entered the Tommasi collection, where it was first recorded in 1857, but there is no evidence that the family ever acquired fifteenth- or sixteenth-century pictures outside Cortona. By the mid-nineteenth century the family owned several pictures by Signorelli, and all of them appear to have been painted for Cortonese families or churches.[29] While these examples suggest that the Tommasi actively acquired pictures that were available in Cortona, the *Bache Madonna* might have entered the collection in another way. Felicia Signorelli married Luca Boscia in 1500.[30] The Boscia line merged with the Tommasi in the early seventeenth century (with subsequent generations of the family tracing themselves to both lines).[31] The *Bache Madonna* might have entered the Tommasi collection if, for instance, Felicia's daughter, Bernardina, had inherited the picture when Gabriella's daughters died without issue. This is, however, pure speculation.

On balance, the unique gilded background, the scale, the date, and the provenance of the *Bache Madonna* all point to its identity with the picture that Signorelli gave to his daughter in 1507. It would, in that case, have been familiar to Signorelli's nephew and artistic heir, Francesco Signorelli (ca. 1490/95–1553).[32] This may help to explain the genesis of another picture which is sometimes attributed to Luca Signorelli but has more recently been assigned to Francesco: the *Virgin and Child* in the Walker Art Gallery, Liverpool (Figure 5).[33] This picture is very badly abraded and was extensively overpainted in the past.[34] Although the Liverpool picture is slightly larger than the *Bache Madonna* (it measures 59.1 by 50.1 cm), the two pictures appear to have been executed on the basis of the same cartoon, and Kanter has suggested that the Liverpool version was probably painted by Francesco Signorelli, possibly before Luca's death and under his supervision (ca. 1515?).[35] The fact that the colors of the Virgin's draperies are identical in both versions also suggests familiarity with the *Bache Madonna*.

Signorelli's painting in the Metropolitan Museum is exceptionally well preserved, although it is slightly abraded and has a few localized repaints. It is a beguiling image and there are few comparable works by other artists. The most unusual elements in the picture are the decorative motifs and the putti (both winged and wingless) of the gold background. These putti are painted in thin red, blue, and green glazes on gold leaf and reflect Signorelli's decorative interest in the first decade of the sixteenth century. Fry suggested that the background is meant to recall a "gilded leather hanging," a type of decoration known to have existed during the Renaissance (e.g., in the Palazzo Medici, Florence).[36] Alternatively this background can be compared to intricate bookbindings or to the *quadratura* of fifteenth-century illuminated manuscripts, but the scale is unusual and this explanation of

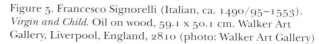

Figure 4. Luca Signorelli. *Virgin and Child* (detail of the central panel of the Arcevia polyptych), 1507. Oil and gold on wood. Collegiata di San Medardo, Arcevia, Italy (photo: Istituto Centrale per il Catalogo e la Documentazione, Rome)

Figure 5. Francesco Signorelli (Italian, ca. 1490/95–1553). *Virgin and Child.* Oil on wood, 59.1 x 50.1 cm. Walker Art Gallery, Liverpool, England, 2810 (photo: Walker Art Gallery)

the picture's appearance is not very satisfactory.[37] Another possibility, which was suggested to me by Keith Christiansen, is that this background recalls a window made out of stained-glass roundels. The way in which these roundels are apparently joined to one another by small loops recalls window construction, and if Signorelli's house had windows of this type there is no reason why he could not have decorated the panes of glass with glazes.[38]

Another unusual feature of the picture is the two coins, or medals, with their wreathed portraits of Roman emperors. The medal in the top left corner shows Domitian (r. 81–96) and is inscribed: s·p·q·r domicianvs ii im / s / c (The Senate and the People of Rome. Domitian Emperor in the Second Year of His Reign, by Decree of the Senate). The medal in the top right corner shows Caracalla (r. 211–17) and is inscribed: s·p·q·r· cha·chali·im·an·iii m·iiii / i / c (The Senate and the People of Rome. Caracalla Emperor in the Third Year and the Fourth Month of His Reign, by Decree of the Emperor). These medals are, however, Renaissance fantasy rather than copies after the antique, and their inscriptions are similarly made up.[39] The proportions of the heads to the fields is also unrelated to ancient Roman coins, and they are no more than generically *all'antica*.

In addition to his sensitivity to the nature of the background, to the role of color and of line, and to the primacy of the *Bache Madonna* over the Liverpool version, Roger Fry was also keenly aware of the simplicity of the Virgin Mary in this picture. She is more plainly dressed than most of Signorelli's other Madonnas—and she has not been given a halo. She is the Mother of God and may have been painted, with loving care, at a moment when Signorelli had lost his wife and the mother of his children.[40] If so, this gift to his surviving daughter was particularly poignant, and the *Bache Madonna*'s charm may have found a partial explanation.

ACKNOWLEDGMENTS

This paper is dedicated to the memory of Guido Tommasi-Aliotti (1926–1996), who was the passionate guardian of his family archive and founder of the Associazione fra i Proprietari di Archivi di Carattere Domestico in Cortona. He facilitated my researches into the provenance of the *Bache Madonna*, which was owned by the Tommasi family in the nineteenth century; I am also indebted for her assistance to his widow, Grazia Tommasi-Aliotti. An earlier version of this paper was presented at the Metropolitan Museum in February 1999, and I am very grateful to Keith Christiansen for inviting me to speak and for welcoming me to New York. My transcription of the document of April 1507 was kindly corrected by Caroline Elam.

ABBREVIATIONS

ASCC
    Archivio Storico Comunale, Cortona
ASF, NA
    Archivio di Stato, Florence, Notarile Antecosimiano
Mancini 1903
    Girolamo Mancini. *Vita di Luca Signorelli*. Florence: Carnesecchi, 1903.
Zeri and Gardner 1980
    Federico Zeri and Elizabeth Gardner. *Italian Paintings, a Catalogue of the Collection of The Metropolitan Museum of Art: Sienese and Central Italian Schools*. New York: MMA, 1980.

APPENDIX

Archivio di Stato, Florence, Notarile Antecosimiano 11417 (formerly L 51), Noferi Laparelli, 1501–7, fol. 271v (10.4.1507). Unpublished (referred to by Girolamo Mancini, *Vita di Luca Signorelli* [Florence: Carnesecchi, 1903], p. 148). New transcription by Tom Henry and Caroline Elam.

Aprilis
[note in margin] Donatio facta domine Gabrielle filie magistri Luce

In dei nomine amen. Anno domini 1507 Indictione X^ma papa Julio ii residente. Die vero X mensis aprilis dicti anni. Actum in apotecha ecclesie sancte Margharite sita in Cortona in terzerio S. Vincenti iuxta rem Nicoli Christofori Gulielmi de dicta civitate, plateam, viam comunis et alios etc. Presentibus ibidem Guidone Antoni Thorelli et Baptista Ser Jacobi Petri Mazzette omnibus de Cortona testibus etc.

Egregius et excellens vir et Pictor magister Lucas Egidii de Signorellis civis Cortonensis ex certa eius scientia etc. omni meliori modo etc. per se et suos heredes et successores causa et titulo donationis facte inter vivos dedit tradidit et donavit domine Gabriele filie dicti magistri Luce et uxori ad presens Mariotti Antoni Mazze et mihi notario infrascripto pro dicta domina Gabriella stipulanti et recipienti ac pro suis heredibus et successoribus unam imaginem Virginis Marie integre cum duabus figuris a latere in uno quadro. Item dicto titulo donavit eidem brachia octo panni viridis ciopi urbevetani. Item eodem titulo unam camurram pavonazii obscuri veterem, unum foderum domine Galitie. Item unum quadrettum cum media imagine Virginis Marie cum puero in ulnis cum campo auri elaborato. Item eodem titulo florenos duos auri larghi vel circa pro ea solutione et pagamento quod apparet in libris quondam Bernardini Mariotti de Thomasiis que omnia et singula suprascripta dictus magister Lucas per se et suos etc. promisit dicte domine et mihi notario pro ea ac suis heredibus et successoribus recipienti per se vel alium aliqua ingratitudinis casu repetere exigere vel cum ea venire sub pena dupli valoris etc. Sed ea mere pure libere e simpliciter donativo titulo inter vivos donavit etc.

April

[note in margin] Gift made to Mistress Gabriella daughter of master Luca

In the name of God amen. Year of our Lord 1507, Tenth Indiction, Pope Julius II residing. On the tenth day of April of the year stated. Enacted in the workshop of the church of Saint Margaret situated in Cortona in the *terzerio* of St. Vincent next to the property of Niccolo Cristoforo Gulielmo of the said city, the square, the common road and other [boundaries], etc. In the presence at the same place of Guido Antonio Thorelli and Battista di Ser Jacopo Pietro Mazzette all from Cortona, witnesses.

Master Luca di Egidio Signorelli, outstanding and excellent man and painter, citizen of Cortona in his sure knowledge, etc., and in every way for the better on behalf of himself and his heirs and successors after he had made a gift of cause and title in his lifetime, gave handed over and granted to Mistress Gabriella the daughter of the aforementioned master Luca and wife for the present of Mariotto Antonio Mazza. And to me the notary named here, requesting and receiving on behalf of the aforementioned Mistress Gabriella and on behalf of her heirs and successors an image of the Virgin Mary, full-length with two figures to the side in a painting. Also by the aforementioned title he has then given eight *braccia* of green cloth from Orvieto. Also in the same title an old dark purple *camurra*, [and] a coverlet belonging to Mistress Galitia. Also a small picture with a half-length image of the Virgin Mary with her son in her lap with an elaborate gold background. Also in the same title two large golden florins as payment and satisfaction of [the debt?] that appears in the accounts of Bernardino Mariotto di Tommaso. Which all together and singly here noted the aforesaid master Luca promised on behalf of himself and his family. And he promised to

the aforesaid mistress and to me as notary through these statements and for his heirs and successors . . . [continues with two lines of legal formula]

NOTES

1. Roger Fry, "The Umbrian Exhibition at the Burlington Fine Arts Club," *Burlington Magazine* 16 (1909–10), pp. 267–74, esp. pp. 268–73. For Fry's particular interest in Signorelli, see Caroline Elam, "Roger Fry and Early Italian Painting" in Chris Green, ed., *Art Made Modern: Roger Fry's Vision of Art*, exh. cat., Courtauld Gallery, London (London: Merrell Holberton, 1999–2000), pp. 87–106, esp. pp. 102–3.

2. It was seen in Cortona by Otto Mündler, September 8, 1857: "Caval^re Luigi (or Luca?) Tommasi has several pictures by Signorelli. . . . A Virgin and Child by the same artist, is more delicate, and preferable; yet extremely dirty, 1 f. 6¼ in. w. 1 f. 8¼ in h." (Carol Togneri Dowd, ed., "The Travel Diaries of Otto Mündler 1855–1858," *Walpole Society* 51 [1985], p. 165). The picture was also described by Charles Eastlake, "Notebook" (in the archive of the National Gallery, London), 1857, vol. 1, fol. 5r–v. It cannot be confidently identified in the "Inventario e stima di tutti i quadri che esistono nel palazzo dei nobili Signori Luigi e Girolamo Tommasi fatta del Prof. Niccola Monti" (20.3.1858), MS in the Tommasi-Aliotti archive, Cortona. But it was recorded as in the Girolamo Tommasi collection by Robert Vischer, *Luca Signorelli und die italienische Renaissance, eine kunsthistorische Monographie* (Leipzig: Veit, 1879), p. 260.

3. Zeri and Gardner 1980, pp. 91–92, with previous bibliography.

4. The document was referred to, but not published, by Mancini 1903, p. 148. The connection with the *Bache Madonna* has not previously been proposed (except in my Ph.D. diss., "The Career of Luca Signorelli in the 1490s," London University, 1996, p. 222).

5. Signorelli's date of birth is unknown. For his death, see Nicola Fruscoloni, "Quattro documenti inediti per la vita di Luca Signorelli," *Annuario dell'Accademia Etrusca di Cortona* 21 (1984), pp. 175–89, esp. p. 188.

6. Mancini 1903, p. 18.

7. Mancini 1903, p. 19 (and ASF, NA 11413 [formerly L 49], Girolamo Laparelli, 1505–7, fols. 279r–283r).

8. ASCC, Lib. Q. 4, fol. 20r (27.12.1490); paraphrased by Girolamo Mancini, *Notizie sulla Chiesa del Calcinaio* (Cortona: Bimbi, 1868), p. 88. For Signorelli in Volterra, see Tom Henry, "New documents for Signorelli's 'Annunciation' at Volterra," *Burlington Magazine* 140 (1998), pp. 474–78.

9. Archivio Comunale, Città di Castello, "Antico libro de' creditori della comune," 1494, fol. 7 (published by Giacomo Mancini, *Istruzione storico-pittorica per visitare le Chiese e i Palazzi di Città di Castello* [Perugia: Baduel, 1832], vol. 2, pp. 68, 69): "1494 Maestro Luca da Cortona depentore deve dare a di I. de febbraro Ducati 6. d'oro larghi, li quali ha auto suo figliolo."

10. ASF, NA 17811 (formerly R 128), Lodovico Ricci, 1494–97, fol. 171r–v (10.2.1497). Unpublished.

11. ASCC, Lib. Z. 7, "Libro di entrate e uscite della Compagnia laicale del SS. Salvatore, 1490–1536," fols. 31v–32r (17.6.1495); published by Fruscoloni, "Quattro documenti inediti per la vita di Luca Signorelli," pp. 175–77: "Antonio, suo figliolo, dia

avere adì dicto lire una et soldi quindice tanti sono per dipintura de uno paio de candellieri, quali depinse per la Compagnia a biacha inbrunita; monta lire 1, soldi 15, denari."

12. Laurence Kanter, "Signorelli, Siena and the Griselda Master," paper given at a conference, "Signorelli, Raphael, and the 'Other' Artists in the Stanze of Julius II," at the Courtauld Institute of Art, London, November 1998.

13. Luca Signorelli was extracted to serve as a Prior on June 23, 1502, but was excused "habebat familiam morbo epidemie oppressam"; ASCC, Lib. Q. 5, fol. 97r (23.6.1502); Mancini, *Notizie sulla Chiesa del Calcinaio*, p. 89. Antonio was still alive at this date, and this probably refers to Luca's daughter Felicia.

14. See Mancini 1903, pp. 137–38, and ASF, NA 20989 (formerly V 142), Cristoforo Venuti, 1497–1516, fols. 61v–62r (23.7.1502).

15. Mancini 1903, pp. 241–42.

16. ASF, NA 15272 (formerly N 178), Paolo Ferrantini, 1499–1502, fols. 133v–135r (14.10.1500); referred to by Mancini 1903, p. 130.

17. Felicia was apparently still alive in June 1501, see ASF, NA 15272 (formerly N 178), Paolo Ferrantini, 1499–1502, fol. 134v (19.6.1501); referred to by Mancini 1903, p. 130.

18. ASF, NA 5596 (formerly C 623), Pietro Coppi, 1497–1504, fols. 57v–59r (1.8.1502); referred to by Mancini 1903, p. 139. Signorelli's wills are the principal source of information about the artist and his family.

19. ASCC, Lib. G. 1, "Libro dei Ricordi di Pavolino di Mariotto Sarto, 1491–1518," fol. 12r (1.12.1492): "Maestro Lucha denpentore di dare adi predetto di sopra per fatura di tre giubarele del filole monta L 20 S 26." Unpublished.

20. ASF, NA 11417 (formerly L 51), Noferi Laparelli, 1501–7, fols. 141r–146r (31.10.1504); referred to by Mancini 1903, p. 144: ". . . unam Cioppam sive vestem lugubrem panni monacchini valoris et comunis exstimationis florenorum septe auri boni et iusti ponderis comunis cortone." For the tondo, see Laurence Kanter and David Franklin, "Some Passion Scenes by Luca Signorelli after 1500," *Mitteilungen des Kunsthistorischen Instituts in Florenz* 35 (1991), pp. 171–91.

21. ASF, NA 1173 (formerly B 161), Niccolò Baldelli, 1507–24 (1523.2), fols. 10r–14r (13.10.1523); referred to by Vischer, *Luca Signorelli*, pp. 365–66.

22. ASF, NA 11413 (formerly L 49), Girolamo Laparelli, 1505–7, fols. 279r–283r (7.9.1506); referred to by Mancini 1903, p. 19.

23. This act is published in full here in the Appendix.

24. "unam imaginem Virginis Marie integre cum duabus figuris a latere in uno quadro"; see Appendix.

25. See Luitpold Dussler, *Signorelli*, Klassiker der Kunst 34 (Berlin and Leipzig: Deutsche Verlags-Anstalt, 1927), pl. 152.

26. Raimond van Marle, *The Development of the Italian Schools of Painting*, vol. 16 (The Hague: Nijhoff, 1937), pp. 28, 32; and Dussler, *Signorelli*, pl. 56.

27. Mario Salmi, *Luca Signorelli* (Novara: Istituto Geografico De Agostini, 1953), pp. 32, 61; Pietro Scarpellini, *Luca Signorelli* (Milan: Edizioni per il Club del Libro, 1964), pp. 59, 135; Zeri and Gardner 1980, pp. 91–92; and Laurence Kanter, *The Late Works of Luca Signorelli and His Followers 1498–1559*, Ph.D. diss., New York University, 1989 (Ann Arbor: UMI, 1991), pp. 139–41. Of course, the picture mentioned in the document could have been painted at any time before April 1507.

28. See Kanter and Franklin, "Some Passion Scenes by Luca Sig-

norelli after 1500," pp. 171–91; and Tom Henry, *Signorelli in British Collections*, exh. cat., National Gallery, London (London: National Gallery Publications, 1998–99), pp. 22–23.

29. E.g., the *Adoration of the Shepherds* (now Accademia Etrusca, Cortona), the *Virgin and Child with Saints Joseph and Onuphrius* (formerly in the Canepa collection, Rome), the *Incredulity of Saint Thomas and a Donor* (formerly in a private collection in Italy but destroyed by fire in 1995), and the *Virgin and Child with Saints Peter, Paul, Benedict, and Vincent* (now Castel Sant'Angelo, Rome). The *Nativity* now in the Galleria Sabauda, Turin, is also said to have come from the Tommasi collection, and pictures by Signorelli with a Tommasi provenance are also to be found in the Uffizi, the Fiocco collection in Padua, and in the Detroit Institute of Arts and the Philadelphia Museum of Art.

30. For documentation of the Signorelli-Boscia marriage, see note 16 above. Luca Boscia's relationship with Signorelli is suggested by several additional references. In May 1497 Boscia acted as *fideiussore* when Signorelli served as a Prior (ASCC, Lib. Q. 4, fol. 319r). In February 1502 he acted as the artist's procurator (ASF, NA 5764 [formerly C 683], Bernardino Cortonesi, 1502, fol. 22v), and Signorelli was his *fideiussore* in May 1504 and again in November 1519 (ASCC, Lib. Q. 5, fol. 183r, and Q. 8, fol. 255v). Boscia was Signorelli's *fideiussore* again in May 1520 (ASCC, Lib. Q. 8, fol. 300v).

31. I could not have made this connection without the assistance of the late Guido Tommasi-Aliotti. According to his "Schema genealogica della famiglia Boscia Tommasi" (Tommasi-Aliotti archive, Cortona), the connection between the families can be dated to the marriage in the early fifteenth century of Francesco di Battista Boscia and Giovanna di Giovanni Tommasi.

32. Laurence Kanter, "Francesco Signorelli," *Arte Cristiana* 82 (1994), pp. 199–212.

33. Fry saw the pictures together in 1910 and was the first to dismiss the Liverpool picture as "merely a school piece"; see Fry, "The Umbrian Exhibition at the Burlington Fine Arts Club," p. 268.

34. Ralph Fastnedge, "A Restored Work by Signorelli at Liverpool," *Burlington Magazine* 95 (1953), pp. 273–74.

35. Kanter, "Francesco Signorelli," p. 206.

36. Fry, "The Umbrian Exhibition at the Burlington Fine Arts Club," pp. 268–73. For the gilded leather wall hangings of the Palazzo Medici, see John Shearman, "The Collections of the Younger Branch of the Medici," *Burlington Magazine* 117 (1975), pp. 12–27, esp. pp. 20, 25.

37. See Anthony Hobson, *Humanists and Bookbinders* (Cambridge: Cambridge University Press, 1989).

38. Signorelli also worked with stained-glass artists: see Giorgio Vasari, *Le Vite . . .*, ed. Rosanna Bettarini and Paola Barocchi (Florence: Sansoni, 1966–87), vol. 3, p. 636; and Girolamo Mancini, *Guglielmo de Marcillat francese insuperato pittore di vetri* (Florence: Carnesecchi, 1909), pp. 29, 32 and passim.

39. The free translations follow Zeri and Gardner 1980, p. 91.

40. The style of the picture is arguably consistent with a narrower range of dates than that proposed above; the period could be shortened to between September 1506 and April 1507 (the dates, respectively, of the death of Signorelli's wife and of this gift to his daughter). If we knew more about the circumstances, a parallel might be found in Piero della Francesca's undertaking to paint the *Madonna del Parto* following the death of his mother, Romana di Pierino da Monterchi, in November 1459.

The Goldschmidt and Scholz Scrapbooks in The Metropolitan Museum of Art: A Study of Renaissance Architectural Drawings

ÉMILIE D'ORGEIX

AMONG THE FEW surviving groups of sixteenth-century architectural drawings, two outstanding examples are held by the Department of Drawings and Prints at The Metropolitan Museum of Art. One, given by Janos Scholz and Anne Bigelow Scholz in 1949, is made up of ninety-four sheets dedicated to Renaissance studies of contemporary Florentine and Roman buildings, known as the Scholz scrapbook.[1] An additional five sheets that are treated here as part of the Scholz scrapbook came into the Museum among a large group of drawings of tomb monuments, fountains, and other subjects purchased from Janos Scholz in 1949.[2] In 1968 these acquisitions were enhanced by the Museum's purchase from Lucien Goldschmidt of sixty-eight sheets of Renaissance architectural drawings devoted to buildings of ancient Rome, known as the Goldschmidt scrapbook.[3] The purpose of this article is to present the drawings of the Goldschmidt and Scholz scrapbooks together, discussing both groups and the aspects that link them. Appendix 1 lists the sheets in the order in which they were apparently organized and numbered by an early collector.

In the late nineteenth century the drawings in the Goldschmidt scrapbook belonged to French collector and interior designer Edmond Lechevallier-Chevignard (1825–1902).[4] Seventy-three drawings were sold with his collection at the Hôtel Drouot, Paris, April 30 and May 1, 1902 (lot 50).[5] They were acquired by architect Georges-Paul Chedanne (1861–1940), who bought them while he was working on a never-realized publication of Roman antique buildings.[6] In 1968 Lucien Goldschmidt sold sixty-eight of these drawings to the Metropolitan Museum. The drawings came to the Museum accompanied by a typescript catalogue written by Howard Burns, which is the basis of my study. Two sheets from the same group were given anonymously in 1966 to the Cabinet des Estampes of the Bibliothèque Nationale, Paris,

where they were catalogued as by Philibert de l'Orme (Figures 11, 13, 14).

The provenance of the Scholz scrapbook before 1947 is unknown. Charles de Tolnay discovered the drawings in Paris in 1947 and published one of them (250r) in 1948.[7]

SIMILARITIES BETWEEN THE GOLDSCHMIDT AND SCHOLZ SCRAPBOOKS

The sheets from the Goldschmidt and Scholz scrapbooks were organized by an early owner, numbered, and bound. Both groups of drawings are composed of single and double-spread leaves (some glued together). Most of the single leaves measure approximately 42.5 by 29 centimeters (16¾ x 11⅜ in.) and the double leaves 42.5 by 58 centimeters (16¾ x 22⅞ in.). The bound scrapbooks must have shared the same format since the larger drawings are neatly folded to fit these dimensions. On sheets in both groups, the remnants of guards—thin strips of paper pasted on the inner edges of the sheets to reinforce the binding—are similar. Several of the guards are recycled pieces of other, unidentified architectural drawings. There are inscriptions on two of the guards: that on Scholz 241[b] has a sentence fragment, followed by *Commandant d'A——court* and a paraph; that on Goldschmidt 70, a small segment of an architectural drawing, is inscribed *Cour*. The handwriting on those fragments is stylistically typical of late seventeenth- or early eighteenth-century penmanship.

In both groups of drawings, the sheets were numbered apparently by the same hand in a similar way: on most, large numbers were written in graphite, usually in the middle of the sheet and apparently by the same hand. The sheets from the Goldschmidt scrapbook are numbered intermittently from 10 to 188, except for one, 206. On the sheets from the Scholz scrapbook, the numbering is unbroken from 208 through 300, except for sheet 120. The five sheets grouped here with the Scholz scrapbook are num-

© The Metropolitan Museum of Art 2001
METROPOLITAN MUSEUM JOURNAL 36

The notes for this article begin on page 194.

Figure 1. Incomplete elevation and cross section of the Tempietto in the courtyard of San Pietro in Montorio (Goldschmidt 206). Pen and brown ink over stylus-ruled and incised compass lines, 44 x 29.3 cm (17⅜ x 11½ in.). The Metropolitan Museum of Art, Purchase, Rogers Fund, Joseph Pulitzer Bequest, and Mark J. Millard Gift, 1968 (68.769.47)

Figure 2. Measured partial elevations of the colonnade in the Forum of Nerva (Goldschmidt 10v). Pen and brown ink over black chalk over stylus-ruled and incised compass lines, 43 x 28.3 cm (16⅞ x 11⅛ in.). The Metropolitan Museum of Art, Purchase, Rogers Fund, Joseph Pulitzer Bequest, and Mark J. Millard Gift, 1968 (68.769.21)

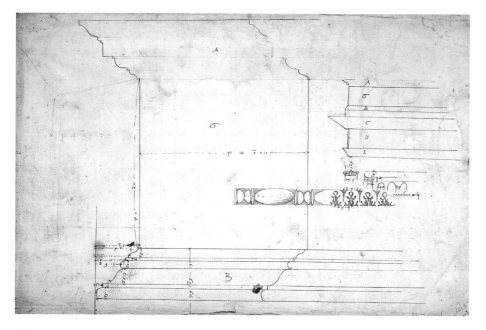

Figure 3. Measured profiles of attic and entablature of the colonnade in the Forum of Nerva (Goldschmidt 20r). Pen and brown ink over leadpoint, stylus-ruled lines, and scattered pin-pricks; 29.5 x 42.2–44.2 cm (11⅝ x 16⅝–17⅜ in.). The Metropolitan Museum of Art, Purchase, Rogers Fund, Joseph Pulitzer Bequest, and Mark J. Millard Gift, 1968 (68.769.19)

Figure 4. Measured elevation of the Arch of Constantine (Goldschmidt 14r). Pen and brown ink over traces of silverpoint and stylus-ruled and incised compass lines, 43.8 x 28.6 cm (17¼ x 11¼ in.). The Metropolitan Museum of Art, Purchase, Rogers Fund, Joseph Pulitzer Bequest, and Mark J. Millard Gift, 1968 (68.769.20)

Figure 5. Measured profile of the entablature of the Arch of Constantine (Goldschmidt unnumbered). Pen and brown ink over black chalk, 19.7 x 21.8 cm (7¾ x 8⅝ in.). The Metropolitan Museum of Art, Purchase, Rogers Fund, Joseph Pulitzer Bequest, and Mark J. Millard Gift, 1968 (68.769.18)

bered, seemingly in the same hand as on the Scholz and Goldschmidt drawings, 127 (49.19.12), 247[a] (49.19.13), 295 (49.19.14), 298[a] (49.19.39), and 298[b] (49.19.40). The drawings of tomb monuments and other subjects are numbered similarly but above 300.[8]

Most of the drawings from the Goldschmidt and Scholz scrapbooks were executed on white or slightly yellow laid paper in pen and brown ink, frequently over an underdrawing in black chalk, charcoal, or metalpoint, and sometimes over stylus-ruled lines and incised compass lines. Ornamental detailing, such as acanthus leaves or bead-and-reel moldings, was often only sketched out in metalpoint or charcoal. Watermarks are visible in many of the sheets of paper in both groups of drawings. The ones that correspond to examples in the compilation of watermarks by Charles-Moïse Briquet are Italian and were in use during the third quarter of the sixteenth century.[9]

By and large the drawings are measured cross sections or elevations of classical architecture and ornamental detailing: in the Goldschmidt scrapbook, Roman triumphal arches and temples, along with studies of antique fragments; in the Scholz scrapbook,

sixteenth-century religious and civic buildings in Rome and Florence. The depiction of supporting—base, shaft, capital—and crowning—cornice, entablature, pediment—elements was especially emphasized. Other sheets show measured partial elevations and architectural details that respect the classical model of orthographic projection: plan, elevation, section. The drawings of ornamentation include *grotteschi*, coffered ceilings, antique stelae, and Roman sculpture.

In most of the drawings from both scrapbooks, precise measurements were annotated on the delineated architectural elements. The abbreviations used can be read in either Italian or French—*p* for *palmi* or *pieds*, *o* for *oncie* or *onces*, and *m* for *minuti* or *minutes*—although comparison with actual measurements or those on other drawings indicates that they mostly signify *palmi*. Exceptions are Goldschmidt sheets 84–95, drawings of the Pantheon, on which measurements are given in *pieds*, and Scholz sheets 247–267, drawings of Florentine buildings, on which measurements are given in *braccia fiorentine*. In addition many of the drawings were inscribed in French or in a mixture of French and Italian, except the sheets representing Michelangelo's Florentine work, which were inscribed

171

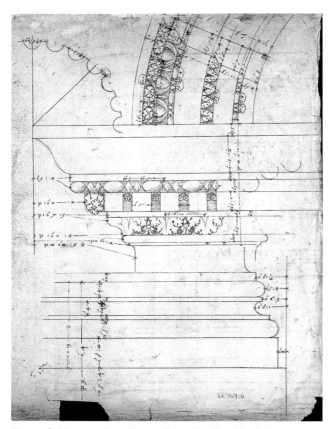

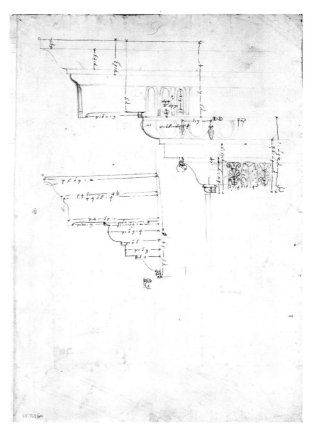

Figure 6. Measured profiles and details of archivolt, impost, and a column of the Arch of Septimius Severus (Goldschmidt 22[a]v). Pen and brown ink over black chalk over traces of stylus-ruled and incised compass lines, 34.5–30.8 x 23.8–12 cm (13⅝–12⅛ x 9⅜–4¾ in.). The Metropolitan Museum of Art, Purchase, Rogers Fund, Joseph Pulitzer Bequest, and Mark J. Millard Gift, 1968 (68.769.11)

Figure 7. Measured elevations in profile of the upper entablature of the Temple of Antoninus and Faustina (Goldschmidt 31v). Pen and brown ink over charcoal, 43.3 x 29.4 cm (17 x 11⅝ in.). The Metropolitan Museum of Art, Purchase, Rogers Fund, Joseph Pulitzer Bequest, and Mark J. Millard Gift, 1968 (68.769.50)

in Italian. The inscriptions give such information as locations of antique buildings or identifications of Renaissance buildings.

The Goldschmidt and Scholz scrapbooks thus seem to represent a dismembered group of drawings that once belonged to a single collector and may well also have included tomb and fountain drawings.

CONTENTS OF THE GOLDSCHMIDT SCRAPBOOK

The sheets from the Goldschmidt scrapbook are devoted to the architecture of Roman antiquity. The exception, sheet 206, is an elevation and cross section of Bramante's Tempietto in the courtyard of San Pietro in Montorio, Rome (Figure 1). It is the only drawing numbered above 188, but since, during the Renaissance, the Tempietto was considered the first modern building in the antique style,[10] the presence of such a representation in the Goldschmidt scrapbook is not

surprising. There are numerous lacunae among the numbered sheets of the Goldschmidt scrapbook, and six sheets of architectural and ornament drawings do not have numbers (see Appendix 1). It is likely that at some time before Lechevallier-Chevignard's ownership, the drawings were unbound and many were sold individually. The large numbers written in graphite in the center of each sheet are too obvious not to have been erased once the work was separated from the main body of drawings. Because of the gaps in the Goldschmidt group, many of the fragments of moldings, bases, and capitals that appear without accompanying elevations cannot be identified.

The Goldschmidt drawings of antique Roman architecture divide roughly into five groups: partial elevations in profile with ornamental detailing of temples and triumphal arches located within the boundaries of Augustan Rome; bases and capitals, probably drawn after other sixteenth-century representations; studies of the Pantheon; studies of buildings located on the

Figure 8. Ornamentation and elevation of a soffit in the Temple of Castor and Pollux (Goldschmidt 67r). Pen and brown ink over black chalk; outlines probably reworked with gray ink; 22 x 15.5–16.2 cm (8⅝ x 6⅛–6⅜ in.). The Metropolitan Museum of Art, Purchase, Rogers Fund, Joseph Pulitzer Bequest, and Mark J. Millard Gift, 1968 (68.769.30)

Figure 9. Sketches of two ornaments with lions, dolphins, and masks (Goldschmidt 67v). Charcoal over stylus-ruled lines, 22 x 15.5–16.2 cm (8⅝ x 6⅛–6⅜ in.). The Metropolitan Museum of Art, Purchase, Rogers Fund, Joseph Pulitzer Bequest, and Mark J. Millard Gift, 1968 (68.769.30)

periphery of Rome; and drawings of ornament, especially in the Domus Aurea.

Temples and Triumphal Arches

The collection starts with several drawings dedicated to the Forum of Nerva. The recto of the first numbered sheet (10) shows studies of a composite capital found near the Arch of Constantine, which is also known in two engravings published by Philibert de l'Orme in his *Premier tome de l'architecture* (1567, fols. 206, 207). On the verso of sheet 10 (Figure 2) is a partial view of the colonnade near the Temple of Minerva. Known as the Colonnacce during the Renaissance, it was a subject drawn frequently by architects. The draftsman of Goldschmidt 10 organized his sheet so that in the upper left there is a partial elevation of the colonnade, and down the right side the entablature and attic are delineated in profile, with details of foliage and beading toward the bottom. The same

profile is partially drawn by another hand on the recto of sheet 21. Linked to these two sheets is the recto of Goldschmidt 20 (Figure 3), which shows several details from the colonnade. Sheets 11 and 57 show architectural details of the Temple of Minerva. These two sheets are both inscribed in the draftsman's hand *fore di traiano*, referring mistakenly to the Forum of Trajan, to the northwest of the Forum of Nerva.

Five drawings are dedicated mainly to the arches of Constantine and Septimius Severus, at opposite ends of the Roman Forum. Sheets 14 (Figure 4) and 20v showing the Arch of Constantine are of lesser quality than many contemporary representations of the same arch.[11] They are probably copies. An annotation on sheet 14v, *la mesure de larque set linpeste,* labeling a small sketch of the arch's impost, attests to the nationality of the draftsman. A drawing by a more confident hand shows a measured profile of the arch's entablature (unnumbered, 68.769.18; Figure 5). A study of the Arch of Septimius Severus (22[a]) shows measured

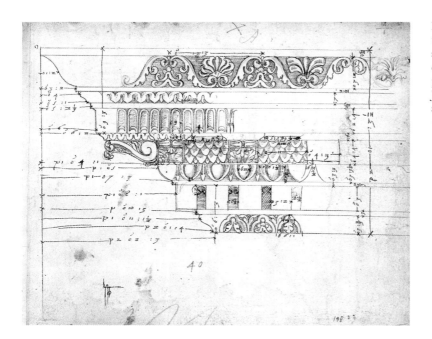

Figure 10. Measured study of antique entablature found near the Arch of Camigliano (Goldschmidt 40[b]r). Pen and brown ink over black chalk, 23 x 29.4 cm (9 x 11⅝ in.). The Metropolitan Museum of Art, Purchase, Rogers Fund, Joseph Pulitzer Bequest, and Mark J. Millard Gift, 1968 (68. 769.17)

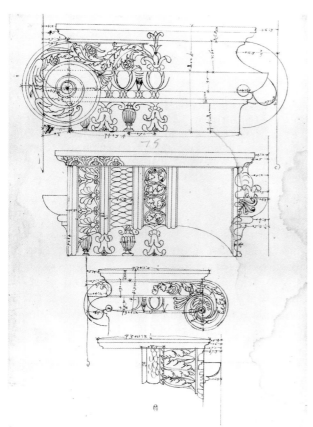

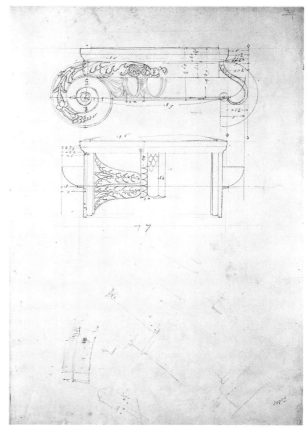

Figure 11. Measured study of two Ionic capitals (sheet 75). Pen and brown ink over stylus-ruled lines, 43 x 28.2 cm (16⅞ x 11⅛ in.). Bibliothèque Nationale de France, Paris, Cabinet des Estampes, don anonyme 15 138, B2a, réserve (photo: Bibliothèque Nationale)

Figure 12. Measured front and side elevations of an Ionic capital and, below, plans and architectural details, possibly of the Temple of Roma and Venus (Goldschmidt 77). Top, pen and brown ink over black chalk and lead point, and ruled and compass lines; bottom, charcoal; 43.6 x 28.5 cm (17⅛ x 11¼ in.). The Metropolitan Museum of Art, Purchase, Rogers Fund, Joseph Pulitzer Bequest, and Mark J. Millard Gift, 1968 (68.769.37)

profiles of the entablature and pediment on the recto, and on the verso details of a column, the impost, and the central archivolt (Figure 6).[12] The drawing on the lower part of sheet 68 repeats *in pulito* part of the study on 22[a]v.

The numbering on the Goldschmidt sheets then skips from 22 to 31. The recto of sheet 31 depicts a measured elevation in profile of the entablature of the Porticus of Octavia—located in the southern part of the Campus Martius—along with a small elevation of its pediment. The notation *A sainct ange en pesquerie*, inscribed below the pediment, refers to its location, the medieval church of Sant'Angelo in Pescheria that was built on the site. The verso of the sheet shows two elevations in profile of the upper entablature of the Temple of Antoninus and Faustina, located on the north side of the Via Sacra (Figure 7). First excavated in 1546, when parts of the frieze and entablature were found, these fragments were recorded by contemporary artists such as Giovanni Antonio Dosio and the draftsmen represented in the codices Destailleur 4151 and OZ 111.[13] Compared to the work of these draftsmen, Goldschmidt 31v lacks precision. It seems to be an unfinished preparatory drawing, for most of the lower part of the sheet was left blank and details were left in charcoal, with no reworking in ink. Another drawing, Goldschmidt 65r, rendering a Corinthian capital, appears also to have been inspired by that temple's ornament,[14] but since it lacks measurements or an inscription, a firm identification is difficult.

Figure 13. Drawing of a volute from an Ionic capital (sheet 71r). Pen and brown ink over black chalk and traces of stylus-ruled lines, 40.9 x 29 cm (16⅛ x 11⅜ in.). Bibliothèque Nationale de France, Paris, Cabinet des Estampes, don anonyme 15 138, B2a, réserve (photo: Bibliothèque Nationale)

Figure 14. Measured sketch of a capital with floral detail of abacus (sheet 71v). Pen and brown ink over black chalk and traces of stylus-ruled lines, 29 x 40.9 cm (11⅜ x 16⅛ in.). Bibliothèque Nationale de France, Paris, Cabinet des Estampes, don anonyme 15 138, B2a, réserve (photo: Bibliothèque Nationale)

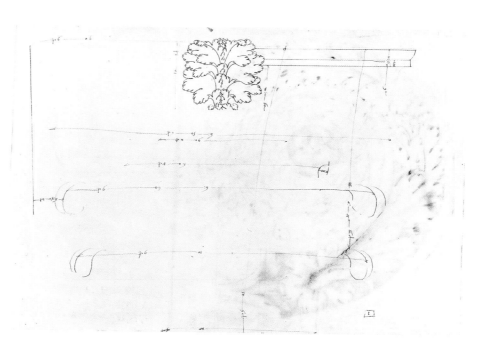

The upper part of sheet 32r, inscribed *Aupres de la / coullonne / troiane,* depicts the cornice of the Basilica Ulpia in the Forum of Trajan. As in the case of sheet 31v, the Temple of Antoninus and Faustina, this classical subject was frequently drawn during the second half of the sixteenth century. Both the Codex Coner and the codex of antique drawings after Alberto Alberti in Sir John Soane's Museum, London, include similar representations.[15] The lower half of sheet 32r and sheet 34 show crudely drawn entablatures found near Sant'Angelo in Pescheria. Sheet 67 depicts a soffit of the entablature of the Temple of Castor and Pollux, rebuilt at the beginning of the first century A.D. and consecrated in A.D. 6, one of the richest of the Augustan era (Figure 8). Sketched with fine strokes of the pen, the drawing shows the interlaces of flowers and acanthus leaves and the double frame of beading and egg-and-dart moldings. On the verso, a freehand sketch in charcoal shows details of two unidentified ornaments decorated with lions, dolphins, and masks (Figure 9).

Unidentified Entablatures and Column Capitals and Bases

Within the Goldschmidt scrapbook, there are several fragments of entablatures. Some—those on sheets 22[b], 34v, 39r, and 40[a]v—are difficult to identify. Others, the ones on sheets 34r, 40[b]v, 43, 47[a]r, 47[b]r, and 51r, bear either specifications or notations that assist in determining their locations in the sixteenth century. For instance, an entablature that was frequently reproduced in Renaissance codices and was referred to as found near the Arch of Camigliano is represented on sheet 40[b]r (Figure 10).[16] Sheet 43 bears the inscription *trouvee a camp de fleur,* indicating the findspot of the cornice represented, the Campo dei Fiori. Sheet 51 presents a measured profile of an entablature and a capital and is inscribed *desoulz campidoil a la prison du pere / de la charite romayne,* probably indicating a location in the Roman Forum, near the Tabularium.

Unidentified column capitals and bases appear on sheets 68 (upper part), 70, 72, 73[a], 73[b], 74, 77, 78, 80, 81, and 82. Clearly organized, the elements on

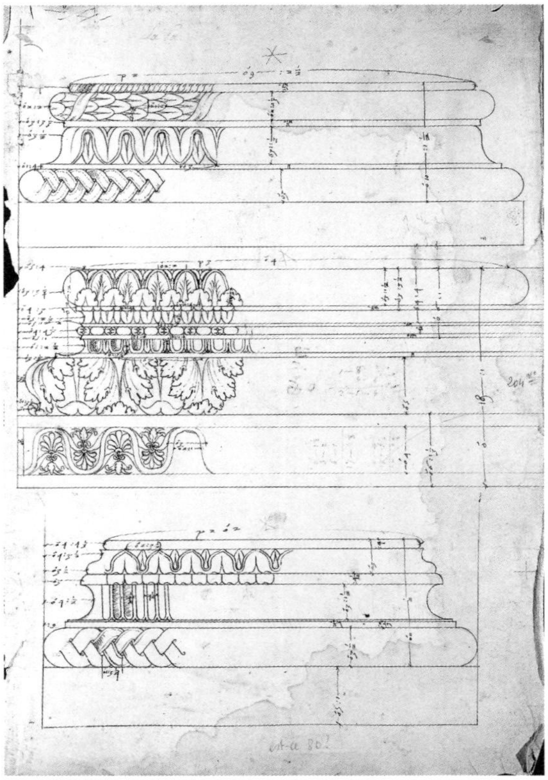

Figure 15. Measured details of three antique column bases (Goldschmidt 80). Pen and brown ink over leadpoint and ruled and compass lines, 43.4 x 28.4 cm (17⅛ x 11⅛ in.). The Metropolitan Museum of Art, Purchase, Rogers Fund, Joseph Pulitzer Bequest, and Mark J. Millard Gift, 1968 (68.769.39)

Figure 16. Measured study of the truss roof and colonnade of the Pantheon's portico (Goldschmidt 84–85r). Pen and brown ink over black chalk, 55.8 x 42.6 cm (22 x 16¾ in.). The Metropolitan Museum of Art, Purchase, Rogers Fund, Joseph Pulitzer Bequest, and Mark J. Millard Gift, 1968 (68.769.1)

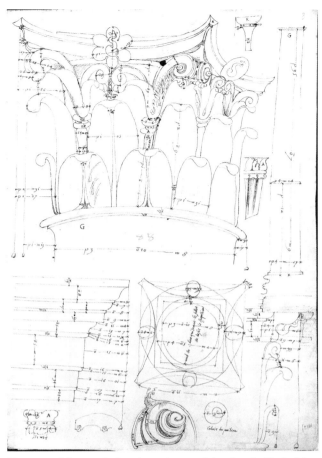

Figure 17. Measured elevation, plan, and details of a Corinthian column of the Pantheon's portico (Goldschmidt 88r). Pen and brown ink over black chalk, 43 x 28.8 cm (16⅞ x 11⅜ in.). The Metropolitan Museum of Art, Purchase, Rogers Fund, Joseph Pulitzer Bequest, and Mark J. Millard Gift, 1968 (68.769.4)

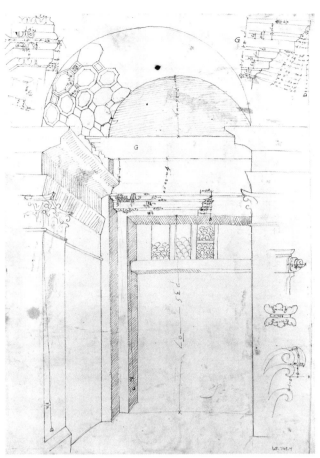

Figure 18. Measured details of the ornamentation of the Pantheon's vaulted entranceway (Goldschmidt 88v). Pen and brown ink over black chalk, 43 x 28.8 cm (16⅞ x 11⅜ in.). The Metropolitan Museum of Art, Purchase, Rogers Fund, Joseph Pulitzer Bequest, and Mark J. Millard Gift, 1968 (68.769.4)

these sheets are placed either one below the other or centered on each page, and most of them are known from earlier representations. The two sheets that are now in the Bibliothèque Nationale have graphite numbers that correspond to sheets missing from the Goldschmidt scrapbook in this group of bases and capitals. One, numbered 75 (Figure 11), rendering two Ionic capitals in elevation and section, is clearly from the same series and drawn by the same drafts-man as sheet 77 (Figure 12). The other sheet, num-bered 71, also by the same hand, details in elevation a volute of an Ionic capital on the recto and a study of a capital on the verso (Figures 13, 14). Goldschmidt sheets 77 and 78 represent Ionic capitals close to those of the Temple of Venus and Roma. Sheet 80 (Figure 15) depicts three antique bases, one of which is also represented on folio 34 of the Larger Talman Album in the Ashmolean Museum, Oxford.[17] Sheet 82 shows another frequently drawn base, identified as being from the Porticus Deorum Consentium, built

beneath the Tabularium and the wall of the Clivus Capitolinus in the Roman Forum. This base is also shown in a drawing in the Uffizi, in the *Frammenti* after Alberti, and in the Codex Coner.[18]

The Pantheon

The group of drawings devoted to the Pantheon stands out in the Goldschmidt scrapbook. The series—almost unbroken—is also the most accurate and complete study of the Pantheon to survive from the sixteenth century. The sheets are numbered from 84 through 100, with 96, 97, and 98 missing, while sheets 84–85, 92–93, 94–95, and 99–100 are double-page spreads. The set is composed of floor plans, cross sections, and partial elevations, as well as many mea-sured details. Within the group, special attention was given to structural and technical details: drains for rainwater, types of workmanship, and construction materials such as marble, serpentine, and bronze.

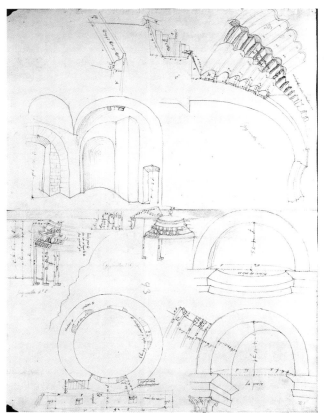

Figure 19. Studies of the Pantheon's rotunda (Goldschmidt 92–93r). Pen and brown ink over black chalk, 58.3 x 42.6 cm (23 x 16¾ in.). The Metropolitan Museum of Art, Purchase, Rogers Fund, Joseph Pulitzer Bequest, and Mark J. Millard Gift, 1968 (68.769.7)

Annotations on these drawings are in French, and measurements are given in French *pieds* on all except sheet 99–100, whose measurements are in Italian *palmi*. The series starts with studies of the Pantheon's portico. Sheet 84–85r shows details of the portico's structure including the bronze girders that have since been lost (Figure 16). On the verso is a measured ground plan of the portico. Sheets 86 and 87 detail on both sides the entablature of the portico along with its cornice, pediment, and elements of the portal. Sheet 88r includes in elevation one of the Corinthian capitals supporting the portico (Figure 17).

The next drawings are devoted to the interior of the Pantheon. Sheet 88v is a perspective elevation of the entrance to the cella as seen from the rotunda. It shows details of the polygonal coffering of the vault that no longer exist (Figure 18). Farther inside the building, sheet 89v presents a half ground plan of the rotunda with a cross section on the verso. On sheet 90 the lower order of the rotunda is carefully analyzed, with many details of the entablature, pilaster capital, and base on the recto, and on the verso a perspective view of one rectangular alcove as seen from the rotunda. Sheet 91 depicts, on the recto, the decorated paneling of the entrance, and, on the verso, two measured plans of the alcoves. The double-spread sheet 92–93 is devoted partly to the upper order of the rotunda and partly to the dome. Unlike those of the beginning of the series, drawn by a single draftsman whose style was rather untidy and disorganized, this

Figure 20. Measured cross section of the Pantheon and, at left, elevation of its portico (Goldschmidt 99–100r). Pen and brown ink over charcoal and silverpoint, 43.8 x 58.3 cm (17¼ x 23 in.). The Metropolitan Museum of Art, Purchase, Rogers Fund, Joseph Pulitzer Bequest, and Mark J. Millard Gift, 1968 (68.769.9)

Figure 21. Measured interior elevation of the Oratorio della Santa Croce (Goldschmidt 115). Pen and brown ink, brush and brown wash over charcoal, leadpoint, and ruled lines; 37 x 33.6 cm (14⅜ x 13¼ in.). The Metropolitan Museum of Art, Purchase, Rogers Fund, Joseph Pulitzer Bequest, and Mark J. Millard Gift, 1968 (68.769.44)

Figure 22. Measured cross section of the rotunda of Centocelle (Goldschmidt 128v). Pen and brown ink, brush and brown wash over black chalk, 22.3–29.3 x 14.2–28.8 cm (8¾–11½ x 5⅜–11⅜ in.). The Metropolitan Museum of Art, Purchase, Rogers Fund, Joseph Pulitzer Bequest, and Mark J. Millard Gift, 1968 (68.769.49)

and the verso of the following double-spread sheet (94–95) are executed by a different hand. Apart from stylistic differences, this draftsmanship is distinguished by the neatly drawn details, which are lacking in the previous sheets. Nevertheless, the objectives of the two draftsmen are similar. In particular, sheet 92–93r presents a freehand sketch of the stairs built onto the exterior of the dome up to the central oculus (Figure 19, top right). The rest of the sheet is composed of plans and details of alcoves including entablatures and ornamentation. The last drawing of this series, double-spread sheet 99–100, is the work of a third draftsman (Figure 20). Although it represents the only complete cross section in the group, this drawing is less informative. Numerous general representations of the Pantheon were available in the sixteenth century and several survive to this day, but technical studies such as the other drawings in the Goldschmidt scrapbook are much rarer and provide far more information on the building's structure.[19]

Other Architecture in Rome and Environs

Sheet 115 from the Goldschmidt scrapbook represents the no longer extant Oratorio della Santa Croce (Figure 21). The drawing, modeled in brown wash, shows the interior of the oratory, focusing on its pilasters and paneling. It is inscribed in a combination of French and Italian: *tempio pres san Joan di Lateran*. An unnumbered sheet (68.769.43) shows the plan and the interior organization of the oratory, and a drawing on sheet 126v delineates the paneling. On the recto of sheet 121 is a plan of the second-century tomb of Annia Regilla in the Valle della Caffarella. The drawing, rather simple and sketchy, is a measured ground plan of the tomb, which has the form of a small temple. On the verso are two ornamental strips with foliage and an eagle drawn in charcoal. They depict the inner pilasters of the Arch of the Argentarii, located near the church of San Giorgio in Velabro. The recto of sheet 128 shows a measured ground plan of the rotunda of Centocelle, in the suburbs of Rome. On the verso, a perspective cross section delineates the interior organization of the rotunda and provides measurements for each window opening (Figure 22). Both sides of the sheet are lightly shaded with brown wash. Sheet 129 shows, on the recto, a partial elevation of the upper story of the interior of Santa Costanza, near Sant'Agnese fuori le mura, and on the verso details of spiral staircases and a doorway.

Figure 23. Details of some stuccoed and painted ceiling *grotteschi* in the Volta Gialla of the Domus Aurea (Goldschmidt 148r). Pen and brown ink over black chalk, 23.4 x 16.3 cm (9¼ x 6⅜ in.). The Metropolitan Museum of Art, Purchase, Rogers Fund, Joseph Pulitzer Bequest, and Mark J. Millard Gift, 1968 (68.769.67)

Ornament Drawings: Grotesques from the Domus Aurea

The last numbered sheets from the Goldschmidt scrapbook include *grotteschi*, grotesque decoration, inspired by the Domus Aurea, the Golden House of the emperor Nero. Sheet 148 depicts the ceiling decoration in the Volta Gialla of the Domus Aurea (Figure 23).[20] Grotesques on two strips of sheet 154 (68.769.60, 61) depict decoration in the cryptoporticus of the Domus Aurea.[21] A washed drawing of a fragment of antique ornament with a head and foliage is on sheet 176. On sheet 188 is a fantastic bull, and on an unnumbered sheet (68.769.54), a winged lion. Another unnumbered sheet (68.769.55) records details of an ancient Roman mural with foliage, griffins, and birds.

180

In the Scholz scrapbook of drawings after sixteenth-century Roman and Florentine architecture, the sheets are numbered in an unbroken sequence from 208 to 300; numbers 241, 247, and 298 are repeated; one detached portion of a sheet is unnumbered; and two sheets, 120 and 127, are numbered below 200 (see Appendix 1). As mentioned earlier, five of the sheets (127, 247[a], 295, 298[a], and 298[b]) came into the Museum separately from the Scholz gift in 1949. Two Scholz drawings are of architecture from antiquity. On the recto of sheet 120 is a structural drawing of a Roman calidarium, which, in view of the number on the sheet and the composition of the rest of the Scholz scrapbook, would more logically belong with the Goldschmidt drawings. The verso of sheet 299 shows an elevation of the Pont du Gard, which

Figure 24. Sketch of Saint Peter's and two blank papal escutcheons (Scholz 208). Pen and brown ink over brush and brown wash over charcoal; 42.3 x 27.3 cm (16⅝ x 10¾ in.). The Metropolitan Museum of Art, Gift of Janos Scholz and Anne Bigelow Scholz, in memory of Flying Officer Walter Bigelow Rosen, RCAF, 1949 (49.92.55)

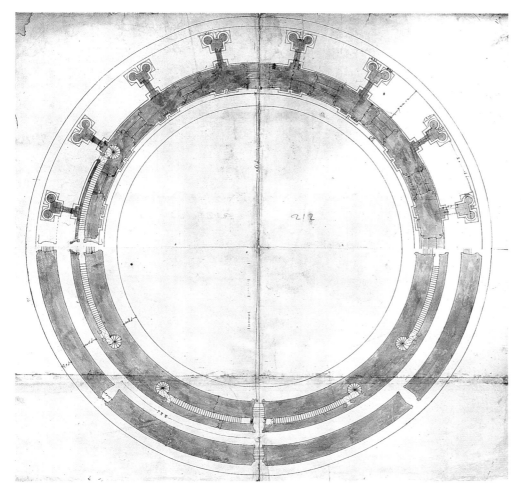

Figure 25. Measured plan of the drum of Saint Peter's, taken at two levels (Scholz 212). Pen and brown ink over brush and gray-brown wash over leadpoint and stylus-ruled and incised compass lines, 55 x 57.8 cm (21⅝ x 22¾ in.). The Metropolitan Museum of Art, Gift of Janos Scholz and Anne Bigelow Scholz, in memory of Flying Officer Walter Bigelow Rosen, RCAF, 1949 (49.92.62)

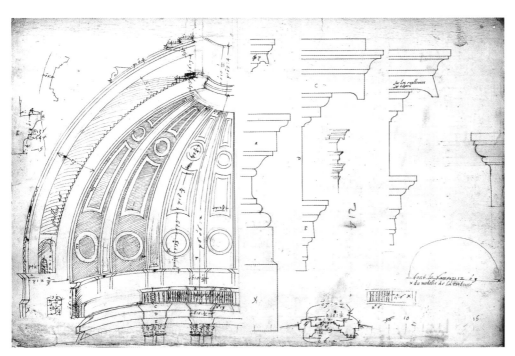

Figure 26. Measured half cross section of the model for Saint Peter's dome (Scholz 214r). Pen and brown ink over charcoal and stylus-ruled and incised compass lines, 29.8 x 44 cm (11⅗ x 17⅜ in.). The Metropolitan Museum of Art, Gift of Janos Scholz and Anne Bigelow Scholz, in memory of Flying Officer Walter Bigelow Rosen, RCAF, 1949 (49.92.92)

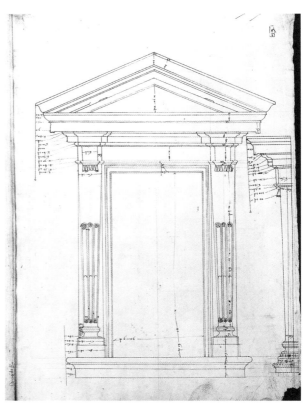

Figure 27. Measured partial elevation of Saint Peter's apse (Scholz 225). Pen and gray-black ink over black chalk and incised compass lines, 41.8–42 x 31.2 cm (16½–16⅜ x 12¼ in.). The Metropolitan Museum of Art, Gift of Janos Scholz and Anne Bigelow Scholz, in memory of Flying Officer Walter Bigelow Rosen, RCAF, 1949 (49.92.45)

Figure 28. Measured elevation and profile, doorway of the Palazzo dei Conservatori, Rome (detail, right side of Scholz 234v). Pen and brown ink over leadpoint and stylus-ruled lines, 57.4 x 43.7 cm (22⅝ x 17¼ in.). The Metropolitan Museum of Art, Gift of Janos Scholz and Anne Bigelow Scholz, in memory of Flying Officer Walter Bigelow Rosen, RCAF, 1949 (49.92.27)

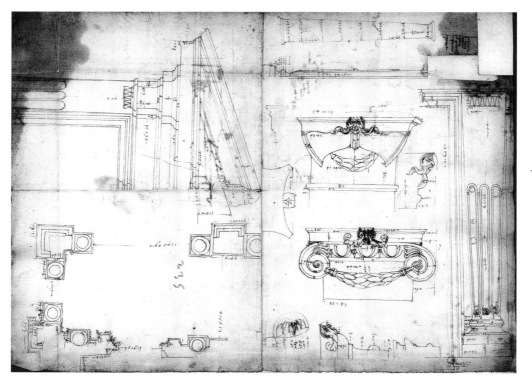

Figure 29. Measured architectural and ornamental details, Palazzo dei Conservatori (Scholz 235r). Pen and brown ink over black chalk, 35.3–34 x 47.3–47.7 cm (13⅞–13⅜ x 18⅝–18¾ in.). The Metropolitan Museum of Art, Gift of Janos Scholz and Anne Bigelow Scholz, in memory of Flying Officer Walter Bigelow Rosen, RCAF, 1949 (49.92.64)

Figure 30. Ionic capital, Palazzo dei Conservatori (Scholz 244r). Pen and brown ink over black chalk and traces of leadpoint, 21.8 x 28.7 cm (8⅝ x 11¼ in.). The Metropolitan Museum of Art, Gift of Janos Scholz and Anne Bigelow Scholz, in memory of Flying Officer Walter Bigelow Rosen, RCAF, 1949 (49.92.10)

seems to be a graphic exercise after one of the numerous existing prints of the bridge.

The studies from the Scholz scrapbook were organized into three principal groups of subjects: Michelangelo's work in Rome, his work in Florence, and Roman palaces. Studies of architectural details from other contemporary buildings in Rome and Florence are interspersed throughout. Because of the relationship of so many of the Scholz drawings with Michelangelo's work, about half of them have been published since they came to light in 1947.

The Architecture of Michelangelo in Rome

The first group of drawings from the Scholz scrapbook is devoted to Michelangelo's designs for remodeling of or additions to buildings in Rome: the Basilica of Saint Peter in the Vatican; the Sforza Chapel in the Basilica of Santa Maria Maggiore; the Piazza del Campidoglio, Palazzo Senatorio, and Palazzo dei Conservatori on the Capitoline Hill; and the Porta Pia. The first sheets describe the ongoing rebuilding of

Figure 31. Elevation of the Porta Pia, Rome (Scholz 239r). Pen and brown ink over black chalk over traces of silverpoint, 55.5 x 41.6 cm (21⅞ x 16⅜ in.). The Metropolitan Museum of Art, Gift of Janos Scholz and Anne Bigelow Scholz, in memory of Flying Officer Walter Bigelow Rosen, RCAF, 1949 (49.92.56)

Figure 32. Measured elevation of Sant'Andrea in Via Flaminia, Rome (Scholz 241[a]). Pen and brown ink over silverpoint, 44 x 29.7 cm (17⅜ x 11¾ in.). The Metropolitan Museum of Art, Gift of Janos Scholz and Anne Bigelow Scholz, in memory of Flying Officer Walter Bigelow Rosen, RCAF, 1949 (49.92.68)

Figure 33. Half elevation of the portico of Santa Maria in Domnica, Rome (Scholz 246). Pen and brown ink over leadpoint and stylus-ruled lines, 44 x 58.4 cm (17⅜ x 23 in.). The Metropolitan Museum of Art, Gift of Janos Scholz and Anne Bigelow Scholz, in memory of Flying Officer Walter Bigelow Rosen, RCAF, 1949 (49.92.78)

Saint Peter's during the second half of the sixteenth century and depict Michelangelo's design for the drum and dome, the apse interiors, and the apse vault. Most were drawn after wooden models of the apse (ca. 1556–57) and the drum and dome (1558–61).[22] Sheet 208, the only perspectival view in the group, shows Saint Peter's dome dominating the surrounding neighborhood (Figure 24). This handsome view is unrelated to the other drawings, for it is later, showing the dome after completion. It may have been added as a visual introduction to the studies of Saint Peter's that follow. Sheets 209, 210v, 211r, and 212 portray plans of the apse and the drum. Two, sheets 211r and 212, are closely related to similar studies by Giovanni Antonio Dosio,[23] particularly sheet 212 (Figure 25), which presents plans of the drum taken at two heights, one half at column base level and one half at shaft level. Numerous drawings depict architectural details of the dome and drum of the basilica (for example, Figure 26). Others are devoted to the apse and show plans, elevations (Figure 27), and architectural details. The only schematic drawing among this group, sheet 218, depicts the centering erected for the dome and is a copy of an engraving of 1561 by Antonio Lafreri.[24] The last of the Saint Peter's sheets, 233, is a geometric-ornament drawing of the coffered ceiling of the Sala Regia.

Among the studies dedicated to Saint Peter's are two, sheets 216v and 217r, which detail a partial interior elevation and a partial plan of Santa Maria Maggiore's Sforza Chapel, designed by Michelangelo for Cardinal Guido Ascanio Sforza about 1560.[25]

Beginning with sheet 234 from the Scholz scrapbook the drawings are devoted to Michelangelo's work on the Campidoglio, initiated about 1550–64.[26] They consist mainly of measured studies of the Palazzo dei Conservatori (sheets 234, 235, 236, 238, 244), focusing on architectural details. Some, such as sheet 234 (Figure 28), depict elevations and details of doorways and windows. Others, such as sheet 235 (Figure 29), show architectural and ornamental elements: on sheet 238, the coffered ceiling of the Palazzo dei Conservatori's colonnade along with a drawing of a sphinx; on sheet 242, a drawing in black chalk—rather schematic and probably copied—of the sculpture of the river god Tigris that adorns the Palazzo Senatorio facade staircase. There is also Michelangelo's oval pedestal (ca. 1560), both an elevation and a plan (sheet 243), executed for the antique statue of Marcus Aurelius.[27] Concluding this group related to the Campidoglio is an Ionic capital (sheet 244r; Figure 30) with festoon, egg-and-dart moldings, horns, and a head with foliate details on its abacus.

Several contemporary Roman structures are depicted in five elevations in well-organized drawings with few measurements, which are distinct from some of the

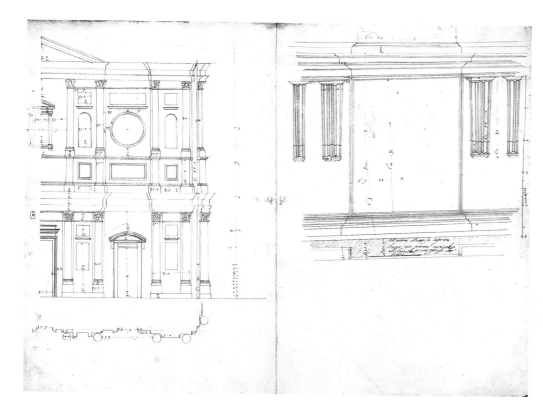

Figure 34. Measured half elevation and plan of the model for the facade of San Lorenzo, Florence (left); measured elevation of the base of a pier and flanking consoles of the Laurentian Library vestibule (right) (Scholz 248). Pen and brown ink over black chalk and leadpoint over stylus-ruled lines, 44.6 x 57.7 cm (17½ x 22¾ in.). The Metropolitan Museum of Art, Gift of Janos Scholz and Anne Bigelow Scholz, in memory of Flying Officer Walter Bigelow Rosen, RCAF, 1949 (49.92.41)

sketchier Campidoglio sheets. Sheet 239r (Figure 31) represents Michelangelo's Porta Pia, erected in the Via Nomentana in 1561–65.[28] It shows an elevation of the portal with its central mask and festooned pediment seen from inside the city wall. Giacomo Barozzi da Vignola's church of Sant'Andrea in Via Flaminia, commissioned by Pope Julius III and completed about 1555, is represented on sheets 240 and 241[a] (Figure 32).[29] And Andrea Sansovino's church of Santa Maria in Domnica, built in the first decades of the sixteenth century, is represented by three bays of its portico delineated on sheets 245 and 246 (Figure 33).

The Architecture of Michelangelo in Florence

After the Roman series comes a group of sheets (247[a]; and 248–266 which are organized and drawn in the same way) dedicated to the architecture of Michelangelo in Florence. Sheet 248 shows at the left an elevation of the right half of the wooden model (ca. 1517) of Michelangelo's never-executed design for the facade of San Lorenzo; at the right are a pier and flanking consoles in the vestibule of the Laurentian Library (Figure 34). Sheet 249 presents an elevation and profile of the north portal of San Lorenzo. Michelangelo's New Sacristy is represented by a ground plan (sheet 250r; Figure 35) and details of a doorway (sheets 251, 252). Sheets 253–263 consist of

measured drawings of the Laurentian Library. These drawings are organized rationally, showing for the architectural element represented a floor plan and an elevation, such as the doorway between the reading room and the vestibule on sheet 254v (Figure 36). Some sheets also include ornamentation on the piers, pediments, or central tablets.

There is on sheet 267 a pen-and-wash elevation of the portal, attributed to Michelangelo, about 1525–35, of Sant'Apollonia in Florence (Figure 37).[30]

Roman Palaces

The first sheet of several devoted to Roman palaces and estates represents another work of Michelangelo's: sheet 268 shows a floor plan of the stairway and semicircle at the upper end of the Belvedere Courtyard in the Vatican Palace (Figure 38). The next three drawings (269–271) represent the Villa Giulia, the casino facade, and the main courtyard with the nymphaeum (Figure 39).[31] This suburban villa, commissioned by Pope Julius III, was built by Giorgio Vasari in collaboration with Vignola and Bartolomeo Ammanati between 1551 and 1553. Michelangelo may have participated since Vasari recalled that he reviewed the project.[32] Sheet 272 presents a ground plan of the Villa Carafa-Este estate on the Quirinal Hill (Figure 40). It was drawn about 1566 during the

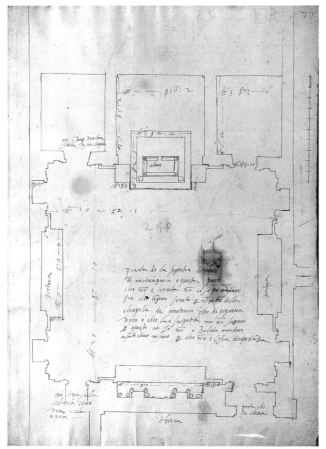

Figure 35. Measured ground plan of the New Sacristy, San Lorenzo (Scholz 250r). Pen and brown ink, 43.6 x 30 cm (17⅛ x 11⅞ in.). The Metropolitan Museum of Art, Gift of Janos Scholz and Anne Bigelow Scholz, in memory of Flying Officer Walter Bigelow Rosen, RCAF, 1949 (49.92.39)

Figure 36. Measured partial elevation and plan of details of the entranceway in the Laurentian Library reading room (Scholz 254v). Pen and brown ink over stylus-ruled lines, 44 x 29.3 cm (17⅜ x 11½ in.). The Metropolitan Museum of Art, Gift of Janos Scholz and Anne Bigelow Scholz, in memory of Flying Officer Walter Bigelow Rosen, RCAF, 1949 (49.92.29)

Este occupancy, and it shows the entire estate with the structures built before 1549.[33]

The next sheets are mostly measured partial elevations or cross sections of Roman palaces: Farnese (sheets 273, 274, 287), Spada (sheets 275, 276; Figures 41, 45),[34] Massimo alle Colonne (sheets 277–281; Figure 42), Cicciaporci-Alberini (sheet 282), Caffarelli-Vidoni (sheet 283), Pirro (also called Palazzo di Angelo Massimo; sheet 285; Figure 43), Giraud-Torlonia (sheet 286), and Salviati-Adimari (sheets 290r, 291, 293v). The last sheets of Roman palaces record the Villa Farnesina, built in 1508–11 by Baldassare Peruzzi for Agostino Chigi (sheets 290v, 292, 293r).[35]

Among the drawings related to Roman palaces, two stand out. Sheet 289, executed on a thinner white laid paper than the other drawings, has on its recto a partial elevation in profile of the side of the fireplace in the Palazzo Massimo alle Colonne (Figure 44). The annotation *tutto illargo d[e]llo architravo p 13 — [o] 4 m 2* is written in an elegant hand unlike that of any other drawings from the scrapbook. Sheet 276, depicting details from the Palazzo Spada, drawn with thick dark strokes of the pen, also gives a very different effect (Figure 45).

Isolated Studies

The final leaves from the Scholz scrapbook do not fit within the previous categories. Sheet 297 is a sumptuous presentation drawing of Santa Maria in Vallicella, or Chiesa Nuova, commissioned by order of the Oratorians and built between 1575 and 1605. Distinct from the other works from the scrapbook in both genre and technique (Figure 46), it is a sophisticated rendering of a project for the church (the facade is

Figure 37. Measured elevation of the portal of Sant'Apollonia, Florence (Scholz 267r). Pen and brown ink over brush and brown wash over black chalk over stylus-ruled lines, 44 x 29.3 cm (17⅜ x 11½ in.). The Metropolitan Museum of Art, Gift of Janos Scholz and Anne Bigelow Scholz, in memory of Flying Officer Walter Bigelow Rosen, RCAF, 1949 (49.92.60)

slightly different from the one that was built), and its late dating—late sixteenth–early seventeenth century—also sets it apart.[36] Sheets 298[a]r (Figure 47) and 298[b]v represent a large Renaissance cabinet with geometric panels.[37] Finally, on sheet 300 are the only military drawings from the scrapbook (Figure 48). Although the sheet is inscribed on the recto *bastidon di sant lorenze di Roma*, it depicts plans of the Bastione Ardeatino, built by Antonio da Sangallo the Younger in 1537–42.[38] On the recto are a general profile of the bastion and a sectional drawing that gives an interior view of two casemates and their openings. For each level, the parts that were filled in with earth are washed with brown. The verso depicts three levels of the bastion and their countermines. These plans also

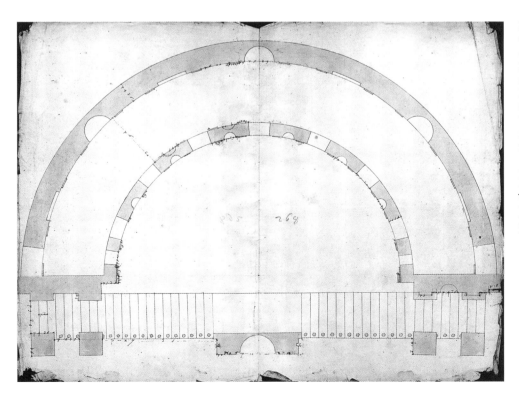

Figure 38. Measured plan of the stairway and semicircle at the upper end of the Belvedere Courtyard, Vatican Palace (Scholz 268). Pen and brown and black ink over brush and gray-brown wash over stylus-ruled and incised compass lines, 44 x 58 cm (17⅜ x 22⅞ in.). The Metropolitan Museum of Art, Gift of Janos Scholz and Anne Bigelow Scholz, in memory of Flying Officer Walter Bigelow Rosen, RCAF, 1949 (49.92.72)

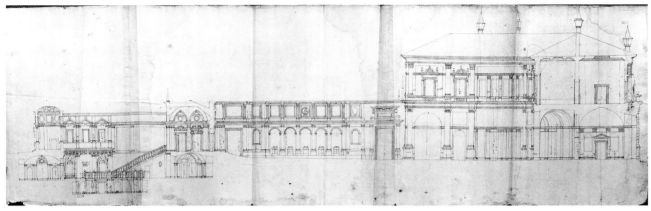

Figure 39. Measured cross section of the Villa Giulia, Rome (Scholz 271). Pen and brown and black ink over brush and gray-brown wash over stylus-ruled and incised compass lines, 43.5 x 138.5 cm (17½ x 54½ in.). The Metropolitan Museum of Art, Gift of Janos Scholz and Anne Bigelow Scholz, in memory of Flying Officer Walter Bigelow Rosen, RCAF, 1949 (49.92.51)

show the location of the casemates, stairs, and emplacements for cannoneers.

THE DRAFTSMEN OF THE GOLDSCHMIDT AND SCHOLZ SCRAPBOOKS

In his typescript catalogue of the Goldschmidt scrapbook, Howard Burns assigned the letters AF to each of the six hands he identified. I adopted this system for the Scholz scrapbook; I also came to different conclusions concerning the classification of several Goldschmidt drawings (see Appendix 1). Based on my assessment, three hands, A, B, and C, seem to have been responsible for drawings in both scrapbooks.

Hand A, the dominant personality in both scrapbooks, could well have been a French architect residing in Italy given his use of French, his knowledge of Italian, and his mixing of the two languages. The presence of work by Hands A, B, and C in both scrapbooks

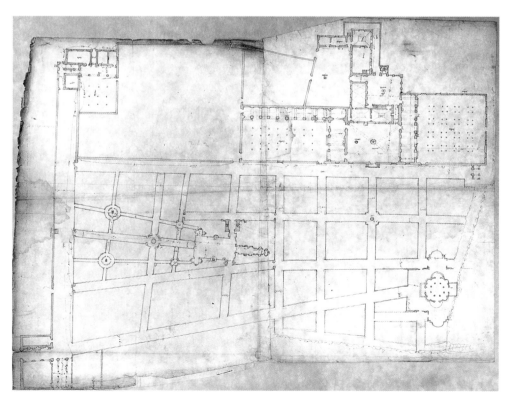

Figure 40. Measured ground plan of the Carafa-Este estate on the Quirinal Hill, Rome (Scholz 272). Pen and medium brown ink over stylus-ruled lines, 58.3 x 78.4 cm (23 x 30⅞ in.). The Metropolitan Museum of Art, Gift of Janos Scholz and Anne Bigelow Scholz, in memory of Flying Officer Walter Bigelow Rosen, RCAF, 1949 (49.92.8)

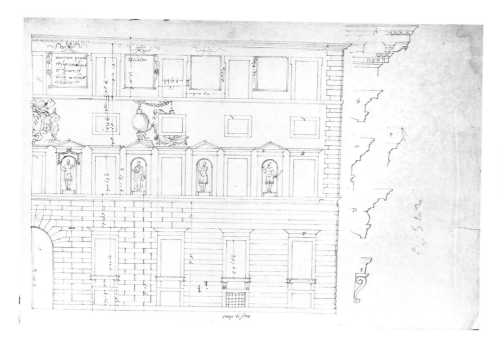

Figure 41. Measured half elevation of the Palazzo Spada, Rome, with profiles of architectural details at right (Scholz 275r). Pen and brown ink over traces of black chalk and ruled lines, 29–30 x 44 cm (11⅜–11¾ x 17⅜ in.). The Metropolitan Museum of Art, Gift of Janos Scholz and Anne Bigelow Scholz, in memory of Flying Officer Walter Bigelow Rosen, RCAF, 1949 (49.92.79)

Figure 42. Measured half elevation of the Palazzo Massimo alle Colonne, Rome (Scholz 278r). Pen and brown ink over brush and brown wash over traces of charcoal over ruled lines, 41.5 x 29 cm (16⅜ x 11⅜ in.). The Metropolitan Museum of Art, Gift of Janos Scholz and Anne Bigelow Scholz, in memory of Flying Officer Walter Bigelow Rosen, RCAF, 1949 (49.92.81)

and additionally in conjunction with other artists on some of the sheets attests to relationships that existed among the sheets before their early organization and numbering. Distinguishing among the hands at work in the Goldschmidt and Scholz scrapbooks allows us to observe that approximately half of the drawings were executed by these three hands, and most of the rest were drawn by draftsmen who also cooperated with the primary three. Several sheets that exhibit two or three hands working together attest to close collaborations among the draftsmen. A few drawings appear unrelated to the others in composition and style and may have been introduced from workshops outside the circle of the Goldschmidt and Scholz draftsmen, for example, the sketch of a hexagonal antique temple (Goldschmidt unnumbered; 68.769.52), the drawing of a fireplace in the Palazzo Massimo alle Colonne (Figure 44), and the project for Santa Maria in Vallicella (Figure 46).

The annotations on the drawings indicate that the draftsmen seem to have been predominantly Frenchmen with a certain knowledge of Italian. The subjects, all Italian architecture except for the Pont du Gard (Scholz 299), suggest that the draftsmen spent a significant amount of time in Italy. Indeed, in publications on the Scholz scrapbook, the draftsmen have most often been considered Frenchmen with strong ties to Italy.

When the drawings from the Goldschmidt scrapbook were in Edmond Lechevallier-Chevignard's collection, he showed them to Viollet-le-Duc, who was particularly taken with some of the ones of the

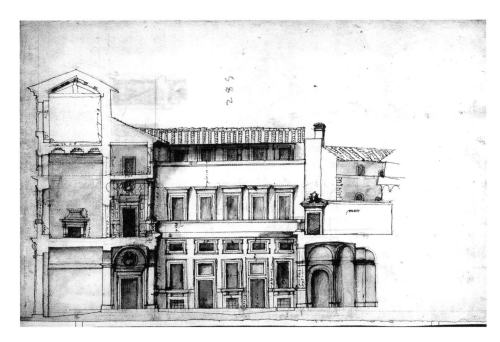

Figure 43. Measured cross section of the Palazzo Pirro (or Palazzo di Angelo Massimo), Rome (Scholz 285r). Pen and brown ink over brush and brown wash over charcoal and stylus-ruled lines, 28.2 x 42.5 cm (11⅛ x 16¾ in.). The Metropolitan Museum of Art, Gift of Janos Scholz and Anne Bigelow Scholz, in memory of Flying Officer Walter Bigelow Rosen, RCAF, 1949 (49.92.54)

Pantheon, notably sheet 84–85 (Figure 16). Lechevallier-Chevignard wrote that Viollet-le-Duc commented: "Ceci, Monsieur, est la signature; plusieurs architectes français pouvaient déjà au seizième siècle, étudier à Rome les édifices antiques, mais un seul, Philibert Delorme le *grand constructeur*, l'inventeur du système qui a gardé son nom, pouvait se livrer à un examen si curieusement approfondi de cette charpente de bronze."[39] The few Goldschmidt sheets that have been published (see notes 4, 5) were attributed to Philibert de l'Orme. Jean-Marie Pérouse de Montclos has demonstrated that de l'Orme probably made a second trip to Rome, about 1560.[40] However, none of the drawings bears his characteristic handwriting, and more than one hand was apparently responsible for them.

Since the acquisition of the Scholz scrapbook by the Metropolitan Museum, the drawings have been associated with the workshops of Étienne Dupérac, Gio-

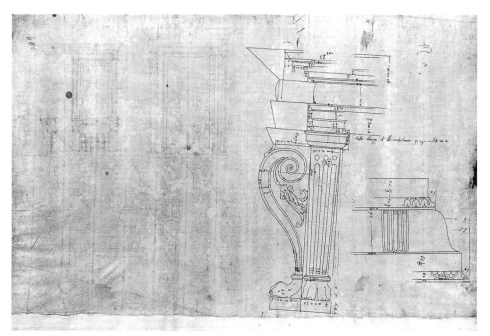

Figure 44. Measured profile and partial elevation of a fireplace on the *piano nobile* of the Palazzo Massimo alle Colonne, with profiles of a cornice at lower right (Scholz 289r). Pen and brown ink, 29.2 x 42 cm (11½ x 16⅛ in.). The Metropolitan Museum of Art, Gift of Janos Scholz and Anne Bigelow Scholz, in memory of Flying Officer Walter Bigelow Rosen, RCAF, 1949 (49.92.4)

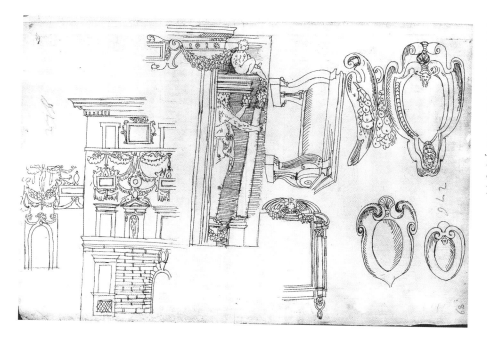

Figure 45. Architectural details of the Palazzo Spada (left) and unidentified ornament (Scholz 276). Pen and brown ink over brush and gray-brown wash over leadpoint and stylus-ruled and incised compass lines, 28.8 x 44.2 cm (11⅜ x 17⅜ in.). The Metropolitan Museum of Art, Gift of Janos Scholz and Anne Bigelow Scholz, in memory of Flying Officer Walter Bigelow Rosen, RCAF, 1949 (49.92.7)

Figure 46. Presentation drawing of Santa Maria in Vallicella, Rome (Scholz 297). Pen and brown ink, brush and gray and brown wash over leadpoint over stylus-ruled and incised compass lines, 57–58 x 43.5 cm (22½–22⅞ x 17⅛ in.). The Metropolitan Museum of Art, Gift of Janos Scholz and Anne Bigelow Scholz, in memory of Flying Officer Walter Bigelow Rosen, RCAF, 1949 (49.92.85)

vanni Antonio Dosio, and Antonio Lafreri. Dupérac (1525–1604), a French printmaker active in Rome from about 1555 to 1578, recorded both antique and contemporary buildings.[41] He published several plates representing the Basilica of Saint Peter in 1569 and 1570, as well as a book on Roman antiquities titled *I vestigi dell'antichità di Roma* in 1575. Some of the Scholz drawings devoted to Saint Peter's have been associated with Dupérac and his circle, particularly by Rudolf Wittkower and by Henry A. Millon and Craig Hugh Smyth.[42]

Dosio (1533–1609) was a sculptor, architect, and printmaker active in Rome from about 1548 to 1579.[43] Seventeen of the drawings from the Scholz scrapbook representing work by Michelangelo in Florence were considered by Charles de Tolnay to be "exact copies of . . . drawings in the Uffizi (nos. 1930–1939 and nos. 1941–1947), where they are attributed to Giovanni Antonio Dosio."[44] In 1977 Carlo Bertocci and Charles Davis compared Scholz 267 (Figure 37), the portal of Sant'Apollonia, with a drawing in the Uffizi, 3018A, and concluded that Scholz 267 was copied from the Dosio studio version. Other works from the Scholz scrapbook are related to the Dosio workshop: Scholz 211r and 212 (plans of Saint Peter's drum) and Uffizi 2031Av and 2032A; and Scholz 277–279 (details of the of Palazzo Massimo alle Colonne) and Uffizi 371A, 372A, and 3244A.

Antonio Lafreri (1512–1577) was a French engraver active in Rome (1540–77) and publisher of the *Speculum romanae magnificentiae*, whose plates were printed

Figure 47. Elevation of a cabinet (Scholz 298[a]r). Pen and brown ink over silverpoint or black chalk over stylus-ruled lines, 43.5 x 28 cm (17⅛ x 11 in.). The Metropolitan Museum of Art, The Elisha Whittelsey Collection, The Elisha Whittelsey Fund, 1949 (49.19.39)

and bound for individual sale between 1545 and 1577.[45] The three drawings from the Scholz scrapbook representing the Villa Giulia (sheets 269–271) were associated by Frances Land Moore with Lafreri's plates, but they "derived ultimately from common or related sources."[46]

As for dates that have been proposed for individual sheets from the Scholz scrapbook, Millon and Smyth assigned the series on Saint Peter's to 1560–70.[47] Drawings of the Villa Giulia (Scholz 269, 270) and the plan of the Villa Carafa-Este on the Quirinal Hill (Scholz 272) have been dated to the 1560s: the Villa Giulia drawings were probably made after 1560–64, when the surplus antique statuary was moved from the villa to the Belvedere,[48] and the drawing of the Villa Carafa-Este, "no earlier than 1561 and more probably soon after 1566."[49] Anthony Blunt, in his discussion of the Palazzo Farnese plans (Scholz 273, 287), dated the building project about 1546–68.[50] Scholz 223, 249, 267, 279, and 300 are on paper with a watermark of about 1566–72 (see note 9). Scholz 242, depicting the river god Tigris at the Palazzo Senatorio facade staircase, shows the sculpture with a tiger lying beneath the god's arm rather than the she-wolf, which replaced the tiger in 1565–88.[51]

The drawings from the Goldschmidt and Scholz scrapbooks were almost certainly assembled long before they were numbered because it is unlikely that a later antiquarian could have put together such a homogeneous collection. Indeed, considering their affinities, the drawings may have been gathered soon after they were executed. It is likely that Hand A, the

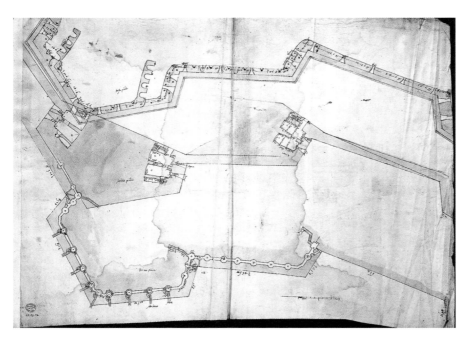

Figure 48. Measured plans of three levels of the Bastione Ardeatino, Rome (Scholz 300v). Pen and brown ink over brush and gray-brown wash over red chalk and leadpoint, stylus-ruled lines, 40.9–41.6 x 57.3 cm (16⅛–16⅜ x 22¼ in.). The Metropolitan Museum of Art, Gift of Janos Scholz and Anne Bigelow Scholz, in memory of Flying Officer Walter Bigelow Rosen, RCAF, 1949 (49.92.76)

dominant figure in the realization and supervision of the drawings from both scrapbooks, had a major role in assembling the original nucleus of sheets, and it would be tempting to consider the hypothesis that Dupérac himself was Hand A and the original collector of the drawings. Although identification both of workshop and of original collector remains elusive, the fortuitous circumstances that brought the Goldschmidt and Scholz scrapbooks together at the Metropolitan Museum provide an opportunity to examine this significant body of late sixteenth-century architectural drawings.

ACKNOWLEDGMENTS

This study of the Goldschmidt and Scholz scrapbooks was made possible through a Sylvan C. Coleman and Pamela Coleman Memorial Fund Fellowship in 1997–98 and a Jane and Morgan Whitney Fellowship in 1998–99 from The Metropolitan Museum of Art, under the supervision of George R. Goldner. The catalogue of the Goldschmidt drawings prepared by Howard Burns, which came to the Museum with the drawings, was immensely helpful to me, particularly in identifying the subjects depicted in those sheets. Janet Byrne shared her knowledge of the drawings with me.

I would also like to thank the following individuals: Carmen Bambach for helping me describe the techniques and media of the drawings; Nicole Dacos for having identified several sheets of grotesques from the Domus Aurea; Mindell Dubansky for advising me on binding terminology; and Beth Holman for pointing out Bramante's plate in Sebastiano Serlio's *Il terzo Libro* (see note 10); Jean Guillaume for his comments on the Pantheon drawings; Claude Mignot for discussing with me the hypothesis of Dupérac's authorship; and for general comments on my manuscript, Dharma Chelikani, Elizabeth Eustis, Bernd Kulawik, Constantine Petridis, Victoria Sanger, and Kristel Smentek.

ABBREVIATIONS

Ackerman 1961; 1986
James S. Ackerman. *The Architecture of Michelangelo.* Vol. 2, *Catalogue.* London, 1961. Rev. Penguin ed. (single vol.). Chicago and Harmondsworth, 1986.
Argan and Contardi 1990
Giulio Carlo Argan and Bruno Contardi. *Michelangelo architetto.* Milan, 1990.

Ashby 1904
Thomas Ashby. "Sixteenth-Century Drawings of Roman Buildings Attributed to Andreas Coner." *Papers of the British School at Rome* 2 (1904).
Bertocci and Davis 1977
Carlo Bertocci and Charles Davis. "A Leaf from the Scholz Scrapbook." *MMJ* 12 (1977), pp. 93–100.
Blunt 1960
Anthony Blunt. "Two Unpublished Plans of the Farnese Palace." *MMAB* 19 (Summer 1960), pp. 15–17.
Briquet
C.-M. Briquet. *Les filigranes.* 4 vols. Paris and Geneva, 1907.
Builders and Humanists 1966
Builders and Humanists: The Renaissance Popes as Patrons of the Arts. Exh. cat. University of St. Thomas. Houston, 1966.
Byrne 1981
Janet S. Byrne. *Renaissance Ornament Prints and Drawings.* New York, 1981.
Coffin 1979
David R. Coffin. *The Villa in the Life of Renaissance Rome.* Princeton, 1979.
Egger 1903
Hermann Egger. *Kritisches Verzeichnis der Sammlung architektonischer Handzeichnungen der K. K. Hof-Bibliothek.* Vol. 1, *Aufnahmen antiker Baudenkmäler aus dem XV.–XVIII. Jahrhunderte.* Vienna, 1903.
Fairbairn 1998
Lynda Fairbairn. *Italian Renaissance Drawings from the Collection of Sir John Soane's Museum.* 2 vols. London, 1998.
Fiore and Tafuri 1993
Francesco Paolo Fiore and Manfredo Tafuri, eds. *Francesco di Giorgio architetto.* Exh. cat. Palazzo Pubblico, Siena. Milan, 1993.
Frommel 1973
Christoph Luitpold Frommel. *Der römische Palastbau der Hochrenaissance.* Vols. 1, text; 2, catalogue; 3, plates. Tübingen, 1973.
Frommel 1981
Christoph Luitpold Frommel. "Sangallo et Michel-Ange (1513–1550)." In *Le Palais Farnèse,* vol. 1, pp. 127–224. Rome, 1981.
Geymüller 1883
Heinrich von Guymüller. *Documents inédits sur les thermes d'Agrippa, le Panthéon et les thermes de Dioclétien.* Lausanne and Rome, 1883.
JSM
Sir John Soane's Museum, London
KB
Kunstbibliothek, Berlin
Keller 1976
Fritz Eugen Keller. "Zur Planung am Bau der

römischen Peterskirche im Jahre 1564–1565."
Jahrbuch der Berliner Museen 18 (1976), pp. 24–56.

Millon 1994
H[enry] A. M[illon]. Cat. no. 231. In Henry Millon and Vittorio Magnago Lampugnani, eds. *The Renaissance from Brunelleschi to Michelangelo: The Representation of Architecture.* Exh. cat. Palazzo Grassi, Venice. Milan, 1994.

Millon and Smyth 1976
Henry A. Millon and Craig Hugh Smyth. "Michelangelo and St. Peter's: Observations on the Interior of the Apses, a Model of the Apse Vault, and Related Drawings." *Römisches Jahrbuch für Kunstgeschichte* 16 (1976), pp. 137–206.

Millon and Smyth 1988
Henry A. Millon and Craig Hugh Smyth. *Michelangelo Architect: The Facade of San Lorenzo and the Drum and Dome of St. Peter's.* Milan, 1988.

Millon and Smyth 1994
H[enry] A. M[illon] and C[raig] H. S[myth]. "The Dupérac Group of Drawings in The Metropolitan Museum of Art and Related Sheets in the National Museum in Stockholm," p. 658, and cat. nos. 381, 386, 388, 390, 392. In Henry Millon and Vittorio Magnago Lampugnani, eds. *The Renaissance from Brunelleschi to Michelangelo: The Representation of Architecture.* Exh. cat. Palazzo Grassi, Venice. Milan, 1994.

Moore 1969
Frances Land Moore. "A Contribution to the Study of the Villa Giulia." *Römisches Jahrbuch für Kunstgeschichte* 12 (1969), pp. 171–94.

Nizet 1902
Charles Nizet. "Les dessins de Philibert de l'Orme de la collection Lechevallier-Chevignard." *L'architecture* (Paris) 15 (1902), pp. 268–70.

Tolnay 1948
Charles de Tolnay. *Michelangelo.* Vol. 3, *The Medici Chapel.* Princeton, 1948; reprinted 1970.

Tolnay 1966
Charles de Tolnay. "Michelangelo a Firenze." In *Atti del convegno di studi michelangioleschi,* Florence and Rome, 1964, pp. 3–22. Rome, 1966.

Tolnay 1967
Charles de Tolnay. "Newly Discovered Drawings Related to Michelangelo: The Scholz Scrapbook in The Metropolitan Museum of Art." In *Stil und Überlieferung in der Kunst des Abendlandes.* Vol. 2, *Michelangelo,* pp. 64–68 and pls. 22–24. Akten des 21. Internationalen Kongresses für Kunstgeschichte in Bonn 1964. Berlin, 1967.

Tolnay 1976; 1980
Charles de Tolnay. *Corpus dei disegni di Michelangelo.* Vols. 2, 4. Novara, 1976, 1980.

UF GDS
Gabinetto Disegni e Stampe degli Uffizi, Florence

Wasserman 1963
Jack Wasserman. "The Quirinal Palace in Rome." *Art Bulletin* 45 (1963), pp. 205–44.

Wittkower 1964
Rudolf Wittkower. *La cupola di San Pietro di Michelangelo.* Florence, 1964.

Wittkower 1978
Rudolf Wittkower. "Michelangelo's Dome of Saint Peter's." In idem, *Idea and Image: Studies in the Italian Renaissance,* pp. 73–89. London, 1978.

Wurm 1965
Heinrich W. Wurm. *Der Palazzo Massimo alle Colonne.* Berlin, 1965.

NOTES

1. Accession numbers 49.92.1–94, Gift of Janos Scholz and Anne Bigelow Scholz, in memory of Flying Officer Walter Bigelow Rosen, RCAF, 1949.
2. Accession numbers 49.19.1–, The Elisha Whittelsey Collection, The Elisha Whittelsey Fund, 1949. The Museum's acquisition of the Scholz scrapbook and these drawings was published by A. Hyatt Mayor, "Prints Acquired in 1949," *MMAB* 8 (February 1950), p. 160.
3. Accession numbers 68.769.1–68, Purchase, Rogers Fund, Joseph Pulitzer Bequest, and Mark J. Millard Gift, 1968.
4. Paul Vitry, "Edmond Lechevallier-Chevignard (1825–1902)," *La revue de l'art ancien et moderne* 12 (October 1902), pp. 297–310.
   When the drawings were in Lechevallier-Chevignard's collection, details of one (Goldschmidt 92–93r) were published: Geymüller 1883, pp. 30–31, figs. 5, 6, 8.
5. According to Nizet 1902, p. 268, the drawings were bought by Chedanne at this sale; Nizet illustrated four: p. 268, figs. 1 (Goldschmidt 188), 2 (Goldschmidt unnumbered [68.769.54]), 3 (Goldschmidt 165 [68.769.65]); p. 269, figs. 4, 5 (Goldschmidt 84–85r). One drawing (Goldschmidt 115) was published in Egger 1903, p. 36 under no. 108, and p. 41 fig. 12.
6. See François d'Hautpoul, "George-Paul Chedanne (1861–1940)," *Monuments historiques,* no. 165 (September–October 1989), pp. 23–26.
   At his death, Chedanne left his academic production, including that manuscript, to the Musée des Beaux-Arts in Rouen, which also has his model of the Pantheon and architectural surveys he drew when he was at the Académie de France in Rome. These drawings were made in the nineteenth century, before he acquired the group of drawings from Lechevallier-Chevignard's sale. Chedanne's collection of Renaissance architectural drawings was subsequently sold (I have not located records of this sale).
7. For his having discovered the drawings in Paris in 1947, see Tolnay 1966, p. 21, n. 13; for his earliest publication of one (Scholz 250r), see Tolnay 1948, p. 269, fig. 165.
8. The sheets numbered above 300 have been partially published by Janet S. Byrne: "A Coronation Drawing," *MMAB* 13 (January 1955), pp. 167–76 (ill. pp. 168, 169: sheet 334 [49.19.115a,

b]); "Design for a Tomb," *MMAB* 15 (February 1957), pp. 155–64 (ill. pp. 156, 157: sheets 322 [49.19.18], 305 [49.19.20]); "Monuments on Paper," *MMAB* 25 (Summer 1966), pp. 24–29 (ill. pp. 24, 26: sheets 318 [49.19.35], 314 [49.19.34]); "Some Sixteenth-Century Designs for Tombs and Fountains in the Metropolitan Museum," *Master Drawings* 21, no. 3 (1983), pp. 263–70, and pls. 12 (sheet 318 [49.19.35]), 13–14 (314 [49.19.34]), 17 (317 [49.19.33]), 18 (320 [49.19.27]), 19 (309 [49.19.24]), 20a (316 [49.19.25]), 20b (308 [49.19.23]), 21a (319 [49.19.36]), 21b (321 [49.19.37]), 22 (315 [49.19.38]), 23 (324 [49.19.29]), 24 (321 [49.19.30]), 25 (323 [49.19.28]), 26 (331 [49.19.9]), 27a (329 [49.19.7]), 27b (332 [49.19.10]).

9. A watermark of a three-rung ladder in a shield surmounted by a cross, close to Briquet 5928 and 5930, appears on Goldschmidt 84–85, 86, 89, 90, 92–93, 94–95, 99–100, unnumbered 68.769.43, and on Scholz 268, 269, 270, 282, 283. The watermark on Scholz 267, a star in a lozenge in a circle, was identified in Bertocci and Davis (1977, p. 98, n. 17) as Briquet 6097. It appears also on Scholz 223, 249, 279, 300.

10. For example, Sebastiano Serlio dedicated several pages to Bramante's Tempietto in *Il terzo Libro di Sebastiano Serlio Bolognese nel qual si figurano, e descrivono, le antiquita di Roma, e le altre che sono in Italia, e fuori d'Italia* (Venice, 1554), fols. XLII, XLIIII, XLVIII.

11. See, for example, fols. 61 and 64 in the so-called *Libro di schizzo di Michelangelo*, attributed to Raffaello da Montelupo, Wicar Collection, Musée des Beaux-Arts, Lille; Frédérique Lemerle, "Livre de dessins de Michel-Ange," in Barbara Brejon de Lavergnée, *Catalogue des dessins italiens: Collections du Palais des Beaux-Arts de Lille* (Paris and Lille, 1997), pp. 310–12, nos. 777, 780.

12. The entablature of the Arch of Septimius Severus is depicted in KB Destailleur OZ 111, fol. 7; Luca Leoncini, *Il codice detto del Mantegna: Codex Destailleur OZ 111 della Kunstbibliothek di Berlino* (Rome, 1993), p. 144.

13. On the frieze and entablature, see Fairbairn 1998, no. 962; for Dosio's drawing, UF GDS, fondo Dosiano, 2006A; for the anonymous draftsmen's drawings, KB Destailleur 4151, fol. 1, and OZ 111, fol. 4 (lower right), in Leoncini, *Il codice*, p. 141.

14. Antoine Babuty Desgodetz published a similar capital in his chapter on the Temple of Antoninus and Faustina in *Les Édifices antiques de Rome dessinés et mesurés tres exactement par Antoine Desgodetz Architecte* (Paris, 1682), p. 115.

15. JSM Coner, fol. 67v, in Ashby 1904, no. 88; JSM *Frammenti* after Alberti, vol. 119, fols. 9v–10r, in Fairbairn 1998, no. 492.

16. For a drawing attributed to Coner, see JSM Coner, fol. 67, in Ashby 1904, no. 87; see also JSM *Frammenti* after Alberti, vol. 119, fols. 43v–44r, in Fairbairn 1998, no. 509.

17. See Leoncini, *Il codice*, p. 239, fig. 28.

18. UF GDS 634A; JSM *Frammenti* after Alberti, vol. 119, fols. 33v–34r, in Fairbairn 1998, no. 504; JSM Coner, fol. 99, in Ashby 1904, no. 132.

19. See those by Dosio, UF GDS, fondo Dosiano, 2020A, 2021A, 2023A, 3212A; and by an anonymous draftsman, KB Destailleur 4151, fols. 103r–v, 105.

20. For a similar composition, see Nicole Dacos, *La découverte de la Domus Aurea et la formation des grotesques à la Renaissance*, Studies of the Warburg Institute 31 (London and Leiden, 1969), pl. 30, fig. 52, anonymous draftsman, UF GDS Orn 1683r.

21. For a composition similar to strip 68.769.60, see Dacos, *La découverte de la Domus Aurea*, pl. 15, fig. 25, fol. 39 of the Sienese sketchbook of Giuliano da Sangallo.

22. Millon and Smyth 1976, pp. 262–68; Millon and Smyth 1994, pp. 658–59.

23. UF GDS, fondo Dosiano, 2031Av and 2032A.

24. Sheet 218 is a copy of an engraving of 1561 by Antonio Lafreri, published in the *Speculum romanae magnificentiae* in 1572.

25. See Paolo Portoghesi, "La cappella Sforza in Santa Maria Maggiore," in Paolo Portoghesi and Bruno Zevi, eds., *Michelangiolo architetto* (Turin, 1964), pp. 683–717.

26. Argan and Contardi 1990, pp. 252–63.

27. Renato Bonelli, "La piazza Capitolina," in Portoghesi and Zevi, *Michelangiolo architetto*, p. 428, n. 9.

28. Elizabeth MacDougall, "Michelangelo and the Porta Pia," *Journal of the Society of Architectural Historians* 19 (1960), pp. 97–103.

29. Wolfgang Lotz, "Die ovalen Kirchenräume des Cinquecento," *Römisches Jahrbuch für Kunstgeschichte* 7 (1955), pp. 35–40.

30. See Bertocci and Davis 1977 for a discussion of Scholz 267.

31. For a discussion of the Villa Giulia and Scholz 269–271, see Moore 1969.

32. Giorgio Vasari, *Le vite de' più eccellenti pittori, scultori ed architettori*, Gaetano Milanesi, ed. (Florence, 1881), vol. 7, p. 694.

33. For a study of the estate, see Wasserman 1963; see also Coffin 1979, p. 188.

34. The inscription *capo di fero* on Scholz 275r (Figure 41) refers to the drawing's original owner, Cardinal Girolamo Capodiferro.

35. Scholz 292v is inscribed, in part, *faciade de gustin guize [Agostino Chigi] transtib[erino] . . . omnipotent—*. Chigi, a wealthy merchant banker and art patron, was known as il Magnifico.

36. A similar drawing by an anonymous draftsman, ca. 1603, is in the Martinelli collection, Milan; it is illustrated on the cover of Costanza Barbieri, Sofia Barchiesi, and Daniele Ferrara, *Santa Maria in Vallicella* (Rome, 1995).

37. See Byrne 1981, pp. 114–15.

38. See Nicholas Adams and Simon Pepper, "The Fortification Drawings," in *The Architectural Drawings of Antonio da Sangallo the Younger and His Circle*, vol. 1, Christoph L. Frommel and Nicholas Adams, eds. (New York, Cambridge, Mass., and London, 1994), pp. 68–71.

39. Undated and unsigned manuscript note of Edmond Lechevallier-Chevignard, Department of Drawings and Prints, MMA.

40. Jean-Marie Pérouse de Montclos, "Philibert de l'Orme en Italie," in *"Il se rendit en Italie": Études offertes à André Chastel* (Rome, 1987), pp. 289–99.

41. For information on Dupérac's engravings of Rome, see *Le antiche rovine di Roma nei disegni di du Pérac*, reprint of *Disegni de le ruine di Roma e come anticamente erono*, facsimile, introduction by Rudolf Wittkower (1963; Cinisello Balsamo, Milan, 1990); Henri Zerner, "Étienne Dupérac en Italie," thesis, École Pratique des Hautes Études, IVe section, Sciences historiques et philologiques, 1963; summary published in the École Pratique's *Annuaire 1963/1964*, pp. 325–26; idem, "Observations on Dupérac and the *Designi de le ruine di Roma e come anticamente erono*," *Art Bulletin* 47 (1965), pp. 507–12.

42. Wittkower 1964, "Appendice II: I disegni del Metropolitan Museum," pp. 101–7, considered Scholz 211, 212, 213, 214, 215, 219, 220, 221 to be preparatory drawings for Dupérac's engravings of Saint Peter's. Most recently, Millon and Smyth 1994, p. 658, discussed Scholz 213, 214, 215r, 219r, 222r, and mentioned the rest of the Scholz scrapbook, "all from the Dupérac circle."

See also Byrne, "Design for a Tomb," p. 162, who connected sheets 305 and 322 with Barthélemy Prieur, noted his and Dupérac's close relationship, and wondered whether "perhaps some [of the numerous drawings of Italian sculpture and architecture in the inventory of Prieur's possessions] had been made in Italy by his friend Étienne du Pérac."

43. For information on Dosio's architectural drawings, see Christian Hülsen, "Dei lavori archeologici di Giovannantonio Dosio," *Ausonia* 7 (1912), pp. 1–78; Eugenio Luporini, "Formazione, cultura e stile di Giovanni Antonio Dosio," in *Studi in onore di Matteo Marangoni* (Florence, 1952), pp. 224–37; idem, "Un libro di disegni di Giovanni Antonio Dosio," *Critica d'arte*, n.s. 4 (1957), p. 442; Franco Borsi et al., *Giovanni Antonio Dosio: Roma antica e i disegni di architettura agli Uffizi* (Rome, 1976); Carolyn Jean Valone, "Giovanni Antonio Dosio: The Roman Years," *Art Bulletin* 58 (1976), pp. 528–41; idem; *Giovanni Antonio Dosio and His Patrons* (Ann Arbor, Mich., 1977); Emanuele Casamassima and Ruth Rubinstein, eds., *Antiquarian Drawings from Dosio's Roman Workshop: Biblioteca Nazionale Centrale di Firenze, N.A. 1159, Catalogue* (Milan, 1993).

44. Tolnay 1967, p. 65.

45. For information on Lafreri's career, see François Roland, "Un franc-comtois éditeur et marchand d'estampes à Rome au XVIe siècle: Antoine Lafréry," *Mémoires de la Société d'émulation du Doubs*, no. 7 (1910), pp. 320–70.

46. Moore 1969, pp. 192.

47. Millon and Smyth 1994, p. 659.

48. Moore 1969, p. 193.

49. Wasserman 1963, p. 207.

50. Blunt 1960, p. 17.

51. Phyllis Pray Bober and Ruth Rubinstein, *Renaissance Artists and Antique Sculpture: A Handbook of Sources*, new ed. (London and New York, 1991), pp. 101–2.

APPENDIX 1: CONTENTS OF THE GOLDSCHMIDT AND SCHOLZ SCRAPBOOKS

GOLDSCHMIDT SCRAPBOOK					
Sheet number	Accession number	Subject	Designation of hand	Watermark	Publications
10	68.769.21	R: elevations, plan, and ornamental detailing of composite capital found near the Coliseum V: (upper left) partial elevation in perspective of the colonnade, Forum of Nerva; (right) elevation in profile with ornamental detailing of attic, cornice, and entablature of the colonnade, Forum of Nerva	Hand B	no watermark	V: Figure 2
11	68.769.22	R: elevation in profile with ornamental detailing of cornice, Temple of Minerva V: partial elevation of capital and profile of base, Temple of Minerva, inscribed in part *fore di traiano*	Hand A	man with halo kneeling before cross, in circle	
14	68.769.20	R: elevation, Arch of Constantine; partial plan V: profiles of base, shaft, and entablature, Arch of Constantine	Hand D	crossbow in circle	R: Figure 4
20	68.769.19	R: profiles of attic and entablature, Forum of Nerva colonnade; ornamental details of architrave V: schematic plan, Arch of Constantine	R: Hand F or G (?) V: unidentified	no watermark	R: Figure 3
21	68.769.10	R: elevations in profile of cornice, entablature, and architrave with ornamental detailing, Forum of Nerva colonnade V: sketched elevation of a capital; sketch of a panel, Temple of Minerva	R: Hand A + Hand E + Hand G + Hand F (?) V: Hand A	no watermark	
22[a]	68.769.11	R: elevations in profile of entablature and pediment with ornamental detailing, Arch of Septimius Severus, inscribed *de larque de septimio mesure au palme romain* V: profiles and details of archivolt, impost, entablature, column, and base, Arch of Septimius Severus	Hand A	eagle in circle	V: Figure 6
[22b]	68.769.12	R: elevation in profile with ornamental detailing of unidentified entablature V: elevation in profile with ornamental detailing of unidentified entablature	Hand A	no watermark	
31	68.769.50	R: elevation in profile of entablature and pediment, Porticus of Octavia, inscribed *A sainct ange en pesquerie* V: elevations in profile, one with ornamental detailing, of upper entablature, Temple of Antoninus and Faustina	Hand A	no watermark	V: Figure 7
32	68.769.24	R: top, elevation in profile with ornamental detailing of cornice, Basilica Ulpia, inscribed *Aupre de la / coullonne / troiane*; bottom, elevation in profile of entablature, Domus Turciorum, inscribed *en pesquerie derie sainct ange* V: unfinished elevation in perspective of the Domus Turciorum, traced from the recto	Hand A	crown surmounted by fleur-de-lis	

Sheet number	Accession number	Subject	Designation of hand	Watermark	Publications
34	68.769.25	R: elevations in profile of two entablatures, inscribed *derier sainct ange / en pesquerie* V: unfinished elevation in profile of unidentified cornice	Hand **A**	no watermark	
39	68.769.51	R: elevations in profile of two unidentified entablatures, with ornamental detailing V: unfinished elevation of unidentified coffered ceiling, with profiles of moldings	R: Hand E + Hand G + Hand A V: unidentified	no watermark	
40[a]	68.769.16	R: elevation in profile with ornamental detailing of cornice, Pantheon V: elevation in profile with ornamental detailing of unidentified cornice	R: Hand G V: Hand A	crossbow in circle	
40[b]	68.769.17	R: elevation in profile with ornamental detailing of an entablature found near the Arch of Camigliano V: sketches of Doric capital; sketched profile of cornice	Hand **A**	no watermark	R: Figure 10
43	68.769.26	Profile and perspective elevation of cornice, inscribed *trouvee a camp de fleur*	Hand **A**	no watermark	
47[a]	68.769.27	R: elevation in profile of curved cornice found on the Palatine Hill V: elevation in profile with ornamental detailing of unidentified base with standing youth and seated woman playing a lyre	R: Hand G V: Hand A	no watermark	
47[b]	68.769.28	R: elevation in profile of cornice found on the Palatine Hill V: elevation in profile of ornamented column base found near the Theater of Marcellus	R: Hand A + Hand G V: Hand E + H and G	no watermark	
51	68.769.29	R: Doric capital, entablature, and panel of a building, inscribed in part *desoulz campidoil a la prison du pere / de la charite romayne* V: capital and shaft, inscribed *A saincte p[re]cedia*	Hand **A**	crown surmounted by star	
[57]	68.769.33	R: column shaft and details of fluting, Temple of Minerva V: elevation in profile of architrave, Temple of Minerva, inscribed *fore di traiano*	Hand **A**	no watermark	
65	68.769.23	R: elevation in perspective of Corinthian capital, Temple of Antoninus and Faustina (?) V: section and plan of unidentified Corinthian capital	Hand **C**	no watermark	
67	68.769.30	R: ornamentation and elevation of soffit, Temple of Castor and Pollux V: sketches of two ornaments with lions, dolphins, and masks	Hand **A**	incomplete cross in circle	R: Figure 8 V: Figure 9
68	68.769.32	(Top) partial elevation in perspective of unidentified Corinthian capital; (bottom) elevations in profile of impost and archivolts, with ornamental detailing, Arch of Septimius Severus	unidentified	no watermark	
70	68.769.34	R: elevation in wash of two solutions to a side view of an Ionic capital V: unfinished elevations in profile of unidentified capitals	unidentified	no watermark	
72	68.769.35	R: elevations of Ionic capital V: sketched profiles and side elevation of Ionic capital	Hand **C**	crossed arrows surmounted by star	
73[a]	68.769.14	R: partial side elevation of Ionic capital V: schematic construction, volute of Ionic capital	Hand **G**	crossbow in circle	
73[b]	68.769.15	R: partial front elevation of Ionic capital V: schematic construction, volute of Ionic capital	Hand **G**	no watermark	
74	68.769.36	R: side and front elevations, section, and profiles of Ionic capital V: partial elevation in perspective of Corinthian capital	Hand **C**	standing human figure	
77	68.769.37	(Top) front and side elevations of Ionic capital; (bottom) sketches of plans and sections of building and details of orders, possibly Temple of Roma and Venus (?)	Hand **A**	three-rung ladder in shield surmounted by star	Figure 12
78	68.769.38	R: front and side elevations of two Ionic capitals V: profile and elevation of entablature, impost, and column details	Hand **C**	no watermark	

Sheet number	Accession number	Subject	Designation of hand	Watermark	Publications
80	68.769.39	Profiles and elevations with ornamental detailing of three unidentified column bases	Hand **A**	crown surmounted by star	Figure 15
81	68.769.40	Profiles and elevations with ornamental detailing of three unidentified column bases	Hand **A**	no watermark	
82	68.769.41	Profile and elevation with ornamental detailing of column base, elevation sketch, and partial study of ornament, Portico of the Dei Consentes	Hand **A**	crossbow in circle surmounted by fleur-de-lis	
84–85	68.769.1	R: detail study of construction of truss roof and colonnade of portico, Pantheon V: plan of portico and entrance, Pantheon	Hand F	close to Briquet 5928, 5930	R: Figure 16 Nizet 1902, p. 269, figs. 4, 5 (R)
86	68.769.2	R: perspective elevation, profile, plan, and details of bronze pilaster of portico, Pantheon; partial plan and elevation of bronze door V: detail studies of portico of Pantheon, inscribed on frieze M·AGRIPPA·L·F·CO / S·TERTIVM·FECIT·, elevation of pediment, profiles and elevations of cornice, and individual moldings	Hand F	close to Briquet 5928, 5930	
87	68.769.3	R: profile and elevation of entablature and details of portico, Pantheon V: elevation of portal and details of panels of bronze pilaster and bronze door, Pantheon	Hand F	no watermark	
88	68.769.4	R: elevation in perspective, plan, profiles, section, and details of capital, shaft, and base of Corinthian column, portico of Pantheon V: perspective view and details of entrance to cella of Pantheon, including polygonal coffering of vault, profile of cornice above door, volutes, and crest	Hand F	no watermark	R: Figure 17 V: Figure 18
89	68.769.5	R: half ground plan of rotunda, Pantheon; details of cella and an alcove V: cross section in perspective of a rectangular alcove and arches of alcove vault, Pantheon	Hand F	close to Briquet 5928, 5930	
90	68.769.68	R: profiles and elevations in perspective of details of lower order of interior, including entablature and pilaster capital, Pantheon V: perspective view of a rectangular alcove, Pantheon	Hand F	close to Briquet 5928, 5930	
91	68.769.6	R: perspective view of entrance with panels, Pantheon; profile of moldings V: plans of a semicircular and a rectangular alcove, Pantheon	Hand F	no watermark	
92–93	68.769.7	R: studies of rotunda, Pantheon: (top right) section in perspective of steps onto dome; (center left) cross section of alcoves; (bottom) various studies of details of alcoves V: elevation and details of upper order of interior of Pantheon, with description of materials	Hand M	close to Briquet 5928, 5930	R: Figure 19 Geymüller 1883, pp. 30–31, figs. 5, 6, 8 (R, details)
94–95	68.769.8	R: elevations in perspective, partial plans, and details of alcoves, Pantheon V: elevations of alcoves and profile and perspective elevations of interior, Pantheon	R: Hand F V: Hand M	close to Briquet 5928, 5930	
99–100	68.769.9	R: cross section of Pantheon; (left) elevation of portico V: partial elevations and plans of a capital, Pantheon	Hand **A** + unidentified handwriting for text	close to Briquet 5928, 5930	R: Figure 20
115	68.769.44	Interior elevation, Oratorio della Santa Croce, inscribed *tempio pres san Joan di Lateran*	Hand F (?)	no watermark	Figure 21 Egger 1903, p. 36, under no. 108; p. 41, fig. 12 (partial)
121	68.769.42	R: plan of tomb of Annia Regilla V: strips with foliate ornamentation and eagle, Arch of the Argentarii	Hand **A**	no watermark	
126	68.769.45	R: front and side elevations and plan of an unidentified funerary altar V: partial elevation of paneling, Oratorio della Santa Croce	Hand **C**	crown surmounted by star	

Sheet number	Accession number	Subject	Designation of hand	Watermark	Publications
128	68.769.49	R: perspective cross section of rotunda, Centocelle V: plan of rotunda, Centocelle	Hand **C**	no watermark	V: Figure 22
129	68.769.48	R: partial elevation in perspective of interior, Santa Costanza; diagrams of column shafts; sketchy elevation of unidentified building V: sketches of spiral staircases and doorway, Santa Costanza	Hand F	six-rung ladder in shield surmounted by cross	
138	68.769.31	Sketches and detail studies of Corinthian capital	Hand **A**	no watermark	
148	68.769.67	R: partial details of ceiling *grotteschi* in the Volta Gialla, Domus Aurea V: unfinished sketch of vault	Hand **A** (?)	crown surmounted by star	R: Figure 23
154	68.769.56–61	Five sheets with details of *grotteschi*; sheets 68.769.59–61 show decoration of the cryptoporticus, Domus Aurea	unidentified	no watermark	
165	68.769.62–66	Six sheets with details of unidentified ornamentation	unidentified	grapes	Nizet 1902, p. 268, fig. 3 (68.769.65)
176	68.769.46	Elevation of unidentified architectural fragment with head and foliage	unidentified	no watermark	
188	68.769.53	Ornamental motif of fantastic bull with foliate details	unidentified	no watermark	Nizet 1902, p. 268, fig. 1
206	68.769.47	Partial elevation and cross section of Bramante's Tempietto, San Pietro in Montorio	Hand **A** (?)	man with halo kneeling before cross, in circle	Figure 1
unnumbered	68.769.13	R: elevation in profile of ornamentation with lion's paws and strapwork V: elevation in profile of unidentified column base	R: Hand D V: unidentified	no watermark	
unnumbered	68.769.18	Elevation in profile of entablature of the Arch of Constantine, with ornamental detailing	Hand **A**	incomplete: crown (surmounted by star?)	Figure 5
unnumbered	68.769.43	R: partial cross section of interior, Oratorio della Santa Croce V: plan of Oratorio della Santa Croce and detail of decoration	Hand **A**	close to Briquet 5928, 5930	
unnumbered	68.769.52	Plan of unidentified temple	unique hand	no watermark	
unnumbered	68.769.54	Winged-lion ornamental motif	Hand **A**	no watermark	Nizet 1902, p. 268, fig. 2
unnumbered	68.769.55	R: portion of Roman mural V: fragment of unidentified partial entablature	unidentified	no watermark	

SCHOLZ SCRAPBOOK

Sheet number	Accession number	Subject	Designation of hand	Watermark	Publications
120	49.92.66	R: plan and cross section of Roman calidarium; icosahedron in perspective and in parallel projection V: projections of polyhedra	unidentified	lily in circle	
127	49.19.12	Exercise in perspective	unidentified	no watermark	
208	49.92.55	Landscape view with Saint Peter's and neighboring buildings and two blank papal escutcheons, the three drawings each on separate sheets, glued together	unidentified (later view)	crown surmounted by star in circle (on landscape view)	Figure 24
209	49.92.71	Partial plan of Saint Peter's showing the crossing and the apse	Hand H	crossed arrows surmounted by star	Ackerman 1961, p. 99
210	49.92.22	R: (left) elevation of window in attic, Saint Peter's; (right) profiles of column bases V: (center) partial plan of the apse, Saint Peter's; (lower right) small sketches of window cornice and architrave	R: Hand **A** V: Hand H	crossed arrows surmounted by star	Tolnay 1967, pl. 24.2 (V); Keller 1976, p. 33, fig. 9 (V); Tolnay 1980, p. 110, ad corpus 616r (R); Ackerman 1986, p. 321
211	49.92.63	R: plan of drum taken at two levels, Saint Peter's V: compass, inscribed SEPTENTRIO / AQUILO / ORIENS / EVRVS / AVSTER / AFRICVS / FAVONIVS / CAVRVS	Hand **A**	no watermark	Wittkower 1964, p. 105, no. 11 (R)

Sheet number	Accession number	Subject	Designation of hand	Watermark	Publications
212	49.92.62	Plan of Saint Peter's drum taken at two levels	Hand **C**	crossed arrows surmounted by star	Figure 25 Wittkower 1964, p. 105, no. 12
213	49.92.1	Half elevation of exterior of Saint Peter's dome	unique hand + Hand H	no watermark	Ackerman 1961, p. 99; Wittkower 1964, p. 101, no. 1; Tolnay 1967, pl. 23.3; Wittkower 1978, p. 82, fig. 85; Ackerman 1986, pp. 321, 322; Millon and Smyth 1988, p. 173, fig. 21; Argan and Contardi 1990, p. 333; Millon and Smyth 1994, cat. 392
214	49.92.92	R: half cross section of dome, with attic, profiles, and details, Saint Peter's, inscribed in part *tout la vane / du modelle de la tribune* V: architectural sketches, Saint Peter's	Hand **A**	no watermark	R: Figure 26 Ackerman 1961, p. 99; Wittkower 1964, p. 102, nos. 2 (R), 3 (V); Tolnay 1967, pl. 24.1 (R); Wittkower 1978, pp. 81 fig. 84 (V), 82 fig. 86 (R); Tolnay 1980, p. 94, ad corpus 595r; Ackerman 1986, p. 321; Millon and Smyth 1988, cats. 16a (R), 16b (V); Argan and Contardi 1990, pp. 329, 330 figs. 442, 443 (V), p. 333; Millon and Smyth 1994, cat. 386
215	49.92.17	R: elevation of the interior of Saint Peter's drum V: (left) elevation in profile of cornice; (right) elevation in profile of pedestal, Saint Peter's drum	Hand **A**	crossed arrows surmounted by star	Wittkower 1964, pp. 104–5, nos. 9 (R), 10 (V); Wittkower 1978, p. 83, fig. 87 (R); Millon and Smyth 1988, cat. 18 (R); Millon and Smyth 1994, cat. 388 (R)
216	49.92.19	R: elevation in profile of cornice and entablature of exterior and interior of Saint Peter's tribune V: partial plan of Sforza Chapel, Santa Maria Maggiore	Hand **A**	grapes with monogram	
217	49.92.23	R: partial elevation of Sforza Chapel, Santa Maria Maggiore V: elevations in profile of column base and entablatures	R: unique hand V: Hand **A**	no watermark	
218	49.92.16	Schematic elevation of centering for arches resting on cornice of entablature, Saint Peter's	Hand **C**	no watermark	
219	49.92.21	R: partial elevation of exterior of Saint Peter's drum V: elevation in profile and details of coffers of entablature of Saint Peter's tribune	Hand **A**	crossed arrows surmounted by star	Wittkower 1964, p. 103, nos. 4 (R), 5 (V); Wittkower 1978, p. 84, fig. 89 (R); Millon and Smyth 1988, p. 177, fig. 26 (R); Millon and Smyth 1994, cat. 390 (R)
220	49.92.18	R: partial details in elevation of one of the exterior bays of Saint Peter's dome V: unfinished section of the model of Saint Peter's drum	Hand **A**	crossed arrows surmounted by star	Wittkower 1964, p. 104, no. 8 (V)
221	49.92.20	R: (left) profile and elevation of Saint Peter's entablature; (right) details of the coffers of entablature and profiles of bases and pedestals, Saint Peter's V: unfinished section of the model of Saint Peter's drum, with elevation in profile of entablature	Hand **I**	lamb with banner in circle	Wittkower 1964, pp. 103–5, nos. 6 (R), 7 (V); Keller 1976, p. 35, fig. 11 (V); Wittkower 1978, p. 85, fig. 91 (V); Millon and Smyth 1988, cat. 17 (V)
222	49.92.89	R: elevation of a window on the apse vault interior, Saint Peter's V: elevation and half plan of the portal of the Palazzo Crivelli (?)	Hand **H**	no watermark	Millon and Smyth 1976, p. 189, fig. 41 (R); Millon and Smyth 1994, cat. 381 (R)
223	49.92.3	(Top) elevation in profile with ornamental detailing of a baluster; (bottom) two profiles of cornice, Saint Peter's	Hand **C** (?)	Briquet 6097	
224	49.92.14	R: elevation in profile with ornamental detailing of Saint Peter's main cornice from the exterior; (right) small profile and elevation of a base V: half elevation of an ornament and a related small plan of the niche	Hand **C** + Hand **I**	kneeling winged man in circle	

Sheet number	Accession number	Subject	Designation of hand	Watermark	Publications
225	49.92.45	Partial elevation of Saint Peter's apse	Hand **A**	crossbow in circle	Figure 27 Tolnay 1980, p. 99, ad corpus 602v
226	49.92.91	Partial elevation of Saint Peter's apse	Hand **A**	crossed arrows surmounted by six-point star	
227	49.92.52	R: partial elevation, profile, and details of a Corinthian capital from Saint Peter's, with profile of base V: elevation of acanthus leaves of a Corinthian capital from Saint Peter's and two profiles of a cornice	Hand J	kneeling man with cross in circle	
228	49.92.13	R: architectural details of column and balustrade in elevation, and studies of cornice seen in profile from the front and from below V: partial elevation in profile of the exterior of Saint Peter's showing details of capitals and arches	Hand H	crossed arrows surmounted by star	
229	49.92.42	R: elevation and plan of a niche on the exterior of Saint Peter's apse V: elevation of a column shaft; elevation and profile of a scrolled console on the niche on the recto	Hand J	man with halo kneeling before cross	
230	49.92.12	R: section of niche on the exterior of Saint Peter's apse, with details in elevation of upper part of niche V: frontal and profile elevations of architectural details of niche on the exterior of Saint Peter's apse	Hand J	no watermark	
231	49.92.15	R: partial elevations of unidentified building in the Doric order V: unfinished section of Saint Peter's drum	Hand **A**	crossed arrows surmounted by star	
232	49.92.87	R: design of a ceiling V: ceiling designs with lilies and masks	Hand **A** (?)	no watermark	
233	49.92.88	Unfinished elevation of the ceiling of Saint Peter's Sala Regia	unidentified	no watermark	
234	49.92.27	R: (left) profile of cornices, pedestal, and base of the Palazzo dei Conservatori; (right) elevation of a column and partial plan of the portico, Palazzo dei Conservatori V: elevation and profile of a portal in the portico of the Palazzo dei Conservatori, Rome	Hand I	lamb with banner in circle	v: Figure 28 Ackerman 1961, p. 55; Tolnay 1980, p. 103, ad corpus 606r; Argan and Contardi 1990, p. 262
235	49.92.64	R: architectural and ornamental details of the Palazzo dei Conservatori V: (left) profiles of bases and pedestals from the Palazzo dei Conservatori; (right) sketchy partial elevation of the Palazzo dei Conservatori's portico and outline of the same sketch in metalpoint	Hand I	blacksmith with hammer and bucket	R: Figure 29 Ackerman 1961, p. 55; Argan and Contardi 1990, p. 262
236	49.92.11	(Left) architectural details in elevation of the bay on the right; (right) partial elevation of one of the bays of the Palazzo dei Conservatori	Hand **A**	unicorn and crest in circle	
237	49.92.69	R: elevation of a second-story window, Palazzo Senatorio, Rome V: plan and profile of window on recto	Hand I	blacksmith with hammer and bucket	Ackerman 1961, p. 55; Argan and Contardi 1990, p. 262
238	49.92.2	Coffered ceiling with military trophies, Palazzo dei Conservatori; an Egyptian sphinx	Hand **A**	lamb with banner in circle	Argan and Contardi 1990, p. 262
239	49.92.56	R: elevation of the portal of the Porta Pia, Rome V: (left) elevation and profile of a window, Porta Pia	Hand **A**	seven-petal flower	R: Figure 31 Tolnay 1980, p. 113, ad corpus 619v (v); Argan and Contardi 1990, p. 351 (v)
240	49.92.67	(Top) cross section and (bottom) plan, Sant' Andrea in Via Flaminia, Rome	Hand **A**	three-rung ladder in circle surmounted by star	

Sheet number	Accession number	Subject	Designation of hand	Watermark	Publications
241[a]	49.92.68	Elevation and (right) profiles of cornices and console, Sant'Andrea in Via Flaminia	Hand **A**	no watermark	Figure 32
241[b]	49.92.70	R: plan of facade staircase, Palazzo Senatorio V: plan of facade staircase, Palazzo Senatorio, showing central niche	Hand **A**	no watermark	Ackerman 1961, p. 55; Argan and Contardi 1990, p. 262
242	49.92.43	Line drawing (tracing?) of sculpture of river god Tigris on the front of the staircase, Palazzo Senatorio	unidentified	no watermark	
243	49.92.65	R: elevation of pedestal for Marcus Aurelius statue, Piazza del Campidoglio, Rome V: plan of pedestal for Marcus Aurelius statue	Hand **A**	lamb with banner in circle	Argan and Contardi 1990, p. 262
244	49.92.10	R: elevation in partial perspectival projection of an Ionic capital, Palazzo dei Conservatori V: plan and partial projection of the capital on the recto	Hand **A**	no watermark	R: Figure 30 Argan and Contardi 1990, p. 262
245	49.92.9	(Top) profile of the main entablature of Santa Maria in Domnica, Rome; (bottom) partial plan of the portico, Santa Maria in Domnica	Hand **A**	cross with dots in circle surmounted by fleur-de-lis	
246	49.92.78	Half elevation of the portico of Santa Maria in Domnica	Hand **A**	cross with dots in circle surmounted by fleur-de-lis	Figure 33
247[a]	49.19.13	(Left) elevation and plan of a bay, San Lorenzo, Florence; (right) perspective exercise with standing figure	unidentified	no watermark	
247[b]	49.92.94	Tracing of allegorical figures of a river god and a nymph with an ideal cityscape in the background	unidentified	grapes with monogram DR	
248	49.92.41	(Left) half elevation and plan of the model after Michelangelo's design for the facade of San Lorenzo; (right) elevation of consoles and base of a pier, vestibule of the Laurentian Library	Hand **L**	blacksmith with hammer and bucket	Figure 34 Millon and Smyth 1988, p. 89, fig. 19; Millon 1994, cat. 231
249	49.92.40	R: elevation of the north portal of San Lorenzo, inscribed *la porta di fiancho D san Lor[en]zo di mano di michellagnoli buonarotti misurata col [s]olito braccio fiorentino* V: profile of the cornice of the north portal, San Lorenzo	Hand **L**	Briquet 6097	Tolnay 1966, p. 21; Tolnay 1967, pl. 22.1 (R)
250	49.92.39	R: plan of the New Sacristy, San Lorenzo, inscribed *pianta de la segrestia dimano / de michelangnolo e questa parte / che no[n] e fornita no[n] ci si po / fre due te[n]gono serato p[er] rispetto della / chapella del pontorno che dipigneua / vero e che la scoperta ma no[n] sap[r]ano / p[er] questo et Io no[n] o voluto mendare / afatichar nisuno p[er] che no[n] e cossa dimportanza* V: frontal and profile elevations of architectural details in the New Sacristy	Hand **L**	face with hat	R: Figure 35 Tolnay 1948, pl. 165 (R); Tolnay 1976, p. 24, ad corpus 178r (R); Argan and Contardi 1900, p. 184
251	49.92.33	R: elevation and plan of a doorway, New Sacristy, San Lorenzo V: partial elevations and profiles of frame, cornice, and base of doorway on recto	Hand **L**	no watermark	
252	49.92.59	R: elevation and plan of the tabernacle above a doorway to the New Sacristy, San Lorenzo V: profiles of entablature, cornice, and base of niche on recto, inscribed *la modanatura In sul Mezo / del frontone e quella piu / abasso segnato B sie et sul / pilastro cioe Cornice fregio et / architraue e chapitello e basso / sono questi modani del pasato / tabernachulo disacrestia de mani / di mich[e]llagnolo buonaroti misurato / to el solito bracio fiorentino*	Hand **L**	face with hat	
253	49.92.90	R: two plans of the Laurentian Library and a detail of the steps V: plan of the vestibule, Laurentian Library	Hand **L**	no watermark	Tolnay 1967, pls. 23.1 (V), 23.2 (R); Tolnay 1980, pp. 54 ad corpus 526r (V), 64 ad corpus 545r (R)

Sheet number	Accession number	Subject	Designation of hand	Watermark	Publications
254	49.92.29	R: elevation of the doorway to the Laurentian Library reading room from the vestibule V: partial elevation of the doorway from the reading room to the vestibule	Hand L	face with hat	V: Figure 36
255	49.92.31	R: two cross sections of the Laurentian Library entranceway from the reading room V: elevation of the entranceway on recto	Hand L	no watermark	
256	49.92.28	R: elevation of the Laurentian Library entranceway from the reading room V: two cross sections of portal on recto	Hand L	no watermark	
257	49.92.32	R: elevation of the Laurentian Library entranceway from the reading room V: cross section and plan of portal on recto	Hand L	face with hat	
258	49.92.25	R: elevation of one of the blind windows flanking the doorway of the Laurentian Library reading room V: two profiles of cornices	Hand L	crossbow in circle	
259	49.92.26	R: elevation of a window in the upper order of the vestibule, Laurentian Library V: partial elevations and profiles of elements in the reading room	Hand L	no watermark	
260	49.92.24	R: profile and detail of the entablature and a pilaster, Laurentian Library V: profile of the entablature, Laurentian Library	Hand L	face with hat	
261	49.92.38	R: (left) elevations of a window in the upper order of the Laurentian Library vestibule; (right) elevation, cross section, and plan of a niche in the vestibule V: (left) profiles, partial elevations, and details of niche on recto; (right) base, column, and entablature of window on recto	Hand L	blacksmith with hammer and bucket	
262	49.92.35	R: elevation and plan of a doorway, Laurentian Library V: section of doorway on recto and elevation in profile of architectural details	Hand L	blacksmith with hammer and bucket	
263	49.92.30	R: profile of entablature on verso V: elevation of a column and entablature, Laurentian Library	Hand L	blacksmith with hammer and bucket	
264	49.92.34	R: elevation and plan of a window, New Sacristy, San Lorenzo V: elevation and plan of a window, New Sacristy	Hand L	blacksmith with hammer and bucket	
265	49.92.37	R: elevation and plan of a bay, Laurentian Library (?) V: profiles, section, and partial elevation of architectural details of a door, Laurentian Library	Hand L	no watermark	
266	49.92.36	R: elevation and plan of a bay, Laurentian Library (?) V: profile, section, and details of a bay, Laurentian Library (?)	Hand L	lamb with banner in circle	
267	49.92.60	R: elevation in perspective of the portal of Sant' Apollonia, Florence, inscribed *Porta di Sta app'lonia Munistirio In fiorenza Di mano Di Michelagnolo buonaroti / Misurato aluso fiorentino cioe el b[raccio] partito In 20 soldi et ogni soldo In denari 12—* V: plan of the portal of Sant'Apollonia	Hand L	Briquet 6097	R: Figure 37 Tolnay 1966, p. 21; Tolnay 1967, pls. 22.2 (R), 22.3 (V); Bertocci and Davis 1977, p. 94, figs. 1 (R), 2 (V); Ackerman 1986, p. 305; Argan and Contardi 1990, p. 201 (R)
268	49.92.72	Plan of the staircase and semicircle at the upper end of the Belvedere Courtyard, Vatican Palace	unique hand	close to Briquet 5928, 5930	Figure 38 Tolnay 1967, pl. 24.3; Ackerman 1986, p. 325; Argan and Contardi 1990, p. 338

Sheet number	Accession number	Subject	Designation of hand	Watermark	Publications
269	49.92.73	Plan of the Villa Giulia, Rome, with some garden features, with three flaps	Hand **B**	close to Briquet 5928, 5930	Moore 1969, pp. 189–90, figs. 18–20; Tolnay 1980, p. 116, ad corpus 623r (2nd flap)
270	49.92.58	Half elevation of the casino facade, Villa Giulia, inscribed *palais de la vigne*	Hand **B**	close to Briquet 5928, 5930	Moore 1969, p. 187, fig. 16
271	49.92.51	Cross section of the Villa Giulia	unique hand	unidentified	Figure 39 Moore 1969, p. 187, fig. 17
272	49.92.8	Plan of the Quirinal Hill, Rome, with the estate of the Villa Carafa-Este	Hand **B**	blacksmith with hammer and bucket	Figure 40 Wasserman 1963, p. 224, fig. 5; Coffin 1979, p. 188, fig. 119
273	49.92.61	Plan of the Palazzo Farnese, Rome	Hand **A**	crossed arrows surmounted by six-point star	Blunt 1960, p. 16, fig. 1; Ackerman 1961, p. 78; Frommel 1973, pl. 56a; Keller 1976, p. 31, fig. 7; Frommel 1981, p. 185, fig. 12
274	49.92.57	Cross section of the Palazzo Farnese	Hand **C**	blacksmith with hammer and bucket	Frommel 1973, pl. 58a; Keller 1976, p. 30, fig. 5; Frommel 1981, p. 217, fig. 60
275	49.92.79	R: half elevation of the Palazzo Spada, Rome, and profiles of architectural details, inscribed *capo di fero* V: details of interior ornamentation, Palazzo Spada	Hand **A**	crown surmounted by fleur-de-lis	R: Figure 41 Frommel 1973, pl. 30b (R)
276	49.92.7	(Left) partial elevation and ornamental detailing, Palazzo Spada; profile of fireplace (?); (right) elevation in perspective of a sarcophagus; window frame with putto; three ornamental shells and profile	unique hand	lily in double circle	Figure 45
277	49.92.83	R: plan of the Palazzo Massimo alle Colonne, Rome, with small studies of architectural details, inscribed *pianta del palas di maxima* V: (left) elevations of cornice, bases, capitals, inscribed *la coroniche di fora*; (right) elevation of a fireplace in the Palazzo Massimo alle Colonne	Hand **B**	star in circle	Wurm 1965, p. 53, n. 86; Frommel 1973, cat. p. 240, nos. 11j, k
278	49.92.81	R: half elevation of the Palazzo Massimo alle Colonne V: partial elevation and profile of the portal, Palazzo Massimo alle Colonne	Hand **B**	no watermark	R: Figure 42 Wurm 1965, p. 53, n. 86; Frommel 1973, cat. p. 240, nos. 11h, i
279	49.92.80	R: partial elevation and cross section of the Palazzo Massimo alle Colonne V: profile of entablature and base, Palazzo Massimo alle Colonne	Hand **B**	Briquet 6097	Wurm 1965, p. 53, n. 86; Frommel 1973, cat. p. 239, no. 11f, g
280	49.92.6	R: profile of the entablature of the Palazzo Massimo alle Colonne, inscribed in part *Au portique du palais des maxime A romme* V: two profiles of an entablature and cornice; the lower one seems to be antique; inscribed *A Santa prosedia*	Hand **A**	no watermark	Wurm 1965, p. 53, n. 86 (R); Frommel 1973, cat. p. 239, no. 11c
281	49.92.5	(Left, top) detail of Palazzo Massimo alle Colonne portal bracket in elevation; (left, center) partial elevation of portico, Palazzo Massimo; (left, bottom) side elevation of Palazzo Massimo fireplace on sheet 277v; (right) elevation of portal with elevation in profile of a cornice, Palazzo Massimo	Hand **A** + Hand **H**	crown surmounted by star	Wurm 1965, p. 53, n. 86; Frommel 1973, cat. p. 239, no. 11b
282	49.92.82	Half elevation of the Palazzo Cicciaporci-Alberini, Rome	Hand **B**	close to Briquet 5928, 5930	Frommel 1973, pl. 6h
283	49.92.49	(Left) half elevation of the Palazzo Caffarelli-Vidoni, Rome; (right) profiles and elevations, inscribed *faciade di caffarelle a rome*	Hand **A**	close to Briquet 5928, 5930	Frommel 1973, pl. 27b
284	49.92.77	Plan of an unidentified palazzo	Hand **A**	face with hat	

Sheet number	Accession number	Subject	Designation of hand	Watermark	Publications
285	49.92.54	R: cross section of the Palazzo Pirro, Rome V: partial cross sections and profiles, Palazzo Pirro	Hand **B**	no watermark	R: Figure 43 Frommel 1973, pls. 101c (R), 102d (V)
286	49.92.47	Half elevation of the Palazzo Giraud-Torlonia; (right) profiles of details, Palazzo Giraud-Torlonia	Hand **B**	crossbow in circle	
287	49.92.74	Schematic plan of the Palazzo Farnese	unique hand	blacksmith with hammer and bucket	Blunt 1960, p. 17, fig. 3; Ackerman 1961, p. 78; Frommel 1973, pl. 56c; Frommel 1981, p. 187, fig. 15
288	49.92.46	Cross section and half elevation of a palazzo, inscribed *faciade del palasso apresso larco di camigliano vescovo*	Hand **B**	six-point star in circle surmounted by cross	
289	49.92.4	R: profile and partial elevation of *piano nobile* fireplace, Palazzo Massimo alle Colonne; profile of a cornice; inscribed *tutto illargo d[e]llo architravo* V: elevation of door and window, Palazzo Massimo; profiles of the same elements	unique hand	dove in shield surmounted by star	R: Figure 44 Frommel 1973, cat. p. 239, no. 11a
290	49.92.44	R: front and side elevations of the Palazzo Salviati-Adimari, Rome, inscribed *faciade dirito a trastevere sopra al jardino del gran priore* V: (left) plan and cross section of the stables, Villa Farnesina, Rome; (right) technical study of a screw	Hand **B**	no watermark	Frommel 1973, pls. 70e (V), 129d (R); Coffin 1979, p. 96, fig. 60 (V)
291	49.92.48	R: partial cross section of the Palazzo Salviati-Adimari V: architectural details and profiles, Palazzo Salviati-Adimari, inscribed *profil palas del grant [tibre?]*	Hand **B**	no watermark	Frommel 1973, pls. 129c (V), e (R)
292	49.92.53	R: elevation of Villa Farnesina north facade, with ornamental detailing V: plan and profiles of the Villa Farnesina, inscribed in part *faciade de gustin guize transtib[erino]*	Hand **B**	fleur-de-lis in circle surmounted by star	*Builders and Humanists* 1966, pp. 55, 149 (R ill.); Frommel 1973, pls. 66c (V), d (R); Coffin 1979, p. 94, fig. 58 (R); Fiore and Tafuri 1993, p. 117 (R)
293	49.92.50	R: front and side elevations of the Villa Farnesina; (above) profiles of moldings, Villa Farnesina V: plans of the Palazzo Salviati-Adimari	Hand **A**	no watermark	Frommel 1973, pls. 69c (R), 129b (V); Coffin 1979, p. 95, fig. 59 (R)
294	49.92.75	Plan of an unidentified building	Hand **A** (?)	crossed arrows surmounted by star	
295	49.19.14	Elevation and partial plan of an unidentified fireplace	Hand **K**	no watermark	
296	49.92.86	(Top) elevation of a window or door with molded frame; small profile of its cornice; (bottom) partial elevation of a window or door with molded frame; profiles of its moldings	Hand **K**	crossed arrows surmounted by star	
297	49.92.85	Presentation drawing of elevation of facade of Santa Maria in Vallicella, Rome; half plan of facade	unique hand	fleur-de-lis in circle surmounted by crown	Figure 46
298[a]	49.19.39	R: elevation of a Renaissance cabinet V: stone calculators from the Sette Sale	Hand **C**	crown surmounted by star	R: Figure 47 R: Byrne 1981, pp. 114, 115, no. 150
298[b]	49.19.40	R: partial plans of unidentified palazzo and church V: elevation of a panel and profile of the Renaissance cabinet on sheet 298[a]r	unidentified	no watermark	V: Byrne 1981, pp. 114, 115, no. 149
299	49.92.84	R: elevation with decorative panels in geometric forms V: unfinished elevation in perspective of the Pont du Gard	unidentified	crown surmounted by star	
300	49.92.76	R: cross section and plan of the Bastione Ardeatino, Rome, inscribed *bastidon di sant lorenze di Roma* V: plans of three levels of the Bastione Ardeatino	Hand **L** + Hand **B**	Briquet 6097	V: Figure 48
unnumbered	49.92.93	Detached flap, fragment of plan with three windows	unidentified	no watermark	

APPENDIX 2: CONCORDANCE OF ACCESSION AND SCRAPBOOK SHEET NUMBERS

GOLDSCHMIDT SCRAPBOOK

68.769.1	84–85	68.769.16	40[a]	68.769.31	138	68.769.46	176
68.769.2	86	68.769.17	40[b]	68.769.32	68	68.769.47	206
68.769.3	87	68.769.18	unnumbered	68.769.33	[57]	68.769.48	129
68.769.4	88	68.769.19	20	68.769.34	70	68.769.49	128
68.769.5	89	68.769.20	14	68.769.35	72	68.769.50	31
68.769.6	91	68.769.21	10	68.769.36	74	68.769.51	39
68.769.7	92–93	68.769.22	11	68.769.37	77	68.769.52	unnumbered
68.769.8	94–95	68.769.23	65	68.769.38	78	68.769.53	188
68.769.9	99–100	68.769.24	32	68.769.39	80	68.769.54	unnumbered
68.769.10	21	68.769.25	34	68.769.40	81	68.769.55	unnumbered
68.769.11	22[a]	68.769.26	43	68.769.41	82	68.769.56–61	154
68.769.12	[22b]	68.769.27	47[a]	68.769.42	121	68.769.62–66	165
68.769.13	unnumbered	68.769.28	47[b]	68.769.43	unnumbered	68.769.67	148
68.769.14	73[a]	68.769.29	51	68.769.44	115	68.769.68	90
68.769.15	73[b]	68.769.30	67	68.769.45	126		

SCHOLZ SCRAPBOOK

49.19.12	127	49.92.20	221	49.92.45	225	49.92.70	241[b]
49.19.13	247[a]	49.92.21	219	49.92.46	288	49.92.71	209
49.19.14	295	49.92.22	210	49.92.47	286	49.92.72	268
49.19.39	298[a]	49.92.23	217	49.92.48	291	49.92.73	269
49.19.40	298[b]	49.92.24	260	49.92.49	283	49.92.74	287
		49.92.25	258	49.92.50	293	49.92.75	294
49.92.1	213	49.92.26	259	49.92.51	271	49.92.76	300
49.92.2	238	49.92.27	234	49.92.52	227	49.92.77	284
49.92.3	223	49.92.28	256	49.92.53	292	49.92.78	246
49.92.4	289	49.92.29	254	49.92.54	285	49.92.79	275
49.92.5	281	49.92.30	263	49.92.55	208	49.92.80	279
49.92.6	280	49.92.31	255	49.92.56	239	49.92.81	278
49.92.7	276	49.92.32	257	49.92.57	274	49.92.82	282
49.92.8	272	49.92.33	251	49.92.58	270	49.92.83	277
49.92.9	245	49.92.34	264	49.92.59	252	49.92.84	299
49.92.10	244	49.92.35	262	49.92.60	267	49.92.85	297
49.92.11	236	49.92.36	266	49.92.61	273	49.92.86	296
49.92.12	230	49.92.37	265	49.92.62	212	49.92.87	232
49.92.13	228	49.92.38	261	49.92.63	211	49.92.88	233
49.92.14	224	49.92.39	250	49.92.64	235	49.92.89	222
49.92.15	231	49.92.40	249	49.92.65	243	49.92.90	253
49.92.16	218	49.92.41	248	49.92.66	120	49.92.91	226
49.92.17	215	49.92.42	229	49.92.67	240	49.92.92	214
49.92.18	220	49.92.43	242	49.92.68	241[a]	49.92.93	unnumbered
49.92.19	216	49.92.44	290	49.92.69	237	49.92.94	247[a]

Some Notable Sabers of the Qing Dynasty at The Metropolitan Museum of Art

PHILIP M. W. TOM

I N ITS SIZABLE collection of Chinese arms and armor, the Department of Arms and Armor at the Metropolitan Museum has a number of hilted weapons of considerable merit that date from the Qing dynasty (1644–1911). In contrast to the swords of classical antiquity and of the early Chinese Empire, this late imperial material has been generally ignored by art historians. This article will highlight four distinctive sabers dating from the seventeenth through the nineteenth century. The weapons display the richness of imperial China's sword tradition during its last dynasty.

The hilted edged weapons of China fall into two large classes, *jian* and *dao*. The former are straight double-edged swords, while the latter are single-edged blades that come in a variety of shapes. *Dao* may be straight, long and curved, short and compact, or broad with angular points, corresponding, respectively, to the European backsword, saber, cutlass, and falchion. This article focuses on the *peidao*, a type of saber designed to be wielded primarily in one hand and to be worn on the left side in a scabbard slung by straps or cords from a waist belt. A portrait of a Qing military officer of the mid-eighteenth century in battle dress shows a *peidao* suspended in its scabbard from the officer's girdle; its hilt is at the rear to keep the encased sword from becoming entangled with the bow carried on the same side (Figure 1). To draw the weapon, the user pushes the lower part of the scabbard rearward with his left hand, pivoting the hilt forward so that it can easily be grasped with the right hand and the blade can be drawn edge up. Such a draw allows faster deployment on a cutting stroke than if the blade were drawn edge down. An edge-up draw was extensively used in Asian and Islamic cultures, particularly in Japan, Vietnam, the Ottoman Empire, and the Caucasus.

HISTORICAL DEVELOPMENT

Throughout China's history, the *dao* has been associated primarily with the military. Its use dates from

several centuries before the unification of the country in 221 B.C. by the first Qin emperor. The earliest examples were made of bronze, but by the third century B.C. most of the *dao* carried into battle were made of iron or steel. Initially, these weapons were issued to the rank and file. Officers seemed to prefer the double-edged *jian*, which has been identified with the nobility since feudal times and was considered one of the emblems of a gentleman throughout the imperial period.[1] The *dao* employed during this time was, with few exceptions, straight. The Chinese term for this blade configuration is *zhibeidao* (straight-backed knife).

The *zhibeidao* continued to be used throughout succeeding dynasties and became increasingly popular with officers and aristocrats. By the Sui dynasty (A.D. 581–618) fine steel blades in sumptuous fittings were produced.[2] The Metropolitan has two examples, both in unrestored condition (Figures 2, 3). During the Tang dynasty (A.D. 618–907) blades of this style, and the metallurgy to fabricate them, were introduced in Japan, either directly from China or via Korea.[3]

The origins of the *peidao* lie in the curved-bladed sabers wielded by warlike steppe horsemen who ranged during the Middle Ages from western Siberia across the Ural Mountains to the south of modern Ukraine (Figure 4). The nomads learned from experience that a curved edge is more efficient for cutting strokes because its arc coincides with the circular sweep of a rider's arm as he slashes his target at a gallop. Quantities of these weapons have been unearthed at various sites, notably in the Kuban region (where the finds date from the eighth to the ninth century A.D.)[4] and the Yenisey watershed (the artifacts there date from the tenth to the twelfth century).[5]

The descendants of these Eurasian tribes served in large numbers in the ranks of the Mongol hordes that overran and occupied much of eastern Europe and the Middle East, and all of China, in the thirteenth and fourteenth centuries. At least one Western observer noted that sabers were widely used by the Mongol aristocracy by the thirteenth century.[6] The Mongol invaders brought the saber not just to China but also to other cultures that had heretofore relied almost exclusively on straight-bladed swords. The

© The Metropolitan Museum of Art 2001
METROPOLITAN MUSEUM JOURNAL 36

The notes for this article begin on page 222.

Figure 1. Unidentified artist (Chinese, 18th century). *Portrait of the Imperial Bodyguard Zhanyinbao*. Hanging scroll; ink and color on silk; painting and inscription 74¼ x 37⁷⁄₁₆ in. (188.6 x 95.1 cm). The Metropolitan Museum of Art, Purchase, The Dillon Fund Gift, 1986 (1986.206)

Figures 2, 3. Two *zhibeidao*, probably ca. A.D. 600, believed to have been recovered from an imperial tomb near Luoyang, Henan Province. Steel with fittings of gilt bronze and silver, overall L. 39¼ in. (99.7 cm), 40¼ in. (102.2 cm). Figure 2 has traces of its silk burial-wrapping attached to its scabbard chape. The Metropolitan Museum of Art, Figure 2: Gift of George D. Pratt, 1930 (30.65.1); Figure 3: Gift of Clarence H. Mackay, 1930 (30.65.2)

Figure 4. Saber, Eurasia, 10th–13th century. Steel, overall L. 48 in. (122 cm). The Metropolitan Museum of Art, Arthur Ochs Sulzberger Gift, 2000 (2000.609)

Figure 5. Leaf from *Shanama, Gustaham Kills Lahhak and Farshidward.* Iran, first half of the 14th century. Colors, gilt, silver, and black ink on paper, 6⅛ x 5 in. (15.7 x 12.7 cm). The Metropolitan Museum of Art, Rogers Fund, 1969 (69.74.4)

adoption of the saber was gradual, beginning not long after the Mongol conquests and lasting well into the fifteenth century. In many Islamic cultures curved blades almost totally supplanted double-edged swords. In China, India, and Europe sabers and swords existed side by side, and the sword continued to evolve until comparatively recent times.

The sabers used by the troops of the Mongol Empire and its successor states had long heavy blades with a slight curvature, fitted to simple hilts with stubby cross guards (Figure 5). In this form sabers were adopted in China early in the Ming dynasty (1368–1644), when the country's armed forces were reconstituted and a number of Mongol traditions borrowed. During the fifteenth and sixteenth centuries,

many thousands of Japanese sabers were imported into China.[7] The Japanese had long since adopted a disk-shaped guard (Japanese *tsuba*) for their hilts. The Chinese eagerly copied this innovation and by the second half of the Ming had practically abandoned the cruciform guards that were favored in the Islamic world. The disklike guard (Chinese *pan hushou*) became a hallmark of the *peidao* hilt. However, Inner Asian antecedents continued to determine blade shapes, fullers and back edges, and the distinctive scalloped collars (*tunkou*) at the fortes of some blades. By the end of the Ming, the *peidao* had eclipsed the *jian* in China's military. The *jian* was to live on until the present day as one of the primary weapons of martial arts practiced by civilians.

209

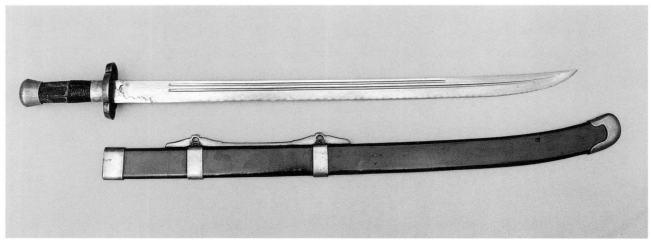

Figure 6. *Yanmaodao* (goose-quill saber) and scabbard, China, 18th century. Blade 29¼ in. (74.3 cm), with heavy brass mounts, lacquered scabbard. Author's collection (photo: author)

Figure 7. Detail of blade of Figure 6, showing lamellar construction, with triple edge plate assembly inserted in a body of pattern-welded iron/steel laminate (photo: author)

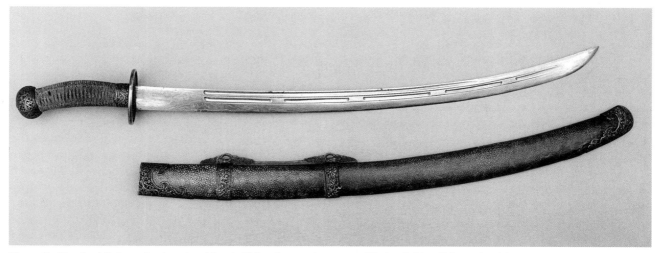

Figure 8. *Piandao* (slicing saber) and scabbard, China, late 19th century. Blade 26⅛ in. (66.4 cm), with segmented fullers inspired by similar effects on some Indian and Persian blades. Mounted in chiseled and pierced brass with rayskin-covered scabbard. Author's collection (photo: author)

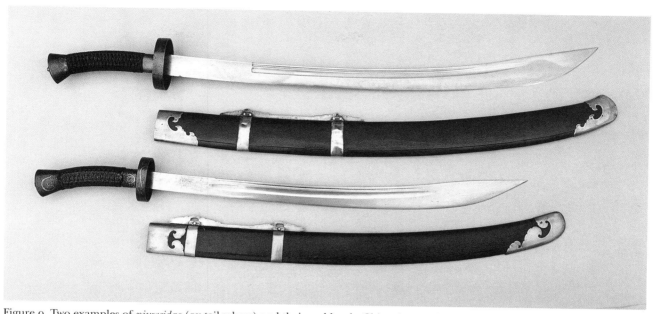

Figure 9. Two examples of *niuweidao* (ox-tail sabers) and their scabbards, China, late 19th–early 20th century. Blades 27½ in. (69.9 cm) and 32¼ in. (81.9 cm), with iron hilt fittings (silver damascening on those of the shorter specimen), brass-mounted scabbards. Author's collection (photo: author)

TYPOLOGY

There are several distinct types of *peidao*, classified and named according to blade shape. The earliest form, which is most closely linked to the ancient and to the medieval *zhibeidao*, is called *yanmaodao* (goose-quill saber). The edge of its blade is straight until the beginning of the back edge and then gradually arches upward to the point (Figures 6, 7). Examples in various collections date from the late Ming to the beginning of the nineteenth century. The *liuyedao* (willow-leaf saber) appeared during the Ming and remained popular until the end of the Qing. The curve of its blade begins gently ahead of the forte and accelerates toward the point (Figures 19, 23). It was the most widely used type of *peidao* during the Qing dynasty; two of the four Metropolitan sabers that are discussed below are *liuyedao*.

A third type of saber is the *piandao* (slicing saber), distinguished by its pronounced curvature (Figure 8). Like the Persian *shamshir*, it was designed for the draw cut at close quarters. Indeed, it is likely that the inspiration for the *piandao*, which saw limited use in China, came from the Middle East. The segmented fullers on the weapon in Figure 8 are strongly reminiscent of motifs found on Indian and Persian sabers.

The last major type is the *niuweidao* (ox-tail saber), which has a distinctive broad blade that widens gradually before terminating in a leaf-shaped point (Figure 9).

It appeared late in the Qing, toward the close of the nineteenth century. This is the only major type of *peidao* that was developed and used mainly by civilians. The shape of its blade suggests that it is derived from peasants' falchions, or even from certain types of pole arms, though some scholars link the broadening tip area with the raised *yelman*, or back edge, seen on many medieval Turkic saber blades.[8]

PEIDAO WITH TWIST-CORE PATTERN-WELDED BLADE

One of the Qing sabers in the Metropolitan Museum has a blade of unusual form and metallurgical sophistication (36.25.1477a, b; Figure 10). The solid understated grace of the weapon's fittings seems to accord with the aesthetic values embodied in the best Yixing teapots and Ming-style hardwood furniture.

The 28¼-inch pattern-welded Damascus blade is made of *huawengang* (flower-patterned steel), forged of six rows of twisted cores of iron and steel laminate; a narrow band of high-carbon steel forms the edge (Figure 11). The curvature of the cutting edge, almost imperceptible near the hilt, increases markedly a few inches from the tip, where the blade widens abruptly. There are two narrow fullers on each side, with small dimples at the forte. The fittings are of blackened iron. The scabbard bands and the flange of the *hushou*

Figure 10. *Peidao* with blade of proto-*niuweidao* form and scabbard, China, probably 18th century. Blade 28¼ in. (72.4 cm), of six-row *huawengang* and stacked edge strip, fitted in iron, scabbard covered in black leather. The Metropolitan Museum of Art, Bequest of George C. Stone, 1935 (36.25.1477a, b). See also Colorplate 3

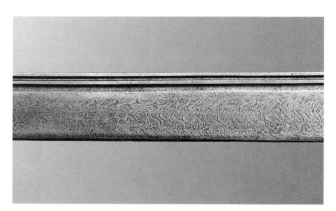

Figure 11. Detail of blade of Figure 10, showing *huawengang* pattern

are hollow-ground. Intricate file-cut decoration on the *tiliang*, or suspension bar, on the scabbard suggests the closely spaced nodes at the base of a bamboo stalk.

This type of blade is rarely encountered. The leaf-shaped point and the pronounced widening toward the tip are features of the more familiar *niuweidao* saber of the late Qing and the early Chinese Republic. The *niuweidao* curves considerably more along its entire length, however, and it broadens over a greater area as well (compare the examples in Figure 9). Per-haps the blade on the Metropolitan's example is a

type antecedent to the *niuweidao*. The near straightness of the blade behind the swelling tip appears indicative of a transitional form: akin to the *yanmaodao*, which seems to bridge the *zhibeidao* and the *liuyedao*. The paucity of examples of this blade type and the absence of textual references preclude a definitive chronology at this time.

Twist-core pattern-welded Damascus blades are sometimes found among weapons produced in China during the Ming and Qing periods. The cores were formed of alternating bars of high- and low-carbon steel forge-welded into a single billet, twisted into a tight spiral, and ground to a square cross section. The smith combined multiple cores when forming the blade. A large nineteenth-century *liuyedao* composed of six cores and a separate back edge is shown in Figures 12 and 13; a stout cutlass blade dating from the seventeenth to the eighteenth century has a four-row twist (Figure 14). Until the early twentieth century twist-core construction was also used for the manufacture of *jian* blades. Normally the cores were simply "stacked," or welded side by side. Often, as in the Metropolitan's example, a separate edge strip of high-carbon steel was added. Sometimes more complex structures were produced, utilizing inserted high-carbon edge plates. Several cores could be stacked to

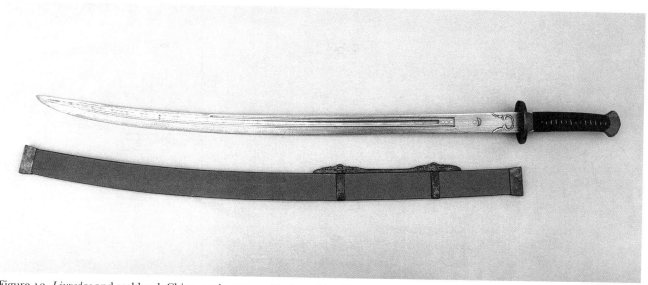

Figure 12. *Liuyedao* and scabbard, China, 19th century. Blade 35⅛ in. (89.2 cm), of six-row *huawengang*, and with a Tibetan inscription and inlays of later date. Author's collection (photo: author)

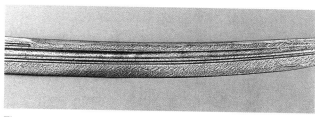

Figure 13. Detail of blade of Figure 12, showing *huawengang* pattern (photo: author)

Figure 14. Detail of blade on a *peidao*, 17th–18th century, showing four-row *huawengang* and inserted edge plate. Courtesy Scott M. Rodell, Great River Taoist Center, Washington, D.C. (photo: author)

form composite plates that were welded to each side of the central edge plate. Such tripartite construction was called *sanmei*. Alternatively, a body of stacked cores could be cleft lengthwise to admit the edge plate; this method was called *qiangang* (inserted steel). Both *sanmei* and *qiangang* were also employed on blade bodies composed of simple lamellar pattern weld, that is, layers of iron and medium-carbon steel folded over and over, with a linear or undulating surface pattern (Figures 7, 28).

Pattern-welded lamellar forging and multiplate structures such as *qiangang* and *sanmei* have been known in China since late antiquity[9] and are the basis of the sword smith's art in Japan and elsewhere. Stacked twisted cores are unknown prior to the Ming dynasty, however. It may be that the manufacture of *huawengang* in China was an outgrowth of Ming connoisseurs' appreciation of blades from Islamic regions.[10] Iran, India, and Central Asia would seem the obvious sources of this technique, given their proximity to China and their well-developed metallurgical traditions. Pattern welding with twisted cores was

widely used in these areas in the production of gun barrels. Such was not the case with blades, though. The most characteristic sabers, daggers, and knives were made of crystalline Damascus steel (*poulad jauhar* or *wootz*). The surface patterns of this material differ from those of pattern-welded steels. They result not from the smith's mechanically combining steels or iron of differing composition but from the formation of a coarse network of iron-carbide structures in the steel.[11] This molecular structure originates during the smelting process.

When pattern welding was used for the manufacture of blades in India and the Middle East, smiths tended not to use twisted structures. The only part of these regions where parallel rows of twisted cores were

Figure 15. *Peidao* with Japanese import blade, the mounts Chinese, ca. 1750–1800. Blade 28¾ in. (73 cm), mounts gilt iron set with gemstones and mother-of-pearl, with polychrome lacquered scabbard embellished with mother-of-pearl. The Metropolitan Museum of Art, The Collection of Giovanni P. Morosini, presented by his daughter Giulia, 1932 (32.75.301a, b). See also Colorplate 3

employed for blades was the Ottoman Empire. There, the technique was sometimes utilized in the manufacture of *yataghan* and *kilij* blades. Examples of these weapons with twist-core blades are almost all from the late eighteenth century or later, however. *Huawengang* seems to have appeared in China at an earlier date.

Twist-core pattern welding was not a universal metalworking tradition in the East and was practically ignored in Japan, Korea, and mainland Southeast Asia. The Indonesian archipelago, though, easily outdid the rest of the non-European world in the production of twist-core blades. The use of this technique among the Moros of the southern Philippines[12] indicates that it was exported northward from Sumatra and Java, probably with the spread of Islam. The rows of star-shaped elements, feathery or flamelike bands, and "barber-pole" structures seen on Moro and Chinese twist-core forging are remarkably similar. Traders, pirates, and émigrés from southern China had extensive contact with Southeast Asian peoples. Indeed, Chinese smiths are known to have made *barong* blades of lamellar *qiangang* structure for export to the Philippines.[13] It is likely that *keris* and other weapons from Southeast Asia made their way to China as trade goods, booty, or travel mementos. Their construction, if not their form, must have held considerable fascination and appeal for Chinese swordsmen and collectors of curiosities.

PEIDAO WITH IMPORTED BLADE AND PRINCELY FITTINGS

Another Metropolitan saber is lavishly decorated (32.75.301a, b; Figure 15). It offers insight into the symbolism underlying the design of the Qing aristocracy's court regalia and illustrates the ongoing appeal of luxury foreign wares to wealthy and sophisticated Chinese. The saber's mountings reflect the opulence verging on decadence that appeared late in the Qianlong period (1736–95) and grew during successive reigns.

The blade is of Japanese manufacture, with a *koshizori* curvature. It is affixed to the hilt by peening at the pommel, and its original surface polish is gone—features that make it difficult to be certain of its age, maker, and school. The forte is engraved and gilded to simulate a *tunkou*. The mounting is in the *fangshi* (squared or angular) style, with the peculiar quadrangular grip and scabbard sections and the squared-off chape that are also encountered on some Tibetan and Timurid weapons. Made of iron overlaid with gold leaf, the fittings are chiseled and inset with round cabochons of red coral, malachite, and lapis lazuli; between the stones and relief elements are small fragments of mother-of-pearl in mosaic patterns (Figure 16). The wooden scabbard is finished with polished black lacquer, embellished with four-clawed dragons (three on each side) amid clouds and auspicious symbols such as the Sacred Mountain, books, coins, and lozenges (Figure 17).[14] The grip is wrapped with blue-green braided silk cord in typical Chinese fashion and fitted with a long ornamental tassel.

Although the Japanese learned the art of sword making from China and Korea,[15] the Chinese developed an appreciation of Japanese sabers as early as the Song dynasty. The renowned poet Ouyang Xiu wrote, about 1060, "From the land of the rising sun come precious swords . . . / With scabbards of fragrant wood, sharkskin-covered, and bearing / Designs in silver and gold, trappings of brass and bronze."[16] During the Ming dynasty, swords were a sought-after luxury import from Japan, and more than seventy-five thousand were shipped to China on eleven "Kango" trade

Figure 16. Detail of Figure 15, hilt and throat area of scabbard, showing position of cabochons, and surrounding mosaic-work of mother-of-pearl

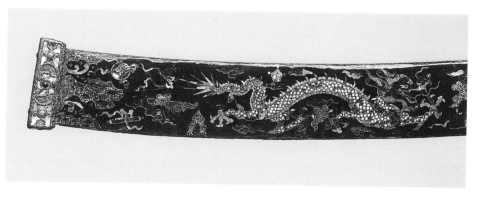

Figure 17. Detail of decoration on lacquered scabbard of Figure 15

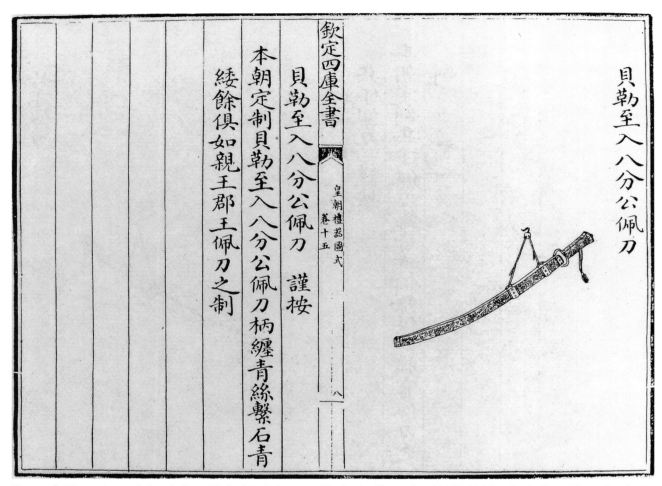

Figure 18. Illustration and description of *beile zhiru bafengong peidao* in the *Huangchao Liqi Tushi* (after facsimile of *Huangchao Liqi Tushi* in *Yingyin Wenyuange siku quanshu*, vol. 656 [Shanghai, 1983], p. 6)

missions between 1432 and 1547.[17] Others were captured as booty from the Wokou coastal pirates after Ming forces under General Qi Jiguang gained the upper hand in the sixteenth century over the large-scale depredations along the China coast. These blades varied greatly in quality, as did those made by the Chinese themselves.

The configuration of the hilt and scabbard of the Metropolitan saber, with a quadrangular cross section and a squared chape, is common in China from the late Ming. The nonmetallic materials that ornament the mountings conform closely to those specified for a *beile zhiru bafengong peidao,* or saber for Princes of the Third Degree (Manchu *doroi beile*) and the Eight Privileged Ranks (*bafengong*), during the Qianlong reign of the Qing dynasty. According to the 1759 *Huangchao Liqi Tushi* (Illustrated Regulations for the Ceremonial Regalia of the Present Dynasty; Figure 18), the deco-

ration of the *beile*'s saber is a carryover from that of the side arm for the next-higher princely ranks, the *Qinwang* and *Junwang* (Manchu *hosoi činwang* and *doroi giyun wang,* respectively).[18] The text states that the sabers for all three ranks are to have fittings set with coral, lapis lazuli, turquoise, and (saltwater) pearls; the polychrome lacquered scabbards are to be decorated with lotus motifs and miscellaneous subjects.[19] The differences are that the hilt and scabbard for the first- and second-degree princes have the *yuanshi,* or rounded cross section and chape, and that the grip is wound with braided cord of golden-yellow rather than blue-green silk.

The silk grip wrapping (*sikou*) of blue green on the Metropolitan's example is consistent with the regulations, as is the polychrome scabbard. Several features of the saber depart from the guidelines, however. For instance, malachite has been substituted for turquoise. This substitution is less drastic than it seems, though, for much of the Tibetan turquoise used during the Qing for ornamental purposes had a greenish tint. More unusual is the replacement of pearls on the metal fittings with small pieces of mother-of-pearl applied in mosaic fashion. (Also of note is the fact that mother-of-pearl ornament on scabbards is atypical for China and more characteristic of Vietnam, until the twentieth century.[20] This decorative technique was fairly widespread in the furniture trade of southern China, however.) A final departure is the presence of dragons on the scabbard—and the absence of lotuses. The regulations neither mandate nor rule out dragons. This may indicate that there was some latitude for individuals, whose regalia were custom-made. The four-clawed dragons depicted seem in any case an appropriate emblem for a *doroi beile*.

The high quality and the sumptuous ornament of this saber's fittings date them to the second half of the Qianlong reign (1736–95), or to the first part of the succeeding Jiaqing reign (1796–1820). Such a weapon would have complemented a suit of armor (the armor of this era later evolved into a military uniform without metal defenses) or a ceremonial robe, jacket, and hat. The armor and dress appropriate to each rank in the Qianlong noble and official hierarchy are detailed in the *Huangchao Liqi Tushi*. Unfortunately, the published regulations for other reign periods are incomplete, inaccessible, or lost.

LIUYEDAO WITH FITTINGS ORNAMENTED WITH LAPIDARY WORK

This saber represents the epitome of the sword maker's art in late imperial China (14.48.2a, b; Figure 19). It is a stunning marriage of elegance and function. Despite its graceful lines and its exquisite and impeccably crafted decoration, it is not a bauble for the parade ground. Its substantial blade has two narrow deep fullers on each side, a peaked *bei* (dorsal) ridge, a well-defined back edge, and a gilt iron *tunkou* at the forte. Distal taper is slight, giving this blade considerable weight and making it well suited for powerful sweeping cuts from horseback. In its current condition, details of the blade's fabrication are not discernible.

The iron mounts are ornamented with pierced fretwork *(loukong)*, chiseling, gilding, and gemstones. The frontal surface of the flanged ogival guard is engraved with floral patterns on a stippled ground. All the fittings are set with coral and malachite; some of the stones are round cabochons, while others are combined in arrangements resembling characters in the archaic "seal" script (Figures 20–22). The wooden grip is wrapped with brown silk braid, and the scabbard is covered with brown morocco-finished leather; both are in the *fangshi* configuration. The chape is missing, and the locket is reversed.

Although the gemstones in the fittings recall the

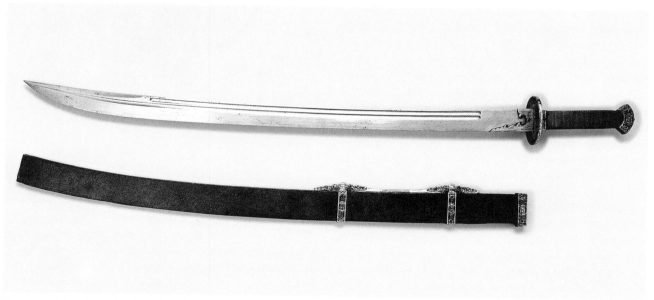

Figure 19. *Liuyedao* and scabbard, China, 17th–18th century. Blade 29⅞ in. (75.9 cm), mounted in gilt openwork iron, embellished with gemstones, with scabbard covered in brown leather. The Metropolitan Museum of Art, Rogers Fund, 1914 (14.48.2a, b). See also Colorplate 3

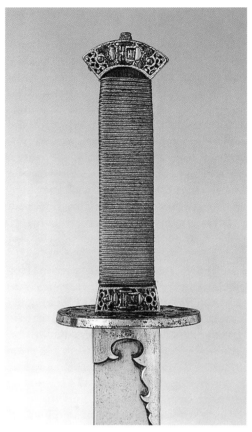

Figure 20. Detail of hilt of *liuyedao* in Figure 19, showing combination of fretwork and inset stones on the iron mounts

Figure 21. Detail of scabbard (*qiao*) of *liuyedao* in Figure 19, showing a suspension band (*tilianggu*) and part of suspension bar (*tiliang*)

Figure 22. Detail of guard (*pan hushou*) of *liuyedao* in Figure 19 from the hilt side

decoration of Figure 15, above, the combination of stones on this saber is not found among the regulation designs set out in the Qianlong-reign *Huangchao Liqi Tushi.* The ornament may have been a prescribed pattern for certain ranks of the nobility or officer corps in an earlier period, one for which published regulations are lacking. Or the saber may have been a specially commissioned nonregulation weapon not authorized for wear during formal court ceremonies or at the grand military reviews in the capital.

The form of the *tunkou* is typical. These collars are often found on *liuyedao* and *yanmaodao* but were frequently omitted from blades produced during the later Qing dynasty. Contrary to popular belief, the *tunkou* is not related to the *habaki* on Japanese sabers and daggers, which performs a similar function. Rather, the shape of the *tunkou* indicates that it is a direct descendant of collars on backswords and sabers made by various Inner Asian peoples during the Middle Ages (see Figure 4).[21] The flaring pommel with radiused end on this and many other *peidao* is also a medieval Eurasian form. Like the *tunkou*, it can be traced back to the sabers of the steppe nomads of centuries past.[22]

Sabers of this style are encountered from the late Ming to just after the mid-Qing. During the late Qing downward-curving grips and *yuanshi* mountings (see Figure 23) became more popular. There was also a tendency toward standardized, pattern-book decoration that was less refined (Figure 8 is an example). As the nineteenth century wore on, the quality of both blades and fittings declined, until production ended in the early twentieth century with gaudy and insubstantial pieces for the curio trade.

LIUYEDAO WITH BLADE SHOWING EUROPEAN DESIGN INFLUENCES

One of the sabers at the Metropolitan exhibits intriguing features analogous to those of Hungarian and Polish blades—while remaining typically Chinese in its curvature and in the design of its fittings (36.25.1473a, b; Figure 23). It is a rare example of limited Western influence on the design of mid-Qing hilted weapons, in contrast to the marked Western imprint on Chinese artillery technology during the same period.

The blade has a somewhat raised back edge with a slight drop at the tip, and deep well-defined fullers. Its dorsal ridge is not typical of a Chinese saber: it has an indented area beginning about ten inches from the guard and ending at the base of the back edge, and this recessed area is cut with a narrow dorsal groove. A brass *tunkou* is fitted to the forte; its frontal portion touches the ends of the fullers, which run farther back than is usual for a *peidao*.

The brass mounts are gilt, the finish much worn. The pommel is associated; the ferrule and the scabbard throat and chape have ornately scalloped borders (Figures 24–26). Quatrefoil in shape, the *hushou* features panels of *loukong* (Figure 25). All these components are engraved with tightly executed floral scrollwork. *Loukong* is also found on the *tiliang* (Figure 26). Yellow silk braid, now faded and worn, is wrapped around the grip. The scabbard is covered with polished green-stained rayskin (the *tiliang* and its supporting bands have shifted position due to shrinkage of the wood). The fittings are in the *yuanshi* style.

With a blade nearly thirty-two inches long, this saber was intended for a horseman. Its overall quality indicates usage by an officer or a member of the nobility, yet its configuration does not conform to the Qianlong-era *Huangchao Liqi Tushi*. This might be a nonregulation item purchased for field or informal use (as has been speculated concerning Figure 19, above), or it might date from a later reign when the regulations were changed or relaxed. Braided yellow silk cord on the grip was generally reserved for the emperor and his armed attendants (*suishi*);[23] a saber such as this would more likely have been carried by the latter.

The unusual features of this blade point to eastern European influence. Saber blades with recessed sec-

Figure 23. *Liuyedao* and scabbard, China, 18th century. Blade 31¾ in. (80.6 cm), with fullers and details of dorsal spine showing European influence, mounted in gilt brass with panels of openwork and with engraved decor, the scabbard covered with polished rayskin. The Metropolitan Museum of Art, Bequest of George C. Stone, 1935 (36.25.1473a, b). See also Colorplate 3

Figure 24. Detail of scabbard throat and forward part of guard of *liuyedao* in Figure 23, showing ornate cusping on ferrule (*binggu*) and scabbard throat (*qiaokou*), and the weave of the *sikou* around the grip

Figure 25. Detail of the guard (*pan hushou*) of the *liuyedao* in Figure 23, revealing its quatrefoil form, engraved decor, and panels of *loukong* (openwork)

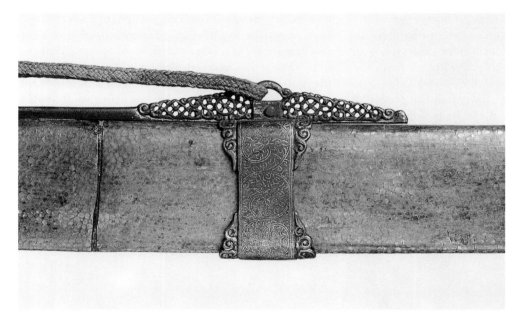

Figure 26. Detail of *tilianggu* and part of *tiliang* on Figure 23

tions of spine, sometimes with a dorsal fuller, were popular in Hungary and Poland during the seventeenth and eighteenth centuries.[24] Chinese sabers with either of these features are extremely scarce. An example in the author's collection features a dorsal groove but lacks a recess (Figures 27–29); its long back edge is flush with the remainder of the spine. It is tempting to conclude that the blade on the Metropolitan's example is an import from Poland or Hungary. The appearance of the fullers and the dorsal area would certainly support this contention. However, the curvature, rather slight compared to that of the European blades, is consistent with Chinese norms. Unfortunately, the blade's surface in its current condition does not reveal any details of lamellar structure or heat treating that would allow us to verify

the blade's origin (by contrast, Chinese *qiangang* lamination and differential hardening are apparent on the author's example; see Figure 28).

The four Metropolitan *peidao* that have been examined above represent an element of Chinese material culture receptive to foreign goods and stylistic concepts, and as such they help to modify the prevailing stereotype of a culturally introspective and isolationist Middle Kingdom. They demonstrate only a small part of the considerable technical and aesthetic repertoire of Chinese bladesmiths and sword fitters during the late imperial period. Yet the weapons reveal much about the tastes of the warrior elite of Qing society—the patrons of the skilled artisans who fashioned these beautiful yet lethal objects.

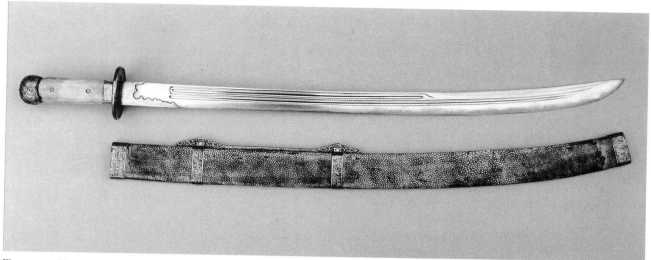

Figure 27. *Liuyedao* and scabbard, China, 18th–early 19th century. Blade of *qiangang* construction, 28⅝ in. (72.7 cm), mounts of engraved brass, with bone grip and scabbard covered in polished rayskin. Author's collection (photo: author)

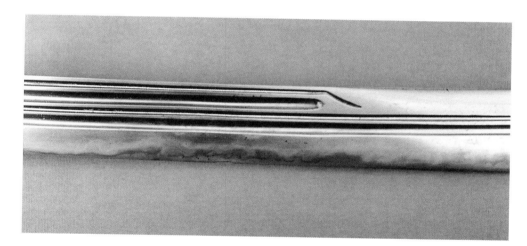

Figure 28. Detail of blade of the *liuyedao* in Figure 27, showing metallurgical details. The central edge plate of highly refined carbon steel is visible as dark gray, along with a white cloudy zone (*shuang-xue*), which is the result of a differential heat-treating process (photo: author)

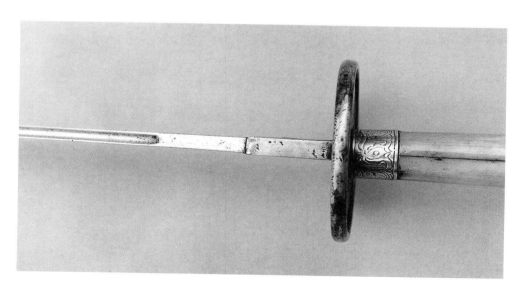

Figure 29. Detail of the dorsal portion of the *liuyedao* in Figure 27, just ahead of the guard. The brass *tunkou* occupies the area just ahead of the guard, and a dorsal groove begins a short distance beyond that. In contrast with Figure 23, this piece has no recessed section on the back of the blade (photo: author)

GENERAL BIBLIOGRAPHY

Allen, James W. *Persian Metal Technology 700–1300* A.D. London: Ithaca Press, 1979.

Clunas, Craig. *Chinese Furniture*. London: Bamboo Publishing, 1988.

Figiel, Leo S. *On Damascus Steel*. New York: Atlantis Arts Press, 1991.

Jacob, Alain. *Les armes blanches du monde islamique*. Paris: Jacques Grancher, 1985.

Mayers, William Frederick. *The Chinese Government*. Shanghai: Kelly and Walsh, 1897.

Nicolle, David. *The Mongol Warlords*. Dorset, England: Firebird Books, 1990.

Rawson, Jessica. *Chinese Ornament: The Lotus and the Dragon*. London: British Museum Publications, 1990.

Richardson, Thom. "The Ming Sword." *Royal Armouries Yearbook* 1 (1996), pp. 95–99.

So, Kwan-wai. *Japanese Piracy in Ming China during the 16th Century*. [East Lansing]: Michigan State University Press, 1975.

Yang, Hong. *Ancient Chinese Weapons*. New York and Beijing: Science Press, 1992.

NOTES

1. Yun Zhang, *The Art of Chinese Swordsmanship* (New York: Weatherhill, 1998), pp. 17–19.

2. Joseph Needham, *The Development of Iron and Steel Technology in China* (Cambridge: W. Heffer and Sons, 1964), p. 26, quotes the historical text *Beiqi Shu,* which describes the legendary backsword blades made by the Taoist adept and sword smith Qiwu Huaiwen for the emperor Gaozi (r. A.D. 543–50). For a sumptuous 8th-century Tang *zhibeidao* preserved in almost pristine condition at the Shôsô-in, Nara, see *The Japanese Sword: Iron Craftsmanship and Warrior Spirit,* exh. cat. (Tokyo: National Museum, 1997), pp. viii, 71–72, 77, no. 58.

3. Stephen V. Grancsay, "Two Chinese Swords Dating about A.D. 600," *MMAB* 25 (September 1930), pp. 194–96.

4. W. Arendt, "Türkische Säbel aus den VIII.–IX. Jahrhunderten," *Archaeologica Hungarica* 16 (1935), fig. 24, pl. VI. For an outstanding specimen from the same cultural sphere and epoch, see Anatolij Kirpičnikov, "Der sogenannte Säbel Karls des Grossen," *Gladius* 10 (1972), pp. 69–70.

5. Iu. S. Khudiakov, *Vooruzhenie yeniseiskikh kyrgyzov, VI–XII vv* (Arms of the Yenisey Kirghiz in the sixth to the twelfth century) (Novosibirsk: Academy of Sciences of the USSR, Siberian Branch, 1980), p. 49. For a rare inscribed example whose contour and other features closely resemble those of Chinese *liuyedao* blades dating centuries later, see Repsime Djanpoladian and Anatolij Kirpičnikov, "Mittelälterlicher Säbel mit einer armenischen Inscriften gefunden in subpolaren Ural," *Gladius* 10 (1972), pp. 15–23.

6. Friar Giovanni di Piano Carpini, *Historia mongalorum quos nos Tataros appellamus,* trans. Erik Hildinger as *The Story of the Mongols Whom We Call the Tartars* (Boston: Branden Publishing, 1996), p. 72.

7. Randolph Caldwell, ed., *The Book of the Sword* (Dallas, Tex.: Tôken Kenkyû Kai, 1972), p. 32.

8. Arendt, "Säbel," p. 64.

9. Needham, *Development*, p. 26.

10. Craig Clunas, *Superfluous Things: Material Culture and Social Status in Early Modern China* (Chicago and Urbana: University of Illinois, 1991), p.110.

11. Oleg Sherby and Jeffrey Wadsworth, "Damascus Steels," *Scientific American*, February 1985, pp. 112–20.

12. Robert Cato, *Moro Swords* (Singapore: Graham Brash, 1996), pp. 20–21.

13. Ibid., p. 21.

14. For an explanation of the various motifs, see C. A. S. Williams, *Outlines of Chinese Symbolism and Art Motives,* 3rd ed. (New York: Dover, 1976).

15. Needham, *Development*, p. 41; Satô Kanichi, "Introduction to the Sword Blades in the Shôsô-in," trans. Shigetaka Kaneko, in *Shôsô-in no Tôken* (Tokyo: Nihon Keizai Shimbun, 1974), p. vi.

16. Needham, *Development*, p. 42.

17. Caldwell, *Sword*, p. 32.

18. Pu Jiang et al., eds., *Huangchao Liqi Tushi,* Palace Edition of 1766 (British Library, 15300.e.1). This version of the text is based on a manuscript of 1759.

19. Ibid., chap. 15, pp. 5a–b, 6a–b.

20. The Metropolitan Museum has two Vietnamese hilted weapons in its collection, a *guỏm* (saber; acc. no. 36.25.1621a, b) and a *kiếm* (sword; acc. no. 36.25.1451a, b). The scabbards of both weapons are decorated with mother-of-pearl in mosaic-like patterns.

21. Khudiakov, *Vooruzhenie*, pp. 38, 41, 43.

22. Ibid., p. 43, pl. VIII, fig. 2; Arendt, "Säbel," pl. III, fig. 5.

23. *Huangchao*, chap. 15, pp. 1a–b—4a–b.

24. Wojciech Zabłocki, *Prawdziwą Cięcia Szablą* (A true cut with a saber) (Warsaw: Wydanictwo Sport i Turystyka, 1988), pp. 206–9.

Weehawken from Turtle Grove: A Forgotten "Knickerbocker" Watercolor by William J. Bennett

KEVIN J. AVERY

Associate Curator, American Paintings and Sculpture, The Metropolitan Museum of Art

AN IMPORTANT EARLY American watercolor in the Metropolitan Museum's collection, *View on the Hudson River,* long attributed to William Guy Wall (1792–after 1863), can now be ascribed instead to Wall's contemporary William J. Bennett (ca. 1784–1844). The picture may also be given back its original title, *Weehawken from Turtle Grove* (Figure 1) and even dated with fair precision to about 1830. In addition, we now know that the watercolor is the source of an engraving (Figure 2) included in one of the earliest New York City publications of American scenery. The picture's subject, the Weehawken bluffs on the New Jersey shore of the Hudson, was a recreational destination favored by New Yorkers of the day, as well as the setting of a "legend" penned by a leading Knickerbocker writer.

The picture represents the view north, upriver, from a peninsula on the western, or New Jersey, shore of the Hudson River. The view across the water—a bay created by the peninsula—shows Hoboken at the extreme left and Weehawken in the center. The time of day is late afternoon. Several large boulders and two conifers that appear to be cedars dominate the foreground and serve as a border to a path partly visible in the lower left corner. At left the bay is only partially seen beyond the trees and boulders, which set off the distant rocky bluffs of Weehawken. In the middle distance at right, fishing boats and sloops plot the Hudson River's recession to the north, with the sails of the sloops serving to close off the composition.

Weehawken from Turtle Grove entered the Metropolitan Museum's collection in 1954 as part of the large bequest of prints, maps, drawings, and documents pertaining to New York City assembled by Edward W. C. Arnold.[1] Since then the watercolor has been regularly exhibited and reproduced.[2] The picture's earlier attribution to Wall was understandable. Wall, an émigré from Ireland, executed the watercolors for *The Hudson River Portfolio,* a series of twenty hand-colored aquatint engravings incised chiefly by John Hill and published in New York by Henry J. Megarey from 1821 to 1825. Additionally, Wall made several handsome watercolor views of New York City, also in the Arnold bequest, two of which (see Figure 3) were engraved by Hill and published by Megarey as a set in 1823.[3] *Weehawken from Turtle Grove,* which is unsigned, is essentially consistent in both subject and style with the Wall watercolors in the Metropolitan's collection, but it is superior to any of them. It possesses a strength of composition, a delicacy of atmosphere, and a painstaking articulation of foreground details that the more schematic works by Wall do not equal. Its special quality seems to have been acknowledged by past commentators. Former Metropolitan curator Albert Ten Eyck Gardner singled out this "Wall," from among others in the collection, for reproduction in his *History of Watercolor Painting in America,* published in 1966, as did Stuart Feld in an article previewing the Metropolitan Museum's 1966 exhibition "Two Hundred Years of Watercolor Painting in America." John K. Howat also illustrated *View on the Hudson River* (along with several authentic Walls) in his 1972 book, *The Hudson River and Its Painters.* Howat remarked on the picture's "greater breadth and luminosity" as compared with other works by Wall.[4]

That the picture lacked its proper title and was so long attributed to Wall testifies to several other factors besides its resemblance to Wall's work. For one thing, the setting is now so altered by urban buildup as to defy identification with Bennett's representation. More to the point, there are relatively few known Bennett watercolors of natural settings with which to compare *Weehawken.*

This is not because the artist produced little work or because his contemporaries ignored it. Bennett had been exhibiting since he was a teenager in his native London, where he had studied watercolor and aquatint engraving at the Royal Academy under Richard Westall. By 1810 his work was earning accolades in the London press, praise that followed him to New York in 1826, where he continued to exhibit his watercolors

The notes for this article begin on page 233.

regularly and was quickly elected to membership in the fledgling National Academy of Design. But in both England and America, Bennett's main livelihood came from producing aquatints after his own and other artists' drawings at a time of rapidly increasing demand for topographical and picturesque views of Europe and the eastern United States.[5] Due to the quality and wide dissemination of copies of his prints, Bennett's reputation as an engraver has persisted and blossomed at the expense of his original watercolors. Most of those were produced as models for his engravings, and probably for that reason few were signed. Undoubtedly, many original Bennett watercolors have not survived, but as had been the case with *Weehawken*, others may remain unrecognized as his work.

Moreover, the majority of Bennett's prints—and consequently the majority of his known watercolors—are of cities. The only other drawing in the Metropolitan's collection that can safely be attributed to him is *View of South Street, from Maiden Lane, New York City* (Figure 4). That picture was executed as the model for one of three aquatints Bennett made for Megarey's *Street Views of the City of New-York*, a projected series of prints of which only the first number was issued, in 1834.[6] *View of South Street* shows few features (except the sky and clouds) readily comparable with the natural forms that prevail in *Weehawken from Turtle Grove*. However, the latter compares well with Bennett watercolors in the collections of the New-York Historical Society and the Brooklyn Museum of Art. The refined rendering of water, sky, sailing vessels, and figures in *Weehawken* strongly resembles corresponding features in *View of the Bay of New York from the Battery, N.Y.C.* (Figure 5), while its treatment of foliage in the foreground and on the background hills closely matches that of comparable motifs in *View on the Potomac, Looking toward Harper's Ferry* (Figure 6); both date probably later than the Metropolitan picture.[7]

Figure 1. William J. Bennett (ca. 1784–1844). *Weehawken from Turtle Grove*, ca. 1830. Watercolor, gouache, and graphite on off-white wove paper, 15⁵⁄₁₆ x 20¹⁄₁₆ in. (38.6 x 51 cm). The Metropolitan Museum of Art, The Edward W. C. Arnold Collection of New York Prints, Maps, and Pictures, Bequest of Edward W. C. Arnold, 1954 (54.90.107). See also Colorplate 4

Figure 2. Asher B. Durand (1796–1886), after William J. Bennett. *Weehawken.* Steel engraving, 4⅛ x 6 in. (11.5 x 15.2 cm), published in *The American Landscape* (New York: Elam Bliss, 1830), pl. [1]. The Metropolitan Museum of Art, Gift of Mrs. Frederick F. Durand, 1930 (30.15.59)

Figure 3. William Guy Wall (1792–after 1863). *New York from Weehawken,* ca. 1823. Watercolor, gouache, and graphite on off-white wove paper, 16⅟₁₆ x 25⅛ in. (40.8 x 62.8 cm). The Metropolitan Museum of Art, The Edward W. C. Arnold Collection of New York Prints, Maps, and Pictures, Bequest of Edward W. C. Arnold, 1954 (54.90.109).

Figure 4. William J. Bennett. *View of South Street, from Maiden Lane, New York City.* Watercolor used with brush and pen on off-white wove paper, 9⅝ x 13⅝ in. (24.4 x 34.7 cm). The Metropolitan Museum of Art, The Edward W. C. Arnold Collection of New York Prints, Maps, and Pictures, Bequest of Edward W. C. Arnold, 1954 (54.90.130)

Figure 5. William J. Bennett. *View of the Bay of New York from the Battery, N.Y.C.,* ca. 1844. Watercolor on paper, 11½ x 17⅜ in. (29.2 x 44.1 cm). The New-York Historical Society, Abbott-Lenox Fund, 1962, 1962.23 (photo: The New-York Historical Society)

The key to the identity of the site depicted in the work formerly known as *View on the Hudson River* is the already mentioned engraving entitled *Weehawken* (Figure 2), the first of the six plates included in *The American Landscape* (1830), a publication project of the engraver Asher B. Durand and the printer E. Wade. Durand (with minor assistance from James Smillie) executed steel engravings from original paintings and watercolors by himself, Bennett, Thomas Cole, and Robert Walter Weir.[8] William Cullen Bryant wrote the bulk of the text (see Appendix 1) accompanying the plates, and the whole was published by Elam Bliss. The engraving was republished in the *New-York Mirror* on April 20, 1833, with an accompanying description (Appendix 2).[9]

Inscribed "Painted by W. J. Bennett" and "Engraved by Asher B. Durand," *Weehawken* derives in virtually every particular from the Metropolitan watercolor

Figure 6. William J. Bennett. *View on the Potomac, Looking toward Harper's Ferry,* ca. 1834. Watercolor over graphite on beige wove paper, 16 x 22¼ in. (40.6 x 57.2 cm). Brooklyn Museum of Art, Dick S. Ramsay Fund, 46.196 (photo: Brooklyn Museum of Art)

formerly attributed to Wall. Its identification with *Weehawken from Turtle Grove* is confirmed by a description of a picture of that title that Bennett exhibited at the National Academy of Design in 1831: "Painted for a work published by Durand & Wade," an obvious reference to *The American Landscape.*[10] (Bryant, in his text for the plate, also identified Turtle Grove as the vantage point.)[11] In the same exhibition, Bennett exhibited *The Falls of the Sawkill, near Milford, Pike County, Pa.* (unlocated), which bore an identical description and was also reproduced in *The American Landscape* (Figure 7) and in the *Mirror,* on May 25, 1833.[12]

In their "Prospectus of The American Landscape," Durand and Wade proposed to publish ten numbers of six prints each, to be issued semiannually.[13] Unlike Wall and Hill, who, in *The Hudson River Portfolio,* had concentrated their talents on the scenery bordering a single watercourse, the collaborators on the later project had more national, nationalistic, literary, and, it might be ventured, pious ambitions. In his preface, Bryant asserted that the features of American scenery were "not less strongly marked than those of the old continent," with its "tamings and softenings of cultivation" and its smaller variety of trees.[14] America's "far-spread wildness," said Bryant, better suggested, especially to visiting Europeans, the idea of divine creation:

Foreigners who have visited our country, particularly the mountainous parts, have spoken of a far-spread wildness, a look as if the new world was fresher from the hand of him who made it, the rocks and the very

Figure 7. Asher B. Durand, after William J. Bennett. *The Falls of the Sawkill.* Steel engraving, 6⁄₁₆ x 4⁄₁₆ in. (15.4 x 11.2 cm), published in *The American Landscape,* pl. [5]. The Metropolitan Museum of Art, Gift of Mrs. Frederick F. Durand, 1930 (30.15.59)

hillocks wearing the shape in which he fashioned them, the waters flowing where he marked their channels, the forests, enriched with a new creation of trees, standing where he planted them; in short, of something which, more than any scenery to which they had been accustomed, suggested the idea of unity and immensity, and abstracting the mind from the associations of human agency, carried it up to the idea of a mightier power, and to the great mystery of the origin of things.[15]

Only the first number of *The American Landscape* ever saw the light of day, yet its importance as an enterprise, and of Bennett's landscape in it, is too easily ignored. It was among the early published manifestations of Knickerbocker culture in New York City, with all its contributors (except James Smillie) members of the Sketch Club, an informal society of New York artists and writers, which was formed in 1829, the year before *The American Landscape* was published.[16] It was the pioneer of New York publications of American landscape views and narratives, anticipating such works as *The Home Book of the Picturesque* (1852; illustrated by several of the same artists, though not Bennett), *A Landscape Book of American Artists and Authors* (1868), and *Picturesque America* (ca. 1872–74), edited by Bryant.[17] And *The American Landscape* was an early step in Durand's transition from printmaking, portraiture, and genre painting to landscape, in which he succeeded Cole as patriarch of the Hudson River School. It may be that *The American Landscape* appeared too early in the history of both American tourism and American landscape art to succeed. Following the opening of the Erie Canal in 1825, the United States witnessed a surge in foreign, especially British, visitors, many of whom published their experiences, in turn stimulating Americans' curiosity about their own countryside.[18] Still, *The American Landscape* reflects the germination of the New York landscape culture that blossomed in the 1840s with increasing tourism among Americans and the proliferation of landscape painters and their patrons.

To be sure, Bennett's *Weehawken* betrays the parochial character of *The American Landscape* compared to later gift books. The view was the first of six that ranged as far north as Lake Winnipesaukee in the White Mountains of New Hampshire (painted by Cole) and as far west as the Sawkill Creek in Milford, Pennsylvania (by Bennett). But half the views, echoing Wall's *Hudson River Portfolio,* were of sites along the Hudson River: the Catskill Mountains (by Durand), Fort Putnam in the Hudson Highlands (by Weir), and Weehawken. Bennett's image, preceding the others, represented the natural refuge—the shores of New Jersey—nearest to New York City. Turtle Grove, the vantage point

of Bennett's view, and the adjacent Elysian Fields of Hoboken, behind the viewer to the south, were already developing into a kind of genteel amusement park and promenade, an ancestor of Central Park, whose inception lay three decades ahead. The area, however, was not a true public park. It was the property of Colonel John Stevens, the owner of Castle Point, a high peninsula on the Hudson at Hoboken (see Figure 3). Stevens owned the steam ferries that began operating between New York and Hoboken in the early 1820s. Once he had established the ferry service, Stevens sought a reason for New Yorkers to use it. He prettified the acreage for a mile on either side of his house with lawns, paths, and willow trees and eventually established refreshment concessions, a circular railway ride, shuffleboard, a camera obscura, and an "incipient ferris wheel."[19] The only price of entry to Stevens's resort was the six-and-a-half-cent ferry ride, and by the 1830s on a given Sunday the Elysian Fields were drawing twenty thousand visitors from Gotham. Stevens or one of his agents gave the resort its pretentious classical name. Turtle Grove was located along the path leading north from Castle Point to Weehawken; its name originated in a club of gentlemen who caught and dined on green turtles at the site.[20]

Walking northward through Turtle Grove, visitors left the Elysian Fields, with the view upriver to the Weehawken bluffs providing a foretaste of the wilder natural beauties north along the Hudson, represented in two of the other plates in *The American Landscape.* One admirer of Bennett's picture conceded that there was little of the fearsomely sublime in the view north from Turtle Grove—"no mountain lifting its icy peak to heaven, no volcano, terrifying the surrounding world with its frightful fires, and no cataract shaking the earth beneath the awe-struck spectator's feet"— but asserted that "almost every other charm which can add attraction to nature may be found from the position chosen by the painter."[21]

As Bryant reminded his readers, the prospect was fraught with history and legend, no less than Fort Putnam and the Catskills miles to the north. Under the farther Weehawken bluff, he wrote, "lies the narrow level called the duelling ground, where [Alexander] Hamilton fell,"[22] mortally wounded by his political nemesis, Aaron Burr, in 1804. The nearer, rockier bluff, on the other hand, supported a natural parapet which Bryant identified as the Devil's Pulpit. He referred readers to a description of it in a recently published tale of the supernatural, a story he happened to have written.[23] The tale—"The Legend of the Devil's Pulpit"—undoubtedly influenced Bennett's selection, and possibly even the composition, of the view from Turtle Grove.

Figure 8. George B. Ellis (active 1821–30), after John Neilson. *The Devil's Pulpit*. Steel engraving, 2¾ x 3¾ in. (7 x 9.5 cm), published in *The Talisman for MDCCCXXVIII* (New York: Elam Bliss, 1827), facing p. 229 (photo: Yale Collection of American Literature, Beinecke Rare Book and Manuscript Library, Yale University, New Haven)

Bryant's story was published in 1828 in *The Talisman*, an annual Knickerbocker anthology that ran to just three volumes (1828–30). *The Talisman* was a direct literary predecessor of *The American Landscape*. Under the pseudonym of Francis Herbert, Bryant and his friends Gulian C. Verplanck and Robert C. Sands collaborated on the varied content, comprising poetry, tales, travel description, and illustrations, many of them landscapes. The volumes were published by Elam Bliss, who later undertook publication of *The American Landscape*. Much of the *Talisman* material was conceived as the friends strolled around New York and at Weehawken and Hoboken, where Sands lived. Sands and Bryant actually wrote the bulk of the anthology: Verplanck preferred to feed them ideas or to dictate his contributions. For "The Legend of the Devil's Pulpit," Sands, the Hoboken resident, is thought to have provided the inspiration, Bryant the expression.[24] A more occasional contributor, Dr. John Neilson, a professor of anatomy at the National Academy of Design and a member of the Sketch Club, supplied an illustration of the site, which was published as the frontispiece of the annual (Figure 8).[25] From a literary point of view, the collaborators were undoubtedly prompted by the tales and legends of the Hudson shores collected in *The Sketch Book of Geoffrey Crayon, Gent.* (London, 1820) by Washington Irving, the dean of the Knickerbocker writers, who had left America for England to become the first native author to be recognized internationally. Another, more contemporaneous, stimulus may have been the moral tales published weekly in the *New-York Mirror.*

Bryant's story relates the misadventures of an improvident tailor of colonial New York who discovers that his only recent customer, a vain and ostentatious rake, has enriched himself in service to the devil, who commands a smuggling ring on the New Jersey shores below the Weehawken bluffs. In his text accompanying the engraving in *The American Landscape*, Bryant attributes the devil legend to the "frightful stories" circulated by actual smugglers of the period.[26] However, from his descriptions of the setting that open the story it is easy to imagine how the tale's fabulous characters and incident could have emerged from the stony, woody recesses of Weehawken's heights. Just as Bryant does later in *The American Landscape*, the narrator of the "Legend" first represents the bluffs from a distance, "striking in their effect . . . from the favourable points on the Jersey side of the river."[27] The narrator then transports the reader to the haunting midst of their forested crests:

> As you stand on the summit of some moss-grown pile of rocks, where some veteran of the forest spreads his gnarled and projecting roots beside you, and extends his enormous and grotesque arms above your head, while monstrous grape vines are twisting and intertwining their serpent and never-ending coils, hanging in fantastic writhings and complications from one trunk or bough to another,—you look down on these woods as they descend to the meadow, and the beams of the sinking sun strike through their winding alleys or glorify their many-coloured masses; and you realize more than is dreamt of in the tales of oriental enchantment.[28]

In this evocative precinct is the famed rock of the title, and it is here that the poor tailor, secretly pursuing his client across the Hudson, discovers the demon holding court from his "pulpit," overlooking the great river and the infant metropolis. The tailor solicits the aid of a city shaman, a Calvinist physician named Magraw, who confronts the devil on his throne and throttles him. In the exorcism's aftermath, the righteous doctor momentarily assumes the pulpit himself. From there he peers down the decades to Bryant's time, musing of New York's citizenry that it "will go the way of all flesh":

> Half a century hence, they will be as wicked as the Londoners. With the same vices they will have more wit. But what of that? So much the worse for them. . . . They will have their Stock Market and their New Market; and there will be bulls and bears, lame ducks, rooks and pigeons in both of them. They will have lotteries and operas and elopements and cracked poets and ballets and burlettas and Italian singers and French dancers. And every second man in a good coat, will be a broker or a lawyer or an insolvent. And there will be no more cash payments; but the women will wear cashmeres, and the men will drink cham-

pagne. . . . And they will run after the heels of every quack who comes among them, and think he is the devil himself, though he has not half the sense of the dirty little devil that I have just discharged.[29]

The divine associations of American scenery expressed in Bryant's preface to *The American Landscape* seem to contradict the imagery of the earlier "Legend of the Devil's Pulpit." There, Bryant's narrator linked the Weehawken bluffs with the origin of New York's presumption to wealth and its concomitant moral decline. That the origin is located outside both city and state seems no accident, and savors of the competitiveness that has traditionally marked relations between New York and New Jersey. Bryant may even be evoking the colonial tradition (originating in the southern Pine Barrens area of the state) of the Jersey Devil: his narrator relates in the closing sentences of the story that "very recently, the people at Weehawken and Hoboken began to talk about a fantastic figure, who was seen upon bright moon-shiny nights, seated on that precipice, especially during sittings of the New Jersey Legislature."[30]

The subtle finger-pointing of Bryant's narrator may be misleading, or at least ambiguous. At the end of the tale he himself assumes Dr. Magraw's place on the Devil's Pulpit and "admits the peculiar metaphysical effect produced by visiting this rock. . . Dreams of wealth, projects of ambition, conceits of vanity, are there engendered in my brain. Visions of pleasure, pomp, and power there come like shadows,—and depart as you descend."[31] Yet, as the narrator reminds us earlier in the story, the pulpit was itself the vantage point of a seductive prospect "of the island of New-York,"

> sprinkled with its villages and villas, and terminating in the city, with all its spires and towers—of the intervening river and the spacious harbour, the green windings of the Jersey shores, and the distant hills of Staten Island. You see the white sails gleaming and gliding to and fro on the broad waters beneath you; you hear the quick heavy beat of paddles from the steam-boats; and when the air is more than commonly quiet, the everlasting murmur and coil of the great city hums drowsily on your ear.[32]

The city prospect is almost precisely the one memorably recorded by Bennett's colleague Wall in one of the two large watercolors (Figure 3) painted a few years earlier and published by Megarey. The narrator's enthralled description of this view, preceding both Dr. Magraw's pessimistic musings on it and his own later demonic enchantment at the Devil's Pulpit, suggests that the powers of the place arose not merely from its haunting ambience but from the God's-eye contemplation of Gotham from its heights.[33]

Figure 9. George B. Ellis, after John Neilson. *Weehawken*. Steel engraving, 2¾ x 4 in. (7 x 10.2 cm), published in *The Talisman for MDCCCXXIX* (New York: Elam Bliss, 1828), facing p. 221 (photo: Yale Collection of American Literature, Beinecke Rare Book and Manuscript Library, Yale University, New Haven)

"The Legend of the Devil's Pulpit" was not the only instance in which Weehawken figured in the pages of *The Talisman*. In the number for 1829, published in 1828, appeared the poem "Weehawken," accompanied by a rather crude image of the bluffs drawn by Neilson and engraved by George B. Ellis (Figure 9). Anticipating Bryant's commentary on the *Weehawken* plate, the poem alluded both to smugglers and to Hamilton's death below the bluffs:

> Spoils, strangely won on distant waves,
> Have lurked in yon obstructed caves. . . .
>
> And here, when Freedom's strife was won,
> Fell, in sad feud, her favoured son. . . .[34]

Bennett, then, had a variety of motivations, pictorial and literary, to portray the Weehawken bluffs. His colleague Wall had already painted (and published) the view of New York from Weehawken; Neilson had represented the bluffs themselves, although in terms feeble enough perhaps to have stimulated Bennett to surpass that image; the bluffs were part of a prospect from a popular New York resort and retained a natural character that evoked the more majestic glories of the upper Hudson; and, thanks to Bryant, Bennett's Sketch Club colleague, Weehawken was redolent with literary associations that reflected on New York City's virtuous colonial past and her licentious commercial future. Among other things, then, Bennett's view was of a fabled standpoint, one made resonant by Bryant's tale. As readily as one may interpret the boulders posed in the foreground of the watercolor as formal analogues of the distant bluffs, one is tempted to imagine that they deliberately intimate the legendary stone perched upon them.

The past truly is a foreign land. Today one looks hard in Hoboken for either Bennett's subject or his point of view. Barge piers, factories, and condominiums fill the bay that washes the concrete shore of the former Turtle Grove and completely block the view north to the Weehawken bluffs. The bluffs are still visible from the heights of Castle Point (now the campus of the Stevens Institute of Technology) but may best be seen from a car or bus on the ramp of the Lincoln Tunnel, commuting to or from Manhattan. And on the once-prominent bluff—until recently miraculously undeveloped—that included the Devil's Pulpit, a latter-day Magraw has just begun building a house with a view for which some might still sell their souls.

ACKNOWLEDGMENTS

The author is grateful to Joelle Gotlib, Vivian Chill, Claire A. Conway, and Kenneth French for their assistance with the research for this article.

APPENDIX 1

W. C. Bryant, "Weehawken," in *The American Landscape*, engraved by Asher B. Durand, printed by E. Wade (New York: Elam Bliss, 1830), pp. 7–8.

The view which bears this name is taken from a fine grove skirting the southern edge of the Weehawken meadows, on the Jersey shore of the Hudson, opposite the northern part of the city of New-York. To arrive at this spot, you proceed from the village of Hoboken, by one of the most beautiful walks in the world. For a considerable distance after leaving the Hoboken ferry, the shore of the river is steep, and covered with forest trees, among which the enterprising proprietors of the soil have formed broad and smooth paths for the convenience of the public, to whom these delightful grounds have been thrown open. The paths wind in various directions along the sides and summit of the steep bank, sometimes coming close to the edge, where it impends over the water, and at other times conducting you to an opening on some elevated point, which commands a view of the city of New-York and the harbour, magnificent for its vast breadth, its varied and populous shores, its scattered islands, its three great passages to the ocean, and the mighty commerce arriving and departing on its bosom. Nothing can exceed the beauty of these walks about the close of May, when the verdure of the turf is as bright as the green of the rainbow; and when the embowering shrubs are in flower, among which the dogwood and the viburnum, white as if loaded with snow, and the sassafras, with its faint yellow blossoms, are conspicuous; and the hum of innumerable bees over the heads of the well dressed throng passing to and fro, mingles with the buzz of voices and the murmurs of the shore. In the sunny nooks of this bank, long before the trees have put forth their leaves, and while the place is yet unprofaned by city feet, the earliest blossoms of the year are found—violets are in bloom before the vernal equinox—

> They come before the swallow dares, and take
> The winds of March with beauty.

During the warm season great numbers of people resort thither from New-York, some of whom cross the ferry for the sake of a purer and cooler atmosphere, and others attracted by the beauty of the spot—

> White muslined misses and mammas are seen
> Linked with gay cockneys glittering o'er the green*—

and the wood-nymphs are astonished at seeing stalls for selling ice cream and various liquid refreshments set up in their sylvan recesses.

231

Having reached the place about a mile above the Hoboken ferry, from which the accompanying view is taken, a striking scene arrests your attention. The river widens to the north of you into a kind of shallow bay, resting on the Weehawken meadows, within which, at most hours of the day, the swell of the tide is perceived only in gentle undulations of the glassy surface. Looking across this bay, you see, rising directly over the meadows, the first of the Weehawken bluffs, on the brow of which is the famous rock called the Devil's Pulpit, described in the first volume of the Talisman. Here, according to an old tradition, the devil used to preach every Friday to a congregation from New-York, until driven off by Dr. M'Graw; the explanation of which is thought to be, that the spot was the haunt of a gang of smugglers, who circulated frightful stories respecting the place, and who were at length discovered and broken up by the eccentric doctor.[†] Further up the river, and rising almost perpendicularly over it, is the second Weehawken bluff, under the east side of which lies the narrow level called the duelling ground, where Hamilton fell. Still further north, along the western shore, you descry the Palisadoes, long, dark and lofty walls of perpendicular rock, diminishing in the distance, until the western shore, with its barren precipices and wild solitudes, and the eastern shore, with its soft declivities, its dwellings and gardens, seem to meet, and the river disappears.

The time for contemplating this scene in all its beauty, is near sunset, when the glorious hues of the sky seem to tinge the very substance of the waters; when the sails of the passing barks are gilded with the horizontal sunshine; when the steam boats of the Hudson are seen majestically furrowing the waters on their departure or their return; when the dwellings on the New-York shore, reflecting the setting sun from their windows, appear like palaces of topaz; and when, if the atmosphere be still, a mighty and multitudinous murmur of human activity reaches you from all parts and streets of the far-off city at once, and the tolling of the hour from its steeples comes softened by distance into the faintest and sweetest of sounds.

APPENDIX 2

"Description of the Plate: Weehawken," *New-York Mirror,* April 20, 1833, p. 329.

To speak of Weehawken to a New-Yorker is to conjure up before his mind's eye a world of agreeable associations; and pleasant indeed will it be in his recollection, if he be far absent from his native city. It will bring before him a picture of beautiful scenery, which, if not the most lovely in the world, the goodnatured reader will pardon him for thinking so. He will remember a bay encircled by blue hills, studded with bright islands, and enlivened with vessels of every description, from the giant war-ship sleeping, like a castle, on the water, to the winged pleasure-boat that sweeps along like a bird, or the steamboat thundering and ploughing on its way, careless of wind and tide. There is here, it is true, no mountain lifting its icy peak to heaven, no volcano, terrifying the surrounding world with its frightful fires, and no cataract shaking the earth beneath the awe-struck spectator's feet, while clouds of foam float away on the breeze, spanned by the rainbow fallen from the sky; but almost every other charm which can add attraction to nature may be found from the position chosen by the painter of the accompanying view. The spectator is supposed to stand on the Jersey shore, about a mile above the Hoboken ferry. It is impossible to confine our pen to the description alone of those two elevations called the Weehawken bluffs. The whole scene which greets the passenger's eye, from the moment when he leaves the city ferry till he arrives at the spot represented in the foreground of the engraving is distinguished for a degree of rich romantic and picturesque loveliness, reminding one of some of the delicious delineations of scenery in the Lady of the Lake.

For the information of distant readers, we are more minute in our details than we should be were we writing only for the eyes of our fellow-citizens; for sluggish indeed must be the foot that has trodden near these tranquil Eden scenes, and not often pressed the grass among their groves. A line of steamboats plies across the river from a central part of the city to the village of Hoboken, conveying passengers from the reflected heat and dust of the crowded streets into the midst of a rural scene, in a few moments and for a few cents. A green swell of land is generally in pleasant afternoons during the summer months, found swarmed with people of every class, among whom always is an agreeable preponderance of women and children. Here are various simple amusements to beguile the time: shuffle-board—a swing—a circular rail-road, most unexceptionable milk-punch, &c. Groups of tired citizens,

---

*Poetry of the Anti-Jacobin.

†On this bluff is also situated the singular rock called *Mambrino's Helmet,* an engraving of which is given on the cover.

seated in chairs, inhale the cool breezes and enjoy the refreshing prospect; and we never remember to have been so exquisitely delighted by a trifle as we were one day here by a large *camera obscura* drawn to the summit of this acclivity, and revealing to the eyes of those who chose to pay six-pence and take their stand within— wonders—fairy wonders—than which, we believe, nothing in all the range of art and nature could be more enchanting. Children who have never beheld this exquisite optical exhibition, should be initiated forthwith into its magical displays; and if we were the enterprising and tasteful proprietors of those delightful pleasure-grounds, which, with a commendable liberality have been thrown open for the gratuitous accommodation of the public, we should have one erected permanently, if it were only to watch and enjoy the surprise and delight so vivid and graceful in the faces of our youthful friends.

From this point, a path, which might have wound through Paradise and allured our first sinless parents, hand in hand, along its tempting and fragrant windings, leads on, over the meadow land, to the rocks and trees visible in the front of the picture. This commands a fine prospect. From elevated banks—overhanging woods—meandering paths—from hedges of scented verdure, and cool sylvan recesses, you come suddenly to the open tract and the low shore—where the water spreads out like a lake, sometimes swollen with the tide, and sometimes sleeping in glassy calmness, or only, at intervals, as some steamboat rushes on its course, heaving the long billow, heavily and beautifully to the beach. Across this bay, to the north, you see the first of the Weehawken bluffs. Further up the river is the other. Under the east side of the latter lies the duelling ground, consecrated, in the pages of history, by the blood of Hamilton. On the brow of the former is the renowned rock, called the Devil's Pulpit. Tradition affirms that his satanic majesty used to preach from this rock every Friday, to a New-York congregation, until driven away by Dr. M'Graw. For the truth of this, however, we shall not be responsible, but rather lean towards the less marvellous accounts which represent the spot as the haunt of a gang of smugglers, whose interest in circulating stories of this nature is obvious, and who were finally broken up by Dr. M'Graw.

The admirer of nature may seek this spot as an appropriate shrine on which to offer up his devotions. At all times of the season—at all hours of the day, it cannot fail to stir up, in the coldest heart, some sparkle of enthusiasm. In the opening spring, in the tranquil, shadowy summer, or the golden, teeming autumn, it is always invested with seducing loveliness. On a still, soft, dewy, summer morning, when every object around is at rest, when the very wind and waters scarcely move—when the sails hang against the masts, and the river-craft lapse along almost imperceptibly with the tide, the view, from the Weehawken hill, may perhaps be seen to most advantage; though probably the sunset hour, with its richer colourings and repose, may exercise over the imagination, an influence more sweet and soothing. At all times, however, the place has been the theme of remark and admiration. The poet and the painter have united their powers to celebrate it; and it will probably afford a subject of illustration to pen and pencil for generations yet to come.

NOTES

1. For Arnold, see the obituary in the *New York Times*, February 8, 1954, p. 23.

2. *Two Hundred Years of Watercolor Painting in America: An Exhibition Commemorating the Centennial of the American Watercolor Society*, exh. cat. (New York: MMA, 1966), p. 13, no. 28; Albert Ten Eyck Gardner, *History of Watercolor Painting in America* (New York: Reinhold, 1966), p. 27, pl. 12; Stuart P. Feld, "Preview of an Exhibition: Two Hundred Years of Watercolor Painting in America," *Antiques* 90 (December 1966), p. 845, fig. 11; John K. Howat, *The Hudson River and Its Painters* (New York: Viking, 1972), p. 162, no. 54; Stephen C. Rubin, ed., *American Watercolors from The Metropolitan Museum of Art,* exh. cat. (New York: American Federation of Arts in association with Harry N. Abrams, 1991), p. 64, no. 25; Tracy Felker, *Master Drawings of the Hudson River School,* exh. cat. (Manlius, N.Y.: Gallery Association of New York State, 1993), pp. 1, 4.

3. Many of Wall's original watercolors for *The Hudson River Portfolio* are in the New-York Historical Society. They are discussed in Donald A. Shelley, "William Guy Wall's Watercolors for *The Hudson River Portfolio*," *New-York Historical Society Quarterly* 31 (January 1947), pp. 25–45. Both *The Hudson River Portfolio* and Hill's aquatints of Wall's pair of watercolors of New York City, published by Megarey, are thoroughly documented in Richard C. Koke, *A Checklist of the American Engravings of John Hill (1770–1850)* (New York: New-York Historical Society, 1961), pp. 29–44; and Gloria Gilda Deák, *Picturing America, 1497–1899* (Princeton, N.J.: Princeton University Press, 1988), vol. 1, pp. 217–19, 228–30. For a more recent discussion of Wall's work, see Edward C. Nygren, *Views and Visions: American Landscape before 1830,* exh. cat. (Washington, D.C.: Corcoran Gallery of Art, 1986), pp. 298–302.

4. Gardner, *History*, p. 27, pl. 12; Feld, "Preview," p. 845, fig. 11; Howat, *Hudson River*, p. 162, no. 54.

5. For Bennett, see the excellent essay in Gloria Gilda Deák, *William James Bennett: Master of the Aquatint View,* exh. cat. (New York: New York Public Library, 1988), pp. 13–64, 67–69 (chronology).

6. For the Metropolitan watercolor, see Rubin, *American Watercolors,* pp. 15, 55. For the print, see Deák, *Bennett,* pp. 32, 74; Deák, *Picturing America,* vol. 1, p. 244; and Elliot Bostwick Davis, "The Currency of Culture: Prints in New York City," in Catherine Hoover Voorsanger and John K. Howat, eds., *Art and the Empire*

City: New York, 1825–1861, exh. cat. (New York: MMA, 2000), p. 201, fig. 158.

7. For *View of the Bay of New York from the Battery, N.Y.C.*, see Richard J. Koke, *American Landscape and Genre Paintings in the New-York Historical Society* (New York: New-York Historical Society, 1982), vol. 1, p. 40, no. 136; for *View on the Potomac, Looking toward Harper's Ferry*, see Linda S. Ferber and Barbara Dayer Gallati, *Masters of Color and Light: Homer, Sargent and the American Watercolor Movement*, exh. cat., Brooklyn Museum of Art (Washington, D.C.: Smithsonian Institution Press, 1999), pp. 6–7.

8. *The American Landscape, No. 1. Containing the Following Views: Weehawken, Catskill Mountains, Fort Putnam, Delaware Water Gap, Falls of the Sawkill, Winnipiseogee Lake. Engraved from Original and Accurate Drawings; Executed from Nature Expressly for this Work, and from Well Authenticated Pictures; with Historical and Topographical Illustrations* (New York: Elam Bliss, 1830).

9. "Description of the Plate: Weehawken," *New-York Mirror*, April 20, 1833, p. 329. The editors of the *Mirror* were Nathaniel Parker Willis, George W. Curtis, and Theodore Fay, all of whom wrote travel literature and any of whom could have authored the text for the plate.

10. *National Academy of Design Exhibition Record, 1826–1860* (New York: New-York Historical Society, 1943), vol. 1, p. 30, no. 99.

11. *The American Landscape*, pp. 8–9.

12. *National Academy of Design Exhibition Record*, vol. 1, p. 30, no. 90; "Description of the Plate: Falls of the Sawkill," *New-York Mirror*, May 25, 1833, p. 369.

13. A. B. Durand and E. Wade, Jun., "Prospectus of The American Landscape," *The American Landscape*, p. 4.

14. William C. Bryant, "Preface," *The American Landscape*, pp. 5–6.

15. Ibid., p. 6.

16. For a description of the Sketch Club, see James T. Callow, *Kindred Spirits: Knickerbocker Writers and American Artists* (Chapel Hill: University of North Carolina Press, 1967), pp. 12–29.

17. *The Home Book of the Picturesque: or American Scenery, Art, and Literature* (New York: G. P. Putnam, 1852); *A Landscape Book of American Artists and Authors* (New York: G. P. Putnam and Son, 1868); *Picturesque America; or The Land We Live In* (New York: D. Appleton, ca. 1872–74); Callow, *Kindred Spirits*, pp. 164–72.

18. The earliest and one of the most influential of this tide of British visitors was Captain Basil Hall, *Travels in North America, in the Years 1827 and 1828* (Philadelphia: Carey, Lea and Carey, 1829); see also Mrs. Trollope, *Domestic Manners of the Americans* (London: Whittaker, Treacher, and Co., 1832); [Thomas Hamilton], *Men and Manners in America, by the Author of Cecil Thornton* (Edinburgh: William Blackwood and T. Cadell, 1833); Tyrone Power, *Impressions of America during the Years 1833, 1834, and 1835* (Philadelphia: Carey, Lea, and Blanchard, 1836); Harriet Martineau, *Society in America* (London: Saunders and Otley,

1837); and *Retrospect of Western Travels* (London: Saunders and Otley, 1838).

19. For Hoboken's Elysian Fields and Turtle Grove, see Charles H. Winfield, *Hopoghan Hackingh: Hoboken, a Pleasure Resort for Old New York* (New York: Caxton, 1895), pp. 33–80 (the "incipient ferris wheel," or "Whirligig," is illustrated and described on pp. 71–72); *The Record of the Progress of the Hoboken Evening News, Together with the History of the City of Hoboken, from Its Settlement to the Present Time* (Hoboken, N.J.: Evening News, 1893), pp. 11–13; Samuel L. Knapp, *The Picturesque Beauties of the Hudson River and Its Vicinity* (New York: J. Disturnell, 1835), pp. 4–24; William H. Shaw, *History of Essex and Hudson Counties, New Jersey* (Philadelphia: Everts and Peck, 1884), vol. 2, pp. 1311–12; G. G. Foster, *Fifteen Minutes around New York* (New York: DeWitt and Davenport, 1854), pp. 52–54.

20. Winfield, *Hopoghan Hackingh*, p. 54.

21. *New-York Mirror*, April 20, 1833, p. 329.

22. Bryant, "Weehawken," *The American Landscape*, p. 8.

23. Ibid., p. 8: "Looking across this bay [on the west side of the Hudson River at Hoboken], you see, rising directly over the meadows, the first of the Weehawken bluffs, on the brow of which is the famous rock called the Devil's Pulpit, described in the first volume of the Talisman."

24. For *The Talisman*, see Henry C. Sturges and Richard Henry Stoddard, eds., *The Poetical Works of William Cullen Bryant* (New York: D. Appleton and Co., 1910), pp. xlix–l, cxii; Callow, *Kindred Spirits*, pp. 25–26; Charles H. Brown, *William Cullen Bryant* (New York: Charles Scribner's Sons, 1971), pp. 164–72, 182–83.

25. Callow, *Kindred Spirits*, p. 15.

26. Bryant, "Weehawken," *The American Landscape*, p. 8.

27. Francis Herbert [W. C. Bryant (and Robert C. Sands?)], "The Legend of the Devil's Pulpit," in *The Talisman for MDCCCXXVIII* (New York: Elam Bliss, 1827), p. 230.

28. Herbert, "Devil's Pulpit," p. 231.

29. Ibid., pp. 283–85.

30. Ibid., p. 288. For a discussion of the Jersey Devil tradition, see Jeremiah Sullivan with James F. McCloy, "The Jersey Devil's Finest Hour," *New York Folklore Quarterly* 30, no. 3 (September 1974), pp. 232–39.

31. Herbert, "Devil's Pulpit," pp. 287–88.

32. Ibid., p. 233.

33. What appears to be an admiring description of the view of New York from Weehawken, evidently prompted by the 1823 publication of Wall's view by Megarey and anticipating Bryant's descriptions of the city from New Jersey in *The Talisman* and *The American Landscape*, was printed in the *New-York Mirror*, September 27, 1823, p. 68.

34. "Weehawken," *The Talisman for MDCCCXXIX* (New York: Elam Bliss, 1828), p. 222, engraving facing p. 221.

A Figure for *Cibola:* Art, Politics, and Aesthetics among the Luluwa People of the Democratic Republic of the Congo

CONSTANTINE PETRIDIS

Postdoctoral Fellow, Fund for Scientific Research—Flanders, Ghent University, Belgium

A PARAGON of female beauty, the maternity figure at The Metropolitan Museum of Art exemplifies a well-known sculpture type of the Luluwa people of the Democratic Republic of the Congo (Figures 1, 2). Luluwa figures that depict a pregnant woman or a mother and her child are generally related to the cult of *Bwanga bwa Cibola,* the goals of which are to prevent infertility and infant mortality and to foster the reincarnation of a deceased ancestor.[1] The Metropolitan Museum's figure offers an opportunity to explore Luluwa notions of fertility and aesthetics, and to investigate the formal and stylistic variety of the Luluwa's figurative carvings in the context of their history and sociopolitical organization.

A few years ago, I contributed an essay on a very similar Luluwa maternity figure at the Art Institute of Chicago.[2] On the basis of the complementary research that I have conducted since, the present article offers some additional data and new interpretations. After a brief introduction to the Luluwa and the core concepts of their traditional religion, I will analyze the *Bwanga bwa Cibola* cult and compare it with a possession ritual of the neighboring Mongo. In passing, I will also shed some light on a cult called *Bwanga bwa Bwimpe.* I will then focus attention on the striking body decorations that grace both male and female figures and discuss the different regional substyles that characterize Luluwa figurative sculpture. In conclusion, I will address the so-called hemp cult, popularized in the last quarter of the nineteenth century, and the iconoclasm it allegedly entailed.[3]

THE LULUWA PEOPLE

The Luluwa, or Beena Luluwa, live in a vast region between the Lubudi and Kasai Rivers in West Kasai Province in the southern central part of the Democratic Republic of the Congo (formerly the Republic of Zaire; Figure 3).[4] Together with the Luntu, the Konji, and the Luba-Lubilanji, the Luluwa, who comprise a number of subgroups, form what might be termed the Luba-Kasai cluster. These peoples all speak Chiluba dialects and share many cultural traits, and they all trace their origins to Nsanga a Lubangu, a mythical place said to be located in Katanga Province in southeastern Congo. There are also many overlappings in these peoples' social and political organization, economy, and religion. The general consensus is that Luba emigrants from Katanga Province settled in their present-day environment in successive waves between the seventeenth and eighteenth centuries. They assimilated with the local population of their new habitat, which consisted of peoples identified as Bindji (or Bindi) and Kete and different pygmoid groups. Although hunting is still considered a prestigious activity by the male population, today the Luluwa are mainly farmers. They have always been active traders, but it was especially their involvement in the long-distance trade at the end of the nineteenth century that had a profound impact on their culture.

About 1875 Chokwe traders from Angola immigrated to Luluwa country; some of them founded villages amid the Luluwa, the traces of which can still be seen today. The traders introduced the Luluwa to products previously unknown in the region and left their mark on the local culture. Body decoration, architecture, and masking are among the aspects of material culture that clearly show Chokwe influence. Elsewhere, I have discussed the diffusion of the Chokwe boys' *mukanda* puberty ritual and associated masks among a number of Luluwa subgroups.[5] Chokwe immigrants also inspired the Luluwa's political organization and social structure. Kalamba Mukenge, of the Luluwa Bakwa Katawa subgroup, and other power-hungry Luluwa chiefs became close allies of the Chokwe chiefs who led the northward migrations. These Luluwa chiefs emulated the Chokwe's more centralized state formation, overruled neighboring Luluwa chiefs, and gradually created a social divide between chiefs and commoners. As we shall

© The Metropolitan Museum of Art 2001
METROPOLITAN MUSEUM JOURNAL 36

The notes for this article begin on page 253.

Figure 1. Maternity figure (*Bwanga bwa Cibola*). Luluwa (Bakwa Mushilu subgroup), Democratic Republic of the Congo, mid to late 19th century. Wood, metal ring; H. 24.7 cm. The Metropolitan Museum of Art, The Michael C. Rockefeller Memorial Collection, Bequest of Nelson A. Rockefeller, 1979 (1979.206.282)

Figure 2. Rear view of Figure 1

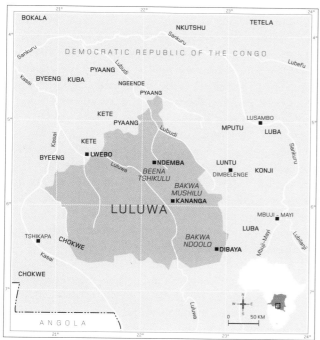

Figure 3. The Luluwa and neighboring peoples in West Kasai Province in the Democratic Republic of the Congo (map: Charles Meur and Marc Felix, Brussels)

see, this class distinction also had an effect on the Luluwa's artistic production in that a number of ritual objects evolved into symbols of status.

The Luluwa and their Luba neighbors believe that both the spiritual and the physical world are permeated with a life-force (*mooyo*). The ritual specialist (*mpaka manga* or *mupaki wa manga*) evokes the life-force's powers by using charms (*manga*; sing. *bwanga*). The term *bwanga* refers to an object that serves as a container or support of power substances or ingredients (*bishimba*). It also refers to the cult associated with this object and the rituals that define the cult. If the container has the shape of an anthropomorphic figure, it may be regarded as a "real" power figure, in which case the term *lupingu* (plural, *mpingu*), a generic name for man-made figures, is also applicable.[6]

The above-mentioned ingredients assure the efficacy of both *manga* and *mpingu*. They are composed of mineral, plant, animal, and human substances and act as mediators or conductors. The ritual specialist determines the composition of the ingredients and the way they are to be introduced into the container. The power of both the *manga* and the ingredients is sustained by recharging the mixture at regular intervals, particularly with the appearance of the new moon. The most powerful substance used to effect this recharging or revitalization is kaolin (*lupemba*).

Manga are diverse in both form and function. Although a distinction is sometimes made between positive and negative *manga,* all may be used both to heal and to harm. There is also a distinction between "large" (or collective) and "small" (or individual) *manga.* They can be of a permanent nature and have a lasting power or be used periodically and have merely a temporary effect. The manipulation of these charms resembles the worship of ancestors in that charms incite the ancestral spirits (*bakishi, bashangi,* or *bankambwa*).[7] People placate and make sacrifices to the ancestral spirits in exchange for their help and protection. Some forms of ancestor worship involve the explicit manipulation of charms.

Bwanga bwa Cibola

The *Bwanga bwa Cibola* fertility cult and the accompanying charms are popular among the Luluwa and their Luntu, Konji, and Luba neighbors.[8] There are many regional and even local differences regarding certain details of the cult. Sometimes, it is called *Mbombo* instead of *Cibola*. Several of the Luluwa's numerous *manga* are concerned with issues of fertility and the protection of pregnant women, newborns, and small children. The *Cibola* cult deals specifically with women who have had a succession of miscarriages or whose newborn children have died shortly after birth. The cult must ensure a successful outcome of the pregnancy and a safe delivery and see to it that the child grows up without problems. Its ultimate goal, however, is to provoke the reincarnation of a deceased ancestor in the newborn child.

Like other *manga*, *Bwanga bwa Cibola* in many ways relates to the veneration of so-called spirit-trees, trees that are believed to inhabit or shelter spirits and are the focus of prayers and offerings.[9] Indeed, as in the *Cibola* cult, a tree altar called *Mulopo* is addressed when a woman's children die after birth. The *Mulopo* also promotes the reincarnation of the deceased child's spirit in a newborn infant. A female and a male spirit-tree, respectively called *mumbu* and *kasambankusu*, are planted to ensure that the ancestors of both lineages watch over the pregnancy and the delivery. A small conical clay mound is erected between them. The whole is consecrated with a mixture of palm wine, rainwater, and water from a pond. This mixture is kept in a bowl, which is later placed on the mound. Another spirit-tree, the *kapulwayi* (*Jatropha curcas*), fulfills a function similar to that of the *Mulopo* and *Bwanga bwa Cibola*. This spirit-tree is planted when a woman suffers from sterility or experiences difficulties during pregnancy, or when a child dies after birth.

As a rule, initiation into the *Cibola* cult follows upon consultation with a diviner. This religious specialist is called in by the unfortunate woman or by her relatives when traditional medical treatments with plant and other vegetal extracts are not effective. Initiation into the *Cibola* cult is the sole effective remedy to the woman's problem. Many potential causes are taken into consideration. Most often, sorcery is thought to be the determining factor in calamities and bad fortune. Sometimes, the diviner will reveal that the woman is the victim of a fickle ancestral spirit or a malevolent *manga* maker. Occasionally, it is believed that the woman is possessed by a metaphysical force identified as *cibola*. However, this kind of possession is often perceived as the result of the transgression of certain behavioral rules and norms. Thus, women who have had premarital sexual relationships are especially vulnerable.

Possession by the *cibola* leads to a relationship of reciprocity and mutual dependence. The relationship of the patient to the *cibola* force is one of ambivalence, ambiguity, and reversibility. Those who do not respect the imposed rules and prohibitions run the risk of being severely punished. *Bwanga bwa Cibola* is therefore sometimes characterized as a double-edged sword (*mwele wa nkanza*). As I have noted elsewhere, *Bwanga bwa Cibola* is clearly related to other healing and fertility cults shared by various Bantu-speaking peoples in central and southern Africa.[10]

At least in some respects, the initiation process into *Bwanga bwa Cibola* resembles a possession ritual called *Zebola*, *Jebola*, or *Yebola*, which is widespread among the peoples of the Mongo complex living north of the Luluwa.[11] *Zebola*—note the homophony with *Cibola*—is a female healing ritual for either purely physical or mental health problems thought to be caused by ancestral spirits that are also called *Zebola*. Through divination the spirit inhabits the woman's body and thus reveals the source of the disease. The ensuing healing ritual entails taking various kinds of medicine and learning the *Zebola* songs and dances. As we shall see, as in *Cibola*, emphasis is placed on the beautification of the patient's body. Unlike *Cibola*, however, *Zebola* has a communal and public character, and choreography and music play a much more important role. *Zebola* also addresses a much wider range of problems.

After having determined the cause of the woman's misfortune, the Luluwa diviner will direct her to a *mupaki wa manga* (ritual specialist). A *mupaki wa manga* who specializes in *Bwanga bwa Cibola* is often a woman. It is the *mupaki* who organizes the initiation into the cult and determines the proscriptions to be respected by the woman. Although the initiation process as such allows for many variations and often reflects the personal preferences of the ritual specialist, it always follows the same basic pattern and consists of a number of essential phases. The prohibitions, which are shared by the ritual specialist, concern both the woman's diet and her behavior. Thus, certain game animals are forbidden to her, and sometimes her food is even restricted to the consumption of manioc porridge. Most often she will be secluded in a special fenced-in house at the edge of the village. The initiation always involves the learning of ritual cult songs, a confession of past sins or crimes, and the sacrifice of chickens. Although intense sexual activity at the beginning of a new pregnancy is believed to stimulate the fetus's growth, a mother-to-be will soon have to abstain completely from sexual intercourse. In the past, the mother had to wait until the child born after her initiation into the *Cibola* cult had reached the age of three before she was allowed to resume intimate relations with her husband.

After the birth of the child, the diviner will be asked to identify which deceased ancestor is reincarnated in the newborn. In order to do so, he—or she—will look carefully for possible congenital signs or handicaps (*misangu*; sing. *musangu*).[12] The identity of the ancestor will later become clearly evident through the child's way of walking and manner of speaking. The first child, boy or girl, born after a successful initiation

Figure 4. Mothers of "special children" (*mapanga*) performing a ceremonial dance on market day near the city of Kananga (formerly Luluabourg), ca. 1900. Luluwa, Democratic Republic of the Congo. Unknown photographer. Frobenius-Institut an der Johann Wolfgang Goethe-Universität, Frankfurt am Main, L1/2360 (photo: Frobenius-Institut)

into the cult is always named Tshibola. Usually, when she—or he—is three months old, the child will be officially presented to the community in a solemn coming-out ceremony called *dyala*, scheduled to take place during the new moon. Prior to the *dyala* ceremony the child may only be approached by other initiates into the *Cibola* cult. As a way of giving thanks to the ancestors, a meal is shared by the ritual specialist and the families of both spouses, and a plantain tree—for a boy—or a banana tree—for a girl—is planted near the parents' house in the village.

The mother and her child will continue to live apart from the village until the child starts to walk. During this postnatal seclusion period, the newborn infant, like its mother, must regularly be rubbed with a mixture of red clay and palm oil. At the rising of each new moon the mother must sing ritual songs in her baby's honor and sacrifice a chicken for her *manga*. Blood of the chicken is poured over her *manga*, and her *Cibola* figure is "fed" a piece of chicken liver or some manioc porridge. At the end of the seclusion period, the ritual specialist will shave the heads of both mother and child, neither of whose hair has been cut since the child was born, and lift the ban on the mother's sexual activity. In exchange for her or his services, the happy couple will present the *mupaki* with money or goods. A final communal meal signals the end of the ritual cycle. Like the birth of other "special children," generally called *mapanga*, that of a *Cibola* child is always accompanied by a public closing ceremony (Figure 4). Mothers of such children will continue to perform ceremonial dances on market days, Sundays, and other holidays.[13] The parents of such a child usually remain cult members until their fifth child is born, after which they are allowed to lead *Cibola* initiations themselves.

POWER OBJECTS AND SYMBOLS OF STATUS

Bwanga bwa Cibola does not often involve the use of carved figurative *manga*. Instead, as is the case in many other cults, horns, snail shells, leather or cloth bags, pouches, or bundles serve as containers for ingredients. Some of the cult accessories are depicted on related figurative *Bwanga bwa Cibola* sculptures, at least on those carved in a naturalistic style. The figure at the Metropolitan Museum bears on its back the carved imitation of a snail shell stuffed with all kinds of ingredients (Figure 2). A snail shell (*nyonga; Achatina marginata swains*) is the central object of the *Bwanga bwa Cibawu*, one of the most popular types of *bwanga*.[14] *Bwanga bwa Cibawu* is a general term that encompasses different important *manga* with multiple functions, combining defensive and offensive powers. It is the most important collective protection of both the community (*ditunga*) and the family's yard (*lubanza*) and is therefore sometimes called *Bwanga bwa Ditunga* or *Bwanga bwa Lubanza*. Its main function is to offer protection against sorcerers in general and so-called lightning senders in particular.[15] Because several primary sources have explicitly linked the cult with problems of infant mortality, there is a direct relationship between the *Bwanga bwa Cibola* and the *Bwanga bwa Cibawu*.

239

Figure 5. Ceramic vessel filled with dirt, medicinal ingredients, and two snail shells (*Bwanga bwa Cibawu*). Luba, Luluwa, or Kete, Democratic Republic of the Congo. 19th–early 20th century. H. 11 cm, Diam. 17 cm. Field-collected by Frederick Starr in the village of Tshimbundu in 1906. American Museum of Natural History, New York, 1910, 90.0/6215 (photo: Craig Chesek, courtesy Department of Library Services, American Museum of Natural History)

Figure 6. Two wrapped snail shells attached to a twig framework (*Bwanga bwa Cibawu*). Luba, Luluwa, or Kete, Democratic Republic of the Congo, 19th–early 20th century. H. 24.5 cm, W. 22 cm. Field-collected by Frederick Starr in or near the town of Lwebo in 1906. American Museum of Natural History, New York, 1910, 90.0/9003 (photo: Craig Chesek, courtesy Department of Library Services, American Museum of Natural History)

Figure 7. Wooden peglike half-figurines inserted in a wrapped fiber ring (*Bwanga bwa Ditunga* or *Bwanga bwa Lubanza*). Luba, Luluwa, or Kete, Democratic Republic of the Congo, 19th–early 20th century. Field-collected by Frederick Starr in 1906. American Museum of Natural History, New York, 1910, 90.1/9033 (photo: Craig Chesek, courtesy Department of Library Services, American Museum of Natural History)

bichromy of many power objects connotes the combination of defensive and offensive powers. The few known figurative *Cibawu* objects usually also combine this partition of the body surface in two opposing colors with a Janus face or multiple heads on a single body.[17] Two singular objects at the American Museum of Natural History, New York, which were collected by Frederick Starr, a professor of anthropology at the University of Chicago from 1892 to 1923, in the mixed area around Lwebo in 1906, are rare examples of *Cibawu* snail shells (Figures 5, 6). Another type of object, identified as a *Bwanga bwa Lubanza* or *Bwanga bwa Ditunga,* of which Starr also collected examples, consists of a ring made of fibers and twigs into which a number of schematically carved half-figures are inserted (Figure 7).

Contrary to the cleaned and polished surface of many Luluwa figures in Western collections, the original powderlike red surface of the figure in the Metropolitan Museum is almost intact and closely resembles the way people beautified their bodies in various rituals and ceremonies. Indeed, the figure's appearance is strikingly similar to that of the conservative elders who opposed the reforms of chief Kalamba Mukenge, described in early travel accounts (see below, p. 248). It is clothed in a small loincloth that imitates those made of red-dyed fiber or banana leaves that constituted a Luluwa woman's only covering. Like the Metropolitan's figure, Luluwa women also typically wore a metal ring or a bamboo stick through the septum. Although

The shell's surface is normally divided into two halves, one red and one white. The white mostly derives from kaolin (*lupemba*) and has essentially positive connotations. The red is obtained either from camwood powder (*kakula*) or from red clay-earth (*mpisha, cilaabu, kamuma,* or *budinda*). This color signals the punishment, even the destruction, of sorcerers.[16] The

Figure 8. A twelve-year-old girl in the village of Katende wearing beads woven into her hair and bamboo sticks through her earlobes and septum, 1905. Luluwa (Bakwa Mwanza subgroup), Democratic Republic of the Congo. Frobenius-Institut an der Johann Wolfgang Goethe-Universität, Frankfurt am Main, SkB XI 3 (after drawing by Hans Martin Lemme, in Leo Frobenius, *Ethnographische Notizen aus den Jahren 1905 und 1906*, Hildegard Klein, ed., vol. 3, *Luluwa, Süd-Kete, Bena Mai, Pende, Cokwe*, Studien zur Kulturkunde 87 [Stuttgart: Franz Steiner, 1988], p. 83, fig. 6)

Figure 9. Half-figure of a woman holding a child (*Bwanga bwa Cibola*). Luluwa (Beena Tshikulu subgroup), Democratic Republic of the Congo, mid to late 19th century. Wood (*Balanites wilsoniana*), metal tack, glass beads; H. 33 cm. Field-collected by Henri Morlighem in 1934. Royal Museum for Central Africa, Tervuren, 1935, RG 35964 (photo: Hughes Dubois, Brussels–Paris)

women undergoing initiation into the *Cibola* cult sometimes had to shave their heads, most related figures are shown with elaborate hairstyles. The example depicted here wears a three-lobed coiffure (*makata*) that resembles the wigs made of vegetable fibers and human hair and adorned with cowrie shells (*mibela*; *Cypraea moneta*) that were woven into the hair (Figure 8). This type of headdress was also smeared with palm oil, red camwood powder, and clay. The central pointed extension on the skull depicts a headdress called *disunga* or *disungu*.[18] The attention devoted to the construction of the hair also recalls the aesthetics of the above-mentioned Mongo *Zebola* possession rituals.

Usually, a woman receives a number of protective *manga* from the ritual specialist, including one or more carved figures and other cult accessories, when she enters seclusion. According to some sources, the figurative carvings are given to the mother-to-be in the course of the eighth month of pregnancy. This month, generally called *cizaba*, constitutes a crucial time in the woman's initiation process. At this time, the many pro-

hibitions enter into force and the *manga* start to work. The *cizaba* month is, accordingly, sometimes also referred to as "the month of the *manga*." The term *cizaba* also refers to a clay container, filled with water and various other ingredients, that the future mother receives from the ritual specialist. Placed at the entrance of her house and, later, near the newborn, this object is meant to offer protection against evil forces. The woman will wash herself daily with the *cizaba*'s contents and drink them regularly to stimulate the growth of the unborn child and ensure a safe delivery.

In times past, it seems that a woman always received two figures. Albert Maesen reported that, traditionally,

Figure 10. Half-figure (*Bwanga bwa Cibola*). Luluwa, Democratic Republic of the Congo, 19th–20th century. Wood; H. 35.7 cm. Ex coll. Henri Pareyn, Antwerp. Etnografisch Museum, Antwerp, 1920, AE 758 (photo: Etnografisch Museum)

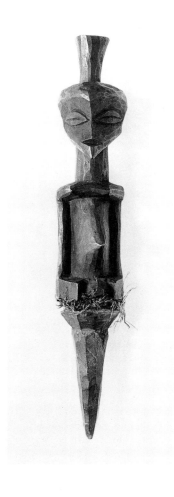

Figure 11. Half-figure. Luba, Luluwa, or Kete, Democratic Republic of the Congo, 19th–early 20th century. Wood, fibers; H. 37.5 cm. Field-collected by Frederick Starr in the village of Tshikoma Pinda in 1906. American Museum of Natural History, New York, 1910, 90.0/8958 (photo: Craig Chesek, courtesy Department of Library Services, American Museum of Natural History)

she would receive the same number of figures as the number of children she had lost.[19] The figures were sometimes identical, but more often one was a replica of the other in miniature. The larger figure was kept at home; the smaller replica was carried around. The maternity figure at the Art Institute of Chicago is perhaps the only standing full-figure with a short wooden peg under the feet that has been preserved. It thus relates formally to some pointed-base half-figures holding a child (Figure 9). However, I have found that at least one other mother-and-child figure at the Royal Museum for Central Africa, Tervuren, shows the remains of a similar peglike extension.[20] This formal characteristic indicates how these carvings were actually used. Both types of *Cibola* figures seem to have been kept in a corner of the house in a clay pot or a basket filled with dirt and several ingredients, into which the pointed base was inserted. The face of the figure was oriented toward the door in order to prevent evildoers and negative forces from entering the house.

As mentioned earlier, true-to-life and elaborately detailed statues like the one at the Metropolitan Museum are rare. The majority of Luluwa carvings,

including those related to the *Bwanga bwa Cibola,* are rough-hewn, even to the point of male figures being indistinguishable from female figures (Figure 10). Luluwa figurative sculpture can thus be classified according to two styles, one realistic, or even naturalistic, the other schematic, or even abstract. This classification would point specifically to the sociopolitical context of the second half of the nineteenth century. Naturalistic images are as much symbols of status as ritual objects. They are related to the development in some parts of Luluwa territory of a class distinction that reached its culmination in the last quarter of the nineteenth century.

This development is strongly reminiscent of the evolution from "process art" to "statement art" that Allen Roberts has described with regard to the Tabwa people of Lake Tanganyika in eastern Congo.[21] An understanding of the distinction between the two may be useful to our discussion of the schematic and the naturalistic styles of Luluwa art. Like ritual, process art is "transformatory" and meant to provoke change or to solve problems connected with change. Statement art, on the other hand, is "confirmatory" and concerned with the celebration of authority and the safe-guarding of an existing order.

Among the Luluwa, the contact with Chokwe tradesmen from Angola and the influence of the slave trade gradually led to the formation of a small elite of noblemen. Some Luluwa chiefs tried to imitate the more centralized political organization of the Chokwe. They attempted to overrule neighboring lesser chiefs, a goal they achieved at least in part thanks to the accumulation of imported Chokwe firearms. Not every Luluwa chief benefited from the newly developed long-distance trade. And because exploration of the region was not extensive, only a few chiefs appear in the travel accounts written by German explorers at the end of the nineteenth century. Among the best-known headmen are Mfwamba, Tshinkenke, and Kalamba Mukenge, all of them reigning in the central Luluwa region.

The sociopolitical evolution must have occurred concurrently with the development of workshops under the direction of master sculptors. It seems obvious that refined sculptures, such as the one at the Metropolitan Museum, were produced by professional carvers in a workshop environment, whereas rudimentary carvings in the schematic style are the work of ritual specialists or even their clients.[22] Figures in the naturalistic style are thus not only less common than those in the schematic style; they are also more recent, since they are the result of the above-mentioned class distinction. A case in point is that some of the oldest Western collections, such as that in the Royal Museum for Central Africa, Tervuren, hold many more Luluwa carvings in the schematic style than in the naturalistic style. Also, some schematically carved figures at the American Museum of Natural History, New York, which Starr collected as "Baluba" around Lwebo in 1906, may in fact originate from the Luluwa, whom Starr, like many other early travelers, considered to be a subgroup of the Luba (Figure 11).[23]

Female figures in the naturalistic style were probably the exclusive property of an elite group of women in positions of authority. Along with the stratification of Luluwa society sketched above, women close to powerful male leaders possibly also gained sociopolitical prominence. Traditionally, a polygynous man's first wife already held control over the other women of her husband's harem in domestic matters, and chiefs turned to their sisters, mothers, and/or wives for political council. When several villages are collectively struck by repeated misfortune or adversity, the chiefs call in the help of elderly women and widows to perform the *Lwendu lwa Mucipu* ritual as a last resource. At night, these women, wearing only a small

Figure 12. Female figure holding a cup and a pounder (*Bwanga bwa Bwimpe*). Luluwa, Democratic Republic of the Congo, mid to late 19th century. Wood; H. 28.4 cm. The Metropolitan Museum of Art, The Michael C. Rockefeller Memorial Collection, Bequest of Nelson A. Rockefeller, 1979 (1979.206.37)

loincloth, their bodies painted white with kaolin, march through the village and secretly sacrifice a dog at a crossroads on the village border. In imitation of the Chokwe example, the advisory role of the female population in public matters must have acquired a new dimension with the emergence of a nobility at the end of the nineteenth century. It is very likely that small rudimentary figures were meant for private use and could be owned by any woman, whereas refined and elaborately carved larger statues in the possession of a select group of wealthy and powerful women were put to the service of the whole community.[24]

BWIMPE, OR THE MORAL BASIS OF BEAUTY

Although their appearance testifies to the fact that naturalistic female *Cibola* figures portray high-ranking women with ritual and political authority, the figures' iconography also reflects the initiation process discussed above. Ultimately, maternity figures and representations of pregnant women are meant to glorify and celebrate fertility and motherhood. It is here that

Figure 13. Female figure holding a cup and a walking cane (*Bwanga bwa Bwimpe*). Luluwa (Bakwa Mbusha subgroup), Democratic Republic of the Congo, mid to late 19th century. Wood; H. 51 cm. Field-collected by Leo Frobenius between the town of Lwebo and the Luluwa River in 1905. Ex coll.: Museum für Völkerkunde, Hamburg, 5854:06; Charles Ratton, Paris; Helena Rubinstein, New York; Comte Jean-Jacques de Launoit, Brussels; Jay C. Leff, Uniontown, Pa. Detroit Institute of Arts, Founders Society Purchase, Ralph Harman Booth Bequest Fund, Abraham Borman Family Fund, Joseph H. Boyer Memorial Fund, Joseph M. DeGrimme Memorial Fund, General Endowment Fund, New Endowment Fund, Mr. and Mrs. Benson Ford Fund, K. T. Keller Fund, Laura H. Murphy Fund, Mary Martin Semmes Fund, Barbara L. Scripps Fund, Edna Burian Skelton Fund, Mr. and Mrs. Conrad H. Smith Memorial Fund, Henry E. and Consuelo S. Wenger Foundation Fund, and Matilda R. Wilson Fund, 1982, 82.49 (photo: Detroit Institute of Arts)

the Luluwa's notions of aesthetics and ethics come into play. Beauty, especially female beauty, is at the core of both the *Cibola* cult and the naturalistic carvings it relies on. The term *bwimpe*, sometimes replaced by *bulenga*, is generally used by the Luluwa and their Chiluba-speaking neighbors to denote beauty, which refers to both physical and moral beauty and thus combines the Western terms "beautiful" and "good." Indeed, physical beauty is a sign of moral integrity. Moreover, emphasis is placed on cultural, or "human," beauty—that is, beauty created by human hands.

This union of aesthetics and ethics also lies at the basis of the production and use of yet another category of female carvings. Female figures holding a little cup filled with white chalk in one hand, a fine example of which can be found in the Metropolitan Museum's collection (Figure 12), are generally related to a cult called *Bwanga bwa Bwimpe*. Accordingly, the figures themselves are called *Lupingu lwa Bwimpe, Bwanga bwa Bwimpe*, or simply *Bulenga*, although the latter name seems to be proper to the neighboring Luba-Lubilanji, who would have imported their sculptures from the Luluwa. The Detroit Institute of Arts has an example of a special subcategory of *Bwimpe* figures measuring some forty centimeters in height and carrying a cup in one hand and a walking cane or stick in the other (Figure 13).[25] The *Bwimpe* cult was meant first and foremost to safeguard and foster the fertility of a young mother and the beauty and health of a newborn. It was specifically concerned with the well-being of those mothers who had given birth to a child with a pale skin, called *mwana mukunse* (literally, "red child"). Such a child was deemed exceptionally beautiful by the Luluwa and required special protection against sorcerers and envious people. Usually, the birth of a pale-skinned child was also accompanied by the planting of a white-barked spirit-tree called *mwabi* (*Sterculia quinqueloba*) next to the mother's house (Figure 14).

The ideal combination of morality and physical beauty, as expressed by the Chiluba terms *bwimpe* and *bulenga*, is widespread in sub-Saharan Africa.[26] Among the Luluwa, it is clearly reflected in the style and iconography of the naturalistic *Cibola* carvings. It is also evident from the time and attention the Luluwa accord to skin care and skin beautification. As mentioned before, the face and body of a woman undergoing initiation into *Bwanga bwa Cibola* are covered with a mixture of palm oil and red clay, sometimes also red camwood powder and white kaolin. The same treatment will be applied to her *Cibola* figure and, later, to her newborn child. Similar concerns of beauty were the basis of the intricate scarification marks on the face and body of both women and carved female

Figure 14. A *mwabi* tree (*Sterculia quinqueloba*) in the village of Kamembele, 1996. Luluwa, Democratic Republic of the Congo. (photo: Constantine Petridis)

figures. In the past, a woman's body had to be perfected and "humanized" through the application of geometric and curvilinear scarifications, true "marks of civilization," in order to be fully appreciated.[27]

Among the Luluwa, cicatrizations are generally known as *nsalu,* a term also applied to decorations in relief on carved objects, such as drums and drinking horns. It seems that the Luluwa practiced two types of cicatrization, one characterized by raised designs in low relief, the other by graphic color patterns that are closer to tattoos in the strict sense of the word. Sometimes the term *ndundu*—referring to the rubber smeared into cuts to cause black lines in the skin, which tend to fade with the passage of time—is used for the latter types; but it is also used to refer to facial scars as opposed to body marks. It is very likely that the two types of scars were used in different parts of Luluwaland, but, as we shall see, like headdresses and other body decoration, scarifications also changed over time.[28]

According to the Luluwa, children with a spotless

and healthy skin run the least risk of falling victim to sorcery, while children with skin disorders and physical handicaps are seen as potential sorcerers. Of course, the value accorded to the smoothness of the skin can only be applied to the unscarified body of small children. It is significant in this regard that the above-mentioned *Bwanga bwa Bwimpe* also dealt specifically with the beauty and health of newborns and infants. Research by Albert Maesen indicates that, as signs of *bwimpe* or *bulenga* and as emanations of the ideal combination of physical beauty and moral virtue, scarification marks and other skin treatments were also thought of as the best protection against sorcery.[29] This is one of the reasons that some of the finest *Cibola* figures, like the one at the Metropolitan, are distinguished by such a careful and naturalistic rendering of these body marks and other physical signs of beauty.

As power objects and mediators between the ancestral spirits and men, designed to protect against misfortune and adversity, the ultimate function of *Cibola*

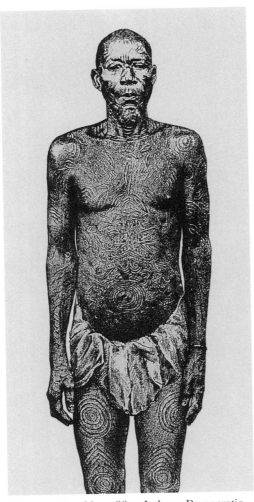

Figure 15. An elder, 1880s. Luluwa, Democratic Republic of the Congo. Unknown photographer (after Hermann von Wissmann et al., *Im Innern Afrikas*, 3rd ed. [Leipzig: F. A. Brockhaus, 1891], p. 166)

Figure 16. Scarifications on a woman's body, 1913–14. Bokala, Democratic Republic of the Congo. Postcard published by Ern. Thill, Brussels, after a photograph by Joseph Maes. The Metropolitan Museum of Art, Department of the Arts of Africa, Oceania, and the Americas, Photograph Study Collection

figures is to seek out and disarm sorcerers. As mentioned earlier, the *Cibola* cult basically serves the same purpose. Other anatomical details also serve to obstruct sorcery. The Luluwa and neighboring Chiluba-speaking peoples in Kasai Province, for example, attribute special meaning to the anterior and posterior fontanels. Like the bichromy of the *Cibawu* discussed above, these body parts signify "double sight"—that is, clairvoyance and the ability to discern the invisible in the visible and the past and future in the present.[30] Often, as is the case with the Metropolitan Museum's figure, the fontanels are visually marked in Luluwa figurative sculpture by means of a pointed hairstyle and usually harbor one or more cavities that are filled with magical substances.

In addition to the realistic depiction of scarification designs, beauty was also expressed in the Luluwa figures' long necks, large heads, and high foreheads. A woman's strong calves were highly esteemed by men, since they indicate her capacity for hard labor in the fields and in the domestic environment. The same positive aesthetic values were expressed by elaborate coiffures and jewelry. Wealthy women wore several blue-and-white-beaded necklaces in parallel rows, as represented in relief in the Metropolitan Museum's figure. Another important sign of beauty and perfection was the naturalistic imitation of an umbilical hernia, at once a symbol of the close relationship between the ancestors and their descendants and of the succession of the generations.

The idealized beauty embodied by female carvings was also meant to invite ancestral spirits to inhabit

Figure 17. Female figure (*Bwanga bwa Cibola*). Luluwa (Bakwa Ndoolo subgroup), Democratic Republic of the Congo, mid to late 19th century. Wood (*Crossopterix febrifuga*); H. 46.5 cm. Field-collected by Jules-Auguste "Tiarko" Fourche, M.D., between 1933 and 1936. Royal Museum for Central Africa, Tervuren, 1946, RG 43850 (photo: Hughes Dubois, Brussels–Paris)

Figure 18. Maternity figure (*Bwanga bwa Cibola*). Luluwa (Bakwa Mushilu subgroup), Democratic Republic of the Congo, mid to late 19th century. Wood (*Crossopterix febrifuga*), fiber; H. 41 cm. Field-collected by Father Constant De Deken ca. 1893. Royal Museum for Central Africa, Tervuren, 1914, RG 18805 (photo: Hughes Dubois, Brussels–Paris)

them. In this regard, Lucien Stéphan speaks of an "esthétique des esprits" in relation to these art forms, which have the realm of the spirits as their main audience and addressee.[31] Judging from extensive research by Mary Nooter Roberts, a similar motivation seems to lie at the heart of the representation of beautiful women in the ritual art of the Luba of Katanga Province.[32] Like carved female figures, Luluwa women themselves are seen as mediators between the natural world of humans and the supernatural world of the spirits. As among the Luba-Katanga, many Luluwa diviners and ritual healers are indeed women.

It is at this point that the parallels with the Mongo *Zebola* initiation become especially apparent. Upon an initial divination session, during which the woman goes into a trance, the *Zebola* healer transforms the patient's body into a kind of shrine for the spirit. With the aim to please and seduce the spirit, her body will be cared for and embellished day after day. Anointment with a red paste signals the bond between the woman and the spirit and advertises her special position. The beautiful dances for the *zebola* spirits, which demand great flexibility, serve the same purpose of spirit seduction. According to Ellen Corin, "the work done on the body during initiation may be interpreted as reshaping several corporal and sensory envelopes and as participating in the recreation of a sense of self; its reconstructive value should be enhanced by its symbolic reference to loving and protective spirits who are the real recipients of what is done to the body."[33] In fact, judging from field photographs, the coiffure, makeup, clothes, and other attributes of the Mongo *Zebola* initiate are strikingly similar to those of a woman undergoing initiation into the *Cibola* cult among the Luluwa.

LULUWA SCARIFICATION AND FIGURATIVE SCULPTURE IN REGIONAL PERSPECTIVE

Scarification, both on people and on figurative carvings in wood, shows a large variety of techniques, forms, and designs. Today, the practice of scarifying one's body is almost extinct. Elderly women occasionally bear traces of small, geometric blackened scars on their face, chest, or abdomen. But in general, these have little in common with the complex curvilinear motifs depicted on naturalistic Luluwa figures such as the Metropolitan's sculpture. Available sources, however, reveal that scarification practices were linked to local fashion trends and foreign influences and have never been equally distributed throughout the vast Luluwa region. Leo Frobenius, for example, writing about his visit in 1905, mentioned that some subgroups in the western part of Luluwa territory adopted scarification patterns from their Chokwe neighbors.[34] As we shall see, certain internal religious reformation movements also had an influence on scarification practices.

Historical field photographs of Luluwa people are scarce, and pictures showing men or women whose bodies are graced with scarification patterns are even more rare. One of the most notable exceptions is a photograph from the 1880s showing a man whose elaborately scarified body seems to indicate that he belonged to the conservative elders who opposed the religious reforms of chief Kalamba Mukenge and his followers (Figure 15). However, the scarified bodies of the male and female carvings in the naturalistic Luluwa style also show some similarity with those of people belonging to the Mongo complex in early field photographs (Figure 16).[35] The parallels are clear in the curvilinear motifs, with a predominance of concentric circles, but also in the fact that Mongo scarifications are usually raised in high relief. Thus, in addition to the affinity between the Luluwa *Cibola* and the Nkundo and other Mongo peoples' *Zebola*, there also seems to be a relationship between the two cultures in terms of their characteristic scarifications.[36]

With the exception of a group of female figures collected in the 1930s by the colonial official and medical doctor Jules-Auguste "Tiarko" Fourche among the Bakwa Ndoolo subgroup near the southern town of Dibaya (Figure 17), naturalistic Luluwa figures appear mainly to have been collected and probably also produced in the northern area of Luluwa territory, close

Figure 19. Female figure holding a cup (*Bwanga bwa Bwimpe*). Luluwa (Bakwa Mbusha subgroup), Democratic Republic of the Congo, mid to late 19th century. Wood; H. 28 cm. Field-collected by Leo Frobenius in 1905. Museum für Völkerkunde, Hamburg, 5858:06 (after drawing by Hans Martin Lemme, courtesy Museum für Völkerkunde)

to the lands inhabited by the peoples of the Kuba confederation. In fact, the naturalistic style encompasses a number of regional substyles, some of which have been identified with particular northern Luluwa subgroups. Along with a number of stylistically related figures at the Art Institute of Chicago, the Brooklyn Museum of Art, and the Royal Museum for Central Africa, Tervuren, the figure at the Metropolitan Museum can be attributed to the Bakwa Mushilu subgroup of the area around the town of Ndemba (Figure 18).[37]

Frobenius's data, however, indicate that naturalistic and schematic figures existed side by side in the same village among the same subgroup at the same time. Indeed, as shown in the accompanying illustrations, he collected stylistically distinct carvings among the

Figure 20. Half-figurine. Luluwa (Bakwa Mbusha subgroup), Democratic Republic of the Congo, mid to late 19th century. Wood; H. 13 cm. Field-collected by Leo Frobenius in 1905. Museum für Völkerkunde, Hamburg, 5921:06 (after drawing by Hans Martin Lemme, courtesy Museum für Völkerkunde)

Figure 21. Female figure holding a cup (*Bwanga bwa Bwimpe*). Luluwa (Bakwa Mbusha subgroup), Democratic Republic of the Congo, mid to late 19th century. Wood; H. 31.5 cm. Field-collected by Leo Frobenius in 1905. Museum für Völkerkunde, Hamburg, 5870:06 (after drawing by Hans Martin Lemme, courtesy Museum für Völkerkunde)

same Bakwa Mbusha (Baqua Mbuscha) subgroup (Figures 19–21).[38] This reinforces the hypothesis that the two Luluwa figure styles were linked to different classes of people. The fact that Frobenius collected far more figures in the schematic style than in the naturalistic style also reinforces the idea that the origin of the naturalistic style is related to the stratification of Luluwa society in the last quarter of the nineteenth century.

Frobenius also collected many refined figures in the naturalistic Luluwa style among neighbors of the Luluwa, such as the Northern Kete and Bakwa Mputu (Beena N'Putu) (Figures 22–27) and the Ngeende (Bangende), Pyaang (Pianga), and Byeeng (Bienge Ndumbi).[39] In this respect, attention should be drawn to the fact that, according to Jan Vansina, small figurines on a pointed end, called *nnoon*, were possibly introduced along with charms among the Pyaang by the neighboring Luluwa.[40] Moreover, the Kuba term for "statue," *iping*, is borrowed from the Luluwa or the Kete, who, as we have seen, use the word *lupingu*. It is also significant that some northern Luluwa subgroups share the Kuba's belief in nature spirits, which are unknown in the southern Luluwa region. Among these northern Luluwa they are referred to as *mingici*, a term that clearly derives from the Kuba word *(mi)ngesh*.[41]

The above-mentioned peoples—Northern Kete, (Bakwa) Mputu, Ngeende, Pyaang, and Byeeng—seem to have acted as mediators between the Luluwa and the Kuba. At the end of the nineteenth century, there existed numerous trade contacts between the Luluwa and the Luba in the south and the Kuba in the north. The Mongo peoples do not typically carve anthropomorphic figures, but the Ndengesh, who are generally viewed as "Kubaized" Mongo, have produced a special type of human statue that is intricately covered with imitations of Mongo-like scarification marks. As such, they show a stylistic kinship with certain Luluwa carvings.[42]

At the beginning of the twentieth century, both the Luluwa and the Luba also intermingled with the Kuba in the area around Lwebo.[43] Frans Olbrechts, who applied Giovanni Morelli's method of morphological analysis to the figure sculpture of Congo, believed that Luluwa art was related to the so-called court art of the neighboring Kuba.[44] And in fact certain scarification designs on Luluwa figurative carvings can also be seen on the remarkable drinking cups in buffalo horn or their wooden replicas that occur among several peoples in southern Congo but are mainly preserved under the name "Kuba" in Western collections (Figure 28).[45] Contrary to what Olbrechts seems to suggest, however, it is the Luluwa and the Kete who influenced Kuba art

Figure 22. Half-figure (*Bwanga bwa Cibola*). Northern Kete, Democratic Republic of the Congo, mid to late 19th century. Wood; H. 30 cm. Field-collected by Leo Frobenius in the village of Kapungu Kalamba in 1905. Museum für Völkerkunde, Hamburg, 5141:07 (after drawing by Hans Martin Lemme, courtesy Museum für Völkerkunde)

Figure 24. Female figure holding a cup (*Bwanga bwa Bwimpe*). Northern Kete, Democratic Republic of the Congo, mid to late 19th century. Wood; H. 23.8 cm. Field-collected by Leo Frobenius in the village of Kapungu Kalamba in 1905. Museum für Völkerkunde, Hamburg, 5138:07 (after drawing by Hans Martin Lemme, courtesy Museum für Völkerkunde)

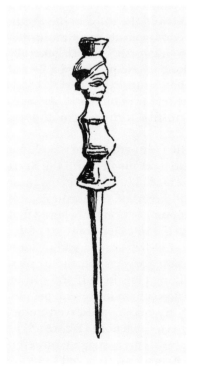

Figure 23. Half-figure (*Bwanga bwa Cibola*). Northern Kete, Democratic Republic of the Congo, mid to late 19th century. Wood; H. 24 cm. Field-collected by Leo Frobenius in the village of Kapungu Kalamba in 1905. Museum für Völkerkunde, Hamburg, 5150:07 (after drawing by Hans Martin Lemme, courtesy Museum für Völkerkunde)

rather than the other way around. Indeed, freestanding anthropomorphic Kuba figures in wood are very rare and practically limited to the famous *ndop* king statues.[46] In the end, the naturalistic Luluwa style constitutes an autonomous entity and shows little if any relationship to the sculptural production of the Kuba and their neighbors.

THE HEMP CULT AND THE ALLEGED END OF LULUWA ART

In the literature, the decline of figurative sculpture among the Luluwa has often been linked to chief Kalamba Mukenge's propagation of a new *bwanga* known as the "hemp cult."[47] As a new *bwanga*, this cult, or religion, was initially aimed at establishing peace, happiness, and friendship. The followers of Kalamba Mukenge's new hemp religion, the *beena dyamba* or "people of the hemp," also expected their new *bwanga* to bring them longevity and even immortality.[48] At the end of the nineteenth century, the explorer Hermann von Wissmann reported how Ka-

250

Figure 25. Female figure holding a cup (*Bwanga bwa Bwimpe*). Bakwa Mputu, Democratic Republic of the Congo, mid to late 19th century. Wood; H. 32.2 cm. Field-collected by Leo Frobenius in 1905. Museum für Völkerkunde, Hamburg, 5284:07 (after drawing by Hans Martin Lemme, courtesy Museum für Völkerkunde)

Figure 27. Female figure holding a cup (*Bwanga bwa Bwimpe*). Bakwa Mputu, Democratic Republic of the Congo, mid to late 19th century. Wood; H. 30 cm. Field-collected by Leo Frobenius in 1905. Museum für Völkerkunde, Hamburg, 5285:07 (after drawing by Hans Martin Lemme, courtesy Museum für Völkerkunde)

lamba Mukenge seized power figures from subjected chiefs and destroyed them publicly in a bonfire.[49]

Wissmann believed that figures covered with scarification patterns were produced by past generations as a result of the ban issued by Kalamba Mukenge on their application. At the time of the explorer's visit to the area, the younger generation had indeed abandoned elaborate marks in favor of simpler motifs, and the *beena dyamba* had copied the forehead scarification marks of the Imbangala.[50] As mentioned above, the scarification of body and face has always been strongly influenced by fashion and foreign influences. Frobenius points out that while certain southern Luluwa subgroups showed the influence of Chokwe scarifications, northern Luluwa subgroups such as the Bakwa Mputu continued to

Figure 28. Drinking horn. Kuba (?), Democratic Republic of the Congo, mid to late 19th century. Buffalo horn, metal wire; L. 50.8 cm. Ex coll. Jeanne Walschot, Brussels. Buffalo Museum of Science, 1938, C12696 (photo: Buffalo Museum)

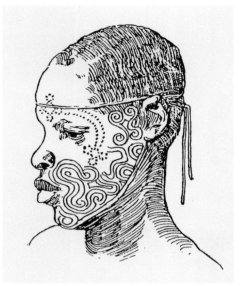

Figure 29. A fourteen-year-old girl with a Chokwe-like cross-shaped scarification motif on her forehead, 1905. Bakwa Mputu, Democratic Republic of the Congo. Frobenius-Institut an der Johann Wolfgang Goethe-Universität, Frankfurt am Main, SkB X 4 (after drawing by Hans Martin Lemme, in Frobenius, *Ethnographische Notizen*, vol. 3, p. 87, fig. 20)

apply "old" *nsalu* scarifications (Figures 29, 30).[51] Consequently, the presence of carved scarification marks on the body of a figure cannot be used as a terminus ante quem.

Although Kalamba Mukenge's privileged relationship with European travelers and explorers gave him wealth and prestige, as well as preeminence over his rivals, his power was limited both geographically and historically, and his religious reform did not affect the entire Luluwa region. Apparently, Kalamba Mukenge's influence did not reach the northern areas of Luluwa country, north of Ndemba, where most of the naturalistic figures seem to have been produced. Nor do the primary sources indicate that his hemp cult actually led to the massive destruction of figurative *manga*.

One should not overlook the fact that basically Luluwa art had an ephemeral status and Luluwa practitioners did not as a rule preserve their cult accessories. They were supposed to relinquish and sometimes even destroy their *manga* statuettes and other cult objects after they retired from the cult—in the case of the *Bwanga bwa Cibola*, after the birth of their fifth child.[52] Perhaps connotations of prestige and status associated with figures in the naturalistic style prevented them from being abandoned or destroyed by their owners, but many figures were

acquired by Westerners before they underwent this irreversible fate.

Kalamba Mukenge's reform, one of many religious renewals, may have entailed the prohibition of existing beliefs and practices, including the use of *manga*, in a limited part of Luluwa territory, but it surely never affected the entire Luluwa region. Moreover, the carving of schematic, rudimentary figures as *manga* has been kept alive up to this day, at least in some villages. It therefore seems more likely that the end of the naturalistic figure style is related to the abolishment of the new stratification of Luluwa society by the colonial powers in the beginning of the twentieth century.

ACKNOWLEDGMENTS

This article is in part derived from my Ph.D. dissertation on the arts of the Luluwa people of the Democratic Republic of the Congo, which I defended at Ghent University, Belgium, in 1997. Library, archival, museum, and field research for my dissertation was sponsored by a predoctoral fellowship from the Fund for Scientific Research—Flanders (F.W.O.—Vlaanderen). The complementary research on which the interpretations and hypotheses proposed in the pre-

Figure 30. Scarified abdomen of an eighteen-year-old woman, 1905. Bakwa Mputu, Democratic Republic of the Congo. Frobenius-Institut an der Johann Wolfgang Goethe-Universität, Frankfurt am Main, SkB X 8 (after drawing by Hans Martin Lemme, in Frobenius, *Ethnographische Notizen*, vol. 3, p. 85, fig. 11)

sent article rest was carried out during two fellowship terms at The Metropolitan Museum of Art, from 1997 to 1999. I am grateful for the Metropolitan Museum's Jane and Morgan Whitney Fellowship, and to the Belgian American Educational Foundation (B.A.E.F.), and the Fund for Scientific Research—Flanders for their support. An earlier version of this article was read at the University Seminar on the Art of Africa, Oceania, and the Americas at Columbia University, New York, on April 15, 1998. Finally, I owe special thanks to Rik Ceyssens for his invaluable suggestions and trenchant critiques of my research.

ABBREVIATIONS

Afrika
 Afrika: Kunst und Kultur. Meisterwerke afrikanischer Kunst. Hans-Joachim Koloss, ed. Exh. cat. Munich: Prestel; Berlin: Museum für Völkerkunde–Staatliche Museen zu Berlin, 1999.
Denolf, *Aan de rand*
 Prosper Denolf. *Aan de rand van de Dibese.* Morele en Politieke Wetenschappen, Verhandelingen 34. Brussels: Koninklijk Belgisch Koloniaal Instituut, 1954.

Fourche and Morlighem, *Communications*
 Jules-Auguste Fourche and Henri Morlighem. *Les Communications des indigènes du Kasai avec les âmes des morts.* Sciences Morales et Politiques, Mémoires 9, no. 2. Brussels: Institut Royal Colonial Belge, 1939.
LF 2, 3, 4
 Leo Frobenius. *Ethnographische Notizen aus den Jahren 1905 und 1906.* Hildegard Klein, ed. Vol. 2, *Kuba, Leele, Nord-Kete.* Vol. 3, *Luluwa, Süd-Kete, Bena Mai, Pende, Cokwe.* Vol. 4, *Kanyok, Songye, Tetela, Songo Meno/Nkutu.* Studien zur Kulturkunde 84, 87, 97. Stuttgart: Franz Steiner, 1987, 1988, 1990.
Maesen, "Statuaire et culte"
 Albert Maesen. "Statuaire et culte de fécondité chez les Luluwa du Kasaï (Zaïre)." *Quaderni Poro* 3 (1982), pp. 49–58.
Maesen, *Umbangu*
 Albert Maesen. *Umbangu: Kunst uit Kongo in het Museum van Belgisch-Kongo.* Kunst in België 3. Brussels: Cultura, 1960.
Petridis, "Of Mothers and Sorcerers"
 Constantine Petridis. "Of Mothers and Sorcerers: A Luluwa Maternity Figure." In *African Art at the Art Institute of Chicago,* pp. 183–95, 198–200. Museum Studies 23, no. 2. Chicago: Art Institute, 1997.
RMCA
 Royal Museum for Central Africa, Tervuren, Belgium
Samain, "Geestenbomen"
 Alidoor Samain "Geestenbomen bij de Baluba's." *Congo* 1, no. 1 (1923), pp. 43–49; 1, no. 2 (1924), pp. 218–29.
Treasures
 Treasures from the Africa-Museum, Tervuren. Gustaaf Verswijver et al., eds. Exh. cat. Tervuren: Royal Museum for Central Africa, 1995.
Wissmann et al., *Im Innern Afrikas*
 Hermann von Wissmann et al. *Im Innern Afrikas: Die Erforschung des Kassaï während der Jahre 1883, 1884, und 1885.* 3rd ed. Leipzig: F. A. Brockhaus, 1891.

NOTES

1. In accordance with the phonetic African alphabet, the "c" in italicized vernacular terms like *Cibola* should be pronounced "ch" as in "cheese." Although I have used the common Anglicized spellings of Chokwe and Chiluba, in toponyms and proper names the sound is spelled "tsh."
2. Petridis, "Of Mothers and Sorcerers." The Art Institute of Chicago's maternity figure also featured in the Metropolitan Museum's recent exhibition "Art and Oracle: Spirit Voices of Africa"; see Alisa LaGamma, cat. no. 42, in LaGamma and John Pemberton III, *Art and Oracle: African Art and Rituals of Divination,* exh. cat. (New York: MMA, 2000), pp. 66–67.

3. In passing, I would like to draw attention to the many erroneous data provided in the German edition of a catalogue that was recently published in conjunction with a traveling exhibition organized by the RMCA; see Boris Wastiau, cat. nos. 62–68, in *Afrikanische Kunst: Verborgene Schätze aus dem Museum Tervuren*, Gustaaf Verswijver et al., eds., exh. cat., Kunstsammlung Nordrhein-Westfalen, Düsseldorf (Munich: Prestel; Tervuren: RMCA, 1999), pp. 166–69. The term *makishi* is common among the Luvale and related peoples of Zambia but is not used among the Luluwa (p. 167); *bakulu* merely points to seniority and eldership but cannot be used to refer to the ancestors or ancestral spirits (p. 167); *bijinga* is clearly a misspelling of the term *bishimba* and certainly not a synonym for *bwanga* (p. 168); there is no field-based proof that wood of the *Hymenocardia acida* is frequently used in connection with Luluwa fertility rituals and medicines (p. 169), and so forth.

4. Rik Ceyssens (personal communication, February 1, 1998) informed me that Luluwa people are also among the Congolese minorities who immigrated to northeastern Angola. It seems that some of these Luluwa immigrants in Angola are called Beena Maayi, or "People of the Water"; see José Redinha, *Os Bena-Mai da Lunda* (Luanda: Fundo de Turismo e Publicidade, 1974). However, according to Ceyssens, the pseudo-ethnonym Beena Maayi is very common in the Kasai region, and the Luluwa themselves use it to denote all their western neighbors.

5. Petridis, "Luluwa Masks," *African Arts* 32, no. 3 (1998), pp. 32–47, 91–94; see also Frobenius, "Bena Lulua," LF 3, pp. 5, 26. Rik Ceyssens (personal communication, September 30, 2000), however, points out that aside from the Chokwe many other influences must be taken into account in order to explain the diversity of Luluwa culture. These various influences have also given shape to Luluwa sociopolitical organization. Thus, it should not be overlooked that several central Luluwa subgroups, such as the Beena Kashiya, Bashila Kasanga, and Bakwa Mwanza, immigrated from the east. Some 18th-century sources also attest that contacts with other than Chokwe peoples living west of the Luluwa's present habitat are much older than scholars generally assume. Moreover, Chokwe immigration occurred sporadically rather than in one monolithic movement.

6. Hermann von Wissmann recorded the terms *bwanga, bishimba,* and *lupingu* in the 1880s; Wissmann, *Unter deutscher Flagge quer durch Afrika von West nach Ost von 1880 bis 1883* (Berlin: Globus, 1889), p. 106; and Wissmann et al., *Im Innern Afrikas*, facing pp. 258, 265. According to Jules-Auguste "Tiarko" Fourche and Henri Morlighem, both makers and users of *manga* had an agreement with the ancestral spirits who lie at the basis of the powers of *manga* and their ingredients (*Communications*, p. 61). Leo Stappers rightfully questions the translation of the term *bwanga* as "fetish" because of its emphasis on aspects of form rather than content; Stappers, "Prières luba-kasaayi datant de 1912," *Cahiers des Religions Africaines* 3, no. 5 (1969), p. 114. In referring to the *Bwanga bwa Cibola* as a "cult," it should be emphasized that this translation cannot be equated with the narrow Christian meaning of the term derived from the Latin verb *colere* (see also note 47).

7. The ancestral spirits are ranked in a hierarchy and are seen as ambassadors of the Supreme Being *Mfidi Mukulu*, who is first addressed in prayers to the ancestors; see Jules-Auguste Fourche and Henri Morlighem, "Conceptions des indigènes du Kasai sur l'homme et la mort," *Journal de la Société des africanistes* 7, no. 2 (1937), pp. 197–98; and David A. McLean, "The Sons of Muntu: An Ethnological Study of the Bena Lulua Tribe in South Central Congo," M.A. thesis, University of the Witwatersrand, Johannesburg, 1962, pp. 156–58. Frobenius—who noted that the southern Luluwa subgroups also called their wooden figures *bashangi*—thought that the term *mukishi* was prevalent among the Luba-Lubilanji but that the neighboring Luluwa preferred the term *mushangi* instead ("Bena Lulua," LF 3, p. 23).

8. According to Albert Maesen (*Umbangu*, pl. 27), an art historian who did some fieldwork among these peoples in 1954–55 during a collecting expedition in southern Congo for the RMCA, the Songye also knew this particular cult. However, other researchers have not been able to confirm this.

9. On spirit-trees and tree altars, see Samain, "Geestenbomen"; Jules-Auguste Fourche and Henri Morlighem, "Mitshi ya m'vidi: Les Arbres-à-esprits au Kasai," *Bulletin des Séances de l'Institut Royal Colonial Belge* 8, no. 2 (1937), pp. 347–77; and Petridis, "Tree Altars, Spirit-Trees, and 'Ghost-Posts' among the Luluwa and Neighboring Peoples," *Baessler-Archiv* 47, no. 1 (1999), pp. 115–50.

10. Petridis, "Of Mothers and Sorcerers," p. 199, n. 7. However, whereas spirit possession used to occur quite frequently in various ritual contexts among the Luluwa, only Maesen and Tshisanda Ntabala-Mweny have mentioned it explicitly in relation to the *Cibola* cult: Maesen, *Umbangu*, pl. 27; and Tshisanda, "Le Thème de la maternité dans l'art luluwa du Kasaï," *mémoire de licence* (M.A. thesis), Université Nationale du Zaïre, Lubumbashi, 1973–74, pp. 64–65.

11. See Edmond Boelaert, "Yebola," *Kongo-Overzee* 1, no. 1 (1934), pp. 16–19; Piet Korse, Mondjulu Lonkongo, and Bongondo Bonje wa Mpay, *Jebola: Textes, rites et signification. Thérapie traditionnelle mongo*, Études Aequatoria 6 (Bamanya and Mbandaka: Centre Aequatoria, 1990); and esp. Ellen Corin, "Refiguring the Person: The Dynamics of Affects and Symbols in an African Spirit Possession Cult," in *Bodies and Persons: Comparative Perspectives from Africa and Melanesia*, Michael Lambek and Andrew Strathern, eds. (Cambridge: Cambridge University Press, 1998), pp. 80–102. The Mongo complex comprises about forty peoples or groups, the Ekonda, Tetela, Nkutshu, and Mbole among them. Although they have their own languages and customs, the forty groups share certain linguistic and cultural traits. Among the Mongo-Ekonda, the *Zebola* healing ritual is known as *Njondo*; see Daniel Vangroenweghe, "Njondo: Therapie voor geesteszieken door muziek en dans bij de Ekondastam," in *De Mongo: Bewoners van het Evenaarswoud in Zaïre*, exh. cat., Stadszalen, Sint-Niklaas (Brussels: Gemeentekrediet van België, 1984), pp. 49–50. Considering the other affinities with Mongo culture, which are discussed later in this article, it seems reasonable to assume that possession by the *Cibola* force as a condition for initiation into the *Cibola* cult was especially prevalent in the northern part of Luluwa territory. For some general information on Mongo culture, see also Gustaaf Hulstaert, *Les Mongo: Aperçu général*, Archives d'Ethnographie 5 (Tervuren: RMCA, 1961); and Luc de Heusch, "La Beauté est ailleurs: Pour en finir avec les masques tetela. Notices d'histoire et d'ethnographie nkutshu," in *Objets-signes d'Afrique*, de Heusch, ed. (Ghent: Snoeck-Ducaju & Zoon, 1995), pp. 175–206.

12. See also Fourche and Morlighem, "Conceptions des indigènes," p. 201; Maesen, "Statuaire et culte," p. 57; and Clémentine M. Faïk-Nzuji, "Les Différentes catégories de noms propres des personnes dans la société luba," *Zaïre-Afrique* 24 (1984), pp. 562–63. Often, children who are born with a physical handicap are

also considered special and are called *mapanga*. The birth of such children is usually accompanied by the planting of a *mumbu* tree; see also Samain, "Geestenbomen," p. 222; Henri Bogaerts, "Onomasticon van 't Luntuvolk," *Congo* 2, no. 2 (1937), pp. 176–81; and Muteba Nzambi Mushipula, "'Mukiya', 'Tshibau' et 'Tshibindi': Sanction sociale et morale chez les Luba du Kasaï," *Zaïre-Afrique* 27 (1987), pp. 277–79.

13. See also McLean, "The Sons of Muntu," pp. xxviii–xxxii; Faïk-Nzuji, "Les Différentes catégories," p. 562; and Diambila Luboya, "La Sage-femme et le couple mère-enfant chez les Beena Luluwà," *Journal de la Société des africanistes* 60, no. 2 (1990), p. 164. Some sources, however, firmly distinguish *mapanga* children from *manga* children; see Samain, "Geestenbomen," pp. 219–21; Bogaerts, "Onomasticon," pp. 176, 181–85; Rafael Van Caeneghem, "Godsgebeden bij de Baluba," *Aequatoria* 7, no. 1 (1944), p. 33; and Mukangala Dibwe Kalombo and Bangi Makombo, "Les Noms circonstanciels comme source diffuse des relations interpersonnelles chez les Luluwa du Kasaï," *Le Mois en Afrique* 22, nos. 253–54 (1987), pp. 122–23. In "Of Mothers and Sorcerers" (p. 189, fig. 6), I published a photograph showing mothers dancing in honor of a son born after three girls or a daughter born after three boys, which Amaat Burssens, a professor of African languages and linguistics at Ghent University from 1926 to 1967, made during fieldwork among the Luluwa in 1937.

14. See also Fourche and Morlighem, *Communications*, pp. 59–60; and Maesen, "Statuaire et culte," pp. 51–52. Frobenius already mentioned that a *tschiboa* is made for protection against sorcerers ("Baluba," LF 4, p. 59). Rafael Van Caeneghem discusses prayers to the Supreme Being near the *Bwanga bwa Cibawu* in case of emergency and distress, but also prior to traveling or embarking on a hunt; Van Caeneghem, "Godsgebeden," pp. 28–29; idem, "Gebeden der Baluba II," *Aequatoria* 10, no. 1 (1947), pp. 8, 13–14; and idem, "Het godsbegrip bij de Baluba van Kasaï," *Zaïre* 3, no. 7 (1949), pp. 758–59.

15. For information on sorcery among the Luluwa and the neighboring Luba-Lubilanji, see esp. August De Clercq, "Mupongo, Buloji," *Congo* 1, no. 1 (1936), pp. 1–10; Rafael Van Caeneghem, *Hekserij bij de Baluba van Kasai*, Morele en Politieke Wetenschappen, Verhandelingen 3, no. 1 (Brussels: Koninklijke Academie voor Koloniale Wetenschappen, 1955); and Mulonda Kadiebwe et al., "Le Mupongo," *Le Mois en Afrique* 21, nos. 239–40 (1985–86), pp. 106–9. For information on the association of "lightning senders" (*beena nkuba*), see Louis De Brandt, "Het heelal van den Muluba," *Congo* 2, no. 2 (1921), pp. 258–60; Amaat Burssens, *Wako—Moyo: Zuidoost-Kongo in de lens* (Antwerp: de Sikkel, 1943), pp. 108–11; Marcel Peeters, "Secte des foudroyeurs: Bena Nkuba," typescript, [1946], Ethnographic file E.D. 1096, RMCA, Ethnography Section; and Kabulampuka Kanyinda, "La Secte Nkuba 1936–1958," in *Symbolique verbale et rituelle chez les Sakata, Lele, Wongo, Kuba, Lulua, Mbole et Vira*, Publications du CEEBA 93 (Bandundu: Centre d'Études Ethnologiques, 1984), pp. 11–28. The *Cibawu* often is kept by a woman whose initiation into the cult is characterized by a possession-trance. These women usually become powerful diviners who specialize in the pursuit of lightning senders and sorcerers.

16. See also Van Caeneghem, "Gebeden," p. 6; Albert Maesen, field notebook no. 30 [1954], RMCA, Ethnography Section, pp. 11–12; and David A. McLean and Ted J. Solomon, "Divination among the Bena Lulua," *Journal of Religion in Africa* 4, no. 1 (1971), pp. 35–36, n. 11. For some general information on the symbolism of the colors red, black, and white among Bantu-speaking peoples, see esp. Anita Jacobson-Widding, *Red—White—Black as a Mode of Thought: A Study of Triadic Classification by Colours in the Ritual Thought of the Peoples of the Lower Congo*, Uppsala Studies in Cultural Anthropology 1 (Uppsala: Acta Universitatis Upsaliensis, 1979); and Allen F. Roberts, "Insight, or Not Seeing is Believing," in *Secrecy: African Art that Conceals and Reveals*, Mary H. Nooter, ed., exh. cat. (New York: Museum for African Art and Prestel, 1993), pp. 65–79.

17. For information on Janus-faced *Cibawu* figures, see Amaat Burssens, field notebook, 1937, University Library, Manuscript Room, Ghent University, nos. 16, 24, 25; Rafael Van Caeneghem, letter of September 13, 1938, Ethnographic file E.D. 678, RMCA, Ethnography Section; and Fourche, typescript, [1946], Ethnographic file E.D. 929, RMCA, Ethnography Section, no. 167. Bichromy is also typical of carved posts that are found among many peoples in Central Africa; see Petridis, "Tree Altars," pp. 138–44. It is not a coincidence that the face of the famous male figure at the Berlin Ethnologisches Museum is also divided into a red and a black half; see Petridis, no. 147, in *Afrika*, pp. 223–24.

18. See Henri Morlighem, "Notes sur quelques fétiches," typescript, [1935], Ethnographic file E.D. 858, RMCA, Ethnography Section; August De Clercq, *Dictionnaire luba. Première partie: luba—français* (Léopoldville [Kinshasa]: Procure des Missions de Scheut, 1937), pp. 57 and 136; and Maesen, field notebook no. 30 (1954), pp. 52–53. The description Hermann von Wissmann (in Wissmann et al., *Im Innern Afrikas*, p. 209) gives of the *bimpulumba*, conservative elders who objected to Kalamba Mukenge's religious reforms, closely resembles the appearance of figures in the naturalistic style, including the beads and cowries woven into the hair; see also Frobenius, "Bena Lulua," LF 3, pp. 13–14; and L. Liétard, "Étude sommaire sur la tribu des Lulua (Kasaï, Congo belge)," *Bulletin de la Société Royale Belge de Géographie* 53, 1 (1929), p. 40.

19. Maesen, "Statuaire et culte," p. 56.

20. See Petridis, cat. no. 111, in *Treasures*, pp. 331–33. Most Luluwa figures in the naturalistic style seem to have been carved from *mutoci* wood (*Crossopterix febrifuga*); see also Roger Dechamps, "L'Identification anatomique des bois utilisés pour les sculptures en Afrique. II: La Sculpture des 'Luluwa,'" *Africa-Tervuren* 17, no. 3 (1971), pp. 79–86. It is noteworthy that such figures are generally in much better condition than pieces made from other kinds of wood.

21. Allen F. Roberts, "Social and Historical Contexts of Tabwa Art," in *The Rising of a New Moon: A Century of Tabwa Art*, Roberts and Evan M. Maurer, eds., exh. cat., University of Michigan Museum of Art, Ann Arbor (Seattle: University of Washington Press, 1985), pp. 10–16, 23. However, contrary to what Annie Vandewiele-Lannoo, a student in art history at Ghent University in the early 1940s, suggested, there is no evidence to identify naturalistic figures as protective charms, on the one hand, and schematically carved pieces as "fetishes," on the other; Vandewiele-Lannoo, "De plastiek der Bena-Lulua," *licentiaatsverhandeling* (M.A. thesis), Rijksuniversiteit te Gent, 1945–46, pp. 12, 36. For general information on the Luluwa's involvement in the long-distance trade, see esp. Ntambwe Luadia-Luadia, "Les Luluwa et le commerce luso-africain (1870–1895)," *Études d'Histoire africaine* 6 (1974), pp. 55–104.

22. This distinction between large and carefully carved figures

made by professional master sculptors for the benefit of the whole community versus small and often rough-hewn figures made by the ritual specialist or the client himself for private purposes, has also been recorded among the neighboring Songye, whose *mankishi* figures are very similar to the *mpingu* of the Luluwa and who also use the terms *bwanga* and *bishimba*; see Dunja Hersak, *Songye Masks and Figure Sculpture* (London: Ethnographica, 1986), pp. 118–22; see also Fourche and Morlighem, *Communications*, pp. 57–60.

23. It is notable, however, that a small elite was able to develop a carving tradition of such a high degree of refinement in a relatively short time span. Unlike the case of the Tabwa of southeastern Congo, there is no indication whatsoever that the Luluwa imported their elite arts from one of their neighbors, nor that they relied on sculptors of foreign origin or that local sculptors imitated the work of others. Curiously enough, in the available sources there is also no mention in relation to the above-cited famous central Luluwa chiefs of their role as patrons of a state art or of the existence of a real court with a distinguished class of professional sculptors.

24. On the *Lwendu lwa Mucipu* ritual, see also Badibanga Kantshiama and Tshishimbi Katumumonyi, "Le Rôle de la femme dans la société luluwa," *Les Cahiers du CEREKA* 1, no. 1 (1988), pp. 93–94. Rik Ceyssens (personal communication, February 1, 1998) questions the social stratification of Luluwa society. Rather, he views the brief and local equation of the power of men and women at the end of the 19th century as resulting from the immigration of traders on traditional matrimonial exchanges. Furthermore, he confirms that some nouveaux riches benefited from the long-distance trade and indeed aggrandized their political status but suggests that the interest of the new bourgeoisie in baubles of foreign origin rather contributed to the degradation of "classical" Luluwa sculpture; see also Ceyssens, *Balungu: Constructeurs et destructeurs de l'état en Afrique centrale* (Paris: L'Harmattan, 1998), pp. 58 n. 54, 155–57.

25. These carvings not only attest to the political power certain women held by the end of the 19th century; they also shed light on a form of spirit-possession not entirely dissimilar to the one that sometimes leads to initiation into the *Bwanga bwa Cibola*. When the eldest daughter of an important chief fell ill and regular treatment brought no relief, a diviner would determine that the woman was being possessed by an illness-inflicting spirit. Initiation into a special cult would free her from possession and lead to her recovery, after which she received the honorary title of *inabanza* and was invested with the highest political power. See Samain, "Geestenbomen," pp. 223–25; and Marcel Lecomte, "Le Rituel de féminisation des sorciers dans la magie de l'accablement lulua et basonge," typescript, n.d., Archives of Jean Willy Mestach, Brussels.

26. Many African languages have a single word that means both beautiful and good. Among the Lega the term *busoga* is close to the classical Greek concept of *kalokagathia*: it denotes the inseparable combination of goodness and beauty that is the ultimate goal of initiation into the Bwami association; see Daniel Biebuyck, *Lega Culture: Art, Initiation, and Moral Philosophy among a Central African People* (Berkeley: Regents of the University of California, 1973), p. 129; and idem, *La Sculpture des Lega*, trans. Brunhilde Biebuyck and Mihaela Bacou, exh. cat. (Paris: Galerie Hélène et Philippe Leloup, 1994), p. 32. For general information on the moral basis of African aesthetics, see also

Susan Mullin Vogel, *African Aesthetics: The Carlo Monzino Collection*, exh. cat. (New York: Center for African Art, 1986), pp. xiii–xiv; and Wilfried Van Damme, *A Comparative Analysis Concerning Beauty and Ugliness in Sub-Saharan Africa*, Africana Gandensia 4 (Ghent: Rijksuniversiteit, 1987), pp. 11–19, 53–57.

27. The expression is borrowed from Susan Mullin Vogel, "Baule Scarification: The Mark of Civilization," in *Marks of Civilization: Artistic Transformations of the Human Body*, Arnold Rubin, ed. (Los Angeles: Museum of Cultural History, University of California, 1988), pp. 97–105. The same ideas of body perfection and humanization through scarification are also reflected in the figure sculpture of the Luba-Katanga; see Mary Nooter Roberts and Allen F. Roberts, "Body Memory," in *Memory: Luba Art and the Making of History*, Roberts and Roberts, eds., exh. cat. (New York: Museum for African Art and Prestel, 1996), p. 98. Rubin, who rightfully remarks that even cicatrizations tend to flatten and are thus not really permanent, draws attention to the fact that the dark pigmentation of many sub-Saharan African peoples lends itself better to the sculptural quality of cicatrizations than to the graphic quality of tattoos; Rubin, "General Introduction," in *Marks of Civilization*, pp. 13 and 15.

28. See also Wissmann et al., *Im Innern Afrikas*, p. 167; Denolf, *Aan de rand*, pp. 121–23; and Albert Maesen, field notebook no. 54 [1955], RMCA, Ethnography Section, pp. 11–12. The term *ndundu* is also used for a specific scarification motif; see Leo Stappers, "'Arbeidsvitaminen' der Bena Luluwa-vrouwen," *Africa-Tervuren* 10, no. 4 (1964), p. 98, n. 30; and Tshisanda, "Le Thème de la maternité," p. 60.

29. Maesen, "Statuaire et culte," pp. 53–54. It seems very likely, however, that, as in the case of the Mongo *Zebola* healing ritual, scarifications were also applied for medical purposes in the context of the *Bwanga bwa Cibola* initiation; see also Diambila, "La Sage-femme," pp. 165, 169.

30. When the anterior fontanel (*kapoba* or *kabankoshi*) of a newborn is sunken, the mother will smear a mixture of red camwood powder, palm oil, and other ingredients on the fontanel in order to prevent the baby's life-force from escaping through it; see Kathryn W. Nelson, "Child Rearing Patterns in a Lulua Village of South Central Congo," Ph.D. diss., University of Michigan, Ann Arbor, 1968, p. 258. On the symbolic significance of the posterior and anterior fontanels and their relationship to the navel, see also Fourche and Morlighem, *Communications*, pp. 62–63; Marcel Lecomte, "Le Thème de l'ésotérisme lulua," *Jeune Afrique* 10, no. 26 (1957), pp. 10–12; Clémentine M. Faïk-Nzuji, *Symboles graphiques en Afrique noire* (Paris: Karthala and Ciltade, 1992), p. 46; and idem, *La Puissance du sacré: L'Homme, la nature et l'art en Afrique noire* (Brussels: La Renaissance du Livre, 1993), pp. 46, 57.

31. Stéphan, "La Sculpture africaine: Essai d'esthétique comparée," in Jacques Kerchache et al., *L'Art africain*, L'Art et les Grandes Civilisations 18 (Paris: Mazenod, 1987), pp. 246–47.

32. See Roberts and Roberts, "Body Memory," pp. 111–12. As among the Luba-Katanga, Luluwa scarifications also had erotic connotations and were meant to heighten a woman's appeal; see also Van Caeneghem, letter of September 13, 1938; and Tshisanda, "Le Thème de la maternité," p. 75. Thus, a lozenge motif on the breasts is called *tunkinda*, meaning "little rat traps," referring to the female genitals which seek to "devour" the male organ, metaphorically called *cya mutu bu mpuku*, "having the head of a rat"; see Clémentine M. Faïk-Nzuji, "L'Art plastique africain comme extension de l'art corporel," in *De l'art nègre à*

l'art africain: L'Évolution de la connaissance de l'art africain des années trente à aujourd'hui (Arnouville: Arts d'Afrique Noire, 1990), pp. 61–62.

33. Corin, "Refiguring the Person," p. 92. The author also notes how the healer traces white marks around the woman's eyes "to represent the 'second look' she will acquire, while entranced, as to what really caused her disease and triggered the spirit's intervention"; ibid., p. 93. Some Luluwa figures, especially those carved in the naturalistic style proper to the Bakwa Ndoolo subgroup, show the same white circles around the eyes (see Figure 17).

34. Frobenius, "Bena Lulua," LF 3, pp. 13–14. One of these Chokwe-inspired motifs is the crosslike mark on the forehead called *kartoza*; see also Tshisanda, "Le Thème de la maternité," p. 60; and compare with Marie-Louise Bastin, *Art décoratif tshokwe*, Subsídios para a História, Arqueologia e Etnografia dos Povos da Lunda Publicações Culturais 55 (Lisbon: Companhia de Diamantes de Angola and Museu do Dundo, 1961), vol. 1, pp. 137–39. Prosper Denolf (*Aan de rand*, p. 121) also recognizes the regional variations in patterns and designs and notes that certain Luluwa and Luba-Lubilanji subgroups shared the practice of raised scars with the Kuba.

35. The same body decorations can be seen in Norman Hardy's 1908 watercolors and sketches of women of the Tetela Sungu subgroup; see Emil Torday and Thomas A. Joyce, *Notes ethnographiques sur des populations habitant les bassins du Kasai et du Kwango oriental*, Ethnographie, Anthropologie, Annales 2, no. 2 (Tervuren: Musée du Congo Belge, 1922), chap. 2. Inspired by Jules-Auguste Fourche and Henri Morlighem's book *Une Bible noire* (Brussels: Max Arnold, 1973), Mubumbila Mfika reads one of Hardy's drawings of a Sungu woman in the light of Luba cosmogony; Mubumbila, *Sur le sentier mystérieux des nombres noirs* (Paris: L'Harmattan, 1988), p. 138, fig. 30. The field photograph by Joseph Maes, on which the postcard reproduced in this article is based, was made during a collecting expedition for the RMCA in 1913–14; see also Maes, *Notes sur les populations des bassins du Kasai, de la Lukenie, et du Lac Léopold II*, Miscellanées, Annales 1, no. 1 (Tervuren: Musée du Congo Belge, 1924), chap. 5.

36. Denolf (*Aan de rand*, pp. 321–23) discusses the political and cultural affinities between the Luluwa and neighboring Kasai peoples, on the one hand, and the Mongo, on the other. Jan Vansina also points to the mediating role that Luluwa and Luba-Lubilanji peoples played in the Mongo influence on cults and religious associations among the Kuba; Vansina, "Miko mi Yool, une association religieuse kuba," *Aequatoria* 22, no. 3 (1959), pp. 84–88; and idem, "Les Mouvements religieux kuba (Kasai) à l'époque coloniale," *Études d'Histoire africaine* 2 (1971), p. 170.

37. On the Bakwa Mushilu and Bakwa Ndoolo substyles, see Paul Timmermans, "Essai de typologie de la sculpture des Bena Luluwa du Kasai," *Africa-Tervuren* 12, no. 1 (1966), pp. 20–22. Although this author equates the substyle of the Bakwa Mushilu with that of the neighboring Beena Tshikulu, the only object collected among the latter, reproduced here as Figure 9, is stylistically quite distinct from the typical Bakwa Mushilu figures. Many of the well-known Luluwa figures collected by Wissmann and his traveling companions in the last quarter of the 19th century, which are now mainly at the Ethnologisches Museum in Berlin, also originate from northern Luluwa subgroups such as the Bakwa Mpika and the Beena Mba(a)la; see Petridis, cat. nos. 147, 148, in *Afrika*, pp. 223–24. Rik Ceyssens (personal

communication, February 1, 1998), however, wonders whether most naturalistic Luluwa figures originated in the northern part of the Luluwa region because until May 25, 1891, the first explorers did not travel south of the 6th parallel, being the southern border of the Congo Free State.

38. Frobenius also collected the above-mentioned (see note 25 and Figure 13) cup-bearing *Bwanga bwa Bwimpe* figure now at the Detroit Institute of Arts among the Bakwa Mbusha (Baqua Mbuscha) in the area between Lwebo and the Luluwa River. Karel Timmermans (personal communication, October 17, 1996), a Belgian art collector and former resident of Kananga (formerly Luluabourg), acquired an almost identical piece in the same Luluwa region north of Ndemba; for illustrations, see *Réceptacles*, exh. cat., Musée Dapper (Paris: Éditions Dapper, 1997), pp. 100–101.

39. The Byeeng belong to the Southern Kuba; it was in one of their chiefdoms, Ndombe, which also encompassed a number of Northern Kete villages, that Starr made some interesting field photographs; see Frederick Starr, *Congo Natives: An Ethnographic Album* (Chicago: Lakeside Press, 1912), pp. 16–17, pls. 10–12; and Jan Vansina, *The Children of Woot: A History of the Kuba Peoples* (Madison: University of Wisconsin Press, 1978), p. 358, n. 4. Frobenius refers to these Kete villages of the Byeeng chiefdom as "Bakete Ndumbis" ("Nord-Bakete," LF 2, pp. 39–45). Frobenius also writes that the Luluwa produced figures for neighboring peoples such as the Luba and the Songye, as well as for certain Tetela enclaves ("Bena Lulua," LF 3, p. 23).

40. Vansina, *The Children of Woot*, pp. 212, 359–60 n. 21; and idem, "Ndop: Royal Statues among the Kuba," in *African Art and Leadership*, Douglas Fraser and Herbert M. Cole, eds. (Madison: University of Wisconsin Press, 1972), pp. 47–48.

41. See Denolf, *Aan de rand*, pp. 197–98; and Vansina, "Les Mouvements religieux," p. 170.

42. See Maesen, *Umbangu*, pl. 20; Joseph Cornet, "À propos des statues ndengese," *Arts d'Afrique Noire* 17 (1976), pp. 6–16; and Faïk-Nzuji, cat. no. 142, in *Treasures*, pp. 344–45. The ethnonyms Songo Meno, Yaelima, and Ohindo are believed to be synonyms for Ndengesh. For field-based data on other Mongo visual art forms, see Gustaaf Hulstaert, "Les Cercueils des Eleku," *Aequatoria* 22, no. 1 (1959), pp. 10–15; idem, "Les Cercueils anthropomorphes," *Aequatoria* 23, no. 4 (1960), pp. 121–29; and esp. de Heusch, "La Beauté est ailleurs," pp. 188–204.

43. See Jan Vansina, "Du Royaume kuba au 'territoire des Bakuba,'" *Études congolaises* 12, no. 2 (1969), pp. 26–27, 32–33, 39. It is interesting to note that the sculptures that Starr collected in the mixed ethnic area around the town of Lwebo for the American Museum of Natural History consist of a large number of rudimentary half- and full-figures but not a single refined and elaborately carved Luluwa figure. These figurative carvings are generally labeled as "Kete" and "Luba"—referring to Luba emigrants from along the Lubilanji River—but their style makes them indistinguishable from schematically carved Luluwa figures. It should be mentioned that many of the objects which Frederick Starr brought back from the Congo were field-collected by Reverend Samuel P. Verner; see Enid Schildkrout, "Personal Styles and Disciplinary Paradigms: Frederick Starr and Herbert Lang," in *The Scramble for Art in Central Africa*, Schildkrout and Curtis A. Keim, eds. (Cambridge: Cambridge University Press, 1998), p. 172.

44. Frans Olbrechts, *Plastiek van Kongo*, with assistance from Albert Maesen (Antwerp: Standaard-Boekhandel, 1946), pp. 52–63;

see also Ivan Lermolieff [Giovanni Morelli], *Die Werke Italienischer Meister in den Galerien von München, Dresden und Berlin: Ein Kritischer Versuch*, trans. Johannes Schwarze (Leipzig: E. A. Seemann, 1880). However, Vansina ("Ndop," p. 50) writes that "to speak of a court style obliterates the major stylistic distinctions observable in Kuba art: those between the various geographical areas and, even more important, that separating masks and other ritual objects . . . from purely secular work"; see also idem, "Kuba Arts and Its Cultural Context," *African Forum* 3, no. 4, and 4, no. 1 (1968), p. 22. Elsewhere, the author emphasizes the important cultural, sociopolitical, and religious differences between the Luba and the Luluwa peoples, on the one hand, and the Kuba, on the other; Jan Vansina, "L'État kuba dans le cadre des institutions politiques africaines," *Zaïre* 11, no. 5 (1957), p. 488; and idem, "Miko mi Yool," p. 92. Not only was there little contact between these peoples until relatively recently, the Kuba even disdained the Luba and the Luluwa, who in turn feared the Kuba.

45. Such drinking horns are also depicted hanging from the shoulder on Luluwa figures that represent high-ranking chiefs; see Petridis, cat. no. 108, in *Treasures*, pp. 330–31; and idem, cat. no. 147, in *Afrika*, pp. 223–24. It remains uncertain whether these objects were made by the Luluwa themselves or were imported from the neighboring Kuba. Among the Kuba, they also serve as status symbols and are used for the consumption of palm wine; see Jan Vansina, cat. nos. 146, 147, in *Kings of Africa: Art and Authority in Central Africa. Collection Museum für Völkerkunde Berlin*, Erna Beumers and Hans-Joachim Koloss, eds., exh. cat., MECC, Maastricht (Maastricht: Foundation Kings of Africa, 1992), pp. 319–20; and David A. Binkley, cat. no. 132, in *Treasures*, p. 341. Curiously, Albert Maesen was told that the piece he collected in the Luluwa village of Mutefu, now at the RMCA (inv. no. RG 53.74.4445), had been carved by a Chokwe sculptor from Tshikapa; Maesen, field notebook no. 30 (1954), p. 57. This drinking horn, which was used for palm wine, was the property of a so-called leopard chief (*mukalenga wa nkashaama*), the highest rank of chieftainship.

46. For a discussion of a well-known Kuba *ndop* figure at the Brooklyn Museum of Art, see David A. Binkley, cat. no. 54, in *Africa: The Art of a Continent. 100 Works of Power and Beauty*, exh. cat., Guggenheim Museum, New York (New York: Solomon R. Guggenheim Foundation, 1996), p. 113. Following Olbrechts, scholars have grouped Luluwa art with the Luba-Katanga rather than the Kuba; see esp. Herman Burssens, "Congo Belga," in *Enciclopedia universale dell'arte*, vol. 3 (Venice and Rome: Istituto per la Collaborazione Culturale, 1958), pp. 777–78; and Albert Maesen, "Styles et expérience esthétique dans la plastique congolaise," *Problèmes d'Afrique Centrale* 44 (1959), p. 84. However, although Luluwa and Luba-Katanga peoples show a predilection for the depiction of female figures, on a purely stylistic level Luluwa art has very little in common with that of the Luba-Katanga.

47. August De Clercq rightfully points out Wissmann's ethnocentric usage of terms such as "cult," "priestess," and "sacred symbol" in relation to the smoking of hemp by Kalamba Mukenge and his followers and underlines the political dimension of the newly established *bwanga*; De Clercq, "Practische wenken over de ethnographische waarnemingen in Kongo," *Onze Kongo* 3 (1912–13), pp. 233–35; and idem, "Le Chanvre chez les Bena Lulua: Origine, signification et influence de l'usage du chanvre," *Congo* 1, no. 4 (1928), pp. 504–5. For an in-depth discussion of hemp use and its various political implications, see Ceyssens, *Balungu*, pp. 152–59, 166–67.

48. Until the 1960s, hemp was related to chieftainship and ancestor worship, which was often accompanied by the smoking of hemp; see Nelson, "Child Rearing Patterns," p. 175. Early sources clearly indicate that, at the end of the 19th century, excessive hemp consumption led to serious health problems. These developments, together with famine and widespread pneumonia, not only led to an antihemp campaign by missionaries and colonials, but also provoked significant internal opposition to the newly established *bwanga*. In a letter of June 12, 1894, published in the journal *Missions en Chine et au Congo* 74 (1895), p. 31, August De Clercq gives a telling, though surely not neutral, account of the state of affairs at the time: "L'usage du chanvre fumé comme du tabac, provoque ici les effets de l'opium dans l'Orient, l'affaiblissement rapide du corps et l'abrutissement de l'intelligence. . . . Des hommes de trente ans ont le visage décrépit d'un vieillard et la physionomie d'un idiot. . . . À ce compte, on comprend aisément que nos fumeurs soient d'une paresse sans égal" (Here, hemp smoking has the same effects as opium in the East, rapid weakening of the body and stupefying of the mind. . . . Thirty-year old men have the decrepit face of an elder and the physiognomy of an idiot. . . . It is therefore easy to understand the unequaled laziness of our hemp smokers); see also Wissmann, *Unter deutscher Flagge*, p. 98; Constant De Deken, *Deux ans au Congo* (Antwerp: Clément Thibaut, 1900), pp. 218, 240; and Leo Frobenius, *Im Schatten des Kongostaates: Bericht der Verlauf der Ersten Reisen der D.I.A.F.E. von 1904–1906* (Berlin: G. Reimer, 1907), p. 238.

49. Wissmann et al., *Im Innern Afrikas*, pp. 266–67. When Ludwig Wolf, one of Wissmann's traveling companions, acquired the famous chief figure now at the Berlin Ethnologisches Museum from a rival of Kalamba Mukenge, he threatened to hand the rival over to Kalamba Mukenge if he refused to give Wolf the figure; see ibid., pp. 265–66. Nevertheless, according to Wissmann, the Bakwa Mpika, among whom he collected a fine *Bwanga bwa Bwimpe* figure holding a walking cane in one hand, also at the Berlin Ethnologisches Museum, were loyal to Kalamba Mukenge and belonged to the *beena dyamba*; ibid., p. 215.

50. See Wissmann et al., *Im Innern Afrikas*, p. 166. Wolf states that both chief Kalamba Mukenge and his ally chief Tshinkenke prohibited scarification as part of their religious reform; Ludwig Wolf, "Anthropologischen Untersuchungen in Central-Afrika," *Zeitschrift für Ethnologie* 16 (1884), p. 424.

51. Frobenius, "Bena Lulua," LF 3, pp. 13–14. Curiously, what is purported to be a portrait of Kalamba Mukenge shows a man who is literally bedecked with complex curvilinear scarifications; see Wissmann et al., *Im Innern Afrikas*, p. 165 (see also Figure 15). But it should be mentioned that according to Prosper Denolf (*Aan de rand*, p. 336), Kalamba Mukenge was not an autochtonous Luluwa chief but a Luba-Lubilanji immigrant of the Bakwa Diishi subgroup who had crossed the Lubi River to overtake the local chief of the Luluwa Bakwa Mushilu subgroup, Mwamba Mputu. Rik Ceyssens (personal communication, September 30, 2000), however, draws attention to the fact that the hemp cult was a very short-lived movement and that scarifications could not simply be erased.

52. See Fourche and Morlighem, *Communications*, p. 55. Henri Morlighem ("Notes sur quelques fétiches," see note 18 above) writes that the half-figure of the Beena Tshikulu subgroup, which is reproduced here as Figure 9, was placed on a grave.

Manuscript Guidelines for the *Metropolitan Museum Journal*

The *Metropolitan Museum Journal* is issued annually by The Metropolitan Museum of Art. Its purpose is to publish original research on works in the Museum's collections and the areas of investigation they represent. Articles are contributed by members of the Museum staff and other art historians and specialists. Submissions should be addressed to:

> James David Draper
> Henry Kravis Curator
> European Sculpture and Decorative Arts
> The Metropolitan Museum of Art
> 1000 Fifth Avenue
> New York, NY 10028

Manuscripts are reviewed by the *Journal* Editorial Board, composed of members of the curatorial and editorial departments. **To be considered for the following year's volume, an article must be submitted, complete including illustrations, by October 15.** Once an article is accepted for publication, the author will have the opportunity to review it in March, after editing, and again in July, after it has been laid out in pages. The honorarium for publication of an article is $100, and each author receives a copy of the *Journal* volume in which it appears.

Manuscripts should be submitted both in hard copy and on computer disk. In addition to the text, the manuscript must include the endnotes and the captions for illustrations. All parts of the type-script—text, quoted material, endnotes, captions, appendixes—must be double-spaced and have margins of at least one inch on all sides. On the disk, each part of the article, including the endnotes, should be in a separate electronic file.

For the style of bibliographic references in endnotes, authors are referred to the Museum's style guide, which in turn is based on the 14th edition (1993) of *The Chicago Manual of Style*. In bibliographic citations, please give the author's full name; the title and subtitle of the book or article and periodical; place and date of publication, including the publisher of a book; volume and page number. For sub-sequent references to cited works, use the author's last name and a shortened form of the title rather than *op. cit. The Metropolitan Museum of Art Guide to Editorial Style and Procedures* is available from the Museum's Editorial Department upon request.

All photographs and drawings must be submitted with the manuscript, each identified according to the list of captions, which should also include photograph credits. We require glossy black-and-white prints of good quality and in good condition. Photographs made from reproductions in books will be considered only when the work to be reproduced is inaccessible; captions for these photographs should include full bibliographic information. Indicate the figure number and the picture's orientation lightly in pencil on the back of the photograph, and mark any instructions for cropping on a photo-copy of the illustration. **The author is responsible for obtaining all photographic material and permission to reproduce all photographs except those of objects in the Metropolitan Museum.**